Baedeker's SWITZERLAND

Cover picture: The Matterhorn from the Winkelmatten Inn

233 colour photographs
83 maps, plans and sketches
1 large road map

Text:
Hans Rathgeb, Rapperswil
Gerald Sawade (Climate)
Christine Wessely (Art)

Editorial work:
Baedeker Stuttgart
English language: Alec Court

Cartography:
Ingenieurbüro für Kartographie
Huber & Oberländer, Munich
Georg Schiffner, Lahr

Design and layout:
Creativ Verlagsgesellschaft mbH, Stuttgart
Ulrich Kolb, Henk Veerkamp

Conception and general direction:
Dr Peter Baumgarten,
Baedeker Stuttgart

English translation:
James Hogarth

© Baedeker Stuttgart
Original German edition

© The Automobile Association
United Kingdom and Ireland

© Jarrold and Sons Ltd
English language edition worldwide

Licensed user:
Mairs Geographischer Verlag GmbH & Co.,
Ostfildern-Kemnat bei Stuttgart

Reproductions:
Gölz Repro-Service GmbH,
Ludwigsburg

In a time of rapid change it is difficult to ensure that all the information given is entirely accurate and up to date, and the possibility of error can never be entirely eliminated. Although the publishers can accept no responsibility for inaccuracies and omissions, they are always grateful for corrections and suggestions for improvement.

Printed in Great Britain by Jarrold & Sons Ltd, Norwich ★★★★★

0–13–056044–8 US and Canada
3–87504–024–4 Germany

Source of illustrations:
Most of the coloured photographs were provided by the Schweizerische Verkehrszentrale (Swiss National Tourist Office) in Zurich and Frankfurt am Main; others by the Liechtensteinische Fremdenverkehrszentrale (Liechtenstein National Tourist Office) in Vaduz (pp. 161, 162); by the cantonal tourist organisations of St Gallen (pp. 54, 55, 98, 248; 310 bottom left), Ticino (pp. 13, 73, 164, 165, 174 bottom left, 175 bottom right, 246 top, 247 bottom) and Valais (p. 53 top); and by the local or regional tourist information offices of Baden (two photographs on p. 61), Basle (pp. 62, 64, 70), Berne (pp. 74, 78), Biel (p. 86), Breiten (p. 92, top left), Brig (p. 90), Chur (p. 102), Crans (p. 101), Davos (pp. 103, 104), Engelberg (p. 112), Glarnerland/Walensee (pp. 256, 257), Grimentz (p. 226 left), Grindelwald (two photographs on p. 139), Interlaken (p. 144), Küssnacht (p. 152), Lausanne (pp. 153, 157), Lauterbrunnen (p. 158), Lucerne (pp. 168–169), Meiringen-Haslital (p. 178), Murten (p. 182), Neuchâtel (p. 184), Pontresina (pp. 7, 188), Riederalp (p. 91), Saas Fee (p. 205), St Gallen (p. 209), St Moritz (p. 111 top; p. 216 top), Schwyz (p. 223 top right), Bad Scuol-Tarasp-Vulpera (pp. 45, 224 bottom left), Vevey (p. 250), Wengen (p. 148), Zermatt (p. 261), Zinal (p. 226 bottom right), Zurich (pp. 266, 272) and Zurzach (p. 192).
Others:
Allianz-Archiv (p. 282); H. Baedeker, Stuttgart (pp. 14, 107, 222); Bahnen der Jungfrau-Region, Interlaken (p. 146); F. Barbier, Braunwald (pp. 11; 138); A. Baumgarten, Stuttgart (p. 58 top); Bergbahnen Engelberg-Trübsee-Titlis (p. 113); R. Bersier, Fribourg (p. 182 bottom); Bürgenstock-Hotels (two photographs on p. 93); Bürgi, Vitznau (pp. 204, 251, 288, left); W. P. Burkhardt, Buochs (pp. 172, 176); J.-D. Demorsier, Geneva (pp. 119, 128, 134); Fetzer, Bad Ragaz (pp. 189, 190, 303); Geiger, Flims Waldhaus (p. 114); Goetheanum, Dornach (p. 72); T. Hiebeler, Munich (p. 235 bottom left); K. Keller, Frauenfeld (p. 245 bottom left); S. Lauterwasser, Überlingen (p. 235); Luftseilbahn Surlej-Silvaplana-Corvatsch (p. 140 top); Musée d'Horlogerie, Le Locle (p. 94); Schweizerische Käseunion, Berne (pp. 239, 294, P. Moeschlin); H. Steiner, St Moritz (p. 186 bottom); Swissminiatur, Melide (p. 175 top right); Werbegemeinschaft Obertoggenburg, Wildhaus (p. 247); Zentral Farbbild Agentur (ZEFA), Düsseldorf (cover picture, V. Phillips; pp. 283, 284); Zwahlen, Lenk (p. 227).

How to Use this Guide

The principal towns and areas of tourist interest are described in alphabetical order. The names of other places referred to under these general headings can be found in the very full Index.

Following the tradition established by Karl Baedeker in 1844, sights of particular interest and hotels and restaurants of particular quality are distinguished by either one or two asterisks.

In the lists of hotels b.=beds, SB=indoor swimming bath and SP=outdoor swimming pool.

The symbol ⓘ at the beginning of an entry or on a town plan indicates the local tourist office or other organisation from which further information can be obtained. The post-horn symbol on a town plan indicates a post office.

Only a selection of hotels and restaurants can be given: no reflection is implied, therefore, on establishments not included.

A Glossary of common German topographical terms and elements in place-names is given on pp. 290–292.

This guidebook forms part of a completely new series of the world-famous Baedeker Guides to Europe.

Each volume is the result of long and careful preparation and, true to the traditions of Baedeker, is designed in every respect to meet the needs and expectations of the modern traveller.

The name of Baedeker has long been identified in the field of guidebooks with reliable, comprehensive and up-to-date information, prepared by expert writers who work from detailed, first-hand knowledge of the country concerned. Following a tradition that goes back over 150 years to the date when Karl Baedeker published the first of his handbooks for travellers, these guides have been planned to give the tourist all the essential information about the country and its inhabitants: where to go, how to get there and what to see. Baedeker's account of a country was always based on his personal observation and experience during his travels in that country. This tradition of writing a guidebook in the field rather than at an office desk has been maintained by Baedeker ever since.

Lavishly illustrated with superb colour photographs and numerous specially drawn maps and street plans of the major towns, the new Baedeker Guides concentrate on making available to the modern traveller all the information he needs in a format that is both attractive and easy to follow. For every place that appears in the gazetteer, the principal features of architectural, artistic and historic interest are described, as are its main areas of scenic beauty. Selected hotels and restaurants are also included. Features of exceptional merit are indicated by either one or two asterisks.

A special section at the end of each book contains practical information, details of leisure activities and useful addresses. The separate road map will prove an invaluable aid to planning your route and your travel within the country.

Switzerland from A to Z

Aarau · Adelboden · Altdorf · Andermatt · Appenzell · Arosa · Ascona · Baden · Basle · Bellinzona · Berne · Bernese Oberland · Bernina Pass · Biel/Bienne · Val Bregaglia · Brig · Brunnen · Bürgenstock · La Chaux-de-Fonds · Chur · Lake Constance · Crans-Montana · Davos · Delémont · Disentis · Einsiedeln · Emmental · Engadine · Engelberg · Entlebuch · Flims · Fribourg · Geneva · Lake Geneva · Glarus · Grindelwald · Grisons · Gruyère · Gstaad · Ilanz · Interlaken · Jungfrau · Jura Mountains · Kandersteg · Klosters · Küssnacht · Lausanne · Lauterbrunnen Valley · Lenzerheide-Valbella · Leukerbad · Liechtenstein · Locarno · Lötschental · Lucerne · Lake Lucerne · Lugano · Lake Lugano · Lake Maggiore · Martigny · Meiringen · Montreux · Mürren · Murten/Morat · Neuchâtel · Nyon · Oberhalbstein · Olten · Pontresina · Bad Ragaz · Rapperswil · Rhine · Rhine Falls · Rhône Valley · Rigi · Rorschach · Saas Valley · Great St Bernard · St Gallen · St Gotthard · St-Maurice · St Moritz · San Bernardino Pass · Sarnen · Schaffhausen · Schwyz · Bad Scuol-Tarasp-Vulpera · Sierre · Simmental · Simplon Pass · Sion · Solothurn · Stein am Rhein · Swiss National Park · Thun · Lakes Thun and Brienz · Thurgau · Ticino · Toggenburg · Valais Alps · Vevey · Walensee · Winterthur · Yverdon · Zermatt · Zug · Zurich · Lake Zurich

Introduction to Switzerland

The Bernina group from Piz Lang

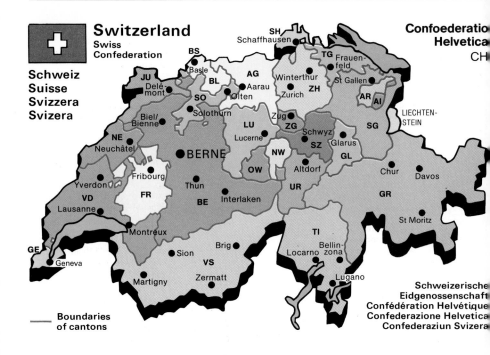

Switzerland
Swiss
Confederation

Schweiz
Suisse
Svizzera
Svizera

Confoederatio
Helvetica
CH

Schweizerische
Eidgenossenschaft
Confédération Helvétique
Confederazione Helvetica
Confederaziun Svizera

Boundaries
of cantons

Cantons		Area in sq. km (sq. miles)	Population (1980)	Religion (%)		Language (%)			Ro-mansh
				Prot.	R.C.	German	French	Italian	
AG	Aargau	1405 (542)	453,442	47·3	50·8	84·0	0·9	11·3	0·2
AR	Appenzell-Ausserrhoden	243 (94)	47,611	69·8	27·7	88·2	0·4	6·8	0·2
AI	Appenzell-Innerrhoden	172 (66)	12,844	4·7	94·9	92·7	0·1	4·6	0·1
BL	Basel-Land	428 (165)	219,822	57·7	39·6	82·9	2·5	10·3	0·2
BS	Basel-Stadt	37 (14)	203,915	52·7	40·7	82·7	3·7	8·3	0·3
BE	Berne	6050 (2335)	912,022	(figures not yet available)					
FR	Fribourg	1670 (645)	185,246	13·4	85·8	32·4	60·3	4·0	–
GE	Geneva	282 (109)	349,040	38·0	53·7	10·9	65·4	10·9	0·1
GL	Glarus	685 (264)	36,718	55·5	43·9	84·5	0·3	12·2	0·3
GR	Grisons	7106 (2744)	164,641	45·9	52·9	57·6	0·5	15·8	23·4
JU	Jura	837 (323)	64,986	15·3	83·9	8·5	82·1	7·0	0·1
LU	Lucerne	1492 (576)	296,159	13·4	85·5	90·9	0·7	5·4	0·2
NE	Neuchâtel	797 (308)	158,368	57·9	38·8	9·2	73·0	12·8	0·1
	Unterwalden:								
NW	Nidwalden	276 (107)	28,617	8·9	90·3	92·0	0·5	4·8	0·2
OW	Obwalden	491 (190)	25,865	4·2	95·4	94·7	0·5	3·2	0·1
SG	St Gallen	2014 (778)	391,995	34·8	63·6	88·4	0·4	7·4	0·4
SH	Schaffhausen	298 (115)	69,413	64·2	32·2	84·4	0·8	9·2	0·2
SZ	Schwyz	908 (351)	97,354	7·9	91·4	90·1	0·3	7·2	0·3
SO	Solothurn	791 (305)	218,102	37·3	60·8	85·5	1·5	10·0	0·1
TG	Thurgau	1013 (391)	183,795	55·0	43·6	85·5	0·5	10·5	0·2
TI	Ticino	2811 (1085)	265,899	7·8	89·9	10·5	1·7	85·7	0·1
UR	Uri	1076 (415)	33,883	6·6	93·1	92·5	0·3	5·6	0·4
VS	Valais	5226 (2018)	218,707	4·4	94·9	32·4	59·4	6·2	–
VD	Vaud	3219 (1243)	528,747	60·7	36·2	8·9	73·6	9·8	0·1
ZG	Zug	239 (92)	75,930	17·4	80·7	86·6	1·0	8·2	0·4
ZH	Zurich	1729 (668)	1,122,839	59·5	37·0	83·0	1·7	10·2	0·4
CH	**Swiss Confederation**	41,295 (15,943)	6,365,960	47·7	49·7	64·9	18·1	11·9	0·8

Percentages correspond to the total population in 1970

Aargau (AG)
Canton since 1803
Area: 1405 sq. km (542 sq. miles)
Population: 453,000
Capital: Aarau

Appenzell-Ausserrhoden (AR)
Half-canton since 1513
Area: 243 sq. km (94 sq. miles)
Population: 48,000
Capital: Herisau

Appenzell-Innerrhoden (AI)
Half-canton since 1513
Area: 172 sq. km (66 sq. miles)
Population: 13,000
Capital: Appenzell

Basel-Land (BL)
Half-canton since 1501
Area: 428 sq. km (165 sq. miles)
Population: 220,000
Capital: Liestal

Basel-Stadt (BS)
Half-canton since 1501
Area: 37 sq. km (14 sq. miles)
Population: 204,000
Capital: Basle

Berne (BE)
Canton since 1353
Area: 6050 sq. km (2335 sq. miles)
Population: 912,000
Capital: Berne

Fribourg (FR)
Canton since 1481
Area: 1670 sq. km (645 sq. miles)
Population: 185,000
Capital: Fribourg

Geneva (GE)
Canton since 1815
Area: 282 sq. km (109 sq. miles)
Population: 349,000
Capital: Geneva

Glarus (GL)
Canton since 1352
Area: 685 sq. km (264 sq. miles)
Population: 37,000
Capital: Glarus

Grisons (GR)
Canton since 1803
Area: 7106 sq. km (2744 sq. miles)
Population: 165,000
Capital: Chur

Jura (JU)
Canton since 1979
Area: 837 sq. km (323 sq. miles)
Population: 65,000
Capital: Delémont

Lucerne (LU)
Canton since 1332
Area: 1492 sq. km (576 sq. miles)
Population: 296,000
Capital: Lucerne

Neuchâtel (NE)
Canton since 1815
Area: 797 sq. km (308 sq. miles)
Population: 158,000
Capital: Neuchâtel

Nidwalden (NW)
Half-canton since 1291
Area: 276 sq. km (107 sq. miles)
Population: 29,000
Capital: Stans

Obwalden (OW)
Half-canton since 1291
Area: 491 sq. km (190 sq. miles)
Population: 26,000
Capital: Sarnen

Unterwalden

St Gallen (SG)
Canton since 1803
Area: 2014 sq. km (778 sq. miles)
Population: 392,000
Capital: St Gallen

Schaffhausen (SH)
Canton since 1501
Area: 298 sq. km (115 sq. miles)
Population: 69,000
Capital: Schaffhausen

Schwyz (SZ)
Canton since 1291
Area: 908 sq. km (351 sq. miles)
Population: 97,000
Capital: Schwyz

Solothurn (SO)
Canton since 1481
Area: 791 sq. km (305 sq. miles)
Population: 218,000
Capital: Solothurn

Thurgau (TG)
Canton since 1803
Area: 1013 sq. km (391 sq. miles)
Population: 184,000
Capital: Frauenfeld

Ticino (TI)
Canton since 1803
Area: 2811 sq. km (1085 sq. miles)
Population: 266,000
Capital: Bellinzona

Uri (UR)
Canton since 1291
Area: 1076 sq. km (415 sq. miles)
Population: 34,000
Capital: Altdorf

Valais (VS)
Canton since 1815
Area: 5226 sq. km (2018 sq. miles)
Population: 219,000
Capital: Sion

Vaud (VD)
Canton since 1803
Area: 3219 sq. km (1243 sq. miles)
Population: 529,000
Capital: Lausanne

Zug (ZG)
Canton since 1352
Area: 239 sq. km (92 sq. miles)
Population: 76,000
Capital: Zug

Zurich (ZH)
Canton since 1351
Area: 1729 sq. km (668 sq. miles)
Population: 1,123,000
Capital: Zurich

Population figures for 1980 (rounded)

Switzerland, for long one of the world's great tourist countries, contains within a relatively small area an extraordinary abundance of natural beauties and other attractions, and at the same time, in spite of the country's varied geographical pattern and the difference in language, religion and way of life among its inhabitants, offers an admirable example of unity in diversity. The 4000 m (13,124 feet) peaks of the High Alps and the lesser summits of the Pre-Alpine regions began to attract the first modern tourists – mainly British – during the 19th century; but Switzerland has developed since then into a Mecca for visitors of every nationality and every age and condition, who find here accommodation to suit every taste from modest to luxurious, modern tourist facilities and a hospitable welcome.

St-Ursanne (Jura)

Geographically Switzerland is made up of three very dissimilar parts. The south-eastern half of the country consists of the Alps; to the north-west are the Jura mountains; and between these two mountain regions is the lower-lying Mittelland, extending from Lake Geneva in the south-west, where the Jura beyond the rift valley of the Rhine abuts on the Alpine chain, to Lake Constance in the north-east, beyond which lies the German Alpine foreland region. The total area of the country is divided fairly equally between the Jura and Mittelland on the one hand and the Alps on the other – one half well cultivated and densely inhabited, the other offering the grandeur and beauty of the high mountains.

The Swiss **Jura** extends in long rolling crests and much-weathered ridges from the south-west, around Geneva, where it adjoins the similarly formed and oriented chains of the French Pre-Alpine region, to Schaffhausen in the north-east, where Randen (912 m – 2992 feet), a peak affording extensive views, and the volcanic Hegau form a transition to the Swabian Jura.

The limestone chains of the Jura reach their highest points in Swiss territory: Mont Tendre, 1679 m (5509 feet); La Dôle, 1677 m (5502 feet) and fall steeply down to the Mittelland. Between the Lac de Neuchâtel and the Doubs valley there are some 20 successive chains, their highest points rising only slightly above the uniform ridges in the form of gently rounded hills. The chains are frequently slashed by gorges, through which the river flowing down a longitudinal valley finds its way into the next valley, continuing through further gorges until it emerges from the mountains. Here the slopes, covered with beautiful forests and the summits with pastureland and scrub, open up to reveal in their light-coloured bands of rock the folding to which the strata have been subjected (most strikingly seen in the Val Moutier and the Gorges de Court).

From the west the Burgundian Jura, lower but still wave-like in form, advances into Swiss territory in the plateaux of La Chaux-de-Fonds and the Franches Montagnes. The long gorge of the Doubs, here forming the frontier, which flows between steep wooded rock walls 400 m (1312 feet) below the edges of the plateau, is particularly beautiful.

Between Basle and Brugg the Jura, only a few hundred metres high, forms tabular plateaux. This "tabular Jura" is also slashed by deep valleys.

The **Mittelland** (c. 400–800 m – 1312–2625 feet), which rises gradually from the Jura to the foot of the Alps, consists of sandstone and, in the area below the Alps, of the conglomerate known as "nagelfluh". Through this conglomerate, originally formed from the detritus deposited by the Alpine streams, these same rivers later cut their way, widening and deepening their channels to form valleys. The hills between them are remnants of the older rocks which have resisted erosion. The Tertiary rocks, however, are covered almost everywhere with a mantle of pasture and arable land, peatbogs and lakes, with small areas of woodland on the hills.

In the western part of the Mittelland the heights have a gently rounded tabular form (the "plateau suisse"), like, for example, Mont Jorat (932 m – 3058 feet) above Lausanne. To the east they are mostly in the form of long and fairly uniform ridges, the flanks of which have been worn smooth by the glaciers of the last Ice Age, such as the Pfannenstiel (853 m – 2799 feet) near Zurich and the Lindenberg (881 m – 2891 feet) in the Aargau. The Napf group (1411 m – 4629 feet) and the Töss hills (Hörnli, 1136 m – 3727 feet) lay outside the glaciated area and were exposed to continual erosion by running water: in consequence they now show a much-dissected pattern of alternating ridges and furrows.

The final Alpine folding movement thrust the adjoining foreland region up into a series of rounded folds, now largely destroyed. Some remnants of these folds, however, survive in the nagelfluh beds which can be seen rising towards the north on the Rigi (1800 m – 5906 feet), Rossberg (1584 m – 5197 feet) and Speer (1954 m – 6411 feet). From the summits of these rocky heights there is a view over the intervening uplands to the distant chains of the Jura. – The wide valley areas around Winterthur, Zurich, Burgdorf, Berne and Geneva are traversed by moraines left by the last great Ice Age, usually running across the valley or along the hillsides and frequently bounding the lower ends of lakes. With its variety of landscape pattern the Mittelland is a region of great attraction, even on cloudy days when the view of the Alps is cut off.

The Mittelland is the most densely settled part of Switzerland, with almost all its larger towns and more than three-quarters of its total population; but it is also a highly developed agricultural region.

The **Alps**, which appear from the distance to be a uniform chain, are in fact deeply indented by valleys and passes. On the north side of the mountain mass are the Pre-Alps, limestone chains which in many places rise above the Mittelland in sheer rock walls; running parallel to one another, they are broken up by wide, deep valleys extending down from the High Alps (e.g. at Montreux, Thun, Lucerne, Rapperswil and Rorschach-Bregenz).

Even the Pre-Alps offer magnificent scenery, with light grey limestone peaks rearing above green upland pastures and dark pine forests. In spite of much erosion and weathering the violent folding of the strata still reveals the gigantic wave-like structure of the rock formations which follow one another in close succession northwards – particularly impressive in the Säntis ridges (2504 m – 8216 feet) and Pilatus (Tomlishorn, 2132 m – 6995 feet). Elsewhere massive limestone mountains tower up, like Tödi (3614 m – 11,858 feet), Selbsanft (3026 m – 9928 feet) and Glärnisch (Bächistock, 2915 m – 9564 feet) which enclose the canton of Glarus. To the south of the Pre-Alps, forming a magnificent backdrop, are the glaciated summits of the High Alps, which fall down on the south, almost without transition, to the North Italian plain. On this side there are no limestone Alps preceding the main massif of ancient rocks.

The Alpine world of Switzerland is brought within reach by a dense network of roads and railways. Nature has created a much-ramified pattern of valleys which provide access to the mountains and make possible the extension of human settlement to considerable altitudes. The *valleys* extend far into the mountains on a fairly gentle gradient. The fall of the rivers is sufficient, however, to enable them when the water-level is high, to bring

Winter in the Glarus Alps

Facts and Figures in Brief

The official (Latin) designation of the Swiss Confederation is CONFOEDERATIO HELVETICA: hence the letters CH to be seen on Swiss cars and in Swiss post codes.

The name of the country (in German *Schweiz*, French *Suisse*, Italian *Svizzera*, Romansh *Svizera*) comes from the canton of Schwyz, and was originally applied only to central or inner Switzerland, i.e. the three cantons of Uri, Schwyz and Unterwalden which laid the foundations of the Confederation when they formed a perpetual alliance on the Rütli meadow by Lake Lucerne in 1291. From the 14th to the 16th century, as the number of cantons joining the alliance increased, the term confederation (*Eidgenossenschaft*) was preferred; but in the end the designation of Schweiz or Switzerland became generally accepted. The official name of the state, Swiss Confederation, combines both forms.

NATIONAL FLAG. – A white cross on a red ground; the arms of the cross are of equal length, each arm being one-sixth longer than it is broad.

AREA. – With an area of 41,295 sq. km (15,944 sq. miles), Switzerland is about the same size as the Netherlands (41,160 sq. km – 15,892 sq. miles), larger than Belgium (30,514 sq. km – 11,781 sq. miles) but rather smaller than Denmark (43,069 sq. km – 16,629 sq. miles), and about a sixth the size of the United Kingdom (244,000 sq. km – 94,208 sq. miles).

FRONTIERS. – Switzerland has a common frontier with five neighbouring countries. The total length of its frontiers is 1882 km (1169 miles) – 363 km (226 miles) with the German Federal Republic, 165 km (103 miles) with Austria, 41 km (25 miles) with Liechtenstein, 741 km (460 miles) with Italy and 572 km (355 miles) with France.

LAND TYPES and LAND USE. – Switzerland is made up of three geographical regions of different size – the *Alps* (some 60% of the total area), the *Mittelland* (30%) and the *Jura* (10%). Of the total area 46% is occupied by meadowland and pasture, 25% by forest and 6% by arable land. Thus 77% of the country's area has been brought into productive use and is densely populated; the remaining 23% is unproductive land in the mountains, but these empty regions provide magnificent recreation areas for holidaymakers and nature-lovers.

HIGHEST and LOWEST POINTS. – The highest point in Switzerland is the Dufourspitze (4634 m – 15,204 feet) in the Monte Rosa group (Valais). The highest permanently inhabited settlement is the village of Juf (2126 m – 6975 feet) in the Avers valley (Grison). The lowest point in the country is Lake Maggiore (193 m – 633 feet) in Ticino.

RIVERS. – The main Swiss rivers – the Rhine, the Rhône, the Aare, the Reuss and the Ticino – rise in the St Gotthard area. The catchment areas of Swiss rivers are as follows: Rhine 36,494 sq. km (14,090 sq. miles) (8531 sq. km – 3294 sq. miles outside Switzerland), Rhône 10,403 sq. km (4017 sq. miles) (3456 sq. km – 1334 sq. miles), Inn 2150 sq. km (830 sq. miles) (358 sq. km – 138 sq. miles), Ticino 1616 sq. km (624 sq. miles), Poschiavino 238 sq. km (92 sq. miles). 67·7% of Swiss waters drain into the Atlantic, 27·9% into the Mediterranean and 4·4% into the Black Sea. The mean annual flow of the Rhine at Basle is 1026 cu. m (36,228 cu. feet) per second.

---

down great quantities of rock debris which cover the whole floor of the valleys. The sides of the valleys are slashed by deep gorges and gullies, filled after heavy rain by rushing mountain streams which also carry down quantities of weathered rock and debris, surging over their banks and any man-made barriers. The hillsides below these gullies, formed by the destructive force of nature, are indebted to nature also for their fertility.

The Alpine valleys were given their characteristic form during the Ice Age. Perhaps 20,000 years ago they were filled with great seas of ice reaching almost to the summit ridges of the mountains, and under the pressure of the ice the rock debris which had been carried down on the floor of the valleys wore away the surface so that the valleys took on a more or less pronounced U shape. Above the steep sides of these trough valleys are found terraces which are probably the remains of earlier valley floors (e.g. the Lauterbrunnen valley, the Urner See). The side valleys were less deeply indented than the main valleys, since the glaciers they contained were smaller, and in consequence their floors lie high above the main valley. The streams flowing down these "hanging valleys" tumble over the edge of the valley in the form of waterfalls (Giétro, in the Valais Alps; Giessbach, near Brienz; Trümmelbach and Staubbach, Lauterbrunnen; Reichenbach, near Meiringen; falls in the Ticino valleys) or emerge from a dark enclosed gorge (Trient gorge, Valais; Medel gorge, Disentis). The floor of the main valley does not fall in a regular gradient but in stages or "steps". The drop between one step and another may be no more than a few metres, but is usually several hundred metres. The head of the valley is frequently a cirque enclosed by high rock walls.

Almost all the larger Alpine valleys have *lakes* near the foot of the mountains. Essentially these are merely elongated basins within the valley, such as the 38 km (24 miles) long Lake Lucerne which is a section of the Reuss valley. The bottom of the lake frequently goes down almost to sea-level; in Lake Maggiore, indeed, to considerably below sea-level. Smaller lakes are found right up to the highest stages in the valleys; sometimes, as on the Engstligenalp, they have been filled up by rock and soil and are now pastureland. The lakes were originally formed either by glacier action during the Ice Age or by a sinking of the mountain mass after the formation of the valleys which reversed the gradient at the mouth of a valley, thus damming the river and creating a lake.

The Swiss lakes, like the mountains, have become popular holiday areas, providing visitors with bases from which they can make excursions into the mountains, the Mittelland and the towns; bathing is possible in most Swiss lakes. Switzerland has a total of 1484 natural lakes, the two largest of which, Lake Geneva and Lake Constance, are shared respectively with France and with Germany and Austria. In addition there are 44 man-made lakes, created for the purpose of producing

Lake Lugano (Ticino)

hydroelectric power, which contribute to the beauty of the landscape in many areas. The largest of these is the Sihlsee in the canton of Schwyz (11 sq. km – 4 sq. miles); and the Grande-Dixence dam in the canton of Valais is the highest gravity dam in the world (285 m – 935 feet).

Switzerland has none of the plateau-like high mountain regions found, for example, in Scandinavia. The various valley systems, each usually meeting on the summit ridge with a corresponding system on the other side, are separated by sharp ridges of variegated profile. The main rock mass is broken up by *Kare* – corries formed on the flanks of the ridge

Geographical Regions of Switzerland

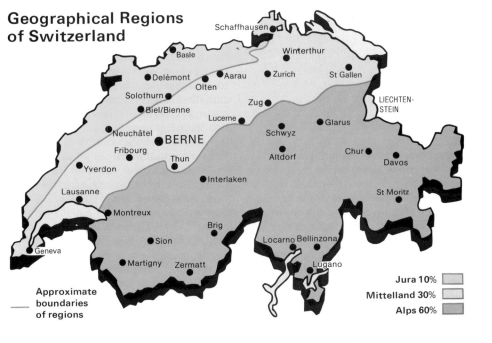

Jura 10%
Mittelland 30%
Alps 60%

Approximate boundaries of regions

Glacier on the Dammastock (central Switzerland)

by small glaciers – into jagged arêtes and rugged towers and pinnacles. Where two corries meet on opposite sides of the ridge they form a breach in the summit line (Lücke, Joch, Furka, Fuorcla) between the towering peaks on either side.

Most of the *high peaks* are pyramids of crystalline rock with sharply defined edges, their varying form reflected in a variety of designations such as Horn, Stock, Dent, Aiguille, Piz, Becca, Poncione, etc. The rugged forms of the mountains are shaped not only by the action of rain and snow but by the daily variation in temperature, which has a particularly destructive effect at the highest altitudes. During the day the rock is heated by the sun and then sharply chilled during the night. In consequence the St Gotthard group, for example, is riven by deep clefts, and many ridges and summits are formed only of loosely bedded blocks, buttresses and tabular formations.

The differences in height between individual peaks in a group appear greater from below than they are in reality: there are only a few giant peaks which stand out from the rest, dominating the landscape. From a high viewpoint, on the other hand, hundreds of peaks fit together into a total picture: at these altitudes the view extends to distances at which differences in height of a few hundred metres are of little significance. Only the very highest peaks, including Mont Blanc, Monte Rosa, the

Weisshorn, the Finsteraarhorn and Bernina, rise commandingly above the mass of mountains which appear to sink down from these few giants.

The geographical centre of the Swiss Alps is the St Gotthard massif, the water-tower of Europe, with the sources of the Rhine, the Rhône, the Reuss and the Ticino. The highest peaks in the Alps, however, are to be found in Valais, the Bernese Oberland and Grisons.

The numerous *passes* in the Alps have since time immemorial provided means of passage through the mountains. During the Ice Age the sea of ice reached up to heights of over 2000 m (6562 feet) in the interior of the Alps, and consequently the glaciers were able here and there to gouge out a passage over the summit ridges and to enlarge it into a broad saddle. The ice-smoothed ridges of rock, the little lakes of clear dark water and the jagged peaks, unaffected by ice action, which rise above them give the St Gotthard, Bernina, Grimsel and other passes an atmosphere of Arctic desolation. Many of the Alpine passes have a long history, which in some cases goes back to Roman times. The San Bernardino pass (Chur-Bellinzona) is almost always open throughout the winter. A drive over one of the great Alpine passes in good weather is a tremendous experience; and with the excellently maintained pass roads day trips are possible over many passes. In winter (November to May or June) many passes are closed. The Swiss Alps can be traversed from east to west by way of the Oberalp and Furka passes, via Andermatt; and the journey from Chur into Valais takes only a few hours, either by road or by rail.

The original sea of ice which many millennia ago covered the whole of the Mittelland and filled the Alpine valleys almost to the summit ridge of the mountains has left behind it about 140 *glaciers*, some of them steadily retreating, others still growing. The total area of all the Swiss glaciers is 1556 sq. km (601 sq. miles). The three largest are in Valais – the Aletsch glacier (area 117·5 sq. km (45 sq. miles), length 23·6 km (15 miles) – the longest in Europe), the Gorner glacier at Zermatt (area 63·7 sq. km (25 sq. miles), length 14·5 km (9 miles)) and the Fliesch glacier (area 39 sq. km (15 sq. miles), length 14·7 km (9 miles)). The great majority of glaciers, however, are no more than a few dozen square kilometres in area.

At altitudes of 3000 m (9843 feet) and above the snow is largely permanent, since in the low air temperatures prevailing at these altitudes there is little melting. The layers of new snow change into the thinner but more compact layers, called "firn" or "névé", which in turn, under the weight of successive annual falls, becomes granular (but still stratified) glacier ice. The snow-line (the lower boundary of perpetual snow) lies between 3200 and 2500 m (10,499 and 8202 feet). The firn accumulates particularly at the heads of the highest valleys, where hundreds of metres of firn and ice may build up, forming the origin of the glaciers in the proper sense. Particularly characteristic of Switzerland are the "valley glaciers", some of which extend over several "steps" in the valley and may reach down almost to the 1000 m (3281 feet) mark (Lower Grindelwald Glacier). Most of these glaciers, however, end at heights of between 1500 and 2000 m (4922 and 6562 feet), although they reach down to more than 1000 m (3281 feet) below the snow-line. More numerous than the valley glaciers, however, are the "mountainside glaciers" or "corrie glaciers" (*Hanggletscher, Kargletscher*) – glaciers occupying hollows in the mountainside which are known as "corries". On warm summer days parts of these overhanging glaciers frequently break off and thunder down into the valley in the form of avalanches.

Variations in the rate of movement in the glaciers (the central part having the fastest pace, up to 200 m (656 feet) a year) lead to the formation of crevasses, which open and close according to the pulling action or the pressure of the ice. At the steeper places the glacier is broken up by large deep transverse crevasses which

The principal Mountains, Lakes and Rivers

transform it into a chaos of vertical ice walls and towers, known by the Savoyard term *sérac*. Where the bed of the glacier becomes wider, on the other hand, longitudinal crevasses open up. Wide glaciers of this kind may bear the designation of Eismeer ("sea of ice"). Such glaciers are usually flanked by lateral crevasses formed by friction against the sides of the valley, which frequently impede access to or return from the glacier. The rock debris which falls into the crevasses is carried down with the stones from the firn area to the melting tip of the glacier, where it emerges together with the ground moraine, material abraded by the movement of the glacier and splintered fragments of the rock bed. Still more rock debris is carried down by the moraines proper which run down the edges, and often also the middle, of the glacier. All this detritus eventually goes to form the horseshoe-shaped terminal moraine or is carried farther down by the melt-water.

Snow is also carried down from the mountains by avalanches. In winter these take the form of dry "dust avalanches" generated by wind; in spring come the real avalanches, in which compact masses of ice break away and hurtle down into the valley. In the steep-sided transverse valleys of the Reuss and the Aare and in the Valais Alps great masses of avalanche snow can still be seen on the valley floor in summer, covered with stones and reddish earth and with the foaming mountain stream running through them in a tunnel. The protective measures taken against avalanches (barriers, walls, lines of posts, belts of trees) can be seen particularly in the Upper Valais, in the Bedretto valley, on the St Gotthard railway and on the Albula railway at Bergün.

The unique panorama of the Swiss Alps is shaped by two dozen peaks over 4000 m (13,124 feet), all first climbed between 1811 (Jungfrau, 4158 m – 13,642 feet) and 1865 (Matterhorn, 4478 m – 14,692 feet), and some 70 mountains rising to over 3000 m (9843 feet). With three-fifths of its area occupied by mountains, Switzerland ranks as Europe's "No. 2 Alpine state", first place being taken by Austria, where the Alps cover more than two-thirds of the country.

Climate

Climatically Switzerland lies in a region of transition. The northern part of the country, outside the Alps, lies in the temperate Central European zone with prevailing west winds and shows a gradual transition from a maritime climate in the west to a more continental climate in the east. The Alps form an important climatic barrier between north and south. In Ticino and much of Grisons strong Mediterranean influences make themselves felt. In the Alps themselves the main factor influencing climate is altitude, but the pattern of relief, with its longitudinal and transverse valleys and numerous sheltered valley basins, also produces many local variations. Other features influencing the climate are the larger lakes, the *föhn* (the warm dry wind which blows down from the Alps in winter) and the temperature reversals which can occur in winter.

In considering **temperature** levels it should be remembered that temperature falls with increasing altitude. The rate of decrease, averaged over the year, is from 0·4 °C (0·7 °F) to 0·5° (0·9°) per 100 m (328 feet); in January it is from 0·04° (0·07°) to 0·5° (0·9°), in July from 0·5° (0·9°) to 0·7° (1·26°) per 100 m (328 feet). The reason for the lower rate of decrease in winter is the frequently observed *temperature reversal*, when the peaks, rising above the low cloud cover, are bathed in warm sunshine, while, if the day is calm, cold air and fog build up in the valley bottoms.

The falling off of maritime influences from west to east is reflected in the temperature levels found at Berne

(619 m – 2031 feet), Zurich (569 m – 1867 feet) and St Gallen (664 m – 2179 feet): January mean respectively −1·2° (30°), −2·3° (28°) and −2·8° (27°), with the July mean about the same in all three places (16·5° (61·7°), 16·5° (61·7°) and 16·2° (61·2°)) but the same falling tendency in the annual mean (8·9° (48°), 7·9° (46·2°), 6·8° (44·2°)) and a corresponding increase in the annual temperature range (17·7° (63·8°), 18·8° (65·8°), 19° (66·2°)). On the high tops the maritime influence increases with altitude: thus Pilatus (2068 m – 6785 feet) and Säntis (2500 m – 8203 feet) have annual temperature ranges of only 14·2° (58°) and 13° (55°) (annual 0·3° (33°) and −2·4° (28°), January −6·2° (20·8°) and −8·5° (16·7°), July 8° (46°) and 4·5° (40°)). Examples of temperate lakeside climates are Rorschach (455 m – 1493 feet) on Lake Constance and Vitznau (440 m – 1444 feet) on Lake Lucerne: annual mean 8·6° (47°) and 9° (48°), January mean 1° (34°) and 1·8° (35°), July mean 16·5° (62°) and 16·5° (62°), annual range 15·5° (60°) and 14·7° (58°). Particularly favoured are Basle (343 m – 1125 feet), at the SE end of the Upper Rhine plain, and Geneva (439 m – 1440 feet), the most south-westerly town of any size in Switzerland, with annual means of 10·1° (50°) and 10·3° (51°) (January 1·2° (34°) and 2° (36°), July 18·5° (65°) and 19° (66°)). South of the Alps, Lugano (276 m – 906 feet) has the highest annual mean (12·0° (54°)) and Locarno-Muralto (239 m – 784 feet) the highest January mean (3·5° (38°)); at both places the July mean is 21·3° (70°). The favoured situation enjoyed, particularly in winter, by resorts on mountain terraces or summits as compared with places in the valleys below can be seen by comparing Sierre (573 m – 1880 feet) in the deeply

indented Rhône valley with Montana (1453 m – 4467 feet) in the mountains above, or Chur (633 m – 2077 feet) in the Rhine valley with Arosa (1865 m – 6119 feet): January mean at Sierre −1·5° (29·3°), at Montana −2° (28·4°) (a temperature decrease of 0·04° (0·07°) per 100 m (328 feet)), annual range 20·5° (69°) and 16° (61°)); January mean at Chur −1·5° (29·3°), at Arosa −4° (24·8°) (annual range 17·8° (64°) and 15·2° (59°)). Davos, St Moritz and Pontresina have similarly favourable winter climates.

In northern Switzerland a periodic rise in temperature is brought about by the wind known as the *föhn*. This occurs during a period of low pressure north of the Alps, when the air is sucked up from south of the Alps to the summit ridge, accompanied by the formation of clouds and heavy rain, and then falls down into the valleys as a warm dry wind, raising the temperature by about 1° (34°) for every 100 m (328 feet).

Precipitation (rain and snow) is distributed over the year in Switzerland as in the rest of Central Europe. It is particularly abundant in summer, reaching a maximum in June or July, more rarely in August. Mediterranean influences produce a maximum in October at many places in Ticino and south-eastern Valais and at Geneva; some places in the Rhône valley (Martigny, Montana, Leukerbad) have their maximum in December. The lowest precipitation is usually in February (January in Ticino, Val Bregaglia, the Engadine, Berne, Murten and other places, June in some parts of the Rhône valley). In northern Switzerland and the Mittelland the level of precipitation rises sharply from February to June and then falls again almost as sharply from June, July or August (e.g. Basle – January and February each 42 mm (1·6 inches), June 97 mm (3·8 inches), December 45 mm (1·8 inches)); elsewhere, particularly on the windward side of the Jura and near the fringes of the Alps, the variation is less marked (La Chaux-de-Fonds 96 mm (3·8 inches) in February, 138 mm (5·4 inches) in June and October; Guttannen, near Meiringen, 115 mm (4·5 inches) in

February, 170 mm (6·7 inches) in August)). Precipitation rises sharply from the plain areas to the mountains, but is relatively low in the Rhône valley, enclosed within high mountain chains, and on the terraces above the valley, as well as in the Engadine.

To illustrate the pattern of precipitation the following examples may be helpful:
1. Geneva (439 m – 1440 feet) 636 mm (25 inches), for Montreux (408 m – 1339 feet) 1058 mm (41·7 inches), Rochers de Naye (1986 m – 6516 feet) 2565 mm (101 inches).
2. Basle (343 m – 1125 feet) 815 mm (32·1 inches), Berne (619 m – 2031 feet) 974 mm (38·3 inches), for Interlaken (568 m – 1864 feet) 1209 mm (47·6 inches), Grimsel hospice (1962 m – 6437 feet) 2070 mm (81·5 inches).
3. Schaffhausen (451 m – 1480 feet) 865 mm (34·1 inches), Zurich (569 m – 1867 feet) 1105 mm (43·5 inches), Zug (429 m – 1408 feet) 1217 mm (47·9 inches), for Schwyz (567 m – 1860 feet) 1756 mm (69·1 inches), Rigi (1775 m – 5824 feet) 2115 mm (83·3 inches), Pilatus (2068 m – 6785 feet) 2300 mm (90·6 inches).
4. Rorschach (455 m – 1493 feet) 1128 mm (44·4 inches), St Gallen (664 m – 2179 feet) 1329 mm (52·3 inches), Säntis (2500 m – 8203 feet) 2875 mm (113·2 inches).
5. Sierre (573 m – 1880 feet) 579 mm (22·8 inches), Grächen (1629 m – 5345 feet) 562 mm (22·1 inches) (lowest figure in Switzerland), Zermatt (1610 m – 5282 feet) 710 mm (28 inches), Pontresina (1805 m – 5922 feet) 815 mm (32·1 inches).
6. Bellinzona (237 m – 778 feet) 1589 mm (62·6 inches), for Lugano (276 m – 906 feet) 1725 mm (67·9 inches), Locarno-Muralto (239 m – 784 feet) 1890 mm (74·4 inches), St Gotthard (2096 m – 6877 feet) 2285 mm (90 inches). In spite of its high level of precipitation, which comes mainly in the form of heavy but relatively short showers of rain (frequently at night), the canton of Ticino records very high figures for hours of sunshine.

Plant and Animal Life

The **plants** of Switzerland are abundant and varied. From the subtropical warmth of Lake Lugano to the snow-clad regions of the High Alps. Switzerland has areas belonging to every zone of plant life in Europe. Particularly notable for its variety of form and splendour of colour is the *Alpine plant life* of Switzerland, which contrives to exist and to flourish in the most rigorous climatic conditions, with temperatures which may rise to 40 °C (104 °F) during the day and freeze hard when the rocks cool down at night. Among the species are rhododendron, gentian, Alpine pansy, primula, globe-flower, silver thistle, soldanella, martagon lily, Alpine aster, edelweiss, Alpine poppy,

glacier buttercup and a variety of saxifrages.

Protected Plants

Of Switzerland's more than 3000 flowering plants and ferns 160 are fully or partially protected by law. A federal law provides for the protection of plants and their habitat, but the executive regulations are the responsibility of the cantons, since the plants vary from area to area. Fully protected plants may not be picked or uprooted; in the case of partially protected plants picking is permitted within reasonable limits, but such plants or flowers may not be sold or supplied commercially.

On account of their rarity the following plants are **fully protected** throughout Switzerland: hart's tongue fern, bristly shield fern, Braun's shield fern, maidenhair fern, Venus's hair fern, ostrich fern, shrubby horsetail, Monte Baldo sedge, snake-root knotgrass, white asphodel, martagon lily, fire lily (both sub-species), fritillary, tulips, dog's tooth violet, summer snowflake, Siberian iris, gladioli, orchids (except early purple, spotted, broad-leaved, vanilla and fragrant orchids), lychnis, wild pink, glacial pink, Cheddar pink, water-lilies, paeony, Alpine columbine, Alpine larkspur, Alpine anemone, pasque flower, pheasant's eye, Alpine poppy, orange poppy, Wulfen's houseleek, burning bush, auricula, downy mezereon, Alpine mezereon, Alpine eryngo, Alpine androsace, Alpine thrift, dwarf scorpion-grass, dragonhead, wormwood (all small Alpine species).

The *Schweizerischer Bund für Naturschutz* (Swiss Association for the Protection of Nature), Wartenbergstrasse 22, CH-4502 Basle, tel. (061) 42 74 42, has published four posters showing the 70 fully protected species.

Rhododendrons

The **animal life** of Switzerland is very similar to that of other Central European countries. The country's stock of game includes some 110,000 roedeer, 70,000 chamois, 20,000 red deer, 9000 ibexes and 100 recently established sika deer from Asia. Stocks of pheasants, hares and partridges are released every year. Marmots are to be found all over the Alps.

Protected Animals

The following species are protected by federal law: hedgehog, beaver, brown bear, otter, wild cat, lynx, ibex, black grouse, capercaillie, hazel hen, eagles, falcons, owls, nutcracker, jackdaw, Alpine chough, turtledoves and rock doves, swans, curlew, black-tailed godwit, sandpipers, rails (except the coot), snow finch and numerous less common species.

Regulations on *shooting* and *fishing* vary from canton to canton. More than half the cantons issue individual shooting licences (some 20,000 of which are in force); the others lease particular areas to shooting clubs.

The height limits for plants, animals and human settlement vary according to climatic conditions. In the northern Alps vines are grown in certain areas up to 550 m (1805 feet), and above this is the zone of deciduous forest, which in these

areas can be regarded also as the highest level of agricultural use of the land. In favourable situations the beech grows at levels of 1500 m (4922 feet) or over; and this is also the height reached by permanent human settlements, mostly small villages, which are more commonly found on the sheltered fringes of the valley floor than on hillsides or hill terraces. The growing of corn, which was once practised in these areas with rather meagre results, was almost completely abandoned in the 19th century. In consequence increased attention has been given to the flower-spangled pastures and the fruit-trees which grow to around 900 m (2953 feet).

The next zone, 1300 to 1700 or 1800 m (4265 to 5578 or 5906 feet), is dominated by coniferous forest, with patches of mountain pasture, which is mown in summer, in the clearings. Deciduous trees are represented by the beautiful maples which grow around the log huts and barns of the mountain-dwellers.

At altitudes between 1600 and 1700 m (5250 and 5578 feet) the dense forest ceases, and only the sturdiest spruces and stone pines survive in proud isolation. The last outposts of the forest are alders and mountain pines. The lower-growing plants flourish in the summer warmth of the soil, the tough short-stemmed species form a vigorous mantle of turf. This is the real *Alp*, the mountain pasture to which the stock is brought in summer and on which the herdsmen have their characteristic huts. Higher still there are only meagre strips of grass between the areas of scree and the rocky crags. Then

Marmot

the patches of firn and the remains of avalanches become increasingly numerous, and between 2800 and 3000 m (9187 and 9843 feet) the snow-line is reached. But even in the zone of perpetual snow plant life does not completely disappear. The glacier buttercup is found at heights of over 3000 m (9843 feet), and even on the high tops lichen cover the sunny rock faces with their patterns of colour.

In Valais and the Engadine all these various zones reach unusually high, thanks to the favoured climate of these areas as a result of the upthrust of the mountain masses and to the warm and dry conditions in their sheltered valleys.

In these areas there are still cornfields as well as pastureland, and, exceptionally, rye and potatoes are grown as high as 1900 m (6234 feet) (Chandolin).

In Ticino vines are grown on stone and timber frameworks up to a height of 600 m (1969 feet). Early flowering almonds and peaches and chestnuts are cultivated up to 1000 m (3281 feet). Above this is a zone of spruce, larch and stone pine; then, as on the north side of the Alps, the mountain pastures begin at 1800 m (5906 feet) and the snow at 2800 m (9187 feet).

The **Swiss National Park**, in the canton of Grisons, is a federal plant and animal reserve with an area of 169 sq. km (65 sq. miles): see p. 236.

Population

The historical development of Switzerland, in the course of which influences from the neighbouring areas of German, French and Italian culture mingled with survivals from the Roman and pre-Roman periods, is reflected in the composition and characteristics of its population.

A striking indication of the heterogenous population structure is the multilingual character of the country. The present-day population of Switzerland is 6·4 million, of whom 5·5 million are natives and 0·9 million foreigners. Some three-quarters of

the Swiss speak German, a fifth French, 4% Italian and 1% Romansh or Rhaeto-Romanic. All four languages are recognised for official purposes throughout the country.

Although in schools and in correspondence in the German-speaking parts of the country standard German is used, with the occasional form peculiar to Switzerland, the spoken language is a quite distinctive tongue, **Schwyzerdütsch** ("Swiss German"), derived from the old Alemannic (West Germanic) language and diversified into a series of local and regional dialects. The use of Schwyzerdütsch is deliberately cultivated, and on radio and television, and even in the political and military fields, it is strongly preferred in speech to standard German at every level including the highest.

Languages of Switzerland

German
French
Italian
Romansh

— Linguistic boundaries

The Swiss forms of **French** (in western Switzerland or *Suisse Romande*) and **Italian** (in the canton of Ticino and some valleys in Grisons) differ only slightly – mainly in intonation – from standard French and Italian. A notable feature of Swiss French (as of Belgian and Canadian French) is the divergent formation of certain numbers (70=*septante* instead of *soixante-dix*, 80=*huitante* or *octante* instead of *quatre-vingts*, 90=*nonante* instead of *quatre-vingt-dix*).

Rhaeto-Romanic or **Romansh**, a language derived from Vulgar Latin which is spoken in a number of dialectal forms in Grisons, has been officially recognised since 1938 as an independent language. The main dialects of Romansh are *Surselvian*, *Sutselvian* and the forms spoken in *Unterhalbstein*, *Oberhalbstein*, *Oberengadin* and *Unterengadin* (the Upper and Lower Engadine).

Another result of differing development in the various parts of the country is the diverse pattern of religious belief. Over the country as a whole there are broadly equal numbers of Roman Catholics and Protestants (professing the form of Protestantism established in Switzerland by Zwingli and Calvin), but there are wide regional variations: see table on p. 8.

In Switzerland as in other countries the flight from the land has become a problem in recent years. Although even the largest cities remain of reasonable size (Zurich 369,000, Basle 180,000, Geneva 151,000, Berne 141,000), half the total population now live in towns of 10,000 inhabitants or more.

The overall population density is 153 inhabitants per sq. km (395 per sq. mile). The most densely populated part of the country is the Mittelland (250 to the sq. km (648 per sq. mile)), while in the Alpine regions, for obvious geographical regions, the density is very low (about 30 to the sq. km (78 per sq. mile)).

Since population growth has not kept pace with economic development Switzerland has had to bring in foreign labour, mainly from Italy and Spain. The Referendum of 1974, which was intended to limit the proportion of foreigners has already failed.

The law of 1980 passed by the Swiss National Council creates a new legal position in Swiss foreign policy. It weakens the argument that foreigners were disadvantaged and makes new regulations for the period during which seasonal workers may stay in the country. In 1981 the so-called Mitenand Initiative, which had as its aim an improvement in the position of foreigners working in Switzerland, suffered defeat after a referendum set up for the purpose.

Government and Society

It may at first appear surprising to an outsider that a state which has developed out of a medley of different ethnic groups should have become the very symbol of stability and harmony; but on closer observation it will be seen that the Swiss communes, the cantons and the Confederation as a whole owe their democratic strength to this very diversity and to the preservation of a federal structure which has eschewed the centralisation of authority. An essential element in Swiss attitudes, too, is the proverbial neutrality of Switzerland, stemming from the Peace of Paris of November 1815.

Extensive rights of self-government, practical participation in the reaching of political decisions and the basic human rights and freedoms are the foundations of Swiss democracy.

The federal constitution of 1848 converted the previous federation of states into a single federal state with a common postal service, army, legislature and judiciary and without any customs or commercial barriers. The new form of union was approved by all the then existing cantons.

The smallest unit in the administrative structure is the **commune** (German *Gemeinde*), of which there are over 3000. They are independent bodies which settle their own budgets and fix their own taxes. The communal or municipal councils are directly elected, usually for a four-year term.

Since 1 January 1979, with the establishment of the new canton of Jura, Switzerland has had 23 **cantons** (26 including the half-cantons: see pp. 8 and 9, whose independence (sovereignty) is enshrined in the constitution. They are real states with their own

Meeting of Landsgemeinde, Appenzell

constitutions, legislatures, executives and judiciaries. Legislative power rests with the people or with a parliament elected by them (Great Council, Cantonal Council, Provincial Council). The executive is responsible to the cantonal government, the members of which change annually.

In the cantons of Appenzell, Glarus and Unterwalden the cantonal assembly (*Landsgemeinde*) still meets annually in the open air to vote on matters concerning the canton.

The cantons are incorporated in the **Confederation** (German *Schweizerische Eidgenossenschaft* or *Bund*), which has a two-chamber legislature, the *Federal Assembly* (German *Bundesversammlung*, French *Assemblée Fédérale*), consisting of the *National Council* (*Nationalrat, Conseil National*), which represents the people, and the *Council of States* (*Ständerat, Conseil des Etats*), composed of representatives of the cantons. The 200 seats in the National Council are distributed among the cantons in proportion to population, with a minimum of one seat for each canton or half-canton. The Council of States has 46 members, two from each canton. The decisions of the Federal Assembly come into effect only after both chambers have approved them by a majority vote.

Executive power is in the hands of the **Federal Council** (*Bundesrat, Conseil Fédéral*), consisting of seven members elected by a joint meeting of both chambers of the Federal Assembly for a four-year term. In the selection of members regard is had to the interests of linguistic, ethnic and geographical minorities. No canton may have more than one member of the Council.

The *Federal President* is chosen from among the members of the Federal Council and holds office for a year, during which he continues to be responsible for his ministerial department. The Federal Council renders an account of its activity annually to the Federal Assembly.

Every Swiss elector (from the age of 20) is entitled to participate in the affairs of his commune in virtue of the basic rights guaranteed by the constitution – equality before the law, freedom of conscience and religious belief, freedom of establishment, freedom of the press, freedom of association and freedom of trade.

The people of Switzerland can exert an important degree of influence on national policy through the mechanisms of the **referendum** and the **initiative**. A referendum can be called for by a petition with a minimum of 30,000 signatures. For an initiative (a proposal for legislation, which may extend to amending the constitution) 100,000 signatures are required.

The **federal army** is a militia based on universal military service between the ages of 20 and 50. After serving their time members of the forces keep their equipment (including weapons) at home and must take part in periodic shooting practice and put in an annual period of training. There is no provision for performing civilian service in place of military service.

A relic of earlier centuries when many Swiss took service with other states is the **Swiss Guard** which still serves as the Papal guard in the Vatican City of Rome.

Numerous *international organisations* have their headquarters in neutral Switzerland. Geneva is the seat, for example, of the International Red Cross, founded by Henri Dunant in 1863, and of the International Labour Office and the World Health Organisation. Geneva is also the European headquarters of the United Nations, although Switzerland itself is not a member of that organisation. It is, however, a member of the European Free Trade Association (EFTA), the Council of Europe and the Organisation for Economic Cooperation and Development (OECD). Since 1977 Switzerland has had a free trade agreement with the European Community.

Education and Science

"Head, heart and hand" were the three elements identified by the Swiss educationalist Johann Heinrich Pestalozzi (1746–1827) as requiring training; and the objectives which he set out so clearly not only influenced the development of the Swiss school system but also aroused wide international interest – forming the basis, for example, of Wilhelm von Humboldt's reform of the Prussian educational system in 1810.

During the early medieval period the main centres of education and culture were the episcopal sees (Sion, Chur, Geneva, Lausanne, Basle; Konstanz, now in Germany) from the 6th c. onwards, followed later by the monastic houses (St-Maurice, St Gallen; Reichenau, in Germany). At the height of the Middle Ages the cultural importance of the towns increased. Powerful new impulses came from the Councils of Constance (1414–18) and Basle (1431–39). Basle was also the centre of Swiss humanism, and Erasmus was active here between 1521 and 1529. The humanists were the first to show an awareness of national identity. The Reformers Ulrich Zwingli (1484–1531) in Zurich and Jean Calvin (1509–64) in Geneva gave fresh stimulus to intellectual and religious life in Switzerland. Later the Enlightenment directed the main currents of thought, in Switzerland as in other countries, towards the exact sciences.

Education was long in reaching the broad mass of the population. In the early days it was in the hands of the Church, and the ability to read and write was until the High Middle Ages a privilege reserved for a small élite. The need for a wide expansion of basic education came to the fore only at the Reformation and Counter-Reformation, with the vigorous new impulses which they gave to human thought. Then in the 18th and 19th centuries the Swiss educational system advanced and developed under the influence of Jean-Jacques Rousseau (1712–78) and the great educationalist Johann Heinrich Pestalozzi

The Swiss constitution assigns the main responsibility for education to the cantons, which share it with the communes. A constitutional amendment making education a joint responsibility of the Confederation and the cantons was rejected by a national referendum in 1972. Only vocational education falls within the competence of the Confederation.

Switzerland also has some 350 *private schools* and *boarding-schools*, many of them with an international reputation. Some of these schools – like some of the Swiss universities – run special holiday courses for both Swiss and foreign students.

Higher education is also, in general, the responsibility of the cantons. The Confederation is responsible only for the Federal Colleges of Technology in Zurich (opened 1855) and Lausanne (opened in 1853 as a private college for road and civil engineers and taken over by the Confederation in 1968). There are cantonal *universities* at Basle (founded 1460), Berne (1834), Fribourg (1889), Geneva (1873), Lausanne (1890), Neuchâtel (1909) and Zurich (1833), together with the School of Economic and Social Sciences in St Gallen (1899). There is also a private Theological Faculty (1878) in Lucerne.

The massive increase in student numbers has strained the resources of the cantons responsible for universities and has led these cantons to put forward claims for federal aid and for contributions from other cantons related to the number of students from those cantons. In addition to the universities there are numbers of technical colleges throughout the country. The total number of students at Swiss higher educational establishments is some 60,000, including 10,000 foreign students.

As the OECD noted in a report, expenditure on research in Switzerland is well above the international average. There is a well-established division of function between public and private agencies, with the state accepting responsibility for the running of academic institutions, while the main costs of research, particularly in the natural sciences, are borne by the private sector. The state is thus unable to exert any major influence on research and development. Here, as in other fields of Swiss life, the trend towards decentralisation can be observed.

Paracelsus, *Theophrastus Bombastus von Hohenheim* (1493–1541)
Natural scientist and theosopher; founder of the modern science of medicine; understanding of the chemical and physical basis of living matter.

Gesner, *Konrad von* (1516–65)
Doctor, scientist and philologist; works on botany, zoology and literary history.

Bürgi, *Joost* (1552–1632)
Mathematician and astronomer; calculated one of the earliest logarithmic tables.

Bernoulli, *Jakob* (1654–1705)
Mathematician and physician; integral and differential calculus.

Amann, *Johann Konrad* (1669–1724)
Doctor and teacher of the deaf and dumb; established the basic method of teaching the deaf and dumb.

Scheuchzer, *Johann Jakob* (1672–1733)
Natural scientist, founder of the study of the Swiss mountains; description of fossil plants and animals.

Euler, *Leonhard* (1707–83)
Mathematician, astronomer and physicist; first analytical solution of mechanical problems, Euler formulas, wave theory of light, development of differential calculus.

Haller, *Albrecht von* (1708–77)
Doctor, natural scientist and poet; works on botany, anatomy and physiology.

Sulzer, *Johann Georg* (1720–79)
Mathematician, philosopher and aesthetician; taught mathematics in Berlin under Frederick the Great.

De Saussure, *Horace-Bénédict* (1740–99)
Scientist; taught in Geneva at the age of 22; studies on the Alps.

Escher von der Linth, *Hans Konrad* (1767–1823)
Statesman, geologist and hydraulic engineer; regularised the course of the River Linth.

Fischer, *Johann Conrad* (1773–1854)
Metallurgist; first production of cast steel in Europe.

De Candolle, *Augustin-Pyrame* (1778–1841)
Botanist; system of classification of plants.

Bodmer, *Johann Georg* (1786–1864)
Engineer and inventor; textile machinery, steam-engines, locomotives, machine tools, etc.

Agassiz, *Louis* (1807–73)
Scientist; theory of Ice Age, research on fossil fishes.

Heer, *Oswald* (1809–83)
Botanist and entomologist; works on the fauna of Switzerland.

Nestlé, *Henry* (1814–90)
Pharmacist and chemist; laid the foundations of the Nestlé business with his powdered milk factory.

Naegeli, *Karl Wilhelm von* (1817–91)
Botanist; work on morphology and physiology of plants, on systematics and heredity.

Riggenbach, *Nikolaus* (1817–99)
Engineer; construction of rack-railways (Rigi, etc.).

Rütimeyer, *Ludwig* (1825–95)
Zoologist and geographer; research on prehistoric fauna of Switzerland.

Balmer, *Johann Jakob* (1825–98)
Physicist; fundamental work on modern spectroscopy.

Favre, *Louis* (1826–79)
Engineer; construction of St Gotthard tunnel.

Kocher, *Emil Theodor* (1841–1917)
Surgeon; Nobel Prize 1910.

Maggi, *Julius* (1846–1912)
Industrialist; development of food concentrates and convenience foods.

Landolt, *E.* (1846–1926)
Ophthalmologist; discovery of Landolt bodies (histological formations in retina).

Forel, *Auguste-Henri* (1848–1931)
Psychiatrist and entomologist; discovery of origin of auditory nerves, studies on insects, control of alcoholism.

De Saussure, *Ferdinand* (1857–1913)
Philologist; fundamental work on phonetics of the Indo-European languages.

Guillaume, *Charles-Edouard* (1861–1938)
Physicist and chemist; discovery of anomalies in nickel-steel alloys; Nobel Prize for physics 1920.

Werner, *Alfred* (1866–1919)
Chemist; Nobel Prize 1913.

Jung, *Carl Gustav* (1875–1961)
Psychologist; development of analytical psychology.

Ritz, *Walter* (1878–1909)
Physicist and mathematician; fundamental contributions to modern spectral theory.

Amman, *Othmar Hermann* (1879–1965)
Engineer; builder of George Washington Bridge, New York.

Niehans, *Paul* (1882–1971)
Doctor; development of cellular therapy.

Piccard, *Auguste* (1884–1962)
Physicist and meteorologist; stratospheric flight in balloon to 16,940 m (55,580 feet), research in ocean depths.

Le Corbusier (*Charles-Edouard Jeanneret,* 1887–1965)
Painter and architect; founder of modern architecture.

Scherrer, *Paul* (1890–1969)
Chemist and physicist; research on structure of crystals with X-rays.

Müller, *Paul Hermann* (1899–1965)
Chemist; inventor of DDT; Nobel Prize 1948.

History

Finds of *Palaeolithic* material in caves (e.g. below the Ebenalp in the canton of Appenzell and at the Schweizerbild crag in the canton of Schaffhausen) point to the presence of primeval hunters in Switzerland during the Ice Age. In the *Neolithic* period the commonest form of settlement was the lake village built on piles, first identified in Lake Zurich in 1853.

In the *Bronze Age* (*c*. 2500–800 B.C.) and *Early Iron Age* the area of human settlement expands, and cultural links are established with the neighbouring regions to the north and east.

About 400 B.C. the CELTS advance into Switzerland from the west. The period takes its name from a Celtic island stronghold at **La Tène**, near Neuchâtel. The HELVETII, a Celtic tribe, seek to move into southern France but are defeated and driven back by Julius Caesar at Bibracte in Burgundy (58 B.C.).

The Romans' campaigns of conquest over the Alps (first roads over the passes) are completed with the subjugation of Rhaetia, in the western Alpine region, in 15 B.C. There follows a period of peaceful colonisation under Roman rule, which comes to an end only about A.D. 455 with the incursion of the ALEMANNI into northern Switzerland and the settlement of the BURGUNDIANS (who soon become Romanised) in western Switzerland.

About the turn of the 5th and 6th centuries the Alemanni and Burgundians are conquered by the Franks. Switzerland now becomes part of the Frankish kingdom and, under Charlemagne, of the Holy Roman Empire. After the fall of the Frankish Empire the noble families of Zähringen, Habsburg, Kyburg and Savoy establish separate domains which seek to achieve independence.

1098 Count *Berthold of Zähringen* is granted the imperial protectorate (Reichsvogtei) of Zurich.

1218 After the death of the last of the Zähringen family, *Berthold V*, the Zähringen possessions fall to the Counts of Kyburg. Berne, Zurich and Solothurn become free Imperial cities.

1231 Uri, an area of importance through its situation on the St Gotthard route, is granted "immediacy" (Reichsunmittelbarkeit: self-government in direct subordination to the Emperor) by Henry, son of the Emperor Frederick II.

1240 Schwyz is also granted immediacy by the Emperor Frederick II.

1264–91 Count *Rudolf III of Habsburg* (German Emperor from 1273) wins power over large parts of Switzerland. Strict rule by governors from outside the area.

1291 After Rudolf's death the forest cantons of URI, SCHWYZ and UNTERWALDEN form the **Perpetual Alliance** which is the germ of the Confederation. By the "Rütli Oath" they promise mutual assistance in the struggle for their traditional rights and against the dynastic policy of the Habsburgs, with the object of maintaining the self-government and independent jurisdiction of the rural communities and towns and achieving the status of immediacy. When the Habsburgs try to bring Switzerland back under Austrian rule in 1439 the Confederation breaks free of the Empire.

The meeting on the Rütli, Wilhelm Tell's great feat and the destruction of the castles of Zwing-Uri, Sarnen, etc., are vividly described in the "Federal Chronicle" of Obwalden – an account which is probably based on historical facts, though we possess it only in a much revised version of about 1470. Later chroniclers, in particular Ägidius Tschudi of Glarus (*c*. 1570), who did not possess the text of the 1291 alliance, erroneously dated the rising to the reign of King Albrecht (1307–08). Schiller's play "Wilhelm Tell" (1804) was based on Tschudi's account.

1315 The forest cantons defeat the Habsburg forces in the Battle of Morgarten, south of the Ägerisee (15 November). – Renewal of the Perpetual Alliance at Brunnen (9 December).

1332–53 The Confederation is enlarged by the admission of the Habsburg territory of LUCERNE in 1332, the Imperial city of ZURICH in 1351, GLARUS and ZUG in 1352 and the Imperial city of BERNE in 1353. The Confederation now has eight members. – Tension with Austria leads to further fighting.

1367–1471 Formation of the **Three Leagues** in Rhaetia. To defend themselves against oppression by the nobility the common people form a series of alliances – the "League of God's House" (1367), in which the lead is taken by the Chur church; the "Upper League" or "Grey League" (1395, renewed at Truns in 1424); and the "League of the Ten Jurisdictions" (1436). In 1471, at Vazerol, they become the "Three Perpetual Leagues".

1386 Victory of the Confederates at Sempach over Duke Leopold III of Austria, who is killed in the battle (9 July). Sacrificial death of *Arnold von Winkelried*.

1338 Defeat of the Austrians at Näfels in the canton of Glarus.

1394 In the "Twenty Years Peace" Austria renounces its claims to sovereignty over the forest cantons, Lucerne, Glarus and Zug.

1403–74 By adroit tactics the Confederation gains additional territories, some of them (Appenzell, Aargau, Thurgau and a number of places between the Walensee and Lake Constance) as "associated territories" which are not admitted to the Confederation but form defensive alliances with it.

Valais breaks away from Savoy and becomes an associated territory. – The Confederation acquires influence in Upper Ticino. – St Gallen, Schaffhausen and Mulhouse in Alsace ask for the Confederation's protection.

1436–50 In the *Old Zurich War*, which arises out of a conflict between Zurich and Schwyz, the Confederation once again finds itself involved in a confrontation with Austria, which now seeks the support of France. On 26 August 1444 the Confederates are defeated at St Jakob an der Birs by an army of French mercenaries (the "Armagnacs"), but defeat the Austrians at Ragaz in 1446. Under a peace treaty in 1450 they retain possession of the territories they hold.

1474 Peace with Austria (March), which once again recognises the territories held by the Confederates. – Alliance between the Confederates and Louis XI of France (October). – Both agreements are directed against Charles the Bold of Burgundy, who is seeking to encircle the Confederates in the Black Forest and Upper Rhine area and in Vaud.

The treaty with France is the first agreement for the provision of Swiss mercenary troops to a foreign power – the beginning of a practice which later, in the Milanese campaigns, leads to Swiss fighting Swiss.

1476–77 Burgundian War, in which the Confederation fights on the side of Austria against Charles the Bold. Charles marches on Berne, but is defeated by the Swiss at Grandson (2 March 1476) and Murten (22 June 1476) and is killed in the Battle of Nancy on 15 January 1477. Swiss mercenaries fighting for Duke René of Lorraine play a considerable part in this victory. Berne and Fribourg acquire territory in Vaud.

1497–98 Grisons enters into a loose association with the Confederation.

1499 Swabian War, in which the Confederation and Grisons are allied against Austria and the Swabian League. – In the Calven defile, near Taufers, a Grisons force of 6000 men defeats an Austrian army of 12,000 (22 May). – Victory of the Confederates over the Swabian League at Dornach (22 July). – In the Peace of Basle (22 September) the Confederation in effect breaks free of the Holy Roman Empire.

1501 BASLE and SCHAFFHAUSEN join the Confederation.

After the admission of APPENZELL in 1513 the composition of the Confederation, which now has 13 members, remains unchanged until 1798.

1500–16 Milanese campaigns. The Confederates, originally involved only as mercenaries (with Swiss fighting against Swiss), later take part in the campaigns as an independent power. After the victory won by Francis I of France at Marignano (13–14 September 1515) the Swiss are left in an untenable position and give up mercenary service. The Confederates assert their possession of Ticino, and Grisons holds on to the Valtellina, conquered by them in 1512, retaining it until 1797.

1516 Peace with France (29 November). The Confederates thereafter abandon their role as a belligerent power and declare their complete **neutrality.**

1523–28 The **Reformation** is adopted in Zurich, Schaffhausen, St Gallen, Basle, Berne and Grisons; the four forest cantons, Zug, Fribourg, Solothurn and Valais remain Catholic.

1529 The *First Kappel War,* arising out of religious conflicts, ends in a peace favourable to the Reformed faith.

1531 *Second Kappel War.* Defeat and death of Zwingli in the Battle of Kappel, north of Zug, against the original (Catholic) cantons (11 October). The peace treaty gives each territory the right to choose its own faith.

1536 Berne is appealed to for help by Geneva, under threat from Savoy. The Bernese conquer the Savoyard territory of Vaud and impose the Reformed faith. The Confederation thus attains approximately the same area as present-day Switzerland.

The theologian Jean **Calvin** (1509–64), having fled from Paris, pursues his work as a Reformer in Geneva. The town becomes the great centre of Calvinism, which then spreads to France, the Netherlands, Brandenburg, Hungary, Britain and North America. (The French term *Huguenot* is a corruption of *Eidgenosse,* "Confederate".)

1548–86 The *Counter-Reformation* and the exacerbation of religious differences lead to an internal split within the Confederation. *Ludwig Pfyffer* (1524–94) makes Lucerne the centre of the Catholic territories.

1618–48 Switzerland remains neutral in the **Thirty Years War.** Only Grisons, disturbed by party strife, is involved in the conflict, since the strategic importance of the Alpine passes within its territory draws Austrian and Spanish forces and a French army commanded by the Duc de Rohan into the area.

18th century. – The patchwork of separate units that makes up the Confederation remains, politically and constitutionally, in the pattern achieved at the time of the Milanese campaigns. The lack of any all-embracing state authority is reflected in the continuing religious, party-political and social tensions. At the same time, however, there is a flowering of intellectual life, linked with that of the neighbouring countries of France and Germany (Haller, Bodmer, Breitinger, Lavater, Pestalozzi, Rousseau, etc.).

1790–97 The influence of the French Revolution makes itself felt: risings against aristocratic and patrician rule. Loss of the Valtellina (1797).

1798 France occupies the whole of Switzerland, dissolves the old Confederation and established the **Helvetian Republic,** a unified state on the French model. Geneva, the Jura and the former free Imperial city of Mulhouse (in Swiss hands since 1515) are annexed to France.

1803 Under the *Mediation Acts* (mainly the work of Napoleon) Switzerland again becomes a confederation of equal cantons, now 19 in number, with the addition of AARGAU, ST GALLEN, GRISONS, TICINO, THURGAU and VAUD to the previous 13. Geneva and Valais remain French. – Napoleon constructs the road over the Simplon pass.

1814–15 At the **Congress of Vienna** the number of cantons is increased to 22 by the addition of GENEVA, VALAIS and NEUCHÂTEL. – Under the Bundesvertrag (Federal Agreement) a new constitution is introduced: the 22 cantons are now recognised as sovereign bodies (August 1815). Peace of Paris (November 1815): the perpetual *neutrality* of Switzerland is guaranteed. Customs-free zones established on the frontiers of Geneva.

1830–39 Liberal movement of "regeneration" in many cantons; attempt to secure a liberal revision of the federal constitution frustrated by conservative resistance.

1845 The Catholic and conservative cantons of Lucerne, Uri, Schwyz, Unterwalden, Zug, Fribourg and Valais form a separate federation, the Sonderbund.

1848 Adoption, by national referendum, of a new federal constitution: the federation of states becomes a **federal state.**

1864 *Geneva Convention.* On the initiative of *Henri Dunant* (1828–1910) an international agreement on the conduct of war on land is signed in Geneva (22 August: formation of Red Cross).

1874 Revision of the federal constitution to increase both the unity of the Confederation and the independence of the cantons. The federal government is assigned responsibility for foreign policy, the army and economic affairs (currency, railways, postal services) and partial responsibility for justice.

1914–18 On the outbreak of the **First World War** the Swiss army is mobilised, but the country's neutrality is fully preserved. During the war Switzerland takes in wounded and sick prisoners of war from both sides.

1920 First meeting of the **League of Nations** in Geneva (15 May). Switzerland becomes a member of the League after a national referendum (16 May).

1939–45 During the **Second World War** Switzerland again remains neutral, but gives aid to those of any nation who need it.

1948 Switzerland becomes a member of UNESCO.

1950 Switzerland becomes a member of the Organisation for European Economic Cooperation (OEEC).

1960 Switzerland joins the European Free Trade Association (EFTA).

1963 Switzerland becomes the 17th member of the Council of Europe.

1971 Women are granted the right to vote and stand for election in federal elections.

1972 Switzerland signs a free trade agreement with the European Community.

1974–75 Regional referenda on the establishment of a new canton of Jura.

1976 A proposal for workers' participation in industrial management is rejected in a referendum.

1978 Economic agreement with the Soviet Union (12 January). – The formation of the new canton of Jura is approved in a national referendum (24 September).

1979 The new canton of JURA becomes a member of the Confederation as the *Republique et Canton du Jura* (1 January).

1980 A national referendum rejects a proposal for the separation of church and state. From June confrontation between the Police and young people again becomes more acute, owing to the closing of a youth centre. In Basle and Berne large demonstrations take place (occupation of property, etc.). On 5 September the new 10 mile (16·3 km) long road tunnel through the St Gotthard is opened to traffic.

1981 In a referendum a majority votes for a constitutional measure by which the equality of men and women will be legally established.

1982 Suppression of the autonomous youth centre in Zurich (20 March). The law intended to alleviate the position of foreign citizens is rejected by a plebiscite (6 June).

1984 Pope John Paul II makes a pastoral visit to Switzerland from 11–17 June. By a plebiscite the Principality of Liechtenstein becomes the last country in Europe to give women the vote. Although Franz Joseph II remains the titular head of the Principality, the business of government is transferred in August to his son, Hans Adam. On 2 October a woman is elected for the first time to the Federal Government of Switzerland.

1985 Following a referendum tolls are introduced for motorways (highways) in Switzerland. Foreign visitors as well as Swiss citizens have to pay 30 Swiss francs per annum to use a vehicle up to 3·5 tonnes in weight on the motorways. In September a majority of Swiss citizens resolves to introduce a marriage law, the object of which is to effect a change from a male dominated union to a partnership. The meeting of the US President Reagan and the Soviet Party Chief Gorbachev in Geneva (19–21 November) creates world-wide interest.

The Romans in Helvetia

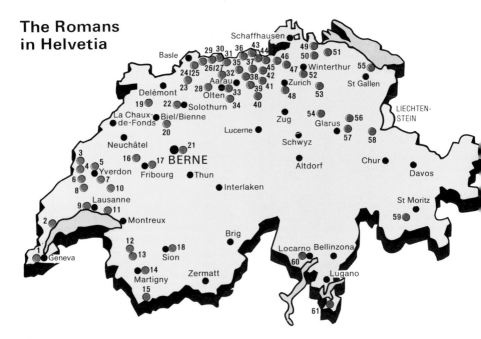

● Roman Remains in Switzerland

1 Geneva *(Genava)*
Town walls, villa; museum

2 Nyon *(Noviodunum)*
Columns; museum

3 Ste-Croix
Roman road

4 Baumes
Columns, altar

5 Yverdon *(Eburodunum)*
Fort; museum

6 Orbe *(Urba)*
Mosaics

7 Ursins
Temple

8 Ferreyres
Kilns

9 Lausanne *(Lousonna)*
Mosaic pavement, remains of fortifications; museum

10 Moudon *(Minnodunum)*
Inscriptions

11 St-Saphorin
Remains of walls, milestone with inscription

12 Massongex *(Tarnaiae)*
Mosaic pavement, inscriptions

13 St-Maurice *(Acaunum)*
Milestone, gateway; museum

Roman columns, Nyon (Lake Geneva)

14 Martigny *(Octodurum)*
Theatre, milestone, remains of columns

15 Great St Bernard *(Summus Poeninus)*
Temple, Roman road; museum

16 Avenches *(Aventicum)*
Theatre, temple, remains of town

17 Fribourg
Mosaic pavement; museum

18 Sion *(Sedunum)*
Milestone, inscriptions; museum

19 Pierre Pertuis *(Petra Pertusa)*
Rock gateway with inscription

20 Studen *(Petinesca)*
Temples, gate tower

21 Berne
Theatre, temples, remains of town; museum

22 Solothurn *(Salodurum)*
Fort; museum, lapidarium

23 Schauenburgerflüe
Temple

24 Liestal
Aqueduct; museum

25 Munzach
Villa, mosaics

26 Augst *(Augusta Raurica)*
Remains of town; museum

27 Kaiseraugst *(Castrum Rauracense)*
Fort

28 Hauenstein
Roman road

29 Pfärichgraben
Watch-tower

30 Bürkli
Remains of fortifications

31 Stelli
Watch-tower

32 Wittnau
Remains of fortifications

33 Olten
Villa, fortifications; museum

34 Zofingen
Mosaic pavement

35 Bözberg
Roman road

36 Schwaderloch
Watch-towers

37 Brugg
Fort; museum

38 Windisch *(Vindonissa)*
Theatre, military camp, aqueduct

39 Lenzburg
Theatre

40 Sarmenstorf
Villa

41 Wettingen
Inscription

42 Baden *(Aquae Helveticae)*
Baths; museum

43 Koblenz
Watch-tower, inscriptions

44 Zurzach *(Tenedo)*
Fort, inscriptions; museum

45 Rümikon
Watch-tower

46 Weiach
Remains of fortifications

47 Seeb
Villa

48 Zurich *(Turicum)*
Remains of fortifications; museum

49 Stein am Rhein
Fort; museum

50 Stuetheien
Villa

51 Pfyn *(Ad Fines)*
Fort

52 Winterthur *(Vitudurum)*
Fort, temple, inscriptions; museum

53 Irgenhausen
Fort

54 Ufenau
Temple

55 Arbon *(Arbor Felix)*
Fort; museum

56 Stralegg
Watch-tower

57 Filzbach
Watch-tower

58 Sargans
Villa

59 Julier (Guglia) pass
Remains of columns

Art and Architecture

The history of Swiss culture is as varied and manifold as the landscape of Switzerland. This region of passage, this land of four languages, has been open at all times to influences from the wider world, and it is not surprising, therefore, to find that its art and architecture in particular show affinities with those of the neighbouring countries of Germany, Austria, France and Italy. But these creative impulses operated in both directions, with architects from Ticino and the Italian-speaking Grisons making a major contribution to the development of Baroque architecture in Rome and South Germany in the 16th and 17th centuries and Austrian and South German architects creating the finest Baroque buildings in Switzerland in the 17th and 18th centuries.

Accordingly Switzerland's numerous works of art and architecture show no distinctively national style; and the country's federal structure, the absence of any princely house to act as patrons and other factors inhibited the development of any major national centre of artistic creation.

The art and culture of Switzerland are predominantly centred on the commune, the valley or the region. With few exceptions (Ferdinand Hodler) Swiss artists of international reputation have established their fame outside Switzerland, for example the Ticinese architects Francesco Borromini and Carlo Maderna (who designed the nave of St Peter's in Rome), Alberto Giacometti and Le Corbusier, who opened up new dimensions of sculpture and architecture while working in Rome, and Othmar Ammann, the engineer who built the George Washington Bridge in New York.

Implements and animal bones dating from the **Palaeolithic** period were found in the Wildkirchli cave on the Ebenalp, and the prehistoric material in the excellent All Saints Museum in Schaffhausen points to occupation during the Ice Age.

The **Neolithic** period (c. 3000 B.C.) is represented in Switzerland by traces of the *Cortaillod culture* and *Michelsberg culture* (belonging to the Western European cultural sphere), probably left by a pre-Indo-European population which already practised arable and stock farming (tulip-shaped cups, mostly black undecorated ware).

In the **Bronze Age** (from c. 2500 B.C.) the Alpine regions, particularly in Grisons, were settled up to altitudes of 2000 m (6562 feet). In sheltered situations on the shores of lakes (e.g. Lake Zurich) pile-dwellings have been found. In the Bronze Age and **Early Iron Age** (the **Hallstatt** culture) there is evidence of cultural links with the regions to the north and east. The Iron Age inhabitants of Grisons and Ticino were the RHAETIANS, while central Switzerland was settled from about 450 B.C. by CELTS. They developed

the Late Iron Age **La Tène** culture (c. 450–50 B.C.), named after the type site at La Tène on the Lac de Neuchâtel. The characteristic feature of La Tène art is its ornament, partly vegetable and partly abstract, and showing strong Etruscan influence. Highly stylised human and animal heads are also found. – In the Late La Tène period art degenerated completely and the decoration of plane surfaces was abandoned.

In 15 B.C. the **Romans** completed their conquest of Rhaetia. Thereafter major Roman settlements were established in many places, particularly in western Switzerland.

Avenches *(Aventicum)*. – The town flourished in the 1st and 2nd centuries A.D. but was destroyed by the Alemanni in 260. Considerable remains survive – a theatre seating 10,000, fragments of the 6 km (4 miles) circuit of walls, the forum baths, the Corinthian column known as the "Cigognier". Finds in local museum.
Lausanne *(Lousonna)*. – Bust of Marcus Aurelius in the Archaeological Museum.
Nyon *(Noviodunum)*. – Columns in the Bourg-de-Rive park.
Geneva *(Genava)*.
St-Maurice *(Acaunum)*.
Martigny *(Octodurum)*. – Remains of a Roman amphitheatre.
Sion *(Sedunum)*.
Windisch *(Vindonissa)*. – Roman camp and remains of an amphitheatre seating 10,000. Rich collection of material in Vindonissa Museum, Brugg.
Kaiseraugst *(Augusta Raurica)*. – Large theatre and remains of several temples, a basilica and an amphitheatre. Museum.

Notable remains of *Roman pass roads* can be seen on the Julier (Guglia), Septimer (Sett), Splügen and Great St Bernard passes.

On the Rütli

With the beginning of the **great migrations** the ALEMANNI penetrated into northern Switzerland in 455, and the BURGUNDIANS, who became Romanised at a very early stage, settled in the south-west (linguistic boundary between French and German). By 534 the FRANKS had conquered the whole country.

During the medieval period the French-, German- and Italian-speaking parts of Switzerland pursued their separate development, influenced respectively by France, Germany and Italy but nevertheless retaining a certain cultural independence.

CHRISTIANITY now became the main cultural force, particularly in Valais and Grisons.

Examples of **pre-Carolingian** architecture can be seen in a number of places, particularly at St-Maurice, Disentis (a Benedictine abbey founded about 720 by St Sigisbert) and Chur (8th century crypt in the 12th century church of St Lucius; St Martin's church, 8th century).

The **Carolingian** period is represented by an abundance of buildings, including the choir of St John's church at Moutier (Grisons). The church, originally founded in 780, was rebuilt in Late Gothic style at the end of the 15th century. It is notable for its frescoes, some of them revealed only about 1950 (now in the National Museum, Zurich), which give some impression of what the original abbey church of St Gallen must have been like.

Also of the Carolingian period are the octagonal baptistery of Riva San Vitale on Lake Lugano; parts of the Augustinian abbey of St-Maurice in Valais, the oldest monastic house in Switzerland, founded about 515 (4th century chapel, devastated by the Saracens about 940; famous treasury, with Merovingian works of art including reliquaries, an Oriental ewer enamelled in gold and a Roman vessel of sardonyx; 11th century Romanesque tower); and St Martin's church at Zillis (Early Romanesque nave and tower, Late Gothic choir; unique painted ceiling of 1140, a magnificent example of very early figural painting).

The Benedictine abbey of Einsiedeln was founded in 934 on the site of the hermitage of St Meinrad (murdered in 861). The library contains very beautiful illuminated manuscripts.

The Benedictine abbey of St Gallen was founded by St Othmar in 719 on the site of a hermitage established by the Irish missionary monk St Gall or Gallus about 612. In the 9th century it rose to considerable economic prosperity and enjoyed a great cultural flowering, with a school and a library which made it one of the leading intellectual centres of the Alpine region (Ekkehart, Notker Balbulus, Notker Labeo).

About 820 the famous **plan of the abbey of St Gallen** (now in the abbey library at St Gallen) was drawn up. This shows the detailed layout of a medieval monastic establishment with a double-choired church and a complete range of conventual buildings. The plan is not to scale, and probably represents the proposed layout for the 9th century abbey, none of which has survived.

The abbey library, with its magnificent interior architecture, contains a rich store of valuable manuscripts and incunabula (ivory book-covers by Tutilo, *c.* 900; "Psalterium Aureum", 9th century; Folchard Psalter, *c.* 860-70; "Casus Monasterii Sancti Galli", by Ekkehart IV, 11th century; 13th century manuscript of "Nibelungenlied", etc.).

The Benedictine abbey on the island of Reichenau, founded in 724, was one of the leading cultural centres of the early medieval period from the 9th to the 11th century (miniatures, wall-painting), the influence of which was particularly strong in northern Switzerland. A notable establishment in this area was the Benedictine abbey of All Saints at Schaffhausen. The minster (1087-1150), a pillared basilica with a single tower, a flat roof and (since its restoration) a sparsely decorated interior, is an outstanding example of **Romanesque** architecture (12th century cloister with elegant arcades). All Saints was a daughter house of the Cluniac abbey of Hirsau in the Black Forest.

Of the Benedictine abbey of Muri (Aargau), founded by the Habsburgs in 1027 (dissolved 1841, largely destroyed by fire in 1889), parts of the east and west ends and the Romanesque three-aisled crypt survive. The "Acta Murensia" are informative on the early period of the abbey, and a Middle High German Easter play has also been preserved.

About the year 1000 a small Romanesque church showing Lombard influence, with fine frescoes, was built at Spiez; and the churches at Amsoldingen and Romain-môtier also date from the 10th to the 11th century. The church of St-Pierre-de-Clages (11th–12th century), in Valais, is one of the finest Romanesque churches in Switzerland.

The Benedictine abbey of Engelberg in the canton of Obwalden, founded about 1120 (church and conventual buildings rebuilt by Kaspar Moosbrugger in 1730–37 after a fire), became noted in the time of Abbot Frowin (1143–78) for its scriptorium and school of painters. The abbey library (open to men only) contains valuable illuminated manuscripts, in-cunabula and miniatures.

Also of the 12th century are the two fine Romanesque churches of Giornico, San Nicolao (three-aisled crypt) and Santa Maria di Castello, and part of the château of Neuchâtel (west wing). The Gross-münster in Zurich was built between the 11th and 13th centuries (fine double crypt of 1100; nave stripped of its interior decoration at the Reformation).

Other examples of Romanesque architec-ture are the 11th century three-aisled pillared basilican church (fine porch) of the Benedictine abbey of Payerne (foun-ded during the Cluniac reform movement of the 10th century, dissolved in 1536); the 12th century church of St-Jean, a pillared basilica with Carolingian work in the nave and a Gothic choir, in the picturesque little town of Grandson; the 12th century collegiate church and the Tour de la Reine Berthe, a relic of the church of St-Martin, in St-Imier; and the Cistercian abbey of Hauterive (Fribourg), showing Burgundian influence, which was founded by Guillaume de Glâne about 1138 and dissolved in 1848 (the church in Romanesque-Gothic tran-sitional style, *c*. 1160; Romanesque cloister; fine stained glass of 1332).

Other examples of the Romanesque-Gothic transitional style of the 12th and 13th centuries are the cathedral of Chur (crypt 6th and 12th centuries); the five-aisled minster of Basle, which dates in its oldest parts from the 9th century and was replaced at the end of the 12th century by a new structure mingling the most varied influences with earlier Ottonian architec-tural traditions (remodelled in Gothic style 1356; richly carved Romanesque capitals; remains of Late Romanesque pavements and frescoes; Late Gothic choir-stalls of the late 14th century); and the church of the former Cistercian abbey of Kappel on the River Albis (13th–14th century).

Impressive examples of Romanesque *sculpture* can be seen in the Grossmünster of Zurich (seated figure of Charlemagne in crypt; copy on south tower). Notable also are the richly varied capitals in the choir of the church of Notre-Dame de Valère (12th–13th century) in Sion, which is built on Roman foundations. The famous St Gallus doorway in the minster in Basle (originally on the west front, now in the north transept: 1170–1200), the earliest major figured doorway in German-speaking territory, has rich sculptured decoration, including figures of the Four Evangelists and the Wise and Foolish Virgins and representations of Christ as Judge of the world and the Last Judg-ment in the tympanum. It appears to have been based on Italian and Provençal models, like the south doorway of the conventual church (12th–13th century) in the little town of St-Ursanne.

The National Museum in Zurich has a large collection of Romanesque sculpture in wood.

During the **Gothic** period the art and architecture of the towns begins to develop, though the appeal of the build-ings of this period frequently lies in their picturesque effect rather than in their architectural quality.

Throughout the 15th century Switzerland remained wide open to influences from outside the country. Only Basle, with its University (founded in 1460), evolved a distinctive intellectual culture of its own. The altar by Konrad Witz in Geneva (1444), with the first representation of the mountains as seen by an artist, marks the beginning of landscape-painting.

The political successes of the Con-federates in the Burgundian wars also created the basis for a distinctively Swiss development of art and architecture. Each town now took on a character of its own, building the town halls, gates and for-tifications still to be seen in Murten, Romont, Solothurn, Schaffhausen and many other towns. The finest urban ensembles which have survived from this period are Berne and Fribourg, the charm of which is enhanced by their situation on peninsulas rising high above river valleys.

Notable among *Gothic churches* is the church of the Cistercian abbey of Wettingen, founded in 1227 and dissolved in 1841 (richly carved choir-stalls of 1604; fine 16th–17th century stained glass in cloister). To this period also belongs the cathedral of Notre-Dame in Lausanne, in Early Burgundian Gothic style, with five towers, fine sculptured decoration in the Apostles' Choir (13th century) and on the main doorway (16th century) and a rose window containing beautiful 13th century stained glass. The cathedral of St-Pierre in Geneva, now a Protestant church, has notable capitals in the Romanesque-Gothic transitional style and beautiful Late Gothic choir-stalls.

The minster in Basle was rebuilt in Gothic style in 1356 after an earthquake. The west front, between St George's tower (1428) and St Martin's tower (1500), is decorated with magnificent 13th century sculpture, including a figure of the Emperor Henry II holding a model of the church. The double cloister, built on Romanesque foundations, dates from the 15th century. – The rathaus of Basle, in Late Burgundian Gothic style with a brightly painted façade and arcades, was built between 1504 and 1521.

The parish church of Winterthur was built between 1264 and 1515, though the towers date only from the 17th and 18th centuries. The cathedral of St-Nicolas in Fribourg, with a tower 76 m (249 feet) high, dates from the 14th and 15th centuries and has magnificent sculpture of that period above the principal doorway (Apostles; the Angelic Salutation; Last Judgment in tympanum); it contains a beautiful choir screen and choir-stalls, stained glass and a famous organ.

The Late Gothic minster of Berne, a three-aisled pillared basilica without transepts, was begun in 1421 to the design of the Ulm architect M. Ensinger. The richly decorated west doorway has a Last Judgment, with numerous figures, in the tympanum. The side walls are embellished with frescoes of 1501 (restored); the nave and choir have reticulated vaulting with fine roof bosses bearing coats of arms; choir-stalls (1523) in Renaissance style; beautiful stained glass by Hans Acker (1441–50). – The Rathaus of Berne was built in 1406–16 in Late Burgundian Gothic style. The clock tower with its astronomical clock of 1530 dates from the 15th century but has undergone much subsequent rebuilding. Also of great interest are the old streets and lanes of Berne with their charming fountains, including the Banner-Carrier fountain of 1542 and the Ogre fountain of 1540.

The cathedral of Notre-Dame-du-Glarier in Sion was rebuilt in the 15th century; it contains fine Gothic tombs. The beautiful Gothic parish church of Moudon has fine choir-stalls of 1502, and the town also possesses three castles, the Tour de Broye (12th century), the château de Rochefort (1595) and the château de Billens (1677).

Other buildings showing the influence of French models are the Gothic castles of western Switzerland – at Champvent (a massive 13th century stronghold), Grandson (Vufflens-le-Château, one of the most imposing castles in Switzerland, 14th–15th century), Lucens (a massive structure of the 15th–16th century, with a 13th century round tower, now the Conan Doyle Museum) and Chillon, near Montreux (founded in 9th or 10th century, present structure 13th century; rock-cut dungeons, large church, court hall, living quarters, etc.: cf. Byron's poem "The Prisoner of Chillon"). At Sion is the ruined Château de Tourbillon, once an episcopal stronghold (built 1294, burned down 1788).

The only structures in southern Switzerland which can be compared with these massive fortresses are the three castles of Bellinzona, built in their present form by the Dukes of Milan in the 15th century and in 1503 given the names of the three original cantons of Uri, Schwyz and Unterwalden. In German Switzerland the castles are on a considerably more modest scale, for example the Habsburg (*c.* 1020), ancestral seat of the Austrian Imperial House, or the Kyburg, which first appears in the records in the 11th century (restored 1925).

The finest examples of *Gothic sculpture* are to be seen in the cathedrals of

Lausanne and Fribourg and in the collegiate church of Notre-Dame-de-Valère in Sion, a three-aisled pillared basilica of the 12th–13th century with its original interior furnishings, a carved wood altar of the 16th century and a 15th century organ still in working order. In the collegiate church in Neuchâtel is the tomb of the Counts of Neuchâtel (1372) with its 15 painted effigies, the most magnificent Gothic funerary monument in Switzerland.

The beautiful *stained glass* produced in Switzerland during this period has unfortunately survived only in a very small number of examples – e.g. in the minster in Berne, the choir of the Gothic conventual church of Königsfelden (14th century) and the cloister of the Cistercian abbey of Wettingen. A secular form of stained glass is represented by the *Schweizerscheiben* (stained glass panels) in the National Museum in Zurich.

After the defeat of Charles the Bold of Burgundy the enhanced political standing of the Confederation was matched by a greater degree of independence in art and architecture. The towns now increased in importance, and secular building played a much more prominent part in comparison with religious building. These developments coincided with the coming of the **Renaissance** to Switzerland.

The architecture of this period can be seen at Murten, with its completely preserved circuit of walls, its timber wall-walk, its arcades and its picturesque fountains; at Romont, also with handsome walls and towers; at Solothurn; and in Fribourg, Berne, Lucerne, Schaffhausen and many other towns.

The *decorative arts* flourished during this period, which has left some beautifully decorated interiors – e.g. in the house built by Georg Supersaxo in Sion in 1505 (panelled banqueting hall with carved and painted ceiling), the richly appointed palace built for Colonel Freuler in Näfels in 1642–47 (panelled rooms, Winterthur stoves: now the Glarus Cantonal Museum) and the Ital-Reding house in Schwyz, and above all in the canton of Grisons.

Many churches were equipped with new choir-stalls and pulpits at this period,

for example at Muri, Wettingen and Beromünster.

The *painting* of the 15th and 16th centuries ranks as one of the high points of Swiss art. A particularly notable figure who worked at Basle in the first half of the 15th century was *Konrad* **Witz** (1400–44), one of the great masters of Late Gothic painting. He broke away from the "soft" style and became the first artist to depict real landscapes (Lake Geneva) and was the founder of Swiss landscape-painting ("St Christopher", *c.* 1435; altar of 1444 in Museum of Art and History, Geneva). Of his 20 surviving panel-paintings 13 belong to the Basle "Mirror of Salvation" altar (*c.* 1435).

Urs Graf (1485–1527), who also worked as a goldsmith, depicts the life of the landsknechts (mercenary soldiers), which he knew from personal observation, in vigorous and often overcharged drawings and woodcuts (Museum of Art, Basle).

Niklaus Manuel, known as *Deutsch* (1484–1530), was a draughtsman of high quality who also depicted scenes from the life of the landsknechts in a rather Mannerist style, as well as altarpieces, mythological pictures and frescoes.

Like Niklaus Manuel-Deutsch, *Hans Leu the Younger* (1490–1531) was one of the early Swiss landscape-painters, showing affinities with the work of the Danube school. *Hans Asper* (1499–1571) was another painter who also produced woodcuts.

Jost Amman (1539–91), who worked mainly in Nuremberg, produced an extraordinary number of woodcuts covering the whole range of subject-matter then in vogue (historical, military and hunting scenes; armorials; illustrations to rhymes by Hans Sachs).

Tobias Stimmer (1539–84) was one of the leading Swiss painters of the Late Renaissance (portraits; vividly coloured paintings on the façade of the Haus zum Ritter in Schaffhausen (1485), the originals of which are now in All Saints Museum).

Hans Fries (1465–1520), working mainly in Basle, Fribourg and Berne, is known principally for his altarpieces, painted in glowing colours. The Berne and Zurich *Masters of the Carnation* also devoted themselves mainly to religious themes.

Hans Holbein the Younger (1497–1543), a native of Augsburg, worked for many years in Basle (Public Art Collection, Basle). In scale and variety his output can be compared only with that of Dürer, and as a portrait-painter he is unequalled. Most of his wall-paintings have, unfortunately, been lost. His woodcuts are also of the highest quality ("Dance of Death", *c.* 1525).

Bernardino Luini painted frescoes in the church of Santa Maria degli Angioli in Lugano in 1529. The cathedral of San Lorenzo in that town, with a marble façade of about 1515, is an early example of Renaissance architecture in Ticino.

After the end of the Thirty Years War there was a great burst of building activity – mainly by the Catholic Church, then concentrating all its resources on the Counter-Reformation, but also by princes and great nobles.

During the **Baroque** period no huge and imposing secular buildings were erected in Switzerland, but mainly fine town houses and small country houses, particularly around Berne, Basle, Geneva, Solothurn and Fribourg. Almost all the house fronts in Berne were rebuilt at this time.

Protestant churches built during this period included a number of small country churches, the church of the Holy Ghost, in French Baroque style, in the Bubenbergplatz in Berne (1726–29), the temple de la Fusterie in Geneva and the temple in Neuchâtel. The parish church in Yverdon was built in 1755–57 (the Town Hall in 1769–73), a beautiful church at Morges in 1776.

The *Catholic Church* did a great deal of building in the first half of the 18th century, and most of the monastic houses were rebuilt or altered. In contrast to Protestant building, however, it followed Italian rather than French models: cathedral of St Ursen, Solothurn (1763–73) and Jesuit churches in Solothurn (1680–89) and Lucerne (1666–77; Rococo interior 1750). The South German type of Baroque hall-church is also found, for example in the church (built 1705, with a sumptuous interior) of the Benedictine abbey of Rheinau (founded in the 9th century, dissolved in 1862).

From the 1680s onwards three families of architects belonging to the *Vorarlberg school* – the Beers, the Thumbs and the Moosbruggers – developed an indigenous form of Baroque which displaced the Italian style. Several generations of these families worked in Switzerland. *Peter Thumb* (1681–1766) and *Johann Michael Beer* built the three-aisled hall-church of St Gallen (1755–66), and Peter Thumb was also responsible for the famous abbey library at St Gallen (1758–61), which already shows strong Rococo influence. The principal work of *Kaspar Moosbrugger* (1656–1723) was the rebuilding of the abbey and church of Einsiedeln (1704–23), a masterpiece of Baroque form and boldly contrasting spatial sequences. The interior of the church was the work of two Bavarian brothers, *Cosmas Damian* and *Egid Quirin Asam*, who had been trained in Rome but cast off the influence of Roman Baroque and created theatrical architectural forms which sought to achieve an indissoluble unity between space, light, colour and plastic and architectural movement.

The Ticinese architects *Carlo* **Maderna** or *Maderno* (1556–1629: nave of St Peter's, Rome) and *Carlo Fontana* (1624–1714) were among the great masters of the Roman Baroque.

Although in the first half of the 18th century sculpture, painting and decorative art were completely subordinate to architecture, towards the end of the century they achieved a greater degree of independence.

The poet and painter *Salomon Gessner* (1730–88) illustrated his famous "Idylls" with delicately etched vignettes, and painted small gouaches and watercolours which depicted mythological scenes and landscapes.

Jean-Etienne **Liotard** (1720–89), who worked in many different countries, produced charming pastels. *Anton Graff* (1736–1813) was exclusively a portrait-painter, notable particularly for his likenesses of leading intellectual figures of the day (Bodmer, Bürger, Gellert, Lessing, Schiller, Wieland, etc.).

Johann Heinrich Füssli (1741–1825), known in Britain as *Henry Fuseli*, worked first in Italy and later became Keeper of the Royal Academy in London. He specialised in the dramatically Baroque and the fantastically horrific ("The Nightmare").

The **Neo-classical** period is represented in Swiss architecture by handsome mansions built for the wealthy middle classes (e.g. Talacker, Zurich), the church at Heiden and the Town Hall of Altdorf (1805–08).

An important Neo-classical painter was **Angelica Kauffman** (1741–1807), most of whose work was on mythological, allegorical and religious themes. She was a prominent member of the group of German artists working in Rome, and produced a famous portrait of Goethe. *Johann August Nahl the Younger*, a pupil of the German artist J. H. Tischbein, painted mythological and historical pictures.

During the second half of the 19th century the Swiss government commissioned a number of major buildings, including the massive Bundeshaus in Berne, in the style known as **Historicism** or **Neo-Renaissance**, with the Bundesterrasse rising 50 m (164 feet) above the Aare on its huge retaining walls, the Swiss National Museum in Zurich and various administrative buildings, railway stations, etc.

The *painting* of this period was of higher quality than its architecture. Among painters working in French Switzerland were *Alexandre Calame* (1810–64), noted for his paintings of the mountains, *François Diday* (1802–77) and *Barthélemy Menn* (1815–93); in German Switzerland *Albert Anker* (1831–1910), *Frank Buchser* (1828–90), *Max Buri* (1868–1915), *Hans Sandreuter* (1850–1901: sgraffito work, stained glass, watercolours) and the etcher *Albert Welti* (1862–1912: stained glass in Bundeshaus, Berne, 1901–03).

A painter who exerted wide influence was *Arnold* **Böcklin** (1827–1901), who alternated between the two extremes of gay joie de vivre and profound melancholy ("Island of the Dead").

Giovanni Segantini (1858–99), a native of Trento, painted the mountains of the Upper Engadine (Segantini Museum, St Moritz), but also produced pictures of symbolic content ("The Dead Mothers").

Ferdinand **Hodler** (1835–1918) gave fresh impulses to painting, developing beyond the naturalism of the late 19th century and setting up in sharp opposition to Impressionism. His pictures are characterised by rhythmic tension of attitude, movement and gesture and by their use of colour, often with symbolic intentions. His monumental murals, "Retreat of the Swiss after the Battle of Marignano" and "Departure of the Jena Students, 1813", gave fresh direction to *historical painting* (National Museum, Zurich; Museum of Art, Berne; Museum of Art and History, Geneva).

The Lausanne-born painter and graphic artist *Félix Vallotton* (1865–1925) worked mainly in Paris (landscapes; Art Nouveau).

In the middle of the First World War the *Dadaist* movement was launched in Zurich, where the pacifist Hugo Ball opened the Cabaret Voltaire in 1916 as a meeting-place for Dadaists.

Cuno Amiet (1868–1961) was influenced by the Impressionists and Neo-Impressionists, and also by Gauguin. Other notable painters of this period were *René Auberjonois* (1872–1957), *Augusto Giacometti* (1877–1947), *Heinrich Altherr* (1878–1947), *Alfred Heinrich Pellegrini* (1881–1958) and *Hans Erni* (b. 1909).

The painter and graphic artist *Paul* **Klee** (1879–1940), who had affinities with the Surrealists and was a member of the "Blauer Reiter" group, worked at the Bauhaus in Weimar, Dessau and Düsseldorf. He created an unreal world of form and colour in which things are set in unexpected relationships to one another ("Wedding Procession on Rails"), using thin lines and delicate colour shadings, in a manner reminiscent of children's drawings, to achieve an effect of fragility and sensitivity. His pictures, usually of small size, often have a droll humour and an enigmatic charm ("The Twittering Machine").

Among *sculptors* of this period are *Carl Burckhardt* (1878–1923: "Amazon", 1923), *Hermann Haller* (1880–1950) and *Alexander Zschokke* (b. 1894).

Alberto **Giacometti** (1900–66) sets his metal figures, lean and emaciated as if eaten away by acid, in empty space, thus emphasising their naked vulnerability ("L'Homme qui marche"). His work carries the ideas of "pittura metafisica" a stage further. After 1930 he became associated with the Surrealist movement.

Jean **Tinguely** (b. 1925) has produced major works in the field of kinetic sculpture ("meta-mechanisms" and "machine sculpture" like the huge "Heureka" in Zürichhorn Park) and self-destroying sculpture ("La Vittoria", a golden phallus over 8 m (26 feet) high). Similarly *Bernhard Luginbühl* (b. 1929)

produces the reductio ad absurdum of modern technology in his wittily contrived machines ("C-Figur", 1960).

Among leading Swiss *architects* of the 20th century are *Karl Moser* (1860–1936: St Anthony's church, Basle, 1927), *Adolf Wasserfallen* (b. 1920) and *Jean-Claude Steinegger* (b. 1930). *Max Bill* (b. 1908) was one of the pioneers of modern architecture in Switzerland; he was also a sculptor, producing abstract plastic works. The architect who left his mark on the century, however, was **Le Corbusier** (*Charles-Edouard Jeanneret*, 1887–1965). Trained under Josef Hoffmann and Peter Behrens, he established a new style of housing and a new pattern of urban living in his "unité d'habitation", a form of residential accommodation which went beyond the normal functions of a house, which he criticised as a mere "machine for living in". Almost all his work was done abroad: in Switzerland there are the Immeuble Clarté in Geneva

The Buildings of Switzerland

Swiss domestic buildings show a carefully cherished individuality of style, with differences and contrasts not only between town and country but also between different parts of the country. Common to all Swiss, however, is the idea that in building a family home they are building for more than one generation, so that the house must be a substantial and durable structure.
Swiss towns and villages are notable for their trim and well-kept appearance, and flowers are much in evidence in squares, on fountains and on houses. Town halls and other public buildings, and private houses as well, match the country's high standard of living, and are almost invariably well maintained and cared for.

Many buildings have paintings, either old or modern, on their façades – a practice which was originally a great specialty of the Engadine. In eastern Switzerland projecting oriel windows have long been a popular feature. Many Swiss towns and villages offer attractive pictures of streets and lanes and sometimes whole quarters built in uniform style. The picturesque little town of Stein am Rhein with its old painted façades is particularly notable in this respect.

The strong sense of local awareness found in the small Swiss communities means that there is wide support for the conservation of their architectural heritage.

Perhaps the most distinctive contribution made by Switzerland to European architecture is its varied range of farmhouses and other rural houses, differing widely from region to region. Local styles are determined mainly by climatic conditions and

local needs, but also by a firm attachment to comfort and cosiness. Local differences are reflected principally in the disposition of the masses, the distribution of the living and working quarters and the roof structure.

The Open-Air Museum of Rural Life now in course of development at Ballenberg, near Brienz, is designed to show the variety of house types by selected examples.

In this connection a word may be added on the effects of modern development – sometimes very questionable – on the most popular tourist attractions and resorts in Switzerland. In the late 19th century and the first half of the 20th many Swiss resorts were disfigured by the construction of hotels, sometimes of enormous size; and in more recent times the development of new types of holiday accommodation and "second homes" in the form of blocks of apartments and chalets, as well as numerous camping and caravan sites, has led many of the most popular resorts to expand far beyond their original bounds, to the detriment of the surrounding countryside.

As in other advanced countries, too, there has been a great expansion of the larger cities through industrial and residential development which has combined with new road developments to make increasing demands on land and to change the environment.

There is also controversy over proposals to construct new mountain railways and cableways, which are designed to make remote mountain regions more easily accessible but involve further encroachments on the natural landscape.

Rural House Types

Travellers in the 17th century were already remarking on the handsome houses of the Swiss peasants and the degree of comfort – extraordinarily high by the standards of the day – which they enjoyed.

Every part of Switzerland, indeed almost every valley, has its own distinctive type of house. It is possible, therefore, to mention here only the most important types out of this wide range.

In *Appenzell*, with its relatively high rainfall, the house and farm buildings are brought together under a single roof. The fronts of the houses, built of timber, are frequently broken by continuous rows of windows.

In *north-eastern Switzerland*, a region of deciduous forests, the houses are predominantly half-timbered, with whitewashed panels in the interstices of the framing.

In the *Jura* the houses are massive stone-built structures, broad-based, with saddle roofs which frequently come far down over the walls.

Half-timbered house, Lützelsee (Zurich)

Around Berne and in the *Emmental* the houses are predominantly of timber, with deep hipped roofs. The barn usually adjoins the living quarters.

In the *Bernese Oberland*, as in other mountain regions with large coniferous forests, the "log-cabin" method of building is preferred, the walls being constructed of horizontally laid tree-trunks. The house is separate from the farm buildings and can thus achieve considerable architectural dignity.

Characteristic of *Valais* are its timber-built houses of several storeys with flat gables and stone-built kitchen premises and its store-houses built on piles, with flat stones at the top of the piles to keep rodents out.

In the area of *Lake Geneva* the rear of the house, with deep eaves, faces on to the street.

The houses of the *Engadine* differ sharply from those of other parts of Switzerland, showing both Germanic and Latin influence. The timber core of the house is surrounded by masonry walls, with sgraffito decoration on the façade.

In *Ticino* the houses are very similar to those found over the frontier in Italy. The walls are of undressed stone, the roof (which projects only slightly over the walls) of stone slabs.

Farmhouse, Emmental (Berne)

(1930–32) and the Centre Le Corbusier in Zurich (1966).

Modern architecture in Switzerland finds expression mainly in churches and schools, but also in offices and industrial buildings. Much use is made of glass and steel as building materials.

Of the artists active in Switzerland since the Second World War, representing a variety of trends which run parallel to one another and influence one another, only a brief selection can be mentioned. *Wilfried Moser* (b. 1914) does collages, assemblages and sculpture intended for walking and climbing on. *André Thomkins* (b.

1930: "holograms"), a strikingly original draughtsman, shows affinities with surrealism. *Roland Werro* (b. 1926) creates coloured objects, monochrome bas-reliefs and mobile sculpture. *Christian Megert* (b. 1936) loves mirror constructions and light-kinetic objects, as does *Christian Herdeg* (b. 1952: "light sculpture"). *Karl Gerstner* (b. 1930) creates "colour sound", pictures with gradations of colour in exactly calculated degrees. *Fritz Glarner* works in the field of "relational painting". *Franz Gertsch* (b. 1930), originally belonging to the "peinture naïve" school, is the only Swiss Hyper-Realist. *Peter Travaglini* (b. 1927) is a Pop artist ("Zip-Fastener", 1970), as is *Urs Lüthi* (b. 1947). *Gérald Minkoff* (b. 1937) produces video tapes, and *Alex Sadowsky* experiments with Surrealist and metaphysical films.

Modern Swiss *graphic art* also has considerable achievements to its credit, and Switzerland occupies one of the leading places in the field of commercial art and advertising. Notable among contemporary graphic artists is *Celestino Piatti* (b. 1922), best known for his expressive book-covers.

Switzerland's rich artistic heritage is studied and interpreted by its art historians and other scholars. The Swiss Society of Art History (Gesellschaft für Schweizerische Kunstgeschichte) publishes a regionally arranged inventory of works of art

and architecture in Switzerland, "Die Kunstdenkmäler der Schweiz".

The protection of historical and artistic monuments (*Denkmalpflege*) is the responsibility of the federal and cantonal authorities, with increasing support from the communes and private sources.

A great wealth of material of artistic and historical interest can be seen in numerous museums, large and small, throughout the country, notably in the Swiss National Museum in Zurich, the Museums of Art in Basle, Berne, Geneva and Zurich and in such private galleries as the excellently arranged Oskar Reinhart Collection in Winterthur, the Abegg Foundation in Riggisberg and the Thyssen Collection in Lugano-Castagnola. Increasingly important, too, are the local and regional museums to be found all over Switzerland.

The Swiss Society of Art History publishes a series of monographs, the "Schweizerische Kunstführer", on places of particular interest.

Literature

The earliest literary activity in Switzerland dates back to the Carolingian period, when the abbey of St Gallen (founded in 613) was a centre of intellectual life. Notable figures who worked at St Gallen were *Notker Balbulus* (*c.* 840–912), whose "Gesta Karoli Magni" is one of the finest narrative works of the Middle Ages, and the historian *Ekkehart* (*c.* 980–*c.* 1060).

The period of chivalry is reflected in the works of the epic poet *Hartmann von Aue* (*c.* 1200) and the minnesingers *Johannes Hadlaub* of Zurich (first half of the 14th century) and *Otau de Grandson*.

In the age of humanism *Ägidius (Gilg) Tschudi* of Glarus wrote his "Helvetian Chronicle", which became a standard work. Some leading figures of the Reformation including *Ulrich Zwingli* (1484–1531), were also writers of some note.

Swiss literature reached its full development, however, only in the 18th century. The Bernese poet, doctor and scientist *Albrecht von Haller* (1708–77) wrote a poem, "Die Alpen", contrasting the beauty of the mountains and the natural life of the mountain people with the unhealthy life of the towns. The Geneva-born *Jean-Jacques* **Rousseau** (1712–78), who spent most of his life in France,

was one of the great revolutionary influences of his day, preaching a "return to nature" and preparing the way for the French Revolution with his doctrine of liberty and equality of men. His ideas on politics, education and literature were equally fertile in stimulation, and influenced both the German "Sturm und Drang" period of the 1770s and the French Romantic movement of 50 years later.

Johann Jakob Bodmer (1698–1783) and *Johann Jakob Breitinger* (1701–76), both of Zurich, ran a moral and aesthetic weekly, "Discourse der Mahlern" ("Discourses of the Painters") which influenced the development of German literature. Other Zurich writers whose reputation extended beyond the bounds of Switzerland were the lyric poet, etcher and landscape-painter *Salomon Gessner* (1730–88), *Johann Caspar Lavater* (1741–1801) and *Heinrich* **Pestalozzi** (1746–1827). *Johannes Muller* (1752–1809 of Schaffhausen wrote "History of the Swiss Confederation" which gave Schiller the inspiration for his play "Wilhelm Tell" *Ulrich Bräker* (1735–98) also achieved some reputation abroad with his autobiography, "Life History and Natural Adventures of the Poor Man in Toggenburg".

Western Switzerland produced three of its notable writers during this period in *Germaine de Staël-Holstein*

(1766–1817), born in Paris but descended from an old Geneva family, who became one of the forerunners of the French Romantic movement under the name of **Mme de Staël**; *Benjamin Constant de Rebecque* (1767–1830) of Lausanne; and *Léonard de Sismondi* (1773–1842) of Geneva. From Italian Switzerland there was *Francesco Soave* (1743–1806).

In the 19th century, under the influence of the Romantic movement, national and regional themes came increasingly to the fore. *Jeremias* **Gotthelf** (*Albert Bitzius*, 1797–1854), a native of Murten who became pastor of Lützelflüh, takes a high place in Swiss literature with his simple but profoundly human stories of peasant life.

The writings of *Gottfried* **Keller** (1819–90) and *Conrad Ferdinand* **Meyer** (1825–98), both of Zurich, are an enduring contribution to literature in the German language.

Johanna Spyri (1827–1901), best known for her children's stories ("Heidi"), also wrote short stories and novels on regional themes.

The historian *Jakob Burckhardt* (1818–97), a native of Basle, achieved wide reputation with his works on the history of art. *Carl Spitteler* (1845–1924) of Liestal was awarded the Nobel Prize for literature in 1919.

The outstanding writers in French and Italian were respectively *Charles-Ferdinand Ramuz* (1878–1947), who collaborated with the composer Igor Stravinsky in writing the "Histoire du Soldat", and *Francesco Chiesa* (1871–1973), of Sagno (near Chiasso), who established his place in Italian literature in spite of the fact that his work was deeply rooted in his native Ticino.

The literature of Rhaeto-Romanic Switzerland began with *Conradin de Flugi* about 1845. The most notable Romansh writer is *Giachen Hasper Muoth* (1844–1906), known principally as an epic poet but also of importance as a lyric poet and a philologist.

Two 20th century writers who have gained reputations extending far beyond the frontiers of Switzerland are *Max* **Frisch** of Zurich (b. 1911) and *Friedrich* **Dürrenmatt** of Berne (b. 1921), authors of both novels and plays. Plays such as Frisch's "Andorra" and "Biedermann und die Brandstifter" ("The Fire-Raisers") and Dürrenmatt's "Der Besuch der alten Dame" ("The Visit") and "Die Physiker" ("The Physicists") and novels such as Frisch's "Stiller" and "Mein Name sei Gantenbein" occupy a high place in contemporary German literature.

Carl Jakob Burckhardt of Basle (1891–1974) made a considerable contribution to international understanding by his work as an art historian and essayist.

A number of younger writers, including *Otto F. Walter* (b. 1928), *Adolf Muschg* (b. 1934), *Beat Brechbühl* (b. 1939), *Urs Widmer* (b. 1938), *Gerold Spät* (b. 1939) and *E. Y. Meyer* (actually Peter Meyer, b. 1946), concern themselves with the problems of contemporary life, usually from a critical point of view. *Hansjörg Schneider* (b. 1938) and *Manfred Schwarz* (b. 1932) have made their mark as dramatists. *Jürg Federspiel* (b. 1931) writes tales and novels.

Jacques Chessex (b. 1934), from French-speaking Switzerland, won the French Prix Goncourt in 1973 for his novel "L'Ogre".

In Grisons literature in the Romansh language has made a considerable breakthrough in the 20th century. Of the numerous writers from this part of Switzerland a few may be taken as representative – the traditionalists *Peider Lansel* (1863–1943), *Alexander Lozza* (1880–1953) and *Gian Fontana* (1897–1935) and the more recent *Gian Belsch* (b. 1913), *Tista Murk* (b. 1915) and *Gion Deplazes* (b. 1918).

In recent years *literature in dialect* has developed with fresh vigour in every part of Switzerland.

Switzerland has given asylum to many foreign writers subject to persecution in their own countries on political or racial grounds. The most prominent of the German authors who found a home in Switzerland during the Nazi period were Thomas Mann and Carl Zuckmayer. More recently writers and scientists from the Soviet bloc have found a refuge in Switzerland, notably Alexander Solzhenitsyn from the Soviet Union and Ota Šik from Czechoslovakia.

During the 19th and 20th centuries, too, many composers came to live in Switzerland in order to escape the censorship or persecution to which they were exposed in their own country (Wagner, Stravinsky, Hindemith, etc.).

Switzerland also has a considerable tradition in the minor literary arts. Notable Swiss cabaret artistes include Elsi Attenhofer, Voli Geiler, Walter Morath, Franz Hohler and "Emil" Steinberger; Bernard Haller, from French-speaking Switzerland, has made a name for himself in Paris.

In this connection mention should also be made of the world-famed artiste and clown *Grock* (real name Adrian Wettach, 1880–1959) and the mimes Dimitri, the "clown of Ascona", and the Mummenschanz group.

Music

An independent school of Swiss music first came to the fore in the 19th century. The names of the composers of this period, however, have largely fallen into oblivion. In the early 20th century the belated Romantic *Othmar Schoeck* (1886–1957) was a composer of some quality, and *Willy Burkhard* (1900–55) – not to be confused with *Paul Burkhard* (1911–77), the composer of musicals – made a name for himself.

The leading Swiss composer is *Arthur* **Honegger** (1892–1955), who was born in France, lived for many years as one of the principal members of the Groupe des Six and died there. Among his chief works are five symphonies (including the "Symphonie Liturgique" and "Deliciae Basilenses"), a number of symphonic poems ("Pacific 231", "Rugby"), the scenic oratorios "Judith", "Jeanne d'Arc au Bucher" and "Le Roi David", and an impressive Christmas Cantata, with a final section in which Christmas carols in various European languages are skilfully mingled.

Frank **Martin** (1890–1974), a native of Geneva, was also an exponent of 12-tone music (dodecaphony), and taught for some years at the Cologne Academy of Music. In addition to symphonic music (Concerto for seven wind instruments, strings and drums) he also composed much choral and chamber music.

Another composer of more than regional significance is *Heinrich Sutermeister* (b. 1910), whose opera "Titus Feuerfuchs" received its first performance during the Brussels Exhibition of 1958. *Volkmar Andreae* (1879–1962), who was conductor of the orchestra of the Tonhalle-Gesellschaft from 1906 to 1949, wrote operas and choral works as well as orchestral and chamber music. – *Rolf Liebermann* (b. 1910), from Zurich, was for many years Manager of the Hamburg State Opera and until 1980 Director-General of the Paris Opéra. As a composer he works mainly in the 12-tone technique. – The world-famous oboist *Heinz Holliger* (b. 1939) has also made a name for himself as an avant-garde composer.

Although Switzerland is a relatively small country, it has a remarkable number of good opera companies, orchestras, conductors and soloists. The Zurich Opera is one of the largest and finest opera-houses in German-speaking territory, and the Grand Théâtre in Geneva and the Municipal Theatre in Basle also enjoy a considerable reputation. The best-known orchestras in Switzerland are the Orchestre de la Suisse Romande, the Tonhalle-Orchester of Zurich, the Basle Symphony Orchestra, as well as the chamber orchestras of Basle, Zurich and Lausanne, the Camerata of Berne and the Festival Strings of Lucerne.

Swiss conductors of international reputation include Ernest Ansermet, Paul Sacher, Edmond de Stoutz, August Wenzinger, Silvio Varviso, René Klopfenstein, Charles Dutoit, Armin Jordan, Michel Corboz and Robert Denzler (1892–1972); among instrumentalists there are Heinz Holliger (oboe), Ursula Holliger (harp), Peter-Lukas Graf and Aurèle Nicolet (flute) and Karl Engel and Adrian Aeschbacher (piano).

In addition many musicians from countries all over the world have made Switzerland their home, among them Paul Kletzki (d. 1973), Andor Foldes and Nikita Magaloff.

In the fields of *light music* and *jazz* a considerable number of individual performers and groups have achieved reputation outside Switzerland, such as Teddy Stauffer, Cedric Dumont, Hazy Osterwald, George Gruntz, Pierre Favre Franco and Flavio Ambrosetti, the Tremble Kids jazz group, Vico Torriani and Pepe Lienhard.

The *folk music* of the Alpine regions – yodelling, Kuhreigen (round dances), dance tunes like the ländler, etc. – is popular, and is performed with committed enthusiasm throughout the whole of Switzerland.

Economy

Switzerland is poorly supplied with minerals and raw materials, and accordingly was compelled from an early stage to turn to the processing industries, commerce and the services sector. In these fields it has been so successful that in 1978 it was the richest nation in the world, with a per-capita income of almost $14,000. It has a very low unemployment figure, the number out of work being about the same as the number of vacancies.

In spite of the difficulty of communication in this mountainous land – a handicap for a country so heavily dependent on imports – Switzerland's principal source of income is **industry**, which employs approximately half the working population. This industry, however, is distributed over the country, and Switzerland has none of the industrial concentrations found in Britain, Germany or Belgium. Even industrial focal points like Basle, St Gallen, Zurich, Winterthur and La Chaux-de-Fonds are poles apart from the traditional idea of dirty and pollution-ridden factory towns. And yet Swiss industry operates in conditions which are unfavourable in comparison with those found in other countries which are Switzerland's competitors. The country's land-locked situation increases freight costs; the high living standard calls for high wages; and production costs are higher because of the lack of local raw materials and fuels. Faced with these difficulties, Swiss industry must compete in foreign markets not by offering lower prices but by the quality of its products. Economically Switzerland is one of the group of Western European industrial countries which depends essentially on exchanging its finished products for raw materials and foodstuffs from other countries.

The main branches of industry are chemicals and pharmaceuticals (concentrated principally in the Basle area), engineering and armaments (Zurich, Winterthur, Oerlikon, Schaffhausen, Baden, Geneva), metalworking, instruments and apparatus, leather, man-made fabrics and textiles, the graphic trades and foodstuffs. The traditional watchmaking industry (concentrated in La Chaux-de-Fonds) is also of great importance, but has been compelled by the tremendous growth of digital electronics to switch over to new methods and accept a temporary fall in output. Industrial products account for some four-fifths of Switzerland's total exports.

Switzerland's Largest Firms

Industry

Nestlé, Cham and Vevey (foodstuffs); **Ciba-Geigy**, Basle (chemicals and pharmaceuticals); **Brown, Boveri & Co.**, Baden (electrical engineering); **Alusuisse**, Chippis and Zurich (metalworking); **Roche**, Basle (chemicals and pharmaceuticals); **Sandoz**, Basle (chemicals and pharmaceuticals); **Sulzer**, Winterthur (engineering); **Oerlikon-Bührle**, Zurich (engineering, armaments); **Jacobs**, Zurich (foodstuffs); **Holderbank**, Glarus (cement).

Commerce

Migros, Zurich (foodstuffs, non-food goods); **Coop**, Basle (foodstuffs, non-food goods); **AMAG**, Zurich (motor vehicles); **Jelmoli**, Zurich (chain of department stores); **Usego**, Egerkingen (foodstuffs, non-food goods); **Globus**, Zurich (chain of department stores); **Siber Hegner**, Zurich (international trading company); **Shell Switzerland**, Zurich (petroleum products); **Denner**, Zurich (foodstuffs); **VOLG**, Winterthur (products for use in agriculture).

Banking

Schweizerischer Bankverein, Basle; **Schweizerische Bankgesellschaft**, Zurich; **Schweizerische Kreditanstalt**, Zurich; **Zürcher Kantonalbank**, Zurich; **Schweizerische Volksbank**, Berne; **Kantonalbank von Bern**, Berne; **Banque Cantonale Vaudoise**, Lausanne; **Luzerner Kantonalbank**, Lucerne; **St Gallische Kantonalbank**, St Gallen; **Crédit Foncier Vaudois**, Lausanne.

Insurance

Zürich, Zurich; **Schweizer Rück**, Zurich; **Rentenanstalt**, Zurich; **Winterthur**, Winterthur; **Winterthur Leben**, Winterthur; **Vita**, Zurich; **Basler**, Basle; **Basler Leben**, Basle; **Helvetia Unfall**, Zurich; **Patria Leben**, Basle.

Transport and services

PTT, Berne (postal and telecommunications services); **Danzas**, Basle (haulage); **Kühne & Nagel**, Pfäffikon (haulage); **SBB**, Berne (railways); **Swissair**, Zurich (air services); **Panalpina**, Binningen (haulage); **Wienerwald Schweiz**, Feusisberg (hotels and restaurants); **Publicitas**, Lausanne (press advertising); **Kuoni**, Zurich (travel agency); **Adia Interim**, Lausanne (temporary employment agency).

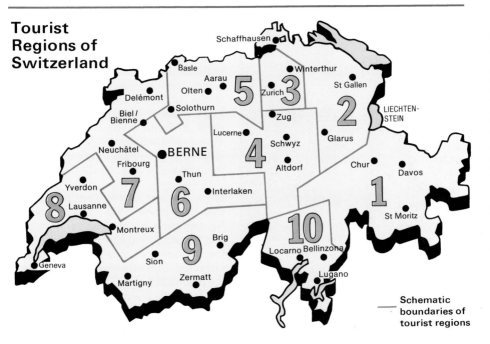

Tourist Regions of Switzerland

Schematic boundaries of tourist regions

1 Grisons
2 Eastern Switzerland
3 Zurich
4 Central Switzerland
5 North-western Switzerland

6 Berne
7 Jura-Fribourg-Neuchâtel
8 Lake Geneva
9 Valais
10 Ticino

In the field of **energy** Switzerland is again almost wholly dependent on imports. Electric power is an exception: 70% of total output comes from hydroelectric power stations, some 28% from the country's four nuclear power stations and only about 2% from oil-fuelled thermal power stations; and roughly a third of the output is available for export. – A legislative initiative aimed at restricting the use of nuclear energy was rejected by a narrow majority in a national referendum on 18 February 1979.

Given Switzerland's high imports and exports, **commerce** is a major element in the economy. The balance of trade is in deficit, but this is made good by income from Swiss-owned businesses abroad.

The country's world-wide trading connections and stable currency, combined with the strict confidentiality maintained by the banks, have given **banking** a dominant position in Switzerland. In addition to the "big five" the cantonal banks also play a major role, with a quarter of the total volume of business; and there are also regional, local and private banks.

– The Swiss banks also trade in precious metals, and have their own gold-refinery (ARGOR).

The **insurance** business, catering for the Swiss desire for material security, plays a large part in the economy. The Swiss insurance corporations have an international reputation, and draw by far the largest part of their premium income from foreign business. In the case of reinsurance – a Swiss speciality – the proportion of income from abroad is almost 90%.

Within the total economic picture **agriculture** is of comparatively small importance. The mountain regions are unfavourable to the development of agriculture, with only a small proportion of usable land, so that reasonably intensive cultivation is possible only in the Alpine foreland. Nevertheless Switzerland contrives to produce more than half its requirements of foodstuffs. In spite of government measures to help agriculture the drift from the land gives rise to problems.

Cattle coming down from the mountain pastures, Bernese Oberland

More than a quarter of the total area of Switzerland is unproductive. A further quarter is covered by forest; pastureland occupies more than two-fifths, and only 4·5% of the country's area is devoted to the growing of corn. These proportions are mainly a reflection of climatic conditions, which are favourable to the growth of meadowland and pasture. Most of the farm holdings are small: only some 30% are larger than 25 acres. Stock-farming is the most important branch of agriculture, and Swiss breeds of cattle are sought after in many countries in the world. The principal type of agricultural produce is milk, and Swiss cheeses (Emmental, Gruyère, etc.) take first place in the country's exports of foodstuffs. Vines grow in the sunniest and mildest parts of Switzerland – Valais, southern Ticino, on Lake Geneva and the Lac de Neuchâtel and in the transverse valley of the Rhine.

Since the end of the 19th century the **tourist trade** has been one of Switzerland's major sources of income, and in more recent years its importance in the economy as a whole has steadily increased. In recent years the decrease in the purchasing power of the dollar has led to a fall in the number of tourists from the USA.

Today visitors from the Federal Republic of Germany are in the majority, followed by those from France, the USA and the Netherlands. In 1980 the Swiss Tourist Board recorded a significant boom in holidays. This continuous upward trend is due to the increase in foreign visitors who spend far more in Switzerland than do Swiss holidaymakers in other countries.

Switzerland
A to Z

Bad Scuol (Schuls), Grison

Aarau

Canton: Aargau (AG).
Altitude: 388 m (1273 feet). – Population: 18,000.
Post code: CH-5000. – Dialling code: 064.

ⓘ **Verkehrsbüro,**
Bahnhofstrasse 20;
tel. 24 76 24.

HOTELS. – *Aarauerhof*, Bahnhofstrasse 68, B, 89 b.;
Stadtturm (no rest.), Ziegelrain, C, 24 b.; *Anker* (no
rest.), Metzgergasse, D, 40 b.; *Glockenhof*, Rain 41,
C, 25 b.; *Kettenbrücke*, Zollrain 18, 28 b. – YOUTH
HOSTEL in Rombach.

EVENTS. – *Maienzug*, youth festival (first Friday
in July); *Backfischet*, children's procession with
Chinese lanterns (second Friday in September);
Mag (Market Aarauer Gewerbetreibender, a trade
fair: autumn).

Aarau, capital of the canton of
Aargau since 1803, lies on the River
Aare under the southern slopes of
the Jura. With Late Gothic houses
dating from the period of Kyburg
rule, their street fronts colourfully
remodelled in Baroque style, it is
known as the "town of gables and
gardens". In addition to its role as
an administrative and cultural centre
it also has a variety of industry
(manufacture of instruments, iron-
and steelworks, optical industry,
bell-casting).

HISTORY. – Founded about 1240 by the Counts of
Kyburg, Aarau soon passed into the hands of the
Habsburgs. In 1415 it came under Bernese rule, and in
1798 became for six months capital of the Helvetian
Republic. In the 18th c. the Swiss national gymnastic,
shooting and singing associations were founded or
held their first meetings in Aarau.

SIGHTS. – The well-preserved OLD
TOWN, built on a prominent rocky hill
above the Aare, has many old gabled
houses with carved decoration (ornamental and figured) on the rooms and
painted shingle fronts. The Rore tower
(1250) is the oldest part of the **Rathaus**
(Town Hall), which was enlarged about
1520 and remodelled in Baroque style in
1762. The Late Gothic **parish church**
(Stadtkirche: Protestant), a pillared basilica, was built in 1471–78. Both these
buildings are in the *Halde*, the best-
preserved old street in the canton, with
houses ranging in date from the 16th to
the 19th c. Here, too, is the **Upper tower**
(Oberer Turm, 1270).

The *Schlössli* was originally a castle keep
(11th c.). The *Grossratsgebäude*, seat of
the cantonal parliament, is the finest Neo-
classical building in Aargau (1826–28). –
Also of interest are the *Municipal Museum* (Stadtmuseum Alt-Aarau) in the
castle and the *Art Gallery*, as well as the

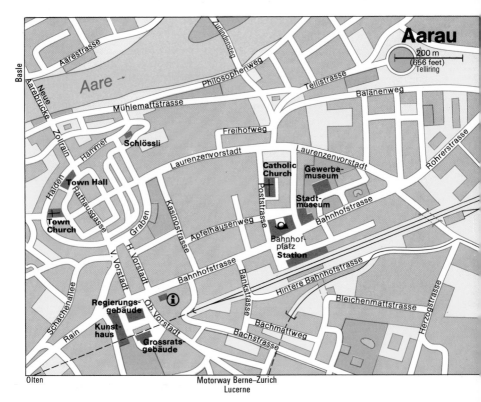

Justice Fountain, Aarau

Aargau Museum of Nature and local interest. – From the new *bridge over the Aare* (Neue Aarebrücke, 1949) there is a fine view of the old town.

SURROUNDINGS. – Good walking in the Aare valley, the Jura and the Mittelland hills. In the wooded Roggenhausen valley are a wildlife park and a nature trail, and in Schachen an interesting aviary.

10 km (6 miles) NE on road 5 lies *Wildegg* (alt. 357 m (1171 feet)), at the foot of the *Kestenberg*, with saline springs containing iodine (water available only bottled). Above the town to the N (1·5 km (1 mile) by road) stands the imposing *Schloss Wildegg* (alt. 433 m (1421 feet): 12th and 17th c.; now open to the public as a museum). On the left bank of the Aare, a little way downstream, is *Schloss Wildenstein*, now an old people's home. – 5·5 km (3 miles), farther downstream we come to **Bad Schinznach** (alt. 355 m (1165 feet): Parkhotel, B, 120 b., SP, SB), an elegant spa established in 1694 (closed in winter), with sulphurous water (34 °C – 93 °F) which is effective in the treatment of rheumatism and metabolic disorders; beautiful park (restaurant). – Beyond Bad Schinznach, on the left, a steep narrow road ascends (2·5 km – 2 miles) to the ruins of the **Habsburg** (alt. 513 m (1683 feet): inn), on the

Wülpelsberg. The castle, built about 1020, was in the 12th and 13th c. the seat of the Counts of Habsburg, one of whom, Rudolf III, was elected King of Germany in 1273 and thus became the founder of the Imperial dynasty of Habsburg. From the 24 m (79 feet) high tower there are superb views. The castle can also be reached from Brugg (see p. 61) on a steep and not very good road (3·5 km – 2 miles).

E of Aarau by way of Buchs is **Lenzburg** (alt. 400 m (1312 feet): Hotel Krone, C, 90 b.), a little town of 7000 inhabitants well known for its food-preserving factories (particularly fruit preserves). Above the old town with its unspoiled 17th and 18th c. houses rises the Burgberg (512 m (1680 feet): road to top), crowned by the large *✱Schloss Lenzberg* (11th–16th c.), now the property of the town of Lenzburg and the canton of Aargau (cantonal historical museum). To the W, on the *Staufberg* (520 m (1706 feet): view), is a Gothic pilgrimage church with 15th c. stained glass. – To the W of the motorway access road are the foundations of a Roman theatre of the 1st c. A.D., discovered in 1964 and restored in 1970–72. – 8 km (5 miles) NE on the Baden road, in the old country church of *Wohlenschwil*, is the Swiss Country Museum (Bauernmuseum: house types, costumes, weapons).

Schloss Lenzburg

Adelboden

Canton: Berne (BE)
Altitude: 1357 m (4452 feet). – Population: 3500.
Post code: CH-3715. – Dialling code: 033.
ⓘ **Kur- und Verkehrsverein,**
Adelboden;
tel. 73 22 52.

HOTELS. – *Nevada-Palace*, B, 125 b., SB; *Parkhotel Bellevue*, B, 70 b., SB; *Huldi & Waldhaus*, C, 80 b.; *Crystal* (no rest.), C, 72 b.; *Beau-Site*, C, 65 b.; *Bristol*, C, 50 b.; *Alpenrose*, D, 50 b.

RECREATION and SPORT. – Riding, tennis, swimming, skittles, fishing; mountaineering school.

CLIMBS. – Via Hahnenmoos up the *Laveygrat* (2254 m (7395 feet): 3½ hours, not particularly difficult); via Schermtanne up the *Albristhorn* (2765 m (9072 feet): 5½ hours, for experienced climbers only); from the

The Habsburg, near Brugg

Engstligenalp in 5½–6 hours, with guide, up the *Wildstrubel* (the E peak, *Grosstrubel*, 3253 m (10,673 feet)), with magnificent views (W peak climbed from Lenk in the Simmental); from the Engstligenalp by way of the *Engstligengrat* to the *Gemmi* pass (4–5 hours, with guide: p. 160).

WINTER SPORTS. – Good downhill runs from the *Fleckli* (1862 m (6109 feet): two lifts from Boden), on the *Engstligenalp* (1940 m (6365 feet): three lifts; accessible by cableway); from the *Kuonisbergli* (1731 m (5679 feet): two lifts from Boden); from the *Schwanfeldspitz* (1950 m (6398 feet): lift; accessible by cableway); from the *Luegli* (2080 m (6824 feet): chair-lift from Geils); and on the *Hahnenmoos* (1957 m (6421 feet): lifts from the Simmental; combined "ski pass" with Lenk; accessible by cableway from Geilsmäder). Also ski-jumping, cross-country skiing, skating (rink with artificial ice) and curling (indoor and outdoor rinks).

The village of Adelboden, a popular altitude and winter sports resort in the Bernese Oberland, lies in a sheltered situation on the W side of the Engstligen valley at the end of a road from Lake Thun. Along the E side of the wide valley with its scatter of huts rises the Lohner chain; to the S is the Wildstrubel.

SIGHTS. – This attractive mountain village is famed for its scenic beauty, its many charming old farmhouses, and its hotels and chalets scattered about on sunny terraces. On the S wall of the *church* (1433) is a late 15th c. painting of the Last Judgment.

SURROUNDINGS. – A chair-lift 1268 m (4160 feet) long ascends in 8¼ minutes to the *Tschentenalp*, on the E side of the **Schwandfeldspitz** (2029 m (6657 feet): restaurant), from which there are magnificent views of the Lohner and Wildstrubel. – A road runs 3·5 km (2 miles) W up the *Allenbach valley* to the *Schermtanne* inn. – A narrow road branches off the road to Frutigen (on right, after the second bend), runs S up the Engstligen valley and passes through *Boden* to the hamlet of *Unter dem Birg*, at the *Lower Engstligen Falls* (6 km – 4 miles), from which a cableway takes us up past the *Upper Engstligen Falls* to the **Engstligenalp** (1940 m (6365 feet): Berghaus Bärtschi, 15 b.), a former lake basin at the foot of the Wildstrubel. – A bus runs SW up the *Gilbach valley* to *Geils*. Cableway from *Geilsmäder* (1707 m – 5601 feet) to the *Hahnenmoos* pass (1957 m (6421 feet): Hospiz Hari, 60 b.; Berghotel, 15 b.). Chair-lift 1650 m (5414 feet) long from Geils to the Laveygrat (2200 m – 7218 feet) and a chair-lift from Geils to Luegli (2080 m – 6824 feet), both operating only in winter. From Hahnenmoos it is a 45 minutes' descent to the Bühlberg restaurant (1660 m – 5446 feet), from which a road leads down (6 km (4 miles), with steep bends) to *Lenk* (p. 228), in the Simmental.

Altdorf

Canton: Uri (UR).
Altitude: 458 m (1503 feet). – Population: 8000.
Post code: CH-6460. – Dialling code: 044.

ⓘ **Verkehrsbüro,**
Rathausplatz 5;
tel. 2 22 03.
Gemeindehausplatz;
tel. 2 47 41.

HOTELS. – *Goldener Schlüssel*, C, 47 b.; *Schwarzer Löwen*, D, 40 b.; *Bahnhof*, D, 46 b.

Altdorf, capital of the canton of Uri, a little town with a long and eventful history, lies 3 km (2 miles) S of the outflow of the Reuss into Lake Uri (the Urner See) in a wide plain at the mouth of the Schächen valley; it is the starting-point of the road over the Klausen pass. It is here that William Tell is supposed to have shot at the apple on his son's head.

HISTORY. – The parish is believed to have been established in the 10th c., though its first appearance in the records is only in 1223. After the struggle to shake off Habsburg rule the place acquired political and economic importance as capital of the territory of Uri, which until 1439 was self-governing in direct subordination to the Emperor.

SIGHTS. – In front of the *Rathaus* (Town Hall, 1805–08) and a medieval *tower house* is the *Tell Monument (by Richard Kissling, 1895). To the E is the *Tell Theatre* (1925), in which Schiller's "Wilhelm Tell" is performed by Altdorf townspeople. Also of interest are the *parish church of St Martin* (rebuilt

Tell monument, Altdorf

1801–10), the *Uri Historical Museum* (founded 1892), the *Suvorov house* and the *Capuchin friary*.

SURROUNDINGS. – 3 km (2 miles) away on the road to the Klausen pass is **Bürglen** (alt. 552 m (1811 feet); pop. 3600), one of the oldest settlements in Uri, built on detritus deposited by the Schächenbach, which here flows into the Reuss. Parish church (1684), with Romanesque crypt and substructure of the tower. Bürglen is supposed to have been the home of the mythical William Tell, whom Schiller's play made the greatest figure in Swiss legend. The Tell chapel (1582) is said to occupy the site of Tell's house, and a stone cross beside the bridge marks the spot where Tell is traditionally believed to have been drowned while rescuing a child from the Schächenbach in his later years. There is a Tell Museum in a Romanesque tower adjoining the church.

1·5 km (1 mile) S of Altdorf, on the left bank of the Reuss, is *Attinghausen* (alt. 469 m (1539 feet); pop. 1200), with the remains of a castle in which Freiherr von Attinghausen (who features in Schiller's play) died in 1321. – From Altdorf a road runs via *Seedorf* (alt. 437 m (1434 feet)), at the SW tip of Lake Uri, and *Isleten* to the delightfully situated village of *Isenthal* (10 km (6 miles): alt. 778 m (2553 feet); pop. 600), the starting-point for the ascent of the *Urirotstock (2932 m (9620 feet): 6–7 hours, with guide); cableways.

14 km (9 miles) S by way of *Erstfeld* (alt. 475 m (1558 feet): station on the St Gotthard line) is **Amsteg** (552 m (1811 feet); Hotel Stern & Post, C, 70 b.), a beautifully situated village and summer holiday resort at the mouth of the Maderanertal, here spanned by a 53 m (174 feet) high viaduct carrying the St Gotthard railway; cableway (1440 m (4725 feet long: 7 minutes) up the *Arniberg* (1392 m – 4567 feet). – A road to the left leads into the *Maderanertal*, one of the most beautiful of the Alpine valleys, watered by the rushing *Kärstelenbach*. A steep mountain road, with many bends, climbs (4 km – 2 miles) to *Bristen* (797 m – 2615 feet), from which there is a cableway to the *Golzernsee* (1410 m – 4626 feet) and a rough track which leads in 2½ hours up to the magnificently situated Hotel Schweizer Alpenclub (1354 m – 4442 feet), a good base for climbers and hill-walkers (e.g. to the *Oberalpstock*, 3330 m (10,926 feet): 8–9 hours, with guide).

Andermatt

Canton: Uri (UR).
Altitude: 1444 m (4738 feet). – Population: 1600.
Post code: CH-6490. – Dialling code: 044.

ⓘ **Verkehrsbüro,**
Bahnhofplatz;
tel. 6 74 54.

HOTELS. – *Krone*, C, 85 b.; *Monopol-Metropol*, C, 60 b., SB; *Drei Könige & Post*, C, 40 b.; *Helvetia*, C, 60 b.; *Kristall*, C, 44 b.; *Badus*, C, 40 b.; *Schlüssel*, C, 35 b.; *Löwen*, D, 40 b.; *Bergidyll*, D, 36 b.; *Alpenhof-Bahnhof*, D, 30 b.; *Sonne*, D, 40 b.; *Alpina* (no rest.), D, 28 b.; *Aurora* (no rest.), D, 50 b.

Andermatt lies in the wide Urseren valley at the junction of four important Alpine roads, which with the

Andermatt and the Urseren valley

exception of the access road from the Reuss valley are closed for between four and six months in the year. The old village has developed into an ideal base for walkers and climbers and a popular winter sports resort.

HISTORY. – The Urseren valley was settled from the Valais, and the oldest parts of Andermatt and Hospental still show Valaisian features. The people of the valley were long subject to the authority of Disentis abbey, but achieved independence in 1382, with their own constitution and their own *ammann* (chief magistrate). Andermatt is still a separate district within the canton of Uri.

SIGHTS. – Baroque *church* (1695), with Rococo interior. On the mountainside is the little 13th c. *church of St Columban* (dedicated to the Irish missionary saint). From the *Mariahilf chapel*, above the village to the S, there are far-ranging views – of the Bäzberg (2550 m – 8367 feet), the Furka pass, with the Muttenhorn (3103 m – 10,181 feet), and Badus (2931 m – 9617 feet).

SURROUNDINGS. – Cableway up the **Gemsstock** (2961 m (9715 feet): length 4030 m (13,222 feet), height difference 1523 m (4997 feet), time 12 minutes), with magnificent views; summer skiing.

Road 2 runs N up the wide *Urseren valley* ("Bear-Hunters' Valley"), a massive Alpine trough flanked by high mountains, some of them snow-capped, and by scree-covered slopes, and watered by the streams which feed the Reuss. The road crosses the *Devil's Bridge* (Teufelsbrücke, 1402 m (4600 feet), built in 1955–56, which spans the Reuss at a waterfall 30 m (98 feet) high. The bridge, 86 m (282 feet) long, inherited its name from an old 15th c. bridle-path bridge at the same spot. A stone cross 12 m (39 feet) high commemorates the fighting in 1799, when General Suvorov's Russians, coming from the St Gotthard pass, defeated the French force which

The Schöllenen bridges on the St Gotthard road

attempted to bar their way. To the right, on the old road, is the Teufelsbrücke restaurant.

The road passes through the Teufelswand ("Devil's Wall") in a short tunnel, and leaving a commandingly situated parking place and five sharp bends (Schöllenen restaurant) returns to the right bank of the river on the *Spengi bridge* (1234 m – 4049 feet). It then enters the *Schöllenen (probably from Latin *scala*, "ladder"), a wild gorge enclosed between precipitous granite walls, and after another four sharp bends (fine views) crosses to the left bank again on the *Vordere Brücke*. Thereafter it crosses the *Göschenen-Reuss* and continues to wind sharply downhill on the St Gotthard road to the village of Göschenen.

Göschenen (alt. 1115 m (3658 feet): Hotel Weisses Rössli, C, 60 b.; St Gotthard, E, 44 b.) is magnificently situated at the junction of the Göschenen-Reuss with the Reuss, which issues from the Schöllenen gorge. It lies near the N entrance to the 15 km (9 miles) long St Gotthard tunnel (see p. 211) and has a large railway station. The builder of the tunnel, Louis Favre, died of a stroke in the tunnel in 1879, shortly before its completion, and is buried in Göschenen churchyard. – To the W an attractive road ascends the beautiful *Göschenen valley* to a reservoir on the *Göschener Alp* (9·5 km – 6 miles). 7 km (4 miles) from Göschenen, on the right, is the Göschener Alp inn (1715 m – 5627 feet), and 2·5 km (2 miles) beyond this, in a magnificent mountain setting, the Damma-gletscher inn (1795 m (5889 feet): E, 13 b.), with a large parking place. Above the inn, from a reservoir (75 million cu. m (2648 million cu. feet)), there is a superb view of the Dammastock and its glacier. The Göschener Alp is the starting-point of a variety of rewarding climbs – the *Lochberg* (3088 m (10,132 feet): $4\frac{1}{2}$ hours, with guide), the *Dammastock* (3633 m (11,920 feet): 5–6 hours, with guide), the *Suster-horn* ($6\frac{1}{2}$ hours, with guide), etc.

The road continues down the bare mountainside and once again crosses to the right bank on the *Schönibridge* (981 m – 3219 feet). Below, on the right, lies the *Teufelsstein* ("Devil's Stone"), a massive boulder which was moved 127 m (417 feet) upstream in 1973, during the construction of the St Gotthard road tunnel. – The road passes the village of *Wattingen* and crosses to the left bank of the Reuss, with the Rienzenstock (2964 m – 9725 feet) on the right and the magnificent Dammafirn (névé) on the left. – 5 km (3 miles) from Göschenen we reach

Wassen (934 m (3064 feet): Hôtel des Alpes, C, 30 b.; Gemsbock, D, 12 b.), a beautifully situated village at the junction with the road over the Furka pass. From the terrace in front of the church (1734), which stands on higher ground, there are superb views of the valley in both directions.

Over the Susten, Grimsel and Furka passes (a round trip from Wassen): This **circuit of three magnificent passes offers a breathtaking experience, combining splendid Alpine scenery with the tremendous technical achievements of the road engineers. – The newest of the three roads, the boldly engineered *Susten road (No. 11), built between 1938 and 1946, runs up from Wassen through the wildly beautiful *Meiental*, goes over the **Susten pass** in a tunnel (2224 m – 7297 feet) just under the summit and descends the *Gadmen valley*, passing close to the *Stein glacier*, to Innertkirchen, where it leaves the magnificence of this high Alpine valley for a gentler landscape of pastureland and orchards. – The *Grimsel road (No. 6), built in 1891–94, which links the Bernese Oberland with Upper Valais (the Upper Rhône valley) and the Furka, starts from Innertkirchen (626 m – 2054 feet), in a beautiful setting of forest and Alpine meadows, and runs up the attractive *Hasli valley*. Above Guttannen this becomes narrower and wilder, until at Handegg the trees disappear altogether and the road continues to climb through a bare rocky wilderness, past massive dams and narrow fjord-like reservoirs. From the **Grimsel pass** (2165 m – 7013 feet), the lowest of the three passes, the road runs down, with many hairpin bends, to Gletsch (1763 m – 5784 feet), in the Upper *Rhône valley*. – From here the *Furka road (No. 19), built in 1864–66, leads up through the bare upper reaches of the valley, passes immediately under the *Rhône glacier* and continues up to the **Furka pass** (2431 m – 7976 feet), the highest point on the trip. It then continues down into the *Urseren valley* through scenery of a different type, with rugged mountains of uncompromising bulk.

All three roads are well built and excellently engineered, particularly the Susten road (minimum width 6 m (20 feet), well-cambered bends, maximum gradient 8%). The Grimsel road, with its many bends, has been modernised (4–7 m (13–23 feet) wide, maximum gradient 9%). The Furka road (improved 1960–63: 4–8 m (13–26 feet) wide) is the steepest of the three (10%); the stiffest gradients are mostly on the bends, and in the thinner air at this altitude they make particularly heavy demands on the engine of a

On the Susten road

car. – The round trip involves an ascent of some 3600 m (11,812 feet) with about 60 sharp bends. Motorists who are unused to Alpine driving should exercise particular care. – All three passes are usually open from mid June to mid October. – Emergency telephones.

The *Susten road, branching off the St Gotthard road at Wassen, runs uphill on a moderate gradient, with an attractive view of Wassen church to the rear. In 0·5 km (about a ¼ mile) it winds its way through two tunnels, between which is another view of Wassen. The road then crosses the gorge of the *Meienreuss* on a high concrete bridge, from where there is a view of Titlis (3239 m – 10,627 feet) ahead. At the Leggistein tunnel on the St Gotthard railway the road takes a left-hand turn, beyond which one has a view of the Fleckistock (3420 m – 11,221 feet) and Stücklistock (3309 m – 10,857 feet). Soon after this it goes through a third tunnel and runs high up on the mountainside above the gorge of the Meienreuss, with a prospect of the valley. After a total of 5·5 km (3 miles) the road comes to the group of houses and the church at *Meien* (1300 m – 4265 feet), beautifully situated at a point where the valley opens out. Beyond this point, in the upper reaches of the *Meiental*, an area of Alpine pasture enclosed by steep mountain walls, the road continues uphill on a moderate gradient above the left bank of the Meienreuss; from here one can see the jagged peaks of the Wendenhorn and Fünffingerstöcke at the head of the valley. – In another 3 km (2 miles) a road goes off on the left and runs down into the valley to the hamlet of *Färnigen*, on the old bridle-path to the Susten pass.

3 km (2 miles) farther on, at *Gorezmettlen*, the road crosses the stream flowing down the Kleinalp valley from the Kleiner Spannort and then climbs higher up the slopes of the Meiental, now wild and desolate, with a view of the summit of the pass and the Sustenhorn, with the Rüttifirn and Kalchtalfirn. The *Sustenstübli* inn is passed on the right of the road. Beyond this, to the left, there is a magnificent panorama, looking backwards down the valley; ahead, to the left, is the summit of the pass, from which the jagged crest of the Fünffingerstöcke extends to the right towards the Wendenhorn (3023 m – 9918 feet) and Grassen (2946 m – 9666 feet). – Then follow two bends and a short tunnel leading up to the *Susten pass (2259 m – 7412 feet), under which the road passes in a tunnel 325 m (1066 feet) long (alt. 2224 m – 7297 feet). Just beyond the far end of the tunnel are a large parking place and a small lake, from which there is a rewarding climb (5 minutes) to the summit of the pass (restaurant), the boundary between the cantons of Uri and Berne, with *views of the imposing chain of mountains N of the Meiental (highest point Titlis, 3239 m (10,627 feet)), the group formed by the Gwächtenhorn (3425 m – 11,237 feet) and the Tierberge (3444 m – 11,300 feet) rearing up above the Stein glacier, the Himmelrank gorge and, in the background, the tunnels on the Susten road and the Gadmerfluh.

Beyond the pass the road – still scenically and technically magnificent but now showing more variety of scenery – runs down in two sharp bends, offering superb close-up views of the Stein glacier and its drainage lake immediately below. It then passes through the *Himmelrank gorge, with seven tunnels or arches in the rock, and takes a left-hand bend down to the *Hotel Steingletscher* (1866 m (6122 feet): C, 70 b.), on the *Alp Stein*. From here there is first a road (3 km – 2 miles) to the *Steinlimmi glacier* (summer skiing centre), and then a footpath

(20 minutes) to the mighty *Stein glacier; also a climb of 7 hours (with guide) to the summit of the Sustenhorn (3504 m – 11,497 feet: superb *views). – From the Steingletscher Hotel the road descends the *Wendental* on the stony slopes of the *Gschletterwald*, through wild and rugged scenery, passing through five tunnels and under a sheer rock face, with a backward view of the Sustenhorn, of which there is a further glimpse after a left-hand bend. It then continues to wind its way down, with continually changing prospects of the Tierberge and Gwächtenhorn to the S and the precipitous walls of the Wendenstöcke and Gadmerfluh to the N. In another 5 km (3 miles) it crosses a stream, and soon after this traverses another tunnel into a left-hand bend (turning-place), and through three more tunnels and round two bends to the *Wendenwasser bridge* over the stream of the same name. It then continues down the *Gadmental*, the valley of the *Gadmer Wasser*. The scenery becomes gentler, with fresh green pastureland and woods of maple and stone pine. Ahead can be seen the Wetterhorn (3701 m – 12,143 feet).

Gadmen (alt. 1207 m (3960 feet): Hotel Alpenrose, E, 36 b.) is a straggling little village in a picturesque situation under the steep rock faces of the Gadmerfluh. – The road continues downhill on a gentle gradient, passes through a tunnel, crosses the gorge of the Gadmer Wasser on the high *Schwendi bridge* and winds its way down to the mouth of the *Trift valley*, from where one can see the Trift glacier. It then crosses back to the right bank of the Gadmer Wasser and comes into the commune of *Nessental* (930 m (3051 feet): Hotel Terrasse, E, 20 b.), which gives its name to the lower part of the valley, where fruit-trees abound. – The road then runs down on a uniform easy gradient to *Mühletal* (837 m – 2746 feet), at the mouth of the *Gental*, a valley running down from the *Engstlenalp (toll road, 11·5 km (7 miles)); the stream is crossed on the Rossweidli bridge. Then on to *Wiler* (4·5 km (3 miles): alt. 740 m (2428 feet)). Beyond this point there is another fine view of the mountains, after which the road winds down into the wide valley of the Aare and comes to **Innertkirchen** (626 m (2054 feet): Hotel Alpenrose, C, 50 b.; Hof & Post, C, 40 b.; Carina, C, 22 b.), a holiday resort surrounded by lush Alpine meadows.

From Innertkirchen the road to the Grimsel goes gradually uphill in the wooded and steadily narrower *Oberhaslital* above the right bank of the Aare, with beautiful vistas of the mountains ahead. In another 2·5 km (2 miles), beyond the huts on the *Äussere Urweid* (716 m – 2349 feet), a narrow stretch of road above the gorge-like valley bears left round a wall of rock and passes through the short *Zuben tunnel*, under a waterfall, into the *Innere Urweid* (760 m (2494 feet): inn). 1 km (about a ½ mile) farther on the road runs through another short tunnel in a rocky spur of the *Tönende Fluh*, after which the valley opens out a little. At the hamlet of *Boden* (876 m – 2874 feet) the road crosses the river and winds its way up the wooded mountainside, with four hairpin bends, to **Guttannen** (1060 m – 3478 feet), the last village in the Oberhaslital, under the precipitous *Ritzlihorn* (3282 m – 10,768 feet), which every year sends its dreaded avalanches tumbling down the *Spreitlaui* valley.

The *Grimsel road proper, which begins at Guttannen, follows a fairly straight and gentle course up the valley for a kilometre or so, begins to climb more steeply through the forest and crosses the river on the *Tschingel bridge* (1140 m – 3740 feet). It then passes rugged black crags and massive accumulations of debris which bear witness to the violence of the avalanches and the rushing torrents, returns by the *Schwarzbrunnen bridge* to the left bank (1217 m – 3993 feet) and continues round the rocky bulk of the *Stäubender*. – The compensation reservoir of the *Handegg I hydroelectric station* is passed on the left (1309 m – 4295 feet). – Then two sharp bends carry the road up through a further stretch of forest to the **Handegg** (Handeck) saddle, 150 m (492 feet) higher up. From a wider length of road there is a *view of the *Handegg falls*, in which the grey-green waters of the *Aare* mingle with the silvery *Aerlenbach*, emerging below the road, and plunge into the chasm 46 m (151 feet) below. – Soon after this, off the road to the right, is the *Hotel Handeck* (1404 m (4607 feet): C, 70 b.). From here a cableway (for industrial use only) ascends the E side of the valley to the *Gelmersee* (1849 m – 6067 feet), an artificial lake formed by a dam 35 m (115 feet) high. – The Grimsel road follows the valley bottom, strewn with boulders, and then winds its way, with sharp bends, up the granite mountainside, worn smooth by the glaciers, to the *Alp Kunzentännlen* (1616 m – 5302 feet), where the last firs disappear, giving place to dwarf pines and rhododendrons. To the right, below, is the Handegg I hydroelectric station with its lake; to the left, higher up, the Gersten glacier; straight ahead the dam of the Räterichsboden reservoir, up to which the road now winds its way (one hairpin bend). – Above, to the right, is the **Räterichsboden reservoir** (1767 m – 5798 feet), which the road skirts, with a view of the Grimselsee dam; near the end of the lake it passes through a short tunnel. – The road then climbs again (to the right, below, a fine view of the Räterichsboden lake), and after two hairpin bends at the massive Seeuferegg dam, reaches the *Grimselsee** (1909 m – 6263 feet), a fjord-like lake extending for 5·5 km (3 miles) to the Unteraar glacier (nature reserve). A road on the right (0·8 km – about a ½ mile) leads by way of the *Seeuferegg dam* (352 m (1155 feet) long, up to 42 m (138 feet) high) to the Grimsel hospice (hotel and restaurant, 1960 m (6431 feet) on the granite ridge of *Nollen*, with a view of the *Spitallamm dam* (258 m (846 feet) long, up to 114 m (374 feet) high) and a magnificent prospect over the lake of the Zinkenstock, the Finsteraarhorn and the Agassizhorn. There is a rewarding walk from the hotel (2–3 hours) to the *Unteraar glacier*.

The *Oberhasli hydroelectric scheme** (1925–54) comprises four separate power stations. The *Handegg I* station (90,000 kW), built in 1925–32, uses the water of the *Grimselsee* (100 million cu. m (3531

million cu. feet)), formed by the Seeuferegg and Spitallamm dams, which is carried in a 5 km (3 miles) long tunnel to a subsidiary reservoir, the *Gelmersee* (13 million cu. m (459 million cu. feet)) and the power station 540 m (1772 feet) below. – The *Innertkirchen station* (192,000 kW) uses water from Handegg I, which is conveyed to it in a tunnel 10 km (6 miles) long. – The *Handegg II station* (60,000 kW), built in 1947–50, gets its water from the *Räterichsboden* lake (27 million cu. m (953 million cu. feet)) and the small *Gauli reservoir* in the Upper Urbach valley. The power station (underground) is at Handegg. – The *Oberaar station* (31,000 kW), built in 1950–54, uses water from the *Oberaarsee*, formed by a dam 525 m (1723 feet) long and 105 m (345 feet) high; the underground power station is between the Grimselsee and Räterichsboden.

From the Seeuferegg dam the Grimsel road skirts the E end of the Grimselsee and then climbs on a moderate gradient (four sharp bends), with magnificent *views to the rear (Grosser Schreckhorn, to the W, 4080 m (13,386 feet)). – 3·5 km (2 miles) farther on is the *Grimsel pass* (2165 m (7103 feet): Hotel Grimselblick, E, 30 b.), on the boundary between the cantons of Berne and Valais, with beautiful views of the Valais Alps, particularly the Gries glacier. Rewarding climb (2½ hours) of the *Kleines Siedelhorn* (2768 m (9082 feet): fine panorama). From the top of the pass a beautiful but narrow private road (alternating one-way traffic) runs 6 km (4 miles) W to the *Oberaarsee* (58 million cu. m (2048 million cu. feet)), with a car park and the Berghaus Oberaar (hotel and restaurant, 12 b., camping site; alt. 2340 m (7678 feet)). – A little farther on, to the right, are the Hotel Grimselpasshöhe (E, 30 b.) and the *Totensee* (2144 m – 7034 feet), whose name ("Lake of the Dead") commemorates the bitter fighting here between Austrian and French forces in 1799. – The road descends the steep slope of the *Meienwang* in six sharp bends, with *views of the Rhône glacier and the windings of the Furka road: to the left the Galenstock and Dammastock, to the SE the Pizzo Rotondo. It then comes to **Gletsch** (1763 m (5784 feet): Hôtel Glacier du Rhône, D, 110 b.), at the lower end of the debris-covered valley, which a century ago was blanketed for more than half its area by the Rhône glacier.

In Gletsch the ***Furka road** crosses the *Rhône* (here also known in German as the Rotten) and then climbs (three sharp bends) up the S side of the valley and follows the slope, with fine views of Gletsch and the windings of the Grimsel road to the rear and of the Rhône glacier ahead. – At the head of the valley the road crosses the narrow-gauge Furka railway, the middle section (completed 1927) of the line from Lake Geneva to Lake Constance by way of the Rhône and Rhine valleys ("Glacier Express" from Zermatt to St Moritz). The road then crosses the *Muttbach bridge* and climbs steeply (five hairpin bends) up the N side of the valley, with beautiful views of the Rhône glacier and of Gletsch far below. – In 7 km (4 miles) the car park of the *Belvedere restaurant* (2272 m – 7454 feet), is reached. From here it is only a few minutes' walk to the *Rhône glacier**, between the *Grosses Furkahorn* (3217 m – 10,555 feet) and the *Gerstenhörner* (3184 m – 10,447 feet), which hangs over the side of the valley in a formidable cataract of ice (charge for access: interesting artificial cave hewn from the glacier). – The road continues to climb (two steep bends), with a magnificent *view of the Rhône glacier to the rear, and to the right, above the Gratschlucht glacier, of the Grosses Muttenhorn (3103 m – 10,181 feet). – In 2·5 km (2 miles) the road reaches the ***Furka pass** (2431 m – 7976 feet). The

The Grimselsee

The Rhône glacier, on the Furka road

Furka ("Fork") is a saddle, falling steeply away on each side, between the *Kleines Furkahorn* (3026 m (9928 feet): 2 hours N) and the *Blauberg* (2757 m (9046 feet): 1½ hours S), both offering easy and rewarding climbs. It forms the boundary between the cantons of Valais and Uri and affords magnificent views, extending NE to the Urseren valley and the Oberalp pass and W to the Bernese Alps (Finsteraar-horn) and Valais Alps (Weisshorn). Rewarding climb, to the N, of the *Galenstock* (3583 m (11,756 feet): 5 hours, with guide), which commands extensive views.

500 m (1641 feet) farther on is the Hotel Furkablick (30 b.). The road then continues downhill, high up on the bare N face of the *Garschental*, a valley constantly threatened by avalanches, with the *Furkareuss* flowing down below. Views of the Siedeln glacier and the sharp pinnacles of the Bielenhorn (2947 m – 9669 feet). – Then by way of the *Tiefentobel* gorge (to the left a waterfall) to the Hotel Tiefenbach (2109 m (6920 feet): 20 b.). – 1·5 km (1 mile) farther on, at the *Ebnetenalp* (2010 m – 6595 feet), where the road takes a sharp bend to the right, there are magnificent views of the Urseren valley and the Wyttenwasser valley, which now opens up to the S, with Piz Lucendro (2964 m – 9725 feet). – Now down the rounded slopes of *Fuchsegg* (nine sharp bends) to the valley bottom and the little village of **Realp** (1547 m (5076 feet): Hôtel des Alpes), the name of which is derived from *riva alpa* (*riva*, "stream"; *alpa*, mountain pasture). To the SE is *Pizzo Rotondo* (3192 m (10,473 feet): 8 hours, with guide), the highest peak

On the Furka road

in the St Gotthard group. – The road now follows an almost level and straight course down the wide *Urseren valley*, between the River *Furkareuss* and the Furka railway, which is crossed in another 3 km (2 miles). From this point the road becomes narrower. Ahead can be seen the square tower of Hospental castle. – 6 km (4 miles) from Realp is **Hospental** (1484 m (4869 feet): Aparthotel Löwen, C, 26 b.; Meyerhof, D, 50 b.; bypass), an old village (from *hospitium*, "hospice") situated at the point where the Furka-Reuss and Gotthard-Reuss join to form the *Reuss*, a popular health and winter sports resort which also has heavy through traffic. Church (1705–11); 13th c. castle tower. – From here on road 2 to **Andermatt**.

Appenzell

Cantons: Appenzell-Ausserrhoden (AR) and Appenzell-Innerrhoden (AI).

ⓘ **Verkehrsbüro Appenzell,**
Hauptgasse 19,
CH-9050 Appenzell (AI);
tel. (071) 87 16 93.
Verkehrsbüro Herisau,
Oberdorfstrasse 1,
CH-9100 Herisau (AR);
tel. (071) 51 44 60.

This attractive Pre-Alpine region in eastern Switzerland, just S of Lake Constance, reaching its highest point in Säntis (2504 m – 8216 feet), in the Alpstein range, is the only Swiss canton which is completely surrounded by another canton (St Gallen). It is subdivided into two independent half-cantons, established in 1597 following democratic votes in the two religious communities, Appenzell-Ausserrhoden being Protestant and Appenzell-Innerrhoden Roman Catholic. The division also reflects a geographical difference: Innerrhoden consists mainly of the Alpstein and Säntis massifs, while Ausserrhoden takes in the upland region to the N of the Säntis range. Both the half-cantons reach their most important political decisions at the Landsgemeinde, the annual meeting of all the men of the community which is held in the open air.

Appenzell is served by good roads and by narrow-gauge railways. The Appenzellerbahn runs from Gossau, in the Unterland, via Herisau and Urnäsch to the town of Appenzell, and from there to Weissbad and Wasserauen; the Gaiserbahn links St Gallen and Altstätten with Appenzell, and there are other lines from Rorschach, St Gallen and Rheineck.

The annual meeting of the Lands-gemeinde is an impressive experience for any visitor who is fortunate enough to be present. On the last Sunday in April all citizens entitled to vote – men over the age of 20 – make their way, wearing swords, to the square where the meeting takes place. The men of Ausserrhoden meet alternately in Trogen, headquarters of the cantonal court and the cantonal police, and in Hundwil. The men of Innerrhoden, carrying their swords as evidence of their right to vote, meet in the cantonal capital, Appenzell. The *landammann* (chief magistrate) and other members of the cantonal government are elected by show of hands and solemnly sworn in on the spot. Every citizen has the right to speak, and can put forward a proposal for legislation or constitutional amendment.

Traditional costume, Appenzell

Folk art is deeply rooted in Appenzell tradition; in Innerhoden in particular an ancient culture characteristic of these upland pastoral regions is still very much alive. Naïve peasant painting is to be seen everywhere in the canton, and other old crafts still practised are the making of bell harness and coopering. Folk music played by string bands (violins, cellos, double basses, dulcimers) and the handsome local costumes also play an important part in the ancient traditions of the sociably disposed people of Appenzell.

HISTORY. – In the Middle Ages Appenzell belonged to the Prince-Abbot of St Gallen, but at the beginning of the 15th c. it broke away after a valiant and determined struggle for independence, and in 1513 became the last canton in the 13-member confederation, which received no further accessions until the French Revolution. The canton owed its prosperity in earlier centuries to its flourishing textile industry, and many villages still have handsome houses with curved gables dating from this period.

The Appenzell "bödeli" (milking-pail)

Around Mt Säntis

The highest peak in the Alpstein massif, which consists of three ranges of hills lying between the Rhine valley, Toggenburg and the Vorderland of Appenzell, is **Säntis** (2504 m – 8216 feet), a mountain much favoured by hill-walkers, climbers and those who prefer to make the ascent by cableway. From the summit there are superb panoramic **views of the Vorarlberg, Grisons, Glarus and Uri Alps and across Lake Constance and far into South Germany (Swabia). To the NW of the peak the boundaries of the two half-cantons and of the canton of St Gallen meet.

From the *Schwägalp* (1283 m (4210 feet): inn, 12 b.) a cableway runs up, with only two intervening supports, to *Säntis (upper station 2476 m (8124 feet); length 2307 m (7569 feet), height difference 1193 m (3914 feet), time 10 minutes; restaurant and inn, 10 b.). The ascent on

Säntis cableway, Schwägalp

The town of Appenzell

foot takes 3½ hours from the Schwägalp and 4–5 hours from Wasserauen.

The railway line from St Gallen via Herisau (11 km (7 miles): change) terminates at Urnäsch (23 km – 14 miles), from which there is a bus to the Schwägalp (11 km (7 miles): 30 minutes). The road from St Gallen to Urnäsch (32 km – 20 miles) passes through Waldstatt (14 km – 9 miles).

Urnäsch (alt. 826 m (2710 feet): pop. 2300; Hotel Krone, D, 40 b.; Bahnhof, D, 30 b.) is the largest in area and one of the oldest communes in Appenzell-Ausserrhoden. The village square with its trim wooden houses reflects the people's attachment to tradition, and Urnäsch is widely known for its rustic dances, New Year celebrations and other traditional observances. It has a museum of Appenzell traditions and a local museum. Footpaths lead into the surrounding hills. – From Urnäsch it is 14 km (9 miles) to Appenzell. The road comes in 4 km (2 miles) to *Jakobsbad* (alt. 876 m (2874 feet): chalybeate spring; Hotel Jakobsbad, C, 60 b.; camping site), from which there is a cableway up the Kronberg (1663 m (5456 feet): length 3223 m (10,575 feet), height difference 772 m (2533 feet), time 8 minutes; restaurant). 2 km (1 mile) beyond this is *Gonten* (alt. 903 m (2963 feet): Zum Bären inn, C, 25 b.).

Appenzell (alt. 789 m (2589 feet): pop. 5200; Hotel Säntis, C, 60 b., SP, SB; Hecht, C, 60 b.) has been since 1597 capital of the Roman Catholic half-canton of Appenzell-Innerrhoden. The town centre is well preserved, with fine old traditional houses. Interspersed among the painted wooden houses are stone buildings dating from the 16th c., including the Town Hall (local museum), the Schloss and the parish church of St Mauritius (nave of 1823). Also of interest are the Landsgemeindeplatz, the square in which the annual meeting of the community takes place, and the churches of the nunnery and Capuchin friary. – Appenzell is the terminus of the Gaiserbahn from St Gallen and a station on the Appenzellerbahn from Gossau, which runs via *Weissbad* (alt. 820 m (2690 feet): pop. 1500; Parkhotel) to *Wasserauen* (alt. 872 m (2861 feet)). There is a cableway to the *Ebenalp* (1644 m (5394 feet): inn), from which it is a 10 minutes' walk down through a 75 m (82 yards) long cavern to the *Wildkirchli* (1477 m (4846 feet): inn), a chapel in a cave which was inhabited by hermits from 1658 to 1853. In 1904 Palaeolithic implements and animal skeletons were found here. – From Wasserauen there is a pleasant walk (1 hour) to the *Seealpsee* (1146 m – 3760 feet), and from there to the *Meglisalp* (1520 m (4987 feet): inn).

Brülisau (alt. 922 m (3025 feet): pop. 700; Hotel Krone), the terminus of a postal bus service (Swiss postal buses convey both passengers and mail), has a cableway up the *Hoher Kasten* (1794 m – 5886 feet), from which there is a *geological trail* to Staubern. A road leads from the *Brühltobel* gorge to the *Sämtisersee* and *Fählensee* (mountain inns). Other good climbs are up *Fähnern* (1506 m – 4941 feet), with a little lake, the Forstseeli, and by way of the steep "Zahme Gocht" up the *Alpsigel* (1662 m – 5453 feet).

In the Vorderland of Ausserrhoden

Herisau (alt. 778 m (2553 feet): pop. 15,000; Hotel Rebstock, D, 21 b.; Sporthotel, D, 48 b.; Landhaus, D, 40 b.; sports centre), capital of the half-canton of Ausserrhoden, lies at the junction of the St Gallen–Wattwil (Bodensee–Toggenburg–Bahn) and Gossach–Urnäsch–Appenzell (Appenzellerbahn) railway lines, and has postal bus connections with Hundwil–Teufen–Speicher–Trogen and Schwellbrunn. The straggling little town, with a beautiful square, is a local market and industrial focal point.

A good impression of the character of the half-canton can be gained on the drive from Herisau to St Margrethen (49 km – 30 miles), via Waldstatt, Teufen (18 km – 11 miles), Trogen (25 km – 16 miles), Heiden (35 km – 22 miles) and Walzenhausen. The road crosses a number of deep gorges, including the Hundwiler Tobel near Waldstatt (concrete viaduct with a span of 105 m (345 feet)).

Hundwil (alt. 793 m (2602 feet): pop. 1000; inn) has handsome old houses in the characteristic local style and a 13th c. church. The *Hundwiler Höhi* (1305 m – 4282 feet), with a mountain inn, is a favourite local excursion. – 1 km (about a $\frac{1}{2}$ mile) beyond Hundwil we turn off the road to Appenzell (8 km – 5 miles) to reach *Stein* (alt. 823 m (2700 feet): pop. 1050; Rose inn), where daffodils (a protected species) bloom in March. Tourists can visit a model cheese factory opened in 1978, the only one of its kind in eastern Switzerland.

Teufen (alt. 837 m (2746 feet): pop. 5500; Zum Ochsen inn), a favourite residential town a few kilometres from St Gallen, is situated on the southern slopes of the *Fröhlichsegg* (1003 m (3291 feet): 20 minutes to top; restaurant). In the handsome square stands an interesting church built in 1778 by the family of a local builder, Hans Ulrich Grubenmann. Domestic industry (embroidery, weaving). – Beyond Teufen lies the pretty village of *Bühler* (alt. 828 m (2717 feet): pop. 1700; Sternen inn), with trim houses in the local style.

Gais (alt. 933 m (3061 feet): pop. 2400; Hotel Krone, D, 65 b.) is a popular health resort with one of the prettiest squares in the region (typical houses with curved gables). This was the first resort to offer the whey cure – medical treatment involving the medicinal properties of the whey of milk. There is a school of folk art. From the top of *Gäbris* (1247 m (4091 feet): 1 hour; inn) there are magnificent views in all directions (road closed on Saturdays and Sundays). – 4 km (2 miles) above Gais, on the *Stoss pass* (938 m (3078 feet): inn), are a chapel and a monument commemorating the victory of 400 Appenzellers over 3000 Austrians in 1405.

5 km (3 miles) NE of Teufen the health resort of *Speicher* (alt 926 m (3038 feet): pop. 3350; Kurhaus Appenzellerhof, C, 26 b.; Krone, C, 20 b., SB), is an idyllic village, to the N of which is the Vögelinsegg (959 m – 3146 feet). Here stands a monument commemorating the Appenzellers' victory over the Abbot of St Gallen in 1403 and there are extensive views of the Lake Constance area.

Trogen (alt. 903 m (2963 feet): pop. 1950; Hotel Krone, D, 20 b.; Schäfli, D, 22 b., SB), the terminus of the St Gallen–Speicher–Trogen tramway, houses the cantonal court and the cantonal school. In the centre of the village is the Landsgemeindeplatz, the elegant square in which the cantonal assembly meets in even-numbered years (in Hundswil in odd-numbered years); the square is surrounded by fine 18th c. houses, a church built by Grubenmann in 1779 and the Town Hall. – SW of Trogen is the Pestalozzi Children's Village for orphans of many nationalities, founded by the Zurich philosopher Walter Robert Corti in 1946. – From Trogen a beautiful minor road leads via the Ruppen (1010 m (3314 feet): inn) into the Rhine valley.

Another winding road (14 km – 9 miles) runs via Wald and Scheidegg (side roads to Rehetobel and Oberegg) to **Heiden** (alt. 806 m (2644 feet): pop. 4000; Kurhotel, C, 100 b., SB; Krone-Schweizerhof, C, 60 b., SP, Kursaal), a popular health resort in a park-like setting high above Lake Constance (rack-railway (cog-railway) from Rorschach, 7 km (4 miles) in 25 minutes), where stands a monument to Henri Dunant, founder of the Red Cross, who lived in Heiden from 1887 until his death in 1910. To the N, via Grub, lies the village of *Wienacht* (alt. 734 m (2408 feet): Kurhaus Landegg, C, 36 b.; Seeblick, C, 41 b., SB), with the Tobel vineyards. – From *Rheineck* there is a rack-railway (1898 m (6227 feet) long; 6 minutes) to *Walzenhausen* (alt. 673 m (2208 feet): pop. 2000; Kurhaus, D, 60 b., SP), 300 m (984 feet) above Lake Constance, and *Oberegg* (alt. 880 m (2887 feet): pop. 2500; Hotel Alpenhof), an enclave of Innerrhoden, 3 km (2 miles) SW of which is the St Anton viewpoint (1121 m – 3678 feet).

Between Herisau and Wattwil, on the Wasserfluh road, is *Schönengrund* (alt. 836 m (2743 feet)), which has a chair-lift up *Hochhamm* (length 1345 m (4413 feet), height difference 328 m (1076 feet), time 15 minutes). On a ridge of hills is the highest holiday village in Ausser-rhoden, *Schwellbrunn* (alt. 966 m (3169 feet): pop. 1200; Kreuz inn).

Arosa

Canton: Grisons (GR).
Altitude: 1740–1890 m (5709–6201 feet). – Population: 4500.
Post code: CH-7050. – Dialling code: 081.
(i) **Kurverein,**
opposite the Kursaal;
tel. 31 16 21.

HOTELS. – NEAR THE TWO LAKES: *Alexandra Palace*, A, 200 b., SB, panoramic restaurant on 9th floor; *Valsana*, B, 170 b. SB, SP; *Eden* (open only in winter), B, 160 b.; *Seehof* (only in winter), B, 120 b.; *Waldhotel National*, B, 160 b., SB; *Raetia*, B, 90 b.; *Post* (no rest.), B, 110 b.; *Mariposa-Residence* (no rest.), B, 32 b.; *Obersee*, C, 40 b.; *Carmenna*, C, 45 b.; *Isla*, C, 80 b.; *Astoria-Furka*, C, 60 b. – Cafeteria *Gloor*.

NEAR THE KURSAAL: *Park-Hotel*, A, 190 b., SB; *Savoy*, A, 220 b., SB; *Hohenfels* (only in winter), B, 90 b.; *Cristallo*, B, 70 b.; *Lamm* (no rest.), B, 40 b.; *Merkur*, C, 65 b.; *Central*, C, 80 b.; *Belvédère-Tanneck*, C, 70 b.; *Hubelsee* (no rest.), D, 40 b.; *Quellenhof*, E, 40 b.

ON THE SE SLOPES OF TSCHUGGEN: *Tschuggen Hotel Arosa*, A, 250 b., SB; *Bellavista* (only in winter), B, 160 b., SB; *Excelsior* (only in winter), B, 120 b., SB; *Streiff*, C, 75 b; *Herwig*, D, 95 b.

INNER-AROSA: *Arosa Kulm*, A, 250 b., SB; *Des Alpes* (only in winter), B, 70 b.; *Bellevue*, B, 110 b.; *Alpensonne*, C, 60 b.; *Brüggli*, C, 72 b.

ABOVE THE TOWN TO THE N: *Berghotel Prätschli*, B, 160 b.; *Golfhotel Hof Maran*, B, 120 b.

YOUTH HOSTEL. – CAMPING SITE.

RECREATION and SPORT. – Riding, golf (Maran), swimming (salt-water, whirlpool and heated outdoor baths at Club-Hotel Altein), tennis (indoor and outdoor courts), walking, climbing; Kursaal (gaming casino), children's crèches (where children may be safely left under supervision), play groups.

CABLEWAYS. – Cableways from Arosa station to the *Mittlere Hütte* (2013 m – 6605 feet) and the *Weisshorn* (2653 m (8704 feet): 15 minutes; restaurant) and from the lower station "Am Wasser" (1830 m – 6004 feet) to the *Hörnligrat* (2493 m (8180 feet): 15 minutes; mountain hut, serviced). – Chair-lifts up *Tschuggen* (2049 m (6723 feet): viewing station, observatory) and from the Mittlere Hütte to the *Brüggerhorn*.

WINTER SPORTS. – Natural and artificial ice rinks (curling); toboggan run; cross-country skiing; ski-bob runs; ski-lifts on Tschuggen, Plattenhorn (2318 m – 7605 feet), Hörnli, Carmenna (2177 m – 7143 feet) and Alp Prätschli. The most popular ski runs are on the *Weisshorn* (2657 m – 8718 feet), *Brüggerhorn* (2429 m (7970 feet): chair-lift) and *Hörnli* (2497 m – 8193 feet); on all three are serviced ski huts.

The popular summer and winter resort of *Arosa seems almost out of this world, lying as it does in a sheltered hollow in the high valley of the Schanfigg, surrounded by mountains, well away from the main traffic routes of the Grisons. The road from Chur, almost 1200 m (3937 feet) below, to Arosa is 30 km (19 miles) long and has many bends; there is also a narrow-gauge railway, opened in 1914, which takes just under an hour to reach the resort. Driving of cars is prohibited in the town after dark.

HISTORY. – The first settlement in the Arosa valley, then accessible only by toilsome bridle-paths, was initiated about 1220 by the monasteries of Churwalden and Sankt Luzi in Chur, and soon afterwards the population was increased by some families brought in from the Valais by the Barons of Vaz. From 1320 to 1851 Arosa belonged to the parish and commune of Davos, but thereafter became an independent commune. In the 15th c. the village had a population of only 150. The little village church was built in 1490. In 1575 most of the mountain pastures were sold to the town of Chur, which still owns some land in the commune. By 1850 the population had fallen to no more than 50. In 1875, however, the post road from Chur to Langwies was constructed, and in 1890 it was extended to Arosa; in 1880 the Seehof Hotel was built to provide accommodation for visitors. By the turn of the century Arosa had made a name for itself as a health resort, and in 1913 it ranked briefly as the leading resort in the Grisons. By 1930 the population

Arosa in winter

had risen to 3724. The first ski school was opened in 1933, and the first three cableways were constructed in 1939.

With excellent facilities for walkers and climbers in summer and skiers in winter, provision for a great variety of sports and more than 150 km (93 miles) of footpaths, Arosa has developed into one of Switzerland's leading resorts. Other features of interest are the little Late Gothic *church* (1493) in Inner-Arosa and the *Schanfigg Local Museum* (history of iron-mining and winter sports). In summer a miniature railway operates at the Arosa Kulm Hotel.

Arosa is an attractive town, with hotels dispersed about the beautiful sheltered valley and numerous small lakes. The tree-line passes through the resort, so that the skiing areas are almost completely open. The road from Chur runs from the *Obersee* (Upper Lake, 1740 m (5709 feet): rowing-boats), beside the **railway station**, above the *Untersee* (Lower Lake, 1694 m (5558 feet)), in a charming wooded setting, past the *Kursaal* (gaming casino) and up above the tree-line to the Alpine meadows of Inner-Arosa, sloping gently uphill. To the N is the mountain village of Maran, a favourite objective of walkers, reached on the "Eichhörnliweg" ("Squirrel's Path"). There are easy mountain walks over the Strela pass to Davos and by way of the Aroser Weisshorn to the Parpaner Weisshorn.

SURROUNDINGS. – Magnificent footpaths through the *pine-forests and flower-spangled *Alpine meadows: N over the *Maran* plateau to *Alp Prätdchli* (2000 m (6562 feet): ski-lift), 1 hour; from Inner-Arosa past the *Schwellisee* (1919 m – 6296 feet) to the romantic *Aelplisee* (2192 m – 7192 feet), 1¾ hours; from the Untersee up the *Welschtobel* gorge to the waterfalls on the *Alteinbach*, 1 hour. The best climbs are the *Aroser Weisshorn* (2653 m – 8704 feet), 2½ hours by way of the Mittlere Hütte, easy, and the *Aroser Rothorn* (2984 m – 9791 feet), 4 hours, rather more difficult, with superb *views.

Ascona

Canton: Ticino (TI)
Altitude: 196 m (643 feet). – Population: 4300.
Post code: CH-6612. – Dialling code: 093.
ⓘ **Ente Turistico di Ascona e Losone,**
   Via B. Papio;
    tel. 35 55 44.

Arosa in summer

HOTELS. – *Eden Roc*, on the lake, A, 80 b., SP, SB; *Delta*, near the airport, A, 90 b., SP, SB; *Castello del Sole*, A, 125 b., SP, SB; *Losone* (no rest.), A, 75 b., SP; *Casa Berno*, high above Lake Maggiore, B, 100 b., SP; *Europe*, on the lake, B, 80 b., SP, SB; *Ascolago*, on the lake, B, 45 b., SP, SB; *Acapulco*, on the lake, B, 80 b., SB; *Ascona*, on the Collina, B, 100 b., SP; *Monte Verità* (nature park), B, 88 b., SP; *Sasso Boretto*, B, 100 b., SB; *Tamaro*, on the lake, C, 70 b.; *Al Porto* (no rest.), on the lake, C, 65 b.; *Schiff* (no rest.), on the lake, C, 30 b.

CAMPING SITE on the Lido. – YOUTH HOSTELS: *Casa Emaus*, Losone; *Casa Moscia*, Ascona-Moscia; *Campo Pestalozzi*, Arcegno.

EVENTS. – *Risotto-feast* in the main squares of Ascona, Losone and Arcegno (Shrove Tuesday); *concerts* in the streets by brass bands (July–September); *exhibitions of pictures* in the Centro d'Arte (summer); *concerts* on summer evenings on the Brissago islands; *International Musical Festival* (August–October).

WATER SPORTS. – Fishing, swimming, sailing, scuba diving, wind-surfing on Lake Maggiore.

RECREATION and SPORT on land. – Billiards, boccia (bowls), flying (sightseeing flights, hire of light aircraft), golf, skittles, mini-golf, riding, tennis, walking (30 km (19 miles) of well-maintained footpaths); skating and curling on the Siberia ice-rink (October–March).

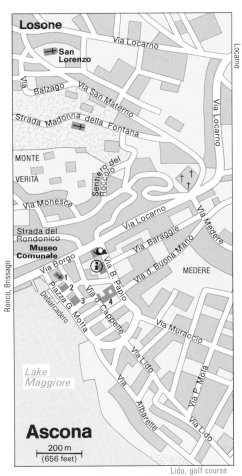

Ascona
200 m
(656 feet)

Lido, golf course

1 Church of S.S. Pietro e Paolo
2 Town Hall
3 Casa Serodine
4 Collegio Pontifico Papio

Ascona, on Lake Maggiore

Thanks to its beautiful situation in a mist-free bay on Lake Maggiore, sheltered from the N winds, and to its subtropical vegetation, *Ascona has developed from a little fishing village into one of Switzerland's most popular holiday resorts, excellently equipped for visitors. It has long hours of sunshine and a mild winter, so that flowers bloom here right through the winter. The main areas of activity from spring into autumn are the picturesque town, a pedestrian precinct with numerous little shops, art galleries and antique dealers, and the piazza on the lake.

HISTORY. – A prehistoric cemetery excavated in 1952 provided evidence of a Bronze Age settlement here (c. 800 B.C.). – The town was "discovered" by a group of vegetarians and nature-worshippers who settled on Monte Verità before and during the First World War. The artists' colony of Ascona attracted such leading figures as Lenin, Leoncavallo, Isadora Duncan, J. C. Jung and Rudolf Steiner, and later residents included the writers Remarque and Hermann Hesse and the painters Paul Klee, M. von Werefkin and Jawlensky. In the 1930s many refugees found a home on Lake Maggiore. The extensive modern development has unfortunately swallowed up the old village.

SIGHTS. – The Collegio Pontificio Papio (1584) has one of the finest Renaissance courtyards in Switzerland (two-storey loggias). – In the church of Santa Maria della Misericordia (1399–1442), belonging to a Dominican monastery, is a cycle of late Gothic frescoes. – Parish church of *SS. Pietro e Paolo* (first referred to in 1264; rebuilt in the 16th c.), a pillared basilica with lateral aisles; "Coronation of the Virgin", a painting by Giovanni Serodine (1633), in the Via Borgo the Museo Comunale with a collection of

Marianne Werefkin. – *Casa Serodine* (1620), now known as Casa Borrani, with a sumptuous façade. – *Casa Berno*, a typical Ticinese Baroque house, since 1978 a craft centre. – In the *Casa Anatta*, Monte Verità, are documents about the history of the mountain. To the south lies the large *lido*, the *Kursaal*, a golf-course and the airport.

SURROUNDINGS. – The road to Verbania (No. 13) follows the steep NW shore of ****Lake Maggiore** (see p. 176). To the right, high above the lake, is the picturesque village of Ronco; to the left are two small islands, the *Isole di Brissago* or *dei Conigli* ("Rabbit Islands"), on the larger of which is an interesting *Botanic Garden with Mediterranean flora. – 3·5 km (2 miles): *Porto Ronco*, where a minor road from Ronco comes in on the right. – 3·5 km (2 miles): **Brissago** (alt. 219 m (719 feet): Hotel Brenscino, C, 160 b.; Mirto au Lac, C, 46 b.), a popular summer resort (bathing lido), also noted for the manufacture of cigars ("Brissago", a long thin Virginia cigar). The town is charmingly situated at the foot of *Monte Limidario* (2189 m – 7182 feet), on the lower slopes of which are beautiful gardens with vegetation of southern type and vineyards. – 2 km (1 mile) beyond Brissago, at the little Lombard-style Renaissance church of the *Madonna del Ponte* (1528), is the *Italian frontier.*

Baden

Canton: Aargau (AG).
Altitude: 385 m (1263 feet). – Population: 13,600.
Post code: CH-5400. – Dialling code: 056.
ⓘ **Kur- und Verkehrsbüro,**
  in Kurpark;
    tel. 22 53 18.

HOTELS. – *Du Parc*, B, 100 b.; *Kappelerhof*. C, 55 b.; *Excelsior* (no rest.), D, 20 b.

SPA HOTELS. – ON LEFT BANK OF LIMMAT: **Staadhof*, A, SB, and *Verenahof-Ochsen*, B, together 150 b.; *Limmathof*, B, 75 b., SB; *Bären*, C, 80 b.; *Blume*, C, 50 b.; *Schweizerhof*, D, 60 b. – IN ENNETBADEN, ON RIGHT BANK OF LIMMAT: *Hirschen*, D, 100 b.

YOUTH HOSTEL. – CAMPING SITE, on the Limmat.

RECREATION and SPORT. – Tennis (indoor and outdoor courts), fishing, open-air swimming pool, indoor thermal baths, little theatre, concerts in Kursaal.

The health resort of Baden has long been an important market town. The picturesque old town, the core of the medieval settlement, lies in the Limmat defile under the Lägern hills; downstream is the spa, with its 19 sulphur springs (48 °C – 118 °F), already used for medicinal purposes

in Roman times, which are efficacious in the treatment of diseases of the joints (rheumatism) and catarrh. To the W of the spa, where the valley opens out, are the newer parts of the town, with large industrial plants (Brown-Boveri).

HISTORY. – Known to the Romans as *Aquae Helveticae*, Baden became in the Middle Ages the country's leading curative resort, the hot sulphurous water (1000 cu. m (35,310 cu. feet) daily) being piped up from a great depth. The town's central situation and its political activity made it a place of importance in the old Confederation, and the Diet frequently met here. The first hydroelectric power station was brought into operation in Baden in 1892.

SIGHTS. – At the entrance to the trim OLD TOWN, to the N, stands the 15th c. *Bruggerturm* (54 m (177 feet) high). A little way SE is the Roman Catholic **parish church** (built 1457–70, remodelled in Baroque style in 1612–98

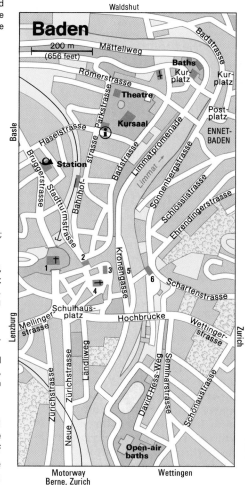

1 Stein Castle, with chapel   4 Parish church (R.C.)
2 Bruggerturm   5 Kornhaus
3 Stadthaus   6 Landvogteischloss

Baden – view over the Limmat to the old town

and in Neo-classical style in 1813–29), and facing it, to the N, the *Stadthaus* (Town Hall), with the Council Chamber (reconstructed in 1497) in which the Diet met between 1424 and 1712. A covered wooden *bridge* (1810) leads across the Limmat to the *Landvogteischloss* (rebuilt 1487–89), the old Governor's residence, which now houses the *Historical Museum*. On a crag to the W of the old town (road and rail tunnel) is the ruined castle of **Stein**, formerly a Habsburg seat.

The SPA is beautifully laid out with gardens (Kursaal, with gaming room and restaurant, inhalatorium (establishment where sulphur vapour can be inhaled), indoor thermal swimming pool). – A high-level bridge crosses the Limmat to *Ennetbaden* (alt. 358 m (1175 feet): pop. 2900), on the right bank.

SURROUNDINGS. – Baden is a good base for walks and climbs in the Lägern hills. 2¼ hours from Ennetbaden rises the *Burghorn* (863 m – 2832 feet), the highest point in these eastern outliers of the Jura (views of the Alps and Black Forest); ½ hour E, above the Limmat bridge, is *Schartenfels* (467 m (1532 feet): restaurant), and 2 km (1 mile) W *Baldegg* (572 m (1877 feet): restaurant), with a view of the Alps. – S of Baden the largest commune in the Aargau, **Wettingen** (alt. 395 m (1296 feet): pop. 19,500), was once a sleepy little wine-growing village, which has developed since the last war into a favourite residential town. In the bend of the Limmat is the best-preserved *Cistercian abbey* in the country, now a teachers' training college. The abbey (founded 1227) has superb Late Renaissance and Rococo decoration, finely carved choir-stalls and in the cloister some of the finest stained glass in Switzerland (182 roundels with coats of arms and figures, 13th–17th c.).

10 km (6 miles) NW of Baden lies **Brugg** (alt. 355 m (1165 feet): Hotel Rotes Haus, D, 36 b.), an old town of 7000 inhabitants and an important traffic junction near the confluence of the Aare, the Reuss and the

Limmat. As the name indicates, it grew up round its bridge, near which are the Black tower (Schwarzer Turm, 11th c.) and the Town Hall. In the old-world main street (No. 39) stands the house in which the educationist Heinrich Pestalozzi (1746–1827) died; his grave is at Birr, 7 km (4 miles) S. The Vindonissa Museum contains a rich collection of material from the Roman fort of Vindonissa.

The Zurich road (No. 3) passes the former convent of *Königsfelden* (on left), founded in 1308 by Elisabeth, widow of the German King Albrecht I, on the spot where he was murdered by Duke Johann of Swabia. The convent was converted into a mental hospital in 1866–72. The choir of the Gothic church has magnificent 14th c. *stained glass. – 1 km (about a ½ mile) beyond this is **Windisch** (alt. 366 m (1201 feet): to the left of road), on the left bank of the Reuss, the site of Roman *Vindonissa*. On the road to Lucerne, which goes off on the left just before the village, are remains of a large amphitheatre which could seat 10,000 spectators.

The ruined castle of Stein, Baden

Basle

Canton: Basel-Stadt (BS).
Altitude: 256–282 m (840–925 feet). – Population:
180,000.
Post code: CH-4000. – Dialling code: 061.
(i) **Verkehrsverein,**
Blumenrain 2,
CH-4001 Basle;
tel. 25 38 11.
Zentrale Unterkunftsvermittlung
(Accommodation Bureau),
in underpass at station,
CH-4021 Basle;
tel. 26 77 00.

HOTELS. – NEAR SBB RAILWAY STATION:* *Euler & Grand
Hôtel*, Centralbahnplatz 14, A, 100 b.;* *Schweizerhof*,
Centralbahnplatz 1, A, 100 b.; *Hilton*, Aeschen-
graben 31, A, 368 b., SB; *Alban-Ambassador*, Jacob-
Burckhardt-Strasse 61, B, 150 b.; *Bernina* (no rest.),
Innere Margarethenstrasse 14, B, 75 b.; *Victoria am
Bahnhof*, Centralbahnplatz 3–4, C, 160 b.; *City-Hotel*,
Henric-Petri-Strasse 12, C, 130 b.; *Jura*, Central-
bahnplatz 11, C, 100 b.; *Greub* (no rest.), Central-
bahnplatz 11, C, 70 b.; *Piccolo* (no rest.), Gartenstrasse
105, C, 140 b.; *Bristol*, Centralbahnstrasse 15, D, 55
b.; *Gotthard-Terminus*, Centralbahnstrasse 13, D, 60
b.; *Vogt-Flügelrad*, Küchengasse 20, D, 40 b.;
Helvetia, Küchengasse 13, E, 35 b.

IN THE TOWN: *Drei Könige am Rhein*, Blumenrain 8, A,
120 b.,* *International*, Steinentorstrasse 25, A, 350 b.,
SB; *Basel*, Münzgasse 12, B, 105 b.; *Drachen* (no
rest.), Aeschenvorstadt 24, C, 62 b.; *Cavalier*,
Reiterstrasse 1, D, 48 b.

ON THE RIGHT BANK OF THE RHINE: *Europe*, Clarastrasse
43, B, 250 b.; *Merian am Rhein*, corner of Rheingasse
and Greifengasse, B, 80 b.; *Alexander*, Riehenring 85,
B, 100 b.; *Krafft am Rhein*, Rheingasse 12, C, 78 b.;
Basilisk, Klingentalstrasse 1, C, 100 b.; *Admiral*,
Rostentalstrasse 5, C, 200 b., SP; *Du Commerce* (no
rest.), Riehenring 91, C, 60 b.; *Hecht am Rhein* (no
rest.), Rheingasse 8, D, 53 b.; *Solitude*, Grenza-
cherstrasse 206, D, 20 b.

IN BIRSFELDEN: *Alfa*, Hauptstrasse 15, C, 70 b.

YOUTH HOSTEL, Elisabethenstrasse 51. – CAMP-
ING SITE: Waldhort, in Reinach, on the road to
Delsberg.

RESTAURANTS. – CITY CENTRE (LEFT BANK OF RHINE):
* *Pfeffermühle*, Grünpfahlgasse 4; *Safranzunft*, Gerbergasse 11; *Stadtcasino*, Steinenberg 14 (Barfüsserplatz); *Steinenpick*, Steinentorstrasse 25;
Méditerranée/Cochon d'Or, Blumenrain 12 (terrace
with view of Rhine; fish dishes); *Kunsthalle*, Steinenberg 7; *Walliser Kanne*, Gerbergasse 50; *Schlüssel-
zunft*, Freie Strasse 25; *Zum Goldenen Sternen*, St
Alban Rheinweg; *Basler Keller*, Münzgasse 12; *Chez
Donati*, St Johanns Vorstadt 48; *Spalenburg Au
Tonneau*, Schnabelgasse 2; *Hasenburg*, Schneider-
gasse.

NEAR THE SBB STATION: *L'Escargot*, Centralbahnstrasse
10; *Steinbock*, Centralbahnstrasse 19; *Bahnhofbuffet
SBB*, in the station; *Schützenhaus*, Schützenmatt-
strasse 56; *Bruderholz*, Bruderholzallee 42; *A la Fine
Bouche*, Centralbahnplatz 14; *Pomodoro*, Steinenvorstadt 71; *Zoologischer Garten*, Bachlettenstrasse
72.

RIGHT BANK OF RHINE: *Mustermesse*, Messeplatz 1;
Taverne Valaisanne, Clarastrasse 27; *Fischerstube*,
Rheingasse 45 (own brewery); *Schnooggeloch*,
Rheingasse 12.

CAFÉS. – *Bachmann*, Eisengasse 1 (at the Mittlere
Rheinbrücke: good view); *Huguenin*, Barfüsserplatz
6; *Komödie*, Steinenvorstadt 63; *Frey*, Centralbahnstrasse 11; *Café zum Teufel*, Andreasplatz (an
artists' haunt); *Schiesser*, Marktplatz; *Pelmont*, Freie
Strasse 82, *Kämpf*, Spalenberg 35 and Clarastrasse
57, all four with good pâtisseries; *Spitz*,
Greifengasse/Rheingasse.

NIGHT SPOTS. – *Atlantis*, Klosterberg (young people
and jazz fans); *Stöckli*, Barfüsserplatz 1; *Club 59*,
Steinenvorstadt 33; *Hazyland*, Heuwaage.

EVENTS. – *Trade Fair*, April–May; *Basler Fasnacht*
(Carnival), beginning at 4 a.m. on the Monday after
Ash Wednesday with a parade of the "cliques" (clubs,
associations).

RECREATION and SPORT. – Golf, riding, tennis
(indoor and outdoor courts), swimming, skittles,
fishing.

*Basle (German Basel, French Bâle),
Switzerland's second largest city,
lying close to the French and German frontiers, has been an independent half-canton (Basel-Stadt)
since 1833, the other half being
Basel-Land. The city is built on both
sides of the Rhine, which here takes
a sharp turn northward between the
Swiss Jura and the Black Forest to
enter the Upper Rhine plain; upstream from Basle the river is known
as the High Rhine (Hochrhein).
Gross-Basel (Great Basle), the city's
commercial and cultural centre, lies
on the higher left bank; Klein-Basel
(Little Basle), where most of its
industry is situated, on the flat right
bank.

In the Rheinhafen, Basle

Situated on the Swiss frontier and at an
important river crossing, Basle soon
developed into an important commercial
town. Its heavy commercial traffic is now
served by two large railway stations and

the Rhine harbour (Rheinhafen) at Klein-hüningen, 3 km (2 miles) N of the city on the right bank of the river (shipping exhibition, "Our Way to the Sea"; viewing terrace on the grain elevator, 55 m (180 feet) high). At St-Louis, 9·5 km (6 miles) NW in French territory, is the Basle-Mulhouse airport (restaurant), with a 5 km (3 miles) long access road (customs). The city's main industries are the manufacture of chemicals and pharmaceuticals, machinery and electrical equipment; it also has numerous banks.

HISTORY. – In the second half of the 1st c. B.C. the hill on which the Minster now stands was occupied by a Celtic settlement, remains of the ramparts of which have been found in the Rittergasse. The proximity of the Roman town of *Augusta Raurica*, founded in 44 B.C. (see below, p. 71), led to the establishment of a Roman military station on the hill in 15 B.C. The name *Basilia* ("royal fortress") first appears in the records in A.D. 374, and soon after that date there is a reference to Basle as the see of a bishop. In the 10th c. the town belonged to Burgundy, and in 1025 it became part of the German Empire. A long history of conflict with the House of Habsburg ended in 1501 when the town joined the Swiss Confederation. In 1529 it went over to the Reformed faith. The University, founded by Pope Pius II in 1460, became, thanks to the presence of Erasmus from 1521 onwards, the principal centre of humanism, and its fame was maintained by a series of distinguished scholars and teachers in later periods: the physician Paracelsus lived in Basle in 1527–28, the mathematicians Jakob and Johann Bernoulli taught in the University in the 17th and 18th c., the cultural and art historian Jakob Burckhardt from 1844 to 1893, the philosopher Friedrich Nietzsche from 1869 to 1879. – Among artists connected with Basle were Hans Holbein the Younger (b. 1497 in Augsburg, d. 1543 in London), who spent many years in Basle between 1515 and 1538, and the 19th c. painter Arnold Böcklin (b. Basle 1827, d. Fiesole 1901).

Museums, Galleries, etc.

Hours of Opening

IN THE CITY

Antiquities, Museum of
(*Antikenmuseum*),
St-Alban-Graben 5;
Tue.–Sun. 10–12 and 2–5.

Art Collection, Public
(*Öffentliche Kunstsammlung*),
St-Alban-Graben 16;
Tue.–Sun. 10–12 and 2–5.

Art Gallery
(*Kunsthalle*),
Steinenberg 7;
daily 10–12 and 2–5,
Wednesdays also 7.30–9.30 p.m.

Basle Mission, Exhibition on
(*Ausstellung der Basler Mission*),
Missionsstrasse 21;
Mon.–Fri. 9–12 and 2–6.

City and Minster Museum
(*Stadt- und Münstermuseum*),
Unterer Rheinweg 26;
Tue.–Sat. 2–5,
Sun. 10–12 and 2–5.

Contemporary Art, Museum of
(*Museum für Gegenwartskunst*),
St-Alban-Tal 2;
Tue.–Sun. 10–12 and 2–5.

Ethnography, Museum of
See Natural History and Ethnography, Museum of

Fire Service Museum
(*Feuerwehrmuseum*),
Kornhausgasse 18;
Sun. 2–5.

Gymnastics and Sport, Swiss Museum of
(*Schweizerisches Turn- und Sportmuseum*),
Missionsstrasse 28;
daily 2–5,
Sun. also 10–12 midday

Historical Museum
(*Historisches Museum*),
(*Barfüsserkirche*),
Barfüsserplatz;
Tue.–Sun. 10–12 and 2–5.

Industrial Museum
(*Gewerbemuseum*),
Spalenvorstadt 2;
daily 10–12 and 2–5,
Wed. also 8–10 p.m.

Jewish Museum of Switzerland
(*Jüdisches Museum der Schweiz*),
Kornhausgasse 8;
Mon. and Wed. 3–5,
Sun. 10–12 and 3–5.

Kirschgarten, Haus zum
Elisabethenstrasse 27;
Tue.–Sun. 10–12 and 2–5.

Kunsthalle
See Art Gallery

Musical Instruments, Collection of Old
(*Sammlung alter Musikinstrumente*),
Leonhardsstrasse 8;
Sun. 10–12 and 2–5.

Natural History and Ethnography, Museum of
(*Natur- und Völkerkundemuseum*)
Natural History Museum (Naturhistorisches Museum),
Augustinergasse 2;
Tue.–Sun. 10–12 and 2–5.
Swiss Folk Museum (Schweizerisches Museum für Volkskunde),
Münsterplatz 20;
Tue.–Sun. 10–12 and 2–5.
Museum of Ethnography (Museum für Völkerkunde),
Augustinergasse 2;
at present closed.

Paper and the Book, Museum of
(*Basler Papier- und Buchmuseum*),
St-Alban-Tal 37.
Mon.–Sat. 2–5,
Sun. 10–12 and 2–7.

Pharmacy, Swiss Museum of the History of
(*Schweizerisches Pharmaziehistorisches Museum*),
Totengässlein 3;
Mon.–Fri. 9–12 and 2–5.

Rathaus
(*Council House*),
Marktplatz;
restoration in progress (seen by appointment).

Sculpture Gallery
(*Skulpturhalle*),
Mittlere Strasse 17;
Tue.–Sun. 10–12 and 2–5.

Stadt- und Münstermuseum
See City and Minster Museum

University Library
(*Universitätsbliothek*),
Schönbeinstrasse 20;
issue of books on loan Mon.–Fri. 10–5,
catalogue and reading rooms Mon.–Fri. 9–8, Sat. 9–5.

IN THE SURROUNDING AREA

Augusta Raurica,
Roman House and Museum,
Augst;
Daily 10–12 and 1.30–6.
Closed Mon. morning

Rhine Shipping Exhibition
(*Rheinschiffahrtsausstellung*),
Rheinhafen,
Kleinhüningen,
Wiesendamm 4;
March–October daily 10–12 and 2–5,
November–February Sat. and Sun. 10–12 and 2–5.

Village and Toy Museum
(*Dorf- und Spielzeugmuseum*),
Riehen,
Baselstrasse 34;
Wed. and Sat. 2–5,
Sun. 10–12 and 2–5.

Sightseeing in Basle

Gross-Basel (Great Basle) and Klein-Basel (Little Basle) are linked by six bridges over the Rhine. From the *Mittlere Rheinbrücke* (Middle Rhine Bridge, 1905), on the position of the first bridge in Basle, built in 1225, there is a fine view of the Minster. Upstream from this bridge are the busy *Wettsteinbrücke* (built 1879, widened 1937), the *Schwarzwaldbrücke* (Black Forest Bridge, 1973), which is designed for through traffic and the *Eisenbahnbrücke* (Railway Bridge), together with the dam of the Birsfelden hydroelectric power station. Downstream are the *Johanniterbrücke* (built 1882, rebuilt 1966) and the *Dreirosenbrücke* (1934). There are also three ferries, driven by the current, with no motors.

GROSS-BASEL, on the left bank of the Rhine, still preserves in the central area some features reminiscent of an old Imperial city, in spite of its many modern buildings and its busy commercial activity. – The Mittlere Brücke leads into the *Marktplatz* (Market Square), which is dominated by the brightly painted **Rathaus** (Council House). The main building, with arcades, is in Late Burgundian Gothic style (1504–21); the new wing to the left and the tall tower on the right are 19th c. additions. The wall-paintings in the attractive courtyard are in part the

Basle – view across the Rhine towards the Minster

work of Hans Bock (1608–11; restored). The statue (1580) on the outside staircase represents the legendary founder of the town, Munatius Plancus. Visitors can see the two council chambers (Regierungsratssaal and Grossratssaal) when they are not in use. – At the corner of the Marktplatz and *Freie Strasse* is the Renaissance *Geltenzunfthaus* (1578), the guild-house of the wine merchants. – A little way W, at Stadthausgasse 13, we find the Rococo *Stadthaus* (Town House, 1771), and at Totengässlein 3 the *Swiss Museum of the History of Pharmacy.* – NW of the Marktplatz is the little *Fischmarkt*, with a Gothic fountain (reproduction: original in Historical Museum).

SE of the Marktplatz the long *Münsterhügel* (Minster Hill) rises above the Rhine (reached from St-Alban-Graben by way of Rittergasse). The spacious *Münsterplatz*, on the site of the Roman fort, is an elegant 18th c. square.

The * **Minster** stands on the highest point of the hill, dominating the city with its two slender spires, its masonry of red Vosges sandstone and its colourfully patterned roof. The oldest parts of the building date from the 9th–13th c. It was rebuilt in Gothic style after an earthquake in 1356, and was a cathedral until the Reformation. The high altar and much of the furnishings were destroyed by militant Protestants in 1529. The church's greatest treasures were concealed in the vaulting of the sacristy and escaped destruction, but were sold when the canton was divided into two in 1833 and are now partly in the Historical Museum in Basle and partly dispersed among other museums throughout the world.

The *W front* and towers are entirely Gothic, with the exception of the lower part of the N tower (St George's tower), which dates from the end of the 11th c. St George's tower, with its elegant upper part and spire, is 64·2 m (211 feet) in height, the S tower (St Martin's), completed in 1500, 62·7 m (206 feet) high.

The sculptured friezes above the main doorway depict Prophets in the outer frieze, roses in the middle one and dancing angels in the inner one. To the right of the doorway is a figure of the "Prince of this world" dallying with one of the Foolish Virgins: from the front he looks a fine young man, but his back is crawling with adders and noxious vermin symbolising corruption. To the left of the doorway are depicted the founder of the church, the Emperor Henry II, with a model of the building, and the Empress Kunigunde. Farther out, under the towers, two mounted saints represent St George (left) and St Martin (right). Above St Martin are a clock and a sundial. On the

Minster   Basle

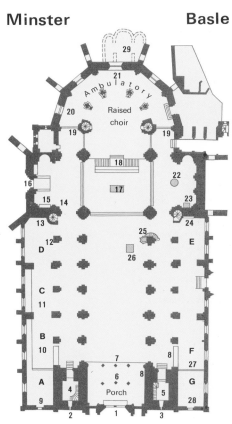

Münsterplatz

A Münch chapel	13 St Vincent panel (c. 1190)
B Neuenburg chapel	14 Tomb of Katharina von
C Aspelt chapel	Baden-Tierstein (d. 1385)
D Schaler chapel	15 Tomb of Georg von Andlau
E Fröwler chapel	(d. 1466)
F Tegernau chapel	16 St Gallus doorway (12th c.)
G Bebelnheim chapel	17 Communion table (1580)
	18 Choir-stalls (late 14th c.)
1 Main doorway (c. 1300)	used as rood-screen
2 St George	19 Entrances to crypt (bishops'
3 St Martin	tombs, 10th–13th c.; ceiling
4 St George's tower	frescoes, early 10th c.;
(1421–28)	lapidarium)
5 St Martin's tower	20 Tomb of Anna von
(1488–1500)	Hohenberg (Habsburg)
6 Organ (1955)	21 Late Romanesque wall-
7 Former choir screen (1381)	paintings and dedicatory
8 Fragments of stalls	inscription of 1202
(c. 1375)	22 Font (1465)
9 Hartung and Johannes	23 Bishop's throne (1380)
Münch monuments (late	24 Apostles panel (11th c.)
14th c.)	25 Pulpit (1486)
10 Monument of R. von	26 Fragment of pavement from
Tierstein (d. 1318); tomb of	an earlier church, with a
Thüring von Ramstein	drawing of a dragon
(d. 1367)	(c. 1170)
11 Tombstones of Oregius de	27 Tomb recess of Walter von
Conflens and Bartolomeo de	Klingen (d. 1380)
la Capra	28 Gravestone of Heinrich von
12 Monument of Erasmus	Flachslanden (d. 1353)
(d. 1536)	29 External crypt (9th c.)

central gable the figures of the founders appear again, and above them, enthroned and bearing the infant Jesus, is the Virgin (to whom the church is dedicated).

The **St Gallus doorway* in the N transept (12th c.), with numerous Romanesque figures showing an archaic severity of style, is one of the oldest figured doorways in German-speaking territory. Between the

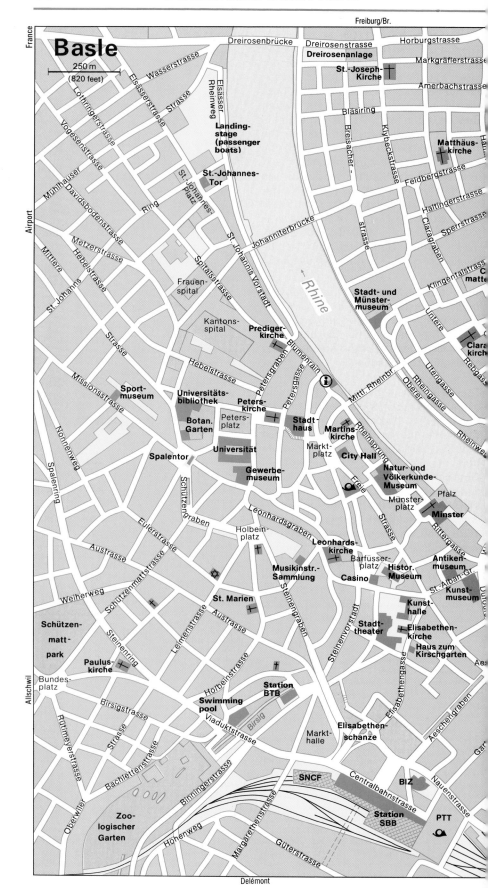

slender columns on either side of the doorway are four figures, two on each side, identified by their symbols (the ox, the lion, the eagle and the angel) as Luke, Mark, John and Matthew. To right and left of the Evangelists are six tabernacles with representations of the Six Works of Mercy; above them are John the Baptist with the Lamb of God (left) and John the Evangelist; and above these figures again are two angels with the trumpets of the Last Judgment. The tympanum above the doorway depicts the Wise and Foolish Virgins, with Christ enthroned above them as the Judge of the world, flanked by Peter and Paul, who present to Him the foundress and the sculptor. The large rose window above the St Gallus doorway symbolises the Wheel of Fortune. The choir, the lower part of which is Romanesque, has round arches borne on capitals with rich foliage decoration surmounted by figures of animals. In the paving E of the choir are lines showing the plan of a 9th c. external crypt which was discovered in 1947.

INTERIOR. – The church, which was carefully investigated and restored between 1963 and 1975, is 65 m (213 feet) long by 32·5 m (107 feet) across, with double lateral aisles; the outer aisles were originally a series of interconnected chapels. The raised choir is surrounded by an ambulatory, and under it is the crypt. The Gothic organ gallery was originally a rood-screen which until 1852 separated the chancel from the nave. In front of the pulpit, under glass, is a piece of the Late Romanesque pavement (12th c.). The Romanesque capitals in the nave and ambulatory are very fine. On the N side of the ambulatory is the sarcophagus of Anna von Hohenberg, wife of Rudolf of Habsburg, and her young son Karl (d. 1276).

Most of the interior furnishings were destroyed in 1529 by Protestants at the Reformation. The elaborately decorated High Gothic altar was the work of Hans von Nussdorf, builder of the Minster (1486). In the outer N aisle are a number of tombs and the monument of Erasmus, who died in Basle in 1536. The panel near here depicting eight scenes from the martyrdom and death of St Vincent of Saragossa and another panel depicting the Apostles in the outer S aisle date from the 11th c. and may be by the same sculptor. The choir-stalls, now at the entrance and the crossing as well as in the choir, are of the late 14th c. The *Crypt*, which can be entered from either side of the choir, contains the tombs of bishops of the 10th to 13th c. and other monuments. The Romanesque frieze on the piers shows fabulous themes, hunting scenes and interlace ornament. The ceiling frescoes depict scenes from the life of the Virgin, the childhood of Christ and the lives of St Martin of Tours and St Margaret. On either side of the altar, formerly dedicated to the Virgin, are life-size Romanesque statues of bishops, dated by an inscription to 1202. On the right-hand side of the altar recess, also identified by an inscription, is Bishop Adalbero, builder of the earlier cathedral of 1019. Under the crossing are a collection of lapidary material and the recently excavated walls of a still earlier church of the early 9th c. – The S tower can be climbed: access from inside the church.

The very beautiful double *Cloister* (entrance from Rittergasse), built in the 15th c. on Romanesque foundations, contains many monuments ranging over a period of five centuries, including that of the mathematician Bernoulli (d. 1705). Behind the Minster is the **Pfalz** ("Palace"), a terrace 20 m (66 feet) above the Rhine with fine views of the river and the hills of the Black Forest.

In *Augustinergasse*, which runs NW from the Münsterplatz, is a Neo-classical building (on left) which houses the rich **Museum of Natural History and Ethnography** (Natur- und Völkerkunde-museum). In the front part of the building is the *Natural History Museum*, to the rear the interesting *Museum of Ethnography*; and the complex also includes the *Swiss Folk Museum* and the *Collection on the History of Paper*. – Augustinergasse is continued by the *Rheinsprung*, which descends to the Mittlere Brücke, passing the old University on the left. In *Martins-gasse*, which runs parallel to the Rhein-sprung on the side away from the river, are two very handsome patrician houses, the *Blaues Haus* (Blue House) and *Weisses Haus* (White House), built between 1763 and 1770 for wealthy silk-merchants. At the W end of the Minster Hill, in a square with a fountain, stands *St Martin's church* (consecrated 1398), the oldest parish church in Basle.

From the Minster, *Rittergasse*, lined by handsome Rococo houses, runs SE into *St-Alban-Graben*. At the corner of Du-fourstrasse in a building designed by R. Christ and P. Bonatz (1932–36), is the ****Public Art Collection** or *Museum of Art* (Kunstmuseum), which contains the finest collection of pictures in Switzerland, including both old masters and modern art, and also a Print Cabinet.

On the first floor are the older masters, from Konrad Witz to Holbein the Younger (both well represented), and a collection of French and Dutch pictures presented by Professor Bachofen. The second floor houses an outstanding collection of 19th and 20th c. art, including Impressionists, Expressionists and Surrealists (Gauguin, Van Gogh, Corot, Corinth, Cézanne, Braque, Kokoschka, Picasso, Kandinsky, Léger, Chagall, Paul Klee, Juan Gris, Dali, Max Ernst), together with 20th c. works, special exhibitions, etc. Items of particular importance include the Heilsspiegel (Mirror of Salvation) Altar by Konrad Witz (d. *c.* 1447), portraits by Holbein (16th c.), a "Crucifixion" by Mathias Grünewald (d. 1528), paintings by Niklaus Manuel-Deutsch (d. 1530) and Rembrandt ("David with Goliath's Head", 1627), Böcklin's "Island of the Dead" (earliest version, 1880) and works by Ferdinand Hodler (1853–1918).

At 5 St-Alban-Graben is the **Museum of Antiquities** (Antikenmuseum), with Greek works of art from 2500 to 100 B.C.

Public Art Collection

Museum of Art, Basle

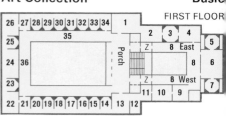

FIRST FLOOR

FIRST FLOOR

1–13 *German and Swiss painting of the 15th and 16th c.*
  1 Romanesque wall-paintings
  2 Konrad Witz
  3 School of Witz (1450–80)
  4 Hans Fries, Hans Holbein the Elder ("Death of the Virgin")
  5 Holbein the Elder, Lucas Cranach the Elder
  6 Hans Baldung, Cranach, Niklaus Manuel-Deutsch ("Judgment of Paris")
  7 Mathias Grünewald, Albrecht Altdorfer, Baldung ("Death and the Maiden", "Death and the Woman"), Hans Leu
  8 Hans Holbein the Younger (selection of drawings)
  9 Ambrosius Holbein, Hans Holbein the Younger (double portrait of Jakob Meyer zum Hasen, burgomaster of Basle, and his wife; portrait of Bonifacius Amerbach; portraits of Erasmus)
  10 Holbein the Younger, religious paintings ("Dead Christ", "Last Supper", panel of the Passion)
  11 Holbein the Younger, late portraits ("Family Group")
  12 Hans Bock the Elder (also Dutch painting of the 15th–17th c.)
  13 Tobias Stimmer, Bock; El Greco

12, 14–21 *Dutch painting of the 15th–17th c.*
  12 Quentin Matsys, Katharina von Hemessen, Frans Floris
  14 Jan Breughel the Elder, Joos de Momper, Tobias Verhaecht, etc.
  15 Rembrandt ("David presenting Goliath's Head to King Saul"), Pieter Lastman, Govert Flinck, Leonhard Bramer, etc.
  16–17 Flemish and Dutch landscapes: David Teniers the Younger, Jan van Goyen, Salomon van Ruysdael, Jacob van Ruisdael, Frans Post
  18 Adriaen Brouwer, Teniers, Adriaen van Ostade, Paulus Potter, etc.
  19 Jan van der Heyden, Pieter de Hooch, etc.
  20 Saburgh, Nicolaes Maes, Caspar Netscher
  21 Jan van de Velde III, Willem van Aelst, Jan Fyt, etc.

22–23 *18th c. painting*
  22 Hyacinthe Rigaud, Anton Graff, Hubert Robert, Johann Heinrich Füssli (Fuseli), etc.
  23 Swiss Alpine and landscape pictures: Caspar Wolf

24–25 *Romantic Neo-classicism*
  24 Peter Birman, Joseph Anton Koch ("Macbeth and the Witches"), Charles Gleyre
  25 Ferdinand von Olivier, Friedrich Overbeck, Moritz von Schwind, Carl Gustav Carus
  26 Early 19th c. Swiss landscapists

27–34 *19th c. French painting*
  27 Théodore Géricault, Eugène Delacroix, Camille Corot ("Italienne à la Fontaine")
  28–34 Gustave Courbet, Edouard Manet, Auguste Renoir, Camille Pissarro, Claude Monet, Edgar Degas ("Le Jockey blessé"), Paul Cézanne ("Montagne Sainte-Victoire"), Paul Gauguin ("Ta Matete"), Vincent van Gogh, Auguste Rodin ("L'Homme qui marche", in porch)

29 *German painting of the 19th c. (second half)*
Hans von Marèes ("Self-Portrait in High Hat"), Anselm von Feuerbach (corridor, 36)

35–36 *19th c. Swiss painting*
  35 Ferdinand Hodler ("The Valiant Wife", "Lake Geneva from Chexbres")
  36 Holler, Feuerbach (see also 19th c. German painting), Arnold Böcklin ("Fight with Centaurs", "Island of the Dead", "Odysseus and Calypso", "The Plague")
  Z Temporary displays of prints, etc.

Public   Museum of Art,
Art Collection   Basle

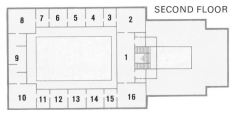

SECOND FLOOR

SECOND FLOOR

20th c. painting and sculpture
Particularly notable for works of Picasso's Cubist period
("Pains et compotier aux fruits sur une table"). Since
there are frequent changes, the arrangement may not be as
shown below. In addition to the artists mentioned, the
Museum also possesses works by Juan Gris ("Le Violon"),
Henri Matisse ("Hommage à Blériot"), Delaunay, Jean
Dubuffet, Serge Poliakoff and Antoine Tàpies.
2 Picasso ("L'Aficionada")
3 Pictures and the Fauves
4 Expressionism, including 20 works by German painters
   which were branded by the German government in 1939 as
   "degenerate" and sold: Paula Modersohn-Becker ("Self-
   Portrait"), Lovis Corinth ("Ecce Homo"), Franz Marc
   ("Destiny of Animals"), Oskar Schlemmer ("Four Figures
   in Space – Roman"), Oskar Kokoschka ("Storm"), Max
   Beckmann, Otto Dix ("The Artist's Parents")
5–7 Marc Chagall, Henri Rousseau, Georges Rouault, etc.
8 Georges Braque ("Violon et Cruche", "Le Portugais")
9 Fernand Léger ("Eléments mécaniques")
10 Alberto Giacometti (sculpture and paintings)
11 Dadaism, Surrealism: Salvador Dali ("The Burning
   Giraffe"), Joan Miró, Max Ernst ("La Grande forêt")
12 Paul Klee ("Villa R", "Ad marginem"), Wassily Kandinsky
13 Hans Arp, Sophie Taeubner-Arp; De Stijl; Constructivism
   (Piet Mondrian, El Lissitzky, László Moholy-Nagy, Georges
   Vatongerloo); Antoine Pevsner (sculpture)
14 Ecole de Paris, Joseph Beuys ("Scene of the Fire")

15–16 *American painting*
   Franz Kline; Barnett Newman, Clifford Still, Mark Rothko,
   Cy Twombly, Jasper Johns ("Voice 2"), Frank Stella
   ("Ifaga II"), Claes Oldenburg, Andy Warhol, Carl Andre
   ("Cedar Piece"), Donald Judd, Sol Le Witt; Sam Francis
   (staircase)
The Museum's large collection of *20th c. Swiss painting
and sculpture* (including Jean Tinguely, etc.) can be displayed
only in selected groups, varying from time to time.
In the entrance courtyard of the Museum is Rodin's "Burghers of
Calais".

and Roman and other Italian art from
1000 B.C. to A.D. 300 (including some
items on loan).

To the W of the Museum of Art, on the
left-hand side of the street called *Steinenberg*, stands the *Art Gallery* (Kunsthalle,
with restaurant), used for special exhibitions. At the far end of the street, on the
right, is the *Municipal Casino* (Stadtcasino: restaurant), with a wall-painting
by A. H. Pelligrini (1940). In Theater-
strasse, to the left, we find the **Municipal Theatre** (Stadttheater, 1975), in
front of which is the unusual "Carnival
Fountain" (Fasnachtsbrunnen), by Jean
Tinguely. – In *Elisabethenstrasse*, to the E
of the Theatre, one of the finest of Basle's
patrician houses, the *Haus zum Kirschgarten* (1780: No. 27), contains 25 rooms

furnished in 18th c. style (including toys,
porcelain, etc.).

In the busy *Barfüsserplatz* is the 14th c.
Barfüsserkirche (church of the Barefoot
Friars), which now houses the * **Historical Museum**, with an important collection on the history of culture and art
(renovated 1975–81; cellars constructed
and reconstruction of the rood screen).
Notable exhibits in the nave of the church
are the Late Gothic tapestries and the
"Lällenkönig" ("Babbling King"), a
crowned head with a movable tongue and
eyes, once the emblem of Gross-Basel
(17th c.). In the aisles are weapons and
furnished rooms, in the choir religious art,
in the crypt the Minster treasury. – Above
the W side of the square rises *St Leonard's
church* (Leonhardskirche), rebuilt between 1480 and 1512 and restored in
1965. The crypt is Romanesque; the choir
dates from the 13th–14th c. The former
monastery adjoining the church, known
as the *Lohnhof*, is now occupied by the
police.

From the Steinenberg we go NW along
Kohlenberg and Leonhardsgraben. To the
left, in Kornhausgasse (No. 8), is the
Jewish Museum of Switzerland. We then
come into the *Spalenvorstadt*, which can
also be reached from the Marktplatz up a
picturesque flight of steps. At the near end
of this street, on the right (No. 2), is the
Industrial Museum (Gewerbemuseum:
periodic special exhibitions). Farther
along, on the left, is the *Spalenbrunnen*, a
fountain also known as the *Holbein
Fountain* (after Holbein and Dürer: original in Historical Museum). In the centre
of this part of the town is the tree-shaded
Petersplatz, on the E side of which stands
St Peter's church (Peterskirche), rebuilt at the time of the Council of Basle
(15th c.), with a gallery running round the
nave and reticulated vaulting in the choir
from an earlier building (14th c.); interesting frescoes in the Eberler chapel and the
nave. In front of the church is a bronze
bust of the poet J. P. Hebel (b. Basle
1760). On the N side of the square is the
handsome *Wild'sches Haus* (1763) and
on the W side the *Botanic Garden* of the
University. Beyond this a concrete building (1965) houses the rich *University
Library* (Universitätsbibliothek), with
numerous incunabula and manuscripts
dating from the time of the Council of
Basle (1431–87).

Spalentor, Basle

On the S side of Petersplatz can be seen the new **University** building (1938–46). At the entrance is a mural painting, in the corridors pictures and busts, including one of Pope Pius II, who founded the University in 1460. The Great Hall (Aula) contains ten stained-glass windows, and there is a beautiful courtyard. To the W of the University is the *Spalentor (1370), a fortified gate which marks the end of the old town. At 28 Missionsstrasse is the *Swiss Museum of Gymnastics and Sport.* – At the foot of Petersgraben, which runs down to the Rhine from Petersplatz, is the *Predigerkirche* (Dominican church), a long building of the 14th–15th c. with a graceful roof turret. Opposite is the house in which the poet Johann Peter Hebel (1760–1826) was born (plaque).

On the S side of the old town is the main **railway station** (*Bahnhof SBB*), with the *Centralbahnplatz* (underground passage with shops, information bureau and café) in front of it. Nearby stands the circular tower block (1975) of the Bank for International Settlements (Bank für Internationalen Zahlungsausgleich, *BIZ*). – To the W, in the valley of the Birsig, is the large and interesting *Zoo (Zoologischer Garten: restaurant), with a vivarium (fishes, penguins, reptiles), an excellent new monkey-house (1970)

and a children's zoo. The zoo has been particularly successful in breeding rhinoceroses. The elephants put on a performance in a special arena and give rides to children.

In the NW of the city *St Antony's church* (1927) was in its day a pioneering example of concrete architecture (fine windows).

To the E of the old town is the St-ALBAN-VORSTADT, which runs E to the *St-Alban-Tor*, an old town gate restored in 1873. From here the Mühlenberg runs down to the old *St Alban's monastery*, under the town walls; part of its Romanesque cloister is preserved in a neighbouring house. To the E, on the Gewerbebach, an old paper-mill with modern extensions now houses the *Museum of Contemporary Art* (Museum für Gegenwartskunst), an annexe of the Museum of Art, with works by Chagall, de Chirico, Dali, Braque, Mondrian, Klee, Arp, Pevsner, Giacometti, Moore and Tinguely. There is an attractive trip across the Rhine to Klein-Basel by ferry.

In KLEIN-BASEL a tree-lined promenade runs along the bank of the river, affording fine views of the old town. At 26 Unterer Rheinweg, a little way NW of the Mittlere Brücke, is the *City and Minster Museum* (Stadt- und Münstermuseum), notable particularly for its collection of sculpture from the Minster. In *Claraplatz* stands the Roman Catholic *Clarakirche* (in part 13th c.). – Near the Wettstein bridge is the St-Theodor-Kirchplatz, in which is the Late Gothic *St Theodore's church* (15th c.). Between the square and the river we find the old *Carthusian monastery*, now an orphanage. – One of the main traffic arteries of Klein-Basel is the *Riehenring*, along which extend the exhibition halls of the **Swiss Trade Fair** (*Schweizer Mustermesse*: restaurant). – A little way E, at Vogelsangstrasse 15, is the *Technical College* (Gewerbeschule, 1961), which has a column by Hans Arp in the courtyard. – 0·5 km (about a $\frac{1}{4}$ mile) NE is the *Baden Railway Station* (Badischer Bahnhof), the German Railways (*DB*) terminus. Beyond the railway line, along the little River Wiese, is situated the popular *Lange Erlen Zoo* (Tierpark: cafés). – In *Riehen* (Baselstrasse 34) is the *Village and Toy Museum*; vineyards.

SURROUNDINGS. – Boats leave from the Mittlere Brücke for trips on the Rhine or around the port installations; boats to Rotterdam from St Johann, Elsässerrheinweg.

To Kaiseraugst. – Leave Basle on the E and join the motorway (N2/N3), which crosses the Rhine on a large bridge. After crossing the River *Birs* we come in 3·5 km (2 miles) to the exit for the Basle suburb of *Birsfelden*, on the N bank of the Rhine. Here there are port installations and a power station built in 1950–55 (visitors' gallery). We continue along the S edge of the *Hard* forest and through a tunnel, beyond which the southern slopes of the Black Forest can be seen on the left. 6·5 km (4 miles): *Liestal-Augst* exit. 6 km (4 miles) S is Liestal; 1 km (about a ½ mile) N is **Augst** (alt. 275 m (902 feet): Hotel Rössli), on the left bank of the *Ergolz*, which here flows into the Rhine and forms the boundary between the cantons of Basel-Land and Aargau.

0·5 km (about a ¼ mile) uphill from the town (signposted) is the site of the Roman colony of *Augusta Raurica*, founded about 27 B.C., with a large theatre and the remains of several temples. At the near end of the site, on the left, is a reconstruction of a Roman house (1953–57) containing a museum. To the right is the theatre (restored: performances in summer), and beyond this to the E the site of a temple,

the main forum and a basilica. On a hill W of the theatre are the remains of a large temple, and to the S a residential district. SW of the main complex is an amphitheatre discovered in 1959.

1 km (about a ½ mile) NE of Augst beyond the Ergolz, beautifully situated on the banks of the Rhine, the little town of **Kaiseraugst** (Gasthaus Löwen; camping site) has the remains of a Roman fortified post and a scrap metal plant (capable of disposing of 70 cars an hour). On the Rhine is the *Augst-Wyhlen* power station (1907–12), which has a dam 212 m (696 feet) long; nuclear power station planned.

Basle via Dornach to Liestal. – Leave from the main railway station on Münchensteiner Strasse and after crossing the railway line take a road on the left; then, soon afterwards, keep straight ahead through the suburb of *Neuewelt* and over the *Birs*. – 6 km (4 miles): *Münchenstein* (alt. 340 m (1116 feet)), where there is an old church. – 2 km (1 mile): **Arlesheim** (alt. 340 m (1116 feet): Hotel Ochsen, 10 b.), with a church built in 1681 and remodelled in Rococo style in 1760 (Silbermann organ of 1761) and many country houses. On the wooded hill above the town are *Burg Reichenstein* (alt. 480 m (1575 feet)) and *Schloss Birseck* (private property), formerly the residence of the Prince-Bishops of Basle. – 1 km (about a ½ mile): *Dornachbrugg* (alt. 295 m (968 feet)),

Basle Zoo

↕ Entrance/exit
← Exit only
P Car parks

1 Main entrance and director's office
2 Kiosk (books)
3 Fishes, penguins, reptiles
4 Aquatic birds
5 Somali wild asses, bongos
6 Brown bears, Malayan bears, spectacle bears, polar bears
7 Zebras, ostriches, flamingos
8 Orangutans, gorillas, chimpanzees, spider monkeys, smaller monkeys
9 Birds from all continents
10 Waterfowl and waders
11 African and Indian elephants
12 Elephant arena
13 Otters, civets, ratels
14 Waders and waterfowl; moorland sheep; ponies
15 Lions, tigers, panthers, fossas, servals
16 Antelopes, giraffes, kudus; kangaroos
17 Rhinoceroses, pigmy hippopotamuses, tapirs
18 Parrots, cockatoos, keas
19 Penguins
20 Barbary sheep, Himalayan thars
21 Père David's deer
22 Birds of prey (golden eagle, bateleur eagle, vulture, raven)
23 Covered seating
24 Sea-lions
25 Owls (snowy owl, eagle-owl)
26 Marmots, wombats
27 Sardinian wild sheep
28 Wolves
29 Camels, llamas, pigmy zebus
30 Wild pigs, musk-oxen, bison
31 Children's zoo (ponies, pigmy goats, domestic animals)

Dorenbachviadukt

Goetheanum, Dornach

with a Capuchin friary. – 1 km (about a ½ mile): **Dornach** (alt. 300 m (984 feet)), a pretty village, to the N of which is the *Goetheanum*, a massive concrete structure built to house the headquarters of the Anthroposophical Society founded by Rudolf

Steiner (1861–1925), with urns containing the remains of Rudolf Steiner, Christian Morgenstern and others (conducted tours). On a hill to the E are the ruins of *Dorneck Castle*. – From Dornach the road winds uphill through wooded country for 7 km (4 miles) to *Gempen* (alt. 672 m (2205 feet)): side road on left ascending the *Gempenfluh (765 m – 2510 feet), with magnificent views of the Jura and of the Rhine, extending beyond Basle to Strasbourg. – From Gempen the road winds its way down for 10 km (6 miles) E to **Liestal** (alt. 330 m (1083 feet): Hotel Engel, C, 60 b.; Radackerhof, C, 51 b.), chief town of the half-canton of Basel-Land. 16th c. Town Hall, with the gold cup of Charles the Bold, Duke of Burgundy, which was captured at Nancy in 1477. ''Dichtermuseum'' (Writers' Museum), with mementoes of the Nobel Prize winner Carl Spitteler (1845–1924), who was born in Liestal, Georg Herwegh (1817–75) and others. At the end of Rathausstrasse is the picturesque Oberes Tor (Upper Gate). NW of the town, at Munzach, are the remains of

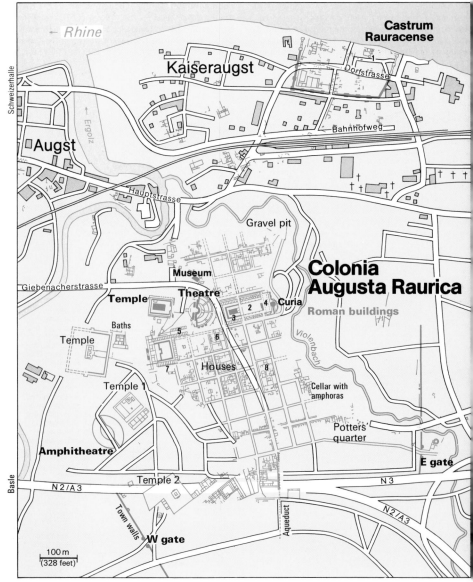

1 Baptistery   2 Principal forum   3 Temple   4 Basilica   5 Subsidiary forum   6 Women's baths   7 S forum   8 Central baths

.iestal

Roman villa (mosaics, etc.). 5 km (3 miles) N via the oliday settlement of *Bienenberg* (alt. 431 m (1414 eet)) is *Bad Schauenburg* (468 m – 1536 feet: :urhaus, Hotel Bad Schauenburg, 42 b.); both places ave brine baths.

3asle to Laufen through the Birsig valley. – .eave Basle by Oberwiler Strasse, passing the Zoo. – : km (1 mile): *Binningen* (alt. 285 m (935 feet): estaurants in Schloss Binningen and Holeeschloss, vith outlook terrace). – 2 km (1 mile): Bottmingen alt. 295 m (968 feet)), has a medieval moated castle enovated in the 18th c.: (restaurant). – 1·5 km (1 nile): *Oberwil* (alt. 315 m (1034 feet)). – 2·5 km (2 niles): *Therwil* (alt. 309 m (1014 feet)), boasts a fine :hurch. – 2·5 km (2 miles): *Ettingen*. – 4 km (2 miles): 'lüh, just on the French frontier, with a chalybeate spring. On a hill beyond the frontier is the ruined castle f *Landskron* (546 m – 1791 feet). – Beyond Flüh the oad climbs sharply. 2·5 km (2 miles): **Mariastein** alt. 515 m (1690 feet): Hotel Post, 20 b.) has a 3enedictine abbey on a steep-sided crag which was ounded in 1645, dissolved in 1874, and reoccupied y Benedictines in 1941; there is also a pilgrimage :hurch (1648–55) and the cave of Maria im Stein. – km (1 mile): *Metzerlen* (alt. 530 m (1739 feet)). – The oad runs up on to the western slopes of Blauen and hen descends steeply to (9 km – 6 miles) **Laufen** (alt. 358 m (1175 feet): Hôtel du Jura), a little town of 3500 inhabitants on the S side of the hill. Two town jates belonging to the old fortifications, the Baslertor nd the Obertor; St Catherine's church (1698); palace)f the Prince-Bishops, now the Prefecture. Large imestone quarry.

Bellinzona

:anton: Ticino (TI).
Altitude: 230 m (755 feet). – Population: 18,200.
ⓘ **Ente Turistico di Bellinzona e Dintorni,**
    Via Camminata;
    tel. 25 21 31.

HOTELS. – *Unione*, Via General Guisan 4, C, 75 b.; Gamper, Viale Stazione 29, D, 50 b.; *Internazionale*, °iazza Stazione, 40 b.; *Metropoli*, Via L. il Moro 5, 25 .; *Croce Federale*, Viale Stazione 12, 24 b. – YOUTH HOSTEL in Bodio (25 km – 16 miles).

RESTAURANTS. – *Grotti Torcett*, Pedevilla; *Della Rocca*, Carasso; *Delcò Raffaelle*, Carasso; *Grottino 'eatro*, Bellinzona.

EVENTS. – Typical weekly market every Saturday 7 to 11.30 a.m.; Carnival, with risotto feast in open air.

RECREATION and SPORT. – Tennis, swimming, fishing, walking.

Three important N–S routes – the roads over the Alpine passes of St Gotthard, San Bernardino and Lucomagno – meet in the valley of the Ticino, and could in the past be closed by a barrier across the road at Bellinzona. The town thus occupied a key strategic situation for many centuries, and this led to its selection as the cantonal capital in 1878. It is now an educational focal point as well as the seat of cantonal administration.

The town is still dominated by its three *castles, an impressive example of a medieval defensive system. The castles and a double circuit of walls were built by the town's Milanese rulers in the second half of the 15th c.

HISTORY. – The region was occupied by Rome for five centuries, from about 30 B.C. to A.D. 450. Bellinzona itself first appears in the records in A.D. 590. In 1242 it fell into the hands of Milan, ruled by the Visconti family and later by the Sforzas. In 1503 the Confederates established the governor's headquarters in the castles. In 1803 Bellinzona became part of the new canton of Ticino.

SIGHTS. – The main features of interest in Bellinzona are the three castles – the **Castello Grande** (13th c.), also known as *Burg Uri* or *San Michele*, with five wards; the **Castello di Montebello** (*Burg Schwyz*), the most interesting of

Bellinzona

Bellinzona

St. Gotthard, San Bernadino

1 Castello Grande
2 Castello di Montebello
3 Castello di Sasso Corbaro
4 Church of SS Pietro & Stefano
5 Government Palace

the three as an example of the art of fortification (originally centred on the keep, with a 13th c. palace and courtyard and further structures built between 1460 and 1480), which now contains a *historical and archaeological museum*; and the **Castello di Sasso Corbaro** (*Burg Unterwalden*), built in 1479, with the *Ticino Museum* (arts and crafts, local costumes). Also worth seeing are the collegiate *church of SS. Pietro e Stefano* (R.C.), a fine Renaissance building with a rich Baroque interior, largely rebuilt in 1517; the former Franciscan *church of S. Maria delle Grazie* has magnificent Renaissance wall-paintings by Lombard artists working in Ticino (16th c.); the

Palazzo del Governo (1738–43, altered 1867–69); and the old town with its picturesque little streets, arcades, old doorways and wrought-iron balconies.

In the outlying district of *Ravecchia* (1·5 km (1 mile) S), off the road to the left, is the Romanesque church of San Biagio (S Blaise), with fine frescoes of the 14th–15th c.

Berne

Canton: Berne (BE).
Altitude: 540 m (1772 feet). – Population: 141,000.
Post code: CH-3000. – Dialling code: 031.
(i) **Offizielles Verkehrs- und Kongressbüro,** Bahnhof (Station),
P.O.B. 2700,
CH-3001 Berne;
tel. 22 76 76.

EMBASSIES. – *United Kingdom*, Thunstrasse 50 (tel. 44 50 21–26); *United States*, Jubiläumstrasse 93 (tel. 43 70 11); *Canada*, Kirchenfeldstrasse 88 (tel. 44 63 81).

HOTELS. – NEAR STATION: *Schweizerhof*, Schweizer hoflaube 11, A, 170 b.; *Alfa*, Laupenstrasse 15 B, 60 b.; *City-Mövenpick*, Bubenbergplatz 7, B 70 b.; *Bristol* (no rest.), Schauplatzgasse 10, B, 130 b.; *Savoy* (no rest.), Neuengasse 26, B, 95 b.; *Bären* Schauplatzgasse 4, B, 91 b.; *Stadthof*, Speichergasse 27, B, 55 b.; *Wächter-Mövenpick*, Genfergasse 4, C, 60 b.; *Krebs* (no rest.), Genfergasse 8, C, 70 b; *National* Hirschengraben 25, D, 42.

BETWEEN THE KÄFIGTURM AND THE NYDEGG BRIDGE *Bellevue-Palace*, Kochergasse 3–5, A, 223 b. *Metropole*, Zeughausgasse 26–28, B, 100 b.; *Kreuz* (Christliches Hospiz), Zeughausgasse 41, C, 160 b.

Berne – panoramic view, with the Minster and the Bundeshaus

Continental, Zeughausgasse 27, C, 65 b.; Arca, Gerechtigkeitsgasse 18, C, 30 b.; Nydeck, Gerechtigkeitsgasse 1, C, 22 b.; Volkshaus, Zeughausgasse 9, D, 110 b.; Hospiz zur Heimat, Gerechtigskeitsgasse 50, D, 60 b.; Goldener Schlüssel, Rathausgasse 72, E, 40 b.

S OF HELVETIAPLATZ: Silvahog, Jubiläumsstrasse 97, B, 85 b.

SW AND NW OF STATION: Touring, Eigerplatz, C, 100 b.; Regina-Arabelle, Mittelstrasse 6, C, 60 b.

YOUTH HOSTEL. – Weihergasse 4.

CAMPING SITES. – Eymatt, 5 km (3 miles) NW on the road to Wohlen; Eichholz, 4 km (2 miles) SE on the road to Belg.

RESTAURANTS. – NEAR STATION: Le Mazot, Bärenplatz 5; Börse, Bärenplatz 27; Bahnhofbuffet, Bahnhofplatz 10; Della Casa, Schauplatzgasse 16; Pizzeria Pinocchio, Aarbergergasse 6; Innere Enge, Engestrasse 54, 1·5 km (1 mile) N on the left bank of the Aare.

BETWEEN THE KÄFIGTURN AND THE NYDEGG BRIDGE: Ermitage, Marktgasse 15/Amthausgasse 10; Du Théâtre, Theaterplatz 7; Chindlifrässer, Kornhausplatz 7; Commerce, Gerechtigkeitsgasse 74; Mistral, Kramgasse 42.

ON THE RIGHT BANK OF THE AARE: Kongress- und Kursaal, Schänzlistrasse 71–77; Rosengarten, Alter Aargauerstalden 31 B (beautiful view); Schönau, Sandrainstrasse 68, at the Dählhölzli zoo.

CAFÉS. – Du Théâtre, Theaterplatz 7; Casino, Casinoplatz; Rudolf, Laupenstrasse 1; Café de Paris, Spitalgasse 22.

RECREATION and SPORT. – Golf, riding, tennis (indoor and outdoor courts), swimming, fishing.

The Swiss capital, *Berne (German spelling Bern), is also capital of Switzerland's second largest canton and a university town. The old town, dominated by the Minster (or basilica), is built on a sandstone ridge encircled on three sides by the Aare, flowing in a valley 35–40 m (115–131 feet) deep. High-level bridges link it with the high ground on the right bank and with the newer parts of the city.

The charming older part of Berne still preserves its original layout. The houses, with their arcades on street level (6 km (4 miles) of arcades altogether) and their projecting roofs, reflect the prosperity of the citizens of Berne in the 18th c. Most of the attractive fountains, painted in lively colours, were the work of Hans Gieng (1540–45). – The industries of Berne include textiles, machinery, chocolate, pharmaceuticals, foodstuffs, the graphic trades and electrical equipment, and it also has a considerable trade in agricultural produce.

HISTORY. – The town is believed to have been founded on its excellent defensive site by Berthold V of Zähringen in 1191. After the Zähringen dynasty died out the Emperor Frederick II granted Berne self-government and its own law court. In the Battle of Laupen (1339) the Bernese, led by Rudolf von Erlach, defeated the Burgundian nobility. In 1353 Berne became a member of the young Confederation, in which the military prowess of its citizens enabled it to play a leading role. In 1528 the Reformation came to the town. Since 1848 Berne has been the seat of the Federal Council and Federal Assembly; it is also the headquarters of important organisations including the Universal Postal Union (since 1874) and the international copyright and railway unions, and of an institute attached to the University for research into tourism. Notable people born in Berne include the 18th c. scholar Albrecht von Haller, the writer Jeremias Gotthelf (1797–1854) and the painters Ferdinand Hodler (1853–1918) and Paul Klee (1879–1940).

Museums, Galleries, etc.

Hours of Opening

Alpine Museum
(Schweizerisches Alpines Museum),
Helvetiaplatz 4;
Tue.–Sat. 9–12 and 2–5,
Sun. 10–12 and 2–5, Mon. 2–5.

Art Gallery
(Kunsthalle),
Helvetiaplatz 1;
Mon.–Sun. 10–12 and 2–5,
Thu. also 8–10 p.m.

Art, Museum of
(Kunstmuseum),
Hodlerstrasse 12;
Tue.–Sun. 10–12 and 2–5,
Tue. also 8–10 p.m.

Bear-Pit
(Bärengraben),
Nydeggbrücke;
April–September 7–6,
October–March 8.30–4.

Bundeshaus
(Parliament),
Bundesplatz;
conducted tours at 9, 10, 11, 2, 3 and 4
(except during sittings of Parliament and on public holidays).

Gewerbemuseum
See Kornhaus

Gutenberg Museum
See Kornhaus

Historical Museum of Berne
(Bernisches Historisches Museum),
Helvetiaplatz 5;
Tue.–Sat. 9–12 and 2–5,
Sun. 10–12 and 2–5.

Industrial Museum
See Kornhaus

Kornhaus
Industrial Museum (Gewerbemuseum),
Swiss Gutenberg Museum,
Zeughausgasse 2;
Mon. 2–5, Tue.–Fri. 10–12 and 2–5,
Sat. 10–12.

Kunsthalle
See Art Gallery

Kunstmuseum
See Art, Museum of

Landesbibliothek, Schweizerische
See National Library

Minster,
Münsterplatz;
daily 10–12 and 2–4
(November to Easter closed Sun. afternoon and
Mon.);
tower daily 10.30–4.

Municipal Archives
(Stadtarchiv),
Junkerngasse 47;
Mon.–Fri. 8–11.30 and 2–5.30.

Municipal and University Library
(Stadt- un Universitätsbibliothek), Casinoplatz;
issue of books on loan Mon.–Fri. 10–12 and 2–6,
Sat. 10–12;
reading room Mon.–Fri. 8–12, Sat. 8–12.

National Library
(Schweizerische Landesbibliothek), Helvetiastrasse;
issue of books Mon., Tue., Thu., Fri. 10–12 and 4–6,
Wed. 10–12 and 4–9, Sat. 10–12 and 2–4;
reading room Mon., Tue, Thu., Fri. 8–12 and 1–6,
Wed. 8–12 and 2–5.

Natural History Museum
(Naturhistorisches Museum), Bernastrasse 15;
Mon.–Sat. 9–12 and 2–5, Sun. 10–12 and 2–5.

Postal Museum
(Schweizerisches PTT-Museum), Helvetiaplatz 4;
Tue.–Sat. 9–12 and 2–5, Sun. 10–12 and 2–5,
Mon. 2–5.

Rathaus
(Council House), Rathausplatz;
seen by prior arrangement Mon., Tue., Thu., Fri.
8–11.45 and 2–5.45 (closed during sittings).

Riflemen's Museum
(Schützenmuseum), Bernastrasse 5;
Wed.–Fri. 10–12 and 2–4, Tue., Sat. 2–4,
Sun. 10.30–4.

Schulwarte, Berner,
Helvetiaplatz 2;
Mon.–Fri. 10–12 and 2–5.30.

Schützenmuseum
See Riflemen's Museum

Stadtarchiv
See Municipal Archives

Sightseeing in Berne

The hub of the city's traffic is the long
Bubenbergplatz. On its N side stands the
handsome *Bürgerspital* (Municipal hospital, 1734–42: now an old people's
home), built round two courtyards. To the
right is the *Heiliggeistkirche* (church of
the Holy Spirit: Protestant), in French
Baroque style, built 1726–29. In between,
to the rear, is the main **railway station**;
the tracks are underground. – From here it
is a short distance S along Christoffel-
gasse into the broad *Bundesgasse,* in
which are the Bundeshaus and the Kleine
Schanze.

In the *Bundesplatz* (vegetable and flower
market on Tuesday and Saturday mornings) is the Renaissance-style **Bundeshaus** (Parliament building), standing

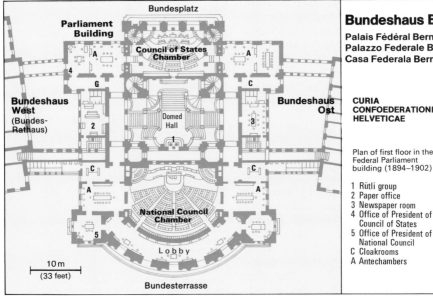

Bundeshaus Bern

Palais Fédéral Berne
Palazzo Federale Berna
Casa Federala Bern

CURIA
CONFOEDERATIONIS
HELVETICAE

Plan of first floor in the
Federal Parliament
building (1894–1902)

1 Rütli group
2 Paper office
3 Newspaper room
4 Office of President of
   Council of States
5 Office of President of
   National Council
C Cloakrooms
A Antechambers

on the edge of the high ground above the river. The domed central block (by H. Auer, 1896–1902) contains the two chambers of the Swiss Parliament (open to visitors), the meeting-places of the National Council and the Council of States; in the E wing (also by Auer, 1888–92) and W wing (by F. Studer, 1851–57) are various Federal agencies and the Federal library.

From the *Bundesterrasse*, which rests on massive retaining walls, there are fine

Minster   Berne
(St Vincent)

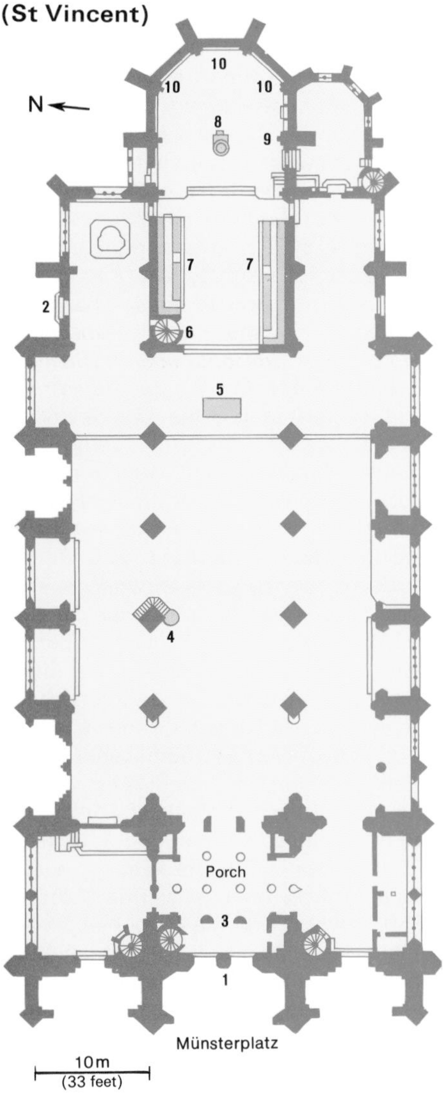

N ◄—

10m
(33 feet)

Münsterplatz

1 Main doorway (1490–95), with 45 figures (copies: originals in Historical Museum)
2 N doorway
3 Organ (1726–30)
4 Pulpit (1470)
5 Communion table from Lausanne Cathedral

6 Stone staircase, a relic of the rood-screen
7 Double rows of choir-stalls (1523–25)
8 Font (1524)
9 Sedilia (c. 1435)
10 Stained-glass windows of choir (1441–50 and 1868)

views of the river Aare 48 m (157 feet) below (funicular into valley) and of the Alps beyond.

Another popular viewpoint, with an orientation table, is the *Kleine Schanze (Little Redoubt: restaurant) to the W, a relic of the old fortifications. In the gardens are a monument to Oskar Bider, who made the first flight over the Alps in 1913, and a monument (1909) commemorating the foundation of the *Universal Postal Union*.

To the E of the Bundesplatz in the *Theaterplatz* are the *Hauptwache* (Guard house), a small pillared hall of 1767, and the *Hôtel de Musique* (1771), once the fashionable assembly rooms of Berne. On the SE corner of the square, at the end of the Kirchenfeld bridge, is the **Casino** (1906–09), an assembly and concert hall with a restaurant and a large outlook terrace; at the NE corner is the *Municipal and University Library* (Stadt- und Universitätsbibliothek), built in 1787–92. From here *Münstergasse* (market for meat and dairy produce on Tuesday and Saturday mornings) leads to the *Münsterplatz*, where stands the *Moses Fountain* (*c.* 1545) and the so-called *Stiftsgebäude* (1748).

The Late Gothic *Minster (dedicated to St Vincent), a three-aisled pillared basilica without transept, was begun in 1421 to the design of Matthäus Ensinger of Ulm, but the tower was not completed until 1893, with the addition of the octagonal upper section and the openwork spire. The *W doorway is richly decorated with sculpture (now copies); in the tympanum is a Last Judgment (originally 1495) containing a large number of figures, and on the side walls are paintings (1501, restored) of the Fall and the Annunciation. The nave and choir have reticulated vaulting with fine 16th c. bosses (coats of arms).

INTERIOR. – The finely carved *choir-stalls* (1523) were the first Renaissance work of art in Berne. In the apse are a Gothic *font* (1524), *sedilia* (15th c.: on right) and beautiful stained glass (1441–50). At the end of the S aisle is a monument to Berthold von Zähringen (1601), incorporating coat of arms; at the end of the N aisle a marble memorial to the 702 men of Berne who died fighting the French in 1798. In the Matter chapel (seventh bay in the S aisle) can be seen the **Dance of Death Window** (1917), with 20 scenes from the "Dance of Death" (1516–19) by

Niklaus Manuel-Deutsch. There is a magnificent Baroque organ (1726–30) with 5404 pipes and fine modern stained glass (1947) in the S aisle.

From the tree-planted Minster terrace (*Plattform*) there is an attractive view down into the Aare valley; and there are fine panoramic views from the gallery on the Minster tower (254 steps).

From here *Junkerngasse*, lined with arcaded houses once occupied by the old patrician families of Berne, runs towards the E end of the old town. At No. 47 is the handsome **Erlacherhof** (1749–52), now occupied by the finance department and the municipal archives. Junkerngasse joins the wide Nydegg-Gasse, at the far end of which is the **Nydegg bridge** (1840–44) over the gorge of the Aare; the principal arch, of stone, has a span of 55 m (180 feet) and stands 26 m (85 feet) above the river. On the left, just before the bridge, is the little *Nydegg church*, built in 1494 on the site of an Imperial stronghold (restored 1956). On the far side of the bridge is one of Berne's great popular attractions, the **Bear-Pit** (Bärengraben), a deep circular den in which bears – the heraldic animal of Berne – have been kept since 1480. From the road running up to the right (Muristalden) there is a fine view of the Minster and the old town. Above the bridge to the left is the beautiful **Rose-Garden** (Rosengarten), with views of the Aare and the old town. Just downstream from the Nydegg bridge at the end of the old *Untertorbrücke* (1461–87), in Läuferplatz are Berne's first town hall and the *Läuferbrunnen* ("Runner Fountain", 1545).

Kramgasse, Berne, by night

From the Nydegg bridge a series of picturesque streets (Nydegg-Gasse, Gerechtigkeitsgasse, Kramgasse, Marktgasse and Spitalgasse), with many antique shops and art galleries, run along the whole length of the old town for a distance of 1700 m (1860 yards) to end in the Bubenbergplatz.

The *Gerechtigkeitsgasse is lined on both sides by arcades and elegant shops. In the middle of the street is the *Justice fountain* (Gerechtigkeitsbrunnen, 1543). At the far end the Rathausgasse, on right, leads to the **Rathaus** (Council House, the seat of the Great Council of the canton and of the Town Council), in Late Burgundian Gothic style, built in 1406–16, much altered in 1866 and restored in the original style in 1939–42. A flight of steps leads up to the entrance. In the square in front of the Rathaus stands the *Banner-Carrier* or *Venner fountain* (1542). – The continuation of the Gerechtigkeitsgasse, the *Kramgasse, also lined with arcaded houses, has three fountains – the *Kramgassbrunnen* (1778), the *Simsonbrunnen* (Samson fountain, 1544) and the *Zähringerbrunnen* (1544). It ends at the *Clock tower (Zeitglockenturm or Zytgloggeturm), a notable Berne landmark, frequently rebuilt – the present stone tower with its pointed spire is 15th c. – which was the W gate of the town until about 1250. On the E side of the tower is an *astronomical clock* (1527–30), with mechanical figures which perform four minutes before every hour. – Beyond this is the busy *Marktgasse (pedestrian precinct), with old guild-houses, arcades, shops and two more fountains, the Schützenbrunnen (Marksman fountain) and Anna-Seiler-Brunnen, both of about 1545. At the far end of the street we find the **Käfigturm** ("Cage tower", 13th and 17th c.), which was one of the town gates from 1250 to 1350. Beyond it is the Bärenplatz, from which the *Spitalgasse* (pedestrian precinct), with the *Pfeifferbrunnen* (Piper's fountain, 1545), continues to the Bubenbergplatz.

This line of streets cuts across two of the town's principal squares. In front of the Clock tower is the *Kornhausplatz*, in which stands the curious *Kindlifresserbrunnen* ("Child-Eater Fountain" or Ogre Fountain, with the figure of an ogre devouring a child) of about 1540. On the

W side of the square we see the handsome **Kornhaus** (1711–16), with high vaulted wine-cellars (restaurant); on the first floor are the *Industrial Museum* and the Swiss Gutenberg Museum. Behind it the *French church* (Französische Kirche), originally a Dominican foundation (13th c.), has frescoes by the Berne "Master of the Carnation". In the NW corner of the square, at the end of the iron bridge called the Kornhausbrücke, is the *Municipal Theatre* (Stadttheater, 1903). – To the S of the Käfigturm the charming little *Bärenplatz* (pedestrian precinct: flower and vegetable market Tuesday and Saturday mornings) was once a bear-pit; to the N is the large *Waisenhausplatz* (partly pedestrianised), at the far end of which stands the handsome old Orphanage (Waisenhaus) of 1782, now the police headquarters.

To the W of this, in the Hodlerstrasse (No. 12), the ***Museum of Art** (Kunstmuseum), built in 1879, with a plain windowless extension of 1935, contains a large collection of Swiss art, pictures by Italian masters of the 14th–16th c. and works by French artists of the 19th and 20th c. Among the older Swiss masters represented are the "Master of the Carnation" (Paul Löwensprung, d. 1499) and Niklaus Manuel-Deutsch (1484–1530), one of the leading Swiss painters of the Early Renaissance; among modern artists Karl Staufer (1857–91) and Ferdinand Hodler (1853–1918). Notable also are the *Paul Klee Collection, with over 2500 of Klee's works, and the Rupf Collection of Cubist art (Braque, Gris, Léger, Picasso, Kandinsky, Feininger, etc.). The Print Cabinet contains works by both Swiss and foreign artists.

The main **Railway Station**, in Bahnhofplatz, below the Grosse Schanze, was completely rebuilt between 1957 and 1974, with the tracks running underground for a distance of 200 m (656 feet) (tourist information office, shopping, restaurants, café, car park, bus station). In the Christoffel underpass are remains of the fourth medieval defensive system (foundations of walls, round towers, remains of a bridge).

Elevators and flights of steps lead up from the station to the **Grosse Schanze**, the principal bastion in the old fortifications (built 1634, demolished 1834), now a park commanding extensive views. On the NW side are the **University**, founded in 1834 (present buildings 1899–1903), with a monument to the Berne doctor and poet Albrecht von Haller (1708–77) in front of it, and the headquarters of the *Swiss Federal Railways* (SBB-Direktion). To the left, beyond Schanzenstrasse, is the *Supreme Court* (Obergericht, 1909).

From Kornhausplatz the **Kornhausbrücke** (1898), a graceful iron bridge 48 m (157 feet) high with a span of 115 m (377 feet), leads over the Aare into the newer part of the town. On a little hill immediately beyond the bridge, on the left, is the **Schänzli**, once an outer work in the town's defences, now occupied by the *Kursaal* (café-restaurant, concert hall, casino, from the terrace of which there is a magnificent *view of Berne and the Alps. Below the hill to the W are the *Botanic Garden* and the *Lorraine bridge*, a concrete structure of 1928–29 which links the Lorraine district of the town with the area around the station.

From the S side of the old town the **Kirchenfeld bridge**, a two-arched iron bridge built 1882–83, crosses the Aare to the residential district of Kirchenfeld, the central feature of which is **Helvetiaplatz**, a large square around the *Telegraph Union Monument* (1922) and surrounded by museums. To the left is the *Art Gallery* (Kunsthalle, 1918), which puts on special exhibitions of contemporary art. To the right are the *Berner Schulwarte* (1933), with a rich collection of teaching material and a library on education, and the ***Swiss Alpine Museum** (1934), which presents a fascinating picture of the Swiss Alps, covering their scientific study, communications, mapping and climbers (large relief model of the Bernese Oberland). In the same building is the *Swiss Postal Museum*, illustrating the history of the Swiss postal service, with a large collection of stamps. Special exhibitions from time to time.

On the S side of Helvetiaplatz the ***Historical Museum of Berne** (1892–94) is built in the style of a 16th c. castle, with collections of prehistoric material, folk art and traditions, ethnography and various types of decorative and applied art. Of particular interest are the *Burgundian Room, with trophies won at the Battle of Grandson in 1476 (weapons,

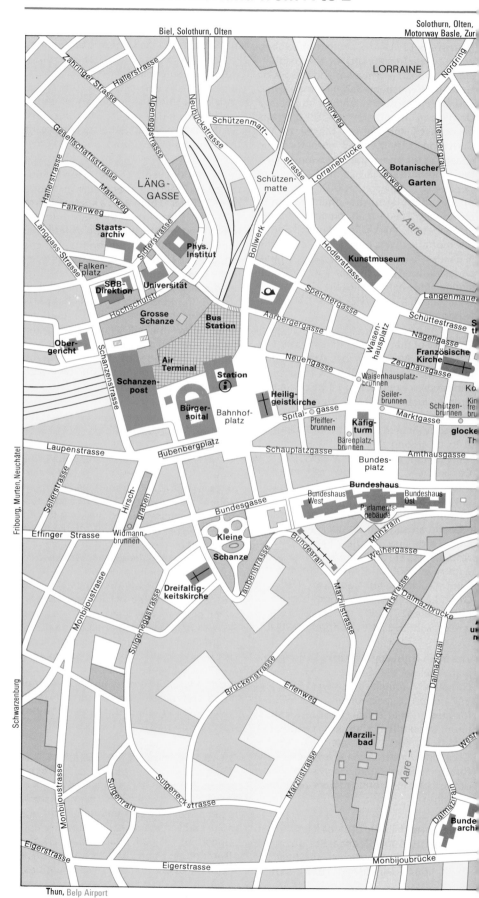

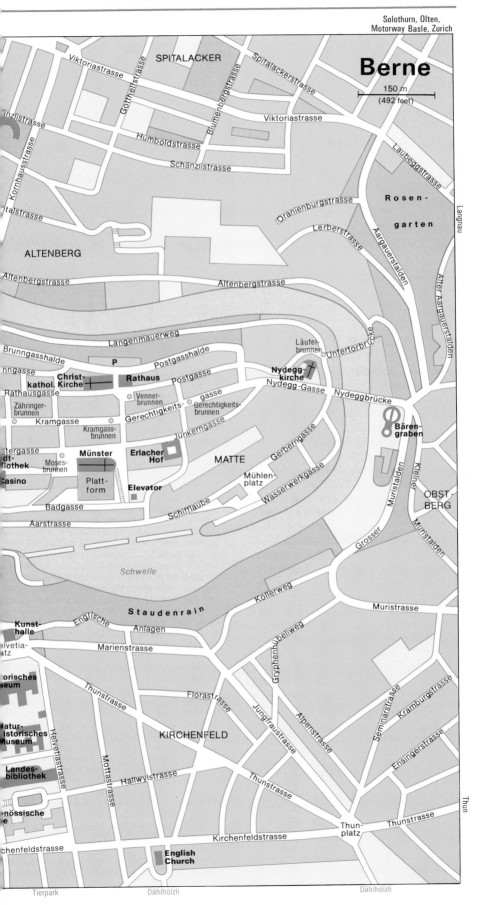

Solothurn, Olten,
Motorway Basle, Zurich

Berne

150 m
(492 feet)

SPITALACKER

Viktoriastrasse

Gotthelfstrasse

Spitalackerstrasse

Blumenbergstrasse

Viktoriastrasse

Humboldtstrasse

Schänzlistrasse

änzlistrasse

Kornhausstrasse

ntalstrasse

Laubeggstrasse

Oranienburgstrasse

Lerberstrasse

Aargauerstalden

Rosen-
garten

Alter Aargauerstalden

Langnau

ALTENBERG

Altenbergstrasse

Altenbergstrasse

Langenmauerweg

Brunngasshalde

nngasse

Postgasshalde

P

Läufer-
brunnen

Untertorbrücke

Christ-
kathol. Kirche

Rathaus

Postgasse

Nydegg-
kirche

Rathausgasse

Venner-
brunnen

gasse

Nydegg-Gasse

Nydeggbrücke

Zähringer-
brunnen

Gerechtigkeits-

Gerechtigkeits-
brunnen

Kramgasse

Gerechtigkeitsstrasse

Junkerngasse

Gerberngasse

Kramgass-
brunnen

stergasse

dt-
liothek

Münster

Erlacher
Hof

MATTE

Wasserwerkgasse

OBST-
BERG

Moses-
brunnen

asino

Platt-
form

Elevator

Mühlen-
platz

Muristalden

Kleiner

Muristalden

Badgasse

Schifflaube

Bären-
graben

Aarstrasse

Grosser

Muristrasse

Schwelle

Kollerweg

Kunst-
halle

Englische

Staudenrain

Anlagen

lvetia-
atz

Marienstrasse

Gryphenhübeliweg

orisches
eum

Thunstrasse

Florastrasse

Jungfraustrasse

Alpenstrasse

Seminarstrasse

Kramburgstrasse

atur-
istorisches
Museum

KIRCHENFELD

Ensingerstrasse

Landes-
bibliothek

Helvetiastrasse

Mottastrasse

Hallwylstrasse

Thunstrasse

nössische
e

Thun-
platz

Thunstrasse

Thun

English
Church

Kirchenfeldstrasse

chenfeldstrasse

Tierpark   Dählhölzli   Dählhölzli

Bernese Oberland

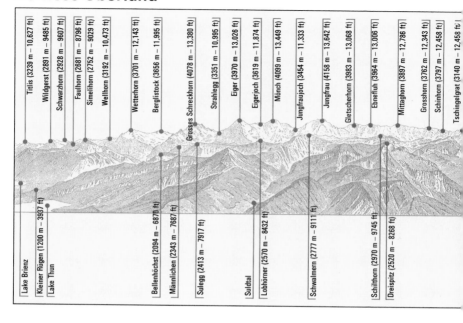

tapestries, embroidery), the Henri Moser Charlottenfels Collection (weapons and objets d'art from the Islamic East), the Lausanne cathedral treasury and late medieval * tapestries. – Beyond the Historical Museum, in Bernastrasse, are (No. 5) the *Swiss Riflemen's Museum* and (No. 15) the **Natural History Museum** (Naturhistorisches Museum, 1933), with excellently displayed collections of geology, mineralogy, palaeontology and zoology (series of dioramas of African mammals in the B. von Wattenwyl Collection; dioramas of the animals of other regions; collection of rock-crystal; collection of antlers; zoological laboratory). – Still farther S rises the massive building occupied by the **National Library** (Landesbibliothek, 1929–32). – Thormannstrasse continues S to the *Dählhölzli*, in a bend of the Aare, with the **Tierpark** (nature park and zoo: restaurant). Footpath along the river (15 minutes) to the *Elfenau* nature reserve.

SURROUNDINGS. – To the NW, between the town and the Aare, is a large wooded area, the **Bremgartenwald**, now encroached on by the motorway. – On the N side of the Aare, near the Halenbrücke, the interesting modern residential development of *Halen* (1959–61), is surrounded by the forest. – To the NW of the Bremgartenwald lies the **Wohlensee**, an artificial lake 15 km long formed by the damming of the Aare (motor-boat trips, rowing-boats).

Ascent of Gurten. – Leave on the road to Belp, which runs SE to the suburb of *Wabern* (alt. 556 m (1824 feet)), 3·5 km (2 miles) away. From here (car park) a funicular ascends in 5 minutes to the summit of the green hill of **Gurten** (861 m – 2825 feet). At the upper station, *Gurten-Kulm* (843 m – 2766 feet), are the Gurten-Kulm Hotel (C, 51 b.), a large garden restaurant (view of Berne) and a miniature railway. From the Ostsignal (857 m (2812 feet): 10 minutes walk E) and the Westsignal (856 m (2809 feet): 3 minutes W) there are superb views of the Bernese Alps.

Through the Gürbe valley. – From Wabern it is 3·5 km (2 miles) to *Kehrsatz* (alt. 573 m (1880 feet) bypass), with a 16th c. Schloss, now a state girls' reformatory. – From here the direct road runs through the beautiful **Gürbe valley** (to the left *Schloss Oberried*, now a boys' school), via the trim little town of **Belp** (alt. 526 m (1726 feet): Hotel Sternen), at the foot of the *Belpberg* (894 m – 2933 feet), which has a picturesque 16th–17th c. castle and a series of Gothic frescoes (1455–60) in the church, then on to *Toffen* (Schloss, 17th c.), *Rümligen* (Schloss, 18th c.) and *Seftigen*, continuing over the ridge between the Gürbe and Aare valleys to *Thun* (p. 239). – Alternatively take a road on the right at Kehrsatz, and after a short distance uphill turn left into a ridge road which runs above the Gürbe valley (extensive views), passing below *Zimmerwald*, where the formation of the Third International (the Communist international organisation) was discussed at a conference in September 1915 attended by Lenin. – The road runs sharply downhill to (12 km – 7 miles) *Riggisberg* (alt. 768 m (2520 feet): Gasthaus Sonne), a little town of 2000 inhabitants (Abegg Collection of textiles and decorative art). From here via *Gurnigel* (alt. 1153 m (3783 feet): winter sports) to *Schwefelbergbad* (see p. 117). Beyond this turn left (road on right to Gurnigel). 4·5 km (3 miles): *Burgistein* (775 m – 2543 feet), under a prominent 16th c. castle (813 m – 2667 feet). – 2·5 km (2 miles): **Wattenwil** (604 m – 1982 feet), below the *Staffelalp* (983 m (3225 feet): far-ranging views; inn; 3 km (2 miles) by road). Continue through the Gürbe valley. – 4 km (2 miles): *Blumenstein* (661 m (2169 feet): Pension Tannenbühl), with a 14th c. church (beautiful stained glass in choir) and a chalybeate spring (impregnated

Panorama from Niesen (2362 m – 7750 ft)

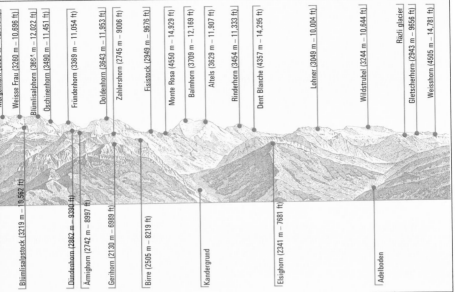

Wildenhorn (3663 m – ...) · Weisse Frau (3260 m – 10,696 ft) · Blümlisalphorn (365¹ m – 12,022 ft) · Oschinenhorn (3490 m – 11,451 ft) · Fründenhorn (3369 m – 11,054 ft) · Doldenhorn (3643 m – 11,953 ft) · Zahlershorn (2745 m – 9006 ft) · Fisistock (2949 m – 9676 ft) · Monte Rosa (4550 m – 14,929 ft) · Balmhorn (3709 m – 12,169 ft) · Altels (3629 m – 11,907 ft) · Rinderhorn (3454 m – 11,333 ft) · Dent Blanche (4357 m – 14,295 ft) · Lohner (3049 m – 10,004 ft) · Wildstrubel (3244 m – 10,644 ft) · Razli glacier · Gletscherhorn (2943 m – 9656 ft) · Weisshorn (4505 m – 14,781 ft)

Blümlisalpstock (3219 m – 10,562 ft) · Dündenhorn (2862 m – 9390 ft) · Arnighorn (2742 m – 8997 ft) · Gerihorn (2130 m – 6989 ft) · Birre (2505 m – 8219 ft) · Kandergrund · Elsighorn (2341 m – 7681 ft) · Adelboden

with iron). – 4.5 km (3 miles): *Oberstocken* (672 m – 2205 feet), at the foot of the Stockhorn, from which there are extensive views.

Berne to Fribourg via Schwarzenburg. – The beautiful road to Schwarzenburg (No. 157) runs SW following the railway. – 4 km (2 miles): *Köniz* (alt. 575 m (1887 feet): pop. 32,000) has a 13th c. castle which belonged to the Teutonic Order and a notable church (Romanesque nave; Gothic choir with 14th c. stained glass and wall-paintings). – 5 km (3 miles): *Niederscherli*, where the road cuts across the deeply slashed valley of the *Scherlibach*. – 10 km (6 miles): **Schwarzenburg** (795 m (2608 feet): Hotel Bären, 18 b.), with a castle of 1573, a little 15th c. church (the "Kappeli") and the Swiss short-wave radio transmitter. – From here road 74 leads W towards Fribourg through an upland region with far-reaching views, crossing the gorge of the *Sense* River on a covered wooden bridge (1·3 km (1 mile) N, above the right bank of the river, the runis of the Imperial castle of *Grasburg*). – 5 km (3 miles) *Heitenried* (760 m – 2494 feet). – 8 km (5 miles): *Tafers* (655 m – 2150 feet) has a notable church (oldest part 9th–10th c.; altered in 16th, 18th and 20th c.). – **Fribourg**: see p. 115.

Bernese Oberland

Cantons: Berne (BE) and Valais (VS).
ⓘ **Verkehrsverein Berner Oberland,**
CH-3800 Interlaken;
tel. (036) 22 26 21.

The ** **Bernese Oberland is that part of the Swiss Alps lying between Lake Geneva and the River Reuss; it rises above the 4000 m (13,124 feet) mark in the Finsteraarhorn (4274 m – 14,023 feet), the Aletschhorn (4195 m – 13,764 feet), the Schreckhorn (4078 m – 13,380 feet), the Mönch** (4099 m – 13,449 feet) and the Jungfrau (4158 m – 13,642 feet).

The massif is drained on the N by the Saane, Simme, Kander and other streams, on the S by the Rhône, which is fed by the Aletsch glacier and Rhône glacier and by its right-bank tributaries. The Rhône forms the southern boundary of the Bernese Oberland until it flows into Lake Geneva. Below the N side are Lake Thun and Lake Brienz (see p. 240). The principal gateway to the mountains of the Bernese Oberland is Interlaken (p. 144).

HISTORY. – The regions bordering the Bernese Oberland have a long history of human settlement, as is shown by the Stone Age and Bronze Age material and the Roman remains which have been found by

The Hörnli and the Eiger above Grindelwald

View from the Jungfraujoch towards the Wengernalp

excavation, as well as by churches dating from before the year 1000. For many centuries the villages in the Bernese Oberland were wholly dependent on their stock-farming and pastoral economy, but the time came when the beauties of mountain scenery began to be appreciated. In the latter part of the 18th c. Goethe visited the Lauterbrunnen valley, and during the Romantic period there was an enthusiastic interest in natural beauty. This period too saw the beginning of modern mountaineering. The Jungfrau was climbed in the early years of the 19th c., and the other peaks represented a challenge to climbers. Perhaps the best known of these is the Eiger, the N face of which was long regarded as unclimbable. The first successful ascent was in 1938 (by Heckmair, Vörg, Harrer and Kasparek), and the first winter ascent in 1961 (by Hiebeler, Kinshofer, Almberger and Manhardt).

The Bernese Oberland has a number of major tourist resorts which are among the oldest established in Switzerland. Lenk, Adelboden and Grindelwald, among others, were already attracting many visitors in the 19th c., and up to the First World War the region became the haunt of the nobility and successful artists from all over Europe. In our own day, too, the Bernese Oberland, with its magnificent scenery and its excellent and steadily expanding facilities for winter sports, is perhaps still the best-known holiday region in Switzerland. The finest mountains, and those affording the best views, are well provided with cableways and elevators – e.g. the Jungfraujoch, the Schilthorn, the Eggishorn, etc. The main N–S route through the Bernese Oberland is the 14·6 km (9 miles) railway tunnel under the Lötschberg; the busiest road is the one which runs over the Grimsel pass from Brienz to Gletsch, at the foot of the Rhône glacier.

The most impressive panoramic** view is to be had from the 2362 m (7750 feet)

high **Niesen**, which rises above the SW side of Lake Thun and can be reached by funicular from Mülenen. From the summit there is a prospect taking in Lakes Thun and Brienz, the 4000 m (13,124 feet) peaks of the Jungfrau massif and the Valais Alps to the S.

Bernina Pass

Canton: Grisons (GR).
Altitude: 2323 m (7622 feet).
ⓘ **Kur- und Verkehrsverein Pontresina,**
CH-7504 Pontresina;
tel. (082)6 64 88.

One of the most rewarding routes through the Alps is the road which runs from St Moritz over the *Bernina pass and down the Poschiavo valley into Italy, and usually remains open through the year for both road and rail traffic. The pass is not only the watershed between the Engadine and the Valtellina but also the boundary between Rhaeto-Romanic (referring to the language and culture peculiar to south-eastern Switzerland and the Tyrol) and Italian culture. The road, already being used in the 13th c. and built in its modern form between 1842 and 1865, traverses magnificent mountain and glacier scenery.

The journey from St Moritz to Tirano in Italy goes over the 58 km (36 miles) long pass road – via Pontresina (8 km – 5 miles) to the Bernina pass (24 km – 15 miles), and then via Poschiavo (17 km – 11 miles) to Tirano (34 km – 21 miles). By rail, on the Rhätische Bahn, the journey takes 3½ hours (the highest railway over the Alps).

The road crosses the plateau via Samedan (airport) and Celerina, and begins to climb at Punt Muragl (cableway up Muottas Muragl: see p. 188). At Pontresina there are views up Val Roseg to the right and Val Languard to the left. 4·5 km (3 miles) farther on a road goes off on the right to the Hotel-Restaurant Morteratsch (45 minutes' climb from here to the Morteratsch glacier, 35 minutes up Chünetta). From the sharp bends at Montebello there are superb views of the Morteratsch glacier, Piz Palü (3905 m – 12,812 feet), Bellavista (3827 m – 12,556 feet), Piz Bernina (4049 m – 13,285 feet) and Piz

Morteratsch (3751 m – 12,307 feet). – Two of Switzerland's finest cableways start from special stations on the Bernina railway.

The * * **Diavolezza** (2973 m – 9754 feet), one of the most popular skiing areas in the Alps, is reached by a cableway starting from just beyond Bernina Suot (length 3625 m (11,894 feet), height difference 883 m (2897 feet), time 10 minutes). The Diavolezza-Haus (2977 m – 9768 feet), situated opposite the giant peaks of the Bernina group, affords views of overwhelming magnificence. From here there are numerous paths leading into the mountains. The "Diavolezza-Tour" is one of the easiest glacier walks (3 hours, with guide), going from the Diavolezza-Haus by way of the Pers and Morteratsch glaciers to the Morteratsch Hotel. Summer skiing.

***Piz Lagalb** (2959 m (9708 feet): lower station Curtinatsch 2090 m (6857 feet), upper station 2896 m (9502 feet): restaurant, with panoramic view): wildlife park, view into the Valtellina. The cableway, 2381 m (7812 feet) long, runs up from Curtinatsch (Bernina-Lagalb) in 8 minutes.

The **Bernina Hospice** (2309 m (7576 feet): 40 b.) is a good walking and climbing base. Two lakes, *Lej Nair* (Black Lake, 2222 m (7290 feet)) and *Lej Pitschen* (2220 m – 7284 feet), fed by springs, drain northward into the Inn; they are separated by a masonry dam from the *Lago Bianco* (White Lake, 2230 m (7317 feet)), an artificial lake supplying the Brusio hydroelectric station. From the *Alp*

Grüm (2091 m (6861 feet): railway station) there is a fine view of the Palü glacier (Alpine garden). – Nature-lovers can observe many species of birds, from the golden eagle to the rock swallow, from the pigmy owl to the snow-finch. – The Bernina road now leaves the railway track, which runs over the Alp Grüm and down into the Val di Pila, and climbs past the Lago della Crocetta to the *Bernina pass (Italian *Passo del Bernina*, 2323 m (7622 feet)), with the desolate landscape of ice-worn rocks commonly found on the high passes and beautiful views on both sides. – From here the road runs sharply downhill in short bends and then descends in four hairpins, with magnificent views down into the valley, into the Val Agoné, the highest part of the Poschiavo valley. At *La Motta* a road branches off on the left over the Forcola di Livigno pass (2315 m – 7596 feet) into the Val di Livigno, in Italy (3·5 km (2 miles) to the frontier, then 15 km (9 miles) to Livigno: large skiing area, customs-free zone). – 5.5 km (3 miles) from the pass is *La Rösa* (1878 m (6162 feet): Hotel Post), a picturesque little mountain village at the foot of Piz Campascio. – Then downhill above a wooded gorge, with beautiful views, followed by two sharp bends down to *Sfazù* (1666 m (5466 feet): restaurant) and over the Wildbach at the mouth of the beautiful *Val di Campo* (on left), a valley gouged out by a glacier (narrow mountain road, 8 km (5 miles), maximum gradient 13%). – 4 km (2 miles) beyond La Rösa, on the left, is the *Pozzolascio* restaurant (1530 m – 5020 feet), near a small lake. – The road continues high up on the wooded mountainside, soon affording an excellent view of the Poschiavo valley. On the opposite slope (view restricted by trees) are the boldly engineered bends of the Bernina railway. – 10 km (6 miles) from La Rösa, at *San Carlo* (1095 m – 3593 feet), the road reaches the floor of the Poschiavo valley (Italian *Valle di Poschiavo*). Before the village is a hydroelectric station belonging to the Brusio complex.

From the Poschiavo valley into the Valtellina. – The 34 km (21 miles) long Poschiavo valley, which descends from the Bernina pass to Tirano in the Valtellina, is a region of southern vegetation and Italian life-style. It remained part of the canton of Grisons after the cession to Italy of the Valtellina, which belonged to the

The Rhätische Bahn at the Lago Bianco

Grisons from 1512 to 1797. – The road on the S side of the Bernina pass is now of a good standard. In 17 km (11 miles) it comes to *Poschiavo* (1014 m (3327 feet): pop. 3600; Hôtel Suisse; Albrici-Posta, in an old patrician house; Altavalla; Croce Bianca; Centrale; camping site), the central area of population in a commune made up of six separate villages. Handsome patrician palazzos; Town Hall with Romanesque tower; church of San Vittore (Late Gothic, 15th–16th c.); church of Santa Maria (Baroque, 17th–18th c. – 4 km (2 miles) beyond Poschiavo is the summer holiday resort of * **Le Prese** (alt. 965 m (3166 feet): Hotel Le Prese, B, 50 b., SP; La Romantica, D, 55 b.), on the Lago di Poschiavo.

The commune of *Brusio* (alt. 740 m (2428 feet): pop. 1340), which takes in the seven villages between the Lago di Poschiavo and the frontier, is an area of lush southern vegetation. The principal village is dominated by the towers of its 17th c. church. – The road continues through tobacco plantations and forests of chestnut-trees to *Campascio* (630 m – 2067 feet) and *Campocologno* (553 m – 1814 feet), the last place in Switzerland (customs), with the Brusio power station (33,000 kW).

From the frontier crossing at Piatta Mala the road leads into the Valtellina. The village of *Madonna di Tirano* (438 m – 1437 feet) has a famous * pilgrimage church (1503–33). – The road now forks. To the right it runs down the Valtellina and continues via Sondrio and around Lake Como to **Lugano** (120 km (75 miles): see p. 174). The road to the left runs up the valley to the old town of *Tirano* (429 m (1408 feet): pop. 8000), straddling the River Adda, with old patrician houses of the 15th–17th c.

Biel/Bienne

Canton: Berne (BE).
Altitude: 440 m (1444 feet). – Population: 58,000.
Post code: CH-2500. – Dialling code: 032.
ⓘ **Offizielles Verkehrsbüro,**
   Hochhaus Kongresshaus,
   Silbergasse 31;
   tel. 22 75 75.

HOTELS. – NEAR THE STATION: *Elite*, B, 100 b.; *Continental*, C, 100 b.; *Club-Hotel*, C, 70 b.; *Touring-Hôtel de la Gare*, D, 95 b. – IN THE OLD TOWN: *Atlantis*, C, 32 b.; *Dufour*, C, 60 b.; *Royal* (no rest.), D, 40 b.;

Bären, D, 24 b. – YOUTH HOSTEL: Solothurner Strasse 137 (5 km – 3 miles).

RESTAURANTS. – *Bahnhofbuffet*, Bahnhofplatz 4; *Kongresshaus*, Zentralstrasse 57; *Sporting*, Neumarktstrasse 14.

RECREATION and SPORT. – Billiard club, boccia, hire of boats, water-skiing, riding, bridge, ice sports, fencing, fishing, golf, go-karting, judo, skittles, rowing, sailing, tennis (indoor and outdoor courts); indoor swimming pool.

EVENTS. – *Fasnacht* (Carnival), February; *100 km (62 miles) run*, June; *Braderie* (fair), July; *Chilbi* in old town, August; Lesesonntag (Vintage Sunday) on the lake, October; concerts in park, Wednesday evenings in summer.

This bilingual town (Biel in German, Bienne in French), with two-thirds of its inhabitants speaking German and one-third French, is the capital of the Swiss watchmaking industry. Several hundred small and medium-sized firms are engaged in the manufacture of watches and watch parts in the town, which is also a place of considerable commercial activity. The residential districts are mainly on the lower slopes of the Jura hills, which here slope down to the lake. In recent years the town has also made a name for itself as a convention capital.

Zunfthaus der Waldleute, Biel

HISTORY. – The town was founded about 1220 by the Prince-Abbot of Basle and remained under the rule of successive Prince-Abbots until 1792. From 1798 to 1815 it belonged to France; thereafter it was incorporated in the canton of Berne. It is now the second largest town in the canton.

SIGHTS. – The UPPER TOWN with its historic old buildings is well preserved.

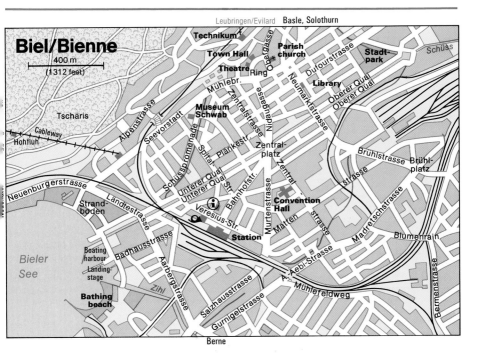

Leubringen/Evilard Basle, Solothurn

Biel/Bienne

400 m
(1312 feet)

Technikum

Town Hall
Theatre Ring
Mühlebr.

Parish church
Stadt-park
Schüss

Tschäris

Alpenstrasse
Seevorstadt
Schüspromenade
Spital-
Plänkestr.
Zentralstrasse
Nidaug.
Obergasse
Neumarktstrasse
Dufourstrasse
Oberer Qual
Oberer Qual

Library

Cableway
Hohfluh

Museum Schwab

Zentral-platz

Neuenburgerstrasse

Ländtestrasse
Strand-boden

Schüs-
Unterer Qual
Unterer Qual

Bahnhofstr.
Veresius-Str.

Murtenstrasse
Matten-strasse
Zentral-strasse

Brühlstrasse Brühl-platz

Convention Hall

Madretschstrasse

Blumenrain

Bieler See

Boating harbour
Landing-stage

Badhausstrasse

Aarbergstrasse

Zihl

Salzhausstrasse

Gurnigelstrasse

Mühlefeldweg

Aebi-Strasse

Bermenstrasse

Bathing beach

Berne

In the Burgplatz are the Late Gothic **Rathaus** (Town Hall: built 1530–34, renovated 1676) and the *Theatre*, originally the armoury (1589–91); in front of the Rathaus stands the *Justice fountain* (1714), and from here the Burggässli leads to the *Ring*, a square surrounded by arcaded houses. The old **Zunfthaus, der Waldleute** (Guild-House of the Foresters, 1559–61) is now occupied by the Kunstverein (Society of Arts). The Late Gothic *parish church* (1451–92: Protestant) has 15th c. stained glass and wall-paintings. In the Obergasse are the 16th c. *Angel fountain* and the former inn *Zur Krone* (1578–82), with a tablet commemorating Goethe's stay there in 1779. In the *Rosiusplatz* are towers and part of the moat belonging to the old fortifications, the old *Clock tower* (rebuilt on this site in 1843) and the *Technikum* (Technical College). In the Seevorstadt, a street running down to the lake, we find the *Schwab Museum* (closed Mondays), with material of the prehistoric period (lake-dwellings), Iron Age and Roman period. To the S are the *railway station* and the modern **Congress Hall** in the Zentralstrasse (1961–66: indoor swimming pool).

SURROUNDINGS. – From the north-western Jura hills above the town there are panoramic views of the Bernese Alps and the Mittelland, with the lakes. – 2·5 km (2 miles) from Biel on the Delémont road (No. 6) a narrow road branches off on the left and comes in 4·5 km (3 miles) to **Magglingen** (French *Macolin*: alt.

875 m (2871 feet: pop. 420; Hôtel Bellevue), with the Federal School of Gymnastics and Sport; easy hill-walking in the surrounding area. – There are cableways from Biel to Magglingen (length 1694 m (5558 feet), time 9 minutes) and to *Leubringen/ Evilard* (length 933 m (3061 feet), time 6 minutes).

In the *Taubenlochschlucht*, a gorge 2 km (1 mile) E of the outlying district of Bözingen, the folding of the strata caused by the geological upheavals of the past can be observed in the rock face.

Around the lake (the wine villages). – The **Bieler See** or *Lac de Bienne* (alt. 429 m (1408 feet): area 39 sq. km (15 sq. miles), length 14·5 km (9 miles), breadth up to 3·5 km (2 miles)) forms the boundary between two geological regions, the limestone formations of the Jura and the molasse (soft greenish sandstone) of the area around the lakes. On the N side of the lake the slopes of the Jura fall steeply down, with the German-speaking villages of Tüscherz, Twann and Ligerz, once belonging to Burgundy, set amid vineyards at the foot. The shore on the S side, less visited by tourists, is flatter, and in prehistoric times was occupied by numerous lake-dwellings built on piles. At the S end of the lake lies St Petersinsel (St Peter's Island), a popular resort of both local people and visitors. The SE side of the island is the haunt of large numbers of waterfowl.

In 1878, as a result of the control of the River Aare, the level of the lake was lowered by some 2 m (7 feet). The Aare, which had previously flowed past the lake 7 km (4 miles) to the E, was then diverted into the lake by the construction of a canal at Hagneck and brought back to its original bed by another canal from Nidau to Büren. As a result soil and debris carried down by the river were deposited in the lake.

A *circuit of the lake* provides an opportunity of seeing the beautiful scenery of its shores and a series of attractive little towns and villages, in the largest vine-growing area in the canton of Berne. Three-quarters of the area is planted with the white Chasselas grape, a fifth with the red Pinot Noir. The local method of wine-making, involving early racking (separation of the wine from the sediment or "lees"), produces fruity wines of high carbonic acid content, mainly sold as Twanner, Schafiser and Erlacher, which are much sought after. Vines are also grown at Ligerz, Tüscherz, Vingelz, Tschugg, La Neuveville and Alfermée and on St Petersinsel. There is a Wine-Growing Museum of Viticulture in Ligerz. Visits to wine-making establishments can be arranged through the Informations- und Propagandastelle für Bieler-See-Weine, CH-2514 Ligerz.

A walk along the "wine route" from Biel to Tüscherz and Twann (2 hours), returning from Twann by boat or continuing on foot to Ligerz ($\frac{1}{2}$ hour), is a memorable experience. – The road round the lake runs SW via Vingelz and the old Burgundian settlement of Alfermée to the wine village of *Tüscherz* (alt. 435 m (1427 feet): pop. 2800; Hotel Bellevue), which has a railway station and landing-stage, and continues to **Twann** (French *Douanne*: 434 m (1424 feet): pop. 900; Hotel Fontana, C, 40 b.; Bären, C, 35 b.), a sleepy little village of narrow winding streets and old houses which has preserved its medieval character. Excavations here in 1974–76 revealed remains of the earliest farming settlements (between 3000 and 2000 B.C.).

Ligerz, on the Bieler See

The next village is **Ligerz** (French *Gléresse*: 433 m (1421 feet): pop. 500; Hotel Kreuz, E, 20 b.; Wine-Growing Museum), from which there is a cableway to Prêles (*Prägelz*), on the *Tessenberg* (length 1200 m (3937 feet), height difference 379 m (1243 feet), time 7 minutes); from the terrace below Mont Chasseral there are superb views. Good walking among the vineyards, through the Twannbach gorge and to Schernelz. – The last Bernese commune on the lake is **La Neuveville** (German *Neuenstadt*: 438 m (1437 feet): pop. 3900; Hôtel J. J. Rousseau, C, 29 b.), the "Montreux of the Jura", with narrow streets, old gates and towers which belonged to the town's fortifications, and a thousand-year-old church, the Blanche Eglise. The road now enters the canton of Neuchâtel.

The first place beyond the cantonal boundary is *Le Landeron* (433 m (1421 feet): pop. 3400), a medieval market town with house fronts of the 16th and 17th c. The largest flea-market in Switzerland, the Fête de la

Brocante, is held here annually in September. – Continuing along the S side of the lake, we come to **Erlach** (433 m (1421 feet): pop. 1050; Hotel Schlossberg), with an old castle which is now a cantonal school hostel. The administrative district of Erlach also includes the farming and vine-growing villages of Vinelz and Lüscherz.

The most popular excursion on the lake is to **St Petersinsel** (alt. 435 m (1427 feet): Hotel St Petersinel), a place of idyllic beauty. Once an island, it can be reached from Biel of La Neuveville by boat, or (since the 19th c. regulation of the River Aare) on foot from Erlach on the "Heidenweg". The inn was originally a Cluniac priory (founded 1120, dissolved 1530); the room in which Rousseau stayed in 1765 is shown to visitors.

The return route from Erlach crosses the Aare canal and comes, just before Biel, to *Nidau* (430 m (1411 feet): pop. 8400; Hotel Schloss), situated at the end of the Nidau-Büren canal and separated from Biel by the Zihl canal. It thus in effect lies on an artificial island. The castle, from 1388 seat of the Bernese Governor, is now occupied by district administrative offices.

Aarberg (alt. 455 m (1493 feet): pop. 3300; Hotel Krone, C, 30 b.) 11 km (7 miles) S of Biel, a unique little medieval town, was founded about 1220, and was for centuries one of the country's most important road junctions. Its main features of interest are the Stadtplatz with its ring of well-to-do citizens' houses and the old wooden bridge over the Aare.

Lyss (alt. 444 m (1457 feet): pop. 8300; Hotel Weisses Kreuz; swimming pool and ice-rink): walks along the Alte Aare, the old course of the river (rich flora and fauna).

Büren an der Aare (alt. 443 m (1453 feet): pop. 2900), a little town, gay with flowers, lying between the Aare and the forest, with many fine old buildings.

Val Bregaglia

Canton: Grisons (GR).
ⓘ **Pro Bregaglia,**
CH-7649 Promontogno;
tel. (082) 4 15 55.

The *Val Bregaglia (in German Bergell) is a wild and romantic gorge, enclosed between towering granite mountains, which descends in a series of terrace-like steps from the Maloja pass (1815 m – 5955 feet) to the Italian town of Chiavenna (333 m – 1093 feet), 32 km (20 miles) SW. The high valley of the River Mera, which eventually flows into Lake Como, begins by falling steeply down from the pass (the watershed between the Val Bregaglia and the Engadine) and then descends to Chiavenna in six stages, the first four of which are within the canton of Grisons. The bizarrely shaped crags, buttresses and pinnacles of this mountain world are a climber's paradise, and the picturesque villages with their old patrician houses are a reminder of the long history of this region, which began in Roman times.

Beyond the pass the road leads down in a series of 13 hairpin bends, one after the other, with gradients of up to 9%, into the green valley below.

The highest village in the valley is **Casaccia** (1458 m (4784 feet): pop. 60), from which the old bridle-path, one of the busiest routes through the Alps in medieval times, crossed the Pass da Sett (Septimer pass) to Bivio in the Sursés (Oberhalbstein) valley. The ruined Turratsch watch-tower and the 16th c. hospice are relics of these earlier days. A cableway 2500 m (8203 feet) long belonging to the hydroelectric station which supplies power to Zurich (available for the transport of visitors by prior arrangement) leads up to the Albigna reservoir (2163 m (7097 feet): dam 115 m (377 feet) high, 67 million cu. m (2366 million cu. feet) of water).

Vicosoprano (1067 m (3501 feet): pop. 400) was originally the chief place in the valley. 16th c. patrician houses; Senwelenturm, a 13th c. tower 23 m (75 feet) high; courthouse, with torture chamber; Town Hall (1584); church (1761).

Stampa (994 m (3261 feet): pop. 180), a village which straggles along the road, was the home of the Giacometti family of artists. In the Ciäsa Granda (the "large house") is a fascinating museum devoted to the Val Bregaglia (collection of minerals, a weaving room, handsome living rooms and domestic utensils). – The following defile, *La Porta*, marks the boundary between the Alpine and the more southerly parts of the valley; it was fortified in Roman times.

The hamlet of *Promontogno* (821 m – 2694 feet) has a church (Nossa Donna), which dates in part from the 12th c., and a ruined castle (Castelmur). – From here a rewarding excursion (3 km – 2 miles) can be made to *Soglio (1090 m (3576 feet): pop. 210) on a road which branches on the right and runs through a chestnut wood. The village was the ancestral home of the Salis family and has three palaces (16th–18th c.) which belonged to them.

Soglio, Val Bregaglia

From the village, huddled round the tall tower of its church on a natural terrace above the valley, there are magnificent views of the Sciora group and the Val Bregaglia.

22 km (14 miles) from the Maloja pass the road reaches the Italian frontier at **Castasegna** (697 m (2287 feet): pop. 220), a trim village of southern aspect surrounded by luxuriant vegetation and the beautiful chestnut wood of Brentan. Underground hydroelectric power station (50 by 25 m (164 by 82 feet)).

The Italian town of **Chiavenna** lies at the junction of the Spluga (Splügen) and Maloja pass routes. The Roman *Clavenna* occupied a key strategic situation, as its name (from *clavis*, "key") implies. From 1512 to 1797 it was in the Grisons. Its principal church, San Lorenzo, has an octagonal baptistery (font of 1156).

Lake Brienz
See Lake Thun and Lake Brienz

Brig

Canton: Valais (VS).
Altitude: 684 m (2244 feet). – Population 9500.
Post code: CH-3900. – Dialling code: 028.
ⓘ **Offizielles Verkehrsbüro,**
Marktplatz;
tel. 23 19 01.

HOTELS. – *Victoria*, C, 80 b.; *Schlosshotel* (no rest.), C, 45 b.; *Alpina-Volkshaus*, C, 90 b.; *Londres-Schweizerhof*, C, 30 b.; *Elite-Touring*, D, 90 b.; *Europe* (no rest.), D, 50 b.; *Sporting* (no rest.), D, 57 b.; *Brigerhof* (no rest.), D, 45 b.; *Simplon*, E, 35 b.; *Du Pont*, E, 30 b.; *Ambassador*, 45 b.

CAMPING SITES. – Brig-Geschina, Brigerbad, Ried-Brig, Glis.

EVENTS. – Concerts in the Stockalperschloss; cellar theatre; Upper Valais Trade Fair (September).

The historic little town of Brig, on the S bank of the Rhône, is capital of the German-speaking Upper Valais (Oberwallis) and an important junction on the Simplon, Lötschberg, Furka–Oberalp and Brig–Visp–Zermatt railways. It is also the starting-point of the great roads over the Simplon, the Furka and the Nufenen passes. It has a number of notable old buildings.

HISTORY. – Brig was already of importance in Roman times as a staging-point on the N side of the Simplon pass. Its name comes from its situation between two bridges (over the Rotten – Rhône – and the Saltina). It later became the see of a bishop, and enjoyed a period of great prosperity in the time of Kaspar Jodok Stockalper (see below).

Stockalperschloss, Brig

SIGHTS. – The most notable building in Brig is the *Stockalperschloss, the finest Baroque palace in Switzerland, which the town bought from the Stockalper family in 1948. Since then it has been thoroughly renovated and restored by a trust, with financial assistance from the Federal government, the canton and the town. This imposing structure, dominated by three square gabled towers, was built by the great Valais merchant prince Kaspar Jodok Stockalper von Thurm (1609–91), who had occupied all the leading positions in the land. The palace, built between 1658 and 1678, pointed the way towards a great flowering of the baroque in Valais. It now houses, in addition to the family library of the "king of the Simplon" and 12,000 documents, the *archives* of the Upper Valais Historical

Society, the *Valais Institute* (Walser-Institut) and the *Museum of the Upper Valais* (May–October). – Near the palace are the collegiate *church of Spiritus Sanctus* (1675–85) and the Gothic *St Antony's chapel*. – W of Brig, on the Glisacker, stands the *pilgrimage church of Unsere liebe Frau (c. 1540), representing the final phase of medieval architecture (Gothic and Renaissance), which contains the finest works of art in this part of Switzerland.

Also of interest are the monument to Dr Ernest Guglielmetti (known as "Dr Goudron" – i.e. "Dr Tar"), inventor of the asphalt-surfaced road (in the Marktplatz, to the N of the Stockalperschloss) and the fountain commemorating the Peruvian aviator Geo Chavez, who flew over the Simplon for the first time in 1910 (in Sebastiansplatz).

SURROUNDINGS. – On the N bank of the Rhône is *Brigerbad* (alt. 655 m (2149 feet): pop. 185; Hotel Simplon (no rest.); Römerhof; camping site), with the first thermal swimming bath in a cave (air-conditioned, 38–42 °C (100–108 °F)) and the largest open-air thermal baths in Switzerland.

9 km (6 miles) SW is **Visp** (alt. 660 m (2165 feet): Hotel Staldbach, C, 30 b.; SP; Vispa, C, 32 b.; City-Rhône, D, 54 b., SB), a little town of 4000 inhabitants picturesquely situated at the mouth of the Vispa valley, up which runs the road to Zermatt and Saas Fee. Remains of town walls; old houses with coats of arms. On a crag above the Vispa is a large church of 1761 with a Romanesque tower, and higher up the hill St Martin's church (1651, altered 1963), with an arcaded porch. A road winds its way up the E side of the Vispa valley, through the highest vineyards in Europe (700–1200 m (2297–3937 feet): "Heidenwein", "heathens' wine"), coming in 10·5 km (7 miles) to the village of *Visperterminen* (1340 m (4397 feet): Hotel Rothorn, D, 32 b.), surrounded by a network of irrigation channels. From the village a path, with Stations of the Cross, climbs to the pilgrimage chapel of the Visitation (17th c.: old organ). Chair-lift from Visperterminen to Giw (1925 m – 6316 feet).

At the foot of the Aletsch glacier

To the N of Brig extends a magnificent glacier region. Between the *Riederhorn* (2230 m – 7317 feet) and the *Eggishorn* (2937 m – 9636 feet), a natural terrace exposed to the sun, from which the land falls steeply away, forms a transition to the Rhône valley. From Brig there are various routes to the Aletsch glacier which offer attractive day or half-day outings, with the help of cableways and lifts.

From Brig-Naters there is a good road up to *Blatten* (1332 m – 4370 feet: pop. 50), a typical little Valais mountain village, from which there is a cableway (length 1780 m (5840 feet), height difference 766 m (2513 feet), time 6 minutes) to *Belalp* (2080 m – 6824 feet). From here a footpath (½ hour) leads to the Belalp Hotel (D, 30 b.), at the foot of the Sparrhorn and above the western tip of the Aletsch glacier.

The Aletsch glacier – view from the Riederalp

7 km (4 miles) up the Rhône valley from Brig is **Mörel** (800 m (2625 feet): pop. 600; Hotel Relais-Walker, C, 40 b.; Bahnhof, D, 34 b.), formerly a post station and now a base for walks and climbs on the Riederalp. There are two cableways, one running up in two stages via *Ried* (length 3055 m (10,023 feet), height difference 1155 m (3790 feet), time 25 minutes) to the *Riederalp*, the other to the *Greicheralp* (length 2798 m (9180 feet), height difference 1141 m (3744 feet), time 15 minutes), with a continuation to the *Moosfluh* (length 1817 m (5962 feet), height difference 451 m (1480 feet), time 12 minutes), directly above the Aletsch glacier. From the Riederalp there is a chair-lift (length 1053 m (3455 feet), height difference 299 m (981 feet), time 7 minutes) to the *Hohfluh*, from which there is a splendid walk down to the *Riederfurka* (2064 m – 6772 feet).

The ** *Aletsch glacier* is a unique natural feature of great magnificence – the largest stretch of firn (ice formed from snow) in the Alps and in Europe (area 170 sq. km (66 sq. miles), length 22 km (14 miles)). Its catchment area extends from the S side of the Bernese Alps, round the Jungfrau, to the almost level Konkordiaplatz (see below), where the ice is some 800 m (2625 feet) deep, and from there southward to the Aletschwald (nature reserve), one of the highest forests of stone pines in Europe.

The Aletsch area offers magnificent opportunities for walkers and climbers. The Villa Cassel on the *Riederfurka* was the first office for the protection of nature established by the Schweizerischer Bund für Naturschutz (Swiss Association for the Protection of Nature: exhibition, Alpine garden).

The real gateway to the Aletsch glacier and the Aletschwald is the * **Riederalp** (1950 m (6398 feet): pop. 180, with the neighbouring hamlets 300; Hotel Art Furrer, B, 100 b., SB; Walliser Spycher, B, 35 b.; Alpenrose, B, 60 b.; Aparthotel Valaisia, Walliserhof, Riederalp, C, 104 b.; Adler, C, 34 b.; Reiderfurka, E, 15

b., accommodation for climbers). – Courses in ski acrobatics. – Particular features of interest are the Riederalp chapel (1679) and the *Blausee* (Blue Lake). – There is a pleasant, almost level, walk to the * **Bettmeralp** (1950 m (6398 feet): pop. 150; Bettmerhof, C, 50 b.; Hotel Aletsch, D, 50 b.; Alpfrieden, D, 96 b.; Waldhaus, D, 60 b.). The picturesque little mountain village, around the chapel of Maria zum Schnee (1679), is a popular resort both in summer and in winter, with excellent walking (walking, fishing and tennis weeks; glacier walks; climbing school). – From the Rhône valley the Bettmeralp can be reached via *Betten* (10 km (6 miles) from Brig) on a cableway (length 2610 m (8563 feet), height difference 1120 m (3675 feet), time 10 minutes).

The Aletsch area can also be reached from **Fiesch**, 18 km (11 miles) E of Brig (1050 m (3445 feet): pop. 700; Hotel Fiescherhof, C, 44 b.; Pension Schmitta (no rest.), C, 24 b.; Kristall, D, 50 b.; Alpenblick, in the Fieschertal; Jungfrau, on the Kühboden; family and youth hostel on the Kühboden). – Fiesch, which first appears in the records in 1203, has a chapel with an altar of 1704. There is a large health and holiday complex for young people, opened in 1966 (1050 b., SE, gymnasium). – From the * **Eggishorn** (2926 m – 9600 feet) there are panoramic views in the Upper Valais. A cableway (length 4795 m (15,732 feet), height difference 1807 m (5929 feet), time 13 minutes) ascends to the Kühboden and from there to the summit (magnificent view of the Aletsch glacier). Under the N face of the Eggishorn is the *Märjelensee* (2345 m (7694 feet): nature reserve). 8 km (5 miles) NE of the Eggishorn is * *Konkordiaplatz* (2840 m (9318 feet): Swiss Alpine Club hut; guide required).

A new-style holiday resort can be found at * **Breiten ob Mörel**, 8 km (5 miles) up the valley from Brig (900 m (2953 feet): pop. 80; Apartmenthotel Salina, B, 70 b.; Hotel Garni in Grünen (no rest.), B, 100 b.; holiday chalets). This centrally managed resort on a sunny

Breiten ob Mörel

terrace above the valley of the infant Rhône is the only brine spa in the Alps (water at 33 °C (91 °F)), with a well-equipped treatment and fitness facility (SB, heated SP) and its own farm (cheese dairy of 1713).

Brunnen

Canton: Schwyz (SZ).
Altitude: 440 m (1444 feet). – Population: 6300.
Post code: CH-6440. – Dialling code: 043.
ⓘ **Kur- und Verkehrsverein,**
   Bahnhofstrasse 32;
   tel. 31 17 77.

HOTELS. – ON THE LAKE: *Seehotel Waldstätterhof*, A, 190 b., SP, SB; *Bellevue au Lac*, B, 100 b.; *Schmid am See* (no rest.), B, 45 b.; *Elite-Aurora*, C, 110 b.; *Eden au Lac*, C, 60 b.; *Hirschen am See*, C, 50 b.; *Alfa au Lac* (no rest.), C, 40 b.; *Metropol au Lac*, C, 25 b.; *Brunnerhof*, C, 100 b. – AWAY FROM THE LAKE: *Parkhotel Hellerbad*, B, 140 b.; *Cabana* (no rest.), C, 30 b., SP; *Weisses Rössli*, C, 50 b.; *Alpina*, D, 35 b. – OUTSIDE THE TOWN: *Hotel Waldhaus Wolfsprung*, on the Axenstrasse; *Fallenbach*, on the road to Gersau.

CAMPING SITE. – To the W of the town.

EVENTS. – "Greiflet" and "Dreikönigsplöder" (old fertility rites), 6 January; National Festival on the Rütli, 1 August.

RECREATION and SPORT. – Bathing beach, sailing school, hire of boats; boat trips (steamers and motor launches) to Treib, Rütli, the Tell Chapel and Lucerne. – Kursaal, with gaming rooms.

The popular summer resort of Brunnen has a magnificent *situation at the right-angled bend in Lake Lucerne formed by the Urner See (Lake Uri) and the Gersauer Becken (Gersau basin), at the beginning of the Axenstrasse on the road over the St Gotthard. Since the construction of a bypass road it is a pleasantly quiet resort, with splendid views of the lake, the Seelisberg (with the Rütli Meadow) and the Bürgenstock.

Above the wide Muota valley rise the two characteristically shaped horns of the Mythen; above the deep rocky trough of the Urner See towers the massive Urirotstock, almost 3000 m (9843 feet) high; and to the rear of the Gersau basin is Pilatus, rising to over 2000 m (6562 feet). – The first reference to the town is in the Einsiedeln chronicles in 1217, but its traditions go much further back. – The Axenstrasse was opened in 1865.

SIGHTS. – The historic *Bundeskapelle* (Federal chapel), built in 1632 by Landammann Heinrich von Reding, has an altarpiece by Justus van Egmont (1642), a pupil of Rubens. Late Baroque *parish church of St Leonhard* (1661, restored 1978) in Ingenbohl. Memorial to the composer Othmar Schoeck, a native of Brunnen (1959). Crypt dedicated to the foundress of the convent of the Sisters of Charity of the Holy Cross (1975).

Brunnen, on Lake Lucerne.

SURROUNDINGS. – From the Axenstrasse a steep road runs up to the natural terrace at the foot of the *Fronalpstock* (1922 m – 6396 feet). – 3 km (2 miles: **Morschach** (alt. 645 m (2116 feet): pop. 550; Hotel Rütliblick, D, 30 b.; Betschart, D, 45 b.) has a superb view of the lake and the mountains, concerts, a forest park and a swimming pool. From here it is 1 km (about a ½ mile) to the *Axenstein* (708 m (2323 feet): nurses' home), an excellent viewpoint.

Bürgenstock

Cantons: Nidwalden (NW) and Lucerne (LU).
Altitude: 878–1132 m (2881–3714 feet).
Post code: CH-6366. – Dialling code: 041.
ⓘ **Bürgenstock-Hotels,**
   CH-6366 Bürgenstock LU;
   tel. 64 13 31.

HOTELS. – *Grand Hôtel*, A, 130 b., *Palace Hotel*, A, 140 b., *Park-Hotel*, B, 100 b., all three only

Bürgenstock – view over the hotel colony to Lake Lucerne

May–October, SP; *Waldheim*, C, 70 b., open through-out the year.

RESTAURANTS. – *Golf-Grill, Swimming Pool Café, Schifflände Kehrsiten, Berghaus Hammetschwand, Bahnhofsrestaurant* (garden café), *Taverne, Night-Club-Spycher.*

RECREATION and SPORT. – Golf, tennis, walking, swimming; concerts, dancing, bridge tournaments (instructor).

The **Bürgenstock is a limestone ridge 10 km (6 miles) long and between 1·5 and 3 km (1 and 2 miles) broad, covered with forests and Alpine meadows, which forms a peninsula in Lake Lucerne. Its N side rises steeply to a height of 500 m (1641 feet) above the lake; the S side slopes more gently down to the Stans valley.

This select health resort and magnificent viewpoint can be reached by road from Stansstad (5 km – 3 miles) or from the landing-stage of Kehrsiten-Bürgenstock (30 minutes from Lucerne) by funicular

(944 m (3097 feet), gradient 45%, 7 minutes). At the upper station of the funicular are the Bahnhofsrestaurant, the Park-Hotel and the Palace Hotel; 300 m (328 yards) SW is the Grand Hôtel. The hotels have a notable collection of pictures.

TOUR (2 hours: strongly recommended). – Starting from the hotels, walk along the *Felsenweg on the Hammetschwand cliffs (30 minutes) to the *Hammetschwand lift*, which runs up the vertical rock face to the upper station (restaurant) at 1115 m (3580 feet). From here it is a 3 minutes' walk to the summit of the **Hammetschwand** (1132 m – 3714 feet), the highest point on the Bürgenstock, with splendid views to the N of the lakes of central Switzerland and to the S of the Uri and Bernese Alps. – Take the lift down again and continue on the Felsenweg, the finest stretch of which begins here: 20 minutes to the *Honegg-Känzeli*, and from there another 30 minutes, past the *Kurhaus Honegg* and the *golf-course*, back to the hotels. – The narrow road which runs from the hotels by way of the Honegg saddle to Ennetbürgen can be used by cars only from the Kurhaus Honegg.

La Chaux-de-Fonds

Canton: Neuchâtel (NE).
Altitude: 997 m (3271 feet). – Population: 45,000.
Post code: CH-2300. – Dialling code: 039.
ⓘ **Office du Tourisme,**
Rue Neuve 11;
tel. 22 48 21.

HOTELS. – *Club*, 90 b.; *Moreau*, 60 b.; *Fleur-de-Lys*, 58 b.; *Motel du Jura*, 22 b.; *Gare et Poste*, 40 b.; *Balance*, 30 b.; *France*, 50 b.

RECREATION and SPORT. – Riding, tennis (outdoor and indoor courts), swimming, walking (nature park).

The Bürgenstock hotels

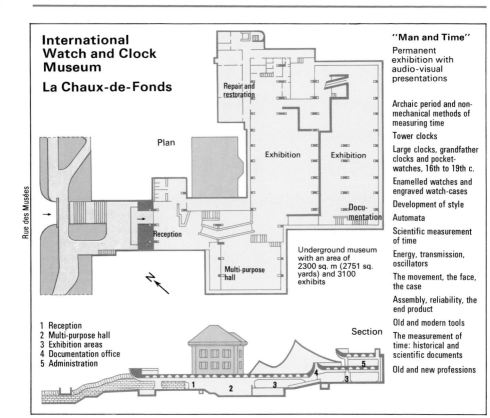

**International
Watch and Clock
Museum**

La Chaux-de-Fonds

Plan

Repair and restoration

Exhibition

Exhibition

Reception

Documentation

Underground museum with an area of 2300 sq. m (2751 sq. yards) and 3100 exhibits

Multi-purpose hall

1 Reception
2 Multi-purpose hall
3 Exhibition areas
4 Documentation office
5 Administration

Section

Rue des Musées

"Man and Time"

Permanent exhibition with audio-visual presentations

Archaic period and non-mechanical methods of measuring time

Tower clocks

Large clocks, grandfather clocks and pocket-watches, 16th to 19th c.

Enamelled watches and engraved watch-cases

Development of style

Automata

Scientific measurement of time

Energy, transmission, oscillators

The movement, the face, the case

Assembly, reliability, the end product

Old and modern tools

The measurement of time: historical and scientific documents

Old and new professions

WINTER SPORTS. – Illuminated ski trails, lifts from town, cross-country skiing, ski-bob run, indoor and outdoor ice-rinks, tobogganing, ski school.

Situated in a high valley in the Jura, the town of La Chaux-de-Fonds (rebuilt on a regular plan after a fire in 1794) is the capital of the Swiss watchmaking industry, which was first established here about 1705 (several hundred firms: visitors can tour some of the establishments). La Chaux-de-Fonds was the birthplace of the famous architect Charles-Edouard Jeanneret, better known as Le Corbusier (1887–1965).

SIGHTS. – In Rue du Progrès is a *Technical College*, with a watchmaking school. At 29 rue des Musées the ****International Watch and Clock Museum** (*Internationales Uhrenmuseum*: partly underground) takes as its theme "Man and Time", displaying the history of timekeeping from the Egyptians to the latest achievements of modern technology. It also has a workshop for the restoration of old watches and clocks which makes its services available to

Pendulum clock in the Watch and Clock Museum, Le Locle

collectors generally, a documentation office and library, audio-visual apparatus and a multi-purpose hall which is used for special exhibitions.

33 rue des Musées houses the *Museum of Art and Ethnography*, and 11 rue de la Loge the *Historical Museum*. Protestant *church*, rebuilt after the 1794 fire. – To the E of the town is a large *sports complex*.

SURROUNDINGS. – 8 km (5 miles) SW is the modern industrial town of **Le Locle** (alt. 925 m (3035 feet): Hôtel des Trois Rois), second only to La Chaux-de-Fonds as a hub of the watchmaking industry, which was founded in 1705 by Daniel Jean-Richard (monument at Post Office). In front of the Watchmaking School stands a monument to the first director of the school, J. Grossmann (1829–1907), a native of the watchmaking town of Glashütte in Saxony. In the Château des Monts are a *Watch and Clock Museum, with an interesting collection of watches and clocks and 35 automata, ranging in date from the 16th to the 19th c., and a small historical museum.

Chur
(Cuera/Cuoira)

Canton: Grisons (GR).
Altitude: 587 m (1926 feet). – Population: 33,500.
Post code: CH-7000. – Dialling code: 081.

ⓘ **Verkehrsverein,**
Ottostrasse 6;
tel. 22 18 18.

HOTELS. – *Duc de Rohan*, B, 60 b., SB; *Chur*, B, 90 b.; *ABC-Terminus* (no rest.), B, 60 b.; *Romantik-Hotel Stern*, C, 85 b.; *Mothotel Sommerau*, C, 95 b.; *Posthotel*, C, 85 b.; *Freieck*, C, 80 b.; *Drei Könige*, D, 60 b.; *Marsöl*, D, 24 b.

YOUTH HOSTEL, Bergstrasse 68. – CAMPING SITE: Touring, Untere Plessurstrasse.

RESTAURANTS. – *Steinbock*, opposite station; *Du Nord*, Bahnhofplatz; *Rätushof*, Bahnhofstrasse; *Hofkellerei* (an old Gothic wine-house).

RECREATION and SPORT. – Obere Au sports centre, indoor and outdoor swimming pools, artificial ice-rink, indoor riding-school, tennis.

Chur, capital of the Grisons canton and oldest town in Switzerland, has developed into a considerable intellectual and cultural attraction thanks to its excellent strategic situation at the end of some of the most important passes through the Alps and also to its mild climate. The town, known in Romansh as Cuera or Cuoira, grew up around the episcopal residence of the bishops of Chur (who are first mentioned in the records in 452), and became an important staging-point on the trade routes through the Alps. It is also the terminus of international railway lines and the starting-point of the Rhätische Bahn (narrow gauge) to St Moritz, the Chur–Arosa line and the "Glacier Express", and the Furka–Oberalp line to Brig. There is a postal bus service from Chur via Lenzerheide to St Moritz.

HISTORY. – Excavation has shown that the site was occupied about 3000 B.C. In 15 B.C., after their conquest of Rhaetia (an ancient Alpine district), the Romans made this the chief town of Rhaetia Prima. The name is derived from the Celtic *kora* or *koria* (tribe,

Bishop's Court, Chur

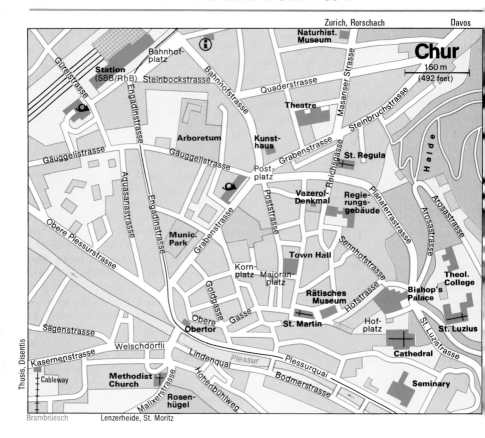

Chur

clan). In 284 Chur became the provincial capital, about 450 the see of a bishop. In the 12th c. the bishops of Chur were granted the status of princes of the Empire, but the Reformation deprived them of their secular authority. When the canton of Grisons was established in 1803 Chur became its administrative capital.

SIGHTS. – The town is situated on the River Plessur, which here flows into the Rhine. It is dominated by the picturesque **Bishop's Court** (*Bischöflicher Hof*), an extensive group of buildings surrounding the *Hofplatz*, on the site of a Roman fort. The * **Cathedral**, dedicated to the Assumption, is a Romanesque and Gothic building of the 12th and 13th c. (choir consecrated 1178, church 1272) with fine monumental sculpture and a richly decorated interior ranging in date from the Carolingian period to the Baroque.

INTERIOR of Cathedral. – The carved **altar**, by Jakob Russ of Ravensburg (1486–92), is the finest Late Gothic altar in Switzerland. There are notable figured *capitals* in the nave and crypt (6th and 12th c.). In one of the aisles is the **tomb** (gravestone), discovered in 1960, of the Swiss patriot **Jürg Jenatsch** (b. 1596, murdered 1639), who fought for the return of the Valtellina region to the Grisons canton. In the choir is a fine *triptych* of 1492.

The * **Cathedral Museum** displays the valuable Cathedral treasury, including the relics of St Lucius (2nd c.) and a 4th c. seal. – The *Bishop's Palace* (1732–33), an elegant Baroque building, has an imposing façade (stucco decoration). In the medieval Marsöl tower are the Bishop's chapel (17th c.) and a library. – Above the Cathedral, to the E, are the former monastic * *church of St Lucius*, with a round Carolingian crypt (8th c.), a seminary for the training of priests and a theological college.

Below the Bishop's Court is the * OLD TOWN, with interesting old buildings of the 15th–17th c. In the Regierungsplatz are the *Vazerol monument*, commemorating the union of the three Rhaetian leagues in 1471, and the *Regierungsgebäude* (Government Building), known as the "Graues Haus" (Grey House), with the cantonal chancery, the chamber in which the Little Council meets, the cantonal library and the state archives. – In the Reichsgasse is the *Rathaus* (Town Hall), built in 1465, with the Citizens' Council Chamber (1583; 17th c. tiled stove) and the Town Council Chamber (1494; collection of precious stones). – At the end of the Reichsgasse *St Martin's church* (Protestant; originally 8th c., rebuilt in Late Gothic style

1476–91) has stained glass by A. Giacometti (1917). – Above the church, to the E, we find the Buolsches Haus (1674–80), now housing the *Rhaetian Museum* (Rätisches Museum: material of the early historical period, cultural history, folk art).

In the middle of the town is the *Postplatz*, from which the Bahnhofstrasse and Grabenstrasse run respectively NW and NE–SW. In the Bahnhofstrasse is the *Art Gallery* (Kunsthaus: pictures of the 18th–20th c., including works by Giovanni, Augusto and Alberto Giacometti and Giovanni Segantini; closed Mondays). In Masaner Strasse is the *Natural History Museum* (Naturhistorisches Museum: also a national park museum; collections of rocks and minerals, etc.). To the NE is the *Grossratsgebäude* (Great Council Building), converted in 1958 from the old Armoury, which also houses the Municipal Theatre (*Stadttheater*) – SE of the Postplatz is the *Fontanaplatz*, with a monument to Benedikt Fontana, leader of the men of Grisons in the Battle of the Calven gorge in 1499.

SURROUNDINGS. – From the S side of the town a cableway ascends in two stages to *Brambrüesch* (1600 m – 5250 feet), from which there is a chair-lift to the *Dreibüdenstein* (2180 m – 7153 feet): walks and climbs on *Pizokel* and up **Calanda** (2806 m (9206 feet): wide views).

4·5 km (3 miles) from Chur on the Lenzerheide road is **Bad Passugg** (alt. 780 m (2559 feet): Hotel Kurhaus – at present closed), which has chalybeate (iron-bearing) springs in the Rabiosa gorge (drinking-fountain). The road continues via *Praden* (1160 m – 3806 feet) to the health resort of *Tschiertschen* (1343 m (4406 feet): pop. 200; Hotel Alpina, D, 60 b.; Carmenna, D, 35 b.; two ski-lifts). From here it is a 2 hours' climb to the *Churer Joch* (2038 m (6687 feet)) and a rewarding 3 hours' walk to Arosa (equally good in the reverse direction). Arosa: see p. 57.

Lake Constance

Within Germany, Switzerland and Austria.
Swiss cantons: Thurgau (TG) and St Gallen (SG).
ⓘ **Verkehrsbüro Kreuzlingen,**
Hauptstrasse 1A,
CH-8280 Kreuzlingen;
tel. (072) 72 38 40.
Verkehrsbüro Arbon,
Bahnhofstrasse 26,
CH-9320 Arbon;
tel. (071) 46 65 77.
Verkehrsbüro Rorschach,
CH-9400 Rorschach;
tel. (071) 41 16 80.

Internationaler Bodensee-Verkehrsverein (*IBV*),
Schützenstrasse 8,
D-7550 Konstanz (Germany);
tel. (07531) 2 22 32.

*Lake Constance (in German the Bodensee), lying below the northern edge of the Alps, with its shoreline shared between Switzerland, Germany and Austria, is by far the largest lake in Germany, the third largest lake in Central Europe (after Lake Balaton and Lake Geneva) and the second largest of the lakes bordering the Alps. From SE to NW it is divided into the Obersee, extending from Bregenz Bay to Eichhorn (Constance), and the much narrower, shorter and shallower Überlinger See, between the Bodanrück and Linzgau, and Untersee.

The Untersee is separated from the main lake by a strip of land which is traversed by the Rhine at Konstanz. At its northern end it splits into the Gnadensee, between the island of Reichenau and the Bodanrück, and the Zeller See, between the Höri and Mettnau peninsulas in Radolfzell Bay.

The whole of the southern shore of the lake is in Switzerland, much the greater part of it (running SE to beyond Arbon) belonging to the canton of Thurgau and the rest (from the vicinity of Rorschach to the Old Rhine) to St Gallen.

HISTORY. – Evidence of the ancient fauna of the region has been found in the form of animals' bones (mammoths, bison, reindeer, deer, wild horses, bears, etc.), and, in caves in the Thayngen area (canton of Schaffhausen), particularly in the Kesslerloch, works of art dating from the Late Palaeolithic period (*c.* 10000 B.C.) – engravings on reindeer antlers, figures of wild horses, a carving of a musk-ox's head, etc. Many traces of human settlement in the Mesolithic period (*c.* 8000–5000 B.C.) have been identified around the lake; and occupation during the Late Neolithic and Early Bronze Age (*c.* 3000–2000 B.C.) is attested by the pile-dwellings – huts occupied by hunters, fishermen and farmers – found, for example, at Ermatingen on the Untersee and between Botighofen and Seedorf on the Obersee. Remains of these houses, built on piles to provide protection from flooding, can be seen at low tide a short distance from the shore of the lake. Since the water level was 2–3 m (7–10 feet) lower at the time the houses were built they would originally have been on dry land. There are also remains of whole villages of pile-dwellings dating from the Early Iron Age (*c.* 800 B.C.).

The land around Lake Constance was originally Celtic territory, into which the Romans penetrated in the

FACTS AND FIGURES. – Geographical, **situation**: *Constance* lat. 47°39' N, long 9°10' E; *Bregenz* lat. 47°30' N, 9°44' E. – Mean **water level**: 395 m (1296 feet) (with fluctuations, so far unexplained, unconnected with season or weather conditions). – **Area**: total 545 sq. km (210 sq. miles) (Obersee and Überlingersee together 480 sq. km (185 sq. miles), Untersee 65 sq. km (25 sq. miles)). – Greatest **length**: between Bregenz and Stein am Rhein 76 km (47 miles) (as the crow flies 69 km (43 miles)), between Bregenz and the mouth of the Stockacher Aach 63 km (39 miles); longest direct line over water, from Hard to near the mouth of the Aach, 60 km (37 miles). – Greatest **width**: between Kressbronn and Rorschach 14·8 km (9 miles). – Greatest **depth**: in the Obersee (between Fischbach and Uttwil) 252 m (827 feet), in the Überlinger See 147 m (482 feet), in the Untersee 46 m (151 feet) (Zeller See 26 m (85 feet), Gnadensee 22 m (72 feet)). – **Circumference** (at half-tide level: total 263 km (163 miles), of which 168 km (104 miles) (64%) are in Germany, 69 km (43 miles) (26%) in Switzerland and 26 km (16 miles) (10%) in Austria. – Average **volume of water**: total 48,430 million cu. m (1,710,063 million cu. feet) Obersee and Überlinger See together 47,600 million cu. m (1,680,756 million cu. feet), Untersee 830 million cu. m (29,307 million cu. feet)). – **Tides** (at Constance tide-gauge): *mean high water* (end June/beginning July) 440 cm (173·2 inches) (highest recorded, beginning September 1817, 623 cm (245·3 inches)); *mean low water* (end February) 280 cm (110·2 inches) (lowest recorded this century, end March 1972, 237 cm (93·3 inches)). – **Visibility** from surface: annual average *c.* 7·50 m (25 feet) (in January down to 12 m (39 feet)). – **Colour** of water: in the Überlinger See and western Obersee blue-green, becoming increasingly yellowish towards the E as a result of the inflow of muddy water from the Rhine. In summer there may be a shimmering greenish layer caused by algae, and in May the water in quiet bays and inlets may have a yellow coating of pollen from coniferous trees.

Romanshorn – a bird's-eye view

1st c. B.C. Among Roman foundations on the Swiss shore of the lake was *Arbor Felix* (Arbon). In the 3rd c. A.D. the Alemanni, a Germanic tribe from the N, thrust into the western Lake Constance area. The region was Christianised by Iro-Scottish monks including Columban and his disciple Gallus, who preached here about the year 610, and the 8th c. saw the foundation of the abbey of St Gallen, which developed into a major cultural hub whose influence extended far beyond the region.

In the Appenzell war (1403–08) the confederation of towns on Lake Constance supported the Abbot of St Gallen against the mountain peasants, who suffered a defeat at Bregenz in 1408. – Constance, a member of the Swabian League, lost all rights of sovereignty in the Thurgau under the Treaty of Basle at the end of the Swabian war (1498–99).

Kreuzlingen (alt. 404 m (1326 feet): pop. 17,000; Hotel Quellenhof; Hotel Emmishofen), sister city to the German town of Constance, is separated from that town only by the line of the frontier, which does not follow the Rhine but runs through the built-up area at some distance from the river. The town's name comes from a relic of the True Cross which is preserved in the conventual church. – In the Hauptstrasse is the former Augustinian convent (since 1844 occupied by the Thurgau teachers' training college) built by Michael Beer in 1640–53 to replace an earlier monastic house destroyed during the Thirty Years War and remodelled in Baroque style in 1765. *St Ulrich's church*, well restored, together with the rest of the conventual buildings, after a fire in 1936, has notable ceiling frescoes, a fine organ and a grille by Jakob Hoffner (1737). A representation of the Agony in the Garden (in the N lateral chapel) preserves 280 of its original 322 figures (1720–40), and a large Gothic cross bears a figure of Christ with natural hair.

To the N of the town, by the lake, lies the trim Seeburg Park, with the ivy-clad *Seeburg*, built in 1598 as a country residence of the bishops of Constance, largely destroyed during the Thirty Years War, rebuilt in 1879–94 and now occupied by the military. The park contains a reserve for fallow deer and wildfowl. 1 km (about a ½ mile) E of the Seeburg, at the Fischerhaus camping site and restaurant, is a waterworks, and just offshore is a *fountain*, visible far and wide when it is working (illuminated at night). – SW of the former convent stands the *Rosenegg Heimatmuseum* (local history and traditions); and still farther SW, in Bernrain, are an *observatory* and a Baroque *pilgrimage chapel.*

The road W from Kreuzlingen towards the **Untersee** comes first to the village of *Tägerwilen* (alt. 406 m (1332 feet)), with the church of SS. Cosmas and Damian. – 1·5 km (1 mile) S, above the village, *Schloss Castell* or *Chastel*, was built in 1661 near the palace of the bishops of Constance, which was destroyed in 1499; it was rebuilt between 1878 and 1894. – Tägerwilen was the birthplace of Hermann Müller (1850–1927), who produced the Müller-Thurgau grape (a cross between Riesling and Sylvaner) which bears his name. – To the N, on the Rhine, in the picturesque *Gottlieben* district of the town (alt. 398 m (1306 feet)), stands a palace built in 1251 as a subsidiary residence of the bishops of Constance (enlarged 1480, rebuilt in Neo-Gothic style 1837–38), in which Jan Hus, his fellow Hussite Jerome of Prague and Anti-Pope John XXIII were imprisoned in 1415; the palace now belongs to the singer Lisa della Casa. There are a number of handsome old half-timbered *houses, including the Drachenburg and the Waaghaus or Weigh-House (both 17th c.), as well as the so-called Burg (Castle) and Haus Rheineck. – A local speciality is the pastry called "Gottlieber Hüppen".

Ermatingen (alt. 397 m (1303 feet): Hotel Seetal), 4 km farther W a fishing village (picturesque half-timbered houses) is also a holiday resort, situated on the Staad or Stad peninsula (on which remains of pile-dwellings have been found). Above the village rises *Schloss Wolfsberg* (16th c.: private property), from which there are fine views.

Farther W again, beautifully situated opposite the island of Reichenau (2 km (1 mile): ferry), is *Mannenbach* (alt. 405 m (1329 feet)), above which stands *Burg Salenstein* (505 m (1657 feet): originally 11th c., restored 1842). On a terrace to the E is *Schloss **Arenenberg** (458 m (1503 feet): Napoleonic Museum, closed November to March), built 1540–46, with later alterations. From 1830 until her death in 1837 this was the residence of Napoleon's stepdaughter Queen Hortense de Beauharnais, whose son Louis Napoléon, later Napoleon III, spent his childhood here. In 1906 the Empress

Eugénie, Napoleon III's widow, presented the castle to the canton of Thurgau as a memorial to her husband. – Above Mannenbach to the W is the ruined castle of *Sandegg* (517 m (1696 feet): views), and 500 m (1641 feet farther S *Schloss Eugensberg* (544 m (1785 feet): private property), built in 1820 for Eugène de Beauharnais, Napoleon's stepson and brother of Queen Hortense.

The road continues through the quiet resort of *Berlingen* (alt. 398 m (1306 feet)), with a Town Hall of 1780, to **Steckborn** (404 m (1326 feet): pop. 4500; Seehotel Romantica, E of the town), an ancient little town on a peninsula in the Untersee which is a popular holiday resort (picturesque half-timbered houses). The *Turmhof*, a castle on the lakeside, built about 1320 (17th c. domed tower and corner turrets) by Diethelm von Castell, Abbot of Reichenau, houses a *local museum* (closed in winter). – *Town Hall* (1667), with a collection of weapons on the first floor (open weekdays). – The *Town church* (1766), a plain Baroque building by F. A. Bagnato; has extensive wide views from the tower. – *Jakobuskirche* (St James's church, 1963: R.C.). – At the SW end of the town is the Bernina sewing-machine factory, with a sewing-machine museum.

The road SE from Kreuzlingen along the **Obersee** comes in 2·5 km (2 miles) to the village of *Bottighofen* (alt. 398 m (1306 feet): Gasthof Schlössli), which is attractively situated amid fruit orchards and has a well-equipped boating harbour. – 1·5 km (1 mile) beyond this is **Münsterlingen** (398 m (1306 feet): Hotel Hecht), a holiday resort situated on a peninsula. The church of the Benedictine convent (rebuilt 1709–16), now a cantonal hospital, has a fine Baroque interior, and since 1963, when the lake last froze, has housed the 16th c. bust of St John Baptist, which traditionally transfers between Hagnau and Münsterlingen whenever the lake freezes.

The road continues through *Kesswil* and *Uttwil*, both with fine half-timbered houses, to **Romanshorn** (399 m (1309 feet): Seehotel, Inseli), a lakeside resort which is also the largest port on Lake Constance and the base of the Swiss lake steamers (shipyard of Swiss Federal

Railways). – To the N of the *Bundesbahn-hafen* (Federal Railways harbour) lies the *Seepark*, with the *Old Church*. The *Schloss* (now a hotel) dates in its present form from 1829. Small *Zoo* (restaurant). – In the lake, to the N, is the *Inseli*, a rocky islet. 1·5 km (1 mile) NW is the lake pumping-station for Amriswil.

The next place of any size is **Arbon** (alt. 398 m (1306 feet): pop. 14,000; Hotel Metropol, Rotes Kreuz), a port town situated on a peninsula, occupying the site of the Celtic settlement of Arbona and the Roman *Arbor Felix*. It is also a busy industrial town. St Gallus died here about 645. From 1285 to 1798 the town was held by the bishops of Constance.

NW of the Alter Hafen (Old Harbour) and the Schlosshafen is the Roman Catholic *parish church of St Martin* (choir 1490, nave 1788; Madonna of 1525). – Farther NW is the 16th c. *Schloss*, built on the foundations of a Roman fort of A.D. 294, with a seven-storey tower originally dating from about 400, which contains a local historical museum (open 10–12 and 2–4; closed in winter). – Other features of interest are the Römerhof (*c.* 1500) and the *chapel of St Gallus* (originally 10th c.; 14th c. frescoes). – Lakeside promenade 3 km (2 miles) long.

From Arbon the road continues to *Steinach* (alt. 400 m (1312 feet)), a fishing village with a Baroque parish church and a large granary (the "Gred") of 1473, *Horn* (398 m (1306 feet): Hotel Bad Horn), an enclave belonging to the canton of Thurgau, boasts a castle which belonged to the Landgrave of Hesse, and **Rorschach** (p. 204), the old port of St Gallen. – Farther E is *Altenrhein*, on the delta of the Old Rhine. Here is to be found the hangar of the FFA aircraft and car factory (Flug- und Fahrzeugwerke Altenrhein: formerly the Dornier works) and the base from which the old Dornier flying-boats took off in the 1920s.

SE of the mouth of the Old Rhine is **Rheineck** (400 m (1312 feet): pop. 3000; Hotel Schiff Buriet), the attractive little Swiss frontier town on the banks of the idyllic *Old Rhine*. Rheineck has arcaded streets, and old town gate, a Town Hall of 1555, a Late Gothic and Baroque church (Protestant), two imposing 18th c. town houses, the Löwenhof and the Custerhof, and a ruined castle (views). – From here a narrow-gauge rack railway runs up (1·9 km (1 mile), taking 6 minutes) to *Walzenhausen* (682 m – 2238 feet), a hillside village in a commanding situation high above Lake Constance which is also a health and winter sports resort.

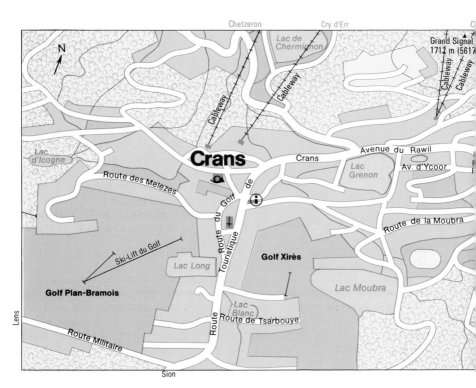

3·5 km (2 miles) SE of Rheineck is **St Margrethen** (402 m (1319 feet): pop. 6000; Hotel Bahnhof), a rail and road junction on the Swiss-Austrian frontier (customs) situated on the Old Rhine in a fertile fruit-growing region. It is also a spa (Kneipp treatment). – St Margaret's chapel, a cemetery church dating from 1090, has frescoes and Late Baroque altars. In the Rheinpark is a large shopping complex. – To the SW is *Schloss Bergsteig*, to the W *Schloss Vorburg* (open to visitors). – Pleasant walks to the hill villages (good views) in the St Gallen and Appenzell areas.

Crans-Montana

Crans in winter

Canton: Valais (VS).
Altitude: 1500–1680 m (4922–5512 feet).
Post code: Crans CH-3963, Montana Ch-3962.
Dialling code: 027.

(i) **Office du Tourisme Crans-sur-Sierre,**
CH-3963 Crans;
tel. 41 21 32.
Office du Tourisme Montana-Vermala,
CH-3962 Montana;
tel. 41 30 41.

HOTELS (mostly closed in October–November and May). – IN CRANS: **Du Golf et des Sports*, A, 160 b., SB; *De l'Etrier*, B, 250 b., SP, SB; *Beau Séjour*, B, 100 b., SB; *Eurotel-Christina*, B, 100 b., SB; *Rhodania*, B, 80 b.; *Royal*, B, 100 b.; *Alpina & Savoy*, B, 100 b., SB; *Belmont*, C, 50 b.; *Carlton*, C, 60 b.; *City*, C, 45 b.; *Serenella*, C, 40 b. – IN MONTANA-VERMALA: **Crans

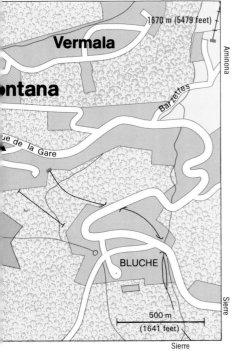
Sierre

Ambassador, A, 100 b., SB; **Supercrans*, A, 50 b., SB; *Mirabeau*, B, 100 b.; *Curling*, B, 70 b., SP; *St-Georges*, B, 75 b., SP; *Grand Hôtel du Parc*, C, 135 b.; *Aida*, C, 60 b.; *Forest*, C, 45 b.; *Primavera*, C, 50 b.; *Vermala*, C, 70 b.; *Helvétia*, D, 30 b.

CAMPING SITE. – On Lac Moubra.

RECREATION and SPORT. – Two beautiful golf-courses (18 and 9 holes), many tennis courts, riding track, swimming, skittles, fishing, walking.

WINTER SPORTS. – Short training lifts in the valley, numerous lifts on the Cry d'Err (2207 m (7241 feet): cableways from Crans and Montana), Chetzeron (2100 m (6890 feet): cableway from Crans) and Bella Lui (2543 m (8343 feet): cableway from Cry d'Err). Summer skiing in the Plaine Morte glacier area (3000 m (9843 feet): cableway from Violettes). Many ski-trails with lifts between Violettes (2208 (7244 feet): cableway from Vermala-Zaumiau) and Petit-Mont-Bonvin (2411 m (7910 feet): cabin cableway from Aminona). Artificial ice rink, curling, tobogganing, cross-country skiing, ski school with 30 instructors.

The popular holiday and winter sports area of *Crans-Montana lies NW of the little town of Sierre in the Rhône valley. It is reached by any one of three roads from the Rhône valley or by a funicular from Sierre.

The attractive resort of **Crans sur Sierre** (1480–1500 m – 4856–4922 feet), to the W, lies round a number of small lakes, the *Etangs de Lens*. From Crans a cableway 4480 m (14,699 feet) long ascends in 25 minutes, via *Merbé* (1900 m – 6234 feet) and Cry d'Err, to **Bella Lui* (2543 m (8344 feet): restaurant), from which there are superb views. Another cableway, roughly parallel to the first, takes 13 minutes to reach *Chetzeron* (2100 m – 6890 feet), from which there is a ski-lift to the Cry d'Err.

The popular mountain and winter sports resort of **Montana** (1500 m – 4922 feet), 1·5 km (1 mile) to the E on *Lac Moubra*, lies on a natural terrace covered with forests and Alpine meadows 1000 m (3281 feet) above the Rhône valley, sheltered by the mountains to the N, and has a mild, dry mountain climate. A cableway 540 m (1772 feet) long climbs in 3 minutes to the *Grand Signal* (upper station 1712 m (5617 feet)), from which there are ski-lifts to *Verdet* (1875 m – 6152 feet) and the Cry d'Err. Another cableway, 2500 m (8203 feet) long, runs up in 12 minutes to the *Cry d'Err* (2263 m (7425 feet): restaurant). – Above Montana, 1·5 km (1 mile) N, is **Vermala** (1670 m – 5479 feet), with a ski-jump. From Vermala-Zaumiau a cableway 2545 m (8350 feet) long goes up via *Les Marolires* to the Swiss Alpine Club's *Cabane des Violette* (2208 m (7244 feet): restaurant), from which another cableway (3243 m (10,640 feet) long) continues to the *Plaine Morte* (2927 m – 9603 feet), above the S end of the Plaine Morte glacier (summer skiing).

10 km (6 miles) NE of Montana is **Aminona** (1437 m – (4415 feet)), a popular winter sports resort with a group of tower-block hotels, from which there is a cabin cableway 2410 m (7907 feet) long to the *Petit-Mont-Bonvin* (2411 m (7910 feet): numerous ski-lifts).

Davos

Canton: Grisons (GR).
Altitude: 1560 m (5118 feet). – Population: 12,300.
Post code: Ch-7270. – Dialling code: 083.
ⓘ **Verkehrsverein,**
Promenade 67,
Davos Platz;
tel. 3 51 35.
Self-Service Hotel Reservation,
Bahnhofstrasse 9,
Davos Dorf.

HOTELS. – DAVOS DORF: *Flüela*, A, 130 b., SB; *Derby*, B, 130 b.; *Seehof*, B, 134 b.; *Montana*, B, 80 b.; *Meierhof*, B, 80 b.; *Des Alpes* (no rest.), C, 100 b.; *Parsenn*, C, 70 b.; *Bristol*, C, 120 b.; *Sonnenberg*, C, 70 b., SB; *Stolzenfels*, D, 65 b.; *Herrmann*, D, 40 b.; *Concordia*, D, 40 b.; *Touring*, E, 40 b. – DAVOS PLATZ: *Steigenberger Belvédère*, A, 255 b., SB; *Morosani's Pöstli*, B, 110 b., SB; *Schweizerhof*, B, 150 b., SB; *Sunstar Park*, B, 400 b., SB; *Central*, B, 100 b., SB; *Cresta*, B, 90 b., SB; *Cresta Sun*, B, 90 b., SB; *Europe*, B, 110 b., SP, SB; *Sunstar*, C, 140 b., SB; *Bellavista*, C, 70 b.; *Terminus*, C, 120 b.; *Angleterre*, C, 80 b.; *Lohner*, C, 65 b.; *Bündnerhof*, C, 48 b. – ON THE SCHATZALP: *Berghotel Schatzalp*, B, 170 b., SB.

CAMPING SITE. – *Waldhaus*, Davos Platz.

YOUTH HOSTELS. – *Davos-Wofgang*; *Berghaus Stafelalp* (1 hour above the Frauenkirch station).

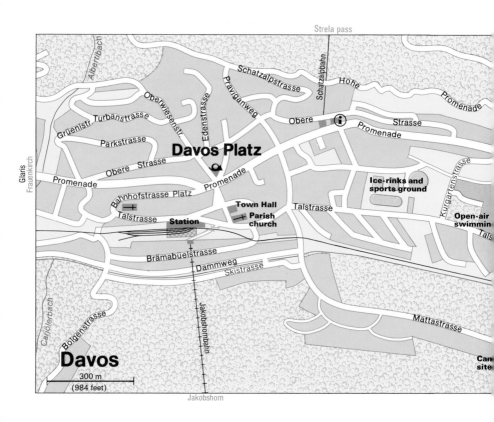

Davos

RECREATION and SPORT. – Bathing beach on the Davoser See; indoor and outdoor swimming pools (Hallenbad, Gartenbad) in the Kurpark. – Golf-course, Davos Platz. – Natural ice-rinks (22,000 sq. m (26,312 sq. yards): the largest in Europe), with areas for figure and speed skating, ice-hockey and curling; artificial ice-rink (1800 sq. m (2153 sq. yards), open in summer as well as winter: curling). – Beautiful Kurpark (bandstand). – 40 cableways and lifts with a total capacity of 30,000 persons, giving access to extensive mountain-walking and skiing areas. – Toboggan run, Schatzalp-Davos.

EVENTS. – *International Ice Hockey Tournament* for the Spengler Cup, *curling tournaments, skating events, ski races, "walking weeks".*

SCIENTIFIC INSTITUTES. – Swiss Research Institute (Physical and Meteorological Observatory and World Radiation Centre, Institute of Medical Climatic and

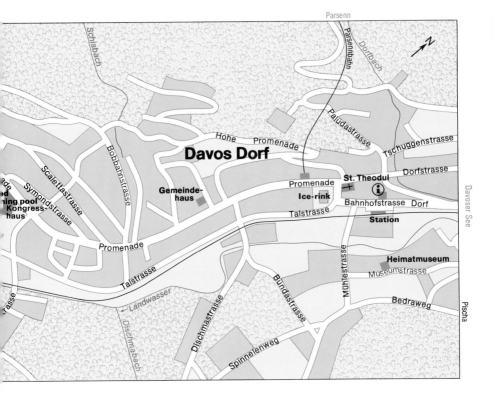

Cableway from the Weissfluhjoch to the summit of the Weissfluh, above Davos

Tuberculosis Research, Laboratory of Experimental Surgery, Osteosynthesis Study Group); Federal Institute of Snow and Avalanche Research, Weissfluhjoch/Davos.

*Davos, a high valley extending 16 km (10 miles) SW from the Wolfgang pass and traversed by the Landwasser, is the second largest commune in Switzerland (254 sq. km — 98 sq. miles) — larger than the canton of Zug. The twin settlements of Davos Platz and Davos Dorf have increased their population fivefold over the last 100 years and have now united to form a built-up area 4 km (2 miles) long. Surrounded by forest-covered mountains and sheltered from rough N and E winds, Davos enjoys a climate (bracing but not excessively so, with plenty of sunshine and dry air) which has made it one of Switzerland's leading summer and winter resorts.

The foundations of Davos's fame as a health resort were laid by a Mannheim doctor, Alexander Spengler, who prescribed mountain air for his tuberculosis patients and brought the first summer visitors here in 1860 and the first winter visitors in 1865.

Since 1890 Davos has been linked with the Rhine valley (Chur) by the Rhätische Bahn (Rhaetian Railway), and since 1909 with the Albula valley and the Engadine.

There are postal bus services from Davos over the Flüela pass to Susch/Süs (only in summer), to Clavadel and Sertig Dörfli (in winter only to Clavadel) and into the Dischma valley (in winter only as far as Teufi), and from Davos Glaris to Monstein. Local bus operators run services between Davos Platz, Davos Dorf, Davos Wolfgang and Dörfji (near which is the lower station of the Pischa mountain railway). There are numerous cableways and lifts and a wide range of facilities for sport and entertainment.

HISTORY. — The name of Davos (in the form *Tavauns*, which later became *Dafaas*) appears for the first time in 1160, in a document in the episcopal archives in Chur. In 1289 14 families from the Valais established households here. After the death of the last member of the Toggenburg family in 1436 the League of the Ten Jurisdictions was formed. In 1649 Davos purchased its freedom from Austrian sovereignty. A large ice-rink (24,000 sq. m — 28,704 sq. yards) for the world figure-skating championships and the European speed skating championships was opened in 1899, and in the same year the Davos-Schatzalp funicular and the Schatzalp toboggan run came into operation.

SIGHTS. — The chief place of the valley is **Davos Platz** (1560 m — 5118 feet), the only old buildings in which are the *parish church of St John the Baptist* (1481; nave 1280–85, restored 1909), with a window in the choir by Augusto Giacometti (after 1928), and the adjoining *Rathaus* (Town Hall: restored 1930), with the panelled "Great Chamber" (Grosse Stube) of 1564. Adjoining the indoor swimming pool (Hallenbad) stands the modern

Congress House (Kongresshaus, 1969). –
In **Davos Dorf** (1563 m – 5128 feet) is
the 14th c. *church of St Theodulus*. At
Museumstrasse 1 is the Old Prebend
House (Altes Pfrundhaus), the only
surviving example of an old burgher's
house, which is now occupied by a *local
museum* (Heimatmuseum). The *Gemeindehaus* (communal house) of Davos Dorf
was built by Jürg Jenatsch in 1634
(altered 1886).

SURROUNDINGS. – A favourite walk from Davos is
to the *Davoser See*, a natural lake (area 0·59 sq. km
(0·23 sq. mile)) which supplies a hydroelectric power
station (walk round the lake $1\frac{1}{2}$ hours). There is a
bathing beach. – The footpath called the Hohe
Promenade (level walk of 2·5 km (2 miles) from Davos
Dorf to Davos Platz) leads to Wolfgang (1631 m –
5351 feet) and Laret (1525 m – 5004 feet), to the NE,
and to Frauenkirch (1532 m – 5026 feet), Spinabad
(1465 m – 4807 feet), Glaris (1443 m – 4734 feet),
Schmelzboden (1590 m – 5217 feet: Mining Museum)
and Wiesen (1421 m – 4662 feet) to the SW.

To Parsenn and the Weissfluhjoch. – This is a
renowned skiing area and also excellent walking and
climbing country. The mountains on the W side of the
Davos valley were made conveniently accessible by
the opening in 1931 of the *Davos-Parsenn-Bahn*,
a funicular 4106 m (13,472 feet) long (height
difference 1106 m (3629 feet), time 25 minutes).
From the *Höhenweg* station (2 km (1 mile): 2219 m
(7281 feet)) there are magnificent mountain walks
without any real climbing. The funicular continues up
to the *Weissfluhjoch* (2663 m (8737 feet): restaurant), with views of the Silvretta and Flüela
groups, from Piz Buin to the Tinzenhorn. From the
upper station there is a cableway to the summit of the
Weissfluh (2844 m (9331 feet): restaurant), from
which there are superb views in all directions. There is
also a cableway from the Weissfluhjoch to the
Parsenn hut (2200 m (7218 feet): restaurant), 2
hours' walk from Wolfgang. One of the finest paths in
the area is the *Panoramaweg*, which runs from the
Parsenn hut through the Meierhoftäli valley to the
Höhenweg funicular station and from there through
the Dorftäli and under the Schiahörner to the Strela
pass. – From the Parsenn hut it is a half-hour's walk to
the Gotschnagrat (2285 m – 7497 feet).

From Davos Platz the **Schatzalpbahn** (funicular,
length 716 m (2349 feet), height difference 301 m
(988 feet), time 5 minutes) ascends to the *Schatzalp*
(1861 m (6106 feet): hotel and restaurant; on foot
$1–1\frac{1}{2}$ hours. 350 m (1148 feet) N of the Berghotel is
the *Schatzalp Alpine Garden (Alpinum)*, which
contains 7500 plants in 550 species and sub-species
(free admission with funicular ticket). – From the
Schatzalp a rewarding walk via the Podestatenalp,
Lochalp and Grüenialp leads to Davos ($2\frac{1}{4}$ hours). –
The Schatzalp-Davos toboggan run is 2·5 km (2
miles) long, with well-cambered bends. – The *Strela
pass* (2350 m – 7710 feet), reached by the Schatzalp-
Strela cableway (length 1760 m (5775 feet), height
difference 488 m (1601 feet), time 10 minutes;
restaurant), passes larches over a thousand years old.
From the Strela pass a cabin cableway (opened 1981)
ascends to the lower station of the Haupteräli Skilift
which goes up to the Weissfluhjoch.

The Jakobshorn and the eastern valleys. – There
are also pleasant walks and climbs on the left side of

the valley. A cableway constructed in 1954 runs up to
the *Ischalp* (1931 m (6336 feet): restaurant), and
from there to the *Jakobshorn (2590 m (8498 feet):
restaurant), from which there are splendid panoramic
views. From here a waymarked path runs down
through groves of rhododendrons to the Ischalp ($1\frac{1}{4}$
hours). Ski-lifts from the Ischalp serve the *Brämabüel*
skiing area (2477 m – 8127 feet). Another footpath
from the Ischalp leads in 45 minutes to the *Clavadeler
Alp* (1971 m – 6467 feet) and from there in another 45
minutes to *Clavadel* (1664 m (5460 feet): postal
bus), one of the sunniest spots in the valley. The walk
from Davos Platz to Clavadel and back takes between
2 and 3 hours. – In summer the postal bus runs up the
Sertig valley to **Sertig Dörfli** (1861 m (6106 feet):
restaurant), in a superb mountain setting (a popular
trip with walkers, plant-lovers and animal-lovers).

The magnificent walking and winter sports area on the
Rinerhorn, a few kilometres S of Davos, can be
reached by taking the chair-lift from Davos Glaris to
Jatzmeder (2045 m (6710 feet): restaurant), from
which it is $1\frac{1}{2}$ hours' climb to the summit of the
Rhinerhorn (2528 m – 8294 feet). – A short distance
beyond Glaris a by-road branches off on the left to the
little village of *Monstein* (1626 m – 5335 feet),
idyllically situated on a sunny terrace on the
mountainside, where the old German dialect of the
Upper Valais is still spoken.

The *Dischma valley* is the longest (12 km – 7 miles) of
the valleys on the left side of the Davos valley. On the
right bank of the Dischmabach is a narrow road, on
the left bank a pleasant footpath. The timber buildings
to be seen here are typical of the older Davos. The last
village in the valley is *Dürrboden* (2007 m (6585 feet):
inn), which can be reached on foot in 3–4 hours from
Davos Dorf. Postal bus in summer to Dürrboden, in
winter to Teufi.

The *Flüela valley* is another good walking and skiing
area (nature reserve). The road from Davos Dorf
crosses the Flüelabach (waterfall, 5 minutes' walk)
and comes in 4 km (2 miles) to *Dörfji* (1803 m (5916
feet): bus station; restaurant), from which the
*Pischabahn (length 2030 m (6660 feet), height
difference 680 m (2231 feet), time 6 minutes) serves
Pischa (2485 m (8153 feet): inn). From there it is a
climb of $1\frac{1}{2}$–2 hours to the summit of the *Pischahorn*
(2980 m – 9777 feet).

Over the Flüela pass into the Engadine. – The
shortest route from the Rhine valley to the Lower
Engadine goes from Landquart through the Prättigau
to Davos Dorf and from there over the Flüela pass to
Susch. The *Flüela pass road* between Davos and
Susch (27 km – 17 miles), opened to traffic in 1867, is
between 5·5 and 7 m (18 and 23 feet) wide, with
gradients of up to 10%; in winter it is usually open
during the day.

From *Dörfji* (1815 m (5955 feet): restaurant), from
which there is a beautiful view to the rear of the
Weissfluh, one can reach *Tschuggen* 7 km (4 miles)
SE (1941 m (6368 feet): holiday centre, 100 chalets –
in summer postal bus service from Davos), amid
magnificent expanses of rhododendrons and stone
pines. 13 km (8 miles) beyond this is the *Flüela pass
(2383 m (7819 feet): mountain inn), the highest
Alpine pass in the Grisons, $3\frac{3}{4}$ hours on foot from
Davos Dorf. Beyond the pass, at the head of the lower
Engadine, *Susch* (1438 m (4718 feet): pop. 200;
Hotel Steinbock; Flüela), straddles the Inn and the
Susaca.

Delémont

Canton: Jura (JU).
Altitude: 430 m (1411 feet). – Population: 12,500.
Post code: CH-2800. – Dialling code: 066.

ⓘ **Office du Tourisme,**
2 Route de Basle;
tel. 22 66 86.

HOTELS. – *La Bonne Auberge*, C, 20 b.; *Victoria*, D,
30 b.; *Central*, D, 20 b.; *Cigogne*, D, 40 b. – YOUTH
HOSTEL. – CAMPING SITE.

**Delémont (in German Delsberg), the
largest town in the Jura and capital
of the newest Swiss canton, is an
important railway junction on the
Berne–Basle and Delle–Paris lines
and the starting-point of many postal bus services. It lies in the wide
valley of the Sorne, which here
flows into the Birs, and is traversed
by two principal streets running
parallel to one another.**

HISTORY. – Delémont first appears in the records in
728 as a market village, and again in 1212 as a town
founded by the Prince-Bishop of Basle. It was granted
a municipal charter in 1289. After the Reformation it
was a favourite residence of the bishops of Basle.
From 1815 it was the chief town of a district in the
canton of Berne, and in 1978 it became capital of the
new canton of Jura.

Delémont
100 m
(328 ft)

SIGHTS. – As an important industrial,
cultural and tourist area Delémont has
developed into a modern town without
losing its old-world character. The main
features of interest are the *church of St-
Marcel* (1762–66), a three-aisled basilica

built over an earlier cruciform structure;
the *château of the Prince-Bishops*
(1716–21); the 13th c. *Archive tower*; the
Grand'Rue, the wide main street; five
large fountains; and the *Musée Jurassien*
(local history, prehistoric and Roman
material).

SURROUNDINGS. – There are many places of
interest in the immediate surroundings of the town,
including the fortress of *Vorbourg*, the *château de
Domont* and the *château de Soyhières*.

The Ajoie Uplands. – To the W of Delémont a hilly
region extends towards the French frontier, a
limestone plateau which falls away towards the
Belfort gap. The road from Delémont to Porrentruy
(28 m – 17 miles) is a section of the through route
from Berne via Belfort to Paris. After passing through
Develier (church with stained glass by Bissière) it
comes in 14 km (9 miles) to the pass of *Les Rangiers*
(858 m (2815 feet): Hôtel Quatre Vents, C, 14 b.), on
the Mont Terri ridge (fine views). – 1 km (about a $\frac{1}{2}$
mile) beyond the pass, on the right, is a military
memorial (by L'Eplattenier, 1924) commemorating
the manning of the frontier during the First World War.
The road then continues through *Les Malettes* (inn),
down the *Combe Maran* and under a high railway
viaduct (5 km – 3 miles) to *St-Ursanne* (alt. 440 m
(1444 feet): pop. 1100; Hôtel Deux Clefs, E, 16 b.), a
romantic little medieval town on the River *Doubs*,
which here describes a sharp bend into Swiss territory.
Founded in the 7th c., the town developed around a
monastic house which succeeded the earlier hermitage of Ursicinus, an Irish monk who accompanied
St Columban. The church, a three-aisled pillared
basilica without a transept (Romanesque chancel,
12th c.; Gothic nave, 13th–14th c., and W tower,
1441), is one of the finest buildings in western
Switzerland. It has a cloister, Merovingian sarcophagi
and a Romanesque crypt. The Romanesque S
doorway is of outstanding quality. – Other features of
interest in the town are the gate towers, the old bridge
and the ruined castle. (Photograph, p. 10.)

The road to Porrentruy continues down from Les
Malettes, passes through the village of *Cornol* (alt.
503 m (1650 feet)), in a narrow defile, and enters the
Ajoie uplands. In 8·5 km (5 miles) it reaches
Courgenay (493 m – 1618 feet), and in another 5 km
(3 miles) **Porrentruy** (426 m (1398 feet): pop. 7800;
Hôtel Terminus, D, 80 b.; Cheval Blanc, D, 50 b.;
Belvédère, E, 10 b.), a town of medieval aspect which
is the commercial, industrial and cultural focal point of
the Ajoie region. The massive castle became after
Basle's adoption of the new faith (1529) the
permanent residence of the Prince-Bishop. Other
features of interest are a round tower of Roman origin,
the Tour Réfouse (from *refugium*), the Porte de
France (1563), the parish church of St-Pierre (1349),
the Jesuit church (16th–17th c.) and several Baroque
buildings. The Botanic Garden attached to the
cantonal school is open daily. – From here it is only 12
km (7 miles) to the Swiss frontier town of *Boncourt*
(375 m (1230 feet): pop. 1700; Hôtel De la Locomotive, E, 12 b.; Lac Rochette, 12 b.), with a 12th–13th c.
church, a tobacco factory of 1814 and stalactitic caves.

The Franches Montagnes. – From Delémont a
road runs SW through the Jura via Saignelégier (33
km – 21 miles) to Neuchâtel and Geneva. The first

stretch of the road follows the *Sorne valley*, passing through the villages of *Courtételle* and *Courfaivre* (bicycle factory; church with stained glass by F. Léger), and comes in 10 km (6 miles) to the watchmaking village of *Bassecourt* (alt. 478 m (1568 feet)). It then runs uphill, high up on the hillside above the *Combe Tabeillon*, into the *Franches Montagnes*, a limestone plateau at a height of between 1000 and 1100 m (3281 and 3609 feet). At *Montfaucon* (1006 m (3301 feet): pop. 450) is the interesting cave system called the Grand Creux. – 5 km (3 miles) farther on we come to **Saignelégier** (982 m (3222 feet): Hôtel Bellevue, C, 100 b.; Hôtel de la Gare et du Parc, C, 60 b.), chief place in the Franches Montagnes and a horse-breeding centre. The National Horse Fair ("Marché Concours") is held here annually on the second weekend in August. – The village of *Noirmont* (alt. 970 m (3183 feet): pop. 1550) lies close to the French frontier; at *Les Bois* (1037 m (3402 feet): Hôtel Couronne) the Tête de Moine cheese factory can be visited. The road continues over the *Col de Bellevue* (1073 m – 3521 feet) to **La Chaux-de-Fonds** (p. 93).

Disentis/Mustér

Canton: Grisons (GR).
Altitude: 1140 m (3740 feet). – Population: 3500.
Post code: CH-7180. – Dialling code: 086.

ⓘ **Kur- und Verkehrsverein,**
  Disentis;
  tel. 7 58 22.

HOTELS. – *La Cucagna*, B, 70 b., SP; *Cristallina*, C, 24 b.; *Oberalp*, C, 25 b.; *Bellavista*, C, 50 b. – CAMPING SITE.

A glimpse of Disentis

The little market town of Disentis (accent on first syllable: Romansh Mustér) lies in a wide green valley at the point where the Medelser Rhein or Mittelrhein (Middle Rhine) becomes the Vorderrhein. It is a health and winter sports resort as well as a spa, with a chalybeate (iron-bearing) spring.

SIGHTS. – Above the town is a **Benedictine abbey** founded by St Sigisbert about 720 and almost completely

rebuilt at the end of the 17th c.; the abbey dominates the valley with its handsome conventual buildings and *St Martin's church* (Vorarlberg Baroque, 1696–1712); it contains a collection of artistic and historical interest.

SURROUNDINGS. – Cableway (2060 m (6759 feet), 5 minutes) from *Funs* (1228 m – 4029 feet) NW to *Caischavedra* (1842 m – 6044 feet); from there ski-lifts to the slopes of *Piz Ault* (3027 m – 9932 feet).

Over the Lucomagno (Lukmanier) pass to Biasca (65 km – 40 miles). – The road runs S from Disentis and climbs, with moderate gradients, through the **Höllenschlucht** (Hell's Gorge), a magnificent wooded defile. It then continues uphill, with numerous bends, and passes through a number of tunnels, between which there are views to the rear of Disentis abbey and later impressive views of the foaming waterfalls in the gorge below.

Curaglia (alt. 1332 m (4370 feet)), with a church of 1672 (Late Gothic altar), situated at the mouth of the *Val Plattas*, which runs down from *Piz Medel* (3210 m (10,532 feet): 7 hours, with guide). To the E there is a rewarding climb (3½–4 hours) up *Piz Muraun* (2897 m – 9505 feet), from the top of which there are extensive views of the central ridge of the Alps, from Monte Rosa to the Ortles (Ortler) group, and of the nearer Tödi group in the Glarus Alps.

Platta (1380 m – 4528 feet), a struggling village (church with Romanesque tower) in an open part of the *Val Medel.* – Beyond this, on the right, is a small waterfall on the Mittelrhein. – *Acla* (1476 m (4843 feet): off the road to the right), with a chapel. The scenery now becomes wilder; *Fumatschfalls*, 30 m (98 feet) high, on the Medelser Rhein. to the rear there is a view of the valley around Platta, with the Tödi massif rearing up beyond the Vorderrhein.

Pardatsch (or *Perdatsch*), 1556 m (5105 feet)), a hamlet with a small chapel. The road continues uphill under Piz Curvet (2248 m – 7376 feet). – *Sogn Gion* (1615 m – 5299 feet), a former hospice. – The road now climbs a lonely Alpine valley, with tumbles of rock, areas of sparse pasturage and rhododendrons. To the right are the pointed summit of Tgiern Sogn Gion (2677 m – 8783 feet) and Piz Ganneretsch (3040 m – 9974 feet). – In 8 km (5 miles) or so the Santa Maria lake (formed by a dam completed in 1967) can be seen below the road on the right. On the old road along the W side of the lake, at *Santa Maria* (1842 m – 6044 feet), was the old hospice of "Sancta Maria in Luco Magno" which gave its name to the pass. Above the W side of the lake is *Piz Rondadura* (3016 m (9895 feet): 3½ hours), to the E the dark slaty peak of *Scopi* (3187 m (10,457 feet): 4–4½ hours).

The **Lucomagno pass** (Romansh *Cuolm Lucmagn*, German *Lukmanierpass*: 1920 m (6300 feet)), with an inn, a large stone figure of the Virgin and a chapel, is the lowest road crossing of the central ridge of the Swiss Alps, over which there was already considerable traffic in medieval times. It is flanked on the left by Scopi and on the right by Scai (2676 m – 8780 feet). The pass marks the boundary between the cantons of Grisons and Ticino.

The road descends from the pass through a rocky valley, following the left bank of the *Brenno*, which is fed by numerous streams flowing down from Scai and

Pizzo Lucomagno. To the left are the rock walls of Pizzo Corvo (2510 m – 8235 feet). Then through an area of high Alpine meadows, past scattered summer chalets. Ahead can be seen the Rheinwaldhorn (3406 m – 11,175 feet). – 4·5 km (3 miles) beyond the pass, on the right, is the *Acquacalda* inn (1780 m (5840 feet): Albergo del Passo, 20 b.), surrounded by a forest of stone pines, with a beautiful waterfall on the Brenno. – The road traverses the Alpine meadows of the *Piano di Segno*, passing above the huts of *Campra*, continues down the N side of the beautiful **Valle Santa Maria**, high above the Brenno, and then through a wooded gorge, passes close to the Albergo Grande Venezia and comes to the former hospice of Camperio. – The road now leaves the Valle Santa Maria and runs down the *Val Blenio*, high up on the S side of the valley, with magnificent * views of the valley itself, the precipitous buttresses of the Rheinwaldhorn, the Cima di Pinaderio and the Cima Giù (2369 m – 7773 feet), and Olivone in its fertile valley, with the jagged granite peak of Sosto rearing above it. – 5·5 km (3 miles) beyond Camperio there is a rewarding drive on a road which branches off on the left and after traversing a road tunnel 1490 m (4889 feet) long, which bypasses the narrow *Gola di Sosto*, reaches the mountain village of *Campo Blenio* (1228 m – 4029 feet), 4·5 km (3 miles) N, situated at the meeting of three valleys. Beyond this, 1·5 km (1 mile) up the Val Camadra, is *Ghirone* (1302 m – 4270 feet), with a very picturesque old church; then 3 km (2 miles) E up the Val Luzzone to a large artificial lake (1590 m – 5217 feet).

The main road continues down to the village of **Olivone** (Romansh *Uorscha*, 893 m (2930 feet)), a summer holiday resort beautifully situated at the junction of the two arms of the Brenno under the massive pyramid of *Sosto* (2221 m – 7287 feet), surrounded by fruit-trees. It has a fine old house, still inhabited, the Casa Cesare Bolla (*c.* 1500), once the residence of the governor, and an interesting local museum. – Beyond Olivone the road to Biasca winds its way down the fertile **Val Blenio**, on the left bank of the Brenno, to the valley floor.

Aquila (788 m – 2585 feet), with trim houses of Ticinese type, lies at the foot of the Colma massif, which reaches its highest point in the *Cima di Pinaderio* (2490 m – 8170 feet). – From here there are alternative routes to Dongio: either on a narrow by-road (5 km (3 miles) longer) which runs above the right bank of the Brenno through a series of pretty villages and chestnut groves (at *Prugiasco*, 7·5 km (5 miles), detour on right, 30 minutes, up to the little Romanesque *church of San Carlo Negrentino*, with 13th–16th c. frescoes); or on the main road, which climbs up the left bank of the Brenno and beyond *Dangio* turns into the *Val Soia*, running down from the Rheinwaldhorn (3406 m – 11,175 feet).

Torre (770 m – 2526 feet) is prettily situated on a terrace. A southern vegetation of vines, mulberries and walnut-trees begins to feature more prominently in the landscape. – Farther down the valley, on the hillside to the left, is the village of *Lottigna* (695 m – 2280 feet), the chief place in the Val Blenio, beautifully situated at the foot of *Simano* (2580 m – 8465 feet), with a church of the 15th and 17th c. – Beyond this there is a superb view down the valley, with a view of the pyramidal peak of Sosto to the rear. – *Acquarossa* (538 m – 1765 feet), a spa (mineral spring, 25·5 °C, 78 °F).

Dongo (470 m – 1542 feet) is a long straggling village surrounded by vineyards and orchards, where the by-road from Aquila comes in. To the SW, on the other side of the Brenno, stands the *chapel of San Remigio*, with Romanesque wall-paintings. – *Malvaglia* (375 m – 1230 feet), lies at the mouth of the deep Malvaglia valley, with the church of San Martino (originally Romanesque, altered in 1603: beautiful campanile). – A narrow mountain road runs 10·5 km (7 miles) up the Val Malvaglia, passing an artificial lake, to *Madra* (1086 m – 3563 feet). – Opposite Malvaglia, on the right bank of the Brenno, is the village of *Semione* (402 m – 1319 feet), with the ruined castle of *Serravalle* (12th–14th c.). – Below Malvaglia the valley becomes wider and more regular, with large areas of tumbled rocks on the valley bottom. – Below the narrow mouth of the *Val Pontirone* the road skirts the *Buzza di Biasca*, a great mass of debris resulting from a tremendous landslide in 1512. The place from which the rock broke away can be seen high above the road on *Pizzo Magno* (2298 m – 7540 feet).

At **Biasca** (305 m – 1001 feet) we join the road from the St Gotthard (p. 211), which runs down the Ticino valley to Bellinzona (p. 73).

Einsiedeln

Canton: Schwyz (SZ).
Altitude: 905 m (2969 feet). – Population: 9600.
Post code: CH-8840. – Dialling code: 055.
ⓘ **Offizielles Verkehrsbüro,**
Einsiedeln;
tel. 53 44 88.

HOTELS. – *Drei Könige*, B, 100 b.; *Storchen*, B, 70 b.; *Bären*, C, 60 b.; *Linde*, C, 50 b.; *Pfauen*, C, 50 b.; *Sonne*, C, 50 b.; *Löwen*, C, 35 b.; *St Georg*, D, 100 b.; *St Johann*, D, 70 b.; *Schiff*, D, 60 b. – YOUTH HOSTEL, Unteriberg.

EVENTS. – *Fasnacht* (Carnival), with throwing of bread; skiing contests and open ski races; *Engelweihe* (Angelic Dedication), 14 September. Every five years (next time 1985) performance of Calderón's "Great Theatre of the World".

RECREATION and SPORT. – Fishing, riding, skittles, sauna in summer; skiing (six ski-lifts) and ski-trekking ("Schwedentritt", 22 km (14 miles)).

The famous Swiss pilgrimage destination of * Einsiedeln, situated in a high valley of the Pre-Alps between Lake Zurich and Lake Lucerne, has been a great focus of religion and culture for more than a thousand years, and its magnificent conventual buildings are one of the peak achievements of Baroque architecture. The Gnadenkapelle (Chapel of Grace) with its Black Virgin, draws large numbers of pilgrims every year, and many visitors are also attracted by the quiet and beauty of the abbey's setting.

Cemetery

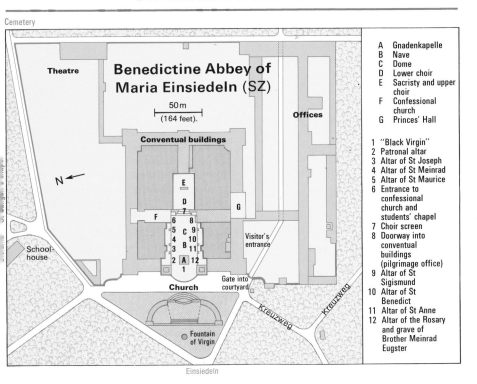

Benedictine Abbey of Maria Einsiedeln (SZ)

50m
(164 feet)

Theatre

Offices

Conventual buildings

N

School-
house

Church

Gate into
courtyard

Visitor's
entrance

Kreuzweg

Kreuzweg

Fountain
of Virgin

A Gnadenkapelle
B Nave
C Dome
D Lower choir
E Sacristy and upper
   choir
F Confessional
   church
G Princes' Hall

1 "Black Virgin"
2 Patronal altar
3 Altar of St Joseph
4 Altar of St Meinrad
5 Altar of St Maurice
6 Entrance to
   confessional
   church and
   students' chapel
7 Choir screen
8 Doorway into
   conventual
   buildings
   (pilgrimage office)
9 Altar of St
   Sigismund
10 Altar of St
   Benedict
11 Altar of St Anne
12 Altar of the Rosary
   and grave of
   Brother Meinrad
   Eugster

Einsiedeln

HISTORY. – In 934 Eberhard, Dean of Strasbourg Cathedral, founded a community of hermits in the "Dark Forest" above the hermitage of a monk from Reichenau, Meinrad, who had been murdered in 861; and Duke Hermann of Swabia and his wife Reginlinde granted the monastic settlement enough land to provide for its maintenance. In 937 Einsiedeln was made a royal abbey, and its abbot became a prince of the Empire. The buildings were destroyed by fire on five occasions, in 1029, 1226, 1465, 1509 and 1577. The Reformer Ulrich Zwingli was for a time a secular priest at Einsiedeln. In 1639 the first peace negotiations between France and Bavaria during the Thirty Years War were conducted here. The building history of the abbey covered the whole range from Romanesque through Gothic to Baroque. Einsiedeln later developed into an important area of intellectual activity, with a flourishing printing and publishing industry. It is the administrative heart of the district of the same name, which comprises the "quarters" of Bennau, Egg, Eutal, Gross, Trachslau and Willerzell.

SIGHTS. – The *Benedictine abbey of Maria Einsiedeln, built by the lay brother Kaspar Moosbrugger (1656–1723) of Au in the Bregenzerwald, is the finest example of Vorarlberg Baroque architecture in Switzerland. The conventual buildings, laid out in a regular square round four courtyards, cover an area of 34,000 sq. m (40,664 sq. yards). The twin-towered *church (1719–35) is a sumptuous Baroque building, 113 m (371 feet) long by 41 m (135 feet) wide, with ceiling frescoes by the Asam brothers of Bavaria (the largest fresco in Switzerland). Wrought-iron choir screen (1684),

designed to give the effect of perspective. The *Gnadenkapelle* (Chapel of Grace), rebuilt in 1815–17 in Neo-classical style after its destruction by the French in 1798, contains the carved wooden figure of the "Black Virgin" (15th c.). The *Library possesses 150,000 volumes, 1300 manuscripts produced in the great medieval scriptorium here and 1200 incunabula. The *Princes' Hall* (Fürstensaal: entrance from the S side of the conventual buildings), with stucco decoration by M. Roncati (1704–05), is used for special exhibitions.

Einsiedeln Abbey

5 minutes away from the square outside the abbey is the *Bethlehem Diorama*, a representation of the manger in Bethlehem with 500 carved wooden figures. A little way beyond this a circular building houses a *Panorama of the Crucifixion* (originally 1893, reconstructed after a fire in 1960).

SURROUNDINGS. – An attractive feature of the surrounding area is the **Sihlsee** (alt. 892 m (2927 feet)), an artificial lake 9 km (6 miles) long and just over 1 km (about a ½ mile) wide on average (area when full 10·85 sq. km (4 sq. miles), depth 25 m (82 feet), capacity 92 million cu. m (3248 million cu. feet)) completed in 1934, the first stage in the Etzelwerk hydroelectric complex. The Willerzell viaduct is 1015 m (3330 feet) long. – The road along the W side of the Sihlsee comes in 13 km (8 miles) to *Unteriberg* (alt. 931 m (3055 feet): pop. 1450; Hotel Rössli-Post, C, 35 b.; youth hostel). 2 km (1 mile) beyond this is *Oberiberg* (1123 m (3685 feet): pop. 550; Hotel Post), and 5 km (3 miles) farther S again *Weglosen* (parking garage), from which there is a cableway up to the holiday and sports facility of *Hoch-Ybrig* (Weglosen-Seebil), at the foot of the Drusberg and the Forstberg, a recently developed walking and skiing area (1600–2200 m (5250–7218 feet): restaurant, chair-lifts, ski-lifts).

11·5 km (7 miles) SW of Einsiedeln in the *Alptal* is the little hamlet of *Brunni* (996 m (3268 feet): pop. 330), from which there is a cableway up *Holzegg*: good walking country, starting-point for the climb of the *Grosser Mythen* (1902 m (6240 feet): mountain inn; wide views), *Ibergeregg*, *Haggenegg* and *Hochstuckli*. From the Ibergeregg pass (1406 m (4613 feet): inn) there is a pleasant walk to *Rickenbach*, from which a cableway 2446 m (8025 feet) long runs up to the *Rotenfluh* (1565 m – 5135 feet).

To the N is the **Etzel pass**, with St Meinrad's chapel (poor road to Pfäffikon), from which a footpath (20 minutes) climbs to the *Etzel-Kulm* (959 m (3146 feet): inn). Near the Teufelsbrücke (Devil's Bridge) in the *Sihl valley* is the house in which the scientist and doctor Theophrastus Paracelsus (1493–1541) was born.

Emmental

Canton: Berne (BE).
(i) **Verkehrsverband Emmental,**
c/o Reisebüro am Hirschenplatz,
CH-3550 Langnau im Emmental;
tel. (035) 2 34 34

RECREATION and SPORT. – Farmhouse holidays for children; weekends on the farm (arranged through Verkehrsverband Emmental); horse-rides in Weier im Emmental, Grosshöchstetten, Trubschachen and Kemmeriboden; trips on steam trains of the Emmental–Burgdorf–Thun line; indoor swimming pools in Burgdorf, Grosshöchstetten, Langnau, Sumiswald and Lützelflüh. CAMPING in Brenzikofen, Burgdorf and Gohl. YOUTH HOSTEL in Langnau.

The Emmental (Emme valley) is a fertile farming region extending E from Berne towards the Napf (1408 m – 4620 feet), with a characteristic way of life which was described in the works of the 19th c. novelist Jeremias Gotthelf (Albert Bitzius), who was pastor at Lützelflüh. It is renowned for its cheese. Until about 1800 it was thought that good cheese could be made only from the milk of the Alps; but the first cheese dairies in the valleys were then established in the Emmental, and the excellent cheese produced there is now exported far and wide.

A typical Emmental farmhouse

The *Kleine Emme* (Little Emme) rises on the Giswilerstock and flows down through the Mariental and Entlebuch valley to join the Reuss after a course of 58 km (36 miles). The *Grosse Emme* (Great Emme) rises on the Hohgant (2197 m – 7208 feet), N of Lake Brienz and flows through the Emmental to join the Aare E of Solothurn after a course of 80 km (50 miles).

The Emmental is a region of gently rolling country with a long tradition of good farming. Many farms have belonged to the same family for centuries. Although traditional values are deeply rooted, the farmers of the Emmental have been among the pioneers of modern agriculture in Switzerland. The farmhouses have a distinctive character – substantial and well built, with arcades, an abundance of flowers and often elaborate carved decoration – as have the barns and the little houses for the grandparents, and the inns with the old traditional names, the "Bear" and the "Lion", the "Star" and the "Crown". When the Federal government has distinguished visitors to entertain they are often taken out from Berne for a good country meal in the Emmental.

The Emmental is the shortest route from Berne to Lake Lucerne. Road 10 runs from Berne to Langnau (30 km – 19 miles) and from there via Wolhusen to Lucerne (92 km – 57 miles).

Burgdorf (alt. 533 m (1749 feet): pop. 16,000; Hotel Touring-Bernerhof, C, 55 b.; Stadthaus, D, 23 b.), a fine town NE of Berne, is the real gateway to the Emmental. 10th c. castle of the Zähringen family, with three towers (now a historical museum); Late Gothic parish church (1490: organ gallery with sandstone tracery); handsome old guild-houses; picturesque arcaded market; old granary; cantonal technical college; ethnographical collection on Kirchbühl. "Planetenweg" from the Binzberg to Wynigen.

Engadine

Canton: Grisons (GR).

Oberengadiner Verkehrsverein,
CH-7504 Pontresina;
tel. (082) 6 65 73.
Verkehrsbüro Zernez,
CH-7530 Zernez;
tel. (082) 8 13 00.

The ****Engadine (in German Engadin, in Romansh Engiadina) is the valley of the Inn (in Romansh En), shut in between mighty mountain chains and flanked by flower-spangled Alpine meadows and magnificent forests of larch and stone pine on the steep hillsides. The village houses are solid white-washed structures, often with sgraffito decoration, painting, handsome oriel windows or elaborate window grilles. The population is Rhaeto-Romanic and predominantly Protestant. Since 1938 the old Ladin place-names have been in official use.**

From the Maloja pass (1815 m – 5955 feet), the boundary between the Engadine and the *Val Bregaglia (p. 88), the road runs NE through the *Upper Engadine, with its clear air and extensive

Champfèr Lake, Upper Engadine

views, to the international resort of *St Moritz (p. 215) and two smaller resorts, popular both in summer and in winter, *Celerina*, where the road to the Bernina pass branches off, and *Samedan*. It then continues to *La Punt* (road on left to Albula pass) and the old-world village of *Zuoz*, once the chief place in the Engadine. Beyond *S-chanf* it runs through a defile at *Puntota* to enter the ***Lower Engadine**, where the valley becomes narrower and more densely forested.

After passing through *Zernez*, where the road through the ***Swiss National Park** (p. 236) to the Ofen pass and the Stelvio pass diverges to the right, the Engadine road turns N for 6 km (4 miles) to reach *Susch*, where the road to Davos over the Flüela pass branches off on the left. From here we continue down the Lower Engadine, running under the S side of the magnificent *Silvretta group*, with a series

The Muottas–Muragl railway near Pontresina

of wild side valleys and picturesque old villages like Lavin, Guarda, Ardez and Ftan nestling on its sunny southern slopes. The valley then opens up again, and the road reaches the **Bad Scuol–Tarasp–Vulpera** group of resorts (p. 224), with Tarasp Castle on its precipitous crag dominating the scene.

Beyond Scuol the valley becomes wilder and more solitary, with the few villages (Sent, Ramosch, Tschlin) perched high above the road on the green meadows on the sunny side of the valley. The scenery becomes still more forbidding in the wooded *Finstermünz defile* beyond the last Swiss village (*Martina*), in which, at the hamlet of Vinadi, the old frontier fortifications can still be seen. Here a boldly engineered road leads into the *Samnaun valley*, where secluded villages attract many visitors both in summer and in winter.

The road now crosses the Austrian frontier into **Tirol** and continues down the Inn valley, between the Samnaun group and the western ridge of the Ötztal Alps. After passing through *Stuben-Pfunds* and *Prutz* it comes to *Landeck*, where it meets the road from the Arlberg pass.

Engelberg

Canton: Obwalden (OW).
Altitude: 1050 m (3445 feet). – Population: 3400.
Post code: CH-6390. – Dialling code: 041.
ⓘ **Kur- und Verkehrsverein,**
Dorfstrasse 34;
tel. 94 11 61.

HOTELS. – *Ring-Hotel*, B, 120 b.; *Bellevue-Terminus*, B, 120 b.; *Europäischer Hof*, B, 140 b.; *Hess*, B, 100 b.; *Edelweiss*, C, 80 b.; *Schweizerhof*, C, 80 b.; *Central*, C, 80 b., SB; *Engel*, C, 70 b.; *Hoheneck*, C, 70 b.; *Engelberg*, C, 55 b.; *Crystal*, C, 45 b.; *Spannort*, C, 36 b.; *Maro*, C, 24 b.; *Marguerite*, C, 65 b.; *Sporthotel Trübsee*, C, 40 b.

YOUTH HOSTEL. – CAMPING SITE: Eienwäldli.

RECREATION and SPORT. – Swimming (indoor and open-air pools), walking (walkers' railcards for mountain railways and cableways), riding, tennis, summer skiing (ski-lift at upper station of Titlisbahn, 3020 m (9909 feet)). – Skating rinks, curling rink, toboggan run from the Gerschnialp (3·5 km – 2 miles), hobby courses.

MOUNTAIN RAILWAYS and CABLEWAYS. – Terminus of narrow-gauge railway from Lucerne via Stans (1 hour); cableways Engelberg–Gerschnialp (length 528 m (1733 feet), height difference 264 m (868 feet), time 4 minutes); Engelberg–Trübsee (length 2195 m (7204 feet), height difference 531 m (1742 feet), time 6 minutes); Trübsee–Stand-Kleintitlis (length 3465 m (11,369 feet), height difference 1220 m (4003 feet), time 14 minutes); Trübsee–Joch pass (length 1459 m (4787 feet), height difference 439 m (1440 feet), time 13 minutes); Engstlensee–Joch pass (length 1631 m (5351 feet), height difference 273 m (896 feet), time 10 minutes); Rindertitlis–Laubersgrat (length 1183 m (3883 feet), height difference 385 m (1264 feet), time 8 minutes); Engelberg–Brunni (length 1193 m (3914 feet), height difference 582 m (1910 feet), time 6 minutes).

The trim little town of ˟Engelberg with its abbey, in a sunny basin under the N face of Titlis, is a popular summer and winter resort lying well away from the main traffic routes. Since 1815 it has been an enclave of the half-canton of Obwalden. It is a region of varied scenery, good walking country with hills and lakes, and with a number of cableways providing easy access to the mountains.

HISTORY. – The Benedictine abbey was founded in 1120, and its abbot held independent sway over the territory. In 1798 the town was released from ecclesiastical authority and became part of the canton of Obwalden.

SIGHTS. – At the upper end of the town is the **Benedictine abbey**, founded about 1120, which ruled the whole valley until 1798. The handsome church, designed by Kaspar Moosbrugger, and the square complex of conventual buildings were rebuilt in 1730–37 after a fire. Rich library (men only admitted), with valuable manuscripts, incunabula and miniatures. To the S, on the left bank of the Aawasser, are beautiful gardens surrounded by forest.

SURROUNDINGS. – ˟Titlis (3239 m – 10,627 feet), covered by eternal snow and ice, is the highest

Engelberg in winter

Cableway on Titlis

viewpoint in central Switzerland, offering a unique panorama of the Alps (ice cave, glacier trail). Restaurants on Titlis and in Stand (2450 m – 8038 feet). Cableway Engelberg–Titlis (45 minutes).

From Engelberg there is a funicular to the *Gerschnialp* (1266 m – 4154 feet), and from there a cableway by way of the steep Pfaffenwand to the *Trübsee Hotel* (1792 m – 5880 feet); descent in 2 hours via the Trübseealp. From Trübsee by chair-lift (or on foot in 1¼ hours) to the *Joch pass* (2215 m (7267 feet): ski hut), and from there a bridle-path (1 hour) to the *Engstlensee* (1852 m – 6076 feet), in a magnificent mountain setting, and on to the *Engstlenalp* (1839 m – 6034 feet), one of the finest areas of Alpine pasture in Switzerland (rich flora, superb views), and the *Melchsee*.

Other rewarding walks are to the *Bergli* (1341 m – 4400 feet); to the *Surenenalp* and *Tätschbach Falls* (1090 m (3576 feet): restaurant); and by the Herrenrüti grazings to the *Nieder-Surenenalp* (1260 m (4134 feet): restaurant and the *Arnialp*.

CLIMBS: *Titlis (3239 m – 10,627 feet), usually starting either from the Trübsee Hotel or from Kleintitlis; *Hutstock* (2680 m (8793 feet): 6 hours; wild goats); *Schlossberg* (3155 m (10,351 feet): 8 hours); *Engleberger Rotstock* (2820 m (9252 feet): 6 hours, with guide); *Urirotstock (2932 m (9620 feet): 8–9 hours, with guide).

Entlebuch

Canton: Lucerne (LU).
ⓘ **Verkehrsverein Zentralschweiz,**
Pilatusstrasse 14,
CH-6002 Luzern;
tel. (041) 23 70 45.

The quickest route between Lucerne and Berne by either road or rail (92 km – 57 miles) is through the valleys of Entlebuch and Emmental. The region drained by the Great and

Little Emme extends from the Brienzer Rothorn to the Napf: a land of many legends, it has preserved much of its traditional character, but what was once the home of woodcutters and charcoal-burners is now a favourite holiday area. From the borders of the cantons of Lucerne and Berne in the Emmental low passes lead through the hills to Lake Thun and Obwalden.

From Lucerne the road follows the Kleine Emme (Little Emme) by way of Emmenbrücke and the old market village of Malters to Wolhusen (20 km – 12 miles), the gateway to the Entlebuch valley. – The picturesque village of **Entlebuch** (alt. 684 m (2244 feet): pop. 3500) lies above the Entlen, a torrential stream which flows into the Kleine Emme here. It has a parish church founded about 900 with an elegant Rococo interior and a tower of the 13th–14th c. The traditional "Wyberschiessen" ("Women's Shooting") is held every three years.

Schüpfheim (719 m (2359 feet): pop. 3800) is the chief town in the district of Entlebuch, with an eventful history as the place of execution of the Governor of Wolhusen. It is the starting-point of the panoramic road which runs via *Flühli* (883 m (2897 feet): pop. 1500), the principal commune in the Mariental, which also includes the holiday resort of *Sörenberg*, on the road to Giswil (1159 m (3803 feet): Hotel Panorama, B, 110 b., SB; Berghaus Viscosuisse, E, 44 b.; ski-lifts). From Sörenberg there is a cableway up the *Brienzer Rothorn* (length 2740 m (8990 feet), height difference 1040 m (3412 feet), time 8 minutes); and access to other walking and skiing areas is provided by a chair-lift from the Eisee to the Rothorn (length 1061 m (3481 feet), height difference 298 m (978 feet), time 11 minutes) and a cableway to the *Rossweid* (length 1457 m (4780 feet), height difference 305 m (1001 feet), time 8 minutes). – *Escholzmatt* (853 m (2798 feet)) marks the watershed between the Entlebuch valley and the Emmental. – A minor road goes off to *Marbach* (871 m (2858 feet): pop. 1300), from which there is a cableway to the *Marbachegg* (1470 m – 4823 feet), with extensive views of the Bernese Alps.

Flims

Canton: Grisons (GR).
Altitude: 1100 m (3609 feet). – Population: 2000.
Post code: CH-7018. – Dialling code: 081.
ⓘ **Kur- und Verkehrsverein Flims,**
CH-7018 Flims Waldhaus;
tel. 39 10 22.
Verkehrsverein Laax,
CH-7031 Laax;
tel. (086) 2 14 23.

HOTELS. – FLIMS DORF: *Albana*, B, 60 b.; *Crap Ner*, B, 96 b., SB; *Bellevue*, C, 65 b.; *Vorab*, C, 65 b.; *Meiler*, C, 52 b. – FLIMS FIDAZ: *Fidazerhof*, B, 110 b.; *Berghotel Haldenhaus*, 20 b. – FLIMS WALDHAUS: *Park-Hotel Waldhaus*, A, 327 b., SP, SB; *Adula*, B, 135 b., SB; *Segnes-Post*, B, 110 b.; *Surselva*, B, 110 b.; *Schweizerhof*, B, 80 b., SB; *Aparthotel des Alps*, B, 160 b., SB; *Schlosshotel*, C, 70 b.; *National*, C, 45 b.

LAAX: *Sporthotel Happy Rancho*, B, 300 b., SP, SB, tennis, fitness and exercise facility; *Signina House*, B, 120 b.; *Sporthotel Larisch*, C, 70 b.; *Berghotel Crap Sogn Gion* (2200 m – 7218 feet), D, 75 b., SB.

CAMPING SITE. – *Prau*, Flims Waldhaus.

RECREATION and SPORT. – Swimming (bathing beach on Caumasee), riding, tennis (outdoor and indoor courts), fishing, walking and climbing.

CABLEWAYS, LIFTS, etc. – Chair-lift (3400 m (11,155 feet) in 20 minutes) by way of Alp Foppa to Alp Naraus; from there cableway (2200 m (7218 feet) in 7 minutes) to Cassonsgrat. – Cableway from Flims Dorf to *Startgels* (1590 m – 5217 feet); from there Graubergbahn at 2230 m (7317 feet), near the *Berghaus Nagiens* (2128 m – 6982 feet). – Cableway (height difference 1100 m (3609 feet), time 10 minutes) to *Crap Sogn Gion* (2228 m (7310 feet): restaurant)).

Cableway from Flims to Crap Sogn Gion

WINTER SPORTS. – Several *ice-rinks*; *curling rink*; *toboggan run* (3 km – 2 miles) from Alp Foppa; *skiing* on *Alp Foppa* (1425 m – 4675 feet) and *Alp Naraus* (1840 m (6037 feet): restaurant), and on *Cassonsgrat* (2678 m (8787 feet): inn) and *Alp Nagiens*; *ski-lifts*; *cross-country skiing*. Flims–Laax–Fellers "Weisse Arena" ("White Arena": see below), with summer skiing on the *Vorab*.

CLIMBS (experienced climbers only, with guides). – *Piz Segnes* (3102 m (10,178 feet): 8 hours) by way of

the *Segneshütte* (2130 m (6989 feet): serviced). – *Vorab* (3030 m (9941 feet): 6 hours), with magnificent views of the Tödi group.

The summer and winter resort of *Flims*, **lying on a south-facing terrace 500 m (1641 feet) above the Vorderrhein, consists of the original mountain village of Flims Dorf and the hotel development of Flims Waldhaus to the S. The high plateau with its extensive forests and its beautiful lake, the Caumasee, is magnificent walking and climbing country.**

This easily accessible resort – reached by leaving the motorway at Reichenau, 10 km (6 miles) W of Chur and taking a road which runs up to Flims in 12 km (7 miles) – lies on the great mass of debris resulting from the biggest landslide of the last Ice Age in Switzerland. The debris covers an area of 40 sq. km (15 sq. miles), reaching 14 km (9 miles) downstream and 6 km (4 miles) upstream, and blocks the Vorderrhein valley for a distance of 15 km (9 miles) between Kästris and Reichenau. The landslide brought down at least 12,000 cu. m (423,720 cu. feet) of rock.

SIGHTS. – The village of **Flims** (Romansh *Flem*), under the *Flimserstein* (Crap da Flem, 2696 m (8846 feet)), has a Late Gothic church (1512). The "Schlössli" (1682) is now the headquarters of the commune (Gemeindehaus). – 2 km (1 mile) E is the old German settlement of *Fidaz* (1178 km – 3865 feet), with wooden houses (an unusual case of the adoption of a Rhaeto-Romanic practice). – 2 km (1 mile) S of Flims Dorf is **Flims Waldhaus** (1103 m – 3619 feet), the modern resort, with its hotels and holiday houses.

SURROUNDINGS. – From Waldhaus beautiful forest tracks run SW (1 hour) to *Salums* (1015 m (3330 feet): restaurant) and SE (1 hour) past the delightful *Caumasee*, in the heart of the forest (1000 m (3281 feet): small funicular to shore), to *Conn* (990 m (3248 feet): restaurant); from both places there are superb views of the gorge of the Vorderrhein. – From Flims Dorf to the *Cresta-See* (850 m – 2789 feet), on the Rhine valley road in the direction of Trin. – Ascent of the **Flimserstein** (4½–5 hours): from Flims Dorf via *Fidaz* and *Bargis* (1550 m (5086 feet): from here bear left uphill) to *Alp Sura* (3 hours: 2102 m (6897 feet)); then over Alpine meadows to the highest point (1¾ hours: 2696 m (8832 feet)), with magnificent views to the N of Ringelspitz (Piz Bargias, 3251 m (10,667 feet)) and the Trinserhorn (Piz Dolf, 3028 m (9935 feet)).

The "Weisse Arena" on Crap Sogn Gion. – 5 km (3 miles) W of Flims on the road to Ilanz (12 km (7 miles): postal bus) is the long straggling village of **Laax** (alt. 1016 m (3333 feet): pop. 610), which in the time of King Rudolf of Habsburg (13th c.) was the seat of a county, with the right to hold a market and self-government. Baroque church (1675). Laax, Flims and Fellers (Romansh Falera, alt. 1213 m (3980 feet)) – where remains of a Middle Bronze Age settlement and cult site were found – together form the famous "Weisse Arena" ("White Arena"), an extensive winter sports region.

The Flims–Laax–Fellers area has recently been developed as a huge skiing complex, one of the largest in the Alps, more than 140 sq. km (54 sq. miles) in extent. Since November 1978, with the provision of facilities for access to the *Vorab* glacier area (3025 m – 9925 feet), it has been possible to ski here all the year round. There are more than 30 trails, with a total length of some 120 km (75 miles), reached with the aid of two cableways, one cabin cableway, six chair-lifts and seven ski-lifts, which have a total capacity of 18,000 persons per hour. From *Mulania* a cableway (length 4200 m (13,780 feet), height difference 1100 m (3609 feet), time 10 minutes) runs up to **Crap Sogn Gion** (2228 m – 7310 feet), the starting-point of the Laax skiing and climbing area, with a modern mountain restaurant seating 600 and an indoor swimming pool.

Fribourg

Fribourg

Canton: Fribourg (FR).
Altitude: 550–630 m (1805–2067 feet). – Population: 43,000.
Post code: CH-1700. – Dialling code: 037.

ⓘ **Office du Tourisme,**
Grand'Place;
tel. 22 11 56.

HOTELS. – *Eurotel*, B, 200 b., SB; *Rose*, B, 80 b.; *Duc Bertold*, C, 63 b.; *Elite* (no rest.), C, 65 b.; *Central*, D, 23 b.; *Touring*, E, 28 b.

RECREATION and SPORTS. – Golf, riding, tennis (indoor and outdoor courts), fishing; hobby courses (pottery, painting, lace-making, china-painting, batik).

EVENTS. – *International Folk Meeting*, beginning of September; displays of yodelling, Swiss wrestling and the game of *hornussen*.

Fribourg (in German Freiburg), capital of the canton of the same name, is the great stronghold of Catholicism in Switzerland, seat of the Bishop of Lausanne, Geneva and Fribourg and of a Catholic University. One of the finest old medieval towns in Switzerland, it lies on the River Sarine (German Saane), which flows in a deep valley through the Mittelland. The Auge and Bourg quarters leading to the upper town are picturesquely situated, like Berne, above the rocky banks of a bend in the river; in the lower town are the districts of Neuveville on the left bank and Planche on the right bank. – Fribourg was founded by Duke Berthold IV of Zähringen in 1157 and joined the Confederation in 1481.

SIGHTS. – In the middle of the old town is the *Place de l'Hôtel de Ville*. The **Town Hall** (*Hôtel de Ville* or *Hôtel Cantonal*), built in 1522, with an octagonal clock-tower (lantern added 1642), has a very fine interior. – NE of the Town Hall stands the *Cathedral of St-Nicolas (Gothic, 14th and 15th c.), with a tower 76 m (249 feet) high. Fine sculpture (14th and 15th c.) above the main doorway (Apostles, the Angelic Salutation; Last Judgment in tympanum). Notable features of the interior are the pulpit, font, choir screen and choir-stalls (15th–16th c.), the chapel of the Holy Sepulchre (1430–33), the stained glass and a famous organ.

In the adjoining Place Notre-Dame (*Samson fountain*, 1547) is the 12th c. **church of Notre-Dame**, the oldest church in the town (altered 1787 and 1853). – Immediately N is the **Franciscan friary**, with a church (*Eglise des Cordeliers*: choir 1281, nave 1745–46) which contains some notable works of art, including an altarpiece by the "Master of the Carnation" (1481), a predella with a painting by Hans Fries, "The Death of the Usurer" (1506), and a carved and gilded wooden triptych (*c.* 1513). – Beyond this, to the NW, the *Musée d'Art et d'Histoire* in the

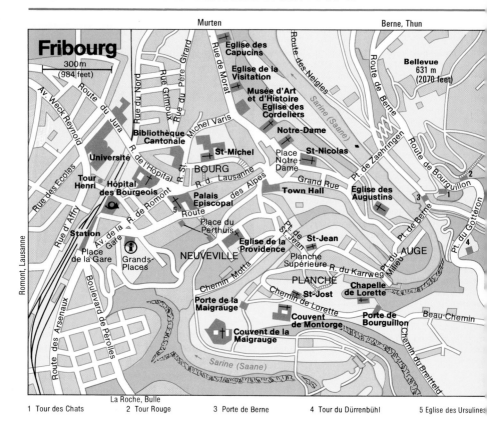

Fribourg

1 Tour des Chats   2 Tour Rouge   3 Porte de Berne   4 Tour du Dürrenbühl   5 Eglise des Ursulines

old Ratzehof houses sculpture and painting from the 10th to the 19th c. At the end of Rue de Morat, which continues NW, is a well-preserved old town gate, the *Porte de Morat* (1414).

From the Place de l'Hôtel-de-Ville we go up the busy Rue de Lausanne or the Route des Alpes (views) to *Place Georges-Python* (610 m – 2001 feet), at the top of a funicular from Neuveville (Place du Perthuis). On the E side of the square stands the *Bishop's Palace* (Palais Episcopal). Higher up, to the N, are the *Albertinum*, a seminary, the *Cantonal and University Library* (Bibliothèque Cantonale) and the Jesuit *church of St-Michel*, with the tomb of St Peter Canisius (Hundlinger, 1521–97), the "first German Jesuit". – To the W, beyond the railway, is the **University** (by Dumas and Honegger, 1941), with an art collection and a museum of natural history and ethnography.

To the SW of the upper town is the newer district around the station, with the *Grands Places*, from which there is a beautiful view of the old town and the Sarine valley. – From the nearby Place de la Gare the *Avenue de Pérolles* runs S

through the Pérolles quarter, with the church of *Christ the King* (1954), to the *Pont de Pérolles*. To the W of Avenue de Pérolles the 16th c. *chapel of St-Bartholomé* (restored 1970) has fine stained glass.

In NEUVEVILLE, in the lower town, are two attractive fountains – in Place du Perthuis (alt. 553 m (1814 feet): funicular to upper town) the *Fontaine du Sauvage* (1627), and at the end of Rue de la Neuveville the *Fontaine de la Prudence* (1550); Gothic house fronts.

In the old-world AUGE quarter, which also has fine 16th c. fountains, is a former *Augustinian convent*, on a peninsula in the bend of the Sarine. The church dates from the 13th to the 17th c. The conventual buildings now house the *Cantonal Archives*, with more than 30,000 parchment documents, the oldest dating from 928. – From Auge a covered wooden bridge, the *Pont de Berne* (1580), leads to the Place des Forgerons, on the right bank of the Sarine, with the *Fontaine de la Fidélité* (by Hans Gieng, 1553). To the N are the *Porte de Berne* (13th–14th c., restored 1660), the *Tour des Chats* (1383) and the *Tour Rouge* (1250).

In the PLANCHE quarter of the lower town, on the right bank of the Sarine, is the *church of St-Jean* (1529; later enlarged). – Above Planche are the *Couvent de Montorge* and two chapels (see below). – SW of Planche, on the banks of the Sarine, is the *Couvent de la Maigrauge*, a Cistercian nunnery with a church built before 1300.

SURROUNDINGS. – **Circuit on the right bank of the Sarine:** from the Cathedral cross the river on the Pont de Zaehringen and turn right past the Tour Rouge; cross the *Pont du Gotteron*, with a fine view of the town, and continue past the *Tour du Dürrenbühl* to the W end of the village of *Bourguillon* (alt. 658 m (2159 feet): church of 15th–18th c.); then sharp right along the Beau Chemin to the *Porte de Bourguillon*, beyond which, to the right, is the *chapel of Notre-Dame de Lorette* (1648), with a view of the town; beyond this, to the right, the *chapel of St-Jost* (1684) and, to the left, the Capuchin friary of *Montorge*, founded in 1626; then down into the Planche quarter, returning to the upper town either by way of the Pont du Milieu and Auge or by the Pont St-Jean and Neuveville.

To Hauterive. – Leave Fribourg by Avenue du Midi. In 3 km (2 miles) the road crosses the Glâne, a short distance above its junction with the Sarine, on a bridge 180 m (591 feet) long and 50 m (164 feet) above the gorge of the river.

2 km (1 mile) beyond the bridge a road goes off on the left and runs 2 km (1 mile) S to the Cistercian abbey of **Hauterive** (inn), in a bend of the Sarine. The church (1160), in the purest Cistercian style, has fine stained glass (1332) and richly carved choir-stalls (1480). – To the *Lac de la Gruyère*: p. 142.

To the Schwarzsee and Schwefelbergbad (28 and 33 km (17 and 21 miles) SE), a beautiful run through the Fribourg Pre-Alps. – The road runs via *Bourguillon* and *Giffers* (alt. 767 m (2517 feet)) to *Plaffeien* (18 km (11 miles): 851 m (2792 feet)), where it enters the valley of the *Sense* and the Fribourg Alps. – 4 km (2 miles): **Zollhaus** (902 m – 2959 feet), at the junction of the Warme and the Kalte Sense. – From here a road to the left leads to Schwefelbergbad (below); the road to the right ascends the valley of the *Warme Sense* to the **Schwarzsee** (1048 m (3438 feet): Hotel Gypsera, D, 25 b.), a lake surrounded by beautiful wooded hills. From the N end of the lake a chair-lift 1436 m (4712 feet) long runs up in 14 minutes to the *Riggisalp* (1500 m – 4922 feet). From *Kaiseregg* (2189 m (7182 feet): 3½ hours from the lake) there are magnificent views; good skiing (ski-lifts).

From Zollhaus the road to Schwefelbergbad leads E up the valley of the *Kalte Sense* by way of the Sangernboden (1005 m – 3297 feet). – 10 km (6 miles): **Schwefelbergbad** (1398 m (4587 feet): Hotel Schwefelbergbad, B, 80 b.), with sulphurous springs, in a beautiful wooded setting at the foot of the *Ochsen* (2190 m (7185 feet): 2½ hours; view) and *Gantrisch* (2177 m – 7143 feet). These mountains are a skiing area much favoured by the people of Berne (many ski huts; ski-lifts from Schwefelbergbad at 1700 m (5578 feet) on the N face of the Ochsen).

Geneva

Canton: Geneva (GE).
Altitude: 337 m (1237 feet). – Population: 151,000.
Post code: CH-1200. – Dialling code: 022.
ⓘ **Office du Tourisme,**
  CH-1211 Genève,
  tel. 28 72 33.

HOTELS. – ON THE N SHORE OF THE LAKE AND THE RHÔNE, with views of the Alps. *Président*, 47 Quai Wilson, A, 500 b.; *Noga-Hilton*, 19 Quai du Mont-Blanc, A, 366 b.; SB *Le Richemont*, Jardin Brunswick, A, 200 b.; *Beau Rivage*, 13 Quai du Mont-Blanc, A, 180 b.; *Des Bergues*, 33 Quai des Bergues, A, 173 b.; *Angleterre*, 17 Quai du Mont-Blanc, A, 110 b.; *Du Rhône*, Quai Turrettini, A, 430 b.; *Ramada*, 19 Rue de Zurich, A, 432 b.; *De la Paix*, 11 Quai du Mont-Blanc, A, 169 b.; *Bristol*, 10 Rue du Mont-Blanc, A, 140 b.; *Ambassador*, 21 Quai des Bergues, B, 134 b.

NEAR THE STATION: *Rotary-PLM*, 18–20 rue du Cendrier, A, 139 b.; *Méditerranée*, 14 rue de Lausanne, B, 314 b.; *Rex*, 44 Avenue Wendt, B, 175 b.; *California* (no rest.), 1 rue Gevray, B, 100 b.; *Amat-Carlton*, 22 rue Amat, B, 190 b.; *Cornavin* (no rest.), 33 Boulevard James-Fazy, B, 175 b.; *Grand-Pré* (no rest.), 35 rue du Grand-Pré, B, 130 b.; *Alba* (no rest.), 19 rue du Mont-Blanc, B, 110 b.; *Royal*, 41 rue de Lausanne, B, 250 b.; *Epsom*, 9 rue Butini, B, 330 b.; *Excelsior*, Rue Rousseau, B, 100 b.; *Suisse* (no rest.), 10 Place Cornavin, B, 120 b.; *Auteuil* (no rest.), 33 rue de Lausanne, B, 220 b.; *Allèves*, 13 Passage Klébert, B, 80 b.; *Balzac* (no rest.), Place Navigation, 14 Ancien-Port, B, 70 b.; *Epoque*, 10 rue Voltaire, B, 100 b.; *Windsor* (no rest.), 31 rue de Berne, B, 90 b.; *De Berne*, 26 rue de Berne, C, 130 b.; *International et Terminus*, 20 rue des Alpes, C, 80 b.; *Astoria* (no rest.), 6 Place Cornavin, C, 95 b.; *Moderne*, 1 rue de Berne, C, 70 b.; *Savoy*, 8 Place Cornavin, C, 80 b.; *Rivoli* (no rest.), 6 rue des Pâquis, C, 104 b.; *Chantilly* (no rest.), 27 rue Navigation, C, 120 b.; *Continental* (no rest.), 17 rue des Alpes, C, 80 b.; *Montana*, 23 rue des Alpes, C, 70 b.; *Strasbourg et Univers*, 10 rue Pradier, C, 100 b.; *Bernina* (no rest.), 22 Place Cornavin, C, 110 b.; *Pâquis-Fleuri*, 23 rue des Pâquis, D, 20 b.; *De l'Union*, 11 rue Bautte, D, 80 b.

NEAR THE INTERNATIONAL ORGANISATIONS: *La Réserve*, 301 Route de Lausanne, A, 105 b., SB; *Intercontinental*, 7–9 Petit-Saconnex, A, 785 b., SB; *Eden*, 135 rue de Lausanne, C, 80 b.; *Mon Repos*, 131 rue de Lausanne, C, 130 b.

NEAR COINTRIN AIRPORT: *Penta*, 82 Avenue Louis-Casaï, C, 65 b.; *Air Escale* (no rest.), 81 Avenue Louis-Casaï, C, 50 b.

ON THE S SIDE OF THE LAKE: *Arbalète*, 3 rue de la Tour-Maîtresse, A, 70 b.; *Les Armures*, 1 Puits-Saint-Pierre, A, 52 b.; *Adriatica* (no rest.), 21 rue Sautter (Plainpalais), B, 62 b.; *Résidence*, 11 Route de Florissant, B, 180 b.; *Century* (no rest.), 24 Avenue de Frontenex, B, 227 b.; *Touring-Balance*, 13 Place Longemalle (lower town), C, 100 b.; *Athénée*, 6 Route de Malagnou, D, 80 b.

RESTAURANTS. – ON THE N SIDE OF THE LAKE: *Auberge "A la Mère Royaume"*, 9 rue des Corps-Saints (near station); *Au Fin Bec*, 55 rue de Berne; *La Cascade*, 19 Quai des Bergues; *Mövenpick Cendrier*, 17 rue du

Cendrier; *Fleur de Ming* (Chinese), 8 rue du Prince, 7 rue du Port; *Buffet de la Gare*, in Cornavin station.

ON THE S SIDE: *Au Plat d'Argent* (historic interior), 7 rue Cherbuliez (Eaux-Vives); *Buffet de la Gare*, in Eaux-Vives station; *Café de la Pointe*, 6 rue de Villereuse; *Le Chandelier*, 23 Grand'Rue (old town); *Les Armures* (fondue, raclette, pizzas), 1 Puits-St-Pierre (old town), with 17th c. Knights' Hall; *Palais de Justice* (old-world atmosphere), 8 Place du Bourg-de-Four; *Auberge de l'Or du Rhône*, 19 Boulevard Georges-Favon; *Le Catalan* (Spanish), 175 Route de Florissant; *Laurent à la Madeleine*, 13 rue de la Madeleine; *L'Aïoli* ("nouvelle cuisine"), Place du Pont (lower town); *Bavaria* (caricatures of politicians), 49 rue du Rhône (lower town); *Café du Centre*, 5 Place du Molard; *Commerce et Molard*, 7 Place du Molard (lower town); *Mövenpick Fusterie*, Place Fusterie (lower town); *Brasserie l'International* (sauerkraut a speciality), Place du Cirque (Plainpalais); *Le Bateau* (floating restaurant), Jardin Anglais.

OUTSIDE THE TOWN: *Restaurant du Parc des Eaux-Vives*, 82 Quai Gustave-Ador; *Auberge du Lion d'Or*, 3 km (2 miles) NE in Cologny, on the lake; *La Perle du Lac* (summer only), in the park of that name, 128 rue de Lausanne (view of the lake and the Alps); *Creux-de-Genthod* (fish a speciality), 21 Chemin du Creux-de-Genthod, 7 km (4 miles) N, on the lake. – AT THE AIRPORT: *Restaurant de l'Aéroport* (Canonica).

CAFÉS. – *La Crémière*, 8 rue du Marché; *Rohr*, 3 Place du Molard; *Stettler*, 20 rue de la Corraterie; *Auer*, 4 rue de Rive; *La Clémence*, 20 Place du Bourg-de-Four (a traditional student haunt in the old town).

JAZZ SPOTS. – *Tube Jazz Club*, 5 rue du Prince; *Aux Vieilles Pierres* (in cellar), 4 rue du Cheval-Blanc; *Au Jet d'Eau*, 90 rue des Eaux-Vives.

RECREATION and SPORT. – Swimming, sailing, water-skiing, fishing, golf, riding, tennis (indoor and outdoor courts), rock-climbing on Mont Salève; skating and curling (indoor and outdoor).

EVENTS. – *International Motor Show* (10 days in March); *Summer Jazz* (jazz concerts in the Jardin Anglais, a week in June); *International Musical Competition* (two weeks in September); *International Inventors' Fair* (November); *Fête de l'Escalade* (12 December, the anniversary of the Duke of Savoy's unsuccessful attack on the town).

BOAT SERVICES (not all operating during the winter). – *Regular steamer services* to places on the lake, run by the Compagnie Générale de Navigation sur le Lac Léman (CGN: head office in Lausanne-Ouchy; branch office in Geneva, "Le Bateau", Jardin Anglais); *round trips and cruises*; shuttle services and short trips in the port area and round about by the *Mouettes Genevoises* (motor-launches).

**Geneva (in French Genève; in German Genf), the city of Calvin and centre of the Reformation, lies in the extreme western tip of Switzerland at the SW end of Lake Geneva (in French Lac Léman). The town is built on morainic hills of varying height on either side of the swiftly flowing Rhône, which here flows out of the lake and is joined on the SW side of

the town by its tributary the Arve, coming down from the Savoy Alps. Lying between the Jura to the NW and the limestone ridges of Mont Salève and the Voirons to the SE, Geneva enjoys a magnificent situation on the largest of the Alpine lakes, within sight of the majestic peak of Mont Blanc. As a hub of European cultural life in which French savoir-vivre and Swiss solidity are happily combined, the venue of international meetings on the highest level, as well as conventions and exhibitions of all kinds, and not least as a major financial, commercial and industrial city, Geneva has a lively and cosmopolitan atmosphere which makes it perhaps the most attractive town in Switzerland and the one that attracts the greatest number of visitors. Evidence of its dynamic growth during the last few decades is provided by the large amount of new building in the city itself and in the surrounding area, where a number of residential suburbs and satellite towns of considerable size have grown up.**

The *townscape of Geneva, though undramatic, is full of variety. On a steep-sided hill on the left bank of the Rhône rises the old town, dominated by the Cathedral, with its picturesque old streets, flights of steps, fountains and historic buildings. On the W, S and E it is surrounded by a ring of imposing buildings and broad streets on the line of the old fortifications. The business life of the city is concentrated in the area below the old town to the N and in Saint-Gervais, formerly an outlying suburb. On both sides of the lake are handsome promenades and extensive parks and gardens. In the northern part of the town are the main railway station, industrial establishments, craft workshops and residential areas. Most of the international organisations have their headquarters still farther N, in spacious park-like grounds. – Geneva is capital of the smallest Swiss canton, the République et Canton de Genève. It is almost entirely surrounded by French territory (free trade zones) and is connected to the rest of Switzerland only by the lake and a narrow corridor along the NW shore of the lake. It has two small enclaves around Céligny in the canton of Vaud.

Geneva – the Jet d'Eau and Mont Blanc

HISTORY. – The first human settlements in this area were established at the foot of Mont Salève at the end of the Ice Age; then about 2500 B.C. a large village of pile-dwellings grew up in the area of the modern port. The first fortified settlement on the hill now occupied by the old town is believed to have been an oppidum (town) belonging to a Celtic tribe, the Allobroges, who were conquered by the Romans in 120 B.C. The first known reference to the town under the name of Geneva occurs in the "Commentaries" (I, 7) of Julius Caesar, who in 58 B.C. caused the strategically important bridge over the Rhône to be destroyed in order to hinder the advance of the Helvetii into Gaul. In 443 the town became the Burgundian capital; in 534 it fell into the hands of the Franks. At the end of the 9th c. it passed to the second Burgundian kingdom, and together with Burgundy became part of the Holy Roman Empire in 1033.

The long continued conflicts between the Bishops (later Prince-Bishops) of Geneva, the Counts of Geneva and the Counts (later Dukes) of Savoy for control of the town were ended by the **Reformation**, to which Geneva firmly adhered. In 1536 Jean **Calvin** (1509–64) fled from Paris to Geneva and joined forces with the Reformer *Guillaume Farel* (1489–1565), who had been preaching the new faith in the town since 1532. Calvin acquired great influence in both ecclesiastical and state affairs, particularly after his return in 1541, when he established a theocratic régime based on strict and often intolerant church discipline. Through his foundation in 1559 of an Academy mainly designed to train Reformed theologians he turned the commercially minded town towards an interest in intellectual matters.

In 1602 Geneva beat off an attempt by the Duke of Savoy to capture the town (the "Escalade", 11–12 December). The town was occupied by the French in 1798, and until 1813 was the administrative capital of the French department of Léman. In 1814 Geneva became the 22nd canton to join the Confederation. The International Committee of the Red Cross was established in Geneva in 1865, and from 1920 to 1946 it was the headquarters of the League of Nations, and thereafter the European headquarters of the United Nations. – Geneva was the birthplace of *Jean-Jacques Rousseau* (1712–78), the writer and philosopher whose ideas had so much influence on the French Revolution.

Museums, Galleries, etc.

Hours of Opening

Cabinet des Estampes
(*Print Room*),
5 Promenade du Pin;
Tue.–Fri. 10–12 and 2–6.

Cathédrale de Saint-Pierre
See Temple de Saint-Pierre

Château de Coppet
March–October daily except Mon. 10–12 and 2–6.

Château de Penthes
See Musée des Régiments Suisses au Service Etranger

Château de Voltaire,
Ferney-Voltaire (France);
Sat. afternoons in July and August only.

Collection Baszanger,
6 Petite Corraterie;
weekdays 10–12 and 2.30–6.

Collections Baur,
8 rue Munier-Romilly;
daily except Mon. 2–6.

Conservatoire et Jardin Botaniques,
Route de Lausanne;
Botanical collections:
Mon.–Fri. 7.45–12.30 and 1–5.
Botanic garden:
daily 7 a.m. to 6.30 p.m., winter 8–5.

Hôtel de Ville,
2–2bis rue de l'Hotel-de-Ville;
conducted visits only as part of organised city tours.
Cantonal Archives Mon.–Fri. 9–12 and 2–5.

Institut et Musée Voltaire,
25 rue des Délices;
Mon.–Fri. 2–5.

Musée d'Art et d'Histoire,
2 rue Charles-Galland;
Tue.–Sun. 9–5.
Salle des Casemates:
special exhibitions.
Cabinet des Dessins:
by appointment (tel. 29 00 11).

Musée de l'Ariana,
10 Avenue de la Paix;
At present closed.

Musée de l'Athénée,
2 rue de l'Athénée;
Tue.–Fri. 10–12 and 2–6, Sat. until 5, Sun. 10–12.

Musée de l'Automobile Jean Tua,
3 rue Pestalozzi;
by appointment only (tel. 33 31 84).

Musée de l'Horlogerie et de l'Emaillerie,
15 Route de Malagnou;
daily 10–12 and 2–6,
closed Mon. mornings.

Musée de l'Ordre de Malte,
Commanderie de Compesières;
by appointment by (tel. 71 10 04).

Musée des Instruments Anciens de Musique,
23 rue Lefort;
Tue. 3–6, Thu. 10–12 and 3–6, Fri. 8–10 p.m., or by appointment (tel. 46 95 65).

Musée des Régiments Suisses au Service Etranger,
Château de Penthes,
18 Chemin de l'Impératrice;
daily except Mon. 10–12 and 2–6.

Musée d'Histoire des Sciences,
128 rue de Lausanne;
April–October daily 2–6.

Musée d'Histoire Naturelle,
11 Route de Malagnou;
Tue.–Sun. 10–12 and 2–5.

Musée du Vieux Genève,
8 rue du Puits-Saint-Pierre
(Maison Tavel);
closed for restoration (collections in Musée d'Art et d'Histoire).

Musée et Institut d'Ethnographie,
65–67 Boulevard Carl-Vogt;
Tue.–Sun. 10–12 and 2–5.

Musée Philatélique des Nations Unies,
Palais des Nations,
Bâtiment E, Porte 39;
Mon.–Fri. 9–11 and 2–4.

Musée Rath,
Place Neuve;
Tue.–Sun. 10–12 and 2–6, Mon. only 2–6.

Observatoire,
Sauverny;
special exhibitions.
Library (tel. 55 26 11).

Palais des Nations (ONU/UNO);
conducted tours only (Entrance 7) every hour, daily
15 May–30 September 9.15–12 and 2–5.15,
1 October–14 May 9.15–12 and 2–4.15.
See also Musée Philatélique des Nations Unies.

Petit-Palais,
2 Terrasse Saint-Victor;
Tue.–Sun. 10–12 and 2–4.30.

Temple de l'Auditoire
(*John Knox Chapel*),
Place de la Taconnerie;
March–October daily 2–5,
November–February 2–4.

Temple de Saint-Pierre
(*Cathedral*),
Cour Saint-Pierre;
daily 9–12 and 2–5;
service on Sunday at 10.

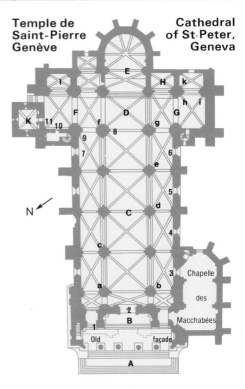

Temple de Saint-Pierre Genève   **Cathedral of St-Peter, Geneva**

Cour Saint-Pierre

A	Steps	F	N transept
B	Porch	G	S transept
C	Nave	H	Rohan chapel
D	Crossing	I	Nassau chapel
E	Choir	K	Sacristy

1 Entrance
2 Organ
3 Gravestone of the Huguenot Théodore Agrippa d'Aubigné (1552–1630)
4 Tablet commemorating the first oecumenical service (20 February 1946)
5 Tablet commemorating the restoration of Genevese independence (31 December 1813)
6 Choir-stalls (from the Chapelle des Florentins, destroyed)
7 Tablet commemorating the Calvinist Reformation
8 Pulpit
9 Calvin's chair
10 Steps to N tower
11 15th c. door

NOTABLE CAPITALS
a Lions, dancers and acrobats
b Daniel in the lions' den
c Angels fighting with dragons
d Salome dancing in front of her father; demons, themes from the Apocalypse
e Melchizedek with bread and wine; Abraham's sacrifice
f Sirens; monks' heads with lions' bodies
g Ornamental motifs with human figures and animals; geometric arabesques
h Partridges billing and cooing, with grapes; acanthus ornament
i Orpheus charming birds
k Christ at Emmaus

Sightseeing in Geneva

One of Geneva's busiest traffic arteries is the **Pont du Mont-Blanc** (1862; rebuilt 1969), the first of its eight bridges over the Rhône, spanning the river at the point where it leaves Lake Geneva. At the S end is the entrance to a car park under the riverbed. Between this bridge and the next one, the *Pont des Bergues*, lies the **Ile Rousseau**, with a statue of Jean-Jacques Rousseau (by Pradier, 1834). Then come the *Pont de la Machine* (pedestrian bridge: under it a dam) and

Pont du Mont-Blanc, Geneva

the double *Ponts de l'Ile* (until the 19th c. the only bridge), crossing an island in the Rhône on which stands the **Tour de l'Ile**, a relic of the medieval fortifications.

THE LOWER TOWN or "Rues Basses", lying between the S bank of the Rhône and the old town, is the city's main business and shopping quarter. The busiest streets are the **Rue du Rhône** and a succession of streets which run parallel to it – *Rue de la Confédération, Rue du Marché, Rue de la Croix-d'Or* (these last two for pedestrians only) and *Rue de Rive*

– with a series of squares (originally landing-stages), passages and cross streets linking the two. Opposite the island in the Rhône is *Place Bel-Air*, around which are a number of banks. Farther E is *Place de la Fusterie*, in the middle of which stands the **Temple de la Fusterie**, a Neo-classical structure built by J. Vennes in 1713–15 as a Protestant church and restored in 1975–77 for use as an oecumenical facility. Along Rue du Rhône, at the corner of Place Molard, is

the *Tour du Molard* (built 1591, several times altered or restored), the remnant of an old arcaded building, with a bas-relief of 1920, "Genève Cité de Refuge".

On the highest point of the OLD TOWN (Vieille Ville: alt. 404 m (1326 feet)), occupying the site of a Roman temple and a number of earlier churches of the 4th–5th c. onwards, rises the **Temple de Saint-Pierre**, the post-Reformation name of the *Cathedral of Saint-Pierre*, a

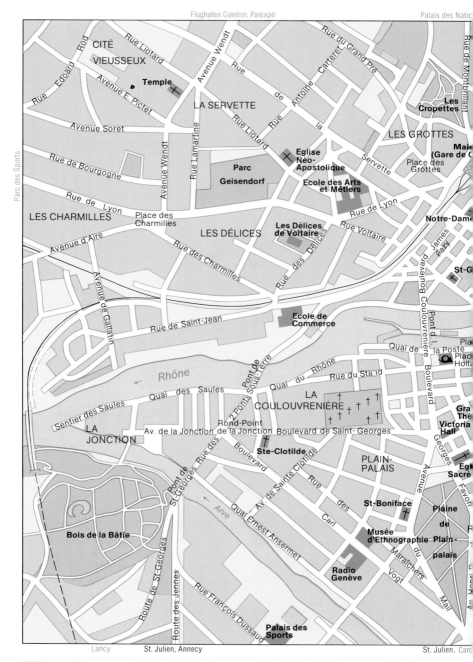

1 Palais de Justice
2 Collège de St-Antoine

3 Musée des Instruments
    Anciens de Musique

4 Musée d'Art et d'Histoire
5 Ecole des Beaux-Arts

6 Athenée
7 Monument de la Réformation

Romanesque church with Gothic elements which was built between about 1150 and 1232, with later alterations, particularly to the exterior. The two principal towers, never completed, date from the 13th c.; the metal spire over the crossing was built only in 1895, replacing a tower destroyed by fire in the 15th c. The original W front and doorway were replaced in 1749–56 by a portico of six Corinthian columns – a piece of stylistic nonconformity which does not, however, interfere with the unity of the interior. Extensive restoration of the church was carried out in 1888–98 and in 1974–79.

The *INTERIOR of the Cathedral (total length 64 m (210 feet)) is of impressive effect with its harmonious proportions and the austere simplicity characteristic of Calvinist churches. The nave, with the aisles divided off by massive clustered piers, has a gallery, blind arcading and triforium; the transepts are short and narrow; the choir, with no ambulatory, ends in a semicircular apse.

Against the walls of the aisles, in the second bay, are the gravestones of ecclesiastical and lay dignitaries of

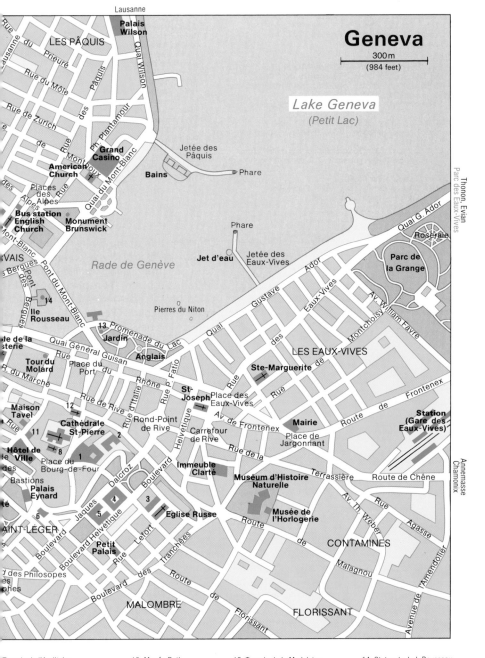

Geneva

300 m
(984 feet)

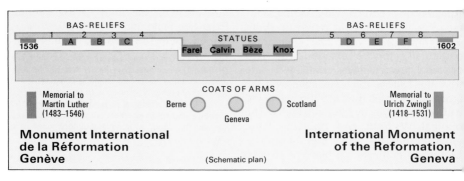

BAS-RELIEFS					BAS-RELIEFS

1536   1 2 3 4   A B C   STATUES   Farel Calvin Bèze Knox   5 6 7 8   D E F   1602

COATS OF ARMS

Memorial to
Martin Luther
(1483–1546)

Berne ◯   ◯   ◯ Scotland

Geneva

Memorial to
Ulrich Zwingli
(1418–1531)

**Monument International
de la Réformation
Genève**   (Schematic plan)

**International Monument
of the Reformation,
Geneva**

On the upper part of the rear wall of the monument, on either side of the central figures, is an inscription in large Roman lettering, POST TENEBRAS LUX ("After darkness comes light"), the motto of the Genevese Reformation. On the plinth of the central group is the Christian emblem IHS. At the ends of the wall are inscribed the two most important dates in the history of Geneva – **1536** (adoption of the Reformed faith and introduction of compulsory schooling) and **1602** (the "Escalade").

STATUES
of the Genevese Reformers **Guillaume Farel** (1489–1565), **Jean Calvin** (1509–64) and **Théodore de Bèze** (1519–1605) and the Scottish Reformer **John Knox** (1505–72)
On either side of the main figures:
A   Frederick William of Brandenburg (1620–88), the Great Elector
B   William I, the Silent, of Nassau-Orange (1533–84)
C   Admiral Gaspard de Coligny (1519–72), leader of the French Protestants
D   Roger Williams (1603–83), the English settler in New England who fought for freedom of conscience in the North American colonies
E   Oliver Cromwell (1599–1658)
F   István (Stephen) Bocskay (1557–1606), Prince of Transylvania, the Hungarian statesman

BAS-RELIEFS of important events in the history of the Reformation:
1   The Great Elector issues the Potsdam Edict of 1685, offering asylum to Protestants driven from France by the Revocation of the Edict of Nantes
2   The States General in The Hague vote for the independence of the Netherlands (26 July 1581)
3   Henry IV of France signs the Edict of Nantes granting religious toleration (13 April 1598)
4   The Reformation is preached to the people of Geneva in the presence of envoys from Berne (22 February 1534)
5   John Knox preaches the Reformation in St Giles' Cathedral, Edinburgh (1565)
6   The Pilgrim Fathers sign a covenant on the "Mayflower" for the righteous colonisation of North America (11 November 1620)
7   The Lords and Commons present the Bill of Rights, providing for the establishment of constitutional monarchy, to William and Mary (13 February 1689)
8   Stephen Bocskay presents to the Hungarian Diet in Košice (Slovakia) the Vienna peace treaty which secures religious freedom for the kingdom of Hungary (13 December 1606)

the 15th and 16th c., originally set into the ground. In the fifth bay are Late Gothic *choir-stalls with delicate carving from the destroyed Chapelle des Florentins. In front of the last pillar on the wall of the N aisle is the "Chaise de Calvin", a triangular chair said to have been used by the Reformer.

In the transepts are chapels: in the NE corner the plain Nassau chapel, NW of the choir the Rohan chapel, with the tomb (1889) of Duc Henri de Rohan (1579–1638), leader of the French Protestants in the reign of Louis XIII.

The simple choir, with blind arcading, dates from the 12th c.; the stained-glass windows are copies of the 15th c. originals, now in the Musée d'Art et d'Histoire (which also has the surviving parts of the high altar, painted by Konrad Witz).

The large gallery above the entrance houses a modern organ (1962–65) with 6000 pipes. The late Romanesque and Early Gothic *capitals on the clustered piers of the nave and the pillars on the walls and windows of the aisles and in the choir and transepts are notable for their high artistic quality and their variety of theme.

Adjoining the SW corner of the Cathedral is the **Chapelle des Macchabées** (1406, with later alterations; restored 1939–40), a superb example of High Gothic religious architecture, with beautiful window traceries.

On the S side of the Cathedral the former *church of Notre-Dame* (originally early 13th c.) has been called since the Reformation the **Temple de l'Auditoire**, in which Calvin, Beza and John Knox preached. Partly rebuilt in the 19th c., it is now used by Scottish, Dutch, Italian and Spanish Protestants (John Knox Chapel; restored 1959; exhibition of historical documents). – To the W of the Cathedral the peaceful tree-shaded *Cour Saint-Pierre* has a number of historic old houses, the most elegant of which is the *Maison Mallet* (Louis XV style, 1721).

SE of the Cathedral in the picturesque *Place du Bourg-de-Four, on the site of the Roman forum, stands the handsome *Palais de Justice*, built 1707–12, which has housed the law courts since 1860. – SW of the Cathedral is the **Hôtel de Ville** (15th–17th c.), seat of the cantonal government, which has a ramp, without steps, leading to the upper floors. The *Tour Baudet* contains the cantonal archives. On the ground floor of the SE wing is the Alabama room, in which the first Geneva Convention (on the Red Cross) was signed in 1864. Facing the

Hôtel de Ville is the *Old Arsenal* (Ancien Arsenal: 15th c., restored 1971), at the beginning of the **Grand'Rue** (pedestrians only), the well-preserved main street of the old town, with house fronts of the 15th–18th c. (at No. 40 the birthplace of Jean-Jacques Rousseau). – SW of the Hôtel de Ville, reached through a pillared gateway, we come to *Promenade de la Treille*, lined with chestnut-trees (views of Mont Salève and the Jura; bench 126 m (413 feet) long). – From the Arsenal the narrow Rue du Puits-Saint-Pierre leads N: at No. 6 is the *Maison Tavel*, the oldest private house in Geneva (first mentioned in the records 1303, rebuilt 1334).

Below the old town, to the SW, is the **Place Neuve** (equestrian statue of General Dufour). On the N side stands the **Grand Théâtre** (Opera House, 1874–79), with the *Musée Rath* (1826: exhibitions) on the right, and the *Conservatoire de Musique* (1858: annual musical competition) on the W side. SE of the square the *Promenade des Bastions*, is graced by old trees and busts of prominent citizens of Geneva.

Against the wall under the Promenade de la Treille can be seen the ***Reformation Monument**** (Monument de la Réformation, 1917). In the middle are figures of Calvin, Guillaume Farel, Théodore de Bèze or Beza and John Knox, and on either side are the statesmen who promoted the cause of the Reformed faith and bas-reliefs with scenes from the history of the Calvinist Reformation. At the ends are memorials to Luther and Zwingli.

On the S side of the Promenade des Bastions is the **University**, housed in its present buildings since 1873, which developed out of the Academy founded by Calvin in 1559 for the training of Reformed theologians. The *Library* in the E wing was founded in the 15th c., and contains some 1,200,000 volumes, a collection of portraits of leading theologians, scholars, writers and statesmen, 6000 valuable manuscripts, a *Rousseau Museum* (manuscripts, books, compositions, etc.) and a *Reformation Museum*. – At the E end of the Promenade des Bastions is the elegant *Palais Eynard* (1821: municipal reception rooms), and to the SE of this the Neo-classical *Athénée* (art gallery). – W of the Uni-

versity, beyond the spacious **Plaine de Plainpalais**, is the **Museum of Ethnography** (65–67 Boulevard Carl-Vogt), with a collection of more than 30,000 items from all over the world, only about a fifth of which can be displayed. Facing the Museum rises a tower block with the headquarters of *Radio Genève* (radio and television). To the SE is the **Palais des Expositions** (40,000 sq. m – 47,840 sq. yards), in which the annual motor show and many other exhibitions and shows are held.

BASEMENT (Sous-Sol)

Salle du Vieux Genève (Old Geneva Room)

Relief model of the town of Geneva in 1850, before the demolition of the fortifications (scale 1:250; by A. Magnin, 1880–96); doors, inn signs and carved shop signs, bells, chairs and other relics of the town's past.

Cour Centrale (Central Courtyard)

Lapidarium, with Roman tombstones and milestones and medieval sculpture; timber from the bridge over the Rhône which was destroyed by Caesar.

LOWER GROUND FLOOR (Rez-de-Chaussée Inférieur)

- 111 Egypt: steles, reliefs, sarcophagi and mummies.
- 112 Near East; gravestones, vessels, bronzes, ceramic and gold articles (various regions).
- 113 Greek sculpture, vases and jewellery.
- 114 Etruscan art – pottery, ceramics and sculptures, urns, small bronzes (figure of Heracles).
- 115 Ancient Rome:
  works of art and everyday objects, mainly from the Geneva area, fine marble head of Augustus.

Musée d'Art et d'Historie Genève	Museum of Art and History, Geneva

Collection of Antiquities

- 218 Prehistoric articles: utensils, weapons, hand-made articles, jewellery, principally from the Geneva region; especially a bronze helmet (950–750 B.C.) from Fillinges, Savoy.
- 213–217 Being converted for special exhibitions.

Applied Art

- 212 Ecclesiastical Art of the Middle Ages: sculptures in wood, stone and ivory; enamel ware from Limoges; windows from the Cathedral of Saint-Pierre, Geneva (end of 15th c.) and from Saint-Fargeau, France (13th c.), capitals from Geneva Cathedral (11th c.), Madonna from Saas, Wallis (early 14th c.).

211 "Salle J.-J. Rigaud": sculptures, furniture, ceiling (15th c.), tapestries from Tournai (c. 1470), Swiss glass (16th c.).
Access to the rooms of the Château of Zizers in the mezzanine, rooms 306–300.
210 "Salle du Conseil d'Etat": carved wooden ceiling (early 18th c.) from the old council chamber of the Hôtel de Ville; furniture, tables (18th c.); Florentine marble table (16th c.).
209 "Salon de Cartigny": carved wooden ceiling (end of 18th c.) from the Château de Cartigny, near Geneva, by the Geneva sculptor Jean Jaquet (1754–1839); furniture, pastel drawing (end of 18th c.).
206/207 "Salle Renaissance": stucco work, articles of marble, bronze and ivory (Italy, France, 14th–16th c.); French embroidery (c. 1580).
205 "Salle d'honneur" of the Château of Zizers (Grisons) (c. 1680): musicians' gallery, painted ceiling, doors, furniture, weapons (15th–17th c.).
204 European Weapons and Armour (15th–18th c.): guns, guillotine (1799), fine collection of pistols; windows from Saint-Pierre (end of 15th c.).
202, 203 Silver from Geneva, the rest of Switzerland and France (18th c.).
201 Contemporary Art: special exhibitions sponsored by AMAN (Association of a Modern Art Museum).

Musée d'Art et d'Histoire Genève — **Museum of Art and History, Geneva**

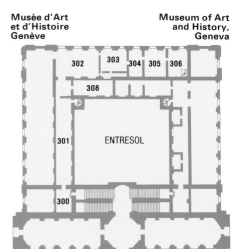

Rhenish school, portraying the "Miraculous Draught of Fishes"; Juan de Flands (d. 1519): "Beheading of John the Baptist"; Fontainebleau school: "Sabina Poppaea" (c. 1570); Andrea Vaccaro (c. 1598–1670): "Triumph of David". Outstanding sculptures: "The Virgin in Majesty" (Auvergne), (c. 1150–80), "St John the Evangelist" (South Germany or Frankish, c. 1480), "Archbishop Giving Blessing" (Rhineland (?), c. 1460).
402 "Fondation Baszanger": Dutch and Flemish painting (15th–17th c.).
403 Dutch painting (16th–17th c.).
404 French and Italian paintings of the 17th–18th c.: Nicolas Régnier (c. 1590–1667), Mattia Preit (1613–99), Charles le Brun (1619–90) and Jean-Baptiste Oudry (1686–1755).
417 Temporary exhibition of the collection of etchings.
418 Room with pictures of the Flemish type and Dutch portraits of the 17th c.
419 Dutch masters, painting in the Italian manner. Notable are two paintings by Nicolaes Berchem (1620–83): "The Miraculous Child" and "Abraham Receives Sarah from the Hands of Abimelech".
420 French paintings of the 17th c.; noteworthy "The Visitation" by Philippe de Champaigne (1602–74).
421 Italian painting of the first half of the 18th c.
422 Pastels by Jean-Etienne Liotard (1702–89), wooden ceiling by the sculptor Jean-Jaquet, sculptures, furniture (18th c.).

Musée d'Art et d'Histoire Genève — **Museum of Art and History, Geneva**

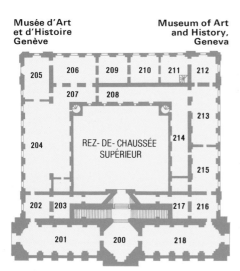

MEZZANINE (Entresol)

300, 301 Special exhibitions.
301, 308 Numismatic collection, Byzantine art.
302 "Salle des étains": pewter from Geneva and other regions of Switzerland (16th–19th c.).
303 "Belle chambre": room from the Château of Zizers, tiled stove.
304 "Chambre peinte": room from the Château of Zizers (Regency style).
306 "Salle Anna Sarasin": coffered ceiling, stove from Winterthur.

FIRST FLOOR (Premier Étage)

Pictorial Art
Paintings and sculpture including panels by Ferdinand Hodler symbolising the Swiss cantons. A commission on the occasion of the National Exhibition of 1896.
400 Peristyle: special exhibitions.
401 Paintings of the German, Flemish, French and Italian schools. Notable paintings: winged altarpiece by Conrad Witz (b. Rottweil c. 1400–10, d. Basle or Geneva c. 1446), a triptych from Maria Stein Monastery, Upper

Musée d'Art et d'Histoire Genève — **Museum of Art and History, Geneva**

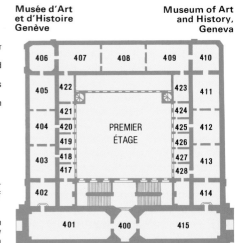

405 First and foremost French portraits of the 18th c. (Nicolas de Largillière, 1656–1746; Maurice-Quentin de La Tour, 1704–88); among them a portrait of Diderot by Levitzky, a likeness of Rousseau by La Tour and a bust of Voltaire by Jean-Baptiste Lemoyne (1704–78).
406 Paintings by Jean-Etienne Liotard; furniture of the 18th c.
407 Paintings from Geneva of the second half of the 18th c.: Jean-Pierre Saint-Ours, Pierre-Louis de la Rive.
408 Paintings and sculpture from Geneva from the end of the 18th and from the first half of the 19th c.: Jacques-Laurent Agasse (1767–1849), Adam-Wolfgang Töpffer (1766–1847), James Pradier (1790–1852).
409 Paintings from Geneva of the 19th c. François Diday (1802–77) and Alexandre Calame (1810–64).
423, 424 Temporary exhibitions of the Cabinet des Dessins.
410 Room entirely devoted to Camille Corot (1796–1875).
425–428 Room devoted to the pioneers of modern painting (Centre Bruno Lussato).
425 Works by Sonja Delaunay, Paul Klee (1879–1940), Fernard Léger (1881–1955) and Le Corbusier (1887–1965).
426 Works by Kurt Schwitters (1887–1948).
427 Works by Hans Richter (1902–69), Hans Arp (1887–1966) and Alexander Rodtschenko (1891–1956).
428 Works by Russian Constructionists.
413 Swiss paintings from the beginning of the 20th c.: Giovanni and Augusto Giacometti, Cuno Amiet (1868–1961), Edouard Vallet, Albert Trachsel and Hans Berger.
414 Paintings by Félix Vallotton (1865–1925).
415 Room devoted to sculpture from the end of the 19th c. and of the present day: Auguste Rodin (1840–1917), August Rodo, Antoine Bourdelle (1861–1929), Henri Laurens (1885–1954), Alexander Archipenko (1887–1964), Hans Arp, Alberto Giacometti, Max Bill (b. 1908), Henri Presset, Jean Tinguely (b. 1925), Robert Müller (b. 1920), César (b. 1921), Bernhard Luginbühl (b. 1929).

The *Cabinet des Dessins*, with about 10,000 drawings and sketches of various schools, can be visited by appointment.

At the SE end of the hill on which the old town is built is the *Promenade St-Antoine*, a former bastion, below which is the *Collège St-Antoine*, founded by Calvin in 1559, now one of the five cantonal secondary schools. Facing it to the S, between the Boulevard Jacques-Dalcroze and Boulevard Helvétique, on a lower level, the *Musée d'Art et d'Histoire* has rich collections of applied art and archaeology, a collection of weapons and a fine picture gallery. In the basement is the Salle du Vieux Genève, with an interesting model (1:250) of the town in the year 1850 and much other material on the history of Geneva. On the lower ground floor Greek and Roman art treasures are displayed, and on the main ground floor the museum's collection of antiquities, with material from Geneva and the surrounding area ranging in date from the Paleolithic and the Iron Age through Roman and Gallo-Roman times to the Middle Ages, together with Middle Eastern and Eastern Mediterranean antiquities, Greek, Roman and Etruscan pottery, Egyptian funerary art and objets d'art of the Gothic and Renaissance periods.

On the first floor the museum's *picture collection includes Italian, Flemish and Swabian old masters, works by Flemish, Dutch and French artists of the 16th–18th c. and pictures of the 18th and 19th c. Geneva school.

The *Ecole des Beaux-Arts* (Art School) behind the Museum to the SW, houses the collection of graphic art of the *Cabinet des Estampes* at 5 Promenade du Pin. A little way S is the *Petit Palais* (2 Terrasse St-Victor), a private museum of modern art. – To the E of the Museum of Art and History, beyond the Boulevard Helvétique, stands the *Russian Church* (1866), with nine gilded domes. Nearby, at 23 rue Lefort, is the *Musée des Instruments Anciens de Musique* (Museum of Old Musical Instruments: Tue., Thu. and Fri. only), and at 8 rue Munier-Romilly the private *Collections Baur* (Far Eastern art: closed Mon.). – Farther E, at 11 Route de Malagnou, the important **Muséum d'Histoire Naturelle** (Natural History Museum) contains informatively displayed collections and a specialised library. Of particular interest are the dioramas of regional fauna on the ground floor and the large fossils and palaeontological and mineralogical collections on the third floor. – Immediately E of the Museum, at 15 Route de Malagnou, is a mansion housing the *Musée de l'Horlogerie et de l'Emaillerie* (Museum of Watchmaking and Enamels). – In a heavily built-up area below the Natural History Museum to the SW rises the *Immeuble Clarté*, the only building of any size in Switzerland designed by the Swiss architect Le Corbusier (along with his cousin P. Jeanneret). The outer walls, mainly of glass, of this block of apartments (1930–32) have no load-bearing function, being merely suspended from a steel skeleton.

On the S side of the lake (the Rive Gauche) the *Promenade du Lac* runs E from the Pont du Mont-Blanc, flanked by the **Jardin Anglais** (large flower clock, café), with the *Monument National* (figures of "Helvetia" and "Geneva"), erected in 1869 to commemorate Geneva's entry into the Confederation (1814). From here *Quai Gustave-Ador* leads NE, following the shore of the lake (commercial and boating harbour). In the lake are two erratic boulders known as the *Pierres du Niton* ("Neptune's Stones"), on the larger of which is a Swiss Ordnance Survey reference point (373·6 m (1226 feet) above sea-level). Beside the *Jetée des Eaux-Vives*, the breakwater enclosing the harbour (beacon), is the *Jet d'Eau, a mighty jet of water which soars up to a height of 145 m (476 feet) (1360 HP pump). – Farther along the lakeside road, on the right, are the *Parc de la Grange* (rose-garden) and the **Parc des Eaux-Vives** (restaurant), both with beautiful mature trees and flower-beds. Beyond this are the *yacht harbour* and the *Genève-Plage* bathing area.

The motor-launch "Elma" in front of the Jet d'Eau

On the N side of the lake (the Rive Droite) the *Quai du Mont-Blanc** extends NE from the bridge, with a* view of the Mont Blanc chain (particularly fine in the late afternoon in clear weather). At the *landing-stage* in front of the Hôtel Beau Rivage the Empress Elizabeth of Austria (b. 1837) was assassinated by an Italian anarchist in 1898. Beyond this is the imposing *Brunswick Monument*, a mausoleum modelled on the Scaliger tombs in Verona, which was built for Duke Karl II of Brunswick (1804–73), who left his money to Geneva; and beyond this again are the modern **Grand Casino** and the *Jetée des Pâquis* (breakwater; bathing area, beacon). From here *Quai Wilson* runs N past the large *Palais Wilson* in which the League of Nations met from 1925 to 1936, to the beautiful lakeside parks of **Mon Repos** and **La Perle du Lac** (Museum of the History of Science, summer only; restaurant).

From the Pont du Mont-Blanc *Rue du Mont-Blanc* goes NW past the *Hôtel des Postes* (on right: the main Post Office, with a special philatelic department) to the main station, the **Gare de Cornavin** (Swiss and French Railways). – S of the station, extending towards the lake, is the old watchmaking quarter of ST-GERVAIS, in the midst of which is the *Temple de Saint-Gervais*; the present church (Protestant) dates from the 15th c. (tower 1435). – To the W of St-Gervais, in the district of LES DÉLICES, we find the little property of the same name where Voltaire lived from 1755 to 1765, when he moved to Ferney, across the frontier in France. The mansion (1730–35, enlarged by Voltaire), set in a small park, is now occupied by the **Institut et Musée Voltaire**, with relics and mementos of Voltaire.

The *Place des Nations*, 2 km (1 mile) N of the Pont du Mont-Blanc, is a busy traffic intersection around which are the headquarters of many INTERNATIONAL ORGANISATIONS. – S of the square are a series of modern buildings occupied by a variety of important institutions. Between the Chemin des Colombettes and the Avenue Giuseppe-Motta are the *United International Bureaux for the Protection of Intellectual Property* (BIRPI: by P. Braillart, 1962) and the *World Meteorological Organisation* (WMO/OMM: by E. Martin, 1956). Between Avenue Giuseppe-Motta and Rue de Vermont is the *International Telecommunications Union* (ITU/UIT), a six-sided tower block by Bordigoni (1958). At the corner of Rue de Varembé and Rue de Montbrillant is the *Centre International*, housing numerous international associations; and closely adjoining are the *European Free Trade Association* (EFTA: by Grand, Praplan and Fischer, 1969), with a beautiful inner courtyard, and the new *International Conference Centre and Press House* (CICG: by A. and F. Gaillard and A. Camenzind, 1971). Also in this area is a modern Roman Catholic church, *Saint-Nicolas-de-Flüe* (by F. Bouvier and V. and J. Malnati, 1967), which was visited by Pope Paul VI in 1969.

NE of the Place des Nations, in a large area of parkland sloping down towards the lake, stands the *Palais des Nations, a monumental complex of buildings clad in light-coloured marble.

This area, which now enjoys extraterritorial status with full judicial, fiscal and postal rights, was formerly part of the *Parc de l'Ariana*, which was bequeathed to Geneva by P. G. Revilliod in 1890. In 1929 the town

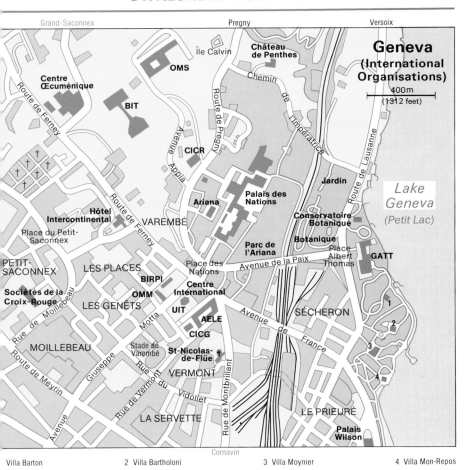

Grand-Saconnex   Pregny   Versoix

Île Calvin   Château
de Penthes

OMS

Chemin

Centre
Œcuménique

BIT

CICR

Jardin

Palais des
Nations

Ariana

Hôtel
Intercontinental   VAREMBÉ

Conservatoire
Botanique

Place du Petit-
Saconnex

Botanique
Place
Albert
Thomas

Parc de
l'Ariana

PETIT-
SACONNEX   LES PLACES

Place des
Nations

Avenue de la Paix   GATT

BIRPI

Sociétés de la
Croix-Rouge   LES GENÊTS

OMM   Centre
International

UIT

AELE

SÉCHERON

1

CICG

MOILLEBEAU

Stade de
Varembé   St-Nicolas-
de-Flüe

VERMONT

2

3

LA SERVETTE

LE PRIEURÉ

Palais
Wilson

Cornavin

Geneva
(International
Organisations)

400m
(1312 feet)

Lake
Geneva
(Petit Lac)

1 Villa Barton   2 Villa Bartholoni   3 Villa Moynier   4 Villa Mon-Repos

made over the area, 200,000 sq. m (239,200 sq. yards) in extent, to the *League of Nations*, which had held an architectural competition in 1927–28 for the design of new headquarters. The most modern and progressive designs were those put forward by Le Corbusier and P. Jeanneret and by H. Meyer and K. Wittwer, but these were rejected and the choice fell instead on the rather ponderous designs submitted by an international group of architects – C. Broggi (Italy), F. Flegenheimer (Switzerland), C. Lefèvre and H. P. Nénot (France) and J. Vago (Hungary). The buildings were erected between 1929 and 1937, and the League of Nations (hitherto housed in the Palais Wilson) was able in 1936 to transfer its headquarters to the new Palais des Nations, which was formally inaugurated in 1938 under the presidency of the Aga Khan. In 1940 the League of Nations ceased to operate, since after the exclusion of the Soviet Union it was no longer an effective international instrument, and it was dissolved in 1946 to give place to the **United Nations Organisation** (UNO/ONU), founded at San Francisco on 24 October 1945. The United Nations Organisation (at present with 157 members) has its main headquarters in New York but has established its European headquarters in the Palais des Nations. – Conducted tours: Entrance 7.

The extensive complex of buildings (25,000 sq. m – 29,900 sq. yards)), the second largest in Europe (after the Palace of Versailles), consists of three main sections. In the middle is the main range of buildings, with a wing at each end enclosing a terraced courtyard facing the lake; in this section are the

Assembly Hall, Council Chamber, conference rooms and library. To the S is the Secretariat Building, and to the N a higher block of offices completed in 1972, with a front wing (conference rooms) topped by two large polygonal domes.

The Palais des Nations has a total of some 30 conference rooms and 1100 office rooms, its own printing office with 36 polycopiers and 6 offset machines, a restaurant, a snack bar and a number of refreshment bars. The interior is comfortable and equipped with the most modern technical services. The large assembly halls have simultaneous interpretation facilities, enabling speeches to be translated into and out of the five official languages of the United Nations (English, French, Spanish, Russian and Chinese). The decoration of the various halls and rooms – usually lavish – was donated by different countries. The following are of particular interest:

Assembly Hall (*Salle des Assemblées*), a square chamber with seating for 2000 – the largest in the Palais – used for meetings of the United Nations and its associated organisations. The curtains, of raw silk, were a gift from India. – It is preceded by the *Salle des Pas Perdus* (Lobby), with a view of the Alps from the E side. The floor is of Finnish granite, and the walls are faced with Swedish marble. The two heavy gilded bronze doors at the ends, brought back from Italy by Napoleon, were presented to the League of Nations by Clemenceau.

International Organisations based in Geneva

A selection in alphabetical order: names and abbreviations in French and English

Accord Général sur les Tarifs Douaniers et le Commerce
General Agreement on Tariffs and Trade (GATT)

Alliance Internationale du Tourisme (AIT)
International Touring Alliance (ITA)

Alliance Réformée Mondiale (ARM)
World Alliance of Reformed Churches

Alliance Universelle des Unions Chrétiennes de Jeunes Gens
World Alliance of Young Men's Christian Associations

Alliance Universelle des Unions Chrétiennes Féminines
World Alliance of Young Women's Christian Associations

Association Européenne de Libre-Echange (AELE)
European Free Trade Association (EFTA)

Bureau International d'Education (BIE)
International Bureau of Education (IBE)

Bureaux Internationaux Réunis pour la Protection de la Propriété Intellectuelle (BIRPI)
United International Bureaux for the Protection of Intellectual Property

Centre Européen de la Culture (CEC)
European Cultural Centre (ECC)

Comité Intergouvernemental pour les Migrations Européennes (CIME)
International Committee for European Migration (ICEM)

Comité International de la Croix-Rouge (CICR)
International Committee of the Red Cross (ICRC)

Commission Economique pour l'Europe
Economic Commission for Europe

Conférence des Nations Unies sur le Commerce et le Développement

United Nations Conference on Trade and Development (UNCTAD)

Conseil Œcuménique des Eglises (COE)
World Council of Churches (WCC)

Fédération Luthérienne Mondiale (FLM)
Lutheran World Federation (LWF)

Haut Commissariat pour les Réfugiés
High Commissariat for Refugees

Ligue des Sociétés de la Croix-Rouge
League of Red Cross Societies

Organisation des Nations Unies (ONU)
United Nations (UN)
(European headquarters: main headquarters in New York)

Organisation Européenne pour la Recherche Nucléaire (CERN=Centre Européen pour la Recherche Nucléaire)
European Organisation for Nuclear Research

Organisation Internationale du Travail (OIT)
International Labour Organisation (ILO)
Executive agency:
Bureau International du Travail (BIT)
International Labour Office

Organisation Météorologique Mondiale (OMM)
World Meteorological Organisation (WMO)

Organisation Mondiale de la Santé (OMS)
World Health Organisation (WHO)

Union Européenne de Radiodiffusion (UER)
European Broadcasting Union (EBU)
Administrative headquarters of EUROVISION (technical services in Brussels)

Union International des Télécommunications (UIT)
International Telecommunication Union (ITU)

Union Internationale des Transports Routiers
International Road Transport Union

Union Interparlementaire (UIP)
Inter-Parliamentary Union (IPU)

Council Chamber (*Salle des Conseils*), with seating for 500. The *wall and ceiling painting* (by J. M. Sert, 1934–36) was a gift from Spain. Done in sepia on a gold ground, it depicts four related themes – technical, social and medical progress and, as a hope for the future, the abolition of war. In the middle (opposite the window side) is "Victors and Vanquished", and on the ceiling "Solidarity of the Five Continents". In this chamber was held the 1955 Four-Power Conference on the reunification of Germany (Eisenhower, Bulganin, Eden, Faure). In the antechamber are three *bas-reliefs* by Eric Gill inspired by Michelangelo. – *Room III:* birch and pearwood panelling; "Ship on a Calm Sea", a picture by the Genevese painter Barraud. – *Room V:* decoration by an English artist, W. Allom; architectural motifs on the doors. – *Room VI:* decoration presented by Switzerland (frescoes by K. Hügin; events from Swiss history on the insides of the doors). – *Room VII:* decoration by Porteneuve. – *Room VIII:* clad with wood inlay by a Dane, Petersen. – *Room IX:* panelled with beautifully grained stinkwood from South Africa. – *Room X:* presented by Latvia (black intarsia oak floor). – *Room XI:* by Mutters (Holland), with leather wall covering. – *Room XII:* presented by Italy (used for showing films) – *Room XIV:* by M. Simon.

The *Library*, donated by John D. Rockefeller Jr, was founded in 1920, and now possesses some 750,000 volumes and numerous manuscripts and letters from outstanding international figures. The *Stamp Museum* displays rare and interesting United Nations issues.

Between the wings of the main range of buildings is the *Cour d'Honneur*, a spacious terrace which merges into the park, with a magnificent view of the lake and the Alps. In the middle is a bronze *armillary sphere* with gilded signs of the Zodiac, presented by the Woodrow Wilson Foundation. On a marble terrace near the Library wing is a *Space Memorial* presented by the Soviet Union symbolising the conquest of space.

Aiguille du Midi 3842 m (12,606 ft)	Mont Blanc du Tacul 4248 m (13,938 ft)	Mont Maudit 4465 m (14,650 ft)	Mont Blanc 4807 m (15,772 ft)	Aiguille de Bionnassay 4052 m (13,295 ft)	Mont Salève 1380 m (4528 ft)

Lac Léman   (Lake Geneva)

View of the Mont Blanc massif from Geneva

The Château de Penthes, 500 m (547 yards) N of the Palais des Nations (18 Chemin de l'Impératrice), houses the *Musée des Régiments Suisses au Service Etranger* (Museum of Swiss Regiments in Foreign Service).

Above the Palais des Nations, to the W, stands the *Ariana, a building in Italian Renaissance style erected in 1877–84 for the Geneva writer and philanthropist P. G. Revilliod (1817–90). With a sumptuously appointed interior, it now houses the International Academy of Ceramics and a rich *collection of ceramics and porcelain* begun by Revilliod.

To the SE, lying between the Route de Lausanne and the Geneva–Lausanne railway line and between the Avenue de la Paix to the S and the Chemin de l'Impératrice to the N, lies the **Jardin Botanique**, a botanic garden established in 1902, with hothouses (exotic plants, etc.), a fine *Alpine garden*, a small animal enclosure (fallow deer, llamas, peacocks, cranes, parakeets) and a refreshment pavilion (summer only). On the E side of the Route de Lausanne is the *Conservatoire Botanique*, with an excellent specialised library and famous *herbaria (in the garden pavilion).

From the Place des Nations the broad *Avenue de la Paix* extends N in a wide curve, passing the Ariana on the right and the Soviet embassy on the left. Opposite the W entrance to the Palais des Nations is the attractive villa, *Vieux-Bois*, which houses the Geneva Hotel School restaurant. On higher ground to the NW is the imposing headquarters of the **International Committee of the Red Cross** (CICR).

The International Red Cross, founded in 1864 on the initiative of Henri Dunant (1828–1910) and managed exclusively by Swiss citizens, is dedicated to pursuing humanitarian aims on the international level (e.g. by the register of prisoners of war and missing persons which it has maintained since 1916). The various national organisations (Red Cross, Red Crescent, Red Lion, Red Sun) belong to the League of Red Cross Societies, which is also based in Geneva.

From the Place des Nations the *Route de Ferney* leads to the NW, coming in 500 m (547 yards) to the *Hôtel Intercontinental* (1964), on left, with a 15-storey tower. Beyond it is the elegant residential development of the *Parc de Budé*. In another 500 m (547 yards) the road comes to a hill (454 m – 1489 feet) where the old road to Ferney goes off on the right. A little way along this road is the **Centre Œcuménique** (Oecumenical Centre), headquarters of the World Council of Churches, the Lutheran World Federation, the Reformed World Federation and other non-Catholic church associations.

Palais des Nations, Geneva

The **World Council of Churches**, first discussed at the Edinburgh World Missionary Conference in 1910 and founded in its present form at Amsterdam in 1948, is composed of more than 220 Protestant, Orthodox, Old Catholic and Anglican churches and maintains contacts with other Christian denominations, in particular with the Roman Catholic Church (Papal visit 1969).

Some 500 m (547 yards) NW of the Oecumenical Centre (1 km (about a ½ mile) from the Palais des Nations) is the headquarters of the **World Health Organisation** (WHO/OMS: 1962–66, by J. Tschumi, P. Bonnard, H. Curchid and P. Cotty), also known as the *Palais de la Santé*.

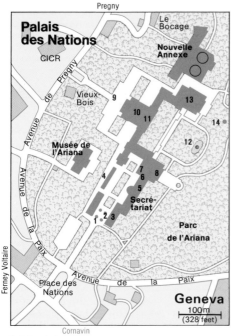

Geneva
100 m
(328 feet)

1 S Gate (main entrance)
2 Porter's lodge (information)
3 First aid post
4 Garage
5 Bank
6 Post office
7 Gate 7: starting-point of conducted tours; Stamp Museum
8 Council Chamber (Salle des Conseils)
9 W Gate
10 Assembly Hall (Salle des Assemblées)
11 Lobby
12 Armillary sphere
13 Library
14 Space Memorial

The World Health Organisation, founded in 1948, succeeded the International Office of Public Health, established in Paris in 1907. It is concerned with health care on an international basis, epidemic control, the training of doctors and other health care personnel, etc., and is active in the field of medical research. Its Geneva headquarters and its six regional offices in Copenhagen, Alexandria, Brazzaville, Manila, New Delhi and Washington have a total staff of almost 5000.

The main building, a rectangular eight-storey block 150 m (492 feet) long built of prefabricated elements, rests on 22 concrete piles and contains 550 rooms. In front of it is a lower structure containing the main assembly hall, surrounded by gardens. The building contains many works of art and other features presented by member nations, notably a large wall decoration (7 m (23 feet) square) presented by Brazil.

To the S of the World Health Organisation, on a previously undeveloped site at Le Grand Morillon rises the new headquarters of the **International Labour Office** (ILO/BIT: 1969–73).

Designed by Beaudouin, Camenzind and Nervi, this has an 11-storey main building 190 m (623 feet) long and 60 m (197 feet) high on a biconcave ground plan borne on two supporting blocks (in the N one various services, in the S one conference rooms and the library). The outer walls (4000 windows) are of aluminium and glass, on a framework of steel and concrete. The building has some 2500 telephone

extensions, facilities for simultaneous interpretation, 23 passenger and 7 goods lifts, a system for the transmission of documents within the office and a four-storey underground garage for 1450 cars.

SURROUNDINGS

Lake Geneva: see p. 133.

To the W of the town, at the "Jonction", the River *Arve* flows into the Rhône, its turbid yellowish water mingling with the clear greenish-blue water of the larger river. Beyond the Arve is the *Bois de la Bâtie* (woodland, meadows, animal enclosure; view of town), and to the SE of this is an artificial ice-rink, the *Patinoire des Vernets* (partly roofed over; seating for 10,000). The suburb of **Carouge**, still farther SE was incorporated in the city in 1816, with the large goods station and bonded warehouses of *La Praille*. Carouge, originally founded by Savoy as a rival to Geneva, has some attractive squares and old houses. – 3 km (2 miles) W of the city is the last of Geneva's eight bridges over the Rhône, the *Pont Butin* (built 1916–27, widened to eight lanes in 1970), spanning the valley at a point where it is fully 50 m (164 feet) deep.

5 km (3 miles) NW of Geneva is *Cointrin International Airport, and 2 km (1 mile) beyond this is the frontier town of *Meyrin*, a large residential suburb with an Alpine garden. Here, too, is the European nuclear research facility **CERN** (Conseil Européen pour la Recherche Nucléaire: partly on French territory), with a 600 MeV synchro-cyclotron, a 28 GeV proton synchrotron, storage rings and a super proton synchrotron (7 km (4 miles) long ring tunnel). – 4 km (2 miles) W of the town, in a bend of the Rhône, is the residential development of **Le Lignon**, a striking example of modern architecture houses a population of 15,000, with two long terraces (together over 1 km (about a ½ mile) long, with a series of offsets) and two tower blocks (26 and 30 storeys), schools, churches, cultural and shopping facilities, swimming pools and a restaurant.

7 km (4 miles) NW, in French territory (bus services, on a road which passes under the runways of Cointrin airport in a tunnel), is **Ferney-Voltaire** (pop. 2000), once a potters' town. To the W of the little town is the *château* which Voltaire acquired in 1758 and later enlarged, where he held court until shortly before his death (mementoes). Above the former chapel is the inscription "Deo erexit Voltaire". In front of the Town Hall is a statue of Voltaire by Lambert.

9 km (6 miles) N (reached by rail or boat) is **Versoix**, an attractive little place on the W side of the Petit Lac, near the border between the cantons of Geneva and Vaud, with a beautiful lakeside promenade. The third Aga Khan, head of the Ismaili sect, died here in his property of *Le Barakat* in 1957 (b. Karachi 1877; buried in Egypt). Near this house is the *Château Rouge* (the property of an Arab ruler). – In **Genthod**, just S of Versoix (fish restaurant on lake), are a number of fine old 18th c. houses, including the *Maison Ami-Lullin*, built in 1723–30 by F. Blondel, which was occupied by the scientist H. B. Saussure. In the *Maison de la Rive* (1730), above the railway line, Goethe stayed in 1779 with the philosopher and naturalist Charles Bonnet (1720–93).

14 km (9 miles) N (reached by rail or boat), in the canton of Vaud, is **Coppet**, a little town on the W shore of the lake, founded in the 14th c., with old

arcaded houses and a 15th c. Gothic church. Above the town, in an extensive park, stands a large *château* on a horseshoe plan, built in 1767–71 by G. de Smethe on the site of an earlier 13th c. castle and purchased in 1784 by the Geneva banker Jacques Necker (1732–1804), later French Finance Minister. In the early 19th c. Necker's daughter Anne-Louise-Germaine, who became the Baronne de Staël-Holstein, better known as the free-thinking writer Mme de Staël (1766–1817), made the château a meeting-place of the leading social and political personalities of the day. Necker and Mme de Staël are buried in the park, in a walled area W of the château (visitors not admitted). The château is open to the public from March to October. – 4 km (2 miles) N, away from the lake, is the pretty village of **Céligny**, in a little enclave belonging to Geneva (Hotel d'Allèves-Beach, B, 25 b.; SP).

Cologny (alt. 450 m (1476 feet)) 14 km (9 miles) NE (No. 9 bus or boat) on the hillside above the E shore of the Petit Lac, has a fine 17th c. country house and a number of modern villas. There is a magnificent *view across the lake to the Palais des Nations and the Jura, particularly from the terrace between the Lion d'Or restaurant and the church and from the "Byron Stone" on the Chemin de Ruth. Byron stayed in the *Villa Diodati* in 1816 and met Shelley, then also living in Cologny. – 1·8 km (1 mile) S, at Chêne-Bougeries, is the handsome modern residential development of La Gradelle, built since 1963.

6·5 km (4 miles) NE, on the lake (No. 9 bus or boat), is **Bellerive**, with the 17th c. Manoir de Bonvent (near the landing-stage) and a 17th c. château.

14 km (9 miles) NE, on the lake (No. 9 bus or boat), is **Hermance**, a pretty little place founded in 1245 close to the French frontier. 12th c. fortifications, château, 15th and 16th c. houses; Stone Age tombs.

*Mont Salève. – A good road ascends to this long limestone ridge S of Geneva, in French territory (good rock-climbing): 16 km (10 miles) to Monnetier, round trip 69 km (43 miles), maximum gradient 6%. – Leave Geneva by the Route de Florissant and road 42, which runs SE via the suburb of *Villette*. 6 km (4 miles): **Veyrier** (alt. 422 m (1385 feet)), on the French frontier (passport and customs control). – Straight ahead is the lower station of a *cableway* 1180 m (3872 feet) long which runs up in 6 minutes to a height of 1143 m (3750 feet) on Mont Salève. Alternatively turn left beyond Veyrier into road 206 and in 3·5 km (2 miles) right into road 206A. 7 km (4 miles): **Mornex** (572 m (1877 feet): Hotel du Château), a summer holiday resort on the southern slopes of the Petit Salève. Almost opposite the Protestant church is a house in which Richard Wagner lived in 1856. – The road continues up the beautiful valley of the Viaison. 3 km (2 miles): **Monnetier** (696 m (2284 feet): Hôtel Chaumière), a health resort in a cleft between the Petit and Grand Salève, from which it is a half-hour climb to the summit of the *Petit Salève* (900 m (2953 feet): beautiful views). – 4·5 km (3 miles) above Monnetier, to the right, is the upper station of the cableway (1143 m (3750 feet): Hôtel Téléférique), with a magnificent *prospect of Geneva, the lake and the Jura. – 1·5 km (1 mile) farther on a road branches off on the right to the *Treize-Arbres* inn (1184 m (3885 feet): modest). From above the inn (1212 m (3977 feet): orientation table) there is a magnificent *view of the Mont Blanc chain, Lake Geneva and the Jura. A footpath leads up (30 minutes) to the *Crêt de Grange-Tournier* (1308 m –

4292 feet), the highest point on the **Grand Salève**. – The road continues along the slopes of the Grand Salève. 5 km (3 miles): *Col de la Croisette* (1176 m (3858 feet): restaurant), with roads running down to Collonges on the right and La Muraz on the left. – Then past the *Grand Piton* (1380 m – 4528 feet), the highest point in the Salève range, and then downhill, with many bends. 16 km (10 miles): *Cruseilles* (781 m – 2562 feet), on the road from Annecy to Geneva (N 201); then N on this road over the little pass of *Mont Sion* (785 m – 2576 feet) and through *Le Châble* and *Saint-Julien* to the Swiss frontier. 28 km (17 miles): **Geneva**.

The *Voirons. – There are two alternative routes (each 37 km (23 miles)) to this long ridge in French territory E of Geneva making an attractive round trip of 74 km (46 miles). – Leave Geneva on the Chamonix road. 7 km (4 miles): **Annemasse** (alt. 436 m (1431 feet)). From here on N 507 to *Bonne-sur-Menoge* and *Pont-de-Fillings* (10·5 km – 7 miles), from which a road to the left climbs (fine views) via *Boëge* to the **Col de Saxel** (12·5 km (8 miles): 945 m (3101 feet)); then a road on the left which winds its way uphill, passing through wooded country. – 7 km (4 miles): Grand Chalet (1400 m – 4593 feet), sanatorium. From here it is a 30 minutes' climb to the *Calvaire* or *Grand Signal*, on the summit of the *Voirons* (1486 m – 4876 feet), with magnificent views (Savoy Alps, Jura, etc.). – 8 km (5 miles): *Bons* (548 m – 1798 feet), on the road from Thonon (N 203); then left along this road via *Langin* and *Saint-Cergues* to *Annemasse* (15 km – 9 miles). – 7 km (4 miles): **Geneva**.

Lake Geneva

Within Switzerland and France.
Cantons: Vaud (VD), Geneva (GE) and Valais (VS).

ⓘ **Office du Tourisme de Genève,**
Tour de l'Ile,
Case Postale 440,
CH-1211 Genève 11;
tel. (022) 28 72 33.
Office du Tourisme du Canton de Vaud (OTV),
10 Avenue de la Gare,
CH-1002 Lausanne;
tel. (021) 22 77 82.
Office du Tourisme de Morges,
80 Grand'Rue,
CH-1110 Morges;
tel. (021) 71 32 33.
Office du Tourisme de Chexbres,
CH-1605 Chexbres;
tel. (021) 56 22 31.

RECREATION and SPORT. – Golf, riding, tennis, swimming, sailing, water-skiing, fishing.

BOAT SERVICES (not all operating during the winter). – Regular steamer services between places on the lake, run by the *Compagnie Générale de Navigation sur le Lac Léman* (CGN: head office Lausanne-Ouchy, branch office in Geneva at Le Bateau, Jardin Anglais); many round trips and cruises (evening trips with dancing on board); shuttle services and round trips in port and on the Petit Lac by the "Mouettes Genevoises"; short round trips on the motor-launches "Elma" and "Star of Geneva". A particular attraction is "Neptune", the last cargo-carrying sailing vessel on the lake, which can be chartered.

"Neptune", a cargo-carrying sailing vessel, on Lake Geneva

** **Lake Geneva (in French Lac Léman or Lac de Genève), the largest of the lakes in the Alps, lies between the Savoy Alps, the Swiss Jura and the Vaud Alps at a mean height of 371 m (1217 feet) above sea-level. Of its total area of 581 sq. km (224 sq. miles) 60% falls within Switzerland and 40% within France. Its maximum depth is about 310 m (1017 feet). The lake, which the River Rhône enters at one end and leaves at the other, extends in a flat arc 72 km (45 miles) long from E to W, with a maximum width of 14 km (9 miles). While the French southern shore of the lake (department of Haute-Savoie) is only thinly populated, with Evian and Thonon as its largest towns, the sunny northern shore in the canton of Vaud, with the vine-growing areas of Lavaux and La Côte, is the Swiss equivalent of the Riviera, a popular holiday and tourist region.**

Along the N side of the lake. – For centuries the beauty of the northern shores of Lake Geneva has been lauded (e.g. by Byron, Voltaire and Rousseau) – the luxuriantly fertile slopes rising gently above the lake, the picturesque towns and old castles, the magnificent backdrop of the Savoy and Valais Alps to the S and E. The climate has a southern mildness in which the vine flourishes.

The road along the shore of the lake from Geneva runs through *Genthod* (restaurant on lake) and the little town of *Versoix* (above p. 132), enters the canton of Vaud (8 km – 5 miles) and comes to

Coppet (p. 132). It then continues via the interesting little town of **Nyon** (p. 185) and *Prangins* (château of 1748) to reach the stretch of land along the lake known as *La Côte*, the fertile slopes descending from the Vaudois plateau, with flourishing vineyards, fruit orchards and farming land: a gentle, prosperous landscape with many old castles and country houses.

Rolle (alt. 376 m (1234 feet): pop. 3600; Hôtel de la Tête Noire, D, 30 b.) is a long straggling little town, an important wine-trading area, with a 13th c. castle (four towers) and old burghers' and vintners' houses lining the main street. On a small island in the harbour is an obelisk commemorating General de la Harpe (1754–1838), who played a part in securing the separation of Vaud from the canton of Berne in 1798. The local speciality is "petits pains au sucre" (sugar rolls). Side road to the * Signal de Bougy. – The road continues to *Allaman* (425 m (1394 feet): 16th c. castle with two towers) and *St-Prex* (373 m (1224 feet): pop. 2000), an old market town with a church which first appears in the records in 885. Cobbled streets; old street signs; Tour de l'Horloge (Clock Tower), the only gate-tower with loopholes in the canton of Vaud. Glassworks; beautiful lakeside gardens and villas.

Morges (381 m (1250 feet): pop. 12,700; Hôtel Du Mont-Blanc au Lac, C, 80 b.; De la Couronne, D, 40 b.; sailing school, annual Tulip Festival, Wine Festival), on a site once occupied by a large village of pile-dwellings, is a town of fishermen, with the headquarters of the World Wildlife Fund. Handsome 18th c. burghers' houses, church (1776), Town Hall (16th–17th c.). In Blanchenay, an old patrician house which once belonged to the engraver Alexis Forel, is the Musée du Vieux Morges (furniture, sculpture and pictures of the Gothic and Renaissance periods). The castle (13th and 16th c.) contains a military museum (Saturdays and Sundays only). – From Morges an excursion can be made (10 km – 6 miles) to **L'Isle** (666 m – 2185 feet), with the little late 17th c. château of Chandieu. Near here are the châteaux of *Chardonney* (18th c.) and *Vufflens-le-Château* (14th–15th c.) – The road continues through the select residential suburb of *St-Sulpice* (Romanesque conventual church, 12th c.) to enter **Lausanne**, capital of the canton of Vaud (p. 153).

To the E of Lausanne is one of the most beautiful parts of Switzerland, with many features of interest. Between *Lutry* (380 m (1247 feet): Hôtel de Ville, B, 60 b.; Au Vieux Stand restaurant) and Vevey the road runs past the *Monts de Lavaux*, the slopes of which are entirely covered with vineyards. There is a magnificent stretch of road on the *Corniche de Lavaux* (Corniche Vaudoise), running high above the lake through the vineyards. From here there are views of the mighty peaks around the upper end of the lake. The road runs via Grandvaux (565 m – 1854 feet) and the wine-growing villages of Riex (450 m – 1476 feet) and Epesses to a superb viewpoint, the *Signal de Chexbres* (655 m – 2149 feet), and the health resort of *Chexbres* (559 m (1834 feet): pop. 1700; Hôtel Signal, B, 132 b., SB; Cécil, C, 45 b.), with good walking in the surrounding area. Then via *Chardonne* (590 m (1936 feet): pop. 1700) to the vine-growing village of *Corsier* (445 m (1460 feet): pop. 3030), which has a fine 12th c. church with a Romanesque tower, the device of the House of Savoy and old bells (1427, 1523). Charlie Chaplin (Sir Charles Chaplin, 1889–1977) is buried here.

The Lavaux vineyards, Lake Geneva

From Lutry the lakeside road continues via Villette to *Cully* (380 m (1247 feet): Hôtel Major Davel, C, 30 b.; Du Raisin, C. 17 b.; Motel Intereurop, 8 km (5 miles) away, C, 140 b.), a vine-growing village with picturesque old streets. Near the landing-stage is a monument to Major Davel, a native of the village, who made an unsuccessful attempt (1723) to free Vaud from Bernese rule. – The main road continues past the famous *Dézaley* vineyards to *Rivaz*, the castle of Glérolles (12th c., rebuilt in the Gothic period: wine-bar) and the vine-growing village of *St-Saphorin* (376 m (1234 feet): pop. 300), with beautiful old houses and a

16th c. church. This was originally a country seat of the bishops of Lausanne. In a house of 1705 opposite the church is the restaurant A l'Onde.

The road then traverses the celebrated resorts of **Vevey** (p. 250) and **Montreux** (p. 178) and comes to *Villeneuve* (378 m (1240 feet): pop. 4500), a little harbour town at the end of the lake which was founded in the 13th c. on the site of earlier Celtic and Roman settlements.

Along the S side of the lake. – Leave Geneva on road 37, which skirts the Parc des Eaux-Vives and passes below the hill of Cologny to Vésenaz, from which the main road to Thonon continues in long straight stretches through attractive rolling country, with the Yvoire peninsula to the left. – Beyond *Corsier* (a former Roman settlement), to the left of the road, the *Swiss-French frontier* is crossed (Swiss passport control). Then on N 5 through a customs-free zone to *Douvaine* (alt. 429 m (1408 feet): French frontier control). – The road continues below the vine-clad *Mont de Boisy* (735 m (2412 feet): on right) and in 5 km (3 miles) reaches *Sciez* (408 m – 1339 feet), where the lakeside road via Yvoire comes in on the left. – Beyond *Jussy*, on a hill to the right of the road, is the village of *Les Allinges*, with two ruined castles and a pilgrimage chapel (beautiful view). – 10 km (6 miles) beyond Sciez is **Thonon-les-Bains** (427 m (1401 feet): pop. 22,000), beautifully situated on the slopes above the lake (carbonated springs). Funicular down to the pretty harbour area and the fishing village of *Rives*.

Beyond Thonon N 5 cuts across the delta of the Dranse. – Interesting detour (2·5 km – 2 miles) to the 15th c. castle of *Ripaille*, on the lake, where Duke Amadeus VIII of Savoy lived as a hermit before his election as Pope (Felix V, 1439–49). – 2·5 km (2 miles) beyond Thonon on N 5 is *Vongy*, where the road from Ripaille joins the main road which then crosses the *Dranse* and continues to *Amphion*, on the shores of the lake. 6·5 km (4 miles) from Vongy is **Evian-les-Bains** (374 m (1227 feet): pop. 6000), a fashionable resort in a beautiful situation on the shores of the lake (alkaline thermal springs). On the broad Quai Baron-de-Blonay are the spa establishment and the Casino (gaming).

From here a funicular ascends to a terrace above the lake, on which are the Pump room and the large hotels.

From Evian to St-Gingolph the road keeps close to the lake. It traverses *Grande-Rive* and *Petite-Rive*, on the outskirts of Evian, and at the *Château de Blonay* (16th c.) passes under the defensive walls. The hills alongside the lake now become steeper and higher. To the right is the *Dent d'Oche* (2225 m (7300 feet): from Evian by road to *Bernex*, 14 km (9 miles), then 4½ hours' climb, with guide). The road then comes to *Meillerie* (386 m – 1266 feet), a picturesque fishing village in a magnificent situation, with large limestone quarries. – Beyond this, on the right, are the steep slopes of *Mont Chalon* (1058 m – 3471 feet); to the left is a superb *view across the lake to Vevey and Montreux, with the villages and villas on the slopes above, and of the peaks of the Vaudois Alps (Pléiades, Dent de Jaman, Rochers de Naye); to the right, on the shores of the lake, is Chillon castle (p. 179).

At *Le Locum* is the French frontier control. The road now crosses a customs-free zone at the foot of the *Pic de Blanchard* (1472 m – 4830 feet) and comes to **St-Gingolph** (391 m – 1283 feet), a picturesque little town straddling the River *Morge*, here flowing through a deep gorge, which marks the *French-Swiss frontier* (Swiss passport and customs control). Then on road 37 beneath the steep slopes of *Le Grammont* (2178 m (7146 feet): wide views; 5–5½ hours from St-Gingolph, with guide). – 4 km (2 miles) from St-Gingolph is **Bouveret** (394 m (1293 feet): Hôtel Bouveret Plage, C, 22 b.), an attractively situated village near the inflow of the Rhône, which creates a wave effect (the "bataillère") reaching far out into the lake. – The road (SP Martigny) now leaves the lake and runs up the broad Rhône valley, keeping close to the foot of the hills. To the left of the road is *Port-Valais*, with the church belonging to Bouveret. – After passing through *Les Evouettes* the road comes to *Porte-du-Secx*, a narrow passage (formerly fortified) between the rock face and the river where a road branches off on the left to *Villeneuve* (8 km – 5 miles) and **Montreux** (p. 178). The main road then continues to the large village of **Vouvry** (384 m (1260 feet): Hôtel de Vouvry, E, 30 b.), with a power station, and **Martigny** (p. 177).

Glarus

Canton: Glarus (GL).

 **Verkehrsverein Glarnerland und Walensee,**
Kirchweg 4,
CH-8750 Glarus;
tel. (058) 61 13 47.

To the S of the picturesque Walensee the little canton of Glarus, occupies the basin of the River Linth, one of the most beautiful transverse valleys in the Alps, with the ridge of Glärnisch (2332 m – 7651 feet) rearing above it on the W and the massive bulk of Tödi (3614 m – 11,858 feet) closing its southern end. Surrounded on three sides by mountains, the canton is linked with the neighbouring canton of Uri by a road which runs SW from Linthal over the Klausen pass.

The 38,000 inhabitants of the canton (area 685 sq. km (264 sq. miles)) – the land of St Fridolin, who appears on Glarus's coat of arms – are an independent-minded race, formed by this rugged mountain world. Industry (in particularly the cotton industry – spinning, weaving, coloured prints) established itself here at an early stage, using the water-power provided by the Linth. The main valley is served by a branch railway line from Rapperswil to Glarus and Linthal, connecting with the main line from Zurich to Chur at Ziegelbrücke. From Linthal there is a cableway to the traffic-free resort of Braunwald, and there is a bus service from Schwanden to Elm in the Sernf valley. – Local culinary specialties are Schabzieger, a herb cheese, and Glarner Pasteten (fruit tarts).

HISTORY. – From 1288 Glarus was under Habsburg jurisdiction, and after repeated threats to its independence became the sixth canton to join the Confederation. Since 1387 the cantonal meeting (Landsgemeinde) has been held every year in the Zaunplatz in Glarus on the first Sunday in May. In 1388 the men of Glarus finally shook off the Habsburg yoke by their victory in the Battle of Näfels. During the Reformation the canton was divided into two half-cantons, one Protestant and the other Catholic, but the two halves were reunited under the 1836 constitution.

Up the Linth valley. – From the broad mouth of the valley at Ziegelbrücke (alt. 428 m (1404 feet)) the road runs S to Linthal (alt. 651 m (2136 feet): 28 km (17 miles)) and from there over the Klausen pass to Altdorf in the canton of Uri. – From *Niederurnen* (432 m (1417 feet): pop. 3500; Hotel Mineralbad) there is a footpath up the Rebberg to the Schlössli (Burg Oberwindegg), with fine views of the Linth plain and the Walensee. – Then on to *Oberurnen* (432 m – 1417 feet), with a view of the Glarus Alps.

Näfels (440 m (1444 feet): pop. 4000; Hotel Schwert), a little market town with a Baroque parish church (1781) is notable for the *Freulerpalast, the finest building in the canton. Built in 1642–47 by Colonel Kaspar Freuler, commander of the famous Swiss Guard in France (who was ennobled by Louis XIII), it has been occupied since 1942 by the Cantonal Museum and contains interesting collections. From here a steep road climbs to a charming little lake, the Obersee (989 m – 3245 feet). – Näfels shares a railway station with its twin town of *Mollis* (444 m (1457 feet): pop. 2800). In the Steinacker is the birthplace of the Glarus humanist Heinrich Loriti (1488–1563), who was crowned as poet laureate by the Emperor Maximilian. On the road up the Kerenzerberg are *Obstalden* and *Filzbach* (sports facility, with a public indoor swimming pool).

Netstal (453 m (1486 feet): pop. 2800) is a long straggling village surrounded by hillocks formed by landslides of the past, with some industry and a hydroelectric power station (50,000 kW) built in 1909. The Late Baroque village church (1811–13) is a statutorily protected ancient monument. From Netstal a road (postal bus in summer) and footpath cross the *Schwammhöhe* (superb views of the Glarus mountains) into the *Klöntal* (850 m – 2789 feet), one of the most beautiful and romantic of Alpine valleys, with the Klöntalersee and a series of tumultuous mountain streams. The lake was almost doubled in size by the construction of a dam. The road passes through *Rhodannenberg* (853 m (2799 feet): 5 km (3 miles), inn) and follows the lake, above the S side of which rear the rock walls of **Glärnisch** (with the peaks of *Vorderglärnisch*, 2331 m (7648 feet), *Vrenelisgärtli*, 2904 m (9528 feet), *Ruchen*, 2905 m (9531 feet), and *Bächistock*, 2920 m (9581 feet)), to *Vorauen* (853 m (2799 feet): inn) and the *Richisau* (1095 m – 3593 feet), an expanse of Alpine pasture at the beginning of the

bridle-path over the Pragel pass (1554 m – 5099 feet) to Muotathal (5 hours' walk). The Klöntal is a popular resort with climbers and hill-walkers (e.g. over the passes into the Sihl and Wägi valleys).

Glarus (481 m (1578 feet): pop. 6200; Hotel Glarnerhof, C, 50 b.), lying at the foot of Glärnisch (Vorderglärnisch, 2331 m (7648 feet)), is capital of the canton, rebuilt in 1861 on a regular grid plan after a devastating fire. The twin-towered Neo-Romanesque church (Protestant) was built in 1866; fine treasury. In the Town Hall is a relief model of the canton on a scale of 1:25,000. The Landsgemeinde (communal assembly) meets every year on the first Sunday in May in the Zaunplatz. In the courthouse are the cantonal archives and cantonal library, with a famous early map of Switzerland by Ägidius Tschudi (1570). The Kunsthaus in the Volksgarten contains a natural history collection and mounts special exhibitions.

Glarus, with Glärnisch in the background

Schwanden (528 m (1732 feet): pop. 2800) lies at the junction of the Sernf and the Linth. Turbine house of the Sernf-Niederenbach hydroelectric scheme. Starting-point of a walk into the Niederental, and from there by cableway to the *Mettmenalp* (mountain inn) and the artificial lake on the Garichte. Good climbing in the Karrenstock and Kärpf area (the oldest wildlife reserve in Switzerland, with numerous chamois, marmots and ibex).

From Schwanden an attractive detour can be made into the *Sernf valley* (also known as the Kleintal). The road runs via Engi and *Matt* (oldest church in Glarus, 1261) and comes in 15 km (9 miles) to *Elm* (977 m (3206 feet): pop. 800; Hotel Sardona, B, 110 b.; Elmer, D, 33 b.), in a quiet and secluded area which offers excellent walking.

The last settlement in the main valley is **Linthal** (653 m (2142 feet): pop. 1400; Hotel Bahnhof, D, 20 b.), with mighty mountains rearing above the little town – Selbsanft (3029 m – 9938 feet), above the artificial lakes supplying the Linth-Limmern hydroelectric scheme, with the Gries glacier; the Bifertenstock (3426 m – 11,241 feet), Clariden (3268 m – 10,722 feet) and Tödi (3614 m – 11,858 feet). *Tierfehd*, 5 km (3 miles) S, is a good base for walks and climbs in the Tödi group.

View of the Ortstock from Braunwald

From Linthal (parking garage) the Braun-waldbahn (length 1314 m (4311 feet), time 10 minutes) ascends to the only traffic-free mountain and holiday resort in eastern Switzerland, **Braunwald** (1256 m (4121 feet): pop. 500; Hotel Alpen-blick, C, 100 b.; Bellevue, C, 100 b., SB; Niederschlacht, C, 80 b., SB; Alpina, C, 65 b.; mountain chalets for groups), an ideal jumping-off point for walking and climbing. Experimental rhododendron nursery. Musical festival in July. Chair-lift to Gumen mountain inn (1900 m – 6234 feet).

Over the Klausen pass to Altdorf. – There is a magnificent drive over the *Klausen pass from Linthal to Altdorf in the canton of Uri (48 km – 30 miles). The road, built in 1893–99 on the line of an old bridle-path, has a maximum gradient of 8·5% (1 in 12) and is usually open from June to November. Before the Second World War an international car race was run over this road.

10 km (6 miles) from Linthal the road crosses the Scheidbächli, a stream which has marked the boundary between the cantons of Glarus and Uri since 1196, and comes to the *Urnerboden* (1313–1400 m (4308–4593 feet): Hotel Wilhelm Tell, C, 32 b.; Unterboden, C, 30 b.), a meadow-covered high valley some 7 km (4 miles) long through which flows the Fätsch-bach, following an almost level course for 4 km (2 miles). A series of ten well-engineered bends leads up to the *Vorfrut* (1812 m – 5945 feet), from which four further bends take the road to the **Klausen pass** (1948 m (6391 feet) chapel, kiosk), 23 km (14 miles) from Linthal. The road then runs down 1·5 km (1 mile) to the Klausenpasshöhe Hotel (1838 m – 6030 feet) and continues down the *Schächen valley*, with the 93 m (305 feet) high Stäubi falls. After passing through *Urigen* (1280 m – 4200 feet) it reaches *Unterschächen* (994 m – 3261 feet), at the mouth of the steep Brunn valley, with a view of the Grosse Wind-gälle (3192 m – 10,473 feet) and the Grosser Ruchen (3136 m – 10,289 feet). Between Spiringen and St Loreto is the *Kinzigpass inn* (640 m – 2100 feet), with the 16th c. Loreto chapel. From *Brügg* a cableway (3·2 km (2 miles) in two stages) runs up in 15 minutes to the Biel mountain inn (1634 m – 5361 feet), below the *Kinzig pass* (2076 m – 6811 feet), over which the Russian General Suvorov was compelled to retreat into the Muota valley in 1799 with 18,000 men, suffering heavy losses. – After passing through the village of *Bürglen* (p. 49) we arrive in **Altdorf** (p. 48).

Grindelwald

Canton: Berne (BE).
Altitude: 1050 m (3445 feet). – Population: 3500.
Post code: CH-3818. – Dialling code: 036.
(i) **Verkehrsbüro**,
    Grindelwald;
    tel. 53 12 12.

HOTELS. – *Grand Hotel Regina*, A, 180 b., SP, SB; *Belvédère*, B, 100 b.; SB; *Parkhotel Schoenegg*, B, 100 b., SB; *Schweizerhof*, B, 80 b., SB; *Silberhorn*, B, 60 b.; *Sunstar*, B, 235 b., SB; *Weisses Kreuz & Post*, B, 90 b., SB; *Adler* (annexe of Sunstar), C, 45 b., SB; *Alpina*, C, 60 b.; *Central Wolter*, C, 60 b.; *Crystal*, C, 35 b.; *Cabana* (no rest.), C, 32 b.; *Bel Air Eden*, D, 40 b.; *Gletschergarten*, D, 50 b.; *Blümlisalp*, E, 12 b. – Several CAMPING SITES.

RECREATION and SPORT. – Tennis, swimming, fishing, walking, climbing (guides' bureau); climbing school.

View towards the Wetterhorn

MOUNTAIN RAILWAYS, CABLEWAYS and LIFTS. – Wengernalpbahn and Jungfraubahn to **Jungfraujoch** (18 km (11 miles): see p. 147) via the *Kleine Scheidegg*. – Cableway (1046 m (3432 feet) long) to *Pfingstegg* (upper station 1387 m (4551 feet): restaurant). – Chair-lift (4354 m (14,285 feet) in four stages) via Oberhaus, Bort and Egg in 30 minutes to **First** (2168 m (7113 feet)), with magnificent views and excellent skiing country (ski-lifts) on the Grindelalp, on the slopes of the Widderfeldgrätli, the ridge between the Faulhorn and the Schwarzhorn. Cableway (6240 m (20,481 feet) long) to the Männlichen (2343 m (7690 feet)).

WINTER SPORTS. – Skiing at Grindelwald and on the First, Kleine Scheidegg and Lauberhorn; tobogganing; ice-rinks (indoor and outdoor); curling.

The "glacier village" of *Grindelwald**, one of the most popular health and winter sports resorts in the Bernese Oberland and a favourite base for climbers, straggles over a considerable expanse of Alpine meadows on the slopes of the Schwarze Lütschine valley. Three towering mountains enclose the valley on the S – the Eiger (3970 m – 13,026 feet), with its sheer N face, the most dangerous mountain wall in the whole of the Alps (first climbed in 1938 by Heckmair, Vörg, Kasparek and Harrer, taking four days), on which the lights in the windows of the Eigerwand station of the Jungfraubahn can be seen twinkling after dark; to the left of the Eiger the Mettenberg (3104 m – 10,184 feet), one of the subsidiary peaks of the Schreckhorn; and the Wetterhorn (3701 m – 12,143 feet), the most characteristic landmark of the Grindelwald valley. Between the three mountains are the two Grindelwald glaciers.

SIGHTS. – The Thalhaus, near the Protestant church, contains a *local museum*.

The best general view is to be had from the *Terrassenweg*, which branches off the road 20 minutes' walk above the church, just before the Mühlbach bridge, and runs along the mountainside above Alpine meadows and through patches of forest to the hamlet of *Duftbach* (30 minutes), from which it is a 20 minutes' walk down to Grindelwald.

SURROUNDINGS. – To the **Upper Glacier** (1½ hours): from the church take a road (closed to cars) to the turn-off of the road to the Grosse Scheidegg, and continue to the end of the glacier, which has recently been advancing again, with an artificial cave hewn from the ice. – To the **Lower Glacier** (1½–2 hours): from the church go down to the bridge over the Lütschine (990 m – 3248 feet), and from there either turn right and continue through the hamlet of *Mettenberg* to the entrance to the impressive *Lütschine gorge* (accessible through a gallery cut through the rock) and so to the end of the glacier; or turn left into a steep path leading up to the Lower Glacier or *Unteres Eismeer* (1650 m – 5413 feet), a large expanse of ice covered with rock debris. – Up the *Faulhorn* (2681 m – 8796 feet), one of the most renowned viewpoints in Switzerland, from which the giant peaks of the Bernese Oberland can be seen in all their magnificence: either by the chair-lift (30 minutes) to the First station and from there an hour's walk N to the *Bachsee* or *Bachalpsee* (2264 m – 7428 feet), or a 3½ hours' walk from Grindelwald to the Bachalpsee; then 1½ hours' climb to the summit (Berghotel, summer only). – A climb of 2½–3 hours up the slopes above the Checklibach leads to the *Grosse Scheidegg* (1961 m – 6434 feet).

Jungfrau: see p. 146.

A mountain lake on the Grosse Scheidegg

The Grisons in winter – the intermediate station of the cableway up Corvatsch (Engadine)

Grisons

Canton: Grisons (GR).
ⓘ **Verkehrsverein für Graubünden** (VVGR),
Hartbertstrasse 9,
CH-7001 Chur;
tel. (081) 22 13 60–61.

**The canton usually known in English
by its French name of** *Grisons
**(German Graubünden, Romansh
Grischun, Italian Grigioni), is a typical mountain region, with its valleys
lying at heights of between 900 and
2000 m (2953 and 6562 feet) and its
highest peak, Bernina, rising to 4049
m (13,285 feet). Two-thirds of its
boundaries lie along the frontiers of
Italy and Austria. Within the canton
are the sources of the Rhine (which
receives the water of three-fifths of
the rivers in the canton) and the Inn
(Romansh En); the rivers in the
south-facing valleys on the Italian
side drain into the Po.**

The climate of the Grisons reflects a
variety of influences. In the catchment
area of the Rhine a continental climate of
northern type predominates, while the
transverse valleys with a southern ex-
posure show Mediterranean characteristics. Magnolias, chestnuts and vines
flourish only a short distance away from
the perpetual snow and ice.

Grisons, the largest canton in Switzerland, owes its name to the Upper or Grey
League (Ligue Grise, Grauer Bund)
formed by the peasants of the region in
1395, like the League of the House of God
and the League of the Ten Jurisdictions,
to defend their interests against the
Habsburgs.

HISTORY. – In 15 B.C. the Romans subjugated the
Rhaetians and began to colonise the region, building
roads over the Alpine passes which have not greatly
altered their course since then. In 536 the Grisons fell
under Frankish rule and, as Chur-Rhaetia, became
part of the Duchy of Swabia. Later the people of the
Grisons formed the three leagues mentioned above,
which at the end of the 15th c. made common cause
with the Swiss Confederation. The Reformation was
adopted by only part of the region. During the Thirty

The Rhätische Bahn at the Bernina pass

Years War it was plunged into bitter internal strife by the conflict between the supporters of France, led by the Salis family, and of the Habsburgs, led by the Planta family. In the 17th c. Jürg Jenatsch freed the Grisons from foreign influence, but the region was not brought together in a single canton until the 19th c. Of the present population of the Grisons 54% speak German, 31% Romansh and 15% Italian.

From very early times the Alpine passes played a vital role in the life of the Grisons. The road over the Septimer pass (Pass da Sett), built in the 14th c., is believed to have been one of the first Alpine roads usable by vehicles. During the 19th c. ten pass roads were built, of which the Julier (Passo dal Guglia), Flüela, Splügen (Passo dello Spluga) and Maloja passes, among others, are still of major importance. The opening of the San Bernardino tunnel in 1967 made available a N–S route open all year round.

The *Rhätische Bahn* (RhB), run by the canton of Grisons, is a narrow-gauge railway system with a total length of 400 km (249 miles). The 6 km (4 miles) long Albula tunnel is the highest railway tunnel in the Alps (1883 m – 6178 feet).

Gruyère

Canton: Fribourg (FR).

ⓘ **Centre Touristique Gruyères-Moléson-Vudalla,**
CH-1661 Pringy;
tel. (029) 6 10 36.

The district of Gruyère (German Greyerzer Land), in the southern half of the canton of Fribourg, is a gently rolling Pre-Alpine region mainly devoted to intensive stock-farming and renowned as the home of Gruyère cheese. Its beautiful scenery, numerous remains of the past and vigorous folk traditions make it an attractive tourist region.

27 km (17 miles) S of Fribourg, on the left bank of the Trême, is **Bulle** (alt. 769 m (2523 feet): pop. 7700; Hôtel Le Rallye, C, 48 b.; Hôtel des Alpes et Terminus, D, 60 b.; Tonnelier, D, 35 b.), chief town and commercial and cultural heart of the Gruyère district, and one of the most important traffic junctions in the canton of Fribourg. From 1196 to 1537 this small market town belonged to the bishops of Lausanne, who built a massive castle here in the 13th c. The town was rebuilt after

fires in 1447 and 1805. It has preserved a number of fine old buildings – the parish church (Protestant), rebuilt in Neo-classical style in 1751, the Capuchin friary and the Town Hall. In the castle is the Musée Gruyérien, with a fine collection of local material; associated with it are the Tissot Collection (works by Corot, Courbet, Poussin, etc.) and a public library (closed Mondays). In the public park is a monument to Abbé Bovet (1879–1952), a composer of lieder. – From Bulle there are roads over the Jaun pass into the Simmental and through the Sarine valley to Château-d'Oex.

Gruyères

6 km (4 miles) SE of Bulle, on a green ridge of hills, is **Gruyères** (alt. 801 m (2628 feet): pop. 1200; Hostellerie St-Georges, C, 34 b.; Hostellerie des Chevaliers, C, 70 b.; Restaurant Le Chalet, Alpine dairy; Les Remparts, cheese dishes; La Halle, fondues). Finely situated and still surrounded by its ancient walls, the town has largely preserved its old-world aspect. From 923 it was the capital of a county which was ruled by a succession of 19 counts; then in 1555 Fribourg and Berne divided the territory between them, and the castle (1493) became the residence of the governors until its acquisition by the Bovy family of Geneva in 1848. Since 1938 the castle has belonged to the canton of Fribourg, and now houses a museum (exhibits of particular interest being three mourning robes belonging to knights of the Golden Fleece, dating from the Burgundian wars). The town lies just off the main road from Bulle to Château-d'Oex but is closed to motor vehicles (car parks outside the town walls). The houses in the main street

are statutorily protected as ancient monuments. At the entrance to the town is a Wax Museum (Musée de Cire: figures from Swiss history).

The commune of Gruyères also includes the villages of *Epagny* (712 m – 2336 feet) and *Pringy* (746 m – 2448 feet). Adjoining the railway station is a famous *model cheese-dairy* making Gruyère cheese (open daily 6 a.m. to 6 p.m.; manufacture of cheese 9–11.30 and 1–3.30).

4 km (2 miles) SW of Pringy is **Le Moléson**, a rounded hill in the midst of the Gruyère district which has become a popular walking and skiing area. From the holiday complex of *Moléson-Village* (1110 m (3642 feet): Hôtel Plan Francey; Pierre à Catillon; camping site) a cableway runs up in two stages to the summit of Le Moléson (2002 m (6569 feet): restaurant), another to *La Vudalla* (1520 m – 4987 feet). From Le Moléson there are far-ranging views, extending from Mont Blanc to Titlis; good walking and climbing.

Between Bulle and Gruyères is the little industrial town of *Broc* (719 m (2359 feet): pop. 1870), with a chocolate factory established by F. L. Cailler in 1898 (conducted tours). Broc lies at the S end of the beautiful *Lac de la Gruyère* (alt. 677 m (222 feet): area 9·6 sq. km (4 sq. miles), greatest depth 75 m (246 feet), capacity 180 million cu. m (6356 million cu. feet)), formed by a dam on the Sarine (Saane).

Gstaad

Canton: Berne (BE).
Altitude: 1050 m (3445 feet). – Population: 2500
Post code: CH-3780. – Dialling code: 030.
ⓘ **Offizielles Verkehrsbüro,**
    Gstaad;
    tel. 4 10 55.

HOTELS. – *Gstaad Palace*, A, 210 b.; SP, SB; *Grand Hotel Bellevue*, B, 85 b.; *Parkhotel Reuteler*, B, 90 b.; SP; *Grand Hotel Alpina*, B, 70 b.; SP; *Arcen-Ciel* (no rest.), B, 20 b.; *Alphorn*, C, 30 b.; SB; *Bernerhof*, C, 90 b.; *National-Rialto*, C, 50 b.; *Posthotel Rössli*, C, 40 b.; *Victoria*, C, 40 b.

EVENTS. – *International Tennis Championship* (July); *Yehudi Menuhin Festival* (August); *International Ski-Jumping Week* (January–February).

Gstaad in summer

RECREATION and SPORT. – Alpine golf, tennis, riding, fishing, clay pigeon shooting, glacier and air-taxi flights, indoor swimming pool, ice-rinks, curling, hill-walking and climbing.

CABLEWAYS. – To *Wasserngrat* (2000 m (6562 feet): length 2585 m (8481 feet), height difference 826 m (2710 feet), time 20 minutes), *Eggli* (1580 m (5184 feet): length 1451 m (4761 feet), height difference 514 m (1686 feet), time 10 minutes) and *Hohe Windspillen* (Höhi Wispile, 1940 m (6365 feet): length 3039 m (9971 feet), height difference 865 m (2838 feet), time 20 minutes). In winter there are helicopter services to the most popular skiing areas in the Bernese Oberland.

The summer and winter resort of *Gstaad in the high valley of the Saane, in the western part of the Bernese Oberland, has for many years enjoyed an international reputation, while still preserving its character as a village of holiday chalets. It is a paradise for walkers and climbers, with cableways providing easy access to the mountains.

The Montreux–Oberland railway (built 1910–11) and the adjacent pass roads make Gstaad easily accessible from both German-speaking and French-speaking Switzerland. – Interesting *St Nicholas's chapel.* In the churchyard is the grave of Count R. Coudenhove-Kalergi (1894–1972), first President of the Pan-European Union.

SURROUNDINGS. – 7 km (4 miles) SE is **Lauenen** (1259 m – 4131 feet), a beautifully situated health resort with a Late Gothic church (1520). An hour's walk S is the *Lauenensee* (1379 m – 4524 feet). – The road to the Col du Pillon leads to the resort of **Gsteig** (1192 m (3911 feet): pop. 870), in the uppermost part of the Saane valley, which has preserved the character of an Alpine farming village. – The road continues over the *Col du Pillon* (1546 m – 5072 feet) to Aigle in the Rhône valley.

3 km (2 miles) NW of Gstaad is **Saanen** (1033 m (3389 feet); *Steigenberger Hotel Sonnenhalde, A, 230 b.; SB, sauna; Hotel Cabana (no rest.), B, 55 b., SP, SB; Saanerhof, C, 45 b.; Boo (no rest.), C, 32 b.; camping site), chief place in the Upper Saane valley, a climatic and winter sports resort (ski-lifts) surrounded by many isolated farms. Church (rebuilt in 15th c.) with a handsome tower and 15th c. wall-paintings in the choir. A prosperous stock-farming and dairy-farming area, notable for its cheese (Saanen, a grating cheese). To the N of the town rises the *Hugeligrat* (1902 m (6240 feet): 3 hours), from which there are superb views. – From Saanen it is possible to continue to Lausanne, by either the Col des Mosses or the Col du Pillon.

Ilanz

Canton: Grisons (GR).
Altitude: 702 m (2303 feet). – Population: 1800.
Post code: CH-7130. – Dialling code: 086.

ⓘ **Verkehrsbüro,**
Ilanz;
tel. 2 24 14.

HOTELS. – *Oberalp & Post*, C, 50 b.; *Casutt*, C, 25 b.

Ilanz (Romansh *Glion*), the "first town on the Rhine", situated in the valley of the Vorderrhein, is the market town of the surrounding district of Surselva.

HISTORY. – The place first appears in the records in 765, when the first church of St Martin was built. In 1395 it became the nucleus of the "Grey League" formed by the Abbot of Disentis together with the local feudal lords and peasants. The people of the Grisons were granted freedom of religious belief following a conference held in St Margaret's church in 1526.

SIGHTS. – Ilanz is a picturesque little town of winding streets with one or two buildings recalling its past greatness. The Late Gothic **parish church of St Margaret** (Protestant) has fine ceiling paintings, Gothic scrollwork and a Rococo organ-loft. There are a number of Baroque mansions, including the *Casa Gronda* (1677), in which the Russian General Suvorov once stayed.

SURROUNDINGS. – A road runs W, climbing steeply up the northern slopes of Piz Mundaun (2067 m – 6782 feet), to *Flond* (1075 m (3527 feet): toboggan run to Ilanz) and *Meierhof* (1302 m – 4272 feet), the principal village in the extensive commune of **Obersaxen**, a German-speaking enclave (skiing).

Through the Lugnez valley to Vrin (22 km (14 miles) SW). – Leave Ilanz on a narrow road which goes through the Obertor and ascends the western slopes of the beautiful *Lugnez valley* (Romansh *Lumnezia*), through which flows the River *Glenner*. The road with a moderate gradient, passes St Martin's church. Below, to the left, can be seen the ruined castle of Castelberg; then, beyond the *Frauentor* defile

(formerly fortified), the St Moritzkapelle (St Maurice's chapel, 1068 m (3504 feet)). – 6 km (4 miles) above Ilanz a road goes off on the left to Peidenbad and the Vals valley. Beyond this point the main road climbs steeply. – 1·5 km (1 mile): *Cumbels* (1145 m – 3757 feet), a large village below the S side of Piz Mundaun. The church has 17th c. sgraffito painting. – 2·5 km (2 miles): **Villa** (1244 m – 4082 feet), with handsome 17th–18th c. houses and a Gothic church (16th c.: frescoes). *Pleif*, below the road on the left, has a church founded in the Carolingian period but much altered in later centuries. Opposite is the mouth of the Vals valley. – The road continues along the side of the Lugnez valley. Below, to the left, is the village of *Igels*, with two Late Gothic churches. – 6 km (4 miles): *Lumbrein* (1410 m – 4626 feet). – After a bend at the mouth of the *Val Miedra* (on right) the road enters the *Vrin valley*, the highest section of the Lugnez valley. – 6 km (4 miles): **Vrin** (1454 m – 4771 feet), a village with a Baroque parish church of 1675, a quiet summer holiday place and a good base from which to climb the numerous neighbouring peaks.

Bad Vals (Grisons)

Ilanz to Bad Vals (21 km – 13 miles). – The road follows the left bank of the Glenner below the road to Vrin. At the ruined 13th c. castle of *Castelberg* it crosses to the right bank and continues through two gorges, the *Rieiner Tobel* (road tunnel) and the *Pitascher Tobel*. – 8 km (5 miles): **Peidenbad** (820 m – 2690 feet), in a wooded setting (chalybeate spring). Above, to the right, is the village of *Peiden*. – 2 km (1 mile): *Uors-Lumnezia* (German *Furth*), where the road enters the beautiful **Vals valley**. To the right, on the mountain spur between the two valleys, is the picturesquely situated little village of *Surcasti* (German *Oberkastels*). – 4 km (2 miles): *St Martin* (1000 m – 3281 feet). The road now traverses a magnificent rocky*gorge, with the river surging and foaming over waterfalls far below; then through the villages of *Lunschania* (1200 m – 3937 feet) and *Bucarischuna* (1170 m – 3839 feet), along another defile and over the Valser Rhein on the *Hohe Brücke* (High Bridge). – 7 km (4 miles): **Bad Vals** (1248 m (4095 feet): pop. 1000; Therme Bad Vals and Häuser Zervreila/Tomül, 300 b.), a little spa which is also frequented by holidaymakers, climbers and winter sports enthusiasts (cross-country skiing). "Stella Maris" spa establishment (spring containing calcium sulphate, 28 °C (82 °F); treatment facility, open-air thermal pool with artificial waves, indoor swimming pool). Church of

1669. The surrounding area has much of geological, botanical and entomological interest (butterflies) to offer. *Piz Tomül* (Weissensteinhorn, 2950 m (9679 feet)) can be climbed in 4½ hours: panoramic *views. – From Bad Vals the road ascends up the right bank of the valley for another 7·5 km (5 miles), passing through a number of tunnels, to the artificial lake of *Zervreila* (1862 m – 6109 feet), beneath the towering bulk of the *Zervreiler Horn* (2900 m – 9515 feet).

Interlaken

Canton: Berne (BE).
Altitude: 568 m (1864 feet). – Population: 13,000.
Post code: CH-3800. – Dialling code: 036.

ⓘ **Verkehrsverein,**
Höheweg 37;
tel. 22 21 21.

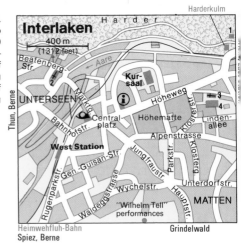

Interlaken
400 m
(1312 feet)

1 Alpine Wildlife Park
2 Protestant church
3 Catholic church
4 Augustinian convent

HOTELS. – ON HÖHEWEG: *Grand Hotel Victoria-Jungfrau*, A, 360 b., SB; *Métropole*, B, 225 b., SB; *Grand Hotel Beau Rivage*, B, 170 b., SB; *Royal-St Georges*, B, 150 b.; *Belvédère*, B, 100 b.; *Du Lac*, B, 80 b.; *Carlton*, C, 80 b.; *Oberland*, C, 100 b.; *Du Nord*, C, 100 b.; *Interlaken*, C, 100 b.; *Weisses Kreuz*, C, 100 b.; *Europe* (no rest.), C, 65 b.; *Hirschen*, D, 32 b.

S OF HÖHEWEG: *National*, B, 70 b.; *Savoy*, D, 80 b.; *Blume* (no rest.), D, 20 b.

N OF HÖHEWEG: *Horn*, C, 80 b.; *Harder-Minerva*, D, 40 b.

IN MARKTGASSE: *Bellevue Garden-Hotel*, B, 100 b.; *Löwen*, E, 35 b.

NEAR THE STATION: *Krebs*, B, 80 b.; *Bernerhof*, C, 65 b.; *Merkur*, C, 60 b.; *Eurotel* (no rest.), C, 75 b.; *Gotthard* (no rest.), D, 20 b.; *De la Paix*, D, 40 b.; *Touriste* (no rest.), E, 28 b.

IN UNTERSEEN: *Goldey*, C, 65 b.; *Beau-Site*, C, 80 b.; *Central*, C, 70 b.; *Chalet Swiss* (no rest.), C, 50 b.; *Hardermannli*, D, 35 b.; *Rössli*, D, 27 b.

IN MATTEN: *Regina*, C, 150 b.; *Sonne*, D, 35 b.; *Alpina*, D, 60 b.

ON ROAD TO LAUTERBRUNNEN: *Park-Hotel Mattenhof*, C, 150 b., SP.

MOTELS. – *Marti Motel*, on road to Brienz, 50 b.; *Strandhotel Golf Motel*, on N side of Lake Thun, 100 b., SP.

YOUTH HOSTEL in Bönigen. – CAMPING SITES at Tiefenau, Neuhaus and Unterseen.

EVENTS. – *Open-air performances of Schiller's "Wilhelm Tell"* (June–September); *Interlaken Musical Festival* (June–August); folk evenings in Kursaal (June–September); evening cruises on Lake Thun and Lake Brienz (July–August).

RECREATION and SPORT. – Bathing beach on right bank of Aare (opposite Kursaal), indoor swimming pool, golf-course at Unterseen, cruises on the lakes, sailing, wind-surfing, riding, tennis, clay pigeon shooting, archery. – Regional Tourist Museum, Unterseen. – Kursaal.

*Interlaken, reached by way of the Berne motorway or the Brünig, Susten or Grimsel/Furka passes, lies between Lakes Thun and Brienz below the N side of the Jungfrau massif and offers an endless variety of walks, climbs and other excursions, particularly in the mountains of the Bernese Oberland, brought within reach by numerous mountain railways, cableways, etc. It is one of the oldest, best known and most popular summer holiday resorts in Switzerland, outstandingly well equipped to cater for the needs of visitors.**

Between the two lakes is an expanse of some 35 sq. km (14 sq. miles) of alluvial soil, deposited over many millennia by mountain streams from the Bernese Oberland such as the Lütschine and the Lombach. On this green and level area, known as the Bödeli, live the 20,000

Interlaken

inhabitants of the separate communes of Interlaken, Bönigen, Matten, Unterseen and Wilderswil.

HISTORY. – The fertile alluvial soil of the Bödeli was probably settled at an early stage by Celtic tribes. Later the main settlers were Alemanni, driven from their homeland by Burgundian incomers. A major influence on the economic and cultural development of the area was the Augustinian house founded here (*inter lacus*) in 1133, joined in 1257 by a nunnery. The monks were pioneers of urban development and soon became the largest landowners in the Bernese Oberland. After Berne's adoption of the Reformed faith in 1528 the monastery was dissolved (and is now occupied by district administrative offices). The first visitors began to come here in the 17th c., and as transport facilities improved – with the coming of the railway, boat services on the lakes and most recently the motorway – Interlaken became the great tourist attraction of the Bernese Oberland. Among the great attractions of the area were its local folk traditions and art. In 1805 and 1808 the peasant stock-farmers of the Alpine pasturelands celebrated their first great pastoral festivals at Unspunnen, near Interlaken; and at this time, too, the painter Franz Niklaus König was living in Schloss Unterseen and painting the pictures of mountains which became so widely popular.

SIGHTS. – The *Höhematte* in the midst of the town is a remarkable example of farseeing town-planning. The area of 14 hectares (35 acres) which had belonged to the Augustinian convent was acquired in 1860 by a group of 37 hotel-owners and private persons and left as an open space, with the **Höheweg**, a splendid avenue running between the E and W stations and affording a magnificent *view of the Jungfrau, surrounded by hotels and flower-beds. Here too is the *Kursaal*, with a theatre, a café, a gaming room and beautiful gardens (flower clock). At the E end is the former *Augustinian convent* (1133–1528: inner courtyard with cloister, restored), with a Late Gothic church (stained glass of 1950) and the adjoining Schloss added in 1750 (now housing cantonal offices).

The *Marktgasse* runs NW from the post office over the Spielmatten islands to the little town of *Unterseen* (569 m (1867 feet): pop. 4700), at the foot of Mt Harder, tourist museum. In the old part of the town stands the parish church, with a Late Gothic tower (1471). – On the SE side of Interlaken is *Matten*, with its old timber houses.

SURROUNDINGS. – Interlaken is an ideal base for day or half-day excursions in the surrounding area. A beginning can be made with the town's "own" hills, Harder and Heimwehfluh. – Beyond the bridge over the Aare on the road to Brienz is the *Harder Alpine Wildlife Park* (Alpenwildpark: marmots, ibexes), is a funicular (length 1447 m (4748 feet), height

difference 725 m (2379 feet), maximum gradient 64% (1 in 1½), time 8 minutes) up *Harder (upper station 1322 m (4337 feet)), with the *Harderkulm* restaurant (1325 m (4347 feet): magnificent views of the Jungfrau area and the lakes). The return can be made by forest paths, via the *Hardermannli* outlook pavilion (1116 m – 3662 feet) and the *Hohbühl* pavilion (memorial to the composers Mendelssohn, Wagner and Weber). – From the S end of Rugenparkstrasse another funicular (length 167 m (548 feet), height difference 120 m (394 feet), time 3 minutes) runs up to the *Heimwehfluh (676 m (2218 feet): café-restaurant; outlook tower; model railway layout), the NW buttress of the *Grosser Rugen* (800 m – 2625 feet).

Another popular trip from Interlaken is to the *Schynige Platte (2101 m (6893 feet): Hotel Kulm, 40 b.), reached from Wilderswil, 3 km (2 miles S of the town, on a rack-railway (cog-railway) opened in 1893 (7 km (4 miles), 50 minutes). From the top there is one of the finest panoramic views of the Alps. Alpine garden with 500 species of flowers.

3 km (2 miles) S of Interlaken is the little holiday town of **Wilderswil** (587 m (1926 feet): Hotel Bären, C, 80 b.; Jungfrau, C, 70 b.; Alpenrose, D, 70 b.; Berghof, D, 60 b.; etc.). NW of the town is the ruined castle of *Unspunnen*, with the Unspunnenwiese, a meadow on which herdsmen's festivals were held at the beginning of the 19th c. – From Wilderswil a road runs 6 km (4 miles) up the Saxeten valley to *Saxeten* (1100 m – 3609 feet), a picturesquely situated mountain village from which *Sulegg* (2412 m (7914 feet)) can be climbed (about 4½ hours).

From the Höheweg a road goes E to reach the S shore of Lake Brienz at **Bönigen** (569 m (1867 feet): pop. 1900; Hotel Seiler au Lac, C, 70 b.; Seehotel, C, 50 b.; Schlössli, C, 60 b., SP; youth hostel near swimming pool). The old part of the town has richly carved timber houses of the 15th to 18th c. The modern resort is well equipped with facilities for the entertainment of visitors. – High above the S side of the lake is the village of *Iseltwald* (567 m (1860 feet): pop. 490; Hotel Bellevue, C, 26 b.; Bernahof, D, 20 b.; Kreuz, C, 20 b.; camping site on lake), on a quiet little peninsula with no through road.

Interlaken to Beatenberg (11 km (7 miles): funicular from Beatenbucht). – From Interlaken station take the Thun road, which crosses the Aare into *Unterseen*, where the road to Thun bears left: continue straight ahead up the Scheidgasse. 2 km (1 mile) from Interlaken is a road junction, with a road on the right which runs up the *Lombach* valley to the prettily situated village of *Habkern* (6·3 km (4 miles), 1067 m (3501 feet): Sporthotel, D, 40 b.). The road to Beatenberg, to the left, begins to climb through wooded country (attractive view of Interlaken to left) and then takes two sharp bends up the hillside. – 3·5 km (2 miles): *Lueglibrückli* restaurant (938 m (3078 feet): car park; with superb *views. – The road continues uphill on a moderate gradient (views of Lake Thun and the mountains to the left) and then takes another two sharp bends. Farther on it passes a number of children's homes under *Amisbühl* (1336 m (4383 feet): *views) and then descends into the *Sundgraben*. – 5·5 km (3 miles): **Beatenberg** (1150 m (3773 feet): Hotel Kurhaus Silberhorn, C, 45 b.; Beau-Regard, D, 30 b.; Oberland, D, 45 b., SB), a popular health and winter sports resort which spreads out along a sunny sheltered terrace high above the N side of Lake Thun, with magnificent views of the

Bernese Alps, from the Schreckhorn to the Niesen. – From the Oberland Hotel (parking garage) a chair-lift runs up in 18 minutes to the *Niederhorn (1957 m – 6421 feet), on the Güggisgrat ridge, with still more extensive views. – At the W end of the town is a funicular (1706 m (5597 feet), gradient 35–40%, 10 minutes) to *Beatenbucht* (p. 241).

Goldswil and *Ringgenberg*: see p. 243.

Jungfrau

Cantons: Berne (BE) and Valais (VS).
(i) **Verkehrsverband Berner Oberland** (VBO), Jungfraustrasse 36, CH-3800 Interlaken; tel. (036) 22 26 21.

HOTELS.–IN WENGEN: *Parkhotel Beausite*, A, 126 b., SB; *Metropole*, B, 168 b., SB; *Victoria-Lauberhorn*, B, 120 b., SB; *Regina*, B, 150 b.; *Berghaus*, B, 30 b.; *Waldrand*, B, 70 b.; *Alpenrose*, C, 90 b.; *Bellevue*, C, 70 b.; *Belvédère*, C, 90 b.; *Brunner*, C, 70 b.; *Eiger*, C, 68 b.; *Falken*, C, 80 b.; *Jungfraublick*, C, 65 b.; *Schönegg*, C, 50 b.; *Silberhorn*, C, 90 b.; *Résidence*, C, 45 b.; *Alpenruhe Kulm*, D, 45 b.; *Bernerhof*, D, 40 b.; *Bristol*, D, 60 b.

RECREATION and SPORT. – In WENGEN: heated open-air swimming pool, indoor pool, tennis, natural and artificial ice-rinks, toboggan run, curling rink, skittle alley, skiing; Valley Museum.

The **Jungfrau massif, with its group of three famous peaks, the Jungfrau (4158 m – 13,642 feet), the Mönch (4099 m – 13,449 feet) and the Eiger (3970 m – 13,026 feet), has long had a powerful grip on men's imaginations. Originally difficult of access, this mighty range of mountains in the heart of the Bernese Oberland has now been brought within easy reach and attracts large numbers of visitors every year.**

The Meyer brothers of Aarau first set foot on the summit of the Jungfrau in 1811; and a hundred years later, in 1912, the rack-railway to the Jungfraujoch was opened. The upper station (3454 m – 11,333 feet) is the highest railway station in Europe.

Mountain railways and cableways. – The area of most interest to visitors extends N from the 4000 m (13,124 feet) peaks of the Bernese Oberland towards Lakes Thun and Brienz (see p. 240).

A railway line connecting the two lakes was opened between Därligen and Bönigen in 1874 (the first steamer on Lake Thun having gone into service nearly 40 years earlier, in 1836). This was followed in 1888 by the Brünigbahn between Lucerne and Interlaken, in 1893 by the Thuner-See-Bahn (Lake Thun railway) and in 1913 by the Lötschberg railway, which provided a link with Italy. The first mountain railways in the Jungfrau area had been built some years previously.

The Jungfrau mountain railways, all under the same management, now have a total length of more than 70 km (43 miles) (all electric), with gauges of either 100 or 80 cm (39 or 31 inches).

Berner-Oberland-Bahnen (BOB)
Opened 1890; from Interlaken Ost (East Station) to Lauterbrunnen (796 m – 2612 feet) and from

Panorama of the Jungfrau area

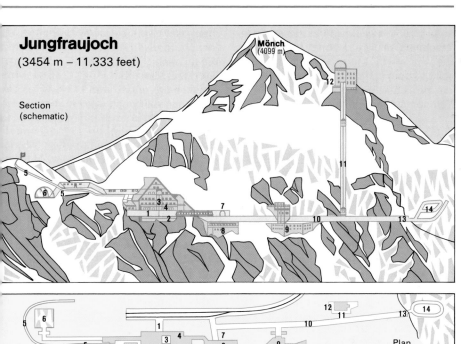

Jungfraujoch
(3454 m – 11,333 feet)

Section
(schematic)

Mönch
(4099 m)

Plan

1 Jungfraujoch station	6 Ice Palace	11 Sphinx elevator
2 Berghaus Hotel	7 Entrance to Sphinx tunnel	12 Sphinx lookout terrace (3573 m –
3 Lift to fourth floor	8 Tourist House	11,723 feet)
4 Restaurant	9 Research station	13 Exit from Sphinx tunnel
5 Road to plateau	10 Sphinx tunnel	14 Ski school and huskies

Interlaken Ost to Grindelwald (1034 m – 3393 feet). Total length 23·5 km (15 miles); gauge 100 cm (39 inches); gradients up to 12% (1 in 8) (partly normal railway line, partly rack-railway).

Schynige-Platte-Bahn
Opened 1893 (associated with the Berner-Oberland-Bahnen since 1895); from Wilderswil (584 m – 1916 feet) to the Schynige Platte (1967 m – 6454 feet). Length 7·3 km (5 miles); gauge 80 cm (31 inches); gradients up to 25% (1 in 4) (rack-railway).

Bergbahn Lauterbrunnen-Mürren (BLM)
Opened 1891; from Lauterbrunnen (796 m – 2612 feet) to the Grütschalp (1487 m – 4879 feet), cableway; Grütschalp-Mürren (1650 m – 5414 feet), railway. Total length 5·7 km (4 miles); gauge 100 cm (39 inches); gradients up to 61% (1 in 1·6) (cableway).

Seilbahn Mürren-Allmendhubel (SMA)
Cable railway opened 1912; from Mürren (1650 m – 5414 feet) to the Allmendhubel (1912 m – 6273 feet). Length 536 m (1759 feet); gauge 100 cm (39 inches); gradients up to 61% (1 in 1·6).

Wengernalpbahn (WAB)
Opened 1893; from Lauterbrunnen (796 m – 2612 feet) to Wengen (1274 m – 4180 feet), the Wengernalp (1873 m – 6145 feet) and the Kleine Scheidegg (2061 m – 6762 feet), and from Grindelwald (1034 m – 3393 feet) to the Kleine Scheidegg (2061 m – 6762 feet). Total length 10 km (6 miles) (the longest single stretch of rack-railway line in Switzerland); gauge 80 cm (31 inches); gradients up to 25% (1 in 4).

Jungfraubahn (JB)
First section, from the Kleine Scheidegg (2061 m –

6762 feet) to the Eiger glacier (2320 m – 7612 feet), opened in 1898; from the Eiger glacier (2320 m – 7612 feet) to the Eigerwand (2865 m – 9400 feet) in 1903; from the Eigerwand (2865 m – 9400 feet) to the Eismeer (3160 m – 10,368 feet) in 1905; and from the Eismeer (3160 m – 10,368 feet) to the Jungfraujoch (3454 m – 11,333 feet) in 1912. Total length 9·3 km (6 miles); gauge 100 cm (39 inches); gradients up to 25%. Tunnel 7·1 km (4 miles) long from the Eiger glacier to the Jungfraujoch. Rack-railway (cog-railway).

Drahtseilbahn Interlaken-Harder (HB)
Cable railway, opened 1908; from Interlaken (567 m – 1860 feet) to the Harderkulm (1322 m – 4337 feet). Length 1·4 km (1 mile); gauge 100 cm (39 inches); gradients up to 64% (1 in 1½).

The best starting-point for a trip into the Jungfrau area is the East station in Interlaken (Interlaken Ost). It is possible to go by car to Grindelwald and Lauterbrunnen. The round trip from Interlaken to the Jungfraujoch and back (either via Lauterbrunnen and Wengen or via Grindelwald) takes between 4½ and 5 hours. It is important to choose a day with favourable weather conditions, to be stoutly shod and to take sun-glasses.

Information from *Bahnen der Jungfrau-Region* (Jungfrau Railways), CH-3800 Interlaken, tel. (036) 22 52 52.

To the Jungfraujoch. – There are two routes from Interlaken to the Kleine Scheidegg, either via Lauterbrunnen or via Grindelwald: the best plan is to go one way and come back the other. The line to both places is the same as far as Zwei-lütschinen, at the junction of two streams, the Schwarze Lütischine (Black Lütischine) coming from Grindelwald and the Weisse Lütischine (White Lütischine) from the Lauterbrunnen valley.

The rail journey from Interlaken Ost to Grindelwald takes 40 minutes, from Grindelwald to the Kleine Scheidegg 35 minutes. The line runs below the dreaded N face of the Eiger, the most dangerous rock wall in the Alps, which claimed many deaths before it was finally climbed in 1938 by an Austrian team of four men (Vörg, Heckmayr, Harrer and Kasparek), who took four days for the ascent. The summit has already been reached by an Englishman, Christopher Berrington, in 1858, following a different route. – The journey from Interlaken Ost to Lauterbrunnen takes 25 minutes, from Lauterbrunnen to the Kleine Scheidegg 42 minutes. There are parking facilities in Lauterbrunnen. The Wengernalpbahn runs up in 14 minutes to Wengen, on a sunny terrace, sheltered from the wind, high above the Lauterbrunnen valley (4 km – 2 miles).

Wengen

Wengen (1275 m (4183 feet): pop. 1350), beautifully situated at the foot of the Eiger, Mönch and Jungfrau, is an ideal base for walks and climbs in the mountain world of the Bernese Oberland. There is a cableway up *Männlichen* (2343 m – 7687 feet), and numerous attractive footpaths. Particularly rewarding is the climb to the *Wengernalp*, either direct (1¾ hours) or by way of the *Mettlenalp* (1700 m (5578 feet): immediately opposite the Jungfrau; 3 hours).

From Wengen the railway continues up for another 4 km (2 miles) to the *Wengernalp* (1873 m (6145 feet): Hotel Jungfrau, November–April, C, 45 b.), from which there are splendid views of the Trümleten valley and the Jungfrau. There is a chair-lift from Wengernalp Wixi to the *Lauberhornschulter* (2310 m – 7579 feet). – 11 km (7 miles) farther on is the **Kleine Scheidegg** (2064 m (6772 feet): Scheidegg Hotels, open December–September, 120 b.), the terminus of the rack (cog)-railways from Lauterbrunnen and Grindelwald and the starting-point of the Jungfraubahn, with tremendous views of the nearby 4000 m (13,124 feet) peaks of the Eiger, Mönch and Jungfrau. Magnificent walks; splendid skiing country (Arven, Honegg and Lauberhorn ski-lifts). Sightseeing flights over the glaciers from Männlichen.

The ****Jungfraubahn**, built 1896–1912, runs up through Alpine meadows and an 87 m (285 feet) long tunnel and comes in 2 km (1 mile) to the *Eigergletscher* (Eiger Glacier) station (2320 m (7612 feet): inn, 10 b.), in magnificently wild scenery (husky-dog kennels), and then enters the long tunnel (7·1 km – 4 miles) which leads up towards the Jungfraujoch. – 4·4 km (3 miles): *Eigerwand* station (2865 m – 9400 feet), with a magnificent view of Grindelwald, 1800 m (5906 feet) below. From here the line runs under the Eiger. – 5·7 km (4 miles): *Eismeer* (Sea of Ice, 3160 m (10,368 feet)), on the S face of the Eiger, 40 m (131 feet) above the Upper Grindelwald-Fiescher Firn (*névé*, or frozen snow), with *views over the much-crevassed surface of the glacier towards the Wetterhorn, the Schreckhorn, the Fiescherhörner and the great crevasse under the Mönchsjoch. – After a journey of 50 minutes and 9·3 km (6 miles) the rack-railway reaches the ****Jungfraujoch** (3454 m – 11,333 feet), the highest railway station in Europe, which together with the accommodation for visitors, the research stations, the underground passages and the elevators forms a little subterranean town of its own. – An outer lobby (post office, shops, restaurants, outlook gallery) leads into the Ice Palace (Eispalast), a cavern hewn out of the glacier, with ice sculpture. From the Sphinx Tunnel an elevator (112 m (367 feet)) ascends to the summit of the *Sphinx* (3573 m – 11,273 feet), with an outlook terrace, a research institute and a weather station. There is also an exit from the tunnel giving access to a summer ski school; here, too, visitors can have a sleigh ride, pulled by husky dogs. – The *views from the Jungfraujoch itself, the saddle of firn (névé) between the Mönch and the Jungfrau, are breathtaking. To the S can be seen the Aletsch glacier, 22 km (14 miles) long, to the N the mountain world of the Alps, the Mittelland and beyond this, on clear days, the Vosges and the Black Forest.

CLIMBS from the Jungfraujoch (only to be undertaken with a guide): the *Jungfrau (4158 m (13,642 feet): 4 hours, difficult), so named (the "Maiden") in honour of the Augustinian nuns of Interlaken; the Mönch (4099 m (13,449 feet): 4 hours, easier), the Finsteraarhorn (4274 m (14,023 feet): 6½–8 hours), the highest peak in the Bernese Alps. There is also a popular glacier walk to *Konkordiaplatz (2840 m – 9318 feet), on the Aletsch glacier.

Jura Mountains

Cantons: Jura (JU), Neuchâtel (NE) and Vaud (VD).
ⓘ Office Jurassien du Tourisme Pro Jura,
16 rue de l'Hôtel de Ville,
CH-2740 Moutier;
tel. (032) 93 18 24.

The *Jura is the range of folded mountains lying NW of the Swiss Alps and extending from Geneva to Schaffhausen. This is the central area of the Swiss watchmaking industry; but, lying as it does on the periphery of the country, has so far played a relatively minor part in the Swiss tourist trade.

The new canton of Jura, the 23rd to become a member of the Confederation, was established on 1 January 1979, following a popular referendum in September 1977. It has an area of 837 sq. km (323 sq. miles) and a population of 65,000, 87·6% of whom are Roman Catholics. The capital is Delémont, and the canton is divided into the three districts of Delémont, Porrentruy and Franches-Montagnes, with a total of 82 communes.

Through the Jura (from Berne). – The road runs through the beautiful *Birs valley* and comes in 41 km (25 miles) to Delémont (p. 106). From here the road to Biel continues S through the picturesque narrow *Val Moutier*, which the River

Cattle grazing in the Jura

Birs has carved through the limestone rock, to *Choindez* and Moutier (alt. 532 m (1745 feet): pop. 8900; Hôtel Oasis, B, 30 b., SP; Suisse, C, 23 b.; De la Gare, C, 4 b.). Watchmaking; manufacture of machine tools. – The road then runs through a picturesque defile, the Gorges de Court, and continues through the villages of Court, Malleray-Bévilard and *Reconvilier* (731 m (2398 feet): pop. 2600; important horse fair), birthplace of the famous clown known as Grock (Adrian Wettach, 1880–1959), to Tavannes (757 m (2484 feet): pop. 4000; Hôtel de la Gare, C, 27 b.), near the source of the Birs. From here the road ascends to the *Pierre Pertuis*, with a passage through the rock 12 m (39 feet) high and 8 m (26 feet) wide (Roman inscription), and then down to *Sonceboz* (656 m (2152 feet): pop. 1370), where the railway line from Biel to La Chaux-de-Fonds branches off. The route then continues through the Vallon de St-Imier, the valley of the River *Suze*, to St-Imier (814 m (2671 feet): pop. 6300; Hôtel des Treize Cantons, C, 22 b.), an important watchmaking capital, with a 12th c. Romanesque church and the Tour de la Reine Berthe, a remnant of the Romanesque church of St Martin. Cableway up the Mont Soleil (1290 m – 4232 feet). – From here there is a direct road to Neuchâtel (30 km – 19 miles), past *Le Chasseral* (1610 m (5282 feet): hotel), from which there are beautiful panoramic views. – The main road continues to La Chaux-de-Fonds (p. 93).

From La Chaux-de-Fonds an attractive excursion can be made via Le Locle (9 km – 6 miles) and the Col des Roches (917 m – 3009 feet), 5 km (3 miles) beyond which is the watchmaking village of *Les Brenets* (849 m (2786 feet): pop. 1200), situated above the *Lac des*

Brenets (753 m – 2471 feet). The lake (length 4 km (2 miles), breadth 100–200 m (328–656 feet), area 0·69 sq. km (0·27 sq. miles)), enclosed by sandstone crags, is a natural formation on the River Doubs, which here forms the frontier between Switzerland and France. It is a 15 minutes' trip by motor-boat or a 45 minutes' walk to the Hôtel du Doubs, from which a 5 minutes' climb leads to a viewpoint opposite the *Saut du Doubs*, a waterfall 27 m (89 feet) high. Immediately downstream from Brenets is the *Lac de Moron* (4·5 km (3 miles) long). – 14 km (9 miles) SW of the Col des Roches we come to *La Brévine* (1046 m (3432 feet): pop. 700), and a further 14 km (9 miles) S, in the Val de Travers, *Fleurier* (743 m (2438 feet): pop. 4100; Hôtel du Commerce). 14 km (9 miles) SW of Fleurier *Ste-Croix* (1092 m (3583 feet): pop. 5300; Hôtel de France) lies in a valley on the slopes of *Le Chasseron* (1611 m (5286 feet): hotel). This little town is famous for its musical boxes. Interesting Musical Box Museum in L'Auberson.

The road from La Chaux-de-Fonds to Neuchâtel (22 km – 14 miles) runs past the *Vue des Alpes* (9 km (6 miles): 1283 m (4210 feet): inn), from which there is a beautiful prospect of the Alps (Mont Blanc). **Neuchâtel**: p. 183. – **Yverdon**: p. 259.

SW of the Lac de Neuchâtel, via *Orbe* (p. 260), is **La Sarraz** (488 m (1601 feet): pop. 1000; Hôtel du Soleil, 10 b.), with a massive 11th c. castle which was given its present form in the 16th c. In the former parish church of St-Antoine (now the Town Hall) can be seen the tomb of Count François de la Sarraz (d. 1363).

NW of La Sarraz, on a by-road to the left of road 9, is the old-world little town of **Romainmôtier** (658 m – 2159 feet) which has a monastery founded in the 5th c. and dissolved in 1537. The *church, built in the 10th–11th c. and enlarged and altered in the 12th–14th c., is one of the most notable buildings in Switzerland.

The by-road continues to the NE end of the *Lac de Joux*. An attractive road follows the S side of the lake, passing through the little village of *L'Abbaye*, dominated by the massive tower of its church. – Just beyond the SW end of the lake is **Le Brassus** (1024 m (3360 feet): Hôtel de France, C, 60 b.; De la Lande, C, 68 b.), a winter sports resort with excellent skiing terrain (ski-lifts up Molard, 1570 m (5151 feet)). – From here it is possible to continue to **Nyon** (p. 185), on Lake Geneva, either by way of the *Col du Marchairuz* (1447 m – 4748 feet) or (passing through French territory) via *La Cure*, the *Col de la Givrine* (1228 m – 4029 feet) and the winter sports resort of

St-Cergue (1043 m (3422 feet): possible detour to the fine viewpoint of La Dôle, 1677 m (5502 feet).

Kandersteg

Canton: Berne (BE).
Altitude: 1170–1200 m (3839–3937 feet). Population: 1000.
Post code: CH-3718. – Dialling code: 033.
(i) **Verkehrsbüro,**
    Kandersteg;
    tel. 75 12 34.

HOTELS (mostly closed in November). – *Royal Hotel Bellevue*, A, 60 b., SP, SB; *Victoria & Ritter*, B, 120 b., SB; *Parkhotel Gemmi*, C, 60 b., SB; *Schweizerhof*, C, 70 b.; *Adler*, C, 35 b.; *Blümlisalp*, C, 40 b., SB; *Alfa-Soleil*, D, 65 b., SB; *National*, E, 20 b.

RECREATION and SPORT. – Riding, tennis, swimming, fishing, walking, climbing.

CABLEWAYS and LIFTS. – Cabin cableway from Eggenschwand to *Beim Stock* (1837 m – 6027 feet) on the Gemmiweg (6 minutes); from there a chair-lift (12 minutes) to 1947 m (6388 feet) on *Sunnbühl*. – Chair-lift from the mouth of the Oeschinental (5 minutes from the church) to *Oeschinen* (1700 m (5578 feet): 9 minutes).

WINTER SPORTS. – Several good skiing areas (ski-lifts); curling (indoor rink), artificial ice-rink, toboggan run. – Ski-trekking school.

Kandersteg is a popular summer and winter resort in the Upper Kander valley, in the Bernese Oberland. The village, with some attractive old peasants' houses and a small 16th c. church, straggles along the meadows of the valley floor for almost 4 km (2 miles), enclosed by towering mountains.

To the NE is the jagged Birrenhorn (2505 m – 8219 feet), to the E the snow-capped Blümlisalp and the Doldenhorn, to the SE the bare slopes of the Fisistöcke (2947 m – 9669 feet) and to the S, closing the valley, the rugged Gellihorn (2289 m – 7510 feet). At Eggenschwand, at the S end of the village, the Lötschbergbahn enters the Lötschberg tunnel, the third longest in the Alps (14·6 km (9 miles): cars carried). – Conference facility.

SURROUNDINGS. – The *Oeschinensee** (1582 m (5191 feet): Hotel Oeschinensee, E, 20 b.) can be reached by a 1¼ hours' walk from the Victoria Hotel up the valley of the Oeschinenbach, or by taking the chair-lift to the Oeschinen station and walking down from there over the *Im Läger* meadows (extensive views: 30 minutes). The lake lies below the Blümlisalp, mirroring the mountain's rugged shape in its

Klosters

Canton: Grisons (GR).
Altitude: 1127–1209 m (3698–3967 feet). – Population: 3500.
Post code: CH-7250. – Dialling code: 083.

(i) **Kur- und Verkehrsverein,**
    Klosters;
    tel. 4 18 77.

HOTELS. – *Pardenn*, A, 130 b., SB; *Silvretta*, A, 180 b.; *Vereina*, B, 170 b., SB; *Chesa Grischuna*, B, 50 b.; *Alpina*, B, 50 b.; *Kaiser's* (no rest.), B, 53 b.; *Kurhotel Bad Serneus*, C, 60 b., SB; *Surval*, C, 30 b., SP; *Sport-Ferienzentrum*, C, 100 b.; *Bündnerhof*, D, 36 b.

RECREATION and SPORT. – Golf, tennis (indoor and outdoor courts), swimming, skittles.

WINTER SPORTS. – Excellent ski-trails in the Parsenn area (several ski-lifts), in the Madrisa area and on the Saaseralp; ice-rink, curling, tobogganing.

The Oeschinensee, at the foot of the Blümlisalp

The popular health and winter sports resort of Klosters, made up of a number of separate groups of houses and hotels, lies in the wide Prättigau valley, through which flows the River Landquart, within a framework of high mountains.

In the main part of the resort, known as *Zentrum* (formerly Klosters Platz, 1209 m (3967 feet)) are the large *hotels* and the *parish church* (restored 1921), which originally belonged to the Premonstratensian (an Order founded at Prémontré, France in 1119) monastery of St Jakob, dissolved in 1528: hence the name of the village (Kloster=monastery). Small local museum in the "Nutlihüsli". – 1·5 km (1 mile) down the valley, at the mouth of the Schlappin valley, is *Klosters Dorf* (1127 m – 3698 feet).

clear water, in a setting of majestic beauty. – From here it is a 3¾ hours' climb to the *Blümlisalp hut* (2837 m – 9308 feet) and a 5 hours' climb (with guide) to the summit of the *Blümlisalphorn* (3664 m – 12,022 feet), the highest peak of the mighty **Blümlisalp.**

Into the Gastern valley (¾ hour to Klus, 2¼ hours to Selden; also possible to drive to Selden on payment of a toll). – The narrow road runs through a tunnel in the rock into the *Klus*, a gorge through which the River Kander rushes and tumbles, and then continues uphill through a second tunnel on the left bank and another on the right bank. In 15 minutes it comes to a magnificent stretch of the valley at *Gasternholz* (1365 m (4479 feet): on the left bank the Waldhaus inn), with the mighty rock walls of the Tatlishorn and Altels towering up on the right. – From here it is a 1¼ hours' walk along the right bank to the huts of **Selden** (1590 m (5217 feet): Hotel Gasterntal), under a grand mountain screen formed by the *Hockenhorn* (3297 m (10,817 feet): 8 hours, with guide), the *Doldenhorn* (3643 m (11,953 feet): 8 hours, with guide, from Kandersteg) and the *Balmhorn*.

To the Gemmi pass (to Schwarenbach Hotel 3 or 1½ hours, to Leukerbad 6½, 5 or 3½ hours depending on route taken). – First a 30 minutes' walk to *Eggenschwand* (road passable for cars for 2·5 km (2 miles) to car park at lower station of Stock cableway); then either by cableway (6 minutes) or on foot (1¾ hours) to *Beim Stock* (1837 m (6027 feet): chair-lift to Sunnbühl). Then a 1¼ hours' walk through wooded country high above the Gastern valley, and up the valley of the Schwarzbach and over the *Spitalmatte* (1900 m – 6234 feet), an Alpine meadow littered with rock debris, to the *Schwarenbach Hotel* (2067 m (6782 feet): E, 20 b.), a good climbing base (climbing school), e.g. for the ascent of the *Balmhorn* (3709 m (12,169 feet): 6–7 hours, with guide). – Then another 1¼ hours through a bleak and rugged region, past the *Daubensee* (2205 m (7235 feet): frozen for 8–10 months of the year) to the **Gemmi pass** (2316 m (7599 feet): Berghotel Wildstrubel, E, 40 b.), with astonishing *views of the Rhône valley and the Valais Alps. – From the pass a cableway descends to *Leukerbad* (p. 160). The walk down to Leukerbad on the old bridle-path (made in 1740) along a rock face which plunges precipitously down for almost 600 m (1969 feet), is to be recommended only to those with a good head for heights (2 hours).

Cableway station on the Gotschnagrat

SURROUNDINGS. – A cableway ascends from Klosters railway station by way of an intermediate station on the *Gotschnaboden* (1780 m – 5840 feet) to the **Gotschnagrat** (2283 m (7491 feet): restaurant; chair-lift down to Laret), with views of the Upper Prättigau and the Silvretta group. From here a footpath leads in 30 minutes to the *Parsenn hut* (2205 m (7235 feet): inn), from which it is another 2 hours' walk to the *Höhenweg* station on the Davos-Weissfluhjoch funicular (2215 m – 7267 feet). There is also a cableway from the Parsenn hut (2400 m (7874 feet), 8 minutes) to the *Weissfluhjoch* (2663 m – 8737 feet). – Another cableway (2280 m (7481 feet), 11 minutes) runs up from Klosters Dorf to the *Albeina* station (1884 m (6181 feet): restaurant) on the *Saaseralp* (several ski-lifts), below the *Madrisahorn* (2826 m (9272 feet): another 3–4 hours, with guide).

The **Prättigau** (Romansh **Val Partens** or *Portenz*), extending NW from Klosters is the fairly narrow valley of the River *Landquart*. Although the trim little villages, situated amid fruit orchards in the wider parts of the valley or on narrow terraces on the steeply sloping meadowland on the hillsides, have Romansh names dating from an earlier settlement they are inhabited by a German-speaking and mainly Protestant population. On the N side of the valley is the **Rätikon** chain (*Scesaplana*, 2967 m (9735 feet)), along which runs the frontier with Austria (Vorarlberg). The numerous summer holiday resorts in the Prättigau are mostly some distance off the road on the hillside (Seewis on the N side, Fideris and Bad Serneus on the S side) or in the side valleys (Valzeina to the S, St Antönien to the N). *Küblis*, with a late Gothic church, and *Schiers*, at the mouth of the Schraubach, are both worth a visit.

From Klosters a narrow road climbs the right bank of the Landquart into the highest part of the Prättigau, with beautiful views of the Silvretta group. – 3 km (2 miles): *Monbiel* (1313 m (4308 feet): restaurant). – From here it is another 4 km (2 miles) (road closed to cars) to the beautifully situated *Alp Novai* (1368 m – 4488 feet), at the point where the Sardascabach and the Vereinabach join to form the Landquart. A bridle-path ascends the Vereina valley (to the right) to the **Berghaus Vereina** (1944 m (6378 feet): inn, with beds), in a magnificent mountain setting (2¼ hours), a good base for climbers. 3½ hours' walk up the Sardasca valley, to the left, is the **Silvrettahaus** (2340 m (7677 feet): inn), in a magnificent situation under the *Silvretta glacier* (1 hour's climb). These are both good bases for climbs in the Silvretta group – the *Silvrettahorn* (3248 m (10,657 feet): 3½ hours, with guide), *Piz Buin* (3316 m (10,880 feet): 4½ hours, with guide), etc.

Küssnacht am Rigi

Canton: Schwyz (SZ).
Altitude: 440 m (1444 feet). – Population: 6250.
Post code: CH-6403. – Dialling code: 041.
ⓘ **Offizielles Verkehrsbüro,**
   Küssnacht;
   tel. 81 33 30.

HOTELS. – *Hirschen*, C, 55 b.; *Engel*, D, 20 b.; *Seehotel Drei Könige*, D, 22 b.; *Seehof du Lac*, D, 30 b.; *Picnic-Motel*. – CAMPING SITE at bathing lido.

RECREATION and SPORT. – Boat trips, bathing, tennis, riding.

Küssnacht, chief town of the district of that name between Lake Lucerne and Lake Zug, famous for its associations with William Tell, lies at the farthest tip of the Küssnachter See, the most northerly arm of Lake Lucerne. It first appears in the records in 870, in connection with a gift to the monastery in Lucerne.

SIGHTS. – The *Gasthaus Engel* (Angel Inn) is a half-timbered building of 1552 with an old assembly hall and a Goethe Room. *Parish church* (rebuilt in Baroque style 1708–10, enlarged 1963); *Town Hall* (1728).

The Hohle Gasse and Tell Chapel, Küssnacht

William Tell, the hero of Swiss legend who, the story goes, refused to recognise the authority of the Habsburg governor Gessler, won his freedom by shooting the apple on his son's head and later killed Gessler in the Hohle Gasse, is a symbolic figure who has been a powerful inspiration throughout Swiss history.
The desire for freedom lay at the root of the striving by this people of herdsmen and forest-dwellers in the heart of Switzerland to achieve independence, and continued in subsequent centuries to inspire the Confederates in their struggle. Switzerland's development into the well-ordered European state of today passed through many troubles and vicissitudes; but the "Perpetual Pact" between the three forest states in 1291 was strong enough to endure and form the basis of the present Confederation of 26 cantons.

SURROUNDINGS. – 2 km (1 mile) NE of Küssnacht on the road to Immensee is the *Hohle Gasse ("Hollow Lane"), where tradition has it that William Tell shot the Austrian governor Gessler with his crossbow. The spot is marked by the **Tell chapel** (built 1638, restored 1895, with paintings by H. Bachmann of "Gessler's Death" and "Tell's Death"). The Hohle Gasse was purchased by the young people of Switzerland and presented to the Confederation. – Above Küssnacht stands the ruined *Gesslerburg* ("Gessler's Castle"), the remains of a medieval stronghold which has no connection with Gessler. – After visiting Küssnacht Goethe suggested the subject of William Tell to Schiller, and Schiller's play in turn inspired Rossini's opera.

5 km (3 miles) above Küssnacht on a narrow and winding mountain road (or 7 minutes by cableway), on the slopes of the Rigi, is the *Seebodenalp* (1030 m – 3379 feet), from which a footpath leads in 1½ hours to *Rigi Staffel* and *Rigi Känzeli*. – 4 km (2 miles) W of Küssnacht is *Udligenswil*, from which there is a footpath up the *Rooterberg* (798 m (2618 feet) St Michaelskreuz chapel). – Just outside Küssnacht on the Lucerne road a Flemish-style memorial chapel is dedicated to Queen Astrid of Belgium, who was killed in a car accident here in 1935.

Lausanne

Canton: Vaud (VD).
Altitude: 380–530 m (1247–1739 feet). – Population: 129,000.
Post code: CH-1000. – Dialling code: 021.
ⓘ **Office du Tourisme et des Congrès,**
   60 Avenue d'Ouchy;
   tel. 27 73 21.
   Branches:
   Railway station (concourse),
   tel. 23 19 35;
   Cointrin airport (arrival hall),
   tel. (022) 98 45 73.

HOTELS. – PLACE ST-FRANÇOIS AND TOWN CENTRE: *Lausanne-Palace*, 7–9 Grand Chêne, A, 300 b.; *De la Paix*, 5 Avenue Benjamin-Constant, B, 230 b.; *Jan*, 8 Avenue de Beaulieu, B, 100 b.; *City*, 5 rue Caroline, C, 120 b.; *Crystal*, 5 rue Chaucrau, C, 55 b.; *Voyageurs*, 19 Grand-St-Jean, C, 50 b.

NEAR THE STATION: *Alpha-Palmiers*, 34 rue du Petit Chêne, B, 270 b.; *Continental*, 2 Place de la Gare, B, 180 b.; *Mirabeau*, 31 Avenue de la Gare, B, 100 b.; *Parking Hotel Motor Inn*, 9 Avenue Rond-Point, B, 210 b.; *Victoria*, 46 Avenue de la Gare, B, 100 b.; *Elite*, 1 Avenue Ste-Luce, C, 53 b.; *Lausanne*, 1 Avenue Ruchonnet, C, 90 b.; *A la Gare-Transit*, 14 rue du Simplon, D, 102 b.

IN OUCHY, on the lake: *Beau-Rivage*, A, 300 b., SP, SB, large park; *Aulac*, Place Navigation, B, 130 b.; *Château d'Ouchy*, Place du Port, B, 85 b.; *Résidence*, 15 Place du Port, B, 80 b., SB; *Navigation*, Place Navigation, B, 78 b.; *Angleterre*, 9 Place du Port, C, 55 b.

IN CROIX-D'OUCHY: *Royal-Savoy*, 40 Avenue d'Ouchy, B, 200 b., SP; *Carlton*, 4 Avenue de Cour, B, 90 b.; *Bellerive*, 99 Avenue de Cour, B, 78 b.; *Orient-Croix d'Ouchy*, 10 Avenue d'Ouchy, B, 32 b.

IN BUSSIGNY, 9 km (6 miles) NW of town centre: *Novotel*, Route de Sullens, B, 300 b.

YOUTH HOSTEL: *Auberge de la Jeunesse*, Avenue de Bellerive/1 Chemin du Muguet, 180 b. – CAMPING SITE at Vidy.

RESTAURANTS and CAFÉS. – PLACE ST-FRANÇOIS AND TOWN CENTRE: *Aux Trois Tonneaux*, Rue Grand-St-Jean; *Grappe d'Or*, 3 Cheneau-de Bourg; *Bonne Auberge*, 32 Avenue Druey; *Brasserie Le Vaudois*, Place de la Riponne; *Nyffenegger*, Place St-François; *Théâtre*, in Theatre; *Chat Noir*, 27 Beau Séjour (near Theatre: an artists' haunt); *Le Mandarin*, 7 Avenue du Théâtre (Chinese); *Manuel*, Place St-François. – STATION: *Buffet de la Gare*.

Lausanne – the old town (Cité)

ON THE LAKE: *Voile d'Or*, club restaurant, with beach.

IN OUCHY, on the lake: *White Horse Pub.* – IN ST-SULPICE: *Débarcadère.* – IN THE HILLS TO THE N: *Chalet Suisse*, Signal de Sauvabelin; *Lac de Sauvabelin*, in Bois de Sauvabelin.

BOAT SERVICES on Lake Geneva (departures from Place de la Navigation, Ouchy): motor launches several times daily to lakeside towns in Switzerland and France; round trips and cruises.

EVENTS. – *Theatre and concert season* (October–March); *International Festival* (May–June); *Festival de la Cité* (June); *"Pour un Eté"* (July–August: free performances for visitors); *Salon des Antiquaires* (November); *Comptoir Suisse* (National Trade Fair: autumn); *International Tourism and Holiday Fair* (March).

RECREATION and SPORT. – Golf, riding, tennis (indoor and outdoor courts), swimming, sailing, rowing, water-skiing, fishing; cross-country skiing, curling (indoor and outdoor rinks), skating.

*Lausanne, the lively capital of the canton of Vaud, is picturesquely situated on the N shore of Lake Geneva, on terraces rising above the lake which are broken by gorges. It ranks with Geneva as a focus of intellectual life in French-speaking Switzerland (Federal Court, University, College of Technology, Hotel School and many other technical colleges), and is also a popular convention and conference hub and the venue of important trade fairs (Comptoir Suisse in Autumn, International Tourism Fair in March). Major elements in the town's economy are the foodstuffs industries, vine-growing and the wine trade.

In the attractive *townscape of Lausanne the modern office blocks and the high-level bridges spanning the gorges (now built over) of the Rivers Flon and Louve form a striking contrast to the narrow lanes and steep flights of steps which run up to the old town (Cité), dominated by the Cathedral (530 m – 1739 feet) and the Château, while to the S pleasant residential districts extend down to the port of Ouchy (380 m – 1247 feet).

HISTORY. – There was a Celtic settlement at the mouth of the River Flon which later became the Roman *Lousonium* or *Lousonna*. After the destruction of this town by the Alemanni about 379 a fortified settlement was built on the hill now occupied by the Cité, and after the transfer of the episcopal see from Avenches to Lausanne (*c.* 590) this became a town of some size which, like Geneva, belonged successively to the Burgundians, the Franks and the second Burgundian kingdom before becoming part of the

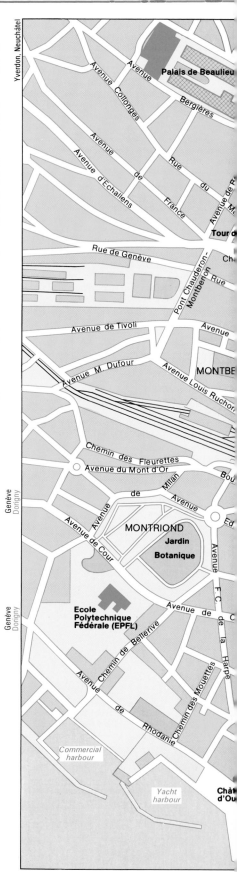

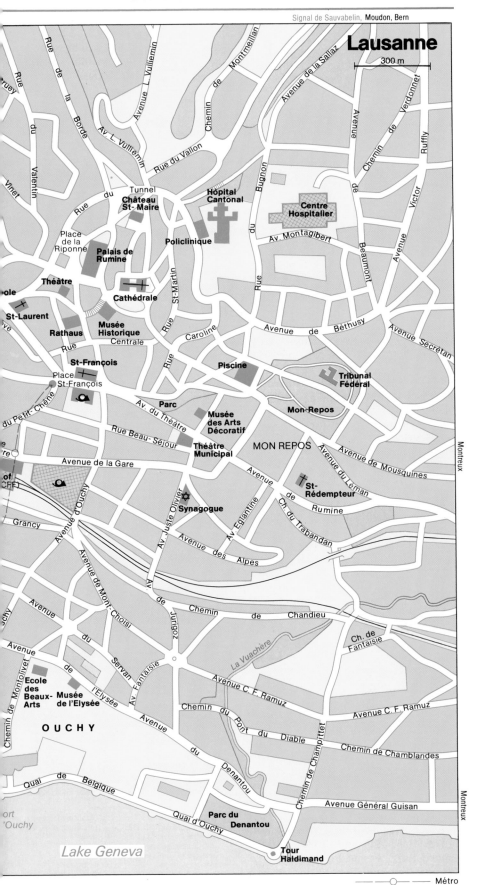

Signal de Sauvabelin, **Moudon, Bern**

Lausanne

300 m

Rue de la Borde

Av. L. Vulliemin

Avenue L. Vulliemin

Rue du Valentin

Vinet

Rue de la Borde

Rue du Vallon

Chemin

de Montmeillan

Avenue de la Sallaz

Avenue

de Verdonnet

Ruffly

Chemin

de

Victor

Avenue

Tunnel

Rue du

**Château
St- Maire**

**Hôpital
Cantonal**

Bugnon

Rue du

**Centre
Hospitalier**

Avenue

Beaumont

Place
de la
Riponne

Policlinique

Av. Montagibert

**Palais de
Rumine**

Rue St-Martin

Théâtre

Cathédrale

ole

✝
St-Laurent

Rathaus

**Musée
Historique**

Centrale

Rue

Caroline

Rue

Avenue

de

Béthusy

Avenue Secrétan

ve

Rue

St-François

Place
St-François

du Petit-Chêne

Piscine

**Tribunal
Fédéral**

👁

Parc

Av. du Théâtre

**Musée
des Arts
Décoratif**

Mon-Repos

Rue Beau-Séjour

**Théâtre
Municipal**

MON REPOS

Avenue de la Gare

re

of.
CFF)

👁

Avenue d'Ouchy

Grancy

Avenue

Avenue du Léman

de

Rumine

Ch. du Trabandan

✝
**St-
Rédempteur**

Avenue du Léman

Avenue de Mousquines

Montreux

Av. Juste Olivier

✡

Synagogue

Av. Eglantine

Avenue des Alpes

Avenue de Mon-Choisi

Av. de Jurigoz

Chemin

de

Chandieu

Ch. de
Fantaisie

Avenue

uchy

du

Servan

Av. Fantaisie

La Vuachère

Avenue

de

l'Elysée

Avenue C. F. Ramuz

Avenue C. F. Ramuz

Chemin de Montolivet

**Ecole
des
Beaux-
Arts**

**Musée
de l'Elysée**

Chemin

du

Pont

du

Diable

Chemin de Champrittet

Chemin de Chamblandes

OUCHY

Avenue

du

Denantou

Quai de Belgique

Quai d'Ouchy

**Parc du
Denantou**

Avenue Général Guisan

Montreux

ort
'Ouchy

Lake Geneva

**Tour
Haldimand**

Métro

Holy Roman Empire in 1033. In the 15th c. Lausanne became a free Imperial city. In 1536 the Vaud region was conquered by the Bernese, who soon afterwards introduced the Reformed faith. In 1798, however, Vaud recovered its independence as the République Lémanique, and in 1803 it became the 19th canton to join the Swiss Confederation.

TOUR OF THE TOWN. – The hub of the town's traffic is the *Place St-François*, surrounded by large office blocks and the *Head Post Office*. In the middle of the square stands the former Franciscan **church of St-François** (13th–14th c.: beautiful stained glass of 1907 in choir), with a tower of 1523. A little way E is the *Derrière Bourg* park (fine views). – From Place St-François take Rue de Bourg (pedestrians only) and Rue Caroline and then turn left over the *Pont Bessières* (1910) to reach the Cathedral (below). – The *Grand-Pont* (1839–44), an arched viaduct 180 m (591 feet) long from which there is an attractive view of the old town and the Cathedral, runs NW from Place St-François into the busy *Place Bel-Air*, with the imposing **Bel-Air Métropole** office block (1932: restaurant and café), crowned by a tower block 67 m (220 feet) high (20 storeys).

From Place Bel-Air, Rue Haldimand runs NE, passing on the right the Protestant *church of St-Laurent* (1719: Baroque façade), into the spacious *Place de la Riponne*. On the E side of the square is the *Palais de Rumine* (1898–1906), which houses the **University**, originally founded as an Academy in 1537. (A new University complex is under construction at Dorigny, 5 km (3 miles) W of the town.) Also in the Palais de Rumine are the *Cantonal and University Library* (700,000 volumes, valuable manuscripts), the *Cantonal Museum of Art* (Musée Cantonal des Beaux-Arts: mainly pictures by 19th c. artists of western Switzerland), the *Natural History Museum* and the *Archaeological Museum* (bust of Marcus Aurelius). – From the church of St-Laurent Rue de l'Ale runs NW to the *Tour de l'Ale*, a round tower 21 m (69 feet) high which is the only remnant of the town's 14th c. fortifications.

A little way S of Place de la Riponne (pedestrian precinct) is *Place de la Palud*, in which is situated the **Hôtel de Ville** (Town Hall, 15th and 17th c.; 16th c. stained glass). From here the *Escaliers du Marché*, a covered flight of steps, lead up

to the Cathedral, in the CITÉ (which can also be reached from Place de la Riponne by a flight of steps to the right of the University and Rue Pierre-Viret).

The * **Cathedral of Notre-Dame** (Protestant), consecrated by Pope Gregory X in presence of King Rudolf of Habsburg in 1275, is an Early Gothic building with five towers (central tower, 75 m (246 feet) high, 1876; a watchman calls out the hours from the bell-cage during the night). The main doorway (16th c.) and the "Apostles' doorway" (13th c.) have very fine sculptured decoration (copies: originals under the rose-window).

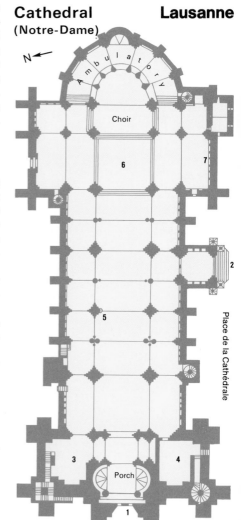

Cathedral   **Lausanne**
(Notre-Dame)

1 W doorway (1515–36; statues restored 1892–1909)
2 Apostles' doorway (13th c.), with coloured statues (restored 1975–76; some are copies)
3 Chapel of Maccabees, with Late Gothic choir-stalls (1509)
4 S tower
5 Pulpit (16th c.)
6 Central tower
7 Rose-window (c. 1240)

The INTERIOR is notable for its noble proportions. In the S transept is a large *rose-window* with beautiful 13th c. stained glass (the Universe); the S aisle has carved choir-stalls of 1509; in the choir are remains of Early Gothic stalls and (on left) the tomb of the minnesinger Otto of Grandson (d. 1328); in the crypt are to be found remains of an 8th c. basilica, with old tombs.

On the terrace to the S of the Cathedral (beautiful view) is the tower (1373–83) of the old episcopal castle, which now houses the *Musée Historique de l'Ancien Evêché* and the *Musée Permanent de la Cathédrale.*

From the Cathedral we go N, past the former *Academy* (1587), to the N end of the Cité and the **Château St-Maire** (1397–1431), originally the bishop's palace, residence of the Bernese governors from 1536 to 1798, and now occupied by the cantonal government. To the left, on the W terrace, is the *Grand Conseil* (the cantonal parliament).

On the E side of the town is the beautiful old park of **Mon Repos** (parking garage; roof terrace with beautiful view). – On higher ground to the N of the park the **Federal Court** (*Tribunal Fédéral:* conducted tours) is housed in a building erected in 1922–27.

Above the town to the N (20 minutes' walk) is the *Signal de Sauvabelin* (647 m (2123 feet): restaurant), with a famous view. – Beyond this a large wooded park, the *Bois de Sauvabelin*, has a small lake (restaurant) and a deer park. To the N of the park, on the far side of the motorway along the banks of the Flon, is the *Vivarium*, with reptiles, insects, birds of prey and small mammals (combined admission ticket which covers also the *Zoo* at Servion, 15 km (9 miles) NW).

On the NW side of the town (1 km (about a $\frac{1}{2}$ mile) from Place de la Riponne) stands the **Palais de Beaulieu** (1920: convention facility, restaurant, theatre), with the show and exhibition halls of the *Comptoir Suisse* and a sports complex. To the S, beyond the Avenue Bergières, the *Château de Beaulieu* (1756) houses a collection of marginal art ("Art Brut") donated by Jean Dubuffet.

On the lakeside 1·5 km (1 mile) S of town's central district (6 minutes by Métro) lies the busy little port of **Ouchy** (380 m – 1250 feet). Between the old and the new harbours is a 12th c. *castle*, the château d'Ouchy, now a hotel and restaurant, in which the peace treaty between Turkey, Greece and the Allies was signed in 1923. To the W is the suburb of VIDY, in Gallo-Roman times the port of Lousonna. On the shores of the lake are a *yacht harbour*, a rowing facility, extensive sports grounds and a camping site. A "Promenade Archéologique" is to be found at the beginning of the motorway. N of the camping site is the *château de Vidy*, headquarters of the International Olympic Committee (founded 1894: museum). To the N of the motorway, in the Chemin du Bois-de-Vaux, is the Vidy *Roman Museum* (Gallo-Roman material).

Convention and Exhibition Centre

Palais de Beaulieu Lausanne

(The **Comptoir Suisse** or National Fair is held here annually in September)

From **Port d'Ouchy**, the old harbour, a beautiful *lakeside promenade* affording attractive views runs 1 km (about a $\frac{1}{2}$ mile) E to the *Tour Haldimand* and the pretty *Parc Denantou*. The *Elysée Museum* in the Avenue de l'Elysée has among its exhibits a collection of graphics. – Above Ouchy to the NW is the *Parc Montriond* (fine views), with the *Botanic Garden*.

To the E of Ouchy the suburb of PULLY has modern bathing facilities and the

The harbour, Ouchy

Château d'Oron (Vaud)

remains of a Roman villa (destroyed in the 2nd c. A.D.). Immediately adjoining is a former monastery, opened to the public only in 1979 (double apse; *wall-painting, 20 sq. m (215 sq. feet)).

SURROUNDINGS. – 25 km (16 miles) NE, off the W side of E 4 the little industrial town of **Moudon** (alt. 513 m (1683 feet): pop. 300) occupies the site of the Roman *Minnodunum.* In the lower town is the beautiful Gothic church of St-Etienne, with richly carved choir-stalls of 1502. In the upper town are attractive old houses, the 12th c. Tour de Broye, the little château of Rochefort (1595: local museum) and the château of Billens (1677).

20 km (12 miles) E of Lausanne on the road to Romont, in *Oron-le-Châtel (above Oron-la-Ville), is the well-preserved château d'Oron* (13th c.: museum).

Lauterbrunnen Valley

Canton: Berne (BE).
(i) **Kur- und Verkehrsverein,**
  Ch-3822 Lauterbrunnen;
  tel. (036) 55 19 55.

HOTELS. – IN LAUTERBRUNNEN: *Staubbach,* C, 60 b.; *Silberhorn,* C, 40 b.; *Jungfrau,* C, 45 b., SB; *Oberland,* D, 60 b. – *Trümmelbach,* 4 km (2 miles) S.

CAMPING SITES: *Jungfrau* and *Schützenbach.* – YOUTH HOSTEL: *Gimmelwald* (alt. 1370 m: 8 km).

RECREATION and SPORT. – Climbing, conducted walks, cross-country skiing (12 km – 7 miles), helicopter flights over glaciers. – Golf-course, natural ice-rink, heated open-air swimming pool and indoor pool in Lauterbrunnen. – Valley Museum, (collection of implements and tools; lace-making).

The *Lauterbrunnen valley to the S of Interlaken extends from Zwei-lütischinen to the foot of the Breit horn, in the Jungfrau massif. The

Trogtal, a typical high Alpine valley through which the Weisse Lütschine flows down to join the Schwarze Lütschine at Zweilütschinen, is enclosed between sheer rock walls over which plunge a number of magnificent waterfalls. The sun does not reach the valley floor until 7 a.m. in summer and 11 a.m. in winter (Central European Time).

From *Zweilütschinen* the road climbs up the valley with a moderate gradient between limestone walls from 300 to 500 m (984 to 1641 feet) high. On the right are the *Sausbach Falls,* and just beyond this, on the left, the *Hunnenfluh* (1334 m – 4377 feet), rearing up like a semicircular tower. Beyond this is **Lauterbrunnen** (800 m (2625 feet): pop. 1000), a popular summer resort and the starting-point of the mountain railways to the Jungfraujoch (p. 147) and Mürren (p. 180). Above the village are the **Staubbach falls,** which plunge down from an

The Staubbach falls above Lauterbrunnen

overhanging crag in a sheer drop of 300 m (984 feet). – A rewarding excursion can be made on a mountain road which runs 3·5 km (2 miles) N to the village of *Isenfluh* (1084 m – 3557 feet), situated on a steep natural terrace, from which there is a superb *view of the mountain giants from the Grosshorn to the Eiger.

The road to **Stechelberg** branches off on the left at the Staubbach Hotel in Lauterbrunnen, bends to the left and runs down to cross the Lütschine; it then continues up the valley through meadows, with a view of the Breithorn, passing two camping sites and the Staubbach falls (on right). In 4 km (2 miles) it comes to the *Trümmelbach Hotel* (on left), from which there is a footpath (5 minutes) to the *Trümmelbach Falls,* which plunge down in five mighty cascades through the

The Birg cableway station on the Schilthornbahn

gorge carved out by the Trümmelbach (charge: electric elevator, stepped paths, floodlighting). – From the hotel the road continues up the Lauterbrunnen valley. In 2 km (1 mile) a side road goes off on the right to the lower station (867 m (2845 feet): car park) of the *Schilthornbahn, a cableway 6967 m (22,859 feet) long which ascends in 34 minutes, via the intermediate stations of *Gimmelwald* (1367 m – 4485 feet), *Mürren* (1638 m (5374 feet): see p. 181) and *Birg* (2677 m (8783 feet): restaurant with observation terrace), to the *Schilthorn (2970 m (9745 feet): revolving restaurant, sun terrace; summer skiing), from which there are magnificent views (telescope). – The road ends, 1 km (about a ½ mile) beyond the turn-off for the cableway station, at the little village of **Stechelberg** (922 m – 3025 feet). – From here it is a 45–60 minutes' walk to the group of huts at *Trachsellauenen* (1263 m – 4144 feet), and from there another 1¼ hours' walk to the *Schmadribach falls* or a 1½ hours' walk to the *Alp Obersteinberg* (1770 m – 5807 feet), which affords a superb *prospect of the mountains and glaciers around the upper part of the Lauterbrunnen valley.

Lenzerheide – Valbella

Canton: Grisons (GR).
Altitude: 1470 and 1540 m (4823 and 5053 feet). –
Population: 2400.
Post code: CH-7078 and 7077. – Dialling code: 081.
(i) **Kur- und Verkehrsverein**
   Lenzerheide – Valbella,
   Ch-7078 Lenzerheide;
   tel. 34 15 88.

HOTELS. – IN LENZERHEIDE: *Schweizerhof*, B, 50 b., SB; *Grand Hotel Kurhaus*, B, 180 b., SB; *Guardaval*, *Sporz*, B, 75 b.; *Sunstar*, B, 170 b., SB; *Central* (no rest.), B, 100 b.; *La Palanca*, C, 70 b.; *Sporthotel Dieschen*, C, 60 b.; *Park-Hotel*, C, 70 b., SP; *Edenhof*, D, 50 b. – IN VALBELLA:* *Valbella-Inn* (no rest), A, 120 b., SB; *Post-Hotel*, B, 160 b., SB; *Waldhaus am See*, B, 55 b., bathing beach; *Chesa Rustica*, C, 37 b.; *Kulm*, C, 56 b.

CAMPING SITE: in Lenzerheide.

CABLEWAYS and LIFTS. – Chair-lift from Lenzerheide via *Tgantieni* (1730 m – 5676 feet) to *Piz Scalottas* (2324 m – 7625 feet); cableway from Valbella (Canols) via *Alp Scharmoin* (1900 m – 6234 feet) to *Parpaner Rothorn* (2865 m (9400 feet): 15 minutes).

RECREATION and SPORT. – Golf, riding, tennis, sailing, fishing, surfing, clay pigeon shooting, walking, climbing.

WINTER SPORTS. – Numerous elevators below the Parpaner Weisshorn and Schwarzhorn (reached by cableway to Alp Scharmoin) and on the slopes of Piz Scalottas and the Stätzerhorn. – Cross-country skiing, tobogganing, skating, curling, horse-drawn sleigh rides. – Three ski schools.

In the park-like and wooded high valley of *Lenzerheide (Romansh Planüra), the beauty of which has long attracted visitors, are the two resorts of Lenzerheide and Valbella, on either side of the Heidsee (the "Lei": 1493 m (4899 feet); bathing beach).

To the E of the two resorts, which are popular both in summer and in winter, rear up the Aroser Rothorn (2984 m – 9791 feet), the Lenzerhorn (2911 m – 9551 feet) and the ridges of the Parpaner Rothorn (2865 m – 9400 feet), Weisshorn (2824 m – 9266 feet) and Schwarzhorn (2683 m – 8803 feet); on the W, Alpine meadows extend up the slopes of Piz Scalottas (2324 m – 7625 feet) and the Stätzerhorn (2574 m – 8445 feet).

Lenzerheide and the Parpaner Rothorn

SURROUNDINGS. – A by-road runs SW from Lenzerheide to Zorten and down into the wild* **Schin gorge** on the River *Albula*.

The main road runs S, past the golf-course, a camping site and the Bual nature park, to *Lantsch* or *Lenz* (1320 m – 4331 feet), with a church dedicated to the Virgin (1505). 2 km (1 mile) beyond Lantsch, below the road on the right, we see the farm of *Vazerol* (1130 m – 3708 feet), where the three Rhaetian leagues agreed to unite in 1471. 6 km (4 miles): **Tiefencastel**, a picturesquely situated village (parish church of 1660) at the confluence of the Julia and the Albula and at an important road junction. From here one road leads S over the *Julier (Guglia) pass* to Silvaplana and another goes E over the *Albula pass* to La Punt-Chamues-ch.

From Valbella the road runs N over the *Acl' Alva pass* (1549 m – 5082 feet), also known as the Valbella saddle or the Lenzerheide pass, which marks the linguistic boundary between German and Romansh (fine view of the Oberhalbstein mountains). The road then reaches *Parpan* (1511 m – 4958 feet), another health and winter sports resort, with a number of fine old houses, including the "Schlössli" (16th–17th c.) of the Buol family, and a 16th c. church with a separate tower. 4 km (2 miles) beyond this is **Churwalden** (1230 m – 4036 feet), a rambling village with a former Premonstratensian abbey (15th c. church, tower-like abbot's lodging). Chair-lifts to the Alp Stätz (1824 m – 5985 feet) and the Pradaschierer Alp (1817 m – 5962 feet).

Leukerbad/Loèche-les-Bains

Canton: Valais (VS).
Altitude: 1411 m (4629 feet). – Population: 1200.
Post code: CH-3954. – Dialling code: 027.
ⓘ **Verkehrsverein,**
　Leukerbad;
　　tel. 61 14 13.

HOTELS. – BADEHOTELS (ALL WITH THERMAL BATHS): *Bristol, A, 180 b.; Des Alpes, B, 90 b.; Regina Therme, B, 100 b.; Grand Bain, C, 150 b.; Bellevue, D, 150 b.; De France, D, 150 b.; Union, D, 150 b. – OTHER HOTELS (WITH RESTAURANTS): Grichting, C, 60 b.; Römerhof, C, 60 b.; Heilquelle, C, 60 b.; Walliserhof, C, 55 b.; Escher, C, 35 b.; Alpina, C, 30 b.; Zayetta, C, 75 b.; Waldrand, D, 30 b.; Gemmi, D, 29 b. – HOTELS WITH NO RESTAURANT: Derby, C, 55 b.; Dala, C, 25 b.; Victoria, D, 35 b.; Paradis, D, 30 b.; Alpenblick, D, 24 b. – Hotel Torrenthorn, 30 b.*

The well-known spa of Leukerbad (in French Loèche-les-Bains) lies amid the green Alpine meadows of a south-facing basin situated in a valley on the N side of the Upper Rhône (Rotten). It lies on the route to the Gemmi pass. This high-altitude resort was known to the Romans; in modern times the earliest reference to the village – then known as Baden – dates from 1315.

The scattered settlement has grown up around its 20 or so thermal springs; the old wooden houses of the village are on the right bank of the River Dala, the hotels and spa establishments on the left.

Leukerbad can be reached by the ordinary motor road from Leuk or by a romantic little by-road which winds its way up from Sierre via Salgesch. From the motor road a daringly engineered path with eight rough wooden ladders up a 100 m (328 feet) high rock face leads to the mountain village of Albinen. – The water (containing lime and sulphur, 51 °C (124 °F); temperature of baths 28–41 °C (82–106 °F)) is efficacious in the treatment of rheumatism, gout and paralysis; there is an open-air pool with thermal water as well as several indoor pools; polio clinic. With its cableways and a magnificent sports centre, Leukerbad is now popular both as a summer and a winter sports resort.

Open-air thermal swimming pool, Leukerbad

SURROUNDINGS. – The Torrentbahn runs from Leukerbad and the Albinen ladders to the *Rinderhütte* (2315 m – 7596 feet). From the Hotel Torrenthorn (2462 m – 8078 feet) it is a 1½ hours' climb to the summit of the *Torrenthorn* (2998 m – 9836 feet), from which there is a superb panoramic view taking in 20 4000 m (13,124 feet) peaks. – The *Gemmiweg*, a path hewn from the rock in 1737–40, runs along a rock face with a sheer drop of 600 m (1969 feet), and is to be recommended only to those with a good head for heights. A cableway (length 1984 m (6510 feet), height difference 935 m (3068 feet), time 5 minutes) runs up to the *Gemmi pass* (2316 m – 7599 feet), from which a bridle-path runs along the shores of the Daubensee and then down to Kandersteg in the Bernese Oberland.

At the mouth of the Dala gorge, above the Rhône, is **Leuk Stadt** (725 m (2379 feet): pop. 2800), a little market town and district administrative capital which was once the summer residence of the Bishop of Sion.

Features of interest include a Late Gothic tower (1541–43) once occupied by a local government official, the *viztum*; the bishop's castle (first mentioned in 1254); the late 15th c. parish church of St Stephan (R.C.); and the former residence of the de Werra family (16th–17th c.). The Ringacker Chapel, on a natural terrace S of the town, is the finest Baroque building in the Valais (1690–94).

Principality of Liechtenstein

Prince's arms

National flag

 Car nationality plate

Arms on car number plates

The Principality of Liechtenstein is an independent state in the Alpine region between Switzerland and Austria with an area of 157 sq. km (61 sq. miles) and a population of rather more than 25,000. It extends from the western slopes of the Rätikon ridge to the Rhine. The most densely populated part of the country and the main agricultural area is the Rhine plain; the hillsides are mainly covered with forest, and in the high valleys Alpine meadows predominate.

The Country of Vaduz, established in 1342, was acquired in 1712 by Prince Hans Adam of Liechtenstein and combined with the lordship of Schellenberg.

Vaduz, capital of Liechtenstein

From 1852 until after the First World War Liechtenstein was joined with Austria in a currency union, but in 1924 it formed an economic union with Switzerland (using Swiss currency and under Swiss customs and postal administration but with its own stamps). Its favourable tax laws have made it the headquarters of numerous holding companies. In proportion to its size Liechtenstein is the most highly industrialised nation in the world, and its per-capita income is also one of the highest in the world. The language of the country is an Alemannic dialect of German.

Vaduz

State: Principality of Liechtenstein (FL).
Altitude: 460 m (1509 feet). – Population: 5000.
Post code: FL-9490. – Dialling code: 075.
(i) **Liechtensteinische Fremdenverkehrszentrale,**
Städtle 37;
tel. 2 14 43.

HOTELS. – *Park-Hotel Sonnenhof*, B, 53 b., SB; *Schlössle*, B, 54 b.; *Real*, B, 15 b.; *Engel*, C, 38 b. – CAMPING SITE. – YOUTH HOSTEL.

RECREATION and SPORT. – Golf, riding, tennis (indoor and outdoor courts), swimming, fishing, walking.

Vaduz, capital of the Principality of Liechtenstein, seat of its government and parliament and its main tourist attraction, lies near the right bank of the Rhine beneath the towering summit of Rätikon.

SIGHTS. – In the middle of the town is the Rathausplatz, with the *Rathaus* (Town Hall). From here the town's main street, *Städtle* (one-way traffic in the opposite direction), runs S for some 500 m (1641 feet) to the Neo-Gothic *parish church* (Pfarrkirche, 1869–73). On the left-hand (E) side of the street, at No. 37, is the *Engländerbau* ("Englishmen's Building"), in which is housed the **Art Gallery** (Gemäldegalerie), particularly notable for the permanent collection in the Prince's Gallery (Rubens, Frans Hals, Van Dyck, Breughel, etc.), also the *Postage Stamp Museum* (Briefmarkenmuseum) and the Tourist Information Office (Fremdenverkehrszentrale). On the opposite side of the street is the *Post Office*. Then follows (No. 43) the *Landesmuseum* (relief model of the Principality on a scale of 1:10,000;

In the centre of Vaduz

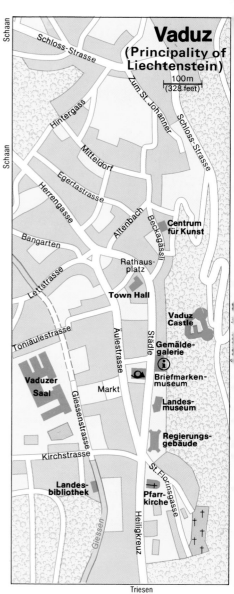

prehistory and the early historical period; weapons; religious art). At the S end of the street, on the left, stands the *Regierungsgebäude* (government offices, 1903–05). – NE of the Town Hall, at 8 Beckagässle, is the *Art Centre* (Centrum für Kunst, 1973: contemporary art, fine books, etc.).

Schloss Vaduz (570 m – 1870 feet) on the E side of the town, the residence of the ruling Prince of Liechtenstein since 1712, was rebuilt in 16th c. style in 1904–10 (no admittance).

OTHER PLACES in Liechtenstein. – The little towns and villages on the hills and in the Upper Samina valley are popular both with summer visitors and winter sports enthusiasts. From Vaduz a hill road winds its way, with steep bends and extensive views, into the Samina valley (14 km (9 miles) to Malbun), going either via the beautifully situated village of **Triesenberg** (884 m (2900 feet): Hotel Bühler; Walser Museum), 6 km (4 miles) from Vaduz, or via *Rotenboden* (1000 m (3281 feet): Hotel Samina), also 6 km (4 miles) from Vaduz, to a road junction at *Gnalp* (8·5 km (5 miles) from Vaduz): left to the Gaflei Hotel, right to Malbun.

The road to the left comes in 1 km (about a $\frac{1}{2}$ mile) to the little village of *Masescha* (1240 m (4068 feet): inn) and in 3·6 km (2 miles) (12 km (7 miles) from Vaduz) to a car park at the *Tourotel Gaflei* (1483 m (4866 feet): 70 b., SB, SP), situated amid Alpine meadows, with extensive views. From here a footpath (the Fürstensteig or "Prince's Path") leads up in $2\frac{1}{4}$–$2\frac{1}{2}$ hours to the *Kuhgrat* (2124 m (6969 feet): magnificent views), the highest peak in the **Drei Schwestern** (Three Sisters) massif.

The road to Malbun, to the right, runs under the *Kulm pass* (1459 m – 4787 feet) in a tunnel 850 m (2789 feet) long to **Steg** (1312 m (4305 feet): Alpenhotel; cross-country skiing centre, ski-lift), in the Upper Samina valley, and continues along a side valley to **Malbun**, 14 km (9 miles) from Vaduz (1650 m (5414 feet): Hotel Malbunerhof, C, 60 b., SB; Montana, 30 b.; several ski-lifts). From here a chair-lift 850 m (2789 feet) long ascends to the *Sareiser Joch* (2014 m – 6608 feet), and the *Schönberg* (2104 m – 6903 feet) can be climbed in $2\frac{1}{2}$ hours.

4 km (2 miles) S of Vaduz is **Triesen** (pop. 3000), with old houses in the upper part of the village and chapels dedicated to St Mamertus and the Virgin. Walks and climbs on the Lavena, Rappenstein and Falknis hills. – 5 km (3 miles) beyond Triesen we reach **Balzers** (pop. 3300), with Gutenberg Castle, the chapels of Mariahilf and St Peter, an old presbytery, a local museum and nature reserves.

3 km (2 miles) N of Vaduz, at the foot of the Drei Schwestern massif, is **Schaan** (pop. 4600), a busy little industrial town with the foundations of a Roman fort. From here a good minor road runs NE to the village of *Planken* (800 m – 2625 feet), situated on a beautiful natural terrace, with good views of the Rhine valley and the Swiss Alps beyond. Planken is an excellent base for walks and climbs in the Drei Schwestern area.

5 km (3 miles) NE of Schaan on road 16 is **Nendeln**. This little town and *Eschen*, a few kilometres W, are

the principal places in the lowland part of Liechtenstein. In both of them remains of the past have been found (in Nendeln the foundations of a Roman villa). The main features of interest are the Pfrundhaus (prebend house), the Holy Cross chapel on the Rotenberg (formerly a place of execution and of assembly) and the chapels of St Sebastian and St Roch in Nendeln. – To the W, on the western slopes of the Eschnerberg, lies the village of *Gamprin-Bendern*, from which the interesting "Eschnerberg History Trail" (Historischer Höhenweg Eschnerberg) runs to *Schellenberg*, with the ruined castle of Neu-Schellenberg. At *Ruggell*, W of Schellenberg in the Rhine valley, is the Ruggeller Riet nature reserve, with interesting flora and fauna.

Locarno

Canton: Ticino (TI).
Altitude: 205 m (673 feet). – Population: 15,000.
Post code: CH-6600. – Dialling code: 093.
ⓘ **Ente Turistico di Locarno e Valli,**
  Via F. Balli 2;
  tel. 31 86 33.

HOTELS. – *La Palma au Lac*, A, 200 b., SB; *Reber au Lac*, B, 130 b., SP; *Parc-Hotel*, B, 125 b., SP; *Esplanade-Hotel*, B, 120 b., SP; *Muralto*, B, 134 b.; *Grand Hotel*, 150 b., SP; *Quisisana*, B, 110 b., SB; *Remorino* (no rest.), 44 b., SP; *Beau-Rivage*, C, 90 b.; *Du Lac*, C, 53 b.; *Excelsior Parcolago* (no rest.), C, 40 b.; *Schloss-Hotel*, D, 60 b., SP; *Navegna au Lac*, D, 30 b.; *Astoria*, D, 92 b.; *Alexandra*, E, 36 b. – IN MONTI: *Olanda*, 14 b. – IN ORSELINA: *Orselina*, C, 150 b., SP; *Stella*, D, 50 b.; *Mirafiori*, D, 40 b.; *Mon Désir*, E, 40 b.

CAMPING SITE: near the Lido.

RECREATION and SPORT. – Golf (at Ascona), riding, tennis (indoor and outdoor courts), sailing, swimming, water-skiing, fishing; curling, ice-rink.

BOAT SERVICES on Lake Maggiore. – Motor-ships (in summer also hydrofoils) to the islands and places on the lake (departure from Lungolago G. Motta).

The old Ticinese town of *Locarno is magnificently situated at the N end of Lake Maggiore, with country villas, gardens and vineyards rising up the hillsides; the newer parts of the town are laid out in a regular pattern on the flat ground at the mouth of the swiftly flowing River Maggia. With its mild climate, in which figs, olives and pomegranates flourish and in August myrtles blossom, Locarno is particularly popular as a holiday resort in spring and autumn.

SIGHTS. – The town's main square is the broad *Piazza Grande*, which extends westward from the landing-stage for some 400 m (1312 feet), with arcades containing shops on its N side. Along the S side are the *Giardini Pubblici* (Public Gardens) and the **Kursaal** (gaming rooms, restaurant). In Via della Pace, which runs S through the gardens to a fountain, is the *Pretorio* (Law Court) or *Palazzo della Conferenza*, in which the Locarno Pact was signed in 1925.

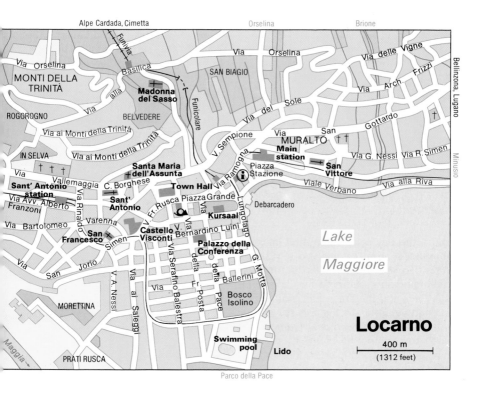

Locarno, on Lake Maggiore, with the pilgrimage church of the Madonna del Sasso in the foreground

The Piazza Grande runs into the curving Via Francesco Rusca, from which four narrow streets lead up to the *Old Town*. On the W side of Via Rusca is the **Castello Visconti**, the old castle of the Visconti Dukes of Milan, which was largely destroyed in 1518; it now houses the *Museo Civico* (closed Mondays), with Roman material recovered by excavations and the Hans Arp Collection (contemporary art). To the SW, on higher ground, is the conventual *church of San Francesco*, a basilica (1528–72) with massive granite columns and wall-paintings, now serving the German-speaking Catholics of the town.

To the N the 17th c. *church of Sant' Antonio* contains painting with perspective effect by G. A. F. Orelli. W of this are the cemetery, and the former *church of S. Maria in Selva* and the tomb of Hans Arp (1887–1966), with sculpture. To the E of Sant'Antonio is the small but fine Baroque *church of Santa Maria dell'Assunta*.

Round the bay runs a beautiful lakeside promenade, the *Lungolago Giuseppe Motta*. To the S this leads to the *Lido* (swimming pool, camping site), the *Parco della Pace* and the Trade Fair grounds on the Maggia delta. To the E is *Rivapiana*, with the 18th c. *church of S. Quirico* (old watch-tower) and the 16th c. *Cà di Ferro*, once a barracks occupied by mercenaries in the employ of the Visconti.

In the MURALTO district to the E of the station stands the *parish church of San Vittore*, originally Romanesque (12th c.) but much altered in later centuries (campanile, completed only in 1932; fine Romanesque *crypt). – Farther NE is the outer district of MINUSIO. In the cemetery (NE entrance in the wall on the right) we find the grave of the German poet *Stefan George* (1868–1933).

The *pilgrimage church of the Madonna del Sasso**, with a Capuchin friary on a wooded crag above Locarno (355 m – 1165 feet) can be reached by funicular from Via Ramogna, between the station and the Piazza Grande, 825 m (2707 feet) in 6 minutes; on foot, by a path with Stations of the Cross, in 30–45 minutes; or by road from Sant'Antonio via Monti or from Muralto via Orselina, 3·5 km (2 miles). The church, founded in 1480, was rebuilt in 1616 and overloaded with decoration in the 19th c. (restored in 20th c.). To the right of the entrance is a major work by Bramantino, the "Flight into Egypt" (1536), and in the second side chapel an "Entombment" by A. Ciseri (c. 1865). Superb *views from the terrace. Cableway to the Alpe Cardada. – On the hillside to the W and E of the Madonna del Sasso, commanding extensive views, are the residential suburbs of MONTI (Monti della Trinità, 404 m (1326 feet)) and ORSELINA (456 m – 1496 feet).

SURROUNDINGS. – From the Madonna del Sasso a cableway 2 km (1 mile) long ascends in 10 minutes to the **Alpe Cardada** (1350 m (4429 feet): Hotel Cardada, E, 30 b.; Colmanicchio, E, 14 b.), with magnificent *views. Chair-lift (869 m (2851 feet), 6 minutes) to *Cimetta* (1676 m – 5499 feet); good skiing, with several ski-lifts. – From Monti a road (6 km – 4 miles) runs steeply uphill through the forest, with many bends, to the little mountain village of *Monte Brè* (1004 m (3294 feet): Hotel Monte Brè, E, 22 b.). 1 km (about a ½ mile) beyond this along the mountainside is *San Bernardo* (1096 m – 3596 feet), with a 16th c. chapel. From both villages there are splendid views.

To Mergoscia (13 km (8 miles): narrow and winding road, but well worth it). – The road runs NE from the Madonna del Sasso along the hillside, with far-ranging views, via Orselina and *Brione sopra Minusio* (433 m (1421 feet): Hotel Dellavalle, C, 85 b.). – 8 km (5 miles): *Contra* (486 m (1595 feet): Hotel Meister, D, 38 b.), high above the mouth of the Val Verzasca. The road continues, through galleries and over bridges, along the W side of the valley. – 5 km (3 miles): **Mergoscia** (735 m – 2412 feet), a beautifully situated village with a view of the Verzasca dam and *Pizzo di Vogorno* (2446 m – 8025 feet). The church has 15th c. wall-paintings.

The Val Verzasca (30 km (19 miles) to Sonogno: reasonably good road, but many bends; its attraction lies in the beauty of this remote and secluded Ticinese valley with its Italian-style houses and churches, many of them with campaniles; good footpaths). – Leave on the Bellinzona road. 4 km (2 miles): *Tenero* (Hotel Stella d'Oro, E, 24 b.), on the W bank of the Verzasca. – 1 km (about a ½ mile): *Gordola* (206 m (676 feet): Hotel La Rotonda, no rest., C, 35 b.), a trim village at the entry of the Verzasca into the Ticino plain (Piano di Magadino). The road now winds its way uphill to the left and continues along the left bank of the river high up on the slopes of the deeply slashed *Val Verzasca, an inhospitable valley which has been considerably changed by the construction of a dam. It has few inhabitants except in summer. – 3 km (2 miles) farther on is the mighty **Verzasca dam**, 220 m (722 feet) high, built 1960–65, which has formed the *Lago di Vogorno*, an artificial lake with a capacity of 105 million cu. m (3708 million cu. feet). Beneath the dam is the hydroelectric power station (235 million kWh annually).

The road continues up the E side of the lake (6 km (4 miles) long), passing through seven tunnels, some of them on sharp bends. Mergoscia can be seen high up on the other side. – 6 km (4 miles): *Vogorno* (490 m (1608 feet): Albergo Pizzo Vogorno, a picturesque village with 13th c. frescoes of saints in the upper church. – 2 km (1 mile): road on left (1 km – about a ½ mile) to the little village of *Corippo* (565 m – 1854 feet). – 2 km (1 mile): **Lavertezzo** (548 m – 1798

Lavertezzo, in the Verzasca valley

feet), at the mouth of the wide Val Lavertezzo, a charming village with a two-arched bridge and a quarry of excellent granite. – The road then climbs through the villages of *Aquino* (574 m – 1883 feet), *Motta* (623 m – 2044 feet) and *Chiosetto* (645 m – 2116 feet) and crosses to the other bank of the river. – 8 km (5 miles): **Brione-Verzasca** (760 m – 2494 feet), another picturesque village at the mouth of the *Valle d'Osola*. The church is the finest in the valley, with a 14th c. figure of St Christopher on the outside and beautiful 14th–15th c. wall-paintings in the interior. The little castle with four towers belonged to the noble Marcacci family of Locarno. – The road continues through the straggling village of *Gerra* (826 m – 2710 feet) and the closely huddled settlement of *Frasco* (885 m (2904 feet): Hotel Efra). – 7 km (4 miles): **Sonogno** (920 m – 3019 feet), a beautifully situated mountain village at the end of the post road. The valley forks into the *Val Vigornesso* (to the right), with a number of other villages, and the *Val Redorta* (to the left).

The *Maggia valley (45 km (28 miles) to Fusio: a good road, almost level as far as Bignasco). – Leave on the Centovalli road and in 4 km (2 miles), at *Ponte Brolla* (260 m – 953 feet) turn off to the right into a road which ascends the left bank of the *Maggia*, in a wide valley enclosed between steep wooded crags. – 7·5 km (5 miles): *church of Santa Maria delle Grazie di Campagna*, with a wooden ceiling and 16th c. frescoes (key in Ristorante Poncini, Maggia). – 0·5 km (less than a ½ mile): **Maggia** (347 m – 1139 feet) has a Baroque parish church above the village and a beautiful waterfall. – 5 km (3 miles): *Giumaglio.* Beyond the village, on the left, is the *Sasso Trolcia*, a rock wall over which the River *Soladino* plunges in a waterfall 100 m (328 feet) high. – 8 km (5 miles): **Cevio** (418 m (1371 feet): Albergo Basodino), the chief place in the Maggia valley, with a 17th c. governor's house (*pretorio*), situated at the mouth of the beautiful Valle di Campo. A road runs up this valley to *Cimalmotto* (14 km – 9 miles) and (in a side valley) *Bosco-Gurin* (15 km – 9 miles), the only German-speaking village in Ticino.

3 km (2 miles): **Bignasco** (441 m (1447 feet): Hotel Posta, E, 30 b.), delightfully situated at the mouth of the *Val Bavona* (characteristic local style of building, beautiful little churches; hydroelectric installations). 11 km (7 miles) up the valley is *San Carlo*, with several cableways. Beyond this point the Maggia valley is known as the *Val Broglio*. – 8 km (5 miles): *Prato* (750 m – 2461 feet), at the mouth of the *Val di Prato*, which runs down from Pizzo Campo Tencia. – 2 km (1 mile): *Peccia* (839 m (2753 feet): inn), with a hydroelectric station. – From here the road climbs in sharp bends to the upper part of the Maggia valley, the *Val Lavizzara* which has interesting flora. – 7 km (4 miles): **Fusio** (1281 m (4203 feet): Hotel Pineta), picturesquely situated on the mountainside (parish church). Above the village lies the *Lago Sambuco*, an artificial lake with a capacity of 63 million cu. m (2224 million cu. feet).

The *Val Centovalli (19 km (12 miles) to Ponte Ribellasca). – Leave Locarno on the Via Vallemaggia, going NW through Solduno. In 4 km (2 miles) the road crosses a bridge (33 m (108 feet) high) over a gorge on the tumultuous River Maggia. At **Ponte Brolla** (9260 m – 30,382 feet), at the mouth of the Valle Maggia (on right), the Centovalli road turns left into the fertile *Pedemonte*, a level area in a wider part of the Val Centovalli. After passing through the picturesque villages of *Tegna* (255 m – 837 feet) and

Verscio (274 m – 899 feet) it comes in 2·5 km (2 miles) to **Cavigliano** (296 m – 971 feet), where a road branches off on the right into the beautiful Val Onsernone. View to the rear of Lake Maggiore.

The road now passes under a railway bridge, over a road bridge (fine *view), through a curving tunnel and over the *Isorno* to enter **Intragna** (342 m (1122 feet): Hotel Antico, E, 50 b., SP), a trim village situated among vineyards on a hill between the Isorno and the Melezza. Church of San Gottardo (1738), with a fine tower (1775) 70 m (230 feet) high – the tallest in Ticino. 2 km (1 mile) beyond the village is a parking place (view).

Now begins the increasingly winding stretch of road through the beautiful *Val Centovalli ("Valley of a Hundred Valleys"), between steep hillsides covered with chestnut trees and slashed by numerous gullies, with a series of picturesquely situated little villages. 2 km (1 mile) along the road is another parking place (view). A road goes off on the left, crosses a dam over the river and comes in 1·5 km (1 mile) to the village of *Palagnedra* which has vivid 15th c. frescoes in the church of San Michele. – Beyond this there are magnificent views down into the valley, with the river swollen into the form of a lake by the dam and Monte Limidario rearing above it. 9 km (6 miles) from Intragna is *Camedo* (552 m – 1811 feet), the last Swiss village (customs). The road then crosses a bridge (with a parallel railway bridge) into the village of *Ponte Ribellasca* (562 m – 1844 feet), on the Italian frontier (Italian customs).

Lötschental

Canton: Valais (VS).
ⓘ **Verkehrsverein Lötschental,**
CH-3903 Kippel;
tel. (028) 49 13 88.

The *Lötschental, surrounded by 17 3000 m (9843 feet) peaks in the Bernese and Valais Alps, has preserved much of its traditional character and customs. It now lies just off one of the great traffic routes through the Alps, the Berne–Lötschberg–Simplon railway. The people of the valley have kept their old local costume and their distinctive dialect, which even their compatriots from other parts of Switzerland find difficult to understand. The subject of study by folklorists, historians and naturalists, the Lötschental now mainly appeals to visitors in quest of peace and seclusion.

From the N the valley is reached by way of Thun and the Kander valley (cars carried by train from Kandersteg to Goppenstein), from the S by way of the Rhône valley and *Gampel* (641 m (2103 feet):

Kippel, in the Lötschental

Hôtel du Rhône, D, 20 b.; camping site), which lies at the mouth of the Lötschental. From Gampel the road winds its way up through the wild gorge of the Lonza to *Goppenstein* (1220 m – 4003 feet).

The Lötschental proper is 10 km (6 miles) long, with magnificent scenery. – Beyond *Ferden* (1389 m (4557 feet): Kummenalp inn) the valley opens out into a wide basin dotted with picturesque villages and hamlets and enclosed by a splendid ring of mountains (to the right the Bietschhorn, 3934 m (12,907 feet), to the left the Petersgrat, 3205 m – 10,516 feet).

Kippel (1376 m (4515 feet): pop. 430; Sporthotel Kippel, E, 30 b.; Lötschberg, E, 40 b.) is the chief place in the valley. In addition to the traditional single-storey houses characteristic of the Lötschental, it has 17th and 18th c. houses of two or more storeys with inscriptions and richly carved decoration. The church dates from 1740. Kippel is the scene of colourful traditional processions. – Cableway to the *Kummenalp.*

Wiler (1421 m (4662 feet): pop. 410) is the only place in the valley with a modern aspect, the old village having been burned down. The little church has beautiful stained glass by Richard Seewald. – Cableway to the *Lauchernalp* (1970 m – 6464 feet), with good skiing and walking.

The last place in the valley is *Blatten* (1542 m – 5059 feet), lying a little off the road which continues up the valley and past the Baroque *Kühmad chapel*, to the **Fafleralp** (1788 m (5866 feet): Hotel Fafleralp, D, 44 b.), a good base for mountain walks and climbs.

Lucerne

Canton: Lucerne (LU).
Altitude: 436 m (1431 feet). – Population: 68,000.
Post code: CH-6000. – Dialling code: 041.

ⓘ **Verkehrsverein,**
Pilatusstrasse 14,
CH-6002 Luzern;
tel. 23 52 52.
SSB Auskunftsbüro
(Railway Information Bureau),
Bahnhof (Station);
tel. 23 21 33.

HOTELS. – ON THE N SIDE OF THE LAKE: *Grand Hotel National*, A, 170 b.; SB; *Palace*, A, 300 b.; bathing beach; *Schweizerhof*, A, 300 b.; *Carlton-Hotel Tivoli*, A, 180 b., bathing beach; *Montana*, B, 120 b.; *Europe Grand Hotel*, B, 300 b.; *Luzernerhof*, B, 116 b.; *Rebstock* (no rest.), B, 50 b.; *Eden au Lac*, C, 70 b.; *Beau Séjour*, C, 50 b.; *Royal*, C, 80 b.; *De la Paix*, C, 70 b., SB; *Kolping*, D, 160 b.

N OF THE REUSS (OLD TOWN): *Balances & Bellevue*, B, 110 b.; *Des Alpes*, C, 80 b.; *Schiff*, D, 30 b.; *Pickwick* (no rest.), D, 25 b.; *Gambrinus*, E, 50 b.

S OF THE REUSS. – NEAR THE STATION: *Monopol & Métropole*, B, 200 b.; *Schiller*, B, 130 b.; *Flora*, B, 280 b.; *Continental*, C, 70 b.; *Park*, C, 60 b.; *Diana*, C, 75 b.; *Bernerhof*, C, 135 b.; *Alpina*, C, 55 b. – ROUND PILATUSPLATZ: *Astoria*, B, 165 b.; *Anker*, C, 65 b.; *Winkelried*, E, 35 b. – ON HIRSCHENGRABEN: *Wilden*

Mann, B, 80 b.; *Rütli–Rheinischer Hof*, C, 100 b.; *Drei Könige*, C, 100 b.; *Rothaus*, C, 85 b.; *Ilge*, C, 62 b., SP.

IN BUNDESPLATZ: *Johanniterhof*, C, 110 b.

ON THE BASLE ROAD: *Untergrund*, C, 90 b.

ON GÜTSCH: *Château Gütsch*, B, 75 b., SP.

IN ST NIKLAUSEN (on lake, 4·5 km (3 miles) from town centre): *St Niklausen am See*, D, 40 b., bathing beach.

YOUTH HOSTEL: on Rotsee, Sedelstrasse 12, 202 b.

CAMPING SITE: at Lido bathing beach.

EVENTS. – *Fasnacht* (Carnival), with masked processions (February–March); *Seenachtsfest* (Lake Festival), with firework display (June); *International Musical Festival*, with choral and symphony concerts (August–September); *Rotsee Rowing Regatta*; *International Horse Races* (September); folk evenings in the Casino (Kursaal); Sunday concerts in Kurplatz (summer).

RECREATION and SPORT. – Climbing school, flying school, parachute jumping, golf-course (on Dietschiberg), tennis, artificial ice-rink (in Tribschen), riding school, indoor and outdoor swimming pools.

*Lucerne (in German Luzern), capital of the canton of the same name, lies at the N end of Lake Lucerne

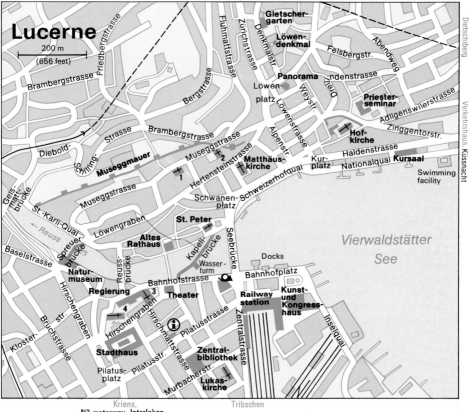

1 Mariahilf Church   2 Church of Christ   3 Jesuit Church   4 Franciscan Church

Lucerne, with the old wooden bridge over the Reuss

(Vierwaldstätter See – Lake of the Four Forest Cantons) at the point where the River Reuss flows out of the lake. For more than a century the town, with its well-preserved medieval core and its handsome and historic old buildings, has been one of the great tourist attractions of Switzerland.

HISTORY. – Lucerne first appears in the records in 840 as *Luciaria*. The name comes from the Benedictine monastery of St Leodegar, founded about 730. After the opening of the St Gotthard pass in the 13th c. it became an important trading town. In 1291 it fell into the hands of the Habsburgs, but in 1332 joined the Confederation. – After the occupation of the whole of Switzerland by Napoleon in 1798 Lucerne was for a brief period capital of the Helvetian Republic.

SIGHTS. – The most characteristic feature of Lucerne is the *Kapellbrücke (Chapel Bridge), a covered bridge 170 m (558 feet) long running diagonally across the Reuss (1333); it is one of the best-preserved wooden bridges in the country. Hanging from the rafters of the roof are more than 100 17th c. pictures depicting local saints and scenes from the town's history. Beside it is the octagonal *Water-Tower* (Wasserturm, 13th c.), once part of the town's fortifications. Farther downstream is another covered wooden bridge, the *Spreuerbrücke* (1408), decorated with scenes from the Dance of Death (17th c.). – Adjoining the Spreuerbrücke, at 6 Kasernenplatz, is the interesting *Nature Museum* (including ecological exhibit with living animals).

The OLD TOWN, on the right bank of the Reuss, still preserves many old burghers' houses and little squares with fountains. In the Kapellplatz is the oldest church in Lucerne, *St Peter's chapel* (1178), which received its present form in the 18th c. In the Kornmarkt is the **Old Town Hall** (Altes Rathaus, 1602–06), in Italian Renaissance style but with a very typical Swiss hipped roof; it contains panelled council chambers (not open to the public). The adjoining tower dates from the 14th c. Immediately E of the Old Town Hall (entrance in Furrengasse) stands the *Am Rhyn-Haus* (17th–18th c.) which houses a collection of important works by Picasso (Rosengart Donation: closed Mondays). To the W of the Kornmarkt is the picturesque *Weinmarkt*; the fountain is a copy (original in the courtyard of the Regierungsgebäude: see below). – Along the N side of the old town runs the *Museggmauer*, a wall built between 1350 and 1408, with nine towers of differing type.

Along the *N shore of the lake*, to the E of Schwanenplatz, extends a series of broad tree-lined **quays** lined with shops and hotels – successively Schweizerhofquai, Nationalquai and Spittelerquai – from

which there is a magnificent panorama of the Alps. To the left is the Rigi group, in the middle the Bürgenstock, to the right the Stanserhorn and Pilatus, and beyond, in the distance, the Glarus and Engelberg Alps. On Nationalquai are the *Kurplatz* and the **Kursaal** (restaurant, gaming rooms).

Above the Nationalquai, on the site of the old monastery of St Leodegar, is the twin-towered **Hofkirche** (R.C.), which was rebuilt in 1634–39 but preserved the towers (1525) of the previous church. On the N tower a Late Gothic sculpture depicts the Agony in the Garden. The church has a carved pulpit and choir-stalls of 1639 and a famous organ (recitals in summer). In the picturesque arcades which surround the church are the tombs of members of old Lucerne families.

From the Kurplatz Löwenstrasse leads N to the Löwenplatz, to the right of which is the *Panorama*, a large circular painting (11,000 sq. m – 118,360 sq. feet) by the Geneva battle-painter Castres, with the collaboration of Hodler and other Swiss painters (1877–79). The painting depicts in highly realistic fashion the retreat of the French Eastern Army into Switzerland in 1871. A little way N, to the rear of a pool is the famous **Lion Monument** (Löwen-denkmal), a huge figure of a dying lion hewn from the face of the living rock. The

monument (1820–21), designed by Thorwaldsen, commemorates the heroic death of the Swiss Guards (26 officers and over 700 troops) who were killed during the attack on the Tuileries during the French Revolution (1792). Above the Lion Monument is the **Glacier Garden** (Gletschergarten), a remarkable relic of the Ice Age which was exposed between 1872 and 1875 (open March–October): glacier-polished rock, erratic boulders and 32 pot-holes, some of them of huge size, with a working model showing the process of formation of a pot-hole. Higher up are an early climbers' hut and a lookout tower. In the museum are relief maps of Switzerland, groups of Alpine animals, specimens of rock, old domestic interiors, etc.

On the outskirts of the town, 1 km (about a ½ mile) farther N, is an elongated lake, the *Rotsee*, on which a well-known regatta is held every year.

On the *S bank of the Reuss*, extending E to the lake and linked with the Schwanen-platz by the busy *Seebrücke* (Lake Bridge), is the *Bahnhofplatz*; here are the **railway station** and the *docks* used by the various boat services. In the gardens stands the *Wagenbach fountain* (1934). At the E end of the square, adjoining the station, is the **Kunst- und Kon-gresshaus** (1932–33), which contains conference and concert halls and the *Museum of Art* (Kunstmuseum: closed Mondays), with a fine collection of Swiss painters of the 16th–20th c., 20th c. European painters and the Rieder Collection (also special exhibitions).

In the part of the old town that extends W from the station along the left bank of the Reuss are the *Municipal Theatre* and the *Jesuit church*, a Baroque building (1666–77) with an elegant Rococo interior (1750). The **Regierungsgebäude** (Government Building) adjoining the church was formerly a Jesuit college, the core of which is the *Ritter palace*, a Renaissance mansion (1557–64 built by Lukas Ritter, a local dignitary who had grown rich in foreign service. In the handsome arcaded courtyard can be seen the original of the Weinmarkt fountain. To the rear of the building is the Neoclassical Chamber of the Great Council (1841–43). Close by are the *Cantonal Archives*. SW of the Regierungsgebäude stands the *Franciscan church* (13th–17th c.), the nave walls of which have paintings of flags and banners (carved pulpit 1628, choir-stalls 1647–51). In front of the church (also known as the Barfüsserkirche or Church of the Barefoot Friars) is the *Barfüsserbrunnen*, a fountain erected in 1546.

SW of the station, at 10 Sempacherstrasse, the *Central Library* (Zentralbibliothek) contains over 400,000 volumes and pamphlets, 2500 manuscripts and over 800 incunabula.

On the N side of the lake, just off Haldenstrasse, is situated the lower station of the funicular to the ***Dietschiberg** (632 m – 2014 feet). There is a fine view of the town and the lake from the top. Near the upper station there are a café-restaurant, a golf-course and a miniature railway (scale 1:10). Below, to the SW, is a park with the interesting *Utenberg Costume and Folk Museum* (Schweizer Trachten- und Heimatmuseum Utenberg).

Beyond the funicular station Haldenstrasse continues to the fascinating ***Verkehrshaus der Schweiz** (*Swiss Transport Museum*, Schweizerisches Verkehrsmuseum: entrance in Lidostrasse). The museum is a large complex of exhibition halls and outdoor exhibits

Aircraft in the Swiss Transport Museum

covering all forms of transport, including air and space travel (Cosmorama), communications and tourism, with railway locomotives and rolling-stock, ships, aircraft, rockets and automobiles (originals or models), together with a *Planetarium*. At the E end of the complex is the *Hans-Erni-Haus* which contains paintings and graphic art by the well-known Lucerne artist of that name, and also a lecture hall.

To the W of the town, on the edge of the extensive *Gütschwald*, is the **Gütsch**, another hill which affords extensive views. It is reached by funicular from Baselstrasse or on foot by way of the Gütschweg (1·5 km – 1 mile).

SURROUNDINGS. – On a hill SE of the town, on the W side of the lake, stands **Tribschen**, a country house in which Wagner lived from 1866 to 1872 and composed the "Mastersingers" and other works. The house is now a museum, with original scores, pictures, prints and a collection of old musical instruments. (Also reached by motorboat from Lucerne.)

SW of Lucerne is the industrial suburb of **Kriens** (alt. 492 m (1614 feet): Motel Luzern-Süd, C, 70 b.; Sonnenberg, D, 30 b.), with the little castle of Schauensee (1595, with a 13th c. round tower). From here there is a funicular up the **Sonnenberg** (780 m – 2559 feet), which affords superb views. Here too is the lower station of a cableway up Mt Pilatus. – 5 km (3 miles) SW of Kriens at *Hergiswald* there is a beautiful 17th c. pilgrimage chapel (flight of 1000 steps; timber *ceiling with more than 300 symbolic images of the Virgin by K. Meglinger, 1654). – The road continues to the mountain resort of *Schwarzenberg* (831 m (2727 feet): Hotel Rössli, C, 60 b.; Weisses Kreuz, C, 40 b., SB).

***Ascent of Mt Pilatus** (a popular round trip, going up by the cableway and down by the cog-railway). – Cableway from *Kriens* (4968 m (16,300 feet), 30 minutes) to the *Fräkmüntegg* (1415 m (4643 feet): skiing), and from there another cableway (1400 m (4593 feet), 7 minutes) to the *Pilatus-Kulm* (2070 m – 6792 feet). – Visitors can also travel by rail, boat or road (16 km (10 miles) on the road to the Brünig pass) to **Alpnachstad** (440 m – 1444 feet). From there

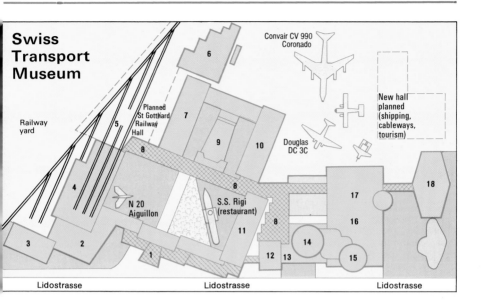

Swiss Transport Museum

1 Entrance, kiosk, Transport Archives
2 Model of St Gotthard railway
3 Modern railway system
4 Locomotives and rolling-stock:
5 Swiss Railways restaurant car of 1914
6 Workshops
7 Road Transport Hall
8 Connecting halls
9 Lecture hall
10 Postal Services Hall
11 Telecommunications Hall
12 Administration
13 Restaurant
14 Longines Planetarium
15 Cosmorama (see No. 16, second floor)
16 Hall of Air and Space Travel
17 Shipping and tourism
18 Hans-Erni-Haus

travel on the *cog-railway* (4·6 km (3 miles), 30 minutes, gradients up to 48% (1 in 2), which runs up through Alpine meadows (orchards) and forest to the passing station at *Ämsigen* (1350 m – 4429 feet) and then continues over the rock-strewn *Mattalp* and up the steep rock face, through four tunnels, to the upper station on *Pilatus-Kulm* (2070 m (6792 feet): Hotel Bellevue, C, 50 b.; Pilatus-Kulm, D, 28 b.). – From here it is a 6–10 minutes' climb to the summit (surrounded by a wall) of the *Esel* (2122 m – 6962 feet), the central but not the highest peak of *Pilatus, from which there are magnificent views of the Alps, from Säntis to the Blümlisalp, Lakes Lucerne and Zug, and the Swiss uplands. The name of the mountain probably comes from the Latin *pileatus*, "covered (with clouds)", although legend ascribes it to Pontius Pilate, said to have been buried in a former lake on the Upper Bründlenalp. Until the 17th c. Pilatus was known as Frakmunt (from *fractus mons*). – From the Pilatus-Kulm it is a 30 minutes' walk to the *Tomlishorn* (2132 m – 6995 feet), the highest point in this rugged limestone massif.

To the W of Lucerne, in the valley of the Kleine Emme, is the industrial town of **Wolhusen** (568 m (1864 feet): pop. 3500). On a hill near the town is situated the convent of *Werthenstein*, which boasts a beautiful pilgrimage church (1608–16) and a fine cloister. – From here road 2 runs NW to the old-world little town of **Willisau** (557 m (1828 feet): pop. 2900), with well-preserved town walls.

To the Sempach, Baldegg and Hallwil lakes. – NW of Lucerne lie three beautiful lakes. Road 2 leads to the S end of the attractive **Sempacher See** (507 m – 1663 feet), on the E side of which is the pretty little town of **Sempach** (520 m (1706 feet): pop. 1500), with a fine half-timbered town hall (1737: old coats of arms in council chamber). On the Kirchbühl N of the town stands St Martin's church (13th and 16th c.). By the lake, to the S of the town, the *Swiss Bird-Watching Station* (Schweizerische

Vogelwarte), houses an ornithological museum. – 2 km (1 mile) N, above the town on the road to Hildisrieden, is the Schlachtkapelle (Battle Chapel), built in 1473 to commemorate the Confederates' victory over Duke Leopold III of Austria on 9 July 1386, a victory traditionally attributed to the self-sacrifice of Arnold von Winkelried.

At the N end of the lake, from which the river *Suhre* flows N, is the tranquil little country town of **Sursee** (507 m (1663 feet): pop. 5000; Hotel Sursee, B, 48 b.; Central, C, 30 b.; Seehotel Bellevue, D, 25 b.) which has a Baroque parish church (1641), a late Gothic town hall (1546) and 18th c. burghers' houses. – From here road 23 runs NE to **Beromünster** (642 m (2106 feet): pop. 1700), with St Michael's church, which belonged to a monastic house founded by Count Bero of Lenzburg about 980. The church, originally Romanesque, was rebuilt in 1606 and remodelled in Baroque style in 1775; fine choir-stalls of 1609, rich treasury. Castle (local museum), in which the first book printed in Switzerland was produced in 1470.

To the E of Beromünster is the Seetal (Lake Valley) in which lie the Baldegger See and Hallwiler See. *Hochdorf*, at the S end of the **Baldegger See**, has a handsome church of 1768. On a hill 3 km (2 miles) E stands a former commandery of the Knights of St John, *Hohenrain* (614 m – 2015 feet), now a special school. – Continue up the E side of the lake on road 26. On the Lindenberg, to the right of the road, is *Schloss Horben* (1701), from which there is a beautiful view of the Alps. – At **Gelfingen** is *Schloss Heidegg* which has a massive 12th c. tower house. – From Gelfingen a road goes off on the right to *Hitzkirch* (473 m – 1552 feet), with a former commandery of the Teutonic Order (main building 1749, church 1680), which now houses a teachers' training college and a lake-dwelling museum. – Road 26 continues to the S end of the Hallwiler See.

Beinwil (522 m – 1713 feet), on the W side of the **Hallwiler See**, lies at the foot of the *Homberg* (792 m (2599 feet): inn), which commands extensive views. – 1 km. (½ mile) NE of Boniswil on the N bank of the lake stands *Schloss Hallwil* (9th–16th c. Museum; local collection). – The road back to Lucerne along the E side of the lake passes *Schloss Brestenberg* (462 m–1516 feet), a country house with a park, built in 1625, which is now a hotel (C, 40 b.; bathing beach). From Gelfingen road 26 returns to Lucerne.

Lugano

Canton: Ticino (TI).
Altitude: 272 m (892 feet)
Population: 29,000 (Greater Lugano 43,000).
Post code: CH-6900. – Dialling code: 091.

(i) **Ufficio Turistico,**
Riva Albertolli 5;
tel. 21 46 64.

HOTELS. – BY THE LAKE: *Splendide-Royal*, A, 125 b., SB; *Commodore*, B, 130 b., SP; *Excelsior*, B, 150 b.; *International au Lac*, C, 120 b.; *Walter*, C, 64 b.; *Plaza* (no rest.), C, 56 b.; *Bellariva*, D, 32 b.; *Felix*, D, 40 b.; etc. – IN THE OLD TOWN: *Cristallo*, C, 120 b.; *Dante* (no rest.), C, 70 b.; *Ticino*, C, 45 b.; *Lux* (no rest.), D, 70 b.; *Cattedrale* (no rest.), E, 30 b. – ROUND THE STATION (on higher ground): *Holiday Select*, C, 80 b.; *Arizona*, C, 100 b., SP; *Scandinavia*, C, 68 b.; *Kocher's Washington*, C, 70 b.; *Montana*, D, 35 b.

IN PARADISO: *Eden Grand*, A, 125 b., SP; *Europa au Lac*, B, 170 b., SB; *Du Lac-Seehof*, B, 90 b., SP; *Admiral*, B, 150 b., SP; *Meister*, B, 130 b., SP; *Beaurivage*, B, 140 b., SP; *Bellevue au Lac*, B, 120 b., SP. – IN CASSARATE: *Villa Castagnola au Lac*, B, 120 b., SB; *Strandhotel Seegarten*, C, 130 b., SP; *La Torre* (on 15th and 16th floors of a high-rise building), C, 50 b. – IN CASTAGNOLA: *Belmonte*, B, 80 b., SP; *Carlton Villa Moritz*, C, 100 b., SP; *Boldt-Arcadia*, C, 90 b., SP. – IN ORIGLIO: *Country Club*, B, 110 b., SP. – IN AGNO: *La Perla*, A, 300 b., SB, SP.

YOUTH HOSTEL: Lugano-Crocifisso, Via Cantonale 13.

RESTAURANTS. – *Bianchi al Cenacolo*, 3 via Pessina; *Locanda del Boschetto*, 40 via Casserinetta (Italian cuisine); *Tavernetta Colorado*, 19 via Maraini (Ticinese specialities); *Al Portone* 3 viale Cassarate; *La Tinera*, 2 via dei Gorini (Ticinese cuisine); many *grotti* (country inns) around the town.

Lugano

EVENTS. – *Carnival*, with open-air risotto feast (February); *morning concerts* (April–October); *Lake Festival*, with firework display (summer); *Summer Risotto Feast* (mid July); *Vintage Procession* (first Sunday in October). – Casino in Kursaal.

WATER SPORTS. – Swimming (bathing beach, heated swimming pools, indoor pools in the Campo Marzio and a number of hotels), water-skiing, sailing, scuba diving, wind-surfing, motor-boats, fishing.

RECREATION and SPORT on land. – Golf (Magliaso), tennis, riding, miniature golf (Comano, Carona), flying (Agno), judo, boccia (ten covered alleys), keep-fit track; skating and other ice sports in Resega Stadium (September–March).

TRANSPORT. – Cars are best parked in the multi-storey parks in the middle of town (signs). Trolley service between Paradiso and Cassarate; funicular (1½ minutes) from the station to the old town (Piazza Cioccaro).

Lugano, the "pearl of Lake Lugano", lies in a bay half-way down the lake, flanked by Monte San Salvatore and Monte Brè. It is the largest and most important town in Ticino, and the beauty of the town and its setting makes it one of Switzerland's most popular holiday resorts during the warmer months of the year.

Lugano has a notably temperate climate, with plenty of sunshine of moderate intensity and mild air temperatures with little variation over the day. The town and surrounding area lie directly on the important N–S traffic route, both road and rail, over the St Gotthard. The architecture and way of life of Lugano show distinctly southern characteristics, as does the plant life.

HISTORY. – Along the shores of Lake Lugano traces of the Etruscans and the Gauls have been found, together with remains of the Roman, Lombard and Frankish periods. During the Middle Ages the town was under the jurisdiction of the Bishop of Como and thus became involved in the conflicts between Milan and Como. After the conquest of Ticino by the Confederates Lugano was from 1512 to 1798 the seat of the district governor. The opening of the St Gotthard railway in 1882 gave fresh impetus to the development of the town, particularly as a tourist and holiday resort.

SIGHTS. – The pulsating activity of Lugano revolves around three squares surrounding the **Town Hall** (Municipio, Palazzo Civico: 1844). – To the N is the *Piazza della Riforma*, with the former Pretorio (Law Court: 15th–18th c.), now occupied by the Cantonal Bank, and a number of cafés. By the lake is the *Piazza*

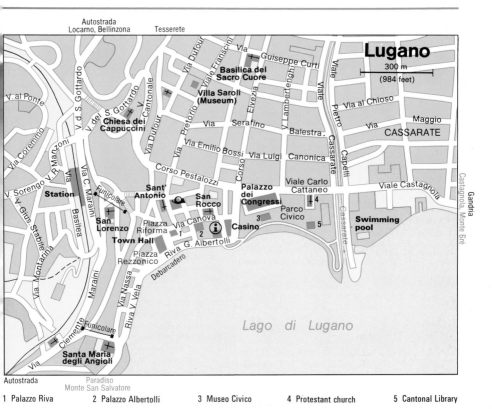

1 Palazzo Riva   2 Palazzo Albertolli   3 Museo Civico   4 Protestant church   5 Cantonal Library

Riziero Rezzonico and the *Piazza Alessandro Manzioni* (gardens), and in front of the 18th c. *Palazzo Riva* is the Debarcadero (dock). The long *lakeside promenade* which runs from Cassarate to Paradiso is unfortunately cut off from the middle of town by traffic on the main road.

The OLD TOWN of Lugano contains a number of historic buildings. Outstanding among the churches is the **cathedral of St Lawrence** (*San Lorenzo*). Originally Romanesque, it was enlarged in the 13th–14th c. and underwent extensive alteration in the 17th and 18th c. It has an imposing Renaissance façade, rich fresco decoration and a Baroque interior.

NE of the Piazza della Riforma in the Via Canova is the handsome *Palazzo Albertolli* (19th c.) and in the adjoining Piazza Maghetti is the 16th c. *church of St Roch* (San Rocco). Still farther E we come to the Piazza Indipendenza, on the S side of which is the *Kursaal*, and beyond this the beautiful *Parco Civico*, with the **Palazzo dei Congressi** (convention facility).

From the Piazza della Riforma the Via Pretoria runs N into Viale Stefano Franscini. On the left-hand side stands the *Villa Saroli*, housing the *Historical and Archaeological Museum* (local history, Etruscan and Roman material).

The conventual **church of Santa Maria degli Angioli** (1499–1515) on the S side of the town contains a fine fresco of the Passion by Bernardo Luini (1529). The nearby pilgrimage church of the *Madonna di Loreto* (1524) has 17th c. frescoes.

In CASTAGNOLA, to the E of the town, is the **Villa Favorita**, which boasts one of the finest private picture galleries in Europe, the *Schloss Rohoncz Collection*, belonging to Baron Heinrich von Thyssen-Bornemisza. Among the paintings are masterpieces by Italian, Flemish, Dutch, Spanish, German and French artists from the Middle Ages to the 18th c.

SURROUNDINGS. – The town's two hills, Monte San Salvatore and Monte Brè, offer attractive day and half-day trips.

Monte San Salvatore (912 m – 2992 feet). – From Paradiso, on the lake, a cableway 1658 m (5440 feet) long, with gradients of 38–60% (1 in $2\frac{1}{2}$–1 in $1\frac{1}{2}$), ascends in 10 minutes to the upper station at 884 m (2900 feet) (inn). From the summit there are magnificent panoramic** views of the town and the lake, the Bernese and Valais Alps (Monte Rosa) and

View from Lugano towards Monte Brè

the N Italian plain. Footpaths to Carona, Melide, Morcote and Figino; return by rail, postal bus or boat.

Monte Brè (933 m – 3061 feet). – From Cassarate, to the E of the little stream of the same name, a cableway 1621 m (5319 feet) long, with gradients of 47–60% (1 in 2–1 in 1½) arrives in 15–25 minutes at the upper station (inn). Fine**views extending to the Valais Alps. This favourite viewpoint can also be reached by car on a narrow and winding road (11 km (7 miles) from Lugano, via Castagnola, Ruvigliana and Aldesago).

There are also a variety of possible excursions farther afield. From 1 March to 31 October a reasonably priced holiday ticket covering travel on all train, boat and postal bus services for a period of 7 days can be obtained from travel agencies and tourist information offices. – For trips on the lake, see under Lake Lugano, below.

The Malcantone district. – An attractive drive through this area between Lugano and the Italian frontier, of about 50 km (31 miles), with *Agno* (6 km (4 miles) W of Lugano) as its starting-point, might take in the health resort of *Cademario* (795 m – 2608 feet), *Breno* (802 m (2631 feet): base for the ascent of Poncione di Breno, 1658 m (5440 feet), 3 hours) and *Miglieglia* (751 m – 2464 feet), from which a chair-lift (2673 m (8770 feet), 18 minutes) goes up *Monte Lema* (1624 m (5328 feet): upper station 1550 m (5086 feet); inn, superb views). Also worth seeing are the villages of *Novaggio* (644 m – 2113 feet), *Banco* (585 m – 1919 feet) and *Astano* (633 m (2077 feet), surrounded by chestnut forests) as well as *Caslano* on

Gandria, Lake Lugano

Lake Lugano, from which the return road runs NE to Agno. SW of Agno on the Swiss-Italian border lies *Ponte Tresa* (motel, 80 b.)

Lugano to Tesserete. – An excursion into the densely populated valley of the Cassarate, running through romantic villages including *Vezia, Cureglia* and **Tesserete** (532 m – 1745 feet), chief place in the hilly *Capriasca* district; then into the *Val Colla*, returning from *Bogno* (963 m – 3160 feet) via *Sonvico, Dino* and *Cadro*. Total distance 20 km (12 miles).

Lugano to Gandria (5 km – 3 miles). – Via Cassarate and Castagnola to the *Gandriastrasse (Gandria road), which runs S to Porlezza and Lake Como (Italy). The last part of the trip must be done on foot, to the picturesque village of *Gandria (alt. 300 m (984 feet): pop. 250; Hotel Moosmann, D, 40 b.), a typical Ticinese settlement clinging picturesquely to a steep slope rising from the lake (narrow lanes, arcades, Baroque church) and surrounded by terraced vineyards.

On the other side of the lake (boat service), to the S, is the *Cantine di Gandria* dock, with an interesting Customs museum, situated near the Italian frontier (containers for smuggled goods, weapons). To the SE is the Italian village of *Santa Margherita*, from which there is a funicular to the *Belvedere di Lanzo* (887 m (2910 feet): good views).

Lake Lugano

Within Switzerland and Italy.
Canton: Ticino (TI).
ⓘ **Ufficio Turistico di Lugano,**
Riva Albertolli 5,
CH-6901 Lugano;
tel. (091) 21 46 46.
Pro Ceresio,
Via Pocobelli 14,
CH-6815 Melide;
tel. (091) 68 63 83.

**Lake Lugano (in Italian Lago di Lugano or Ceresio), on the southern edge of the Alps, lies mainly within the Swiss canton of Ticino, the remainder being in the Italian provinces of Varese and Como. Lying at an altitude of 270 m (886 feet), it has an area of 48·7 sq. km (19 sq. miles), with a maximum depth of 288 m (945 feet). From the W end of the lake the River Tresa flows into Lake Maggiore. The climate already shows distinct Mediterranean characteristics.

Very pleasant round trips on the lake are run by the motor-ships of the Lake Lugano Shipping Company (SNL: head office in Lugano, information in harbour).

The principal town on Lake Lugano is *Lugano (p. 172), on the N shore of the lake. From there a road runs S alongside the lake to **Melide** (alt. 277 m (909 feet): Hotel Park-Palace, C, 110 b.; Seehotel Riviera, C, 39 b.; Generoso Strandhotel, D, 50 b.), situated on a peninsula from which a causeway crosses the lake. A feature of interest here is *"Switzerland in Miniature"*, which reproduces many of Switzerland's principal tourist attractions (towns, castles, monuments, transport) on a 1:25 scale.

Across the causeway, to the N, is the Italian enclave of **Campione d'Italia** (Gran Hotel Campione d'Italia, 75 b.; Bellevue, 17 b.), with the 14th c. church of the Madonna dei Ghirli and a gaming casino.

Lake Lugano from Monte Brè

S of Melide, on the southern slopes of *Monte Arbostora* (839 m – 2753 feet), a promontory projecting into the lake, is the old-world little town of *Morcote (277 m 909 feet): pop. 650; Hotel Olivella au Lac, A, 150 b.; Carina, C, 35 b.), one of the most picturesque places in Switzerland and a great tourist attraction, with its beautiful setting and its well-preserved old houses and streets. In a commanding situation above the village stands the pilgrimage church of the Madonna del Sasso (originally 13th c., rebuilt 1462, remodelled in Baroque style 1758), with a separate campanile; it contains fine 16th c. frescoes. From the church a flight of 408 steps goes down to the village on the shores of the lake. Cemetery with the graves of Moissi, Eugen d'Albert and Baklanoff; Parco Scherrer.

Facing Morcote across the lake is Brusino-Arsizio, which can be reached

"Switzerland In Miniature", Melide

from Melide by way of Melano and Capolago.

From Melide we cross the causeway and go S along the far side of the lake to **Melano**, at the foot of Monte Generoso. – Beyond this, at the S end of the lake, is **Capolago** (277 m – 909 feet), from which a rack-railway (cog-railway) serves ****Monte Generoso** (1704 m (5591 feet): restaurant), with superb views of the Alps and the Lombard plain, including Milan. – 1 km (about a ½ mile) W of Capolago in the village of *Riva San Vitale* there is an octagonal *baptistery (5th c.) and the church of Santa Croce (16th c.).

Beyond this is **Brusino-Arsizio** (277 m (909 feet): pop. 370), which is within the administrative district of Lugano but from the tourist point of view belongs to the fertile and densely populated Mendrisiotto area, at the southernmost tip of Switzerland. This picturesque village lies at the foot of Monte San Giorgio, on which is the little resort of *Serpiano* (645 m (2116 feet): extensive views), reached by cableway or by road from Mendrisio.

Morcote, on Lake Lugano

Lake Maggiore

Within Switzerland and Italy.
Canton: Ticino (TI).
Altitude: 194 m (637 feet).

(i) **Ente Turistico di Ascona e Losone,**
CH-6612 Ascona;
tel. (093) 35 55 44.
Ente Turistico di Brissago e Ronco,
CH-6614 Brissago;
tel. (093) 65 11 70.
Ente Turistico di Locarno e Valli,
Via F. Balli 2,
CH-6600 Locarno;
tel. (093) 31 86 33.

HOTELS. – See under Ascona and Locarno.

****Lake Maggiore, known to the Romans as Lacus Verbanus, is the second largest of the North Italian lakes (area 212 sq. km (82 sq. miles), length 60 km (37 miles), breadth 3–5 km (2–3 miles), greatest depth 372 m (1221 feet)). Less intricately patterned than Lake Como and without the sheer rock faces of the northern part of Lake Garda, it nevertheless offers scenery of southern splendour.**

The N part of the lake, with the town of Locarno, is in Switzerland, but the greater part of it is in Italy, the E side belonging to Lombardy and the W side to Piedmont. The lake's principal tributaries are the *Ticino* and the *Maggia* to the N and the *Toce* on the W side. The river which flows out of the S end, having carved a passage through massive morainic walls, preserves the name of Ticino. – The northern part of the lake is enclosed by mountains, for the most part wooded, while towards the S the shores slope down to the plain of Lombardy. In clear weather the water in the northern part of the lake is green, in the southern part deep blue.

The climate is mild. From midnight until morning the *tramontana* blows, usually coming from the N; from midday until the evening the *inverna* blows from the S. The plant life of Lake Maggiore, like that of Lakes Garda and Como, includes many subtropical species: figs, olives and pomegranates flourish in the mild climate, and in August the myrtle blossoms. On the Borromean Islands lemons, oranges, cork-oaks, sago palms and carob-trees grow. The fisheries are very productive.

The most popular tourist areas are around Ascona (p. 58) and Locarno (p. 163), and on the western arm of the lake between Pallanza and Stresa, where the ***Borromean Islands* with their subtropical gardens are the main attraction. One very attractive excursion is a boat trip from Locarno to Arona (service through the

Lake Maggiore – the Isole di Brissago, off Ronco

year, twice daily in summer; also hydrofoil services), calling alternately at places on the E and W sides of the lake.

Martigny

Canton: Valais (VS).
Altitude: 477 m. (1565 feet). – Population: 11,000.
Post code: CH-1920. – Dialling code: 026.
ⓘ **Office Régional du Tourisme,**
Martigny;
tel. 2 10 18.

HOTELS. – *Du Rhône*, C, 90 b.; *Central*, C, 50 b.; *De la Poste*, C, 65 b.; *Forclaz-Touring*, C, 75 b.; *Forum*, C, 60 b.; *Kluser*, D, 70 b.; *Du Grand St-Bernard*, E, 65 b. – YOUTH HOSTEL.

The ancient little town of Martigny, the Roman Octodurum, situated on the great bend in the Rhône at the inflow of the River Drance, lies on the important through route from Lake Geneva to the Simplon and on the roads to the Great St Bernard and the Col de la Forclaz (Chamonix – Mont Blanc tunnel).

Verbier (Valais)

SIGHTS. – In the newer part of the town, MARTIGNY VILLE, is the attractive Place Centrale, with the 19th c. *Hôtel de Ville* (Town Hall). 2 km (1 mile) S is the old-world MARTIGNY BOURG, with the *Old Town Hall*. – On the vine-clad hillside above the town (30 minutes from Martigny Ville) can be seen the ruins of the 13th c. castle (destroyed in 1518) of *La Bâtiaz*, which belonged to the bishops of Sion; the tower was restored in 1898. – To the SE are remains of a Roman amphitheatre.

SURROUNDINGS. – From the end of Martigny Bourg a narrow winding road runs E through the forest on the slopes of *Mont Chemin*. – 3 km (2 miles): *Chemin-Dessous* (774 m – 2539 feet). – 3·5 km (2 miles): *Chemin-Dessus* (1154 m – 3786 feet). – 2·5 km (2 miles): **Col des Planches** (1409 m – 4623 feet), with fine views which is the starting-point for the ascent of the *Pierre à Voir* (2476 m (8124 feet): 4 hours), the highest peak between the Rhône and the Drance and a commanding viewpoint. From here there is also a beautiful footpath along the mountain-side, level for most of the way, to *Isérables* (4 hours). – From the Col des Planches the road descends steeply, with many sharp bends, to **Sembrancher** (9 km – 6 miles), in the Drance valley, which has a parish church of 1676 with a fine Late Gothic tower.

From Sembrancher (which can also be reached from Martigny on the excellent main road, No. 21) it is 15 km (9 miles) to the well-known winter sports resort of **Verbier**, situated on a natural terrace facing S, with views of the Grand Combin and the Mont Blanc group (1420 m (4659 feet): Hôtel Rhodania, B, 80 b.; Résidence du Parc (no rest.), B, 60 b.; Grand Combin, C, 52 b.; De Verbier, C, 60 b.; De la Poste, C, 60 b.; Mirabeau (no rest.), C, 50 b.). Access to the skiing areas is provided by numerous lifts.

Val de Trient (11 km – 7 miles). – This is a short valley W of Martigny, gorge-like in places, through which the Trient flows to join the Rhône. – The steep and narrow mountain road runs NW through La Bâtiaz, crosses the Trient on the *Gueuroz viaduct* and turns SE. – 7 km (4 miles): **Salvan** (927 m – 3041 feet), a health resort, from which a daringly engineered road climbs by way of *Les Granges* (1044 m – 3425 feet) to the *Lac de Salanfe* (8 km – 5 miles), an artificial lake 2 km (1 mile) long formed between 1947 and 1952 (1914 m (6280 feet): hotels; skiing). From Les Granges there is a footpath to the impressive *Gorges du Dailly*. – 1·5 km (1 mile) SW of Salvan is the summer and winter resort of **Les Marécottes** (1100 m (3604 feet): "Reno Ranch" Alpine zoo, natural swimming pool, from which a chair-lift 1470 m (4823 feet) long (lower station 1140 m (3740 feet)) goes up to *Creusaz* (1780 m – 5840 feet). – The Val de Trient road continues beyond Salvan to *Le Trétien* (4 km – 2 miles), from which it is possible to reach *Finhaut*, higher up the valley, but only by rail.

Over the Col de la Forclaz to Chamonix (France) – Just S of Martigny on the road to the Great St Bernard (see p. 207) turn right into a road which winds its way up, with a number of sharp bends, through the villages of *La Fontaine* and *Le Fays* to the **Col de la Forclaz** (1527 m – 5010 feet), between the *Croix de Prélayes* and the *Mont de l'Arpille* (2089 m (6854 feet): chair-lift; extensive views). It then runs down, with attractive views of the Trient valley and the *Trient glacier*, to Trient (1305 m – 4282 feet), a summer and winter sports resort in a more open stretch of the valley. After passing through **Le Châtelard** (1120 m (3675 feet): Hotel Suisse, C, 28 b.) it comes to the *French frontier*, from which it continues over the *Col des Montets* to Chamonix.

Meiringen

Canton: Berne (BE).
Altitude: 600 m (1969 feet). – Population: 4000.
Post code: CH-3860. – Dialling code: 036.
ⓘ **Verkehrsverein Meiringen-Haslital,**
tel. 71 31 31.

In the Aare gorge, near Meiringen

HOTELS. – *Du Sauvage*, B, 97 b.; *Rebstock*, C, 30 b.; *Löwen*, C, 30 b.; *Sherlock Holmes*, C, 94 b.; *Victoria*, C, 30 b.; *Baer*, D, 50 b.; *Adler*, D, 30 b.; *Rössli*, D, 20 b.; *Weisses Kreuz*, D, 55 b. – YOUTH HOSTEL.

EVENT. – *International Musical Festival* (July).

RECREATION and SPORT. – Rosenlaui climbing school; indoor and outdoor swimming pools; tennis, riding, fishing.

Meiringen, the chief place in the Hasli valley, lies on the Aare, which flows into Lake Brienz a few kilometres W of the town. It is a popular summer holiday resort and a good base for excursions into the Bernese Oberland, and has a long tradition of wood-carving and hand-weaving.

SIGHTS. – The *parish church*, on higher ground, was built in 1684 on the remains of an earlier church (13th c.), and has an 11th c. crypt. The tower, with round-arched windows, dates from the 14th and 17th c. There is also an interesting local museum, the *Haslimuseum*.

SURROUNDINGS. – 2 km (1 mile) SE is the *Aare gorge, 1400 m (4593 feet) long, through which there is a footpath (½ hour, through tunnels and galleries) to the *Lammi inn*, on the road to Innertkirchen. – From the left bank of the Aare (car park) a funicular takes 5 minutes to reach the *Upper Reichenbach Falls*. From the upper station (836 m – 2743 feet) there is a good view of the falls, which plunge down in two stages. Footpath (20 minutes) to the Zwirgi inn.

To the **Schwarzwaldalp** (13 km – 8 miles). – A narrow road branches off the Grimsel road in the hamlet of *Willigen* and winds its way up through the forest. – 3 km (2 miles): *Schwendi* (779 m – 2556 feet). – 2 km (1 mile): *Zwirgi inn* (976 m – 3202 feet), with a fine view to the rear of the Hasli valley and Hasliberg. The road then continues high above the Reichenbach on the slopes of the *Hohbalm* (1371 m – 4498 feet). Straight ahead is the Wellhorn, with the Wetterhorn and Eiger to the right. – 4·5 km (3 miles): *Gschwandenmaad* (1298 m – 4259 feet), from which there is a celebrated *view of the Engelhörner (2781 m – 9124 feet), the Rosenlaui glacier and the Wetterhorn (3703 m – 12,150 feet). – 1 km (about a ½ mile): **Rosenlaui** (1330 m – 4364 feet), in a magnificent setting. A footpath, largely hewn from the rock, winds uphill (½ hour) through the *Rosenlaui gorge*, carved out by the Weissenbach. – The road climbs in a sharp bend and comes in 2·5 km (2 miles) to the **Schwarzwaldalp** (1467 m – 4813 feet). From here a bridle-path leads in 2–2½ hours to the **Grosse Scheidegg** or *Hasli-Scheidegg* (1961 m – 6434 feet), from which there is a *view of the Grindelwald basin (descent, 2 hours).

Hasliberg: see p. 221.

Montreux

Canton: Vaud (VD).
Altitude: 375 m (1230 feet). – Population: 20,000.
Post code: CH-1820. – Dialling code: 021.
ⓘ **Office du Tourisme,**
   42 Grand'Rue;
   tel. 61 33 84.

HOTELS. – *Le Montreux Palace*, A, 420 b., SP; *Hyatt Regency Montreux*, A, 300 b., SB; *Du Cygne*, A, 50 b., SP; *Excelsior*, B, 140 b., SB; *Eden au Lac*, B, 210 b., SP; *Eurotel*, B, 270 b., SB; *National*, B, 100 b.; *Suisse et Majestic*, B, 250 b.; *Golf-Hôtel René Capt*, C, 100 b.; *Bon-Port*, C, 62 b.; *Arizona*, D, 20 b. – IN CLARENS: *L'Ermitage*, C, 29 b.; *Chailly*, D, 65 b. – IN VEYTAUX-CHILLON: *Bonnivard*, C, 100 b.; *Bristol*, D, 110 b. – IN CAUX: *Hostellerie de Caux*, C, 18 b.; *Les Rosiers*, E, 27 b. – IN GLION: *Victoria*, B, 80 b., SP; *Des Alpes Vaudoises*, C, 90 b., SP; *Bellevue*, C, 200 b.; *Righi Vaudois*, C, 100 b.; *Mont Fleuri*, D, 60 b.; *Placida*, E, 50 b., SP.

YOUTH HOSTEL: *Haut Lac*, 8 Passage de l'Auberge, Territet.

RECREATION and SPORT. – Golf, riding, swimming, sailing, water-skiing, fishing; skiing on the Rochers de Naye and Pléiades.

EVENTS. – *Golden Rose Television Festival* (spring); *International Jazz Festival* (June–July); *Musical Festival* (September).

With a magnificent*situation and an unusually mild climate which make it the most popular resort on Lake Geneva, Montreux extends for some 6 km (4 miles) along the shores of the lake, incorporating a number of smaller places which were formerly independent communes.

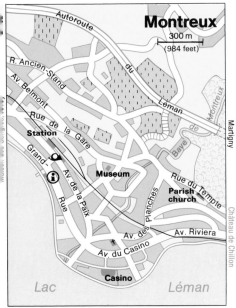

in front of the *parish church* (1507), higher up, there is a beautiful view of the lake.

To the W, in Vernex, stands the modern *Maison des Congrès*, and beyond this lies the attractive residential suburb of **Clarens**. – To the E the district of **Territet** is situated on a narrow coastal strip below the steep slopes of Glion. At the *station* a marble monument (1902) commemorates the Empress Elisabeth of Austria, murdered in Geneva in 1898.

1·5 km (1 mile) beyond Territet, in the outlying district of **Veytaux**, is a popular tourist sight – ****Chillon Castle**, a stronghold of the Counts and Dukes of Savoy. Situated on a rocky islet close to the shore, it commanded the road from Burgundy over the Great St Bernard into Italy.

The charm of the town's setting depends on its variety of geography and vegetation, ranging from the gardens on the lakeside, through the Alpine meadows and forests around Caux and Les Avants, to the lofty peaks of the Rochers de Naye.

SIGHTS. – The main part of the resort, **Montreux Ville**, lies on the steep slopes above the *Baye de Montreux*, a swiftly flowing mountain stream. On the shores of the lake is the *Casino*. From the terrace

The castle, which now belongs to the canton of Vaud (conducted tours), was built in the 9th or 10th c., enlarged in the 11th–12th c. and given its present form in the 13th c. In the basement are large dungeons cut from the native rock. Many Genevese were confined here for expressing their views too freely, among them François de Bonivard, Prior of St Victor's in Geneva and the hero of Byron's poem "The Prisoner of Chillon". He was incarcerated here by the Duke of Savoy in 1530, fettered to an iron ring which is still shown to visitors, but was released in 1536 when the Bernese conquered Vaux and, with the help of ships from Geneva, took the castle. On the ground floor are the large kitchen and the court-room, on the upper

Montreux, on the shores of Lake Geneva

Château de Chillon

Chillon Castle

LEVEL I　　　LEVEL II　　　LEVEL III　　　LEVEL IV

1 Entrance	12 Museum (formerly Banqueting Hall)	23 Count's Great Hall
2 Guard-room	13 Bedroom	24 Torture chamber
3 First courtyard	14 Guest-room	25 Bedroom
4 Magazine	15 Heraldic Hall	26 Latrine (13th c.)
5 Arsenal	16, 17 Duke's apartments	27 Clerks' room
6 Dungeon	18 Latrine (13th c.)	28 Museum (models, sculpture)
7 Gallows	19 Living-room (14th c.)	29 Fourth courtyard
8 Prison	20 Old living quarters (13th c.)	30 Keep
9 Bonivard Column	21 Chapel	31 Defensive towers
10 Castellan's Hall	22 Third courtyard	32 Exit
11 Second courtyard		

floor the Knights' Hall, the living quarters, the chapel, the sentry-walk and a restaurant.

SURROUNDINGS. – **Les Avants** (9 km – 6 miles): From the station take Rue de la Gare; then left along Avenue de Belmont and into a road which climbs up in sharp bends (daffodils in flower in May), passing on the left the massive *Château de Châtelard*; cross N 9 and continue uphill in long bends, via the villages of *Fontanivent* (559 m – 1834 feet), *Chernex* (603 m (1978 feet): Hôtel Les Iris, D, 37 b.; De la Grotte, D, 25 b.), *Sonzier* (664 m – 2179 feet) and *Chamby* (752 m (2467 feet): Narrow-Gauge Railway Museum; light railway to Vevey); then, still climbing, along the E side of *Mont Cubly*, towering above the *Gorge de Chauderon*. – 9 km (6 miles): **Les Avants** (974 m (3196 feet): Hôtel Chalet Hélioda, D, 20 b.), a summer and winter resort high above the valley of the Baye de Montreux. – 3 km (2 miles) farther on is the *Col de Sonloup* (1158 m (3799 feet): Hôtel de Sonloup; view), which can also be reached from Les Avants by funicular.

To the Col de Jaman (14 km – 9 miles). – Leave by Rue de la Gare and the district of *Les Planches*; then a road which runs uphill in a wide curve. – 3 km (2 miles): **Glion** (692 m – 2270 feet), with beautiful

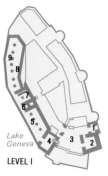

Chillon Castle on Lake Geneva

views of the lake and the Alps; funicular down to Territet. – The road now climbs steeply, with numerous sharp bends. – 3·5 km (2 miles): **Caux** (1054 m – 3458 feet), a health resort in a magnificent *situation, with extensive views; meeting-place of the "Moral Rearmament" movement. From here there is a cog-railway to the popular skiing area (ski-lift) on the *Rochers de Naye, and from the upper station (1973 m (6473 feet): Hôtel des Rochers de Naye, 15 b.) it is a 10 minutes' climb to the summit (2045 m – 6710 feet), which has superb views of the Alps and Lake Geneva; Alpine garden. – From Caux a mountain road runs up 7·5 km (5 miles) to the *Col de Jaman (1516 m (4974 feet): restaurant), with far-ranging views.

To the Pléiades (15 km – 9 miles) to Lally: mountain road). – Leave on the Lausanne road, and in Clarens turn right into a road which crosses the N 9 and winds its way uphill via *Chailly* (485 m – 1591 feet) and comes in 6 km (4 miles) to **Blonay** (623 m (2044 feet): Hôtel Bahyse, D, 25 b.), where Paul Hindemith (1895–1963) spent his last years. The castle dates from the 12th c. The town (which for administrative purposes is part of Vevey: p. 250) is noted for its almost champagne-like wine. From here there is a cog-railway to the Pléiades (4·7 km (3 miles), 25 minutes). – The road from Blonay to the Pléiades climbs in sharp bends, passing a side road on the right to the spa (sulphurous water) of *L'Alliaz* (1044 m – 3425 feet). – 9 km: *Lally* (1237 m – 4059 feet), at the end of the road. – From here it is 4 minutes on the cog-railway from Blonay or 20 minutes on foot to the *Pléiades (1364 m (4475 feet): pension and restaurant), from which there is a famous view.

Mürren

Canton: Berne (BE).
Altitude: 1650 m (5414 feet). – Population: 430.
Post code: CH-3825. – Dialling code: 036.

ⓘ **Kur- und Verkehrsverein,**
　　Mürren;
　　tel. 55 16 16.

HOTELS. – *Mürren*, B, 90 b.; *Eiger*, C, 90 b.; *Jungfrau-Lodge*, C, 35 b.; *Jungfrau*, C, 56 b.; *Bellevue*, C, 35 b.; *Sporthotel Edelweiss*, C, 50 b.; *Alpina*, D, 55 b.; *Touriste*, D, 30 b. – YOUTH HOSTEL.

EVENTS. – *Inferno International Ski Race* (12 km – 7 miles); *International High Alpine Balloon Weeks* (June–July); *Summer Ski Races* (June).

RECREATION and SPORT. – Conducted glacier walks, tennis, climbing, skating, curling, helicopter skiing.

The traffic-free holiday and winter sports resort of Mürren lies on a sunny terrace 700 m (2297 feet) above the Lauterbrunnen valley, with magnificent *views of the Jungfrau massif.

Mürren, with the Eiger and the Mönch

HISTORY. – First mentioned in the records in 1257, Mürren developed during the 19th c. into a popular resort, particularly favoured by the British. The Mürrenbahn (narrow-gauge railway) was opened in 1891, the Allmendhubelbahn (funicular) in 1912.

Mürren is reached from Lauterbrunnen by the funicular (6·5 km – 4 miles) to the *Grütschalp* (1490 m – 4889 feet) and from there by the narrow-gauge railway (5·5 km – 3 miles), or from Stechelberg by cableway (the Schilthornbahn to Gimmelwald (1367 m – 4485 feet) and Mürren. For the continuation of the Schilthornbahn see below.

SURROUNDINGS. – To the NW is a mountain commanding panoramic views, *Allmendhubel* (1938 m (6359 feet): restaurant), which can be reached either by the funicular or by walking (30 minutes). – From *Gimmelwald* (1367 m – 4485 feet), which is accessible either by the Schilthornbahn or on foot (30 minutes), there is a footpath (1½ hours) along a mountain terrace into the Sefinental and to the *Gspaltenhorn* glacier.

The upper sections of the Schilthornbahn lead by way of *Birg* (2676 m – 8780 feet) to the *Schilthorn (Piz*

Gloria, 2970 m (9745 feet): revolving restaurant), from which there are ski trails (moderate and difficult) to Mürren.

Murten/Morat

Canton: Fribourg (FR).
Altitude: 450 m (1476 feet). – Population: 4600.
Post code: CH-3280. – Dialling code: 037.
ⓘ **Verkehrsbüro,**
Hauptgasse 6;
tel. 71 51 12.

HOTELS. – *Schiff*, B, 30 b.; *Krone*, C, 65 b.; *Des Bains*, C, 52 b., SP; *Weisses Kreuz*, C, 53 b.; *Murtenhof*, D, 18 b.; *Stadhaus*, D, 45 b.; *Enge*, D, 44 b. – IN MURTEN-MEYRIEZ: *Vieux Manoir*, B, 40 b. – CAMPING SITE.

EVENTS. – *Carnival* (Fastnacht), with processions; *Schlachtfeier* (festival commemorating the victory of 1476: children's celebrations with flower parade, 22 June); *Murtenschiessen* (shooting contest, June).

RECREATION and SPORT. – Riding, tennis, swimming, sailing, fishing; motor-launch trips on the lake, and the "Three Lakes Trip" (Murtensee, Lac de Neuchâtel, Bieler See).

***Murten (the German form: French Morat) lies on a ridge of hills marking the linguistic boundary between French and German, on the SE side of the idyllic Murtensee (Lac de Morat). This beautiful little medieval town has preserved, more completely perhaps than anywhere else in Switzerland, the old-world character derived from its many surviving buildings of the 15th–18th c. The old town is still surrounded by its circuit of walls (with wall-walk).**

HISTORY. – In 515 King Sigismund of Burgundy presented a property at Murten, on the road into Valais, to the monastery of St Maurice. In 1013 Murten was a stronghold held by King Rudolf III of Upper Burgundy. The real foundation of the town was the work of the Zähringen dynasty between 1157 and 1177. Murten's main claim to fame is the battle fought here in 1476 in which the Confederates defeated the troops of Charles the Bold of Burgundy. The field of battle ranged from Cressier (572 m – 1877 feet) to Greng (449 m – 1473 feet), where a memorial now stands.

SIGHTS. – The ***town walls** (12th–15th c.) are a remarkable example of a medieval defensive wall; access to the wall-walk is by flights of steps at the German church and the Käfigturm (Cage tower). From the walls there are fine views of the roofs of the town. – At the western tip of the old town stands the **Castle**, built by Peter of Savoy in the 13th c. – At the NE end of the picturesque *Hauptgasse* is the *Berne*

Murten

gate (Berntor, 1777–78), a later Baroque reconstruction, with one of the oldest tower clocks in Switzerland (1712).

The *Town Hall* was rebuilt after 1416, and was given a Neo-classical façade in 1832. Also of interest are the Late Gothic *French church* (1478–80) and the *German church* (1710–13). Opposite the German church is the birthplace of the writer Jeremias Gotthelf (whose real name was Albert Bitzius, a pastor, 1797–1854).

One of the town's most picturesque old buildings is the Late Gothic *Rübenloch*, with a frontal gable. The old town mill now houses a *Historical Museum*, opened in 1978 (weapons, banners and uniforms from the Burgundian wars and an old oil-mill). In Schulhausplatz a "world sundial" shows the time in different parts of the world.

SURROUNDINGS. – From the Bodenmünsi hill S of Murten there are magnificent panoramic views of the lake and the Jura mountains. The *Muntelier Riding Centre* contains the largest riding-hall in Europe.

Murten to Avenches. – Leave on the Lausanne road, which runs through the suburb of Meyriez and begins to climb. 2 km (1 mile) from the middle of town, at the junction with the bypass road (on right), is the *monument to the Battle of Murten*, an obelisk erected in 1823 on the site of an ossuary destroyed by the French in 1798. It commemorates the decisive victory of the Confederates over Duke Charles the Bold of Burgundy on 22 June 1476.

The road runs close to the SE shore of the **Murtensee** or **Lac de Morat** (alt. 433 m (1421 feet): area 27 sq. km (10 sq. miles), length 9 km (6 miles), greatest depth 46 m(151 feet)), which is linked with the Lac de Neuchâtel by the River *Broye* (motor-boat traffic). To the right is the flat-topped *Mont Vully* or *Wistenlacher Berg* (657 m – 2156 feet) which lies between the Murtensee and the Lac de Neuchâtel.

2 km (1 mile) beyond the monument is *Faoug* (pronounced Foo; German *Pfauen*; Hôtel Les Rochettes), from which a road descends on the right to a beach station and camp site (inn), 2·5 km (2 miles) W on the wooded shores of the lake. – The Lausanne road now leaves the lake and follows a fairly straight and level course to Avenches, passing the remains of the Roman town just before reaching the modern town.

Avenches (alt. 474 m (1555 feet): Hôtel de la Couronne; bypass), a little town of 2000 inhabitants is situated on a hill, with a medieval castle (remodelled in Renaissance style) and attractive old houses. It occupies the site of the old capital of the Helvetii and the Roman town of *Aventicum*, which had its heyday in the 1st and 2nd c. A.D., when it had a population of some 20,000, and was destroyed by the Alemanni

Roman amphitheatre, Avenches

about 260. The excavated remains of the Roman town can be seen to the E of modern Avenches – a theatre (semicircular in form, with a diameter of 106 m (348 feet)) which could seat 10,000 spectators; the "Tornallaz", the only surviving remnant of the town's 6 km (4 miles) circuit of walls; the remains of the Forum baths; and a 12 m (40 feet) high Corinthian column, probably from the Forum, known as the Cigognier from the stork's nest which formerly crowned it. The numerous finds from the site are displayed in a museum adjoining the amphitheatre.

Neuchâtel

Canton: Neuchâtel (NE).
Altitude: 430 m (1411 feet). – Population: 35,000.
Post code: CH-2001. – Dialling code: 038.
ⓘ **Office Neuchâtelois du Tourisme,**
   Place Numa-Droz 1;
   tel. 25 42 42.

HOTELS. – *Beaulac*, B, 100 b., bathing beach; *Eurotel*, B, 200 b., SB; *City*, C, 55 b.; *Touring*, C, 80 b.; *Beaux-Arts*, D, 46 b. – IN THIELLE: *Novotal*, B, 180 b. – YOUTH HOSTEL.

EVENTS. – *Vintage Festival* (first weekend in October).

RECREATION and SPORT. – Bathing beach, golf-course. – Motor-launches on the lake; trips on the three lakes (Lac de Neuchâtel, Bieler See, Murten-see).

Neuchâtel (German Neuenburg), capital of the canton of the same name, lies on the N shore of the Lac de Neuchâtel (Neuenburger See), below the Jura mountains. It is the

seat of a University and has a Commercial College and the Swiss Watchmaking Research Laboratory. The public buildings are mainly on the shores of the lake around the harbour; the residential districts, with their houses of yellow Jurassic limestone, rise above the lake on the foothills of the Chaumont, surrounded by parks and vineyards.

HISTORY. – The town first appears in the records in 1011 under the name of *Novum Castellum*, and in the course of the 11th c. it became part of the Holy Roman Empire. Thereafter it changed hands several times. The Counts of Neuchâtel gave place to the Counts of Freiburg im Breisgau, who in turn were succeeded by the Counts of Hochberg. From 1504 to 1707 the town belonged to the Dukes of Orléans-Longueville, and then passed to the Crown of Prussia. In 1848 a federal and republican constitution came into force, and in 1857 King Frederick William IV of Prussia renounced his claim to Neuchâtel. – During the 18th c. the town developed into a commercial and industrial hub (watchmaking, fabric printing) and in 1815 it became the cantonal capital.

SIGHTS. – On the long *quays* which extend on either side of the harbour are a series of handsome late 19th c. buildings. In Place du Port is to be found the *Post Office*, in Place Numa Droz (to the S) the **Collège Latin** (1835), with the *Municipal Library* and the *Natural History Museum* (zoology, mineralogy, geology, birds of Switzerland). At the near end of Quai Léopold-Robert, NE of the harbour, is the **Museum of Art and History**

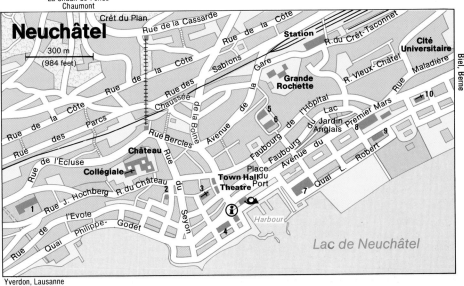

1 Museum of Ethnography
2 Market Hall
3 Temple du Bas (Protestant church)

4 Collège Latin (Municipal Library, Natural History Museum)

5 Archaeological Museum
6 Hôtel du Peyrou
7 Museum of Art and History

8 University
9 Commercial College
10 Catholic church

(closed Mondays), which houses a comprehensive collection of 19th c. Swiss painting and collections of antiquities, automata (mechanical figures) and clocks and watches.

Parallel to Quai Léopold-Robert is the broad Avenue du Premier-Mars, which runs past the *Jardin Anglais* to the **University** (1909), successor to an Academy founded by King Frederick William III of Prussia in 1838. Behind the University, on the shores of the lake, stands the *Commercial College* (Ecole Supérieure de Commerce).

To the N of the Jardin Anglais lies a select part of the town, the *Faubourg de l'Hôpital*, with handsome 18th c. patrician houses, including the *Hôtel du Peyrou* (1764–70, with a beautiful garden), which is now used for receptions and banquets, and the *Grande Rochette* (1730: private property). Behind the Hôtel du Peyrou the *Archaeological Museum* (Musée d'Archéologie) contains an interesting collection of excavated material from La Tène (see below).

The OLD TOWN lies NW of the harbour, rising up the hillside towards the Château. On its E side are the **Town Hall** (Hôtel de Ville, 1784–90), with a pillared portico, and the *Theatre* (1775). The main street, *Rue du Seyon*, occupies the bed of a stream which was diverted in 1844. Side streets on the left lead to the elegant Renaissance *Market Hall* (Maison des Halles, 1570–75). There are also a number of handsome 16th and 17th c. fountains – the *Banner Carrier fountain* (1584), the *Griffin fountain* (1664), the *Justice fountain* (1547) and the *Lion fountain* (1655; the lion itself 1664).

From Rue du Château a stepped lane and a street lead up to the **Château**, which belonged to the Counts and Princes of Neuchâtel and is now occupied by cantonal government offices. The W wing dates from the 12th c., the remainder from the 15th to the 17th c.; the interior has undergone much alteration. The **Collegiate church** was built in the 12th–13th c. (W towers 1867–75). Until 1530, when it was taken over by the Reformed faith, it was the Catholic *Col. légiale Notre-Dame*. In the very dark Romanesque choir the *monument of the Counts of Neuchâtel (1372) has 15 painted effigies and is the finest Gothic memorial in the whole of Switzerland. On the N side of the church is a Romanesque cloister (restored). Outside the W front of the church stands a statue of the Reformer *Guillaume Farel* (1489–1565); from the terrace there are extensive *views.

SW of the church, in a park in Rue St-Nicolas, is the *Museum of Ethnography*, with an excellent permanent collection and occasional special exhibits from time to time. – From Rue de l'Ecluse, on the edge of the old town, a funicular ascends to the *Crêt du Plan** (598 m – 1962 feet), from which there are extensive views of the lake and of the Alps.

SURROUNDINGS. – 5 km (3 miles) NE, in *La Coudre*, is a funicular to the summit of* **Chaumont** (1177 m – 3862 feet), which can also be reached on a steep road from Neuchâtel. From the top there áre far-ranging views of the Mittelland with its lakes and a panorama of the Alps from Säntis to Mont Blanc.

Near *St-Blaise*, at the N end of the lake, in the hamlet of **La Tène**, is a famous Late Iron Age site first excavated in 1858.

*Neuchâtel to Yverdon. – The road (39 km – 24 miles) skirts the NW side of the Lac de Neuchâtel, the largest of the three Swiss lakes on the fringes of the Jura (39 km (24 miles) long, up to 8 km (5 miles) wide). The hillsides are mostly covered with vineyards.

Leave Neuchâtel by way of Quai L.-Perrier and road 5. In the suburb of *Serrières* are the Suchard chocolate factory (1826) and a tobacco factory (visitors admitted).

Auvernier (alt. 460 m (1509 feet)) is a vine-growing village with a school of viticulture. It has a number of handsome patrician houses (16th c.) with Renaissance doorways.

Colombier (460 m (1509 feet): pop. 4000; Hôtel de la Couronne, E, 14 b.) has a massive castle, built in the 12th c. on Roman foundations and rebuilt and enlarged in the 14th and 16th c. From 1754 it was occasionally used as a residence by the Prussian governor of Neuchatel. It now contains a military

The Château, Neuchâtel

museum and a collection of pictures. The surrounding vineyards produce an excellent wine.

Boudry (470 m (1542 feet): pop. 3000; Hôtel Lion d'Or, E, 13 b.) is a picturesque little town at the mouth of the *Gorges de l'Areuse*. The 16th c. castle houses a museum of viticulture. Boudry was the birthplace of the French politician Jean-Paul Marat (1743–93) and of Philippe Suchard. – The road continues, with beautiful views, to *Bevaix* (476 m – 1562 feet), which has a Gothic church and a 1722 mansion-house. – *Gorgier* (518 m – 1700 feet) has a castle of the 14th and 16th c., restored in Romantic style in the 19th c. (view).

St-Aubin (474 m (1555 feet): Hôtel Pattus, E, 9 b.), is the most important town in the district of *La Béroche* on the slopes of the *Montagne de Boudry*, which has picturesque villages and country houses. – Beyond this, to the right, stands the castle of *Vaumarcus*; and, on the left, the former Carthusian house of *La Lance*, with a beautiful Late Gothic cloister. – The road continues via *Grandson* (p. 260) to **Yverdon** (p. 259), at the SW end of the lake.

Nyon

Canton: Vaud (VD).
Altitude: 404 m (1326 feet). – Population: 11,000.
Post code: CH-1260. – Dialling code: 022.

ⓘ **Office du Tourisme,**
7 Avenue Viollier;
tel. 61 62 61.

HOTELS. – *Du Clos de Sadex*, C, 30 b.; *Des Alpes*, C, 55 b.; *Du Nord* (no rest.), C, 26 b.; *Beau-Rivage*, D, 70 b.; *De Nyon* (no rest.), D, 45 b.; *Hostellerie du Seizième Siècle*, D, 29 b.

EVENT. – *International Documentary Film Festival*, held annually.

RECREATION and SPORT. – Riding, tennis (indoor and outdoor courts), swimming, fishing.

The old-world little town of Nyon is beautifully situated on the NW shore of Lake Geneva, at the end of a mountain road over the Col de la Givrine to La Cure.

HISTORY. – There was a settlement of the Helvetii here (*Noviodunum*), and Julius Caesar established the Roman station of *Civitas Iulia Equestris*. The town enjoyed a period of prosperity, under Bernese rule, in the 16th c., when many handsome burghers' houses were built. From 1781 to 1813 there was a porcelain manufactory in Nyon. It was the birthplace of the writer Edouard Rod (1857–1910) and the pianist Alfred Cortot.

SIGHTS. – The town, with its old houses and its *church* (12th and 16th c.: Roman walling in substructure), is picturesquely situated on the slopes of a hill which is crowned by the five-towered **Castle** (14th and 16th c.). The Castle now houses the *Historical Museum* and the

Roman columns, Nyon

Musée du Léman and contains an interesting collection of antiquities (including Roman material) and an exhibition of Nyon porcelain (1781–1813). From the castle terrace there is a magnificent view of the lake and the Alps, with Mont Blanc. In the *Bourg-de-Rive* park are *Roman columns. The newer parts of the town, with high-rise apartments and industrial installations, extend northwards towards the highways.

SURROUNDINGS. – 3 km SW is the *château de Crans*, an elegant 15th c. residence. – 9 km NW is the former Cistercian abbey of *Nonmont*.

Oberhalbstein/Sursés

Canton: Grisons (GR).
ⓘ **Kur- und Verkehrsverein Savognin,**
CH-7451 Savognin;
tel. (081) 74 12 67.

Oberhalbstein (Romansh Sursés) is the name given to the valley of the River Julia, which flows down from the Julier (Guglia) pass to join the Albula at Tiefencastel. There was already a road here in Roman times, running from the Engadine over the pass and down the successive levels of the valley. The language of the valley is Romansh.

Over the Julier pass into the Engadine. – The road from Chur (p. 95) and Lenzerheide (p. 159) was built between 1820 and 1840 and later improved. – At

Savognin, on the road to the Julier pass

above which the next stage of the valley opens up – Oberhalbstein ("above the rock").

Cunter (1182 m – 3878 feet) is a beautifully situated village frequented both by summer visitors and by winter sports enthusiasts. From here a narrow road (8·5 km – 5 miles) runs SW via *Riom* up to *Radons* (1864 m (6116 feet): also reached by cableway from Savognin), from which *Piz Caquiel* (2970 m – 9745 feet) can be climbed (4 hours).

Savognin (1210 m (3970 feet): pop. 950; Hotel Cresta, B, 140 b.; Alpina, C, 44 b.; Danilo, C, 70 b.; Sporthotel Planta, D, 30 b.) is the primary town in the Oberhalbstein, situated at the mouth of the *Val Nandro*, which runs down from the SW to join the Oberhalbstein. The village has three 17th c. churches and numbers of attractive old houses. At the upper end of the village, on the left, is a tablet commemorating the residence of the painter Giovanni Segantini (1886–94). Savognin is also a popular winter sports resort (many ski-lifts; "snow cannon" for producing artificial snow for the ski trails). – To the W of the village is *Piz Curvèr* (2972 m (9751 feet): 6 hours, with guide). Chair-lifts via *Tigignas* to *Somtgant* (2143 m – 7031 feet) and via *Malmigiucr* to *Radons* (see above).

the N end of the Oberhalbstein valley is **Tiefencastel** (Romansh *Casti*, alt. 851 m (2792 feet): pop. 350; Posthotel Julier, D, 90 b.; Albula, D, 60 b.), situated at a road junction on the site of the Roman station of *Imacastra*. On a rocky hill between the Rivers Julia and Albula stands the parish church of St Stephen (1660), with a richly decorated interior. – To the SW lies the village of *Mon* (1227 m – 4026 feet); in the church are 15th c. frescoes. The road continues to climb for 30 km (19 miles) via the old village of *Begun* (1376 m – 4516 feet) to the Albulapass (2312 m – 7588 feet).

The road to the Julier pass runs up from here to the limestone wall of *Crap Sès*,

Farther up the valley is *Tinizong* (1232 m (4042 feet): pop. 360), on the site of the

Stumps of Roman columns on the Julier pass

Roman station of *Tinnetio*. In the parish church (1647) is a carved altar (Late Gothic, 1512) by Jörg Kändel of Biberach in Swabia. – At *Rona* (1420 m – 4659 feet) the road reaches the next "step" in the valley, and continues via *Mulegns* to the step above this, on which is **Lai da Marmorera** (1680 m (5512 feet): parking lot), an artificial lake with a capacity of 60 million cu. m (2118 million cu. feet). Farther along the road, on the left, the new village of *Marmorera* replaces the old village which was submerged by the lake.

In the highest part of the valley is **Bivio** (1776 m (5827 feet): pop. 250; Hotel Post, C, 70 b.; Solaria, C, 65 b.; Grischuna, D, 80 b.), so called (Lat. *bivium*, "road-fork") because a busy medieval road, now represented only by a bridle-path, branched off here and ran over the Septimer pass (Pass da Sett, 2311 m (7582 feet)). In Bivio four different languages are spoken: German, an Italian dialect from the Val Bregaglia, Ladin and the Surmeirian dialect. – Beyond the village the road climbs to the *Julier Hospice* (2244 m – 7363 feet) and the **Julier pass** (Passo dal Guglia, 2284 m (7494 feet)), with the stumps of two columns which probably belonged to a Roman shrine on the pass. To the right, is a small lake. – The road now descends the rocky valley of the *Ova*, past *Piz Julier* (3385 – 11,106 feet), on the left, to a * lookout with a magnificent view of the Bernina massif (4049 m – 13,285 feet). It then continues down to Silvaplana, where it enters the Engadine (p. 111).

Olten

Canton: Solothurn (SO).
Altitude: 396 m (1299 feet). – Population: 22,000.
Post code: CH-4600. – Dialling code: 062.
ⓘ **Verkehrsbüro,**
Bahnhofpassage;
tel. 22 35 35.

HOTELS. – *Astoria*, C, 55 b.; *Schweizerhof*, D, 60 b.; *Löwen-Zunfthaus*, D, 10 b. – IN HAUENSTEIN: *Froburg*, D, 9 b.

RECREATION and SPORT. – Tennis (indoor and outdoor courts), swimming; cross-country skiing; skating, curling (indoor rink).

Olten, an important railway junction, with the main workshops of the Swiss Federal Railways, and a considerable industrial town (engineering), lies astride the River Aare at the foot of the Hauenstein (824 m – 2704 feet), which commands extensive views.

HISTORY. – The place was founded by the Froburg family on the site of a Roman castrum. It first appears in the records as a town in 1201.

SIGHTS. – The handsome twin-towered *parish church* dates from 1806, the modern *Stadthaus* from 1966. An old covered wooden bridge leads into the OLD TOWN, the most notable landmark in which is the Late Gothic *tower* of St Martin's church (demolished in 1844). The *Old Town Hall* (1701) now houses the municipal library. At Kirchgasse 10 is the *Museum of Art* (Kunstmuseum), with works by the Olten-born painter Martin Disteli (1802–44), and to the N, in Konradstrasse, the *Historical Museum*.

SURROUNDINGS. – N of the town is the ruined castle of *Froburg* (excavations). – Road 2 runs S up the *Aare valley*, enclosed between wooded hills, and comes in 4 km (2 miles) to **Aarburg** (415 m (1362 feet): Hotel Krone), a picturesque little town of 6000 inhabitants situated above the junction of the Aare and the *Wigger*, with an 11th c. castle much altered in later centuries, now a penal establishment for young offenders. – On the Engelberg (667 m – 2188 feet) is the "Säli-Schlössli", the ruined castle of Wartburg-Säli. A fire-watching post was established here in 1547, and remained the responsibility of the Säli family for 300 years.

SW of Aarburg via Rothrist and Roggwil-Wynau stands the former Cistercian *abbey of St Urban* (founded 1184), in the NW corner of the canton of Lucerne. The Baroque church (completed 1716) has a fine organ and richly carved choir-stalls, which were acquired by a foreign purchaser in 1854 but were later bought and returned to St Urban by the Gottfried Keller Foundation.

Pontresina

Canton: Grisons (GR).
Altitude: 1800 m (5906 feet). – Population: 1800.
Post code: CH-7504. – Dialling code: 082.
ⓘ **Kur- und Verkehrsverein,**
Pontresina;
tel. 6 64 88.

HOTELS. – *Kronenhof-Bellavista*, A, 230 b., SB, SP; *Walther*, B, 120 b.; *Schweizerhof*, B, 140 b.; *Sporthotel Pontresina*, C, 140 b.; *Bernina*, C, 75 b.; *La Collina & Soldanella*, C, 70 b.; *Engadinerhof*, C, 150 b.; *Müller-Chesa Mandra*, C, 80 b.; *Roseg* (no rest.), C, 120 b.; *Post*, C, 100 b.; *Rosatsch*, C, 70 b.; *Atlas*, C, 150 b.; *Steinbock*, D, 60 b.

CAMPING SITE: in Pontresina-Morteratsch.

EVENTS. – *Engadine Concert Weeks* (July–August); open-air concerts (summer).

RECREATION and SPORT. – Climbing school; conducted glacier walks and botanical and geological excursions; golf, fishing, tennis; winter sports and summer skiing; skating, curling; toboggan run.

Pontresina (Romansh Puntras- chigna), once a mere village on the road to the Bernina pass and now a popular health resort, climbers' base and winter sports capital, lies in a sheltered spot in the highest side valley of the Upper Engadine, on a natural terrace facing SW. It is surrounded by forests of stone pines and larches and enclosed by the majestic peaks of the Alps.

Pontresina (Grisons)

HISTORY. – Pontresina first appears in the records in 1129, but evidence has been found of human settlement here dating back to the Bronze Age. The name has been thought to derive from one Saracenus who built a bridge here (*Pons Sarasinae*).

SIGHTS. – In the LARÈT district is the village *church* (Protestant: 1640). Between Piz Rosatsch and Piz Chalchagn a beautiful glimpse of the Roseg valley and Roseg glacier can be enjoyed. – On the hillside above Ober-Pontresina are the ruins of the pentagonal *Spaniola tower* and the little Romanesque *church of Santa Maria*, with a ceiling of stone pine (1497) and frescoes of the 12th–15th c. – Near here is a plant reserve with an *Alpine garden*.

SURROUNDINGS. – **Ascent of Muottas Muragl**: 3 km (2 miles) from Pontresina on the St Moritz road a funicular (length 2200 m (7218 feet), gradient 13–54%) takes 15 minutes to reach ****Muottas Muragl** or *Muottas Muraigl* (2453 m (8048 feet: restaurant), which commands the finest view of the Bernina group and the lakes of the Upper Engadine. – A good return route is by a path which skirts the Schafberg to the Unterer Schafberg restaurant (1 hour: see below) and on to the *Alp Languard* (2250 m (7382 feet): 45 minutes); then by chair-lift (ski-lift) or on foot (45 minutes) to Pontresina.

The ***Schafberg** (*Munt della Bes-cha*, 2731 m (8960 feet)) is reached from Pontresina in 2¾ hours by way of the *Unterer Schafberg* restaurant (2230 m – 7317 feet), from which there are magnificent views. On the summit, which has a prospect embracing the whole of the Bernina group, is the *Segantini hut*, with a tablet commemorating the painter Giovanni Segantini, who died here in 1899.

***Roseg glacier** (*Vadret da Roseg*). – A narrow road (6 km (4 miles): closed to traffic; horse-drawn cars) leads up the Roseg valley to the *Roseg-Gletscher restaurant* (2000 m – 6562 feet), from which it is a 30–45 minutes' walk under a fine grove of stone pines to the end of the glacier, now much reduced in size. There are more extensive views from the ***Alp Ota** (2257 m (7405 feet): 1¼ hours from the restaurant) and the *Tschierva hut* (2573 m (8442 feet): 2 hours). From the Roseg glacier it is a 2¼ hours' walk to the *Fuorcla Surlej* and the Murtél station on the Corvatschbahn (see p. 217).

Morteratsch glacier (*Vadret da Morteratsch*). – Leave Pontresina on the Bernina road and in 4·5 km (3 miles) take a little road on the right to the *Morteratsch Hotel* (1908 m – 6260 feet), from which it is an hour's walk to the end of the glacier. A finer view of the glacier can be had by climbing *Chünetta (2096 m (6877 feet): 35 minutes). 2 hours beyond this is the **Boval hut** of the Swiss Alpine Club (2495 m (8186 feet): inn with 60 beds), from which there is a superb *view of the Bernina group.

Possible CLIMBS from the Boval hut (to be undertaken only with a guide) include *Piz Morteratsch (3751 m (12,307 feet): 4½–5 hours; easy, for those with a good head for heights), with superb panoramic views; *Piz Palü* (3905 m (12,812 feet): 6–7 hours), a beautifully shaped peak; and **Piz Bernina** (4049 m (13,285 feet): 7–8 hours, very strenuous). – Ascent of the **Diavolezza (on foot from the Morteratsch Hotel or by cableway from Bernina-Suot): see p. 85. – Another rewarding climb from Pontresina is the ascent of *Piz Languard, to the E (3268 m (10,722 feet): 4 hours), with superb views. There is a restaurant 15 minutes below the summit.

For the cableways to the *Diavolezza* (summer skiing) and *Piz Lagalb* see p. 85.

Bad Ragaz

Canton: St Gallen (SG).
Altitude: 517 m (1696 feet). – Population: 4000.
Post code: CH-7310. – Dialling code: 085.
ⓘ **Kur- und Verkehrsverein,**
   Haus Schweizerhof;
   tel. 9 10 61.

HOTELS. – *Quellenhof, A, 200 b., *Grand Hotel Hof Ragaz*, B, 170 b., both connected by corridors with the spa establishment; *Cristal*, B, 90 b., SB; *Lattmann*, B, 130 b.; *Sandi*, C, 100 b.; *Badhotel Tamina*, C, 105 b.; thermal baths. – IN PFÄFERS: *TM Schloss Ragaz*, C, 120 b., SP; *Wartenstein*, C, 50 b.; *St Gallerhof*, D, 50 b.; *Rössli* (no rest.), D, 36 b. – CAMPING SITE.

RECREATION and SPORT. – Golf, tennis (indoor and outdoor courts), riding, boccia, fishing, walking, climbing, swimming bath; concerts, dancing.

The Tamina gorge, near Bad Ragaz

Bad Ragaz

WINTER SPORTS. – Descents in all grades of difficulty on Pizol; cross-country skiing, ice-rink, ski school.

Bad Ragaz, attractively situated in the Rhine valley at the mouth of the Tamina gorge, is one of Switzerland's leading spas. The warm radioactive springs (37 °C – 99 °F), with a flow of 3000 to 10,000 litres (660 to 2200 gallons) a minute, are used in the treatment of rheumatism, paralysis, metabolic disorders and injuries of all kinds. The springs rise in the Tamina gorge and the water has been piped down to Ragaz since 1840.

SIGHTS. – On the left bank of the Tamina stands the *parish church* (1703), with the grave of the German philosopher Friedrich Wilhelm Schelling (1775–1854) in the churchyard. On the right bank we find the Kurgarten, the *Kursaal* and the *Spa Establishment*; to the N is the Giessen Park, with a lake.

SURROUNDINGS. – A road (4 km (2 miles): closed to motor vehicles) climbs the left bank of the Tamina between schist walls almost 250 m (820 feet) high to **Bad Pfäfers** (685 m (2247 feet): public baths), the buildings of which present something of the aspect of a monastery and date from 1704. In the spa (Badehaus) tickets are issued for admission to the *Tamina gorge. Long passages run down to the gorge (500 m (1641 feet) long), at the end of which is a narrow steam-filled gallery where the principal spring emerges from a deep chamber in the rock. In 1242 a gangway was constructed on the rock face, supported on projecting beams, and about 1465 a chamber was contrived above the spring, from which patients were let down on ropes. – Another road parallel to the Bad Pfäfers road runs W up the valley to the developing spa of *Bad Valens* (915 m (3002 feet): Kurhotel, C, 37 b.).

3 km (2 miles) SE of Ragaz we come to the **Wartenstein** (see below), with the *Hotel Wartenstein* (751 m – 2464 feet), from which there is a beautiful view of the Churfirsten. Below the hotel are the ruins of *Wartenstein Castle* (13th c.) and *St George's chapel*. – W of Ragaz, above the right bank of the Tamina, is the **Guschakopf** (751 m (2464 feet): ¾ hour), from which there is a fine view. – SW of Ragaz *Pizol (2848 m – 9344 feet), can be reached by way of a cableway (3·5 km (2 miles), 22 minutes) to *Pardiel* (1630 m (5348 feet): mountain inn), from which a chair-lift leads up to the *Laufböden* (2222 m – 7290 feet), near the Pizol hut (2229 m (7313 feet): cableway from Wangs; first-rate ski trails).

Ragaz to Vättis (15 km – 9 miles). – The road winds its way up to the *Wartenstein*. – 4 km (2 miles): **Pfäfers** (822 m (2697 feet): several inns), with the former Benedictine monastery of St Pirminsberg (founded *c.* 740, rebuilt 1672–93), now a cantonal home. The road continues along the E side of the deep *Tamina valley*, via *Ragol* and *Vadura*. – 11 km (7 miles): **Vättis** (951 m (3120 feet): Hotel Calanda), a quiet and beautifully situated summer resort under the W side of the towering *Calanda* (2806 m – 9206 feet). – From here a very narrow road (excursions by minibus from Ragaz to St Martin, 1350 m (4429 feet), beyond this jeeps only: information from Verkehrs verein, Vättis) runs W up the beautiful *Calfeisental* to the *Alp Sardona* (1742 m (5716 feet): 12 km (7 miles), from which **Piz Sardona** (3059 m – 10,037 feet) can be climbed (4¼ hours, with guide) by way of the *Sardona hut* (2161 m – 7090 feet).

Rapperswil

Canton: St Gallen (SG).
Altitude: 409 m (1342 feet). – Population: 9000.
Post code: CH-8640. – Dialling code: 055.
ⓘ **Verkehrsbüro,**
　Am Seequai;
　tel. 27 70 00.

HOTELS. – *Schwanen*, C, 42 b.; *Speer*, D, 35 b. – YOUTH HOSTEL.

The old-world little town of Rapperswil is picturesquely situated on a peninsula on the N side of Lake Zurich, which is crossed at this point by a causeway 1000 m (3281 feet) long.

HISTORY. – The town appears to have been founded about 1200, and first appears in the records in 1229. The line of the Counts of Rapperswil died out at an early stage. In 1358 Duke Rudolf built a wooden bridge over the lake, which stood until 1878, when it was replaced by a masonry-walled causeway carrying the road and railway. From 1415 to 1464 Rapperswil was a free Imperial city. In 1803 it was incorporated in the canton of St Gallen.

SIGHTS. – In the main square stands the tall *Town Hall* (1471), with a richly carved door at the entrance to the council chamber. From the square a broad flight of steps leads up to the *Schlossberg* (Castle

Hill) or Endingerhügel (436 m – 1431 feet), with the 15th c. *parish church* (restored 1887: two massive E towers) on the right and the imposing 13th c. **Castle** on the left. The Castle, on a triangular plan, with a keep and two other towers, was built by the Counts of Rapperswil, and now houses the interesting *Castles Museum* (Burgenmuseum) of the Swiss Castles Association (Schweizerischer Burgenverein). The museum contains numerous models, plans and documents illustrating life in the age of chivalry (heraldry, the feudal system, arms and armour, hunting). The Castle also houses the *Polish Museum* (Polenmuseum: the Renaissance, the Turkish wars, Chopin, the struggle for freedom). From the tree-shaded W bastion, the *Lindenhof*, there are charming views of the town and the lake. On the N side of the hill is the Hirschgarten (Deer Park), on the S side a vineyard.

Rapperswil, on Lake Zurich

On the Herrenberg, E of the parish church, is the *Heimatmuseum* (local museum), in the 15th c. *Brenyhaus* (formerly Haus Landenberg: restored). – There is an attractive little harbour with a dock for the lake boat services. On the western promontory is a *Capuchin friary* (founded 1605), with a rose-garden. Nearby is a small vineyard which is first referred to in 972. – On the Strandweg (lakeside road) S of the station, is a *Children's Zoo* belonging to the **Knie National Circus**, which is based in the town (trained dolphins, etc.).

SURROUNDINGS. – A road runs over the causeway (*Seedamm*) along the **Hurden peninsula**, via the fishing village of *Hurden* (chapel of 1497), to *Pfäffikon*, on the S side of the lake (see p. 277). – It is a

10 minutes' trip by motor-boat or motor-launch to the island of **Ufenau** (nature reserve: restaurant in old farm), which belonged to Einsiedeln abbey from 965 onwards (church and chapel of 1141). On Zwingli's advice the humanist Ulrich von Hütten sought refuge here in 1523, but died two weeks later; he is buried in the churchyard of the old parish church. – A lakeside road (10 km – 6 miles) runs SE from Rapperswil through the commune of *Jona* to *Busskirch*, with an old church and continues to *Wurmsbach*, which has a former convent of Cistercian nuns (16th–17th c.), now housing a girls' boarding-school. – The road then continues via *Bollingen* to *Schmerikon*, at the E end of the lake.

From Rapperswil road 8 runs E over the *Ricken pass* (805 m (2641 feet): beautiful view) into the **Toggenburg** district (p. 247).

The Rhine

Cantons: Grisons (GR), St Gallen (SG), Thurgau (TG), Schaffhausen (SH), Zurich (ZH), Aargau (AG), Basel-Land (BL) and Basel-Stadt (BS).

ⓘ **Verkehrsverein für Graubünden** (VVGR),
   Hartbertstrasse 9,
   CH-7001 Chur;
   tel. (081) 22 13 60.
   Verkehrsverband Ostschweiz (VVO),
   Bahnhofplatz 1A,
   CH-9001 St Gallen;
   tel. (071) 22 62 62.
   Verkehrsbüro des Kantons Thurgau,
   Rathausplatz 1,
   CH-8500 Frauenfeld;
   tel. (054) 7 31 28.
   **Verkehrsverein Kanton und
   Stadt Schaffhausen**,
   Freier Platz 7,
   CH-8202 Schaffhausen 2;
   tel. (053) 5 42 82.
   Verkehrsverein Zurich,
   Bahnhofplatz 15,
   CH-8023 Zurich;
   tel. (01) 2 11 12 56.
   Verkehrsverein Aarau,
   Bahnhofstrasse 20,
   CH-5001 Aarau;
   tel. (064) 24 76 24.
   **Nordwestschweizerische
   Verkehrsvereinigung**,
   Blumenrain 2,
   CH-4001 Basle;
   tel. (061) 25 38 11.
   Verkehrsverein Baselland,
   Rathausstrasse 51,
   CH-4410 Liestal;
   tel. (061) 91 07 21.

The Rhine (a name probably of Celtic origin: Latin Rhenus, German Rhein, French Rhin, Romansh Reno, Dutch Rijn) is Europe's most beautiful river and most important waterway. The first 375 km (233 miles) of its total length of 1320 km (820 miles) are in Switzerland. Its source is in the eastern part of the St Gotthard

massif, from which the two principal arms of the river flow separately westward for the first 60 km (37 miles).

The **Vorderrhein** flows out of the Tomasee (2345 m – 7694 feet), at the foot of Mt Badus (2928 m – 9607 feet). The **Hinterrhein** originates in the névé of the Rheinwaldhorn (3402 m – 1116 feet). 9 km (6 miles) W of Chur, at Reichenau, the two streams join to form the **Alpenrhein** (*Alpine Rhine*), which flows N into *Lake Constance*. Emerging from the W end of the lake, the river plunges over the **Rhine Falls** at Schaffhausen and, as the **Hochrhein** (*High Rhine*), continues W to Basle. In its passage through Switzerland to this point the Rhine drains two-thirds of the country's total area, including 548 sq. km (212 sq. miles) of glaciers. At Basle the river leaves Switzerland, with an average flow of 1027 cu. m (36,263 cu. feet) of water per second, and turns N, flowing through the Upper Rhine Plain as the **Upper Rhine** and through the Rhenish Uplands as the **Middle Rhine**. Below Bonn it is known as the **Lower Rhine**. In Holland it splits up into a number of arms which flow into the North Sea.

> In this section, for the convenience of visitors coming from the West, the routes along the Rhine valley are described from W to E, going upstream.

The High Rhine (Basle to Lake Constance). – From *Basle (p. 62) the road runs along the N bank of the swiftly flowing High Rhine (navigable to above Basle), which supplies power to many hydroelectric stations. The pleasant valley is bounded on the N by the Black Forest and on the S by the Swiss Jura.

The first place of any size is **Rheinfelden** (alt. 277 m (909 feet): Hotel Eden Solbad, B, 75 b.; Schwanen-Solbad, B, 75 b.; Park-Hotel, C, 90 b.), a little town of 7000 inhabitants beautifully situated on the left bank of the river facing the southern slopes of the Black Forest. It is a popular salt-water spa, with two indoor salt-water baths. The water has one of the highest salt contents in Europe. The waters of the two springs are drunk for medicinal purposes. – The attraction of Rheinfelden lies in its picturesque old town, with ancient walls and towers rising above the

rapidly flowing river. Notable features are the Town Hall (16th–18th c.) and St Martin's church (15th c., with Baroque interior). In the Haus zur Sonne (12 Marktgasse) is the Fricktaler Museum (local history).

At Rheinfelden we cross the Rhine and take a secondary road which runs N of the motorway to *Möhlin* and the village of *Stein* (opposite Säckingen on the N bank of the river), where it joins road 7. This road continues E to **Laufenburg** (318 m (1043 feet): pop. 2000; Hotel Adler, E, 24 b.), opposite the German town of Laufenburg on the N bank (bridge, with border control), at one of the most beautiful spots in the Rhine valley between Basle and Lake Constance, framed by wooded hills. The town has a tall Late Gothic parish church (1489) with a beautiful interior. – After an attractive bend in the valley the road continues via *Leibstadt* (to the N of which a nuclear power station is under construction) to a *bridge over the Aare* (5·5 km – 3 miles), just above its junction with the Rhine. Opposite, on the N bank, is the German town of *Waldshut*. Beyond the bridge a road goes off on the right to Brugg (Berne, Lucerne). – The Schaffhausen road continues to **Koblenz** (321 m – 1053 feet), an important road junction near the confluence (hence its name – Latin *Confluentia*) of the Aare and the Rhine. From here road 7 runs via Winterthur and St Gallen to Rortschach. The Schaffhausen road turns left over the Rhine bridge (border control) into Germany.

Thermal swimming pool, Zurzach

Road 7 comes in 6 km (4 miles) to **Zurzach** (342 m (1122 feet): pop. 3500; Hotel Zurzacherhof, B, 80 b.; Turmhaus & Turmpavillon, C, 130 b., SP), on the site of the Roman fort of *Tenedo*, a little town which was formerly a considerable river port, noted for its fairs, and is now a well-known spa. The hot springs (40 °C – 104 °F), the spa facilities (including three outdoor swimming pools) the Turm Hotel and the rheumatic clinic lie W of the town. Zurzach has a number of handsome old burghers' houses and a church of the 10th and 14th c. (sarcophagus of St Verena, 1603, in crypt; tombstone of a Roman legionary of 1st c. A.D. built into wall). Swimming pool at Oberfeld. Opposite Zurzach (bridge) is the German village of Rheinheim.

The road, signposted to Winterthur, continues along the left bank of the Rhine and in 12 km (7 miles) reaches the old-world town of *Kaiserstuhl* (350 m – 1148 feet), with a massive 13th c. tower and a Gothic church, picturesquely situated above the Rhine opposite the German village of Hohentengen (bridge). Road 7 then leaves the Rhine and comes to **Glattfelden** (359 m – 1178 feet), on the River Glatt just above its junction with the Rhine. This was the home town of the Swiss writer Gottfried Keller and is frequently referred to in his novel "Der grüne Heinrich". – At a crossroads 2 km (1 mile) farther on, where the right-hand road runs S to Zurich, turn left to cross the Rhine on a stone bridge into the picturesque old town of *Eglisau* (360 m – 1181 feet), which has 18th c. church situated on higher ground. – The road then cuts across the *Rafzer Feld*, an area surrounded on three sides by Germany, and a projecting finger of German territory linked with the district of Waldshut only by a narrow corridor. To the E of the German village of Jestetten is the small Swiss town of *Rheinau*, almost completely enclosed within a loop in the river, where there is a dam on the Rhine (motor-boats to the Rhine Falls). The sumptuously appointed Baroque church (1705) belonged to a Benedictine abbey founded in the 9th c. and dissolved in 1862.

From Jestetten the road runs NE into Switzerland again to the industrial town of *Neuhausen*, at the * *Rhine Falls (see p. 202). 3 km (2 miles) farther on is **Schaffhausen** (p. 221).

From Schaffhausen take road 13, which runs 10 km (6 miles) E to **Diessenhofen** (416 m (1365 feet): Hotel Schupfen), a medieval town of 3000 inhabitants, once a free Imperial city, with handsome old burghers' houses, old town walls, the Siegelturm, a church of 1602 and conventual buildings of 1571. On the opposite side of the river is the German

village of *Gailingen*. – Then along the river to *Stein am Rhein** (p. 235).

2 km (1 mile) beyond this, at Eschenz, the Rhine opens out into the *Untersee*, the most westerly arm of Lake Constance. – For places on the lake, see under Lake Constance.

The Alpine Rhine. – From the SE end of Lake Constance road 13 leads up the wide valley of the Rhine to the village of *Heerbrugg*, with an old castle, and **Altstätten** (457 m (1499 feet): pop. 10,000; Hotel Sonne), an ancient town with attractive arcaded houses (Marktgasse), a *parish church* of 1794 and a *Heimatmuseum* (local museum) in Prestegg, an old burgher's house (restaurant). Here a road goes off on the right and over the Stoss pass to Gais (Appenzell, St Gallen), and another road crosses the Ruppen pass, through beautiful scenery, to Trogen (p. 56) and St Gallen.

The road continues through Oberriet and comes in 29 km (18 miles) to **Buchs** (450 m (1476 feet): pop. 8000; Hotel City, D, 27 b.), chief town of a district and a road and rail junction. Buchs is a busy town (many haulage firms) on the route into Austria (Feldkirch–Innsbruck–Vienna). – An attractive excursion can be made from here on a mountain road which runs 8 km (5 miles) SW, with numerous sharp bends, to the *Kurhaus Buchser Berg* (1120 m – 3675 feet), in a magnificent forest setting, with extensive views.

From Buchs the route continues either through the **Principality of Liechtenstein** (see p. 161) or on road 13, which runs along the W side of the valley to *Balzers* (p. 162). Then either on the motorway via **Bad Ragaz** (p. 188), or via **Maienfeld** (525 m (1723 feet): pop. 1500; Hotel Heidihof, D, 23 b.), an ancient Grisons town, with handsome patrician houses, the medieval Schloss Brandis ("Roman Tower"; inn) and Schloss Salenegg (17th–18th c.). In the cemetery is the grave of the writer John Knittel (1891–1970).

From Maienfeld there are two possible routes to Landquart. The direct road (expressway) traverses the Rhine plain in a straight line (5 km – 3 miles) to the bridge which crosses the River Landquart into the town. The alternative route, 2 km

(1 mile) longer, is on an attractive minor road which follows the hillside through the orchards and vineyards of the old "Bündner Herrschaft" (Grisons Lordship) to the old-world village of *Jenins*, famous for its wine, and then continues below the ruined castles of *Aspermont*, *Wyneck* and *Klingenhorn* and past the lower station (1 km (about a ½ mile) before Malans, on left) of a cableway which runs NE to *Aelpli* (1802 m – 5912 feet), under the summit of *Vilan* (2376 m (7796 feet): 1½ hours), to the vine-growing village of *Malans* (568 m – 1864 feet), with handsome old patrician houses, under Burg Bothmar (16th and 18th c.).

Landquart (527 m (1729 feet): Hotel Falknis; camping site) is a busy road and rail junction (paper-making).

The motorway to Chur continues S between the railway and the right bank of the river (with strong side winds when the föhn is blowing). – On the hillside to the E (not visible from the road) is *Schloss Marschlins*, with its four towers (538 m (1765 feet): 13th and 17th c.), commanding the entrance to the Prättigau (p. 152). It can be reached by a side road (1 km – about a ½ mile) off the old road via Zizers. – Beyond this, to the E of the road, lies the village of *Igis*, with a college of agriculture in the Plantahof. – In another 5 km (3 miles) the road passes *Zizers station*, serving the old market town of **Zizers**, Romansh *Zizras* (540 m (1772 feet): Hotel Johannesstift), which lies off the road to the left and has two churches and two 17th c. mansions which belonged to the Salis family (the Unteres Schloss and the smaller Oberes Schloss, in the upper part of the town).

The road then comes to **Chur** (p. 95) and continues, bearing W, to the village of *Domat Ems* (583 m (1916 feet): Hotel Sternen, D, 80 b.), with a church of the Assumption in Italian Baroque style (1730–38). On a rocky hill are the Late Gothic St John's church (1515; carved high altar of 1504) and the Romanesque St Peter's chapel. – 3 km (2 miles) farther on we leave the motorway at the Reichenau exit, just before it comes to an end. To the left is **Reichenau** (603 m – 1978 feet), picturesquely situated on a rocky hill at the confluence of the *Vorderrhein* and the tumultuous *Hinterrhein*, with an old castle (altered in 1775 and 1820) belonging to the von Planta

family; from the beautiful castle gardens there is a view of the junction of the two branches of the Rhine.

The Vorderrhein. – From *Reichenau* road 19 (signposted to Flims and Disentis), after crossing the Rhine, goes up to the village of **Tamins** (Romansh *Tumein*, "hill", alt. 668 m (2192 feet): bypass), dominated by the prominent spire of its 16th c. parish church. – The road then curves round to cross the *Lavoi-Tobel* (gorge) and winds its way up the hillside with views to the left of the Domleschg (valley of the Hinterrhein) and Schloss Rhäzüns, one of the many old castles in the valley, and of the gorge carved by the Vorderrhein through the great Flims landslide. – Shortly before Trin the highest point on this section of road (895 m – 2936 feet) is reached. On a crag to the left is the old tower of *Hohentrins castle*.

4 km (2 miles) from Tamins is **Trin**, German *Trins* (890 m (2920 feet): Hotel Mirada, E, 20 b.), attractively situated on a terrace above the gorge of the Vorderrhein. The road then continues downhill with a view to the rear of the tower of Hohentrins. In 1 km (about a ½ mile) it bends to the right, and one can see on the left the hamlet of *Digg*, picturesquely situated on the hillside. – Then follows a fairly level stretch of road under the sheer cliffs of the *Porclas* defile, with meadow land and forest on the valley floor below. At the *Trinsermühle* (Romansh *Trin Mulin*, 833 m (2733 feet): restaurant), an old mill, there are beautiful waterfalls. – The road then climbs again, with many bends, along the edge of the gigantic masses of rock debris which tumbled down from the Upper Segnes valley during the Ice Age, covering some 52 sq km (20 sq. miles) of the Rhine valley. Off the road to the left is the little *Cresta-See* (850 m – 2789 feet). Beautiful view of the valley below.

6·5 km (4 miles) beyond Trin is **Flims** (p. 114). The road then passes a parking place (on right) for two cableways and bends to cross the Neue Stennabrücke (new Stenna bridge) over the *Flembach* (*Segnesbach*). – After passing through the park-like landscape of the hotel settlement of Flims Waldhaus (p. 114) the road winds its way through a beautiful stretch of woodland and meadowland. 1 km (about a ½ mile) farther on a side road goes off on the left to a camp site; then in another 1 km (about a ½ mile), at *Mulania* (on right), is the lower station of a cableway 4045 m (13,272 feet) long to *Crap Sogn Gion* (upper station 2220 m (7284 feet): large restaurant; ski-lifts) and *Crap Masegn* (2477 m – 8127 feet). The road then runs downhill and uphill again on a moderate gradient, crosses the Laaxer Bach and descends again above the deeply slashed *Laaxer Tobel* (gorge).

The road continues via *Laax* (p. 115) to **Ilanz** (p. 143). From here it follows a fairly straight and level course to Disentis along the left bank of the Vorderrhein, close to the Rhätische Bahn, through a stretch of the valley known as the *Pardella*. – 2 km (1 mile) beyond Ilanz is *Strada* (720 m (2362 feet): bypass), with the charmingly situated little village of *Schnaus* higher up on the right. – 2·5 km (2 miles) farther on is *Ruis station* (736 m (2415 feet): the village is above the road on the right). The road crosses the *Panixer Bach*, with the ruins of *Jörgenberg Castle* (495 m – 1624 feet) on a wooded crag on the right. – 4 km (2 miles) beyond Strada a road goes off on the right and winds its way up (3 km – 2 miles) to *Waltensburg* (Romansh *Vuorz*, 1010 m (3314 feet)), where there is a church containing fine 14th and 15th c. frescoes. From Waltensburg a by-road, with extensive views, runs along a natural terrace to Brigels (5 km (3 miles): see below). – The main road continues along the left bank of the Vorderrhein and then crosses to the other bank, curves under the railway and reaches (12 km (7 miles) from Ilanz).

Tavanasa (800 m – 2625 feet), at the narrow mouth of the *Tscharbach valley*, above which are two ruined castles, *Schwarzenstein* to the left and *Heidenberg* to the right. Here a side road on the right crosses the river to *Danis* and winds its way up (6 km (4 miles) N) to the village of *Brigels*, Romansh *Breil* (1283 m (4210 feet): Hotel Kistenpass, C, 66 b.), a popular summer and winter sports resort in a sunny expanse of Alpine meadows, with the Late Gothic parish church of S. Maria (restored 1963–66) and the Late Gothic church of St Martin. In the surrounding area (good walks, with far-ranging views) are a number of pretty chapels, including the chapel of St Eusebius, with 14th c. frescoes on the exterior. Route over the *Kisten pass* (2638 m – 8655 feet) to *Tierfehd* (9–10 hours).

From Tavanasa the road to Disentis continues along the wooded slopes above the right bank of the Vorderrhein.

Off the road to the left is *Zignau*, at the mouth of the wild *Val Zavragia*, and the ruins of *Ringgenberg Castle*. – Then on a stretch of concrete road to a bridge over the Vorderrhein and past *St Anne's chapel* (1716, on right), on the spot where the "Upper" or "Grey" League of the people of the Grisons against the oppressions of the nobility was renewed in 1424. – 6 km (4 miles) from Tavanasa is **Trun**, German *Truns* (855 m – 2805 feet), a village of 1600 inhabitants at the mouth of the *Val Punteglias*, which runs down from the *Brigelser Hörner* (3250 m (10,663 feet): 10 hours, with guide). In the village are the parish church of St Martin (1660–62), with a Romanesque tower, and the former residence of the Abbots of Disentis (1675), now housing the district court and a museum, with handsome rooms (interesting coat of arms of the communes belonging to the Grey League and of all district judges since 1424). Above the village stands the 17th c. church of S. Maria della Glisch.

The road now climbs gradually to the village of *Rabius* (955 m – 3133 feet), where a road on the left crosses the Rhine to *Surrhein* (892 m – 2927 feet) and climbs the wooded *Val Sumvitg* (*Somvixer Tal*) to 6·5 km (4 miles) S) *Tenigerbad*, Romansh *Bagn Sumvitg* (1273 m – 4177 feet) (indoor pool). From Tenigerbad the road continues 1·7 km (1 mile) to *Runcahez* (1300 m – 4265 feet), on a small artificial lake.

The main road continues from Rabius to **Somvix**, Romansh *Sumvitg* (*summus vicus*, "highest village": 1050 m (3445 feet)), with the Gothic chapel of St Benedict. Below, on the Rhine, lies the village of *Compadials* (965 m – 3166 feet). Beyond this is a beautiful stretch of road high up on the hillside, running through a defile and then over a new bridge (to the right the old covered wooden bridge) spanning the deep gorge of the *Val Russein*, which runs down from Mt Tödi. The road then ascends the rocky hillside and comes to **Disentis** (p. 107), 7·5 km (5 miles) from Somvix.

From Disentis road 19 leads up the **Val Tavetsch** on a moderate gradient, high above the river, with picturesque views of Disentis and its white abbey to the rear and the villages on the slopes of the valley downstream. Ahead can be seen, on the hillside to the right, the villages of *Acletta* (chapel), *Segnes* (1336 m – 4383 feet) and *Mompé Tujetsch* (1397 m – 4584 feet). – The road then continues, with expanses of coniferous forest, passes close to a high viaduct on the Furka–Oberalp railway and curves round to cross a mountain stream, the *Bugnei*.

9 km (6 miles) from Disentis is **Sedrun** (1401 m (4597 feet): Hotel Oberalp, C, 65 b.), chief place in the Val Tavetsch (Val Tujetsch), beautifully situated on gently sloping Alpine meadows and popular both with summer visitors and winter sports enthusiasts (ski-lift); enclosed swimming pool. The church of St Vigilius (1693), has a Romanesque tower and a carved altar (1491). Chair-lift to the spring pastures of *Cungieri* (1900 m (6234 feet): restaurant). To the S is *Piz Pazzola* (2582 m (8472 feet): 4 hours), from which there are magnificent views. – Farther up the valley there is a fine view of Mt Badus (Six Madun). – At *Camischolas* the road crosses a stream flowing down from the *Val Strim*. From here a narrow road (closed to traffic) runs up 8 km (5 miles) to the *Lai da Nalps*, an artificial lake (1909 m – 6263 feet).

Rueras (1450 m – 4757 feet) is a little village in the *Val Milar*, with a small church and fine wooden houses. The road then winds its way up again from the valley floor to the hillside and crosses streams flowing down the Val Milar and Val Giuf. To the left can be seen a tower of the ruined castle of *Pontaningen* (Pultmenga) and beyond this the chapel of St Brida. – 1·5 km (1 mile) before Tschamut a road branches off on the left via the village of *Selva* to the hamlet of *Sut Crestas* (1540 m – 5053 feet) lying in the valley, and which has a charming little church. On the hillside to the right is a wall built to provide protection from avalanches.

The road then comes to the beautifully situated hamlet of **Tschamut** (1648 m (5407 feet): Hotel Rheinquelle), opposite the mouth of the Val Curnera (on left), crosses the *Gämmerrhein*, which flows down from the Val de Val (on right), and bears right at the foot of Mt Calmot into the *Val Surpalix*. To the left the Vorderrhein flows out of the *Tomasee*, at the foot of Mt Badus.

The Hinterrhein. – The road S from *Reichenau*, where the Vorderrhein and Hinterrhein join, crosses the Hinterrhein and runs along a terrace above the left bank of the river to **Bonaduz** (660 m (2165 feet): Hotel Weisses Kreuz, D, 30 b.), a village of some 1000 inhabitants. Here a road goes off on the right via Versam to Ilanz and Disentis. Here a road goes off on the right via Versam to Ilanz and Disentis. The main road (signposted to Thusis) continues S on the terrace above the river. High up on the left can be seen the Late Romanesque *chapel of St George*, with fine wall-paintings of the 14th–15th c. and a Late Gothic carved altar (key at Rhäzüns station). The road then comes to **Rhäzüns** (648 m (2126 feet): Hotel Rätus). To the right is the village, with the Romanesque church of SS. Peter and Paul and another church of 1702. To the left, on a steep crag above the Hinterrhein, stands the imposing *Rhäzüns Castle* the oldest parts of which date from the 13th c., and which commands the entrance to the Domleschg (below). At the end of the village, on left, is the lower station of a cableway, 2100 m (6890 feet) long, to Feldis.

The road follows the railway on the wooded hillside above the Hinterrhein, whose broad stony bed is enclosed between massive levees. On the opposite bank is a tower of the ruined *castle of Nieder-Juvalta*. 2 km (1 mile) beyond this, on the right, is the Rhäzüns mineral spring ("Rhätisana" table water: visitors can tour bottling plant). – In another 2 km (1 mile), just before the *Rothenbrunnen* railway station (625 m (2051 feet): to left), the valley opens out and the road forks. The valley floor and the gentle lower slopes on the E side are known as the **Domleschg**, the steeper W slopes as the Heinzenberg. On both sides are vineyards, and cornfields reaching high up on the hillsides. The main road to Thusis skirts the left bank of the river under the Heinzenberg; the very attractive side road to the left passes through the numerous villages in the Domleschg and rejoins the main road at Thusis. The castles built on projecting spurs of rock were almost completely destroyed at the end of the 15th c.

Through the Domleschg to Thusis (11 km (7 miles): well worth the extra 1·5 km (1 mile)). – The road to the left crosses the Hinterrhein and comes to the village of **Rothenbrunnen**, under high rock walls, with the ruined castle of *Ober-Juvalta*. It has a chalybeate (iron-bearing) spring containing iodine (bottling plant). – Farther on, beyond the bridge over the Scheidbach (on right), is the large *Ortenstein castle* (754 m – 2474 feet), with an early medieval keep and 15th c. domestic quarters. 350 m (1148 feet) S is the ruined *pilgrimage church of St Lawrence*. – 3 km (2 miles) from the road junction a mountain road (not dust-free, with some steep gradients; in winter open only as far as Scheid) runs up on the left via the village of **Tomils** or *Tumegl* (800 m (2625 feet): Late Gothic church with an altarpiece of 1490 and 16th c. wall-paintings) and continues, with many bends, through *Unterscheid* and *Oberscheid* to (8 km (5 miles) NE) **Feldis** or *Veulden* (1472 m – 4830 feet), a health resort in a sunny·spot commanding extensive views (cableway from Rhäzüns). – The Thusis road continues to **Paspels**, with St Lawrence's chapel (Romanesque wall-paintings) and *Alt-Sins Castle* (restored). Beyond this, higher up on the left, is the ruined castle of *Neu-Sins* or *Canova*.

Rodels (700 m – 2297 feet) has attractive 17th and 18th c. houses. Above the village, to the E, can be seen the 12th c. castle of *Rietberg* or *Rätusberg*, which features in Conrad Ferdinand Meyer's "Jürg Jenatsch". – Beyond this is *Pratval*, with the ruins of Hasensprung castle.

At *Fürstenau* are two castles which belonged to the Planta family; the Haus Stoffel has 15th and 16th c. wall-paintings. Higher up, on the left, is the beautiful village of *Scharans* (780 m – 2559 feet), where Jürg (Georg) Jenatsch was pastor in 1617–18. – The road then crosses the *Zollbrücke* over the *Albula*, which emerges from the Schin gorge a little higher up the hill and flows down to join the Hinterrhein. To the left are *Baldenstein castle* and *St Cassian's chapel* (13th c.).

At **Sils** (*Seglias*, 683 m (2241 feet)) we join the road from Tiefencastel through the Schin gorge and turn right along this to reach **Thusis** (722 m – 2369 feet).

The main road to Thusis (No. 13) continues from *Rothenbrunnen station* along the left bank of the Hinterrhein under the *Heinzenberg*, with views of the villages and castles of the Domleschg. To the left are Alt-Sins castle and the ruins of Neu-Sins. In 5·5 km (3 miles) the road reaches **Cazis** (600 m (1969 feet): Hotel Adler), where we find an old Dominican nunnery (1504) (church with wall-paintings in choir) and the Romanesque chapel of St Wendelin.

Beyond this is an attractive view, to the left, of the mouth of the Schin gorge, with the village of Scharans (on left) and Baldenstein castle (on right), the Tinzenhorn (3179 m – 10,430 feet) rearing up above the gorge and in front of it the snow-capped *Piz Curvèr* (2972 m – 9751 feet). – 1 km (about a ½ mile) beyond Cazis a road goes off on the right to Präz. –

Farther on, above the road on the right, are the little village of *Masein* and Tagstein castle. Ahead, barely discernible, is the entrance to the Via Mala, with the ruined castles of Hohen-Rhätien and Ehrenfels. – 3·5 km (2 miles) from Cazis we come to **Thusis**, Romansh *Tusaun* (722 m (2369 feet): Hotel Adler), a handsome market village at the junction with the road through the Schin gorge to Tiefencastel. The village was almost completely destroyed by fire in 1845. The Protestant parish church dates from 1506, the new Catholic church from 1965. – All round Thusis are the ruins of medieval castles. On a steep crag at the entrance to the Via Mala, 246 m (807 feet) above the river, perches the 12th c. castle of *Hohen-Rhätien* or *Realta* (950 m (3117 feet): 45 minutes' climb from the village); at Sils are *Ehrenfels* and *Baldenstein*; to the left, above the entrance to the Nolla valley, is *Ober-Tagstein* (1130 m (3708 feet): 1¼ hours on a forest track) from which there are fine views; and on the slopes of the Heinzenberg stands the castle of *Tagstein* or *Nieder-Tagstein* (848 m (2782 feet): ½ hour).

From Thusis the road to Splügen and the San Bernardino pass continues past the end of the Tiefencastel road, crosses the River *Nolla*, which flows into the Hinterrhein here. The road then enters the *Via Mala, a magnificent gorge on the Hinterrhein, enclosed between limestone walls 500 m (1641 feet) high; the lowest section of the gorge, the *Verlorenes Loch* ("Lost Hole"), is particularly wild and has been passable only since the construction of a road in 1822. The medieval bridle-path bypassed the gorge, running up from the Nolla valley to the right of the wooded crag of *Grapteig*; the road follows the windings of the gorge. The present road runs through a short tunnel and soon afterwards, high up on the hillside, enters a gallery leading into the 500 m (1641 feet) long *Rongellen Tunnel*. 2·5 km (2 miles) from Thusis at the little hamlet of **Rongellen** (863 m – 2832 feet), the gorge opens out into a small basin. It then closes in again, and in this narrower section – the real Via Mala of medieval times – the old road branches off the new road (N 13) just after a short tunnel.

The *new road* (distances about the same as on the old road described below) runs through a gallery, beyond which the old road, going in the opposite direction, comes in on the left. It then traverses a winding tunnel, crosses the Hinterrhein on a pre-stressed concrete bridge 170 m (558 feet) long and runs through another curving tunnel 400 m (1312 feet) long, beyond which the old road, with the bridge at Rania, can be seen lower down on the right. Then through a gallery and a short tunnel to an access road to the expressway, 5·3 km (3 miles) from Rongellen and 1 km (about a ½ mile) N of Zillis.

The *old road through the Via Mala* (closed to large cars) branches off 1 km (about a ½ mile) beyond Rongellen, immediately before a gallery. – 800 m (2625 feet) farther on, beyond the second gallery, is the *Erste Brücke* (First Bridge), built in 1941 on the site of an earlier bridge of 1738. Immediately beyond the bridge, on the right, are a parking place and a kiosk, from which a flight of 257 steps leads down to a gallery 120 m (394 feet) long running above the tumultuous river (admission charge). – 300 m (984 feet) beyond this, after the third gallery, is the *Zweite Brücke* (Second Bridge: 800 m (2887 feet), built 1941), alongside the old bridge of 1739, 50 m (164 feet) above the river. – Above, to the right, can be seen the new road. – In 1·3 km (1 mile) is the *Dritte Brücke* (Third Bridge: 885 m (2904 feet)), at the end of the Via Mala, beside the little restaurant at *Rania* (on right). – The road now enters the pleasant open valley of *Schams* (Romansh *Sassám*), with the pointed summit of *Hüreli* or Hirli (2855 m – 9367 feet) in the background. – 1 km (about a ½ mile) before Zillis is an access road to the N 13 expressway.

1 km (about a ½ mile) S is the village of **Zillis**, Romansh *Ciraun* or *Ziran* (933 m (3060 feet): Hotel Alte Post, 16 b., with the very interesting church of St Martin. The nave and tower are Early Romanesque, the choir Late Gothic; the whole structure was carefully restored in 1938–40. Its most notable feature is the 12th c. *painted wooden ceiling, made up of 153 square panels depicting Biblical scenes – a unique example of very early figural painting. Under the ceiling is a Romanesque frieze revealed in 1940.

STRUCTURE and ICONOGRAPHY

The 153 panels, each roughly 90 cm (35 inches) square, are arranged in rows nine across and seventeen long.

The individual panels, usually made up of three pieces of wood, are framed within decorated transverse and longitudinal battens and cover the entire roof structure. The central row of panels in each direction is enclosed within double battens, thus creating the effect of a cross over the whole length of the church.

The panels were originally painted on the ground and then mounted on the ceiling. They are believed to have been the work of two painters, a "master" and an "apprentice", both probably from Rhaetia. The accepted dating is to about the year 1160.

Thematically the panels fall into two groups: the *marginal panels* (Nos. 1–48) running round the edge and facing the walls, and the *inner panels* (Nos. 49–153), which are arranged in rows from E to W. The marginal panels, linked to one another by a strip of water as on a medieval map of the world, depict allegorical figures – strange fabulous creatures which give the water the double significance of the primeval sea and the sea of the Apocalypse. The inner panels depict scenes from the life of Christ.

The best way of seeing the paintings is to start at the chancel arch and go towards the W door.

Romanesque painted ceiling in St Martin's Church (12th c.)   **Zillis (GR)**

E (chancel)

1	2	3	4	5	6	7	8	9
48	49	50	51	52	53	54	55	10
47	56	57	58	59	60	61	62	11
46	63	64	65	66	67	68	69	12
45	70	71	72	73	74	75	76	13
44	77	78	79	80	81	82	83	14
43	84	85	86	87	88	89	90	15
42	91	92	93	94	95	96	97	16
41	98	99	100	101	102	103	104	17
40	105	106	107	108	109	110	111	18
39	112	113	114	115	116	117	118	19
38	119	120	121	122	123	124	125	20
37	126	127	128	129	130	131	132	21
36	133	134	135	136	137	138	139	22
35	140	141	142	143	144	145	146	23
34	147	148	149	150	151	152	153	24
33	32	31	30	29	28	27	26	25

S (left)   N (right)

W (entrance)

☐ 140 original panels   ☐ 13 panels restored 1939–40

MARGINAL PANELS (including some copies)

1 Auster, the S wind
2 Dragon
3 Fish-tailed cock
4 Nereid with horn
5 Nereid with harp
6 Nereid with fiddle
7 Eagle
8 Dragon
9 Aquilo (written in mirror script), the N wind
10 Fisherman
11 The prophet Jonah
12 Part of a ship

13 Naked woman riding on a fish-tailed bird
14 Fish-tailed goose
15 Fish-tailed fox swallowing a fish-tailed cock
16 Monkey riding on a fish
17 Siren and fish-tailed stag
18 Naked man with axe riding on a fish
19 Fish-tailed wolf
20 Fish-tailed bear
21 Fish-tailed camel
22 Fish-tailed wolf
23 Fish-tailed lion
24 Fish-tailed ram
25 Angel
26 Dragon-tailed bird with snake
27 Dragon
28 Nereid with horn
29 Nereid with harp
30 Nereid with fiddle
31 Fish-tailed goose
32 Dragon-tailed bird with snake
33 Angel
34 Fish-tailed cock
35 Dragon
36 Fish-tailed boar
37 Fish-tailed he-goat
38 Dragon swallowing a winged fish
39 Dragon
40 Fish-tailed animal with small nereid
41 Two dragons biting one another
42 Fish-tailed unicorn
43 Fish-tailed elephant
44 Fish-tailed lion
45 Fish-tailed wolf
46 Fish-tailed boar
47 Fish-tailed ram
48 Sea-horse biting the tail of a fish-tailed roebuck

INNER PANELS

49–51 Kings David, Solomon and Rehoboam
52, 53 The Synagogue and the Church
54, 55 Annunciation
56, 57 Joseph's Doubts
58 Visitation
59 Annunciation to the Shepherds
60–62 Nativity
63–66 The Three Kings on their way to see Herod
67–69 The Three Kings before Herod; three horses in waiting
70–73 Adoration of the Infant Jesus by the Three Kings
74–76 The Three Kings returning home
77 The Three Kings
78 Purification of the Virgin
79 Presentation in the Temple
80 Joseph's Dream
81–83 Flight into Egypt
84 Holy Family
85–90 Slaughter of the Innocents
91 The Child Jesus gives life to clay birds
92, 93 The 12-year-old Jesus in the Temple
94–97 John the Baptist preaching in the wilderness
98 Baptism of Christ
99–101 Christ tempted by the Devil
102 Christ with two angels
103, 104 Marriage in Cana
105 Christ and the centurion of Capernaum
106, 107 Christ healing the sick
108 Christ casts out a devil
109 Christ heals the Canaanite woman
110, 111 Christ heals the impotent man at the pool of Bethesda
112 Christ heals a paralytic
113–115 Raising of Lazarus
116 Christ and the woman of Samaria
117, 118 Christ teaching in the school of Nazareth
119 Christ and the children
120–122 Mission of the Apostles
123–125 Transfiguration
126–130 Entry into Jerusalem
131, 132 Cleansing of the Temple
133–134 Judas's betrayal
135 Washing of the Feet
136, 137 Last Supper
138, 139 Agony in the Garden
140–143 Christ taken prisoner; Judas's kiss
144 Christ before Pilate
145 Mocking of Christ
146 Christ is crowned with thorns
147, 148 St Martin with the beggar
149 St Martin consecrated as an acolyte by St Hilary
150 St Martin raises a man from the dead
151–153 The Devil appears to St Martin in the guise of a king

Ceiling paintings, Zillis (Nos. 136–137 and 143–144)

From Zillis a narrow and winding road runs 2 km (1 mile) SW up the *Schamserberg*, on the left bank of the Hinterrhein, to the village of *Donath* (1033 m – 3389 feet). Above the village are the ruins of *Fardün castle* (1214 m – 3983 feet), famous for the story of a 15th c. castellan who, during a peasant rising, spat into the dinner of a peasant named Johannes Calcar, who thereupon thrust his head into the bowl and suffocated him, with the words, "Maglia sez il pult cha ti has condüt" ("You've salted the dish: now eat it!"). From Donath the road climbs another 6 km (4 miles) W to the quiet little mountain village of *Mathon* (1521 m – 4990 feet), from which *Piz Beverin* (2997 m – 9833 feet) can be climbed in 5 hours.

The N 13 expressway continues S up the Hinterrhein valley, coming in 3 km (2 miles) to the village of *Clugin*, on the left bank of the river (to right of road), with a picturesque little Romanesque church. 500 m (1641 feet) SW of the village are the ruins of *Cagliatscha castle*. – Beyond this, also on the right of the road, in the hamlet of *Bad* (Romansh *Bogn*), there is an alkaline chalybeate (iron-bearing) spring, the water of which is piped to Andeer. On the bridge over the *Pignieuer Bach*, which flows down from Piz Curvèr (2976 m – 9764 feet), is a 15th c. Latin inscription. – 5 km (3 miles) from Zillis is the exit for **Andeer** (979 m (3212 feet): pop. 1000; Hotel Fravi, E, 75 b.), chief place in the Schams area, in medieval times an important trading station and now a health resort (mineral swimming pool) and winter sports facility, with a large parish church (1673: Protestant) and a number of fine 16th c. houses with sgraffito decoration, notably the Haus Padrun. The old road continues through the Rofla gorge to join the new road: the distance is much the same. From Andeer there are rewarding, and fairly easy, climbs – to the W *Piz Vizan* (2472 m (8111 feet): $4\frac{1}{2}$ hours), to the SE *Piz la Tschera* (2632 m (8636 feet): 5 hours).

The new road (N 13) continues above Andeer in a wide curve, twice crossing the old road on bridges and passing below the village of *Bärenburg* (1042 m – 3419 feet). Through the trees can be seen the ruined castle of the same name; to the right is an artificial lake. – The road then traverses a tunnel of some length and crosses the *Averser Rhein* to reach the junction, at Avers, with the old road coming up from Andeer on the right, which gives access to the Rofla gorge and the Avers valley.

For the *Rofla gorge*, bear right into the old road, from which the road to Avers soon branches off on the left. 1 km (about a $\frac{1}{2}$ mile) farther downhill is the *Roflaschlucht inn* (1097 m – 3599 feet), at the entrance to the *Rofla gorge (or *Rofna*: access to gallery hewn from the rock). – Beyond this is a *reservoir* (maximum capacity 1 million cu. m (35 million cu. feet), a compensation basin for the reservoir at Sufers, from which water is carried down under pressure through a tunnel 13 km (8 miles) long to a power station at Sils in the Domleschg. – The old road then crosses under the new one twice and comes in 2 km (1 mile) to *Andeer*.

A rewarding excursion can be made into the beautiful high valley of the tumultuous *Averser Rhein*, which is divided into two parts by a narrow defile – the Romansh-speaking Val Ferrera and the German-speaking Averser Tal (Avers valley). It is reached on a good minor road (18 km (11 miles) to Cresta) which branches off the old road to the Rofla gorge, passes under the expressway and then continues up the wild **Val Ferrera**, first on the left bank and then on the right bank.

3·5 km (2 miles) up this road is **Ausserferrera** (1321 m – 4334 feet), in a wider part of the valley.· – The road then runs through the *Ragn da Ferrera* defile. To the right are the Ferrera turbine house (185,000 kW), hewn from the rock, and a

compensation basin (230,000 cu. m – 8 million cu. feet) for the reservoir in the Valle di Lei. – Then, opposite the mouth of the *Val d'Emet* or *Val Niemet*, the village of **Innerferrera** (Romansh *Canicül* or *Calantgil*, 1480 m (4856 feet)) is reached.

The road next crosses the Averser Rhein, runs through a tunnel (200 m – 656 feet) and another grandiose defile (natural rock arch), with a waterfall at the mouth of the *Val Starlera* on the left. After another tunnel (500 m – 1641 feet) it comes to the new bridge (lower down, the old bridge) over the *Reno di Lei*. This river issues from the Italian *Valle di Lei*, in which a dam was built in 1957–61 as a joint Swiss-Italian enterprise (Valle di Lei-Hinterrhein hydroelectric scheme). – 100 m (328 feet) beyond the bridge the road goes through another tunnel (250 m – 820 feet), and 1·3 km (1 mile) farther on a road branches off on the right to the dam. This runs uphill, with two sharp bends, and in 2·5 km (2 miles) reaches a tunnel 1 km (about a $\frac{1}{2}$ mile) long (traffic lights; closed in winter), at the far end of which are the Swiss-Italian frontier, the Swiss customs (on right) and beyond this the dam (car park). The dam rises to a height of 138 m (453 feet) above the foundations and is 635 m (2083 feet) long at the top. The artificial lake formed by the dam, the *Lago di Lei* (alt. 1931 m (6336 feet), capacity 197 million cu. m (6956 million cu. feet)), lies in Italian territory. The water is carried down under pressure in a tunnel 6·9 km (4 miles) long to the Ferrera turbine house (above).

The main road continues past the turning for the dam along the **Avers valley**, whose German-speaking population originally came from the Valais (Wallis) and adopted the Reformed faith as early as 1530. – After passing through the hamlet of *Campsut* (1670 m – 5479 feet) the road comes to *Cröt* (1720 m (5643 feet): inn), at the mouth of the *Madriser Tal*, with the Cima di Lago (3082 m – 10,112 feet) and Piz Gallegione (3135 m – 10,286 feet) rearing up in the background. It then climbs the wooded hillside in sharp bends, crosses the Rhine once again and after a number of other sharp bends reaches the highest part of the valley.

Cresta (*Avers*, 1960 m (6431 feet): Kur- und Sporthotel), beautifully situated amid flower-spangled Alpine meadows, attracts many visitors as a mountain resort and a climbing base, and also offers good skiing. Outside the closely huddled village of brown wooden houses is the picturesque little 17th c. parish church. On the E side of the valley are the three peaks of the *Weissberg* (3057 m (10,030 feet): 3 hours) and the bold pyramidal silhouette of *Piz Platta* (3398 m (11,149 feet): 4–5 hours). – From Cresta the road continues for another 6 km (4 miles), past the *Podestatshaus* (2042 m (6700 feet): built 1664), to **Juf** (2133 m (6998 feet): Pension Edelweiss; youth hostel), the highest permanently inhabited settlement in the Alps. From here it is possible to walk to Casaccia over the Septimer pass (Pass da Sett) or to Bivio.

Beyond the junction with the old road to Andeer, N 13 continues through a long gallery above the Rofla gorge, and then through two tunnels, one fairly long, the other shorter. Below, to the right, is the Hinterrhein. – The road then crosses to the left bank on a high arched concrete bridge. Farther up the valley, on left, is the *Sufner-See* (alt. 1401 m (4597 feet): capacity 18·3 million cu. m (646 million cu. feet)), formed by a dam 58 m (190 feet) high (viewing platform), which is linked with the reservoir in the Valle di Lei. Beyond this, on the right (exit road from expressway), is the little village of *Sufers* (1387 m – 4551 feet). – The road continues through a beautiful expanse of forest. Soon afterwards the magnificent prospect of the **Rheinwald valley** opens up, with its backdrop of mountains: on the left the pyramid of Pizzo Tambo, to the right of this the blunt summit of Guggernüll (2886 m – 9469 feet), beyond this the sharp peak of the Einshorn (2944 m – 9659 feet) and in the background the Hohberghorn (3005 m – 9859 feet).

Farther on is the exit for the Splügen pass and the village of **Splügen** (1450 m (4757 feet): Posthotel Bodenhaus, C, 80 b.; Piz Tambo, C, 25 b.; bypass), in a wide valley at the foot of the Kalkberg, above which rears the Teurihorn (2973 m – 9754 feet). The village, with handsome stone-built houses and a parish church of 1690, is a popular summer and winter resort (ski-lifts to the Danatzhöhe, 2160 m (7087 feet)), and also attracts considerable through traffic as a result of its location on the route to the Splügen and San Bernardino passes. From the "Burg"

(1527 m (5010 feet): 15 minutes NE), a remnant of the old fortifications of the village, there is a fine view of the valley and the Tambohorn. There is an attractive walk (2½ hours SE) to the three *Suretta lakes* (2270 m – 7448 feet), in a grandiose mountain setting at the foot of the Surettahorn (3031 m – 9945 feet); and *Guggernüll* (2886 m – 9469 feet) offers a rewarding climb (4½ hours, with guide). – For the continuation of the road over the Splügen pass to Chiavenna see p. 218.

The road to the San Bernardino pass (p. 218) continues past the village of Splügen and runs up through the meadows of the *Hinterrhein valley*, following a fairly straight and almost level course, with beautiful views. In 2·5 km (2 miles) it comes to the little village of *Medels in Rheinwald* (1533 m – 5030 feet), consisting of three groups of houses (to right: exit from expressway). – 4 km (2 miles)· beyond this, also on the right (expressway exit), is the trim village of *Nufenen* (1568 m (5145 feet): Rotes Haus inn), opposite the mouth of the *Areuetal*, which runs down from the Tambohorn, with Guggernüll (2886 m – 9469 feet) to the left and the Einshorn (2944 m – 9659 feet) to the right.

3·5 km (2 miles) farther on, to the right, is **Hinterrhein** (1624 m – 5328 feet), the last village in the Rheinwald valley, which comes to an end beneath the snow-capped peaks and glaciers of the *Rheinwald* or *Adula massif*. There is a rewarding walk up the valley to the *Zapport hut* (2276 m (7468 feet): 4 hours), at the lower end of the *Rheinwald glacier*, the source of the Hinterrhein. From here there are many possible climbs (for experienced climbers only) – e.g. the *Rheinwaldhorn* (3406 m (11,175 feet): 4 hours), the *Güferhorn* (3396 m (11,142 feet): 3½–4 hours, with guide), the *Zapporthorn* (3149 m (10,332 feet): 4 hours), etc.

Rhine Falls

Cantons: Schaffhausen (SH) and Zurich (ZH).
ⓘ **Verkehrsbüro Neuhausen,**
   Industriestrasse 39,
   CH-8212 Neuhausen am Rheinfall;
   tel. (053) 2 74 55.

HOTELS. – *Bellevue*, 100 m (328 feet) above the Rhine Falls, C, 55 b.; *Löwenbräu*, in Neuhausen, D, 44 b. – YOUTH HOSTEL: in Schloss Laufen.

The Rhine Falls, Schaffhausen

c., restored: youth hostel), on the S bank. From the balcony there is a good general view of the falls; and a short walk through the park leads down to a number of *viewpoints – the "Pavillon", "Känzli" and the "Fischez", an iron structure which brings the spectator almost within touching distance of the surging river. From the lower gate of the park a ferry can be taken across the river to the little **Schloss Wörth** (restaurant), with the best general view of the falls. From here it is a 10 minutes' walk up the right bank of the Rhine, past the Park Restaurant and then up a flight of steps to the left, to the car park. – From Schloss Wörth a (perfectly safe) boat trip can be taken to the rock in the middle of the falls.

The **Rhine Falls (Rheinfall) at Schaffhausen, the mightiest falls in Central Europe, surge over a ledge of Jurassic limestone 150 m (492 feet) across and between 15 and 21 m (49 and 69 feet) high, with two higher rocks standing in the middle of the river. The flow of water is at its greatest in June and July, after the melting of mountain snow.**

The falls can be reached from Schaffhausen (see p. 221) on either side of the river. To reach the N side, leave Schaffhausen by way of Mühlenstrasse and road 4, which runs SW to **Neuhausen**. A footpath from the car park leads to the *Rheinfallbrücke* (192 m (630 feet) long), which carries the Schaffhausen–Winterthur railway line. From here it is a 15 minutes' walk to *Schloss Laufen* (16th

Rhône Valley

Cantons: Valais (VS), Vaud (VD) and Geneva (GE).
ⓘ **Union Valaisanne du Tourisme,**
15 rue de Lausanne,
CH-1950 Sion;
tel. (027) 22 31 61.
Office de Tourisme du Canton de Vaud,
10 Avenue de la Gare,
CH-1002 Lausanne;
tel. (021) 22 77 82.
Office du Tourisme de Genève,
Tour de l'Île,
CH-1211 Genève;
tel. (022) 28 72 33.

The Rhône rises in the Bernese Oberland, flows through Swiss territory for 260 km (162 miles) and then enters France, eventually reaching the Mediterranean after a total course of 810 km (503 miles).

The source of the Rhône is the *Rhône glacier, which comes down from the Dammastock, near Andermatt (see p. 49). The river, also known as the *Rotten* in its passage through German-speaking territory, flows SW along the southern margin of the Bernese Oberland, with the Valais Alps on its S side, draining both these massifs through tributaries on either bank. At Martigny (p. 177) it turns sharply NW, almost at a right angle, and flows into **Lake Geneva** (p. 133). After passing along the whole length of the lake it emerges again at Geneva (p. 117), leaves Switzerland and in a few kilometres makes its way into the French Jura.

The best way of seeing the Rhône valley is to travel upstream. In this direction the

Rhine Falls

Schaffhausen

500 m
(1641 feet)

Waldshut

Singen

Konstanz

Neuhausen

Flurlingen

Zürich

Rhein-fall

Schloß
Wörth

Schloß
Laufen

Laufen-

Uhwiesen

Winterthur

route passes through a great variety of scenery, rising to a culmination in the majestic landscapes of the High Alps. – The **Rhône valley**, which with its lateral valleys occupies the whole of the canton of *Valais* (German *Wallis*), is a longitudinal trough up to 3 km (2 miles) wide between the steeply scarped southern slopes of the Bernese Alps, from which tumble a succession of short and swift mountain streams, and the main ridge of the Valais Alps, some 30–40 km (19–25 miles) away, the deep side valleys of which originate for the most part on terraces above the Rhône valley. The valley floor, originally littered with rock debris, has mostly been brought into cultivation through the regulation of the river and is now covered with fields of maize and vegetables and fruit orchards. At the bottom and on the lower slopes of the hills are vineyards, on the higher slopes and terraces fields, forests and Alpine meadows. Irrigation is necessary due to the shortage of rain and is provided by a network of channels (*bisses*), mostly fed by glacier water.

Gampel, in the Rhône valley

town of *Visp*, where the road to Zermatt goes off, we soon come to the old town and road junction of **Brig** (p. 89), where the towers of the Stockalperschloss form a distinctive landmark at the beginning of the road over the Simplon pass.

The character of the landscape now gradually changes. Although there are still walnut-trees and chestnuts to give something of a southern air, the rock faces now come closer, wooded gorges and steeper gradients make it clear that we have entered the region of high mountains. Beyond *Fiesch* the road leads through the thickly populated Goms valley, with its brown wooden houses and gleaming white churches, and after passing through Oberwald climbs up into the highest part of the valley, with the hotel complex of *Gletsch*, at the foot of the famous Rhône glacier.

From here there are magnificent passes over the Grimsel into the Bernese Oberland and over the Furka to the St Gotthard road.

Rigi

Cantons: Schwyz (SZ) and Lucerne (LU).
ⓘ **Offizielles Verkehrsbüro,**
CH-6356 Rigi-Kaltbad;
tel. (041) 83 11 28.

HOTELS. – IN RIGI-KALTBAD: *Hostellerie Rigi*, A, 115 b., SB; *Bellevue*, B, 95 b.; *Bergsonne*, C, 40 b. – IN RIGI-STAFFEL: *Rigi-Bahn*, D, 40 b. – IN RIGI-STAFFELHÖHE: *Edelweiss*, D, 20 b. – ON RIGI-KULM: *Rigi Kulm*, C, 100 b.

EVENTS. – *Alp parade, wrestling gala* (July–August); *National Festival*, with bonfires on hills (1 August).

The ****Rigi, the most famous mountain viewpoint in Switzerland, 1800 m (5906 feet) high, rises in isolation above Lake Lucerne, Lake Zug and the Lauerzer See, and is brought within easy reach by two cograilways and a cableway. The roads from Küssnacht, Weggis and Gersau terminate half-way up the mountain.**

View of the Rhône valley from Chandolin

The ***Rhône valley road** runs NE from the old town of **Martigny** (p. 177), from which roads run S to the Great St Bernard and the Col de la Forclaz, and then up the left bank of the river, traversing a region of fruit orchards on the valley floor, flanked by rocky hillsides, and often passing between long rows of poplars. It then crosses to the right bank and continues through a famous wine-growing region to the old episcopal and cantonal capital of **Sion** (p. 230), dominated by its two old castles, and the little town of **Sierre** (p. 225), situated amid a jumble of hills created by a huge prehistoric landslide, in an area offering numerous attractive excursions.

Beyond Sierre the road returns to the left bank and enters the German-speaking *Upper Valais* (*Oberwallis*), passing within sight of the interesting little towns of *Leuk* and *Gampel* on the sunny right bank. – After passing through the picturesque little market

The Rigi massif is an extensive range with a summit ridge some 50 km (31 miles) long. The fashion for climbing the Rigi to watch the sunrise began in the 18th c.

The most popular viewpoints are the *Kulm* (1800 m – 5906 feet), the *Rotstock* (1662 m – 5453 feet) and the *Scheidegg* (1665 m – 5463 feet). The many attractive footpaths and the mountain air, however, make it well worth while spending more time on the Rigi than a brief period for the sake of the view. – The best places for winter sports are the sheltered hotel settlements of Kaltbad, with the excellent facilities provided by the Hostellerie Rigi, and Klösterli (several ski-lifts). The view from the Rigi-Kulm is impressive both for the nearer view of the three surrounding lakes and the more distant panorama of the Alps; this prospect extends for some 200 km (124 miles) from end to end, with Säntis and Glärnisch, preceded by the Mythen, standing out with particular prominence in the E, Tödi in the SE and the giants of the Bernese Oberland in the SW; Pilatus closes the range of mountains in the W, and farther right one sees the Mittelland with its lakes, and beyond this the Jura and the Black Forest. On Rigi-Kulm, too, are the high tower antenna (the "Rigi-Nadel" or "Needle of the Rigi") and other installations of the Swiss Post Office.

MOUNTAIN RAIL- and CABLEWAYS. – **Vitznau to Rigi-Kulm**, the first cog-railway in Europe, built 1871 and electrified 1937 (length 7 km (4 miles), maximum gradient 25% (1 in 4), time 35 minutes). During periods of heavy snow in winter it runs only as far as Staffelhöhe. – The line climbs up through Alpine meadows, the views becoming more and more extensive. 4·5 km (3 miles): **Rigi-Kaltbad** (1440 m – 4725 feet) lies in a sheltered hollow. Footpath to the *First*, and in 20 minutes to the *Känzeli* (1470 m – 4823 feet), with fine views of the mountains and a prospect of Weggis, 1000 m (3281 feet) below. – 5 km (3 miles): *Staffelhöhe* (1552 m – 5092 feet). Beyond this the view of Lake Zug appears. – 6 km (4 miles): *Staffel* (1606 m – 5269 feet), the station for the *Rotstock (1662 m (5453 feet): 15 minutes), with a view similar to that from the Kulm. – 7 km (4 miles): **Rigi-Kulm** (1750 m – 5742 feet). – In summer there are also some steam trains.

Weggis to Rigi-Kaltbad: cableway (7 minutes).

Arth-Goldau to Rigi-Kulm: cog-railway, opened 1875, electrified 1906 (length 9 km (6 miles), maximum gradient 21% (1 in 5), time 35 minutes). The best views are on the right-hand side. – The line runs uphill in a wide curve to the passing station at *Kräbel* (766 m (2513 feet): cableway to Scheidegg, 6 minutes) and then continues up the *Kräbelwand*, with views of the Rossberg and Lake Zug. – 6 km (4 miles): **Klösterli** (1315 m – 4315 feet), in a sheltered hollow, with the pilgrimage church of *Maria zum Schnee* (Our Lady of the Snow: founded 1689, rebuilt 1721; pilgrimages on 2 July and 8 September). – 7·8 km (5 miles): *Staffel*, where the view to the N and W opens up. The line then runs close to the Vitznau line. – 9 km (6 miles): **Rigi-Kulm**.

WALK from Kaltbad or Klösterli to Rigi-Scheidegg (2 hours). – The initial stage is to the *Rigi-First* (1454 m (4771 feet): 20 minutes); then by the "Felsenweg", with superb views, to *Unterstetten* (1440 m (4725 feet): 25 minutes); and from there either on the "Kammweg" (extensive views) by way of the *Nollen* and *Dossen* (1688 m – 5538 feet) in 1¼ hours or on the "Seeweg" (fine view down to the lake) to the ridge between the Dossen and Scheidegg (45 minutes) and from there another 30 minutes to the **Scheidegg** (1665 m (5463 feet): inn, with terrace café, from which there are good views to the S.

Rorschach

Canton: St Gallen (SG).
Altitude: 398 m (1306 feet). – Population: 10,800.
Post code: CH-9400. – Dialling code: 071.
ⓘ **Verkehrsbüro,**
Hauptstrasse 53;
tel. 41 16 80.

HOTELS. – *Waldau, A, 70 b., SB, SP; *Anker*, C, 55 b., bathing beach; *Münzhof*, E, 55 b.

The old port town of Rorschach, lying at the foot of the Rorschacher Berg in a wide bay, the most southerly in Lake Constance (Obersee), was once an important trading post for the town of St Gallen. Its principal industries are textiles and metalworking.

HISTORY. – The development of Rorschach was closely bound up with the economic prosperity of the abbey of St Gallen. As early as A.D. 947 it was granted the right to hold markets, coin money and levy tolls by the Abbot of St Gallen. The old dock was enlarged in 1484, enabling the town to carry on a considerable transport trade, particularly in corn. In the 18th c. the linen trade also flourished. In 1803, on the dissolution of the abbey, Rorschach passed to the canton of St Gallen.

Panoramic footpath near Rigi-Kaltbad

SIGHTS. – In the main street, near the harbour, are a number of handsome 18th c. houses. To the N of the main street lies the beautiful *Seepark* (Lake Park), with a lakeside promenade. At the **Harbour**, near almost all the hotels, the **Kornhaus** (Granary: built 1746, restored 1956–58), now houses a local museum (closed Mondays: well-displayed collection of pre-historic material). SE of the harbour stands the Roman Catholic **parish church** of St Columban (Baroque, 1645–67; nave altered 1783). On the hillside above the town is the former *monastery of Mariaberg* (alt. 440 m (1444 feet)), a teachers' training college since 1805, with a beautiful cloister (1519) and a Gothic chapter-house (music room).

The Saas valley in winter

SURROUNDINGS. – **Rorschacher Berg**: Continue uphill past the Mariaberg monastery and turn left to reach, 2 km (1 mile) from Rorschach, St *Annaschloss* (568 m (1864 feet): private property), with extensive views; then to the top of *Rossbühl* (964 m (3163 feet): 1 hour). – From Mariaberg monastery take the Goldach road, which runs 3 km (2 miles) E to *Wilen*, with **Schloss Wartegg** (1557; beautiful park). – 4 km (2 miles) SW of Rorschach by way of *Goldach* is **Schloss Sulzberg** or the *Möttelischloss* (550 m (1805 feet): private property), with a 13th c. tower.

7 km (4 miles) S of Rorschach in the canton of Appenzell is the popular health resort of **Heiden** (806 m (2644 feet): pop. 3500; Hotel Krone-Schweizerhof, C, 60 b.; Linde, C, 30 b.), which can also be reached by cog-railway in 20 minutes. In this little town, lying high above Lake Constance in a park-like setting, Henri Dunant, founder of the Red Cross, lived from 1887 until his death in 1910 (monument, 1962).

Saas Valley

Canton: Valais (VS).

ⓘ **Verkehrsverein,**
    CH-3906 Saas Fee;
    tel. (028) 57 14 57.

HOTELS. – IN SAAS GRUND: *Touring*, C, 40 b., SB; *Adler*, D, 45 b.; *Sporthotel*, D, 45 b. SB; *Alpha*, D, 45 b.; *Bergheimat*, D, 40 b.; *Primavera*, D, 60 b.; *Rodania*, D, 50 b.; *Moulin*, D, 30 b.; *Eden*, D, 30 b. – CAMPING SITE.

IN SAAS FEE: *La Collina* (no rest.), B, 30 b.; *Saaserhof* (apartments), B, 100 b.; *Beau-Site*, C, 106 b.; *Grand Hotel*, C, 100 b.; *Derby*, C, 60 b.; *Alphubel*, C, 70 b.; *Eden*, C, 40 b.; *Europa*, C, 55 b.; *Etoile*, C, 37 b.; *Mistral*, C, 15 b.; *Waldhotel Fletschhorn*, C, 20 b.; *Du Glacier*, D, 100 b.; *Gletschergarten*, D, 46 b.; *Soleil*, D, 48 b. – CAMPING SITE.

IN SAAS ALMAGELL: *Atlantic*, C, 40 b.; *Kristall*, C, 55 b.; *Mattmarkblick*, C, 60 b.; *Portiengrat*, C, 60 b.; *Christiania*, D, 50 b.; *Lärchenheim*, D, 35 b.

RECREATION and SPORT. – Walking; sports facility with indoor swimming pool; ice-rinks, curling, toboggan run, winter sports.

The narrow *Saas valley, through which the Saaser Vispa flows down to join the Rhône, extends for some 28 km (17 miles) to the S of the little town of Visp, on the Rhône, at heights of between 1000 and 2000 m (3281 and 6562 feet), with the popular resorts of Saas Grund, Saas Fee and Saas Almagell. The starting-point of the valley is the village of Stalden, where the Zermatt and Saas valley roads separate.**

HISTORY. – The name of Saas Fee first appears in the records in 1217, in a document in which the Bishop of Sion disclaims responsibility for the protection of the Antrona pass road. About 1400 the commune of Saas became an independent parish, and in 1893 Fee was also made a separate parish. The local priest, Johann Josef Imseng (1806–69), began to experiment with skis in 1849, and is honoured as the pioneer of winter sports in Switzerland.

In the Saas valley. – The lowest part of the commune of Saas is **Saas Balen** (1487 m (4879 feet): pop. 470), which has a round church (Baroque). – 24 km (15 miles) higher up is the chief place in the valley, **Saas Grund** (1562 m – 5125 feet), situated in meadowland on the valley floor, with a large parish church (1939). Lying between the Mischabel group (the main peak of which is concealed behind lower mountains) to the W and the Fletschhorn (3996 m (13,111 feet), not visible from valley floor) and Weissmies (4023 m – 13,199 feet) to the E, it is a popular base for climbers. Indoor swimming pool in Touring Hotel.

From Saas Grund a minor road (4 km (2 miles) long, gradient 8% (1 in 12) with two hairpin turns) runs up to the "road terminus", just below Saas Fee (car park, parking garage, service garages: no cars beyond this point). The village of **Saas Fee** (1798 m – 5899 feet), in a magnificent *location facing the great Fee glacier, with the peaks of the Mischabel group towering above it in a wide arc, is a popular health resort, with winter sports (indoor swimming pool, ski-lifts, ice-rinks, curling, toboggan run) and climbing. The modern church (1963), with a separate tower, is well adapted to its setting. In the churchyard is the grave of the writer Carl Zuckmayer (1896–1977), an honorary citizen of Saas Fee. – A cableway 3400 m (11,155 feet) long runs SW (23 minutes), via an intermediate station at *Spielboden* (2450 m (8038 feet): marmots), to the *Längfluh (2865 m (9400 feet): restaurant, climbers' hostel), which can also be reached on foot from Saas Fee via the *Gletscheralp* (2135 m – 7005 feet) in 2½–3 hours (from Gletscheralp chair-lift 560 m (1837 feet) long, winter only).

The Längfluh is the starting-point for the ascent of the *Allalinhorn* (4027 m (13,213 feet): 4 hours, with guide), the least difficult peak in the *Mischabel group*, the highest point of which is the *Dom* (4545 m – 14,912 feet), the highest mountain entirely in Swiss territory. – A cableway runs SE from Saas Fee (12 minutes) to the *Plattjen* (2567 m (8422 feet): restaurant, chair-lift; Berghaus Plattjen 30 minutes lower down), from which it is a 2½ hours' climb to the *Britannia hut* (3029 m – 9938 feet). – Cableway from Saas Fee to the *Hannig-Alp* (2400 m – 7874 feet), to the W. – From Saas Fee to Kalbermatten a cableway 3652 m (11,982 feet) long runs S (9 minutes) to the *Felskinn* (2990 m (9810 feet): restaurant, ice cave, geological trail; skiing area, with summer skiing).

From Saas Grund the road continues SE up the valley, with moderate gradients, passing through *Zenlauenen* and *Moos*, and in 4 km (2 miles) reaches **Saas Almagell** (1679 m – 5509 feet), the highest village in the valley, a health resort, winter sports (ski-lifts, ice-rink) and climbing base. Chair-lift to 1950 m (6398 feet) on the *Furggstalden* (good skiing; ski-lift). Walk to the *Almageller Alp* (2225m (7300 feet): 1¼ hours).

The road continues for another 7·5 km (5 miles), past the hamlet of *Zermeiggern*

(1716 m – 5630 feet) and the huge moraine of the *Allalin glacier*, to the dam (115 m (377 feet) high, 780 m (2559 feet) long at the top), completed in 1967, which has formed the *Mattmarksee*. A massive fall of ice from the Allalin glacier crashed down on the construction site in August 1965, killing 88 workmen. – From the dam it is a 45 minutes' climb to the *Monte Moro pass* (2862 m – 9390 feet), which until the construction of the Simplon road was the principal route from the Valais into Italy (Swiss-Italian frontier). From the pass a cableway (large cabins) descends to **Macugnaga** (1307 m – 4288 feet), in the Val d'Anzasca.

Great St Bernard

In Switzerland and Italy.
Canton: Valais (VS).
Height of pass: 2469 m (8101 feet).

The *road over the Great St Bernard pass, between the Mont Blanc group and the Valais Alps, the highest pass road in the Swiss Alps after the Umbrail road, is for the most part excellently engineered (maximum gradient 11%), but is usually open only from the middle or end of June until October. The drive through the defiles of the Drance valley on the N side and above all the descent from the rugged world of the mountains into the southern beauty of the Aosta valley is a great scenic experience.

The construction of the *St Bernard tunnel* (5828 m (19,122 feet) long, carriageway 7·5 m (25 feet): toll) in 1959–63 made the road passable throughout the year and shortened the distance between western Switzerland and Italy in winter by several hundred kilometres.

HISTORY. – This ancient and historic traffic route was used by the Celts, from 105 B.C. onwards by the Ro₁₁ans, in 547 by the Lombards and later by many German emperors travelling to Italy (Charlemagne in 773, Henry IV on his journey to Canossa in 1077, Frederick Barbarossa in 1175). In May 1800 Napoleon led an army of 30,000 men over the pass to Aosta and Milan in order to expel the Austrians from Italy (Battle of Marengo).

From Martigny the road climbs the wild narrow valley of the *Drance*, passing through the village of Sembrancher at the mouth of the Val de Bagnes, to Orsières, and then up the featureless Vallée d'Entremont to **Bourg-St-Pierre** (1634 m (5631 feet): Hôtel Le Relais-Frontière, E, 14 b.; Du Vieux Moulin, E, 25 b.; bypass), a little market town in a wider part of the valley at the mouth of the *Valsorey*. The parish church (1739) has an 11th c. tower. Beside the church is a Roman milestone (4th c. A.D.). From here a number of difficult climbs can be undertaken – e.g. *Mont Vélan* (3765 m (12,353 feet): 7–8 hours, with guide) and the *Grand Combin (4317 m (14,164 feet): 11 hours, with guide).

From Bourg-St-Pierre a covered concrete road (8 m (26 feet) wide, maximum gradient 6% (1 in 16)) runs up the E side of the valley above the *Défilé de Saraire* and past the *Lac des Toules* (1800 m – 5906 feet), an artificial lake (capacity 20 million cu. m (706 million cu. feet)) formed by a dam 80 m (262 feet) high (short tunnel).

The road then reaches *Bourg-St-Bernard*, at the entrance (station, 1915 m (6283 feet); passport and customs control; toll charge) to the ***Great St Bernard tunnel**. To the left are the Petit Vélan (3233 m – 10,607 feet) and the snow-capped summit of Mont Vélan. Cableway (2530 m (8301 feet), 14 minutes) to the *Col de Menouve* (2753 m (9033 feet): Super-St-Bernard winter sports centre; magnificent ski trails).

From here the route continues either through the tunnel (maximum speed in tunnel 60 km p.h. (37 m.p.h.)) and on a covered road (9·5 km (6 miles) long, 9 m (30 feet) wide) to beyond St-Rhémy, or on the old road over the Great St Bernard.

The road *over the Great St Bernard* runs SW over the Alpine meadows, strewn with rock debris, of the *Plan de Proz* to the *Cantine d'en Haut* (1905 m – 6250 feet), and from there through a wild gorge, the *Pas de Marengo*, to the huts of Hospitalet (2100 m – 6899 feet). After crossing the Drance on the *Pont Nudry* (2190 m – 7185 feet) it winds its way up to the pass through the desolate *Combe des Morts*, which is filled with snow right into the height of summer.

The ***Great St Bernard** (2469 m (8101 feet): Hôtel de l'Hospice), a pass used since ancient times, crosses the main

ridge of the Alps, between the Mont Mort (2867 m – 9407 feet) on the left and the Pic de Drona (2950 m – 9679 feet) on the right. In summer the Swiss customs control takes place here. The famous **Hospice** founded about 1049 by St Bernard of Menthon (d. 1081) to succour distressed travellers is now occupied by Augustinian Canons. In the old buildings (16th c.) are the monks' quarters and the guest-rooms of the hospice, which now accommodate only groups of young people. The new building (1898) has been occupied by a hotel since 1925. In the *church* (1676–78) is the tomb of the French General Desaix, who was killed in the Battle of Marengo. The *Museum* contains Celtic and Roman antiquities from the Plan de Jupiter, relics of Napoleon, a natural history collection and a library of 30,000 volumes. The Hospice is famous also for the St Bernard dogs bred by the monks and used to scent out travellers lost in the snow. One particularly famous dog, Barry, saved more than 40 people from freezing to death in the early 19th c. – Chair-lift (10 minutes) to *La Chenalette* (2800 m – 9187 feet), from which there are superb *views.

A St Bernard in the snow

The road to Aosta skirts a small lake, rarely ice-free even in summer, through which runs the *Swiss-Italian frontier* (Italian customs control in summer). To the right is the *Plan de Jupiter*, with a stone cross (1816) and a bronze statue of St Bernard (1905). The name Plan de Jupiter, like the earlier name of the pass, Mont Joux (Mons Jovis), recalls a Roman temple to Jupiter Poeninus which stood here. – The road now descends in a wide curve past the hamlet of *La Baux* and a large crag, the *Gour des Fous*, to the *Cantine de Fonteintes* or *Cantine d'Aoste* (2217 m (7274 feet): Italian customs), in a green hollow. From here it winds its way down the right bank of the **Vallée du Grand-St-Bernard**, which it follows down to Aosta. To the left is the exit from the tunnel (1875 m (6152 feet): Italian and Swiss passport and customs control for entry to Switzerland). The road then crosses the expressway coming from the tunnel and descends, with two sharp turns, to the left bank of the *Torrente Artanavaz* and the village of *St-Rhémy* (1632 m – 5355 feet) which is situated in a wooded defile. The expressway by-passes the village to the W. The road then bears right through the deeply slashed *Combes des Bosses*, and in another 2·5 km (2 miles) is joined by the expressway from the tunnel exit (9·5 km – 6 miles).

St Gallen

Canton: St Gallen (SG).
Altitude: 670 m (2198 feet). – Population: 76,000.
Post code: CH-9001. – Dialling code: 071.
ⓘ **Verkehrsverein der Stadt St Gallen,**
Bahnhofplatz 1A;
tel. 22 62 62.

HOTELS. – *Hecht am Marktplatz*, Marktplatz, B, 100 b.; *Im Portner*, Bankgasse 12, B, 25 b.; *Metropol*, Bankhofplatz 3, B, 52 b.; *Walhalla beim Bahnhof*, Poststrasse 27, B, 82 b.; *Continental*, Teufenerstrasse 95, C, 55 b.; *Dom* (no rest.), Webergasse 22, C, 65 b.; *Ekkehard*, Rorschacher Strasse 50, C, 50 b.; *Sonne-Rotmonten*, Guisanstrasse 94, C, 50 b.; *Elite* (no rest.), Metzgergasse 9–11, D, 40 b. – YOUTH HOSTEL. – CAMPING SITE: in Bernardzell.

RECREATION and SPORT. – Golf, riding, tennis (indoor and outdoor courts); skating-rink, curling (indoor rink).

EVENTS. – *Spring Trade Fair* (end of May); OLMA (Agricultural and Dairy Show: October); *International Race Meeting* (alternate years – 1981, 1983, etc. – in September) on the Breitfeld; *Children's Festival* (every three years – 1983, 1986, etc.), held regularly since 1824.

St Gallen (the German form of the name: French St Gall), capital of the canton of the same name and the see of a bishop since 1846, lies in a narrow high valley in the Pre-Alps, here dissected by numerous streams (the Goldach, the Steinach, the Sitter, etc.) flowing through con-

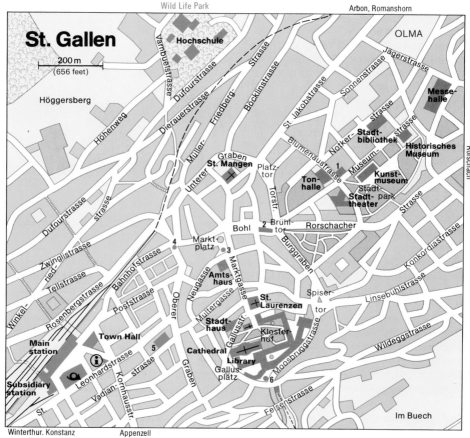

1 Kirchhoferhaus Museum 2 Weigh-House 3 Vadian monument 4 Schibener Tor 5 Gewerbemuseum 6 Müllertor

St Gallen – a bird's eye view

1507. Still farther N is *St Mangan's church* (founded *c*. 900 but much altered in later centuries), with a 16th c. tower.

From the Marktplatz the Marktgasse runs S past *St Lawrence's church* (St Lorenzen: restored 1851–54) to the spacious *Klosterhof* (Abbey Yard), around which is the former ***Benedictine abbey**. The extensive range of buildings, dating from the 17th and 18th c., now accommodates the bishop's palace, the residences of the Cathedral clergy and cantonal government offices. The abbey, believed to occupy the site of St Gall's hermitage of about 612, was founded about 720 and dissolved in 1805.

stricted gorges. The town is the economic capital of north-eastern Switzerland, with a School of Economic and Social Sciences and a number of other technical colleges.

HISTORY. – The town takes its name from the Irish missionary monk *Gall* or *Gallus* who established a hermitage here about 612. This developed into the Benedictine abbey which became a flourishing seat of religion and scholarship in the 9th c.; its school and library made it one of the focal points of European culture N of the Alps. In the 10th c. St Gallen, until then no more than a settlement of craftsmen and tradesmen which had grown up around the abbey, achieved the status of a town which in the 15th c. shook off the authority of the abbey and, in 1524, under a burgomaster named Vadian, adopted the Reformed faith. In the 16th–18th c. the town became exceedingly prosperous through its linen industry and grew considerably in size. The craft of embroidery, introduced in the 18th c., developed about 1830 with the advent of the hand-operated embroidery machine and later the shuttle embroidery machine into a considerable export industry (Textile Museum). Other industries, in particular metalworking, were established later.

SIGHTS. – In the northern part of the old town, which has handsome 17th and 18th c. burghers' houses with oriel windows, is the Marktplatz. At the corner of Marktgasse and Neugasse stands a statue of the 16th c. burgomaster Joachim von Watt (Vadian). To the E of the Marktplatz is the broad street known as the *Bohl*, at the E end of which is the 16th c. *Weigh-House* (Waaghaus); this has a crowstep gable, and houses the Council Chamber. To the N of the Bohl the *St Katharinenhof*, a relic of the former Dominican nunnery, has a cloister of

St Gallen

School of Economic and Social Sciences

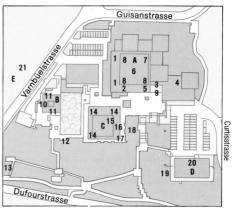

WORKS OF ART

A Main building
1 Joan Miró, ceramic frieze
2 Etienne Hajdu, beaten lead reliefs
3 Soniatta, wood relief on ceiling
4 Georges Braque, mosaic

First floor
5 Pierre Soulages, tapestry

Second floor
6 Alexander Calder, aluminium mobile

Third floor
7 Alberto Giacometti, bronze sculpture
8 Antoni Tàpies, wall decoration (18 wooden panels)
9 Jean Arp, bronze sculpture

B Mensa (Refectory)
10 Walter Bodmer, iron and glass sculpture
11 Jean Baier, coloured reliefs (enamelled aluminium)
12 François Stahly, bronze sculpture on fountain

13 Carl Burckhardt, bronze sculpture

C Great Hall and Chapel
14 Coghuf (Ernst Stocker), three four-part reliefs (iron and glass)
15 Coghuf, ceiling relief of wood and concrete
16 Coghuf, tapestry

Inter-denominational chapel
17 Otto Müller, interior of chapel, with brass cross, bronze relief, lead relief, gilded brass sculpture
18 Alicia Penalba, reinforced concrete sculptures

D Economic research institutes
19 Umberto Mastroianni, coloured aluminium sculpture
20 Zoltan Kemeny, brass relief

E Sports ground
21 Max Oertli, bronze sculpture

The three-aisled **Cathedral** (*Dom-kirche*), rebuilt 1755–66 in Late Baroque style, is mainly the work of the Vorarlberg architects Peter Thumb and Johann Michael Beer, with the help of G. Bagnato of Ravensburg and Gabriel Loser of Wasserburg.

The INTERIOR of the Cathedral was thoroughly restored and renovated in 1962–67, making the old *ceiling paintings* in the choir visible again. The most notable features are the delicate *stucco work*, the colourful ceiling-paintings by Christopher Wenzinger of Freiburg im Breisgau, the ceiling-paintings by J. Wannenmacher (1722–80), the wrought-iron *choir screen* (1772) and the *choir-stalls* by Josef Feicht-mayr, with carved scenes from the life of St Benedict. Under the organ gallery is a 10th c. *crypt*, with the tombs of bishops since the foundation of the see in 1847.

In the inner courtyard is the entrance to the famous ***Abbey Library** (*Stiftsbib-liothek*), with a fine interior and a rich and valuable collection of 100,000 volumes, 1635 incunabula and 2000 manuscripts.

Abbey Library   **St Gallen**

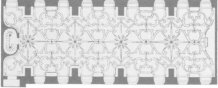

Wooden mosaic flooring in library hall

The ***Abbey Library**, housed in a charming Rococo *Library Hall by Peter Thumb (1758–67), with stucco work by the Gigl brothers and ceiling-paintings by Josef Wannenmacher, possesses works which belonged to the old abbey school, one of the leading European capitals of learning in the 9th–11th c., notable particularly in the fields of book illumination, poetry and the translation of Latin works into Alemannic. The finest items in the library are displayed in rotation. They include the 9th c. *Psalterium Aureum*, the *Casus Monasterii Sancti Galli* by Ekkehard IV (11th c.) and *Manuscript B of the Nibelungenlied* (13th c.). The famous **plan of St Gallen abbey in 820*, displayed under glass, presents the model of a large monastic establishment, a plan which was followed until the end of the Middle Ages. There is also a sarcophagus containing a mummy from Upper Egypt (700 B.C.).

In *Gallusplatz* and *Gallusstrasse*, to the W of the Cathedral, are handsome old burghers' houses of the 17th and 18th c., such as the *Haus zum Greif* (House of the Griffin, Gallusstrasse 22), with a carved oriel window. There are other old houses in neighbouring streets. – In Moosbrugg-strasse, immediately S of the abbey, are two remnants of the old town walls, the *Karlstor* (reliefs of 1570) and a round tower. – SE of Gallusplatz, at the falls on the Steinach, is a terrace with a memorial to St Gall.

NE of the Bohl is Museumstrasse, in which are (on left, at the corner of Blumenaustrasse) the **Tonhalle** (1907 concert hall) and (on right) the **Municipal Theatre** (*Stadttheater*, 1966–68) in modern style. Beyond Blumenau-strasse, at Museumstrasse 27, is the *Kirchhoferhaus Museum* (prehistoric material from caves; Züst collection of silver 16th–19th c., etc.). Beyond this, on the N side of the Stadtpark (Museumstrasse 32, on right), stands the *Museum of Art* (Kunstmuseum, or Altes Museum, founded 1877, at present closed: selection of items displayed in Kirchhoferhaus). Beyond this again (No. 50) is the **Historical Museum** or *Neues Museum* (New Museum), with prehistoric, historical and ethnographic collections, domestic interiors and utensils, porcelain, etc. – NW of the Historical Museum, at Notker-strasse 22, the *Municipal Library* (Stadt-bibliothek Vadiana), founded in 1551, houses the Municipal Archives. To the NE are the exhibition grounds where the annual Agricultural and Dairy Show (OLMA) is held. – At Vadianstrasse 2 is the *Industrial and Craft Museum* (Gewerbemuseum), with a fine collection of embroidery and lace covering five centuries.

To the N of the town, on higher ground, is situated the ***School of Economic and Social Sciences** (Hochschule für Wirtschafts- und Sozialwissenschaften: conducted tours by appointment Mon.–Sat. mornings), a fine example of modern architecture (1960–63), with the *Institute of Tourism and Transport*. Within the buildings and in the grounds are numerous works by leading contemporary artists, including Joan Miró, Alexander Calder, Alberto Giacometti, Antoni Tàpies, Georges Braque, Otto Müller, Hans Arp and Carl Burckhardt (see plan).

The *Botanic Garden* lies NE of the town.

SURROUNDINGS. – 3 km (2 miles) S of the town (from the abbey along St Georgenstrasse to the suburb of *Mühlegg* – also underground elevator – then left along Bitzistrasse and Freudenbergstrasse) is the **Freudenberg** (887 m (2910 feet): restaurant), from which there is a magnificent view of the town, Lake Constance and Säntis. – 3·5 km (2 miles) N (along St Jakobstrasse and in 1 km (about ½ mile) left

p the steep Gerhaldenstrasse) is the **Wildpark
'eter und Paul** (Wildlife Park: 800 m (2625 feet),
estaurant), with Alpine animals (chamois, ibexes,
marmots, etc.). – Cableway up Säntis: see p. 54.

7 km (17 miles) (motorway) is **Wil** (574 m (1883
eet): pop. 16,000; Hotel Schwanen, C, 18 b.; Derby
Hotel, C, 33 b.), an industrial town which at one time
was a favourite summer residence of the Prince-
Abbots of St Gallen. The beautiful old town lies
around the Hofplatz (also known as the "Goldener
Boden" or "Golden Ground"), with the former
Abbot's palace (the Hof), now housing a local
museum, and the Baronenhaus (1795). Nearby is the
Parish church of St Nicholas (1429–78) and to the
W the (originally Gothic) church of St Peter.

St Gotthard

The St Gotthard pass road (S side)

Cantons: Uri (UR) and Ticino (TI).
Height of pass: 2108 m (6916 feet).
Offizielles Verkehrsbüro Andermatt,
  CH-6490 Andermatt;
  tel. (044) 6 74 54.

The ** St Gotthard massif in central
Switzerland is one of Europe's most
important watersheds, with the
sources of the Rhine, the Rhône, the
Reuss and the Ticino (Tessin). This
rugged mass of crystalline schists
and granite was for many centuries
an obstacle to transit through the
Alps, and it was only the bold road-
building operations of the 18th and
19th c. and the construction of the
St Gotthard railway that opened up
this shortest route from N to S for
modern traffic. In 1980 after 11
years' work the St Gotthard road
tunnel was completed.

HISTORY. – There was already a bridle-path over the
St Gotthard pass in the 13th c. The first section of the
modern road, between Andermatt and Airolo, was
constructed in 1819–30, and this was later extended
further S. – The construction of the * **St Gotthard
Railway** (*Gotthardbahn*) in 1874–82 was an outstanding technical achievement for its day, costing
the lives of 177 men, including the engineer in charge,
Louis Favre.

The railway tunnel (15 km (9 miles) long)
runs under the summit of the St Gotthard
massif at a height of 1154 m (3786 feet).

The new ** **St Gotthard Road Tunnel**
(toll-free) is the longest road tunnel in the
world (16·3 km – 10 miles), passing
through the mountains at a height of 1175
m (3855 feet). Its completion means that
the St Gotthard route is now open all year
round. It runs from Göschenen, N of
Andermatt, to Airolo in the canton of
Ticino.

*Andermatt to Bellinzona over the
St Gotthard pass (85 km – 53 miles).
– From **Andermatt** (alt. 1444 m (4138
feet): see p. 49) the road to the St
Gotthard at first follows an almost level
course through the wide Urseren valley,
with views of the Furka.

Hospental (1484 m (4869 feet): Aparthotel Löwen, C, 26 b.; Meyerhof, D, 50
b.; bypass), an old village (Lat. *hospitium*,
"hospice") situated at the point where the
Furka-Reuss and Gotthard-Reuss join to
form the *Reuss*, is now a health and winter
sports resort (ski-lift to 2000 m (6562
feet) on the Winterhorn) with heavy
through traffic. Church (1705–11); tower
of 13th c. castle. – The road to the Furka
pass (p. 50) goes off on the right.

The St Gotthard road, bearing left, now
climbs up into the desolate valley of the
Gotthard-Reuss with five hairpin turns.
The view to the rear of the Urseren valley
and the chain of mountains to the N, from
the Spitzigrat (2560 m – 8399 feet) to the
Galenstock (3597 m – 11,802 feet), like
the later views towards the pass, reveals
the landscape of the St Gotthard massif in
all its austerity – bare gneiss and granite
crags, sometimes containing rare minerals, which have been little affected by
glacier action but have been worn smooth
by earlier ice, with many small lakes
gleaming between the hills. – The road
continues up the long stretch of valley
known as the *Gamsboden* (1640 m –
5381 feet), subject to dangerous avalanches in winter, climbing at a moderate
gradient. To the left is the *Guspis valley*,
below the Pizzo Centrale and the Guspis
glacier.

4 km (2 miles)) farther on we reach the *Mätteli* (1791 m (5876 feet): inn), at the foot of the *Winterhorn* or *Piz Orsino* (2661 m (8731 feet): 3½ hours' climb from Hospental), to the right. The road then climbs more sharply in a double hairpin turn. – At the *Brüggloch* (1908 m – 6260 feet) the cantonal boundary between Uri and the mainly Italian-speaking Ticino is crossed. Ahead can be seen La Fibbia (2742 m – 8997 feet). – The road continues, following a fairly straight course, past the Capanna di Rodont (1966 m – 6450 feet) to the *Lucendro bridge* (2015 m – 6611 feet) over the Reuss, which flows out of the *Lago di Lucendro* (2077 m (6815 feet): 30 minutes up on the right; detour recommended), an artificial lake supplying a power station at Airolo. From the lake it is a 3½ hours' climb (with guide) to the summit of the *Piz Lucendro* (2964 m – 9725 feet), from which there are superb views.

The road then climbs in a series of sharp bends to the *St Gotthard pass (2108 m – 6916 feet), a bare flat depression with a number of small lakes. To the left is *Monte Prosa* (2471 m (8107 feet): 2½ hours), to the right *La Fibbia* (2742 m (8997 feet): 2½ hours, with guide), sloping down sharply into Val Tremola. The St Gotthard group of mountains, forming a link between the Valais and the Grisons Alps, lies in the centre of Switzerland – the core around which the Confederation grew up. Here the valleys carved out by the Reuss and the Ticino have prepared the way for this magnificent route over the central ridge of the Alps. – 100 m (328 feet) beyond the pass is a road fork at which the old road continues straight ahead and the new road bears right.

500 m (1641 feet) beyond the pass, on the *old road*, is the St Gotthard Hospice (2095 m – 6874 feet), founded in the 14th c. but frequently rebuilt and now a protected national monument, with a weather station. Adjoining it is the *Monte Prosa Hotel* (30 b.), from which it is a 45 minutes' walk to the *Sellasee* (2231 m – 7320 feet) and a 3½ hours' climb (with guide) to the summit of the *Pizzo Centrale* (3003 m – 9853 feet). – Beyond the hotel the road descends the slopes of the wild *Val Tremola* ("Valley of Trembling") in 38 well-engineered bends, some of them supported on retaining

walls. In 5·5 km (3 miles) it comes to the *Cantoniera Val Tremola* (1695 m – 5561 feet), from which the *view down into the Val Bedretto and the Valle Leventina opens up.

The *new road*, 7·8 km (5 miles) long, bypasses the Val Tremola on the W, with some remarkable examples of road engineering (three tunnels). It then crosses the old road and later joins it. – Continuing down in 13 sharp bends, the road comes to **Airolo** (1154 m (3786 feet): pop. 2000; Hotel delle Alpi, C, 57 b.; Motta & Poste, C, 50 b.), a summer and winter sports resort in a magnificent mountain setting in the upper valley of the Ticino, known above the town as Val Bedretto and below it as Valle Leventina. To the W is the Rotondo group (Pizzo Rotondo, 3192 m (10,473 feet)). After a great landslide from the Sasso Rosso in 1898 the place was rebuilt and provided with a protective wall. In the Gotthardbahn station, just outside the tunnel, is a bronze relief commemorating the men killed during the construction of the tunnel. Above the bridge over the Ticino stands the *Lucendro power station* (completed 1945). SW of Airolo is the lower station of a cableway up the *Sasso della Boggia* (2065 m (6775 feet): skiing area).

From Airolo a road, narrow in places, goes W up the Val Bedretto, passing through a number of small villages which offer quiet summer holiday accommodation. The road through *Fontana* is particularly constricted. – *Villa* (1358 m – 4456 feet)) has a five-sided church tower designed to resist avalanches. – 1 km (about a ½ mile) farther on we come to the picturesque mountain village of *Bedretto* (1405 m – 4610 feet)). – **All'Acqua** (1605 m – 5266 feet)). From here it is a 3 hours' walk to the *San Giacomo pass*, which leads into the Toce valley (Domodossola). – The road continues over the *Nufenen (Novena) pass* (2478 m – 8133 feet *view) into the Rhône valley.

From Airolo to Biasca the Bellinzona road descends the valley of the Ticino, here known as the **Valle Leventina**: a superb Alpine valley which drops down in a series of stages, its slopes at first clad with green meadows and mountain forests, which soon give way to chestnuts and walnut-trees (many waterfalls). – At the mouth of the wild *Val Canaria* the road traverses the *Stretto di Stalvedro*, passing under four natural rock arches, to **Piotta**

(1012 m – 3320 feet), in a wider part of the valley. To the left, beyond the Ticino, is the *Ritom power station* (50,000 kW), which supplies the St Gotthard railway. From here a funicular 1360 m (4462 feet) long (average gradient 72% (1 in 1·3)) serves the cantonal *Gotthard Sanatorium* (1177 m – 3862 feet) the picturesque mountain village of *Altanca* (1346 m (4416 feet): also reached by road from Piotta; beautiful church of 1603) and *Piora* (1795 m (5889 feet): 24 minutes). From the funicular station it is a 15 minutes' walk to the *Ritomsee* (1830 m – 6004 feet), an artificial lake which supplies the Ritom power station; from here it is a 3 hours' climb to the summit of * *Taneda* (2670 m (8760 feet): magnificent views).

From *Ambri* (980 m – 3215 feet) a narrow mountain road winds up to a number of villages high in the mountains (1·5 km (1 mile) to Quinto, 6 km to Ronco, 7 km (4 miles) to Altanca).

Rodi-Fiesso (945 m – 3101 feet) is a double village beautifully situated between steep hillsides clad with larches and firs (summer holiday accommodation). From here there is a pleasant walk up to the *Lago Tremorgio* (1828 m (8998 feet): 2 hours), to the SW, nestling picturesquely in a deep rocky hollow. – There is also a narrow mountain road from Rodi to the little village of *Prato* (1030 m (3379 feet): 2 km (1 mile) SE), on a natural terrace high above the Ticino valley, with a beautiful Romanesque campanile. 4 km (2 miles) beyond this is the village of *Dalpe* (1140–1200 m – 3740–3937 feet)), above the Piumogna gorge, from which it is a $2\frac{3}{4}$ hours' climb to the Campo Tencia hut (2140 m – 7021 feet) and another $3\frac{1}{2}$ hours (with guide) to the summit of * *Campo Tencia* (3072 m – 10,079 feet), the highest peak in Ticino.

Just beyond Rodi-Fiesso, at the old customs post of *Dazio Grande* (949 m – 3114 feet), the road enters the wild * **Piottino gorge**, with a number of tunnels through the rock, between which (on right) the waterfalls on the River Ticino can be seen.

Faido (725 m (379 feet): pop. 1500; Hotel Milano, C, 70 b.), in a beautiful location, is the primary town in the Valle Leventina, and attracts many summer visitors. The stone-built houses of Ticinese type which now appear alongside the 16th c. timber houses with carved decoration, together with the first chestnuts and mulberry-trees, are the first intimations of a more southern landscape. On the W side of the valley the *Piumogna* plunges down in three beautiful waterfalls to join the Ticino.

Chiggiogna (668 m – 2192 feet). Beyond the railway line stands the parish church of the Madonna di Ascente (13th c., rebuilt in the 16th c.). – The road continues through wooded country, with waterfalls on both sides. Just before Lavorgo, on the right, are the *Cribiasca falls*, pouring down in a cloud of spray.

Lavorgo (622 m – 2041 feet) lies in a magnificent setting, with the long crest of the Monte di Sobrio on the left and a series of ridges running down from Campo Tencia and the Cima Bianca (2630 m – 8629 feet) on the right. – Below Lavorgo a narrow road goes off on the right, crosses the Ticino and runs up (4 km – 2 miles) to *Chironico* (800 m – 2625 feet), a beautiful mountain village with a fine Romanesque church (12th c.) and the 14th c. Torre dei Pedrini. – Beyond this, in the **Biaschina gorge**, the Ticino bursts through into the lowest part of the Valle Leventina (beautiful waterfall).

The village of **Giornico** (378 m – 1240 feet) straddles the Ticino, with handsome old stone houses and two fine Romanesque churches on the right bank. To the right of the road the church of * San Nicolao (12th c.), has a beautiful three-aisled crypt; higher up, amid vineyards, is * Santa Maria di Castello. At the end of the village stands a monument commemorating a victory by 600 men of the Valle Leventina and the canton of Uri over a force of 10,000 Milanese on 28 December 1478.

Beyond this, after crossing the railway, a beautiful waterfall on the *Cramosina* is seen on the right. After the next crossing of the railway, also on the right, is the *Biaschina power station* (30,000 kW). – The vegetation now takes on an increasingly southern character (figs, mulberries); the vines are grown on pergolas, in the manner characteristic of the south.

Biasca (305 m (1001 feet): pop. 3500) lies in a fertile basin in the Ticino valley, at the mouth of the Val Blenio (the valley of the Brenno), through which a road descends from the Passo del Lucomagno (Lukmanier pass); granite quarries, timber trade, railway workshops. On the hillside is the beautiful Romanesque church of Santi Pietro e Paolo (11th–13th c.; interior remodelled in 1685), from which a path with Stations of the Cross runs up to the Petronilla Chapel (384 m – 1260 feet) and a waterfall on the Frodalunga. To the E is the Pizzo Magno (2298 m – 7540 feet).

The road to Bellinzona now continues down through the wide and almost straight valley of the Ticino, which from here to Bellinzona is known as the **Riviera**, with purely southern vegetation (vines, chestnuts, walnuts, mulberries, figs).

At *Osogna* (280 m (919 feet): bypass), above the village, is the chapel of Santa Maria del Castello (altar of 1494, 17th c. frescoes).

At *Claro* (253 m – 830 feet), on the slopes of the *Pizzo di Molinera* (2293 m), to the left, stands the Benedictine monastery (founded in 1490), of *Santa Maria* (650 m – 2133 feet). – 4 km (2 miles) beyond Claro the road from Chur over the San Bernardino pass (p. 207 comes in on the left.

Arbedo (283 m (929 feet): bypass), which has a fine 15th c. parish church (the "Chiesa Rossa" or Red church), lies at the mouth of the *Valle d'Arbedo* (on left): there was a landslide here in 1929 from the *Motto d'Arbino*, which had been in gradual motion since 1888. – In a battle at Arbedo in 1422, during the war with the Duchy of Milan, a force of 3000 Confederates was defeated by an army six times their number, 2000 of them being killed in the battle.

At **Bellinzona** (230 m (755 feet): see p. 73) the road divides: straight ahead for Lugano (p. 172), to the right for Locarno (p. 163).

St-Maurice

Canton: Valais (VS).
Altitude: 420 m (1378 feet). – Population: 3500.
Post code: CH-1890. – Dialling code: 025.
ⓘ **Office du Tourisme,**
Place Val-de-Marne;
tel. 3 77 77.

HOTELS. – *Motel Inter Alps* (no rest.), E, 76 b.; *De la Gare*, 28 b.; *Des Alpes*, 25 b.

The little town of St-Maurice is picturesquely situated in a narrow pass in the Rhône valley, some 25 km (16 miles) S of the E end of Lake Geneva, at the end of a road which runs via Monthey to Champéry. This was the site of the Celtic settlement of Agaunum, where legend has it that St Maurice and his companions of the Theban Legion were martyred by Roman soldiers about the year 300.

SIGHTS. – At the N end of the town is an **Augustinian abbey** founded about 515 in honour of the martyrs, the oldest monastic house in Switzerland. The present church dates from 1611 to 1627; the beautiful Romanesque tower (11th c.) survives from an earlier building. The *conventual buildings* (now occupied by a secondary school and commercial college) were largely rebuilt in 1707–13. In the courtyard, between the abbey buildings and the cliffs, foundations and catacombs belonging to the earliest church on the site, including a 4th c. chapel, have been brought to light. The famous **Treasury* contains some outstanding works of art, largely of the Merovingian period, including several reliquaries, a gold-enamelled jug of Oriental origin and a Roman vessel of sardonyx.

To the N, above the town (footpath from the bridge over the Rhône), is a stalactitic **cave, the** *Grotte aux Fées*, with a restaurant and a view of the town.

SURROUNDINGS. – 6 km (4 miles) NW is **Monthey** (428 m (1404 feet): Hôtel Pierre des Marmettes, C, 40 b.), a busy little town of 11,000 inhabitants with a medieval castle (rebuilt in the 16th and 18th c.: museum). From here a road runs SW into the *Val d'Illiez*, first climbing up the steep hillside in sharp bends and then continuing up the slopes of the valley high above the left bank of the *Vièze*. Amid the vineyards and woods of chestnut-trees are many large boulders brought here by glacial action, including the *Pierre à Dzo*, resting on a base no bigger than a man's hand, and the *Pierre des Marmettes*, with a small

Les Diablerets

house on the top. In 6 km (4 miles) the road comes to *Troistorrents* (760 m – 2494 feet), a prettily situated village at the mouth of the *Val de Morgins*, through which a road runs up to *Morgins*.

The road continues beyond Troistorrents ascending the beautiful valley (many waterfalls) alongside the cog-railway, with views of the Dents du Midi and the Dents Blanches. 3·5 km (2 miles) farther on is *Val d'Illiez* (952 m (3124 feet): Hôtel Télécabine des Crosets, C, 50 b.), a village which attracts summer visitors. – The road continues up the valley, dotted with huts, and in another 3·5 km (2 miles) reaches **Champéry** (1052 m (3452 feet): Hotel de Champéry, C, 100 b.; Beau-Séjour Vieux Chalet, C, 45 b.), a village of 1000 inhabitants at the upper end of the Val d'Illiez, surrounded by forests and flanked by imposing peaks, popular as a health resort and especially for winter sports (heated swimming pool, tennis, golf, climbing school; curling, with an indoor rink; cross-country skiing). Two cableways, one (1·7 km (1 mile) long, 7 minutes) leaving from the S end of the village, the other (2·2 km (1 mile), 10 minutes) 1·5 km (1 mile) N on the Monthey road, go up to the skiing area of *Planachaux* (1800 m (5906 feet): several restaurants, mountain inn; many ski-lifts; beautiful views). – There are many attractive walks and climbs from here. Walks: 1¼ hours SW to the *Chalets d'Ayerne* (1473 m (4833 feet): good general view of the valley), 1¾ hours S to the *Chalets de Bonaveau* (1556 m (5105 feet): inn), etc. Climbs: *Croix de Culet* (1966 m (6450 feet): superb views), 2½–3 hours W (30 minutes from Planachaux); *Dents Blanches* (2645–2764 m – 8678–9069 feet), 7 hours S (with guide); *Dents du Midi* (Haute Cime, 3260 m (10,696 feet)), 7–8 hours E (with guide); etc.

Les Diablerets. – Leave St-Maurice on road 9 (E 2), which runs N down the Rhône valley, and in 13 km (8 miles) turn right into a steep and winding but very beautiful mountain road which comes in 3 km (2 miles) to *Ollon* (15th c. church). From here the road continues uphill, with beautiful views into the Rhône valley, curves round to enter the *Gryonne* valley and climbs in several sharp bends to the village of *Huémoz*; it then runs along the hillside, with a view of Villars, and climbs again in a double hairpin turn to the health resort of *Chesières* (1220 m (4003 feet): Hôtel Richemont, D, 50 b.). 10 km (6 miles) from Ollon is **Villars-sur-Ollon** (1256 m (4121 feet): Grand Hôtel du Parc, A, 140 b., SB; Elite, B, 120 b.; Eurotel, B, 250 b., SB), a popular health resort (salt-water swimming pool, golf-course, climbing school) and winter sports resort (several ski-lifts; cross-country skiing trail 25 km (16 miles) long; ski-bobbing run; artificial ice-rink; curling; ski-flying school), magnificently set on a sunny terrace high above the Rhône valley, with

*views extending to the Mont Blanc group. It is the terminus of an electric mountain railway from Bex (1¼ hours), connecting with the line over the *Col de Soud* (1523 m – 4997 feet) to the *Col de Bretaye* (1850 m (6070 feet): Hôtel du Col de Bretaye (no rest.), 20 b.), which is reached in 20 minutes: beautiful views and good skiing (lift to the *Petit Chamossaire*, 2030 m (6660 feet)). From the Col de Bretaye a chair-lift (12 minutes: on foot ¾ hour) ascends *Chamossaire* (2118 m – 6949 feet), from where there is a famous panoramic view embracing the Bernese, Valais and Savoy Alps and Lake Geneva, and (summer only) a chair-lift to the *Lac Noir* and the *Chaux Ronde* (2027 m – 6651 feet). – From Villars there is a cableway (2400 m (7874 feet), 12 minutes) to the Roc d'Orsay (2000 m – 6562 feet).

The narrow road continues E over the *Col de la Croix* (1780 m – 5840 feet) and comes in 16·5 km (10 miles) to **Les Diablerets** (1163 m (3816 feet): Grand Hôtel & Meurice, B, 180b., SB; Eurotel, B, 248 b., SB), a magnificently situated health resort and winter sports resort (climbing school, ski-lifts, toboggan run) in the *Vallée des Ormonts*, a high valley surrounded by wooded hills and dotted with huts. The valley is bounded on the S by the *Creux de Champ*, a semicircle of rock under the peaks of the *Diablerets* (Teufelshörner, 3246 m (10,650 feet); 7–8 hours, with guide; cableway from the Col du Pillon), with numerous waterfalls which join to form the *Grande-Eau* (pleasant walk, 1½ hours, up the valley). Cableway (2·4 km (1 mile), 15 minutes) to *Isenau* (1770 m (5807 feet): ski-lift). – From Les Diablerets it is possible to continue over the *Col du Pillon* (1546 m – 5072 feet) to Gsteig, Gstaad and Saanen (p. 142).

St Moritz

Canton: Grisons (GR).
Altitude: 1853 m (6080 feet). – Population: 6000.
Post code: CH-7500. – Dialling code: 082.
(i) **Kur- und Verkehrsverein,**
    CH-7500 St Moritz;
    tel. 3 31· 47.

HOTELS. – *Palace, A, 350 b., SB; *Suvretta-House, A, 380 b., SB; *Carlton, A, 200 b., SB; *Kulm, A, 300 b., SB; Schweizerhof, B, 140 b.; Monopol-Grischuna, B, 120 b., SB; Park-Hotel Kurhaus, B, 250 b.; Chantarella, B, 160 b.; Crystal, B, 160 b.; Europa St Moritz, B, 220 b., SB; La Margna, B, 100 b.; Belvédère (no rest.), B, 120 b., SB; Hauser (no rest.), B, 70 b.; Neues Posthotel, C, 120 b.; Steffani, C, 130 b.; Edelweiss, C, 100 b.; Chesa sur l'En, C, 30 b.; Waldhaus, C, 60 b.; Salastrains, C, 54 b.; San Gian (no rest.), C, 96 b.; Sonne (no rest.), D, 50 b. – YOUTH HOSTEL and CAMPING SITE in Moritz Bad.

CAFÉ. – *Hanselmann*, old-established.

IN SILVAPLANA: *Hotel Albana*, B, 50 b.; *Chesa Guardalej*, B, 210 b.; *Sonne*, B, 95 b.; *Julier*, C, 50 b.; *Arlas*, D, 23 b. – IN SILS MARIA: *Waldhaus*, A, 220 b., SB; *Edelweiss*, B, 130 b.; *Schweizerhof*, C, 130 b.; *Maria*, C, 60 b.; *Seraino*, D, 60 b. – IN SILS BASELGIA: *Margna*, B, 110 b.; *Chesa Randolina*, C, 62 b.; *Chasté*, E, 24 b.

RECREATION and SPORT. – Golf (Samedan), riding, tennis, clay pigeon shooting, archery, sailing, fishing.

St Moritz

FUNICULAR, CABLEWAYS, etc. – From St Moritz Dorf a funicular (2·1 km – 1 mile) ascends in 20 minutes via an intermediate station at *Chantarella* (2005 m (6578 feet): hotel) to **Corviglia** (2486 m (8157 feet): restaurant), with fine *views and excellent skiing; from there a cabin cableway (2450 m (8038 feet), 10 minutes) up *Piz Nair (3057 m (10,030 feet): magnificent view). – From St Moritz Bad the *Signalbahn* (cabins: 1460 m (4790 feet), 5 minutes) serves the *Signalkuppe* (2150 m (7054 feet): several ski-lifts).

WINTER SPORTS. – *Eisstadion* (Ice Stadium) and several *ice-rinks*; *curling*; *toboggan run*, the famous Cresta Run or Skeletonbahn (1400 m – 4593 feet); *bobsleigh run* to Celerina-Cresta (1600 m – 5250 feet); *Olympic ski-jump*. – Two international horse-races every year on the frozen lake. – Excellent *skiing country* (downhill, cross-country), easily accessible by the funicular, cableways and numerous lifts.

The world-famed winter sports resort (Winter Olympics 1928 and 1948) of *St Moritz (Romansh San Murezzan), in the midst of the Upper Engadine, is in two parts. St Moritz Dorf – a "village" which has all the appearance of a town, with its large and palatial hotels – is situated on a sunny terrace, sheltered from the N wind, above the St Moritzer See (Lake of St Moritz, 1768 m (5801 feet)), through which the River Inn flows from S to N. St Moritz Bad, on the valley floor at the SW end of the lake, has iron-bearing springs of

high carbonic acid content which were already being used in Bronze Age times.

The magnificent *view from St Moritz embraces the mountains from Piz Languard in the E to Piz Julier in the W, the most prominent peaks being Piz Rosatsch with its glacier, above the lake, to the right of this Piz Surlej and Piz Corvatsch, and in the distance the beautiful Piz della Margna.

SIGHTS. – The heart of ST MORITZ DORF is the Schulplatz (Pl. da Scoula), in

On the bobsleigh run, St Moritz

which stands the *Town Hall*. To the SE, lower down, is the *Tourist Information Office*, to the N, on higher ground, the **Protestant church** (1786), and beyond this, in the idyllic Old Cemetery, the **Schiefer Turm** (Leaning Tower), all that remains of the old Romanesque church of St Maurice.

On the road to Champfèr, to the S, is the *Segantini Museum*, a domed granite building (1911) containing pictures by Giovanni Segantini, including an unfinished triptych with an Alpine setting, "Coming into Being, Being and Passing Away" (1897–99). Opposite the museum stands a monument commemorating the victors in the Winter Olympics of 1928 and 1948. The *Engadine Museum* in the Badstrasse contains domestic interiors, implements and utensils.

In ST MORITZ BAD (1·5 km (1 mile) S of St Moritz Dorf), with its high-rise buildings, is the *Roman Catholic church* (1867), with a separate tower. On the eastern fringe of the forest are the **Spa Establishment** (1973–76), an open-air swimming pool and the *Kurhaus*. – Attractive paths run along the wooded slopes.

SURROUNDINGS. – There are very fine views from *Ober Alpina* (1990 m (6529 feet): 30 minutes SW of St Moritz Dorf), *Alp Nova* (2185 m (7169 feet): 1 hour W) and *Alp Laret* (2101 m (6893 feet): 1 hour N). From Ober Alpina there is a ridge path by way of the Chantarella funicular station to the Alp Laret (1 hour). – 2 km (1 mile) from St Moritz Dorf on the E side of the lake are the *Meierei* hotel-restaurant and café. From there it is another kilometre to the *Staz* hotel and restauran on the eastern shore of the *Lej Staz* (Stazer See, 1808 m (5932 feet): swimming pool), from which it is an hour's walk on forest paths to Celerina or Pontresina. – From St Moritz Bad it is an hour and a half's walk on beautiful forest paths by way of the *Quellenberg* (1920 m – 6300 feet) or the *Johannisberg* (2002 m – 6569 feet) to the **Hannensee** (2159 m (7084 feet): restaurant), and a further 2 hours along the slopes of *Piz Surlej* (3192 m – 10,473 feet) to the *Furcla Surlej (2755 m – 9039 feet), from which there is a breathtaking view of the Bernina group and the Engadine lakes. From here a 2½ hours' climb brings the walker to the summit of *Piz Corvatsch (3451 m (11,323 feet): cabin cableway from Silvaplana; superb views; summer skiing on the glacier (3303 m (10,837 feet), with two ski-lifts). – To the W of St Moritz there is a rewarding climb (not difficult for experienced climbers) by way of the *Alp Suvretta* (2211 m – 7254 feet) to the summit of *Piz Julier (3385 m (11,106 feet): 5 hours), which offers magnificent distant views.

7 km (4 miles) SW, at the junction with the road over the Julier pass, is **Silvaplana** (1815 m (5955 feet): bypass), a health and winter sports resort situated on the green alluvial fan of the *Ova dal Vallun*, with a

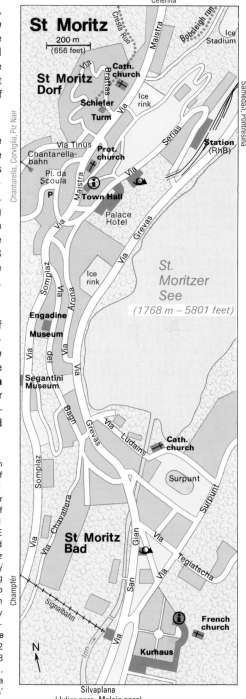

St Moritz

200 m
(656 feet)

St Moritz
Dorf

Cath. church
Schiefer
Turm

Ice
rink

Celerina

Cresta Run
Via Maistra
Via Brattas

Bobsleigh run
Ice
Stadium

Via Tinus
Chantarella-
bahn
Pl. da
Scuola

Prot.
church

Serlas

Station
(RhB)

Via
Samedan, Pontresina

Town Hall

Palace
Hotel

Via Grevas

St.
Moritzer
See
(1768 m – 5801 feet)

Via Somplaz
Via Arona

Ice
rink

Engadine
Museum

Segantini
Museum

Via del
Bagn
Grevas

Via Ludains

Cath.
church

Surpunt

Somplaz

St Moritz
Bad

Via Charatiera
San

Gian

Via

Via Tegiatscha

Surpunt

Champfèr
Signalbahn

Inm

French
church

Kurhaus

N

Silvaplana
(Julier pass, Maloja pass)

Chantarella, Corviglia, Piz Nair

Late Gothic parish church (1491). A bridge crosses the narrow neck of the lake on which it lies to a 19th c. baronial mansion, the *Crap da Sass* (private property), and the houses and chalets of *Surlej* ("above the lake"). 15 minutes' walk farther up is the lower station (1870 m (6135 feet): car park, restaurant) of the Corvatsch cableway. – 5 km (3 miles) farther SW on the road to the Maloja pass, lying to the left of the road between the Silvaplana lake (**Silvaplaner See**, 1794 m (5886 feet): area 2·6 sq. km (1 sq. mile), depth 77m (253 feet)) and the **Silser See** (Romansh *Lej da Segl*,

1797 m (5896 feet): area 4·2 sq. km (2 sq. miles)), is the popular summer and winter sports resort of **Sils** (Romansh *Segl*). This is in two parts – *Sils Maria* (the "Maria" is actually a corruption of a word meaning "farm"), the main tourist attraction, at the mouth of the Val Fex, and *Sils Baselgia* at the outflow of the River Inn from the Silser See. In both parts of Sils there are handsome houses in the style of the Engadine. Sils Maria has a Baroque church (1764), and beside the Edelweiss Hotel is a modest museum devoted to Nietzsche, who spent the summer months here from 1881 to 1889 (commemorative tablet). Sils Baselgia has a church dating from 1446.

From both parts of Sils there are pleasant footpaths (15 minutes) to the wooded peninsula of *Chasté* (1838 m (6030 feet): nature reserve), with scanty remains of an old castle and a Nietzsche quotation carved in the rock. – On the SE shore of the Silser See (45 minutes' walk) lies the hamlet of *Isola* (inn), which is abandoned in winter: behind it, in the gorge of the *Fedozbach*, is a beautiful waterfall. From here it is another 45 minutes' walk to the Maloja pass. – From Sils Maria a narrow road (closed to cars) runs S up the * **Val Fex** to *Crasta* (3 km (2 miles), alt. 1948 m (6391 feet): Hotel Sonne) and *Curtins* (6 km (4 miles), alt. 1976 (6483 feet): Hotel Fex), from which there is a beautiful view of the mountains framing the Fex glacier. – E of Sils Maria (1¼ hours) is the **Marmorè** (2203 m (7288 feet): ski-lift), with a magnificent view into the Upper Engadine. – A good footpath (3½ hours) leads E to the *Fuorcla Surlej* (2756 m – 9042 feet). – To the S of Isola (4–4½ hours, with guide) is the * **Piz della Margna** (3159 m (10,365 feet feet): superb views). – A cableway ascends to the *Alp Prasüra* (2311 m – 7582 feet), giving access to the Furtschellas (2800 m (9187 feet): ski-lifts).

San Bernardino Pass

Canton: Grisons (GR).
Height of pass: 2065 m (6775 feet).

The San Bernardino pass is the highest point on the San Bernardino road, a very convenient link between Lake Constance and Ticino. From Thusis onwards it is now mostly of expressway standard, and since the construction of the San Bernardino tunnel (1961–67) it has been the fastest all-year-round route from Lake Constance through eastern Switzerland to North Italy.

From Chur the road follows the Rhine and Hinterrhein valleys to Thusis, and from there takes a new line by way of the famous * Via Mala (see p. 197) to **Splügen** (bypass). – From here a road leads S over the **Splügen pass** (2113 m – 6933 feet), on the Italian frontier, and continues to *Chiavenna*, from where one can drive E into the * *Val Bregaglia* (p. 88).

The **San Bernardino road** to Bellinzona (69 or 76 km (43 or 47 miles)) continues past Splügen up the Hinterrhein valley. Beyond the village of Hinterrhein (p. 201) the old road branches off to cross the pass, while the expressway (N 13) passes a parking place (on right: kiosk-restaurant) and over the Hinterrhein, here still quite small, to the northern entrance (1613 m – 5292 feet) of the **San Bernardino tunnel** (length 6·6 km (4 miles), width of carriageway 7·5 m (25 feet), highest point 1644 m (5394 feet): emergency telephones; maximum speed 80 km p.h. (50 m.p.h.), overtaking prohibited; toll-free). The tunnel runs in an almost straight line under the pass, emerging just to the W of the village of San Bernardino. The route through the tunnel is 7 km (4 miles) shorter than the road over the pass.

The *road over the pass* climbs in 18 hairpin turns (maximum gradient 9% (1 in 11·1) up the steep slope below the Mittaghorn (2609 m (8560 feet): on left), with beautiful and constantly changing views to the rear of the Rheinwald valley and the peaks rising to over 3000 m (9843 feet) on its N side. – In 4 km (2 miles) it reaches the bare high valley of the Thälialp (1920 m – 6300 feet) and then ascends in nine hairpins to the pass.

The **San Bernardino pass** (2065 m (6775 feet): simple hospice), which may have been used as early as the Bronze Age as a route through the Alps, was originally known as the Vogelberg ("Bird Mountain"). It takes its present name from San Bernardino of Siena, who is said to have preached here in the early 15th c. On the pass, with its rocks worn smooth by the ice, is the *Lago Moèsola*, in which is a small rocky islet. To the E is the pointed summit of *Pizzo Uccello* (Bird Mountain, 2716 m (8911 feet)), to the W the blunt top of the *Marscholhorn* (2902 m – 9521 feet), beside which the Zapporthorn, with the Muccial glacier, comes into view as the road continues S.

The road skirts the lake and then continues down in 21 hairpin turns, following the course of the River *Moèsa*, through a rugged landscape, with magnificent views of the surrounding peaks, particularly of the precipitous Pan de Zucchero (2600 m – 8531 feet) and (to the rear, on the left) Pizzo Uccello, which towers up ever more imposingly as the road descends. To the E are Piz Lumbreda (2977 m – 9768 feet) and Piz Curciusa (2875 m – 9433 feet). After the last hairpin the southern exit from the tunnel (1631 m – 5351 feet) is seen on the right.

Just beyond this point is the village of **San Bernardino** (1607 m (5273 feet): Hotel Brocco & Posta, B, 65 b., SB; Bellevue, D, 35 b.; Ravizza-National, D, 70 b.), the highest place in the Val Mesocco and now a developing holiday and winter sports resort. There are many attractive footpaths through the meadows and woodland of this high valley below Pizzo Uccello (3½–4 hours). Cableway from the Alpe Fracch (1630 m – 5348 feet) to Confin (1953 m (6405 feet): restaurant), ski-lifts to 2500 m (8203 feet), ice-rink, cross-country skiing. – 2 km (1 mile) S, on the old road, is the *Lago d'Osso* (1646 m – 5401 feet), surrounded by forest.

From the tunnel exit N 13 continues S over the moorland plateau, passing on the right an artificial lake (1604 m – 5263 feet), curves round to cross the old road and then continues downhill, passing through two tunnels and two galleries. – In 11 km (7 miles) it passes (on right) the scattered houses of *Pian San Giacomo* (1172 m – 3845 feet), from which the old road runs down on the right to Mesocco. – N 13 then goes down in wide curves and several hairpins (* beautiful views) into the Val Mesocco, which descends in a series of steep steps, with several hydroelectric stations. To the SE are the twin peaks of Cima di Pian Guarnei (3015 m – 9892 feet) and Piz Corbet (3026 m – 9928 feet). – Just before Mesocco N 13 crosses the old road, which traverses the village, while N 13 passes above it (short tunnel) and then descends to the valley floor in a hairpin turn.

Mesocco or *Misox* (769 m (2525 feet): pop. 1500), formerly known as *Cremeo*, is a village of handsome stone houses, the chief place in the * **Val Mesocco** or **Mesolcina** (*Misoxer Tal*), and, like the Val Calanca which runs parallel to it on the W, belongs to the canton of Grisons but is inhabited by an Italian-speaking and Roman Catholic population. The two valleys together are known as the *Moèsano* (from the River *Moèsa* which flows down the Val Mesocco).

Santa Maria del Castello, in the Val Mesocco

Below Mesocco the road passes under a crag crowned by the ruined * **Castello di Misox** (748 m – 2453 feet), the ancestral castle of the Counts Sax von Misox, which was purchased by the Trivulzi family of Milan in 1483, destroyed by the people of Grisons in 1526 and restored by Swiss students in 1922–26 (magnificent view of the deep trough of the Val Mesocco). At the foot of the hill on which the castle stands is the 12th c. church of Santa Maria del Castello, with 15th c. wall-paintings. – Farther down the valley is *Soazza* (bypass), where the expressway comes to an end.

Sarnen

Canton: Unterwalden.
Half-canton: Obwalden (OW).
Altitude: 476 m (1562 feet). – Population: 7300.
Post code: CH-6060. – Dialling code: 041.

ⓘ **Verkehrsverein Sarnen-Wilen-Stalden,**
Sarnen;
tel. 66 40 55.

HOTELS. – *Wilerbad*, D, 120 b.; *Kreuz*, D, 20 b. – CAMPING SITE.

Sarnen, capital of the half-canton of Obwalden, lies at the N end of the Sarner See, on the road from Lucerne to Interlaken over the Brünig pass. The Landsgemeinde, the communal assembly, meets on the Landenberg here on the last Sunday in April.

SIGHTS. – In the **Town Hall** (Rathaus, 1729–32) is kept the "White Book" (Weisses Buch), containing the earliest account (*c.* 1470) of the history of the

Confederation. At the N end of the town is the *Heimatmuseum* (local museum) which houses a collection of prehistoric material, weapons, religious art, furniture, etc. Adjoining the Town Hall is the church of the *monastery of St Andreas* (17th–18th c.). On a hill to the SW stands the twin-towered Baroque *parish church* (by the Singer brothers, 1739–42). To the W, on the *Landenberg*, is the Baroque Schützenhaus (Riflemen's Clubhouse, 1752). – 2·5 km (2 miles) SW, on the sunny western shore of the lake, lies the attractive outlying district of WILEN, from which a road follows the lake via Oberwilen to Giswil.

SURROUNDINGS. – **To Schwendi-Kaltbad** (11 km – 7 miles). – A beautiful road which leads up the hillside – known as Schwendi – above the lake 3 km (2 miles): **Stalden** (797 m – 2615 feet), a small health resort. The road continues through the hamlet of *Gassen* and over the Alpine meadows on the *Schwendiberg*; then road on right to (8 km – 5 miles) **Schwendi-Kaltbad** (1445 m – 4741 feet), with an iron-bearing spring. – Beyond the turning for Schwendi-Kaltbad the road goes on into the **Entlebuch** valley (p. 113).

Into the Melchtal (22 km (14 miles) to Melchtal-Frutt). – Leave Sarnen on the road to Stans, which runs E, crossing N 8. – 2 km (1 mile): **Kerns** (569 m – 1867 feet), a village frequented by summer visitors. Turn right into a road which climbs the E side of the valley of the *Grosse Melch-Aa*. – 3 km (2 miles): *Zuben*. Here a road branches off on the right, crosses the Melch on a bridge 97 m (318 feet) high and reaches *Flüeli* (2 km (1 mile: road recommended as return route from the Melchtal), a hamlet commanding extensive views, and which boasts a pilgrimage chapel of 1618 and a house said to have belonged to the 15th č. hermit Nikolaus von der Flüe. His hermitage is lower down on the slopes of Mt *Ranft* (close by, a chapel of 1700). – 3 km (2 miles): *St Niklausen* (839 m – 2753 feet), with a 14th c. chapel and the old Heidenturm ("Heathens' Tower"). – 4 km (2 miles): **Melchtal** (894 m (2933 feet): Alpenhof-Post, D, 50 b.), a beautifully situated mountain village and health resort. Cableway (1200 m – 3937 feet) to the *Rütialp* (1350 m (4429 feet): restaurant; view). The road continues uphill over the *Balmatt*, at the foot of the precipitous *Rämisfluh* (1866 m – 6122 feet)). – 4 km (2 miles): *Stöckalp* (1070 m – 3511 feet), from which there is a cableway (3333 m – 10,936 feet) to Melchsee-Frutt. The road (alternate one-way traffic) continues, with many bends, up the valley of the Keselnbach, below the rock walls of the *Brünighaupt* (2315 m – 7396 feet). – 6 km (4 miles): **Melchsee-Frutt** (1920 (6300 feet): Sporthotel Kurhaus Frutt, C, 100 b.; Reinhard am See, C, 130 b., bathing beach; Glogghuis, C, 80 b., SB), a popular mountain resort and winter sports resort magnificently situated in a green valley (on the shores of an Alpine lake, the *Melchsee* (1838 m – 6030 feet), from where an unobstructed view of the whole Titlis chain may be enjoyed. A good base for climbs, e.g. to the *Erzegg* (2176 m (7139 feet): 1¼ hours; ski-lift) and the *Hochstollen* (2484 m (8150 feet): 2–2½ hours): easy and pleasant footpath to the Engstlenalp (3 hours). Chair-lift from the S end of the Melchsee (1900 m

Pilgrimage church, Sachseln

(6234 feet), 20 minutes) to the *Balmeregghorn* (2230 m – 7317 feet).

Over the Brünig pass to Brienz. – Leave Sarnen on road 4, which runs S along the E side of the Sarnen See to **Sachseln** (475 m (1558 feet): Mot-Hotel Kreuz, C, 130 b., SB), a prettily situated lakeside village which is popular with summer visitors. In the choir of the church (rebuilt 1672–84; lower part of tower Romanesque) is a glass sarcophagus containing the remains of St Nikolaus von der Flüe (1417–87), popularly known as "Bruder Klaus", whose conciliatory approach brought about the admission of Fribourg and Solothurn to the Confederation in 1481.

Giswil (488 m (1601 feet): Motel Landhaus, C, 85 b. SB, SP; Krone, C, 200 b.), in a green hollow in the valley surrounded by fine mountains, has a church (above the village) and the ruins of an old castle. A winding mountain road runs W, affording fine views over the *Moerli-Alp* (1100 m (3609 feet): restaurant) a popular skiing area.

Kaiserstuhl (701 m (2300 feet): Hotel Kaiserstuhl, E, 45 b., bathing beach): view on right of the picturesque **Lungernsee** (692 m – 2270 feet). – The road runs along the lake (viewpoints, on right), to which water is conveyed from the valleys of the Grosse and the Kleine Melch in a tunnel 10 km (6 miles) long, producing some 50,000 kW of electricity (power station between Giswil and Kaiserstuhl). To the S can be seen the Schwarzhorn chain, to the left the three peaks of the Wetterhorn (3701 m – 12,143 feet).

Lungern (715 m (2346 feet): Hotel Bären, D, 46 b.; Löwen, D, 80 b.; Alpenhof, D, 60 b.), a popular summer holiday place beautifully set at the S end of the lake in a setting of steep wooded hills, with a neo-Gothic church above the village. In 1323 the town of Berne and the three original cantons of Uri, Schwyz and Unterwalden formed an alliance against the Habsburgs here (commemorative tablet at the near end of the village, on left). From Lungern-Obsee a cableway runs up W via the intermediate station of *Turren* (1531 m – 5023 feet) to *Schönbüel* (2010 m (6595 feet): skiing), from which there is a path (4 km – 2 miles) to the Brienzer Rothorn and a ski-lift to the *Hohe Gumme* (2209 m – 7248 feet).

The road now comes to the **Brünig pass** (1007 m – 3304 feet), on the wooded ridge between the

Wilerhorn (2006 m (6582 feet): 3–3½ hours), to the W, and the *Giebel* (2039 m – 6690 feet). To the left is the Brünig-Hasliberg station (restaurant). The view embraces the Engelhörner (2783 m – 9131 feet) and the *Faulhorn* chain; below, to the left, is the Aare valley, extending W from Meiringen to Lake Brienz, with its beautiful waterfalls.

From the Brünig pass it is worth while taking a well-engineered panoramic road branching off on the left along the **Hasliberg**, a sunny mountain terrace high above the Aare valley which is a popular holiday area, with good skiing in winter. The road comes first to the health resort of *Hohfluh* (1049 m – 3442 feet), with far-ranging views, and then continues past the lower station (1150 m – 3773 feet) of a cableway to *Käserstatt* (1826 m (5991 feet): restaurant; chair-lift to Hochsträss, 2120 m (6956 feet); ski-lift to Hohbühl, 2037 m – 6683 feet) to *Goldern* (1053 m – 3455 feet). It then passes through Alpine meadows and crosses the gorge of the *Alpbach* in a wide bend to reach the health resort of **Reuti** (1045 m (3429 feet): extensive views). From here there are cableways via *Bidmi* to Käserstatt or *Planplatten* (2245 m – 7366 feet) and down to Meiringen.

From the Brünig pass the road to Brienz leads down through wooded country, with attractive glimpses to the left of the Hasli valley (the valley of the River Aare) and the Faulhorn chain. 1·5 km (1 mile) below the pass is a road junction, where an excellent road goes off on the left and winds its way down the slopes of the Hasliberg to **Meiringen** (8 km (5 miles): see p. 177), in the valley of the canalised Aare. The Brienz road bears right and descends, with a very fine view of the Aare valley, to the village of **Brienzwiler** (709 m – 2326 feet), on a terrace above the Aare. It then continues along the Aare valley below the *Ballenberg* (727 m (2385 feet) Swiss Open-Air Museum, p. 244) to the hamlet of *Kienholz* (570 m – 1870 feet), where *Lake Brienz comes into sight. Then beneath the *Brienzer Rothorn to **Brienz** (p. 243), on the lake of the same name.

Schaffhausen

Canton: Schaffhausen (SH).
Altitude: 404 m (1326 feet). – Population: 34,000.
Post code: CH-8200. – Dialling code: 053.

ⓘ **Verkehrsverein,**
Fronwagplatz 3,
CH-8202 Schaffhausen;
tel. 5 42 82.

HOTELS. – *Bahnhof*, C, 80 b.; *Kronenhof*, C, 50 b.; *Parkvilla & Schwyzerhüsli*, D, 50 b.; *Schaffhauserhof*, D, 45 b. – YOUTH HOSTEL. – CAMPING SITE.

Schaffhausen, capital of the canton of that name which lies N of the Rhine and is enclosed on three sides by Germany, is an important hub of communications. Its industries include iron and steel works, chemical plants and engineering works.

HISTORY. – Schaffhausen grew up as a transhipment point for traffic on the Rhine, here interrupted by the Rhine Falls. In 1045 the Emperor Henry III granted

Donaueschingen, Singen

Schaffhausen

1 Fronwagplatz
2 Schwabentor
3 Obertor
4 Stadthaus (Town Hall)
5 Diebsturm (Thieves' Tower)
6 Kornhaus
7 Municipal Theatre
8 Rathaus (Council House)
9 Haus zum Ritter
10 St John's church
11 Government Building
12 All Saints Museum

Count Eberhard von Nellenburg the right to mint coins here, and about 1050 the Benedictine abbey of All Saints was founded. From 1330 to 1415 the town was mortgaged to the Habsburgs, and thereafter, until 1501, was a free Imperial city. In 1454 Schaffhausen concluded an alliance with the Confederation, of which it became a member in 1501. From 1798 to 1803 the town and canton were part of the Helvetian Republic.

SIGHTS. – In the heart of the old town is the Fronwagplatz, with two fountains, the *Moor's fountain* (Mohrenbrunnen, originally 1520) and the *Butcher's fountain* (Metzgerbrunnen, 1524), which has a striking figure of a landsknecht (mercenary). Also in the square is the *Fronwagturm*, an old tower remodelled in Baroque style. The three finest old streets in the town radiate from the Fronwagplatz: to the N the *Vorstadt*, with a whole series of houses with oriel windows and coats of arms on the façade, which ends at the *Schwabentor* (Swabian Gate, 14th–16th c.); to the W the short *Oberstadt*, at the far end of which is the *Obertor* (upper Gate, originally 13th c.); and to the E the long *Vordergasse*, which opens out into a square. On the right-hand side of the Vordergasse stands the 15th c. **Rathaus** (Council House), with the fine Chamber of the Great Council (Grossratssaal, 1632) and the Council Arcade (Ratslaube, 1586). Beyond this, at the corner of Münstergasse, we find the colourful *Haus zum Ritter* (1485), with paintings on the façade by Tobias Stimmer (originals, 1570, removed in 1935, now in All Saints Museum; reproductions

Schaffhausen, with Kastel Munot

of 1938–39, restored 1943). Diagonally across the street the Late Gothic *St John's church* (Protestant) has an imposing tower.

In a spacious square S of Fronwagplatz, Herrenacker, are the old *Kornhaus* (Granary, 1679) and the *Municipal Theatre* (rebuilt 1956). In a small square immediately E, the Beckenstube, is situated the *Cantonal Government Building* (Regierungsgebäude), a skilful conversion of the old Arsenal (17th c.), with a magnificent doorway.

The **Minster*, a pillared basilica with a single tower (1087–1150), was originally the church of the Benedictine abbey of All Saints and is now the Protestant parish church. The spacious nave, flat-roofed (restored 1950–58), is a fine example of Romanesque religious architecture. The sparse furnishings are modern; near the altar, a simple wooden table, stand the bronze font and wooden pulpit. In the apse are three stained-glass windows and a large tapestry. The choir contains remains of old wall-paintings. – Outside the Minster, on the N side, is a bronze figure of David with Goliath's head (by K. Geiser, 1959). On the S side the *cloister* (freely accessible) has delicate 12th c. arcades; and in the forecourt of St Anne's chapel, adjoining it on the E, is the famous *Hosanna Bell* (Osannaglocke), cast in 1486, with a Latin inscription ("Vivos voco, mortuos plango, fulgura frango" – "I call the living, I mourn the dead, I quell the lightning") which inspired a well-known poem by Schiller, the "Song of the Bell" ("Das Lied von der Glocke").

The handsome conventual buildings of the abbey now house ***All Saints Museum** (*Museum zu Allerheiligen*), one of the richest local museums in Switzerland, with collections of prehistoric material (mainly from the Kesslerloch at Thayngen), works of religious art (the finest of them in the "Treasury" in the Abbot's Room), a series of rooms furnished in period style, weapons, relics of the old guilds, traditional costumes, etc., and a large *picture gallery*, notable in particular for the works by modern Swiss artists. – Of the old conventual buildings *St Erhard's chapel* (1104), *St John's chapel* (1064), a Romanesque loggia (1200) and the Kreuzsaal (c. 1620) are noteworthy.

To the E, dominating the town on a vine-clad hill is ***Kastel Munot** (1564–85), a circular structure designed in accordance with Dürer's principles of fortification. The walls are more than 5 m (16 feet) thick, with vaulted gunports below. The principal tower has a spiral ramp in place of a staircase to allow supplies to be carried up to the artillery. From the battlements there is a fine view of the town.

***Rhine Falls**: see p. 201.

Schwyz

Canton: Schwyz (SZ).
Altitude: 517 m (1696 feet). – Population: 12,000.
Post code: CH-6430. – Dialling code: 043.
ⓘ **Verkehrsbüro,**
Rickenbachstrasse 1;
tel. 21 34 46.

HOTELS. – *Wysses Rössli*, B, 46 b.; *Ochsen*, C, 32 b.; *Hirschen*, D, 35 b.

The old town of Schwyz, which gave its name to the whole country, is capital of the canton of the same name. It is charmingly situated on the edge of the orchard-covered plain between Lake Lucerne and the Lauerzer See, under the towering twin horns of the Mythen (1815 and 1902 m (5955 and 6259 feet)).

SIGHTS. – Schwyz has many handsome 17th and 18th c. patrician houses. In the main square is the richly decorated Baroque *parish church of St Martin* (1774), and opposite it the **Rathaus** (1642–43), its façade decorated with frescoes (1891) of scenes from Swiss history. The Great Council Chamber contains a series of portraits of Landammänner (cantonal presidents) from 1544 to 1850; the Little Council Chamber has beautiful panelling and a carved ceiling of 1655. In a tower S of the Rathaus is the *Cantonal Historical Museum*. In the Bahnhofstrasse (the road to Seewen) can be seen the **Bundesbriefarchiv**, in

Rathaus, Schwyz

b.), situated on a terrace commanding extensive views, with a large area of excellent skiing terrain. 8 minutes' walk SW of the Kurhaus a chair-lift (in winter a ski-lift) takes 15 minutes to reach the *Karrenstöckli* (1740 m – 5709 feet). From here it is a 10 minutes' walk to the *Luegi* viewpoint. Another chair-lift goes to the summit of the *Fronalpstock* (1922 m (6325 feet): inn), from where superb views of Lake Lucerne and the mountains can be enjoyed.

From Schwyz it is a 4 hours' walk by way of the *Holzegg* inn (1407 m (4617 feet): cableway from Brunni) to the summit of the *Grosser Mythen* (1902 m – 6240 feet), with a splendid view of central Switzerland.

1·8 km (1 mile) SE of Schwyz is *Rickenbach*, from which a cableway 2466 m (8025 feet) long ascends in two stages by way of *Husernberg* to the upper station (1565 m – 5135 feet) on the *Rotenfluh*.

Bundesbriefarchiv, Schwyz

which the original deed of confederation (*Bundesbrief*) between Schwyz, Uri and Unterwalden, signed on 1 August 1291, is displayed as well as other historic documents and mementoes. – Above the town is the *Kollegium Mariahilf*, a large Roman Catholic seminary, rebuilt after a fire in 1910.

SURROUNDINGS. – *Stoos:* Take the road which runs SE up the Muota valley and comes in 4 km (2 miles) to *Schlattli*. From there a funicular (1·5 km (1 mile) long, gradient up to 77%, time 8 minutes) climbs the steep wooded hillside to **Stoos** (1290 m (4232 feet): Sporthotel, B, 110 b., SB; Klingenstock, C, 45

The Muota valley (20 km (12 miles) to Bisisthal). – The road (in good condition as far as Bisisthal) climbs through flourishing fruit orchards to the foot of the *Giebel* (918 m – 3012 feet), where it enters the wooded gorge of the *Muota*. – 4 km (2 miles): *Schlattli* (573 m – 1880 feet), with the lower station of the Stoos funicular. – The road continues past a number of beautiful waterfalls, running through the hamlets of *Ried* (chair-lift via *Illgau* to the *Oberberg*, 1150 m – 3785 feet) and *Föllmis*. – 8 km (5 miles): **Muotathal** (612 m – 2008 feet) has a beautiful parish church (1792) and the picturesque nunnery of St Joseph (1684–93). – 2 km (1 mile): *Hinterthal*, where a road goes off on the left into the Starzlenbach valley. – 6 km (4 miles): *Bisisthal* (870 m – 2854 feet), in a beautiful setting.

The road up the *Starzlenbach valley* comes in 1 km (about a ½ mile) to the entrance to the *Höllochgrotten*, a cave system with extensive branches (total length of passages about 93 km (58 miles); 1 km (about a ½ mile) open to visitors), and ends in 5 km (3 miles) at the *Gutentalboden* (1281 m – 4203 feet), from which it is a 2¾ hours' walk on a bridle-path over the *Pragel pass* (1554 m – 5097 feet) to *Richisau* in the Klöntal (see p. 137).

Brunnen: p. 92. – **Rigi: p. 203. – **Lake Lucerne: p. 251.

Bad Scuol/Schuls-Tarasp-Vulpera

Canton– Grisons (GR).
Altitude: 1203–1268 m (3947–4160 feet). – Population: 1900.
Post code: CH-7550. – Dialling code: 084.
ⓘ Kur- und Verkehrsverein Bad Scuol,
    CH-7550 Bad Scuol;
    tel. 9 13 81.
    Kur- und Verkehrsverein Bad Vulpera,
    CH-7552 Bad Vulpera;
    tel. 9 04 46.

HOTELS. – BAD SCUOL: *Belvedere Kurhotel*, B, 90 b.; *Guardaval*, B, 90 b.; *Engadinerhof*, C, 110 b.; *Bellaval*, C, 55 b.; *Astras*, D, 40 b.; *Hohenfels*, D, 40 b.; *Kurhotel Lischana*, D, 40 b.; *Quellenhof*, E, 70 b. – CAMPING SITE.

BAD TARASP: *Tarasp*, C, 48 b.; *Chasté*, D, 24 b..

BAD VULPERA: *Waldhaus*, B, 300 b., SP; *Schweizerhof*, B, 240 b., SB, SP; *Villa Maria*, C, 35 b.

EVENTS. – *Hom Strom* (the "Driving Out of Winter": first weekend in February); *Chalandamarz* (Spring Festival: 1 March).

RECREATION and SPORT. – Walking, golf, tennis, hang-gliding, boccia, fishing; winter sports.

The village of Scuol, situated on the left bank of the Inn along the main road from St Moritz to Landeck by-

Bad Scuol (Schuls)

Motta-Naluns cableway

pass), combines with Bad Tarasp, only a short distance upstream, the summer holiday village of Vulpera, a little way S above the right bank of the river, and the village of Tarasp-Fontana below Schloss Tarasp to form the leading resort in the Lower Engadine. Scuol is a spa (recommended for diseases of the liver and bile ducts, stomach disorders, etc.), a health resort and a winter sports resort.

The heart of the resort area is the lively little town of **Bad Scuol** or **Schuls** (1244 m – 4094 feet), in a beautiful sunny setting on a gently sloping area of Alpine meadows (photograph, p. 45). In the spa quarter, OBERSCHULS (Scuol-sura), is the *Badehaus* (Pump room), to which the water of Vi, Sotsass and Clozza springs (high carbonic acid content) is piped. In the old village of UNTERSCHULS (Scuol-sot) are richly decorated old Engadine houses, the Protestant *parish church of St George* (1516) and the *Lower Engadine Museum*. – On the SW side of Scuol the Inn gorge is spanned by the Gurlaina viaduct (40 m (131 feet) high). From here it is a half-hour walk to Vulpera.

Bad Tarasp, 2 km (1 mile) SW of Scuol, has sodium sulphate and chalybeate (iron-bearing) springs which are similar in their action to those of Karlsbad. On the left bank of the Inn stand the large Kurhaus and the Kurhotel, on the right bank the Trinkhalle (Pump room). – From here a road climbs 1 km (about a ½ mile), with sharp turns, to **Bad Vulpera** (1268 m – 4160 feet), a quiet little place beautifully situated on a narrow terrace above the river, amid attractive parks and woodland.

From Vulpera a road winds up for 3 km (2 miles) to the little village of *Tarasp-Fontana* (1444 m – 4738 feet), delightfully set on a small lake. Perched on a high schist crag is an imposing medieval castle, ***Schloss Tarasp** (1505 m – 4938 feet), which became the residence of Austrian governors and was much altered during the 16th–18th c. (restored 1907–16 by a Dresden industrialist and made habitable: private property). – To the E is the *Kreuzberg* (Munt la Crusch, 1477 m – 4846 feet), from which the best view of the castle is to be had.

SURROUNDINGS. – From Bad Scuol a cableway 2·3 km (1 mile) long leads up the *Motta Naluns* (2136 m (7030 feet): restaurant; winter sports area), to the NW.

Val Sinestra (11 km (7 miles) to Bad Val Sinestra). – From the E end of Bad Scuol a road on the left climbs to (4 km – 2 miles) **Sent** (1440 m (4725 feet): Hotel Lischana, D, 25 b.; Rezia, E, 34 b.), a village with handsome Engadine houses and the picturesque ruins of St Peter's chapel (12th c.), originally belonging to the castle. It is also a winter sports resort (ski-lift, toboggan run). The road continues (turn left beyond the village) into the deep and narrow *Val Sinestra*, running high above the River *Brancla*. – 7 km (4 miles): **Bad Val Sinestra** (1471 m – 4826 feet), in a sheltered setting among beautiful forests, with arsenical chalybeate (iron-bearing) springs.

Ftan (6 km (4 miles) W). – From Oberschuls a road runs up the valley past the open-air swimming pool and the lower station of the cableway, and then climbs steeply, with many turns, to the village of **Ftan** or **Fetan** (1648 m (5407 feet): Haus Paradies, B, 45 b.; Engiadina, C, 34 b.; Pradatsch, 18 b.), a summer holiday place and winter resort (chair-lift, ski-lift) on a high terrace of meadowland on the N side of the valley, opposite Tarasp.

Val da S-charl (12 km (7 miles) S). – After crossing the Gurlaina viaduct a narrow road, straight ahead, winds its way through the forest. – 2 km (1 mile) from Scuol a road branches off on the left (1 km – about a ½ mile) to the farm of *San Jon* (1469 m – 4834 feet), with fine views of the Inn valley and the Lischanna group. – The road to S-charl continues along the right bank of the *Clemgia* through the beautiful *Val da S-charl*, the eastern boundary of the Swiss National Park (see p. 236). – 10 km (6 miles): **S-charl** or **Scarl** (1813 m (5948 feet): Hotel Crusch Alba, D, 35 b.), a tiny village in a remote and beautiful setting.

Sierre

Canton: Valais (VS).
Altitude: 538 m (1765 feet). – Population: 11,000.
Post code: CH-3960. – Dialling code: 027.
ⓘ **Office du Tourisme de Sierre et Salquenen,**
Avenue Max Huber 2;
tel. 55 85 35.

HOTELS. – *Atlantic*, C, 80 b., SP; *Arnold*, D, 50 b.; *Terminus*, D, 50 b.; *Central*, D, 30 b.; *La Grotte*, D, 30 b.; *Victoria & Jardin*, E, 25 b. – Several CAMPING SITES.

RECREATION and SPORT. – Riding, tennis, fishing; skating, curling (indoor and outdoor rinks).

The little town of Sierre (German name Siders) in the Rhône valley, lies near the linguistic boundary between French and German. It is set amid vine-clad hills formed by a gigantic rock-fall in prehistoric times, facing the gorge-like mouth of the Val d'Anniviers. On the left bank of the Rhône, at Chippis, is a large aluminium plant.

SIGHTS. – In the main street is the 16th c. **Château des Vidomnes**, with four corner turrets, residence of the episcopal bailiffs (*vice domini*). Close by stands the church of *Notre-Dame-des-Marais*, which dates in its present form from the 15th to the 16th c. The Baroque *parish church* is 17th c. (restored 1947). The *château de Villa* (16th–17th c.: restaurant), in the NW of the town, contains a Wine Museum and mementoes of the German poet Rainer Maria Rilke (1875–1926). – On a commanding crag (590 m – 1936 feet) above the town to the E is the massive *Tour de Goubing* (13th c.). To the S, on a rocky hill above the two *Lacs de Géronde* (bathing lido), stands the former Carthusian monastery of *Géronde*.

SURROUNDINGS. – To the *Val d'Anniviers (German *Eifischtal*: 26 km (16 miles) to Zinal, on a good road). – Leave Sierre on the road up the Rhône valley to Visp and in 2 km (1 mile), at *Pfynwald*, turn right into a road which climbs steeply uphill, with numerous hairpin turns. Below, to the right, is the Chippis aluminium plant.

Niouc (900 m – 2953 feet), situated high above the River *Navigenze* or *Navisence*, which flows down through the Val d'Anniviers. – The road then skirts the mouth of the Pontis gorge (short tunnel), beyond which is the Sentier de Sussillon viewpoint (1029 m – 3376 feet). From here a steep and narrow road on the left climbs up (3 km – 2 miles) to *Sussillon* (1386 m – 4547 feet), from which it is a 2 hours' walk to *Chandolin* (1936 m – 6352 feet), one of the highest mountain villages in Switzerland, with a superb view (road from St-Luc). – The road up the Val d'Anniviers continues to the hamlet of *Fang* (1095 m – 3593 feet), above the road on the right. Beyond this Chandolin can be seen high up on the left.

Vissoie (1221 m (4006 feet): Hôtel d'Anniviers) is the chief place in the valley (pop. 400); it has a square stone tower dating from the 14th c. – From here it is worth making an excursion on a road to the left which runs steeply up in seven hairpin turns (gradients of up to 12%, 1 in 8) to the village of **St-Luc**, 6 km (4 miles) E (1643 m (5391 feet): Hôtel Bella Tola & St-Luc, C, 60 b.; Favre, E, 35 b.; parking garage), situated on a steeply sloping expanse of Alpine meadows. This is a popular health and winter sports resort (several ski-lifts) with magnificent views of the Val d'Anniviers and its ring of mountains and over the Rhône valley to the Bernese Alps. Above the village is the *Pierre des Sauvages* (1714 m – 5624 feet), with prehistoric engravings. Chair-lift to the *Alm Tignousa* (2050 m (6726 feet): restaurant). Rewarding climb (4 hours) to summit of *Bella Tola* (3028 m – 9935 feet), with a superb view over the Bernese and Valais Alps to Mont Blanc. From St-Luc a road runs 5·5 km (3 miles) N to Chandolin.

Grimentz in winter

From Vissoie a side road on the right (8 km – 5 miles) descends to a bridge over the Navigenze and continues along the left bank to the little village of **Grimentz** (1570 m (5151 feet): Hotel Marenda, C, 85 b.; De Moiry, E, 70 b.; bypass), picturesquely situated on a little mountain stream, the Marais, above the mouth of the *Val de Moiry*. The village is a popular summer vacation spot, and also attracts winter sports enthusiasts (ski-lift). – The road continues S and in 5 km (3 miles) reaches the artificial *Lac de Moiry* (capacity *c.* 75 million cu. m (2648 million cu. feet): parking place by the lake, beyond a short tunnel; restaurant near the dam). It then follows the E side of the lake to the *Moiry glacier* (2350 m – 7710 feet), 4 km (2 miles) from the dam. From here it is a 1½ hours' climb SE to the *Moiry hut* (2850 m – 9351 feet).

The road up the Val d'Anniviers continues from Vissoie along the right bank of the Navigenze to the hamlets of *Quimet* and *Mission* (1307 m – 4288 feet), opposite the mouth of the Val de Moiry. It then climbs with a double hairpin to **Ayer** (1484 m – 4869 feet), a large village of Valais-style houses preserved intact, which is surrounded by forest and Alpine meadows. From here it is 5 km (3 miles) up the highest section of the valley, the **Val de Zinal**, to **Zinal** (1678 m (5506 feet): Hôtel Les Erables, apartments, C, 450 b., SB; Le Trift (no rest.), D, 28 b.; Pointe de Zinal, E, 35 b.), a popular climbers' base, health resort, winter sports centre (ice-rink, toboggan run) in a magnificent mountain setting. At the head of the valley is the *Zinal* or *Durand glacier* (1¾ hours), and above it tower the *Zinal-Rothorn* (4221 m (13,849 feet): 12 hours, with guide), the jagged twin peaks of *Besso* (3668 m (12,035 feet): 9 hours, with guide), the *Pointe de Zinal*

(3806 m (12,487 feet): 9 hours, with guide) and the *Dent Blanche* (4357 m (14,295 feet): 15 hours, with guide, very difficult). To the W of the Zinal-Rothorn is a Swiss Alpine Club hut, the *Cabane du Mountet* (2886 m (9469 feet): 5 hours from Zinal). Easier climbs are to the *Alpe de la Lex* (2188 m (7179 feet): 2 hours) and the *Roc de la Vache* (2587 m (8488 feet) 3 hours), which both afford splendid views; 1½–2 hours NE of the Roc de la Vache is another SAC hut, the *Cabane de Tracuit* (3256 m – 10,683 feet). From the near end of Zinal a cabin cableway (2000 m – 6562 feet) ascends to the *Alpe de Sorebois* (2470 m (8104 feet): restaurant), a good skiing area (two ski-tows up to 2900 m – 9515 feet).

Sierre via Montana-Vermala to Crans. – A funicular goes up via St-Maurice-de-Laques (change cars) to Montana (4·2 km (3 miles), gradient 49% (1 in 2), 30 minutes). There is also a well-engineered road to Crans (15 km – 9 miles) which winds its way up the steep hillside through vineyards and forest. From the first bend there is a view of the little *château de Muzot* (not open to the public), in which the German poet Rainer Maria Rilke lived at one time. – 4 km (2 miles): *Venthône* (813 m – 2667 feet), a picturesque village with a Gothic church. – 5 km (3 miles): *Randogne* (1250 m – 4101 feet), with the Montana sanatoria (pulmonary tuberculosis, tuberculosis of the bones and joints). – 4·5 km (3 miles): **Montana** (1500 m (4922 feet): see p. 102). 1·5 km (1 mile) N, higher up, is **Vermala** (1680 m – 5512 feet): p. 102). – 1·5 km (1 mile) W of Montana is the separate resort of **Crans sur Sierre** (1480–1500 m (4856–5922 feet): p. 101). – From here an excellent road, with extensive views, runs SW to **Lens** (5 km – 3 miles), a small health resort in a commanding situation, and from there to **Sion** (p. 230).

Sierre to Vercorin (16 km – 10 miles). – The road runs S from Sierre and over the Rhône to *Chippis* (2 km – 1 mile: 534 m – 1752 feet), at the entrance to the Val d'Anniviers, where there is a large aluminium plant

Zinal, in the Valais Alps

(Alusuisse). From here a road runs 3·5 km (2 miles) down the Rhône valley to *Chalais* (521 m – 1709 feet), at the near end of which village, on left, is a cableway up to Vercorin (1820 m – 5971 feet, 7 minutes). – From Chalais a winding mountain road, with sharp bends and two tunnels, continues up 10·5 km (7 miles) to *Vercorin (1342 m (4403 feet): Hôtel Orzival, C, 30 b.; Victoria, D, 30 b.), a beautiful old village 800 m (2625 feet) above the Rhône valley. A cableway runs S to *Sigeroula* (1865 m – 6119 feet). Still farther S is *Mont Tracuit* (2332 m – 7651 feet).

Simmental

The Simmental

Canton: Berne (BE).

ⓘ **Verkehrsverein Zweisimmen,**
Lenkstrasse,
CH-3770 Zweisimmen;
tel. (030) 2 11 33.
Kur- und Verkehrsverein Lenk,
CH-3775 Lenk im Simmental;
tel. (030) 3 10 19 and 3 15 95.

HOTELS. – ZWEISIMMEN: *Krone*, C, 50 b.; *Rancyl-Sternen*, C, 25 b.; *Residence*, C, 30 b.; *Sport Motel*, C, 50 b.; *Hüsi Blankenburg*, E, 6 b.

LENK: *Kurhotel Lenkerhof*, B, 160 b.; *Kreuz*, B, 160 b., SB; *Parkhotel Bellevue*, B, 100 b.; SP; *Wildstrubel*, B, 80 b., SB; *Crystal*, B, 50 b.; *Residence*, C, 40 b.; *Waldrand*, C, 50 b.

The Upper Simmental extends down from Lenk in the Bernese Oberland by way of Zweisimmen to Weissenbach, going almost due N; the Lower Simmental then turns E, bounded on the NW by the steep limestone crags of the Fribourg Alps. At Spiez the valley opens out and the River Simme flows into Lake Thun. With its handsome timber houses, its typically "Oberland" church towers, its herds of cattle (the famous Simmentaler breed) and its Alpine meadows dotted with huts, the Simmental is a very characteristic stretch of Bernese farming country.

At the W end of **Spiez** (see p. 242) turn off the lakeside road to Thun into road 11 (on left), which climbs, with a fine view of the Niesen (2367 m – 7766 feet), to *Spiezwiler* (652 m – 2139 feet), where the Kandertal road goes off on the left via *Mülenen* (7 km (4 miles): funicular up the *Niesen) to Kandersteg and Adelboden.

Road 11 continues straight ahead and then curves down to enter the valley of the *Kander*, which it crosses (to the left a view of the Blümlisalp, 3671 m – 12,045 feet). It then continues through wooded country to **Wimmis** (631 m (2070 feet):

Hotel Löwen), below the N side of the Niesen (5–5½ hours: see p. 242), with attractive old wooden houses and a 10th c. church. Above the village on the Burgfluh stands the imposing *Weissenburg Castle* (14th c.), which now houses the Nieder-Simmental communal offices (on the ground floor a room furnished in Simmental style). – Beyond Wimmis the road passes the end of a section of motorway and crosses the Simme to join a road coming in from Thun on the right. It then continues alongside an artificial lake, the *Simmensee*, and through the *Port*, a narrow passage between the high rock walls of the Burgfluh (990 m – 3248 feet) and the *Simmenfluh* (1456 m – 4777 feet). Now in the **Lower Simmental**, it ascends on a moderate gradient, with a view of the Jungfrau area to the left, to *Latterbach* (703 m – 2307 feet), in the commune of Erlenbach. – From here an attractive detour can be made on a narrow road to the left which runs through *Oey* and then 14 km (9 miles) SW up the Diemtigtal to the *Grimmi-Alp* (1222 m – 4009 feet), with far-ranging views, from which the *Seehorn* (2283 m (7491 feet): 3 hours) and the *Männlifluh* (2654 m (8708 feet): 4½ hours) can be climbed (fine views from both peaks).

Erlenbach (707 m (2320 feet): Hotel Alpina) is a typical Simmental village, with 18th c. timber houses. Situated on high ground is its old church (11th–13th c.), with an octagonal steeple (fine wall-paintings, mainly 15th c., with some late 13th c. work at the SE corner of the nave). Important cattle markets. A cableway 4040 m (13,255 feet) long runs N, via an intermediate station at *Chrindi* (1640 m (5381 feet): restaurant), to the *Stockhorn* (2190 m (7185 feet): upper station 2160 m (7087 feet); restaurant; mountain hut, magnificent view) in 15 minutes (on foot 4½ hours). – 5 km (3 miles) beyond Erlenbach lies the village of *Därstätten*, also with handsome 18th c. timber houses on the S bank of the Simme (in particular Haus Knutti, 1756). 2·5 km (2 miles) NW, in *Nidfluh* (920 m – 3019 feet), is the oldest farmhouse in the Simmental (1642).

Weissenburg (776 m (2546 feet): Hotel Weissenburg & Alte Post, D, 25 b.). – 1·5 km (1 mile) NW is *Weissenburgbad* (844 m – 2769 feet), a former spa (sulphurous spring, 31 °C (88 °F)) which no longer operates as such. – From Weissenburg the main road continues steadily uphill through a wooded valley, with villages situated on a terrace higher up on the right. It then comes to **Boltigen** (830 m (2723 feet): Hotel Bären), in a wider part of the valley, with the precipitous limestone peak of the *Mittagfluh* (1890 m – 6201 feet) rearing above it. Beyond this, at *Reidenbach* (840 m – 2756 feet), a road goes off on the right over the Jaun pass to Bulle and Lausanne. The main road continues up through the green Alpine meadows of the Simmental to *Weissenbach* (846 m – 2776 feet), and 2 km (1 mile) beyond this through a narrow passage which separates the Lower from the Upper Simmental. Beyond the crag of *Laubeggstalden* (ruined castle; waterfall on the Simme) the valley opens out again. The road passes the ruined castle of *Mannenberg* (1016 m – 3333 feet), on the left, and comes to **Zweisimmen** (954 m (3130 feet): pop. 3000), the chief place in the Upper Simmental, situated in a wide expanse of meadows at the junction of the Grosse and the Kleine Simme. The little town attracts many summer visitors, but is particularly favoured by winter sports enthusiasts (30 km (19 miles) of cross-country skiing; toboggan run; indoor tennis courts). It has a fine church·with a typical Simmental tower (15th c.; 15th–16th c. stained glass). Cableway (5·1 km (3 miles), 30 minutes) up the Rinderberg. To the W is the *Hundsrück* (2049 m (6723 feet): 4 hours), with extensive views.

From Zweisimmen the main road continues to Saanen (see p. 143), while the road to Lenk through the **Upper Simmental** branches off on the left, running alongside the *Grosse Simme* to *Betelried* (960 m – 3150 feet), with the 18th c.

Schloss Blankenburg (local government offices). It then continues to *St Stephan* (996 m (3268 feet): 15th c. church), with the Wildstrubel (3253 m – 10,673 feet) in the background, and to Matten (1026 m – 3366 feet), at the mouth of the Fermelbach valley. 5 km (3 miles) farther on (views of the Wildstrubel) is **Lenk** (1068 m (3504 feet): pop. 2000), in a beautiful setting of woodland and meadows at the head of the Upper Simmental, with the grandiose bulk of the *Wildstrubel* closing the valley to the S. Lenk is a health and winter sports resort (ice-rink, curling, cross-country skiing) and also a spa (sulphurous springs). The spa establishment lies to the SW of the village. Cableway (3698 m (12,133 feet), 26 minutes) via intermediate stations at *Stoss* and *Betelberg* (1650 m (5414 feet): restaurant) to the *Leiterli* station on the *Mülkerblatten* (2000 m – 6562 feet), with beautiful views and good skiing. – From the Wallbach a chair-lift (3241 m (10,634 feet), 28 minutes) also provides access to the Mülkerblatten via an intermediate station at *Wallegg* (1580 m – 5184 feet).

A narrow road (8 km (5 miles): alternate one-way traffic) runs S from Lenk up the *Pöschenried valley*, past the *Iffigen Falls (130 m (427 feet) high) to the **Iffigenalp** (1618 m – 5309 feet). From here there are rewarding climbs (not difficult for experienced climbers, with guide) by way of the Wildhorn hut (2315 m – 7596 feet) up the *Wildhorn (3248 m (10,657 feet): 6 hours) and by way of the Wildstrubel hut (2793 m – 9164 feet) up the *Wildstrubel (W peak 3251 m (10,667 feet), E peak 3253 m (10,673 feet): 7 hours), from both of which there are magnificent views of the Valais Alps and the Mont Blanc group. – A new road (N 6) is planned to run SW from the Iffigenalp through a tunnel 4 km (2 miles) long into the Valais.

Another road leads SE from Lenk up the Simme valley, past a cableway to *Metsch* (1480 m – 4856 feet), to *Höhenhaus* (5 km – 3 miles: 1103 m – 3619 feet), at the head of the valley. From here a footpath (1 hour) ascends past the *Simme Falls* to the huts on the *Räzliberg* (1404 m (4607 feet): restaurant), near which the **Siebenbrunnen** (1446 m – 4744 feet), the main source of the Simme, gushes out of seven clefts in the rock walls of the *Fluhhorn* (2139 m – 7018 feet).

Finally a road running E from Lenk climbs with steep bends to the *Bühlberg* restaurant (6 km – 4 miles: 1660 m – 5446 feet), from which it is an hour's climb to the **Hahnenmoos pass** (1957 m – 6421 feet).

Simplon Pass

Canton: Valais (VS).
Height of pass: 2005 m – 6578 feet.
ⓘ **Verkehrsverein,**
CH-3901 Simplon Dorf;
tel. (028) 29 11 34.

The road over the *Simplon pass (Italian Passo del Sempione), constructed on Napoleon's orders between 1801 and 1805, is the shortest route between Valais and southern Ticino or northern Italy. The road is usually open throughout the year; but it is always possible for motorists to avoid the pass by loading their cars on to the train which runs through the 19·8 km (12 miles) long Simplon tunnel between Brig and Iselle (Italy).**

The road, which offers a tremendous scenic experience, ascends from the old town of Brig (p. 89), at an important road junction in the Upper Rhône valley, with numerous turns and constantly changing views of the deep tributary valleys of the Saltina and the magnificent peaks of the southern Bernese Alps, and continues over the pass and down to Domodossola (Italy) and Locarno.

The *Simplon road* (64 km (40 miles) to Domodossola) branches off the Rhône valley road at **Brig** and winds its way up towards the towering Glishorn (2528 m – 8294 feet), with beautiful views of Brig to the rear. It then climbs the *Briger Berg* in the direction of the Klenenhorn (2695 m – 8842 feet), affording an attractive view, to the left, of Brig and the Rhône valley. Ahead is the Belalp, with the Sparrhorn (3026 m – 9928 feet) rearing above it; to the left the Nesthorn (3820 m – 12,533 feet), and, to the right, higher up, the conical peak of the Eggishorn (2934 m – 9626 feet).

Ried-Brig (938 m (3078 feet): Hotel Chavez, D, 30 b.). – The road continues uphill through wooded country, passing under a cableway to *Rosswald* (2000 m

(6562 feet): Hotel Klenenhorn, D, 38 b.), to the SE.

Schallberg Refuge Hut (Schutzhaus II, 1320 m (4331 feet)): the view of the pass, with the Bellevue Hotel, now opens up. To the rear are the Bernese Alps, from the Bietschhorn to the Aletschhorn. – The road now curves round into the wooded *Ganter valley*, beyond which (from left to right) are the Bortelhorn (3194 m – 10,480 feet), Furggenbaumhorn (2991 m – 9813 feet) and Wasenhorn (3246 m – 10,650 feet).

Berisal (1526 m – 5007 feet), a little hamlet with accommodation for summer visitors. – The road continues to wind its way up the mountainside through forests of larch, with beautiful views of the Bernese Alps.

The Simplon pass road at Berisal

At *Rothwald* (1750 m (5742 feet): inn) the magnificent summit of the Fletschhorn (3996 m – 13,111 feet) comes into view above the pass (to right). – 100 m (328 feet) farther on a side road on the left runs up through the forest (0·5 km – about a $\frac{1}{4}$ mile) to the commandingly situated Taferna Hotel (E, 22 b.). The main road now makes straight for the pass, running high above the *Taverbach*, with beautiful views down into the valley on the right. – *Schallbett Refuge Hut* (Schutzhaus V, 1934 m (6345 feet)).

The *Simplon pass** (2005 m (6578 feet): Hotel Bellevue, D, 70 b.; Simplon-Blick, D, 30 b.) is a ridge covered with Alpine meadows at the foot of the much-glaciated *Monte Leone* (3553 m (11,657 feet): 7 hours, with guide) and the black rock walls of the *Hübschhorn* (3192 m – 10,473 feet), lying closer to the pass. – The road now crosses a fairly level stretch of ground, passing a large stone eagle on a mound to the right which commemorates the manning of the frontier by Swiss troops during the Second World War. Beyond this, on the left, is the *Simplon Hospice* (2001 m – 6565 feet), established by Napoleon, which has been occupied since 1825 by monks from the Great St Bernard (see p. 207). – The road then descends the wide valley of the *Krummbach*, enclosed by snow-covered mountains, with fine views of the magnificent Fletschhorn. Below the road on the right can be seen the tall building of the *Altes Spital* (Old Hospice: 1872 m – 6142 feet), established about 1660 by Kaspar Stockalper, the great merchant prince of Brig (see p. 90). – At the *Engeloch* (1795 m – 5889 feet) the road leads down to the valley floor, crosses the Krummbach (1617 m – 5305 feet) to *Eggen* (1660 m – 5250 feet), at the mouth of the *Rossboden* or *Sengbach valley*, from which there was a devastating rock fall and avalanche from the *Rossboden glacier* in 1901.

Simplon Dorf (Italian *Sempione*, 1479 m (4853 feet): Hotel Fletschhorn, E, 18 b.) is beautifully situated in an expanse of green Alpine meadows in a wider part of the valley. To the E is *Monte Leone*, to the S the *Fletschhorn* (3996 m – 13,111 feet) and *Weissmies* (4023 m – 13,199 feet).

Gabi or *Gstein* (1232 m (4042 feet): Hotel Weissmies-Gabi, E, 30 b.) is situated at the confluence of the Krummbach and Laggienbach, forming the *Diveria* or *Doveria* River, which the road now follows downstream. – Beyond the *Gabi gallery* is the rugged *Gondo gorge*, one of the wildest and deepest ravine roads in the Alps. – The road continues through the *Gondo gallery* and crosses the *Alpienbach*, which flows down from the Alpien glacier on Monte Leone, forming beautiful waterfalls.

Gondo (858 m – 2815 feet), picturesquely situated below the rock walls of the ravine opposite the mouth of the *Zwischenbergen valley* (waterfall), is the last village in Switzerland (customs; Swiss passport control). The church dates only from 1968, but has an older choir. The high square tower was built by the Stockalper family of Brig about 1660 for the protection of travellers.

1 km (about a ½ mile) beyond this is the *Swiss-Italian frontier* (800 m (2625 feet): Italian passport and customs control). From here the road runs down the valley, now known as the **Val Divedro**, to **Iselle** (657 m – 2156 feet). At *Iselle station*, 1 km (about a ½ mile) beyond the village, the railway emerges from the S end of the Simplon tunnel; cars loaded here for Brig. – After passing through *Crévola d'Ossola* the road runs in a long straight stretch through the wide and fertile valley of the Toce, here known as the **Valle d'Ossola**, in which the vegetation already has a southern character (chestnut, fig and mulberry trees, fields of maize, vineyards), and comes to **Domodossola** (278 m – 912 feet), a town of 20,000 inhabitants, with an attractive market square, the Piazza del Mercato. From here a road runs E through the *Val Centovalli* to **Locarno** (p. 163).

Sion

Canton: Valais (VS).
Altitude: 520 m (1706 feet). -- Population: 22,000.
Post code: CH-1950. – Dialling code: 027.
ⓘ **Office du Tourisme de Sion et Environs,**
   6 rue de Lausanne;
   tel. 22 28 98.

HOTELS. – *De la Gare*, Place de la Gare, C, 60 b.; *Du Rhône*, 10 rue du Scex, C, 80 b.; *Touring*, 6 Avenue de la Gare, C, 40 b.; *Treize Etoiles*, 3 Avenue de Tourbillon, C, 60 b.; *Du Cerf*, 10 rue des Remparts, D, 42 b.; *Du Castel* (no rest.), 38 Rue du Scex, D, 60 b.; *Du Soleil*, 17 rue des Remparts, E, 50 b. – YOUTH HOSTEL. – Several CAMPING SITES.

RECREATION and SPORT. – Riding, tennis (indoor and outdoor courts), swimming, fishing; climbing school; skating.

Sion (German Sitten), capital of the canton of Valais, occupies the site of the Roman town of Sedunum and has been the see of a bishop since the 6th c. It is now an important market town for the wine (Provins Valais depot: conducted tours), fruit and vegetables of the fertile Rhône valley, with many features of interest. The old town is built on the detrital fan of the River Sionne, dominated by two picturesque castle-crowned crags. Here the River Borgne, coming from the Val d'Hérens to the S,

flows into the Rhône, carrying down boulders and scree which the Rhône has thrust against its northern bank.

SIGHTS. – In the spacious Place de la Planta are the *Palais du Gouvernement* (cantonal offices) and a monument commemorating the centenary of Valais' admission into the Confederation (1815). At 7 rue de Conthey stands the **Maison Supersaxo**, built by Georg Supersaxo, the provincial governor, in 1505; it has a fine hall with an elaborately carved and painted *ceiling. In the main street, *Rue du Grand-Pont*, which is built over the conduited River Sionne, is the **Hôtel de Ville** (Town Hall, 1660), with an astronomical clock. Built into the hall on the ground floor are a number of Roman inscribed stones, including one of A.D. 377 which is the earliest evidence of Christianity in Switzerland. – To the NE the **Cathedral** of *Notre-Dame-du-Glarier*, was rebuilt in the 15th c. and has a 12th c.

Romanesque tower. It contains 15th c. bishops' tombs and 17th c. choir-stalls; among the many valuable items in the treasury are a number of reliquaries of the 8th–10th c. – Facing the Cathedral, to the SW, is the *church of St-Théodule*, a sober building of 1516. The *Bishop's palace* (Evêché) on the W side of the square was built in 1840. – From here the narrow Rue de la Tour runs N to the *Tour des Sorciers* (Wizards' tower, 12th c.), a relic of the medieval fortifications. Close by, at the junction of Rue de Gravelone and Avenue St-François, stands the Muli (Mule) monument (by M.-E. Sandoz, 1966).

From the Town Hall another narrow street, Rue des Châteaux (at No. 12 a *Museum of Antiquities*), leads up to the castles. (It is possible to drive as far as the All Saints chapel and park there.) On the left are the remains of the *château de la Majorie*, which now houses the *Valais*

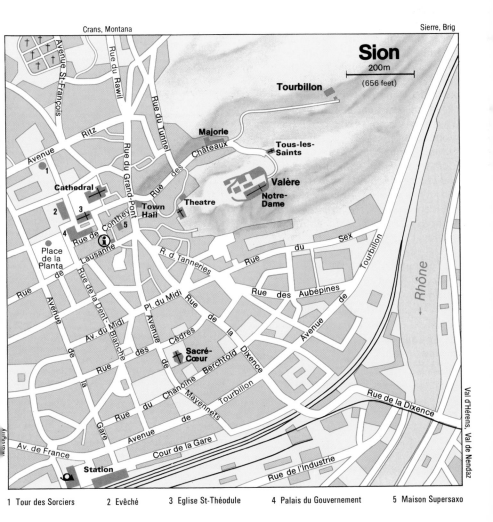

1 Tour des Sorciers   2 Evêché   3 Eglise St-Théodule   4 Palais du Gouvernement   5 Maison Supersaxo

Château de Valère, Sion

Museum of Art. In front of the castle is a monument to St Theodulus (Bishop of Valais. Beyond this is *All Saints chapel* (Tous-les-Saints), still in Romanesque style though it was built as late as 1325 (with some 17th c. rebuilding) From here it is a few minutes' walk to the château de Valère (15 minutes to the château de Tourbillon). The **château de Valère** (621 m – 2038 feet) and the former collegiate church of *Notre-Dame-de-Valère* (12th–13th c.), built on Roman foundations, combine to form an impressive architectural group (floodlit on summer evenings). The church is a three-aisled pillared basilica, with fantastically decorated capitals in the choir; the carved wooden altar is 16th c., the beautifully carved choir-stalls 17th c., the stone rood-screen 13th c., and the organ, in a painted loft, 15th c. (one of the oldest that can still be played). – Beside the church is the cantonal *Musée de Valère* (closed Mondays), with Roman antiquities and medieval sculpture.

On the higher of the two hills above the town (655 m – 2149 feet) are the imposing ruins of the **Château de Tourbillon** (built 1294, destroyed by fire

Romanesque church
(founded c. 407;
earliest doc.
reference 1152)

Saint-Pierre-de-Clages
(VS)

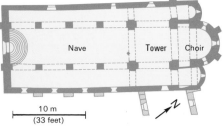

10 m
(33 feet)

1788), from which there is a view embracing the Rhône valley from Leuk in the E to Martigny in the W.

SURROUNDINGS. – Road 9 runs down the Rhône valley via the wine-producing village of *Vétroz* to **St-Pierre-de-Clages** (526 m – 1726 feet), which has a *church of the 11th–12th c. with an octagonal tower, one of the finest Romanesque churches in Switzerland (stained glass of 1948).

To the Val de Nendaz (16 km (10 miles) to Haute-Nendaz, 27 km (17 miles) to the Lac de Cleuson). – Leave Sion on the Val d'Hérens road and after crossing the Rhône take a road on the right which leads gradually uphill and comes in 5 km (3 miles) to *Arvilard* (684 m – 2244 feet), where a road branches off on the left to Mayens de Sion. – 1 km (1 mile): *Baar* (738 m – 2421 feet), beyond which the road turns S into the narrow *Val de Nendaz*. – 2 km (1 mile): *Brignon* (895 m – 2936 feet). – 2 km (1 mile): *Beuson* (972 m – 3189 feet), where the road crosses the *Printse* to the W side of the valley. Side road to *Veysonnaz* (see below). – 2 km (1 mile): *Basse-Nendaz* (992 m – 3255 feet). The road climbs up the open hillside in three large turns. – 4 km (2 miles): **Haute-Nendaz** (1370 m (4495 feet): Hôtel Sourire, C, 58 b.), a holiday and skiing resort high above the Rhône valley. Cableway (2270 m (7448 feet), 12 minutes) to *Tracouet* (2200 m (7218 feet): skiing), at the foot of the *Dent de Nendaz* (2463 m (8081 feet): 2–3 hours). – The road continues S up the valley above an irrigation channel (*bisse*). 2 km (1 mile): *Le Bleusy* (1412 m – 4633 feet), with a chapel. – 3 km (2 miles): *L'Antie* (1565 m – 5135 feet). – 3 km (2 miles): **Super-Nendaz** (1736 m (5696 feet): apartment hotel; several ski-lifts. From here a road (2 km – 1 mile) runs to the *Alpe de Tortin* (2039 m – 6690 feet), from which there is a cableway (2280 m (7481 feet), 12 minutes) to the *Col de Chassoure* (2734 m – 8970 feet); from there chair-lift to the Lac des Vaux. – The road continues climbing, with sharp bends. 3 km (2 miles): **Lac de Cleuson** (2115 m – 6939 feet), an artificial lake 1200 m (3937 feet) long created in 1958.

From Beuson a steep and narrow mountain road climbs 3·5 km (2 miles) to *Veysonnaz* (1233 m – 4045 feet), from which a cableway ascends to the holiday and winter sports resort of **Thyon 2000** (2068 m (6785 feet): Hôtel Résidences Thyon; blocks of flats; indoor swimming pool, ski-lifts), which can also be reached by road (13 km – 8 miles) from Vex via *Les Collons* (1800 m – 5906 feet).

To Mayens de Sion (15 km – 9 miles). – At Arvilard (5 km – 3 miles) on the Val de Nendaz road turn left into a road which climbs in large bends via *Salins* (847 m – 2779 feet) to (13 km – 8 miles) *Les Agettes* (1030 m – 3379 feet). – 2 km (1 mile): **Mayens de Sion** (1300–1400 m – 4265–4593 feet), a summer village of chalets widely dispersed over the Alpine meadows, which are supplied with water by irrigation channels (*bisses*). Magnificent views of the Bernese Alps, in particular the Wildhorn (3248 m – 10,657 feet), due N above Sion.

To the Lac de Tseuzier (23 km (14 miles): the Rawil road). – The road runs N up the Sionne valley and then climbs in sharp turns up the E side of the valley. – 3·5 km (2 miles): *Champlan* (714 m – 2343 feet), a village surrounded by vineyards. – 2·5 km (2 miles): **Grimisuat** (881 m – 2891 feet), on a rocky spur.

From here a narrow mountain road ascends steeply to *Arbaz* (1146 m – 3760 feet), immediately above Gromisuat to the N. – 3·5 km (2 miles): *Ayent* (978 m – 3209 feet), a widely scattered settlement made up of a number of separate villages. Road to Crans via Lens. – 2·5 km (9 miles): *La Giète* (1154 m – 3786 feet), where a road goes off on the left to *Anzère* (see below). The main road now climbs up through the forest in two large bends. – 7 km (4 miles): *Praz Combeira* (1620 m – 5315 feet), beyond which the road passes through three tunnels. – 4 km (2 miles): **Lac de Tseuzier** (1777 m – 5830 feet), an artificial lake (1956–58) 1 km (about a ½ mile) long and 600 m (1969 feet) across, in wild and lonely country. A footpath follows the W side of the lake. – A new road (N 6, the Rawil road) is planned to run under the Rawil pass (2429 m – 7970 feet) in a tunnel 4 km (2 miles) long into the Upper Simmental (see p. 228).

From La Giète a road (5 km – 3 miles) goes up to **Anzère** or *Antsère* (1500 m (4922 feet): Hôtel de la Porte), a developing winter sports resort beautifully set on a mountain terrace (ski-lifts). Cableway (2180 m – 7153 feet) to the *Pas de Maimbré* (2362 m (7750 feet): view; ski-runs). To the N is the *Wildhorn* (3248 m – 10,657 feet), the highest peak in the western Bernese Oberland (5½ hours, with guide). Several chair-lifts.

To the Col du Sanetsch (27 km (17 miles); to the Sanetschsee 32 km (20 miles). Road 2–6 m (7–20 feet) wide, maximum gradient 18% (1 in 5½); closed in winter. – The winding road runs NW from Sion through vineyards. 5 km (3 miles): *St Germain* (820 m – 2690 feet). The road then passes through the commandingly situated villages of *Granois* (857 m – 2812 feet) and *Chandolin* (818 m – 2684 feet) and turns N above the wild valley of the *Morge*. – 6 km (4 miles): *Pont du Diable* (919 m – 3015 feet), where it crosses to the right bank. It then continues winding its way uphill, crosses the Morge again and later the *Nétage*, and climbs, with many turns to (16 km – 10 miles) the **Col du Sanetsch** or *Col de Senin* (2243 m (7359 feet): Hotel du Sanetsch), on a ridge between the *Arpelistock* (3035 m – 9958 feet) to the E and the *Sanetschhorn* (*Mont Brun*, 2942 m (9653 feet)) to the W. From both of these peaks (respectively 3½ and 2½ hours' climb from the pass) there are magnificent views. – The road continues for another 5 km (3 miles) to the dam (42 m (138 feet) high) at the N end of the *Sanetschsee*, a reservoir (2·7 million cu. m (95 million cu. feet)) on the upper course of the River *Saane* (*Sarine*).

The Val d'Hérens (32 km (20 miles) to Les Haudères). – The road runs SE from Sion over the Rhône, turns right and in 800 m (2625 feet) left (road on right to Nendaz). At the foot of the hill, on the right, is the old Chandolin power station of the Grande-Dixence Company. The road now climbs sharply in hairpin bends, with beautiful views to the rear.

Vex (957 m (3140 feet): pronounced Veh) is commandingly situated high above the gorge of the *Borgne*, which flows down through the Val d'Hérens. A narrow road goes off on the right and ascends the Val d'Hérémence, running above the Val d'Hérens road to the picturesque village of *Hérémence* (1236 m – 4055 feet), with the church of St-Nicolas (by W. M. Förderer, 1963–71). – The road continues up the **Val d'Hérémence** via *Pralong* (1608 m – 5276 feet) to **Motôt** (1925 m – 6316 feet), with a parking place (1970 m – 6464 feet). From here it is a 2 hours' walk

(also private road, 5·5 km (3 miles)) to the *Grande-Dixence dam* (2365 m (7760 feet): completed 1961: 284 m (932 feet) high; top 748 m (2454 feet) long, 15 m (49 feet) wide), in the *Val des Dix*. Its water is carried in underground tunnels to the Fionnay power station and beyond this, under pressure, to the main power station at Nendaz in the Rhône valley. At the end of the road, beneath the dam, is a hotel and restaurant with a large car park. From here a cableway runs up to the lake (motor-boat). At the S end of the lake is an iron suspension bridge. Prominent among the peaks forming the magnificent mountain setting of the lake are the *Rosablanche* (3336 m – 10,945 feet), *Mont Blanc de Cheilon* (3871 m – 12,701 feet) and the *Aiguilles Rouges d'Arolla* (3650 m – 11,976 feet). Walks: along the lake (2½ hours); to the Cabane des Dix (4 hours; by boat 2 hours); to the Col de Riedmatten (4 hours); to Arolla (6 hours).

The road to Les Haudères continues along the hillside, following an almost level but winding course. On the opposite side of the valley is the pretty village of *Vernamiège*. – After crossing the River *Dixence*, coming from the Val d'Hérémence, the road turns into the *Val d'Hérens* (German *Eringertal*) and passes through a tunnel under a series of *earth pillars*, columns of morainic debris which have been protected from erosion by a large boulder or capstone.

Euseigne or *Useigne* (970 m (3183 feet): Hôtel des Pyramides, E, 20 b.): road on right into Val d'Hérémence. On the opposite side of the valley is the village of *St-Martin*.

La Luette (1020 m – 3347 feet), beyond which the road crosses the grey waters of the Borgne on a high bridge, the *Pont Noir de Lugnerez* (1001 m – 3284 feet). 1 km (about a ½ mile) farther up the valley, at *Praz-Jean* (1100 m – 3609 feet), a narrow road goes off on the left and passes through a number of hamlets and the villages of *St-Martin* and *Mase*, standing high above the right bank of the Borgne and offering fine views. The road then runs down in steep bends to *Bramois* and across the Rhône to Sion (25 km – 16 miles). – The Val d'Hérens road continues to **Evolène** (1378 m (4521 feet): Hotel d'Evolène, D, 75 b.; Hermitage, D, 50 b.), the chief town in the valley (pop. 1500) and a popular holiday resort, lying in the wide green stretch of valley between *Sasseneire* (3259 m (10,693 feet): 5½ hours, with guide) to the E and the *Pic d'Arzinol* (3001 m (9846 feet): 5–5½ hours) and the *Mont de l'Etoile* (3372 m (11,064 feet): 6 hours, with guide) to the W. Higher up the valley the view is dominated by the bold outline of the Dents de Veisivi and the massive Dent Blanche (to left). – The road continues along the right bank of the Borgne and in 4 km (2 miles) reaches **Les Haudères** (1433 m (4702 feet): Hôtel des Haudères, D, 55 b.; Edelweiss, D, 38 b.), a health resort. It is the highest village in the Val d'Hérens, which divides at this point into the Val d'Arolla and the *Combe de Ferpècle*. A good road ascends the *Val d'Arolla* to *Arolla*, properly *Mayens d'Arolla* (1962 m (6437 feet): Grand Hôtel & Kurhaus, D, 100 b.; Mont-Collon, D, 100 b.), winter sports and mountain resort (ski-lifts, cross-country skiing, toboggan run, curling) magnificently set facing the *Pigne d'Arolla* (3801 m (12,471 feet): 5–6 hours) and *Mont Collon* (3644 m (11,956 feet): 7 hours, with guide).

A narrow and sometimes steep road runs up the *Combe de Ferpècle* from Les Haudères to the huts of **Ferpècle** or *Salay* (6·5 km (4 miles), 1800 m (5906 feet): Hôtel du Col d'Hérens, E, 25 b.), near the end of twin glaciers, the *Glacier du Mont Miné* and the *Glacier de Ferpècle*. From here it is a 2 hours' climb to the *Alpe de Bricolla* (2462 m – 7960 feet), with superb views of the mighty Glacier de Ferpècle, with the *Dent Blanche* (4364 m (14,318 feet): 9–10 hours, with guide) rearing above it on the left, and the Glacier du Mont Miné, with the *Dents de Bertol*, the *Aiguille de la Za* (3673 m – 12,051 feet) and the *Dents de Veisivi* (3425 m (11,237 feet): 5½–6 hours).

Solothurn/Soleure

Cathedral of St Ursen, Solothurn

Canton: Solothurn (SO).
Altitude: 442 m (1450 feet). – Population: 18,000.
Post code: CH-4500. – Dialling code: 065.
ⓘ Verkehrsbüro,
69 Hauptgasse, Kronenplatz;
tel. 22 19 24.

HOTELS. – *Krone (Couronne)*, B, 50 b.; *Roter Turm*, C, 40 b.; *Astoria*, C, 70 b. – YOUTH HOSTEL.

EVENTS. – *Film Festival* (January); *Swiss Jazz Days* (January); *Fasnacht* (Carnival, Shrovetide); *Vorstädter Chilbi* (fair, July).

Solothurn (French Soleure), capital of the canton of the same name, lies astride the River Aare at the foot of the Jura hills. Numerous Renaissance and Baroque buildings bear witness to the one-time splendour of the town, which in the 16th, 17th and 18th c. was the residence of the French ambassadors to the Confederation.

HISTORY. – The town of *Salodurum* ranked with Trier in Germany as one of the oldest Roman settlements N of the Alps. In A.D. 303 two members of the Theban Legion, Ursus and Victor, were martyred here. Solothurn joined the Swiss Confederation in 1481.

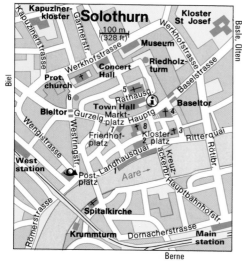

1 Landhaus
2 Theatre
3 St Peter's church
4 Cathedral of St Ursen
5 Franciscan Church
6 Buristurm
7 Clock Tower
8 Jesuit Church

SIGHTS. – Just inside the *Baseltor* (Basle Gate, 1508), where the Baselstrasse enters the old town, stands the *Cathedral of St Ursen* (St Ursus: 1763–73), in Italian Baroque style, which has been the cathedral of the diocese of Basle since 1830. On the ground floor of the 60 m (197 feet) high tower is the rich *Treasury*. On the steps leading up to the Cathedral are two fountains with figures of Moses and Gideon. – The *Old Arsenal* (Altes Zeughaus, 1610–14), NW of the Cathedral, contains a rich collection of *arms and armour of the 16th and 17th c. Almost opposite is the **Rathaus** (Town Hall), of the 15th and 17th c., with a handsome Renaissance doorway; in the N tower a cantilevered winding staircase dates from 1632. – In the nearby Marktplatz is the 12th c. *Clock tower* (Zeitglockenturm), with mechanical figures (1545) of a king flanked by Death and a soldier. In Hauptgasse, which runs between the Marktplatz and the Cathedral, is the **Jesuit church** (1680–89). At No. 2 Klosterplatz is the *Nature Museum*. From the Marktplatz the Gurzelngasse leads W to the *Bieltor* (Bielgate, originally 12th c.) and a 16th c. tower, the Buristurm. At No. 30 Werkhofstrasse, in the old town, is the Museum of Art, housing works by old masters (including a Madonna by Hans Holbein the Younger) and by 20th c. artists. Farther N, at Blumensteinweg 12, is the *Schloss Blumenstein Historical Museum,* with collections of applied art (patrician domestic interiors of the 18th c.). – On the western outskirts of the town *St Mary's church* (1953), has the largest stained-glass windows in Switzerland (some 100 sq. m (1076 sq. feet)), by H. Stocker.

SURROUNDINGS. – **To the Weissenstein** (10 km – 33 feet): Leave Solothurn by the Bieltor and

Bielstrasse and bear right along Weissensteinstrasse
into a road which runs through the watchmaking
town of *Langendorf* (artificial ice-rink in winter) to
Oberdorf. – 4·5 km (3 miles): *Oberdorf station* (658 m
– 2159 feet), from which a chair-lift (2369 m (7773
feet), 16 minutes) ascends to the Weissenstein. – The
road then climbs in steep bends up the *Nesselboden*
(1051 m – 3448 feet), with a celebrated view of the
Alps extending as far as Mont Blanc. Marked
footpaths lead to various viewpoints in the hills,
which offer excellent skiing in winter.

Stein am Rhein

Canton: Schaffhausen (SH).
Altitude: 413 m (1355 feet). – Population: 2700.
Post code: CH-8260. – Dialling code: 054.

ⓘ **Verkehrsbüro,**
Rathausplatz;
tel. 8 94 21.

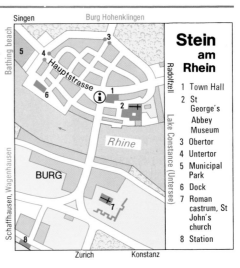

Stein am Rhein

1 Town Hall
2 St George's Abbey Museum
3 Obertor
4 Untertor
5 Municipal Park
6 Dock
7 Roman castrum, St John's church
8 Station

HOTELS. – *Rheingerbe*, 18 b.; *Grenzstein*, 80 b.;
Rheinfels, 15 b.; *Motel Adler*, 30 b. – YOUTH
HOSTEL. – CAMPING SITE.

RECREATION and SPORT. – Bathing beach, water
sports, track. – In summer regular boat services to
Constance and Kreuzlingen.

The little town of *Stein am Rhein,
**situated at the western tip of the
Untersee, the arm of Lake Constance
by which the Rhine leaves the lake, is
the best-preserved medieval town in
Switzerland.**

Stein am Rhein – a bird's-eye view

HISTORY. – The first Roman bridge over the Rhine
was built near the town. The Benedictine abbey of St
George was erected here in 1001–07, and in 1083 the
Benedictine house of Wagenhausen was founded on
the left bank of the Rhine. The town, first mentioned in
the records in 1094, received its municipal charter in
1385 and became part of the canton of Schaffhausen
in 1803.

SIGHTS. – In the very picturesque *Marktplatz (fountains) stands the **Rathaus**

(Town Hall, 1538), which contains the
town's *historical collections*. – From the
Marktplatz the *Hauptstrasse* (with an old
house, the *Weisser Adler* or White Eagle,
at No. 14) runs NW to the *Untertor*
(Lower Gate). On the N side of the old
town is the *Obertor* (Upper Gate). – SE of
the Rathaus the former conventual *church
of St George*, a 12th c. Romanesque
basilica, is now the Protestant parish
church; it has old frescoes in the choir.
The former Benedictine abbey adjoining
the church (transferred here from Hohen-
twiel in 1005, dissolved 1524) now
houses the **St George's Abbey Museum** (*Klostermuseum St Georgen*), with
fine wall-paintings (1516) in the Great
Hall and old gravestones in the Late
Gothic cloister.

On the left bank of the Rhine is the district
of BURG. On the hill (views) are remains
of the Roman castrum of *Tasgaetium* (A.D.
294). Within the castrum is the *parish
church of St John* (originally built *c.* 800),
with frescoes of about 1400. – 1 km
(about a ½ mile) W is the outlying district
of *Wagenhausen*, with a *Benedictine
monastery* built in 1090–92 and dissolved
in 1529.

SURROUNDINGS. – On the *Klingenberg* (593 m –
1946 feet), a wooded hill N of the town, is a well-
preserved 12th c. castle, **Burg Hohenklingen**
(armoury, 16th c. stained glass; restaurant), once the
home of the minnesinger Walther von Klingen (*c.*
1350); fine views.

At *Eschenz*, SE of Stein at the end of the Untersee, is
the commandingly situated *Freudenfels castle*. – On
the nearby island of *Werd*, in the Rhine, is the
pilgrimage church of St Othmar (15th c.).

Swiss National Park

Canton: Grisons (GR).

ⓘ **Verkehrsbüro Zernez,**
CH-7530 Zernez;
tel. (082) 8 13 00.
**Kur- und Verkehrsverein
Bad Scuol-Tarasp-Vulpera,**
CH-7550 Bad Scuol (Schuls);
tel. (084) 9 13 81.
Kur- und Verkehrsverein S-chanf,
CH-7525 S-chanf;
tel. (082) 7 22 55.
Verkehrsbüro Zuoz,
CH-7524 Zuoz;
tel. (082) 7 15 10.
Verkehrsverein Val Müstair,
CH-7531 Santa Maria;
tel. (082) 8 55 66.
Information Office:
Nationalpark-Haus,
CH-7530 Zernez.

HOTELS. – ZERNEZ: *Baer & Post*, C, 55 b., SB;
Sporthotel, C, 43 b.; *Filli*, D, 26 b. – SCUOL: *Belvedere
Kurhotel*, B, 90 b.; *Guardaval*, B, 90 b.; *Engadinerhof*,
C, 110 b.; *Hohenfels*, D, 40 b. – S-CHANF: *Parc-Hotel
Aurora*, C, 80 b.; *Scaletta*, D, 40 b. – ZUOZ: *Engiadina*,
B, 73 b.; *Castell*, C, 126 b.; *Crusch Alva*, C, 41 b., SP.

The **Swiss National Park (Schweizerischer Nationalpark, Parc National Suisse, Parco Nazionale Svizzero, Parc Naziunal Svizzer) lies in
the Lower Engadine to the NW of the
Ofen pass (Pass dal Fuorn), covering
an area of 168·7 sq. km (65 sq. miles),
or about the same as the canton of
Appenzell. In the S it borders on Italy
for a distance of 19 km (12 miles). It
is a mountainous region of Eastern
Alpine character, with some Dolo-
mitic features. The highest peak in
the National Park is Piz Pisoc (3174
m – 10,414 feet), to the N, closely
followed, in the S, by Piz Quattervals (3164 m – 10,381 feet) from
which radiate the four valleys referred to in its name. The permanent
snow level lies between 2900 and
3000 m (9515 and 9843 feet).

The only area of habitation in the park is
the Il Fuorn Hotel on the busy Ofen pass
road (Ofenberg road), which runs from
Zernez into Val Müstair. Along this road
are nine parking places, from which
radiate a network of footpaths (marked
white–red–white) with a total length of
80 km (50 miles). Visitors must not leave
the marked paths: the National Park is
subject to strict regulations designed to
ensure that the natural conditions are not
disturbed in any way.

PLANT LIFE. – Something like a third of the park's
area is covered by forest. The characteristic tree is the
mountain pine: larches and stone pines, forest pines
and spruces feature less prominently, and deciduous
trees (birch, aspen, willow) play a very minor role.
Above the tree-line dwarf shrubs predominate
(rhododendrons, dwarf willows, junipers, crowber-
ries, etc.). On the dry limestone crags the commonest
form of grass cover is the brownish type of turf known
in Switzerland as "crooked sedge turf" (Krummseg-
genrasen, *Caricetum curvulae*). On the sunnier
hillsides the predominant type is blue grass (*Sesleria
semperviretum*). The type known as "milk-grass

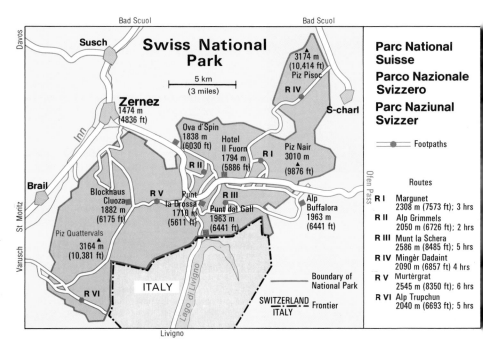

pasture" (Milchgrasweide), which includes a wide variety of species, prefers wetter ground, while on poor soil the mat grasses form a thick felt-like carpet. Particularly attractive flowers are found in small hollows on shaded slopes which become impregnated with melt-water. The brilliantly yellow Rhaetian Alpine poppy manages to find a foothold even on steep scree slopes.

ANIMAL LIFE. – Reptiles and amphibians are represented by the grass frog, Alpine newt, viviparous lizard and adder. The commonest rodents are the marmot, the blue hare and the squirrel. Altogether thirty species of mammals are found – among the larger game are red deer, chamois, ibex and small numbers of roe-deer, among the predators the fox, the marten and the ermine. There are more than a hundred species of birds, the commonest being nutcrackers, ring ouzels, Alpine titmice and greater spotted woodpeckers; the game birds include capercaillie, black grouse, rock partridge, ptarmigan and hazel hen; and the crags provide nesting-places for ravens, Alpine choughs and, in many places, golden eagles.

In the Swiss National Park

*WALKS IN THE PARK. – Marked footpaths run through some of the most beautiful parts of the National Park, with opportunities for observing the wildlife. The animals are wary of man, so that they can usually be seen only at distances of 500 or 1000 m (1641 or 3281 feet): observers should therefore be properly equipped (field-glasses, telephoto lens).

Route I: to Margunet. – From parking place 7 on the Ofen pass road through the wooded *Val dal Botsch* to the first rest area (Rastplatz), from which chamois can be observed; then on to the large rest area at *Margunet* (2308 m – 7573 feet), with a beautiful view (Munt la Schera, Piz Nair, Piz dal Fuorn; red deer); down from here to another rest area (red deer) and the Stabelchod hut (park-keeper's house; colony of marmots); then back to the Ofen pass road and along a path parallel to the road, past parking places 9 and 8, to parking place 7. The path continues to Il Fuorn. Time about 3 hours.

Route II: to Alp Grimmels. – From Il Fuorn NW over Plan Posa and through Val Ftur; then climb to the Champlönch dry valley and the Alpine meadows of *Grimmels* (2050 m (6726 feet): marmots, sometimes in the early morning red deer hinds), with a beautiful view (Ofen pass, Munt la Schera, Piz dal Fuorn). Then either back to Il Fuorn or down (W) to parking place 1, 2 or 3 on the Ofen pass road. An easy walk of 2–2½ hours.

Route III: to Munt la Schera. – The route starts from Buffalora, just outside the National Park boundary: from there S through a forest of stone pines to Marangun, then W over the flower-spangled meadows of Fop da Buffalora to enter the park beneath Munt Chavagl. After about 2 hours' walking bear right up *Munt la Schera* (2586 m – 8485 feet), with magnificent views of the Ortler group (3900 m – 12,796 feet) to the SE, the snow-covered Bernina group (4000 m – 13,124 feet) to the SW and the whole area of the National Park. Then down the S side of the hill to the Alp la Schera (rest area: marmots; red deer may be seen on the southern slopes of Munt la Schera). From there on the upper forest path to Il Fuorn; then either back on the postal bus to Stradin

Buffalora or on the footpath to the right of the road (1¼ hours). A day's outing of about 5 hours.

Route IV: to Alp Mingèr Dadaint. – The route starts from the parking place at the junction of the Mingèr with the Clemgia on the road from Scuol to S-charl. After crossing the Clemgia the path leads SW through tall spruce forest to Mingèr Dadora, past a sandstone crag known as the Hexenkopf ("Witch's Head") and on to the Alpine meadow of *Mingèr Dadaint* (2090 m (6855 feet): good opportunities of observing red deer and marmots). At the head of the valley are the precipitous peaks of Piz Plavna Dadaint (3166 m – 10,388 feet). Return by the same route, or alternatively continue W to Il Foss and then via Alp Plavna to Tarasp. A half-day outing of about 3½ hours.

Route V: by way of the Cluoza hut to the Murtèrgrat. – Starting from Zernez, cross the covered bridge over the Spöl at the E end of the village and continue over the Selva meadows to a clearing at Il Pra (beautiful view from the Bellavista viewpoint). Then down to the valley floor and a short climb on the other side to the *Cluoza hut* (Blockhaus Cluoza, 1882 m (6175 feet): food, dormitory accommodation – to book tel. 8 12 35). Then up the hillside to the left and by way of Alp Murtèr to the Murtèrgrat (2545 m – 8350 feet), with fine views of Piz Quattervals and Piz del Diavel to the S and the Fuorn valley and Piz Terza to the N, and an opportunity to see chamois and marmots. Descend by way of Plan dal Poms to the Praspöl meadows, then over the Spöl and up to the Ofen pass road at Vallun Chafuol (postal bus stop). Time about 6 hours.

Route VI: to Alp Trupchun. – From the bridge over the Inn NE of S-chanf make for Mulins Varusch; then continue along the stream in the direction of Val Casana and at the next junction take a path on the left through Val Trupchun. Along the park boundary and opposite the mouth of Val Müschauns there are opportunities for observing wildlife (chamois, ibex, eagles' nest). Then climb to the hut on Alp Trupchun (2040 m – 6693 feet), with numbers of animals (including ibexes) in almost every direction. Return along the right bank, past the mouth of Val Müschauns, to reach the National Park boundary at Chanels; then on to the Varusch hut (refreshments), and from there back to the parking place. A day's outing of about 5 hours.

Over the Ofen pass into Val Müstair. – The village of **Zernez** (1474 m – 4836 feet), situated in a broad valley basin, is the best base from which to visit the National Park (of which a good general impression can be had in the National-parkhaus). Part of the village was burned down in 1872 and rebuilt in rather urban style. In the older part, standing on higher ground, is the parish church (1607), with rich stucco decoration. Another old building that has survived is the Schloss Planta-Wildenberg (17th–18th c.). – From here take the Ofen pass road, which runs E from the main road through the Engadine to St Moritz, following the *Spölbach* upstream through the wooded gorge of *La Serra*; then a well-engineered stretch of road up the rocky wooded hillside, passing through three galleries designed to provide protection from avalanches. – In 3·5 km (2 miles) there is a fine view down to the right of the wild Val Cluozza, the oldest part of the National Park, with the glacier descending the slopes of Piz Quattervals (3164 m – 10,381 feet) in the background. – The road then follows a fairly level course over the forest-covered *Champ Sech*, beyond which the Piz del Diavel (3072 m – 10,079 feet) comes into sight, and then descends down in a wide curve to the *Wegerhaus Ova d'Spin* (on left: car park), at the W entrance to the National Park.

The road runs downhill, crosses the *Ova d'Spin* (parking place) and continues along the wooded slopes above the river, then above the Spölbach (parking place) and the *Ova del Fuorn*, flowing down from the Ofen pass, and comes to the *Punt la Drossa* (1710 m (5611 feet): Swiss customs; parking place), in a narrow pass, where the road crosses to the left bank of the Ova del Fuorn. On the right is the entrance to a road tunnel 3·3 km (2 miles) long, belonging to the Munt la Schera hydroelectric complex, which reaches the Italian frontier at the *Punt dal Gall* (1963 m – 6441 feet) over the River Spöl, at the N end of an artificial lake 8 km (5 miles) long (dam, alt. 1805 m (5922 feet), 540 m (1771 feet) long, 130 m (427 feet) high, 10 m (33 feet) thick; capacity 164 million cu. m (5791 million cu. feet)). A road runs down the W side of the lake through a customs-free zone to *Livigno* (19·5 km (12 miles), alt. 816 m (2677 feet): large skiing area, four ski-lifts). – Beyond the Punt la Drossa the road to the Ofen pass climbs gradually; then comes a fairly level stretch, in which the road emerges from the forest; and finally it returns to the right bank of the Ova dal Fuorn and reaches the Parc Naziunal Hotel, in the lonely high valley of *Il Fuorn* (German *Ofen*, 1804 m (5919 feet)), named after an iron-smelting works which once stood here. From here a marked footpath ascends *Munt la Schera* (2590 m (8498 feet): 2½ hours), from the limestone summit plateau of which there is a fine general view of the National Park.

From the hotel the road continues uphill through the coniferous forests in the high valley of the Ova dal Fuorn, past the mouths of the wild Val dal Botsch and Val da Stabelchod, at the foot of Piz Nair (3010 m – 9876 feet); several parking places. In 4·5 km (3 miles) it comes to the *Alp Buffalora* (1963 m – 6441 feet), in a marshy valley bottom, with Val Nüglia running down from Piz Tavrü (3168 m – 10,394 feet) on the left and Munt da Buffalora (2629 m – 8626 feet) on the right. – The road then climbs more steeply to the **Ofen pass** (Romansh *Süsom-Givè* or *Pass dal Fuorn*, 2149 m (7051 feet): hotel), from which there is a *view of the Ortler group. – It then winds its way down, with three hairpin turns, first over Alpine meadows and then along the slopes of the valley, through stretches of forest, with fine views.

Tschierv (1664 m (5460 feet): Hotel Sternen; camping site) is the highest village in **Val Müstair**, the valley of the *Rom*. Here the road crosses the river and runs down the S side of the valley, with patches of woodland, on a moderate gradient.

Fuldera (1641 m (5384 feet): bypass) is a little hamlet at the foot of Piz Turettas (2958 m – 9705 feet). Beyond this a road goes off on the left to *Lü* (3·5 km – 2 miles, 1920 m – 6300 feet), the highest village in its valley. The main road now runs down more steeply to *Valchava* (1435 m (4708 feet): bypass), where the first fruit-trees appear. Beyond this, on the right, is the mouth of the beautiful *Val Vau*.

Santa Maria (1388 m (4554 feet): Hotel Schweizerhof, C, 50 b.; Stelvio, C, 72 b.), the chief town in Val Müstair (pop. 350; Prot.), lies at the mouth of Val Muraunza, which runs down from the Umbrail pass.

It has pretty painted houses, a church of 1491 and a local museum. Down the valley the view embraces the castles of Taufers and the Ötztal Alps, with the snow-capped peak of the Weisskugel. – From Santa Maria a road goes off on the right to the Umbrail and Stelvio (Stilfserjoch) passes. The main road continues down Val Müstair, through the village of Müstair, into the Upper Adige valley.

Thun

Canton: Berne (BE).
Altitude: 565 m (1854 feet). – Population: 33,000.
Post code: CH-3600. – Dialling code: 033.
ⓘ **Verkehrsverein,**
Bahnhofplatz;
tel. 22 23 40.

HOTELS. – *Krone*, Rathausplatz, B, 70 b., SB; *Elite*, Bernstrasse 1, B, 80 b.; *Holiday*, Dürrenast, B, 114 b.; *Freienhof*, Freienhofgasse 3, B, 110 b.; *Beau-Rivage*, Aare-Quai, C, 50 b., SB. – CAMPING SITE at Gwatt.

RECREATION and SPORT. – Riding, tennis (indoor and outdoor courts), swimming, fishing; sailing school, based at Hilterfingen/Oberhofen and Spiez; skating, curling (indoor and outdoor rinks).

The old-world town of Thun (French Thoune), which has belonged to the canton of Berne since 1384, lies on the River Aare just below its outflow from Lake Thun. Charmingly situated on both banks of the swiftly flowing green river and on an island (1 km (about a ½ mile) long) in the middle, with its castle on a hill 30 m (98 feet) high dominating the town, it is the gateway to the Bernese

Oberland. An unusual feature of the old town is the flower-decked pedestrian walkways running along above the arcades containing the shops on ground level in the main street (Hauptgasse).

SIGHTS. – From the *Rathausplatz*, with the handsome **Rathaus** (Town Hall: 1589, rebuilt 1685), a covered flight of steps leads up to the **Castle**, whose massive keep with its corner turrets is a prominent landmark of the town. It was built in 1191 by Duke Berthold V of Zähringen, later became the seat of the Counts of Kyburg, and in 1492 was enlarged by the addition of an official residence for the Chief Magistrate of Berne. It now houses the *Historical Museum*, with arms and armour and 14th and 15th c. tapestries in the large Knights' Hall, prehistoric and Roman material, furniture and ceramics in the three lower rooms and a collection illustrating 19th c.

Old cheese dairy, Kiesen

Swiss military history in the upper hall. From the Castle and from the Protestant *parish church* (rebuilt 1738, with an older tower) on the SE slopes of the castle hill there is a superb *view of Lake Thun and the Alps (the Stockhorn chain, the Niesen and, to the left, the snow-covered Blümlisalp). – In the Thunerhof (Hofstettenstrasse) is the *Municipal Art Gallery*, with works by modern artists (Hodler, Amiet, etc.). – The composer Brahms lived in the town in 1886–88. – On the Oberes Inseli, a small islet SE of the station, stands the *Kleisthaus* (private property), in which the dramatist Heinrich von Kleist stayed in 1802 while working on his play "Robert Guiscard".

SURROUNDINGS. – 1·5 km (1 mile) S, on the lake the village of *Scherzlingen*, has a little 12th c. church (frescoes) and *Schloss Schadau* (1852: special exhibitions of works by Swiss minor masters). In the

Berne

Thun

200 m
(656 feet)

Bernstr.
Burgstrasse
Hauptgasse
Hofstettenstrasse
Bälliz
Aarestrasse
Scherzligweg
Aare
Bleichestr.
ⓘ **Station**
Seestrasse
Mönchstr.
Waisenhausstr.

Interlaken

Thuner See

Spiez, Interlaken

1 Rathaus (Town Hall)
2 Castle (Historical Museum)
3 Parish church
4 Municipal Art Gallery
5 Catholic church

castle park is the Wocher Panorama, a large circular painting (38 by 7·5 m (125 by 25 feet)) by Marquard Wocher (1760–1830) of the town of Thun as it was about 1810. – 5 km (3 miles) NE is the resort of **Goldiwil** (1010 m (3314 feet): Hotel Jungfrau, E, 50 b.). – 6 km (4 miles) SW is the village of *Amsoldingen* (644 m – 2113 feet), on the shores of a small lake, with a castle and a fine Romanesque church of the 10th or 11th c.

8 km (5 miles) NW on the Berne road in *Kiesen* (546 m – 1791 feet) there is a reconstruction of an old Bernese cheese dairy.

Lake Thun and Lake Brienz

Canton: Berne (BE).

ⓘ **Verkehrsverband Thunersee/ Verkehrsverein Thun,**
Bahnhofplatz,
CH-3600 Thun;
tel. (033) 22 23 40.
Verkehrsbüro Spiez,
Bahnhofstrasse 12,
CH-3700 Spiez;
tel. (033) 54 21 38.
Verkehrsverein Interlaken,
Höheweg 37,
CH-3800 Interlaken;
tel. (036) 22 21 21.
Verkehrsverein Brienz am See,
CH-3855 Brienz;
tel. (036) 51 32 42.

BOAT SERVICES. – Regular services during the season (April–September) from Interlaken-West to Spiez and Thun and from Interlaken-Ost to Brienz; numerous round trips, cruises and excursions.

RECREATION and SPORT. – Pedal-driven, rowing and motor boats for hire at many places; sailing, swimming, fishing, riding, tennis, golf (at Unterseen , near Interlaken); hobby courses.

* **Lake Thun (Thuner See) and** * **Lake Brienz (Brienzer See), in the Aare valley between the towns of Thun and Brienz, were originally a single lake, which was divided into two at Interlaken by the debris deposited from the River Lütschine and other mountain streams.**

> * **Lake Thun** (alt. 560 m (1837 feet)) is 18 km (11 miles) long and between 2 and 2·8 km (1 and 2 miles) wide, with an area of 48 sq. km (19 sq. miles); its greatest depth is 217 m (712 feet). There are roads from Thun to Interlaken along both the N and the S banks.

The *road along the N side of the lake* (23 km – 14 miles), which affords a succession of beautiful views, leaves Thun by way of Hofstettenstrasse along the banks of the *Aare*, passing on the right the Municipal Art Gallery in the Thunerhof and on the left the Kursaal. – It then follows the northern shore of Lake Thun (trolley-bus to Beatenbucht). Sheltered from N and E winds, the lake has an unusually mild climate. Many southern plants including laurels and fig-trees flourish in the gardens of the charming little towns and villages strung along its shores, which attract many visitors in spring and autumn as well as in summer. – Almost all the way along the lake there are magnificent *views of the giants of the Bernese Alps. At the entrance to the Kandertal and Simmental the conical Stockhorn (2190 m – 7185 feet) can be seen on the right and the pyramidal peak of the Niesen (2362 m – 7750 feet) on the left, with the three peaks of the Blümlisalp (3664 m – 12,022 feet) farther to the left. To the right of the Blümlisalp a series of summits come gradually into view – from left to right the Fründenhorn (3369 m – 11,054 feet), Doldenhorn (3643 m – 11,953 feet), Balmhorn (3709 m – 12,169 feet), Altels (3629 m – 11,907 feet) and Rinderhorn (3453 m – 11,329 feet). In the direction of Interlaken the most prominent peaks are (from right to left) the Ebnefluh (3960 m – 12,993 feet), Jungfrau (4158 m – 13,642 feet), Mönch (4099 m – 13,449 feet) and Eiger (3970 m – 13,026 feet), and beyond these the Schreckhorn (4078 m – 13,380 feet) and Wetterhorn (3701 m – 12,143 feet).

3·5 km (2 miles): **Hilterfingen** (562 m (1844 feet): Hotel Schönbühl, C, 30 b.; Bellevue, D, 75 b.) has a small church of 1470 and the 18th c. Schloss Hünegg. Thuner See sailing school. – Adjoining Hilterfingen is **Oberhofen** (575 m (1887 feet): Hotel Montana, C, 45 b.; Moy, C, 90 b.; Kreuz, D, 50 b.), with a picturesque castle on the lake (12th c., enlarged in the 17th–18th c.; museum). – Beyond this, to the right, is a fine view of the Niesen.

3 km (2 miles) farther on we reach **Gunten** (567 m (1860 feet): Hotel Hirschen am See, B, 110 b.; Eden-Elisabeth, C, 50 b., SP; water-skiing school), at the mouth of the Guntenbach, which emerges from a gorge just above the village. Road on left to the little

Sailing-boats off Hilterfingen, Lake Thun

summer vacation spot of *Sigriswil* (3 km (2 miles), 800 m (2625 feet): Hotel Bären, B, 60 b.; Adler, C, 45 b.), from which a narrow but very beautiful road (high toll charge; alternate one-way traffic) continues up to Beatenberg (12 km (7 miles): see p. 145). – 3·5 km (2 miles) from Gunten on the lakeside road *Merligen* (568 m (1864 feet): Hotel Beatus, A, 140 b., SB) lies in a very sheltered situation at the mouth of the Justistal. The road continues to **Beatenbucht**: dock; terminus of the trolley-bus from Thun; funicular to *Beatenberg* (1150 m (3773 feet): p. 145).

The lakeside road now changes its character. The gently sloping shore with its villages and gardens gives place to a steep wooded scarp, along which the road climbs in a series of bends. 1·5 km (1 mile) farther on it passes in two tunnels through a rocky promontory, the *Nase*. A kilometre (about a ½ mile) beyond this there is a beautiful glimpse of the lake to the right. – The road then comes to the parking place for the **Beatushöhlen** or **St Beatus's caves** (623 m (2044 feet): 8 minutes' walk from the road), an extensive complex of stalactitic caves (2 km (1 mile) accessible to visitors) which according to the legend were occupied by St Beatus (d. 112) and until the Reformation were a place of pilgrimage (conducted tour, 1 hour; Waldhaus restaurant).

The route continues through three tunnels and around a sheer rock face which in places actually overhangs the road, to *Sundlauenen* (615 m (2018 feet): Hotel Beatus, E, 10 b.). It then runs along below the crag, above the lake; in another 1·5 km (1 mile) passes a camping site (on right); and at the *Neuhaus* bathing station (on right: Strandhotel, C, 100 b.; camping site on the left) comes to the end of Lake Thun. 2 km (1 mile) farther on the road passes the Hotel Beau-Site and crosses the "Bödeli", an area of alluvial soil deposited by the *Lombach*, to *Unterseen* (old church), an outlying district of Interlaken, where a road branches off on the left to Beatenberg (p. 145). – The road then bears right and crosses the *Aare* to enter **Interlaken** (p. 144).

The *road along the S side of the lake* offers two alternative routes between Thun and Interlaken, One way is to go S from the old town over the Aare and continue under the railway and then SW for 3 km (2 miles) to join the motorway from Berne (N 6), which runs at some distance from the lake to Spiez (10 km – 6 miles). – Alternatively, after passing under the railway turn left along Frutigenstrasse and continue past the bathing beach at the end of the town (on left: beautiful gardens, camping site). This road, at some distance from the lake, comes in 4·5 km (3 miles) to *Gwatt* (564 m – 1850 feet), beyond which a turn on the right leads to the Simmental. – Then over the River *Kander* and up a winding stretch of road, with beautiful views of the bay of Spiez and the Niesen. Below the road, on the left, is the village of *Einigen* (Motel Hirschen), with a Romanesque church (11th and 13th c.). 5·5 km (3 miles) from Gwatt is **Spiez** (630 m (2067 feet): Hotel Belvédère, B, 55 b.; Edenhotel, B, 80 b., SP; Des Alpes, 60 b.). At the near end of the town a road goes off on the right to the *Simmental* (p. 227) and via Mülenen (8 km (5 miles): funicular up the Niesen) to Frutigen (Kandersteg, Abelboden). – The picturesquely situated town of Spiez (pop. 10,000) is a popular health and water sports resort (sailing school), and it is also an important junction for the roads and mountain railways into the Kandertal and Simmental. – From an intersection in the upper part of the town, near the parish church (1907), a street runs down to the medieval castle (massive 12th c. tower) which was owned by the Erlach family from 1516 to 1875 (museum; concerts). Beside the castle stands a small Romanesque church (11th c.), with fine frescoes. – From Spiez an attractive path runs along the lake to *Faulensee* (30 minutes).

6 km (4 miles) SE of Spiez is the village of **Aeschi** (860 m (2822 feet): Hotel Baumgarten, C, 40 b.; Niesen, E, 60 b.), a popular summer resort on the hill between Lake Thun and the Kander valley. Church (Protestant) dating in part from the 12th to the 13th c., with frescoes in the choir (probably 14th c.) which were exposed in 1966.

To the Niesen. – From Spiez take the Kandersteg road to *Mülenen* (8 km – 5 miles), from which a funicular (3·5 km (2 miles), maximum gradient 68% (1 in 1·4), 30 minutes) serves the *Niesenkulm Hotel* (2362 m (7750 feet): mountain inn, 16 b.), a few minutes below the summit of the **Niesen** (2362 m (7750 feet): see p. 84), with superb ** views of Lake Thun and Lake Brienz, the Jungfrau massif and the Blümlisalp. Descent to Wimmis on foot, 2 hours.

To the Griesalp (22 km – 14 miles). – From Spiez take the Kandersteg road to *Reichenbach* (9 km – 6 miles); then turn left into a narrow road which winds its way up to the village of *Scharnachtal* and continues through the narrow wooded *Kiental*. – 6 km (4 miles): **Kiental** (906 m (2973 feet): Hotel Bären, E, 32 b.; Kientalerhof, E, 50 b.), a village which attracts many summer visitors, with a

beautiful view of the Blümlisalp. From here a chair-lift (1405 m (4610 feet), 18 minutes) ascends to a skiing area (1500 m – 4922 feet) on the E side of the *Gerihorn* (2133 m – 6998 feet). – The road (now a very narrow private road: toll) continues up the Gornerengrund, the upper part of the Kiental, and comes in 4 km (2 miles) to the *Alpenruhe Hotel* (1140 m (3740 feet): 12 beds). Then on to the *Tschingelalp* (1151 m – 3776 feet), and beyond this a series of narrow turns up the wooded hillside (gradients of up to 20% (1 in 5)) and past the *Pochten Falls* (curious rock forms resulting from erosion) to the *Pochtenalp* (1400 m – 4593 feet). – 3 km (2 miles): **Griesalp** (1407 m (4616 feet): Kurhaus, 26 b.), which attracts summer visitors and skiers (interesting nature reserve). From here it is a 3 hours' climb to the *Blümlisalp hut* (2837 m (9308 feet): see also p. 151), to the S.

The Interlaken road continues straight ahead through the upper part of Spiez, with parking places 1 km (about a $\frac{1}{2}$ mile) and 1·5 (1 mile) km from the town which afford beautiful views of the bay of Spiez and its picturesque castle. It then skirts a wooded promontory projecting into the lake and comes to **Faulensee** (587 m (1926 feet): Strandhotel Seeblick, C, 40 b.; Bellerive (no rest.), C, 20 b.), attractively set in a bay (bathing beach). On the left, above the road, is the church of St Columban (1962). – There follows a beautiful but winding stretch of road closely following the lake (parking places). 2 km (1 mile) farther on an expressway from Spiez comes in on the right. Just before Leissigen an attractive road branches off on the right to Aeschi (6·5 km – 4 miles). – 6·5 km (4 miles) from Spiez is **Leissigen** (573 m (1880 feet): Hotel Kreuz, C, 70 b.), among beautiful orchards, with an old church. – The road now runs along above the lake, with a view of Beatenberg (p. 145) high up on the opposite side.

Beyond *Därligen* (564 m (1850 feet): Strandhotel du Lac, D, 60 b.; bypass to S of village) the road climbs up the hillside above the lake and then descends again (railway to left of road), after which it leaves the lake and continues along the edge of the wide Aare valley, passing at one point along the rocky wooded slopes of the *Rugen* (see p. 145). In the outskirts of Interlaken, on the right, is the lower station of the cableway up the *Heim-wehfluh (p. 145); straight ahead is the road to Grindelwald and Lauterbrunnen, bypassing Interlaken; to the left the road to the town of **Interlaken** (p. 144).

---

*Lake Brienz** (alt. 567 m (1860 feet)) is 14 km (9 miles) long and between 2 and 2·5 km (1 and 2 miles) wide, with an area of 29 sq. km (11 sq. miles); its greatest depth is 259 m (850 feet). The lake, which is in effect an enlargement of the valley of the River Aare, lies between the limestone ridge of the Brienzer Grat and the Jurassic Faulhorn group.

Lake Brienz was originally connected with Lake Thun, but now lies 7 m (4 miles) higher. The clear water of the lake has a light greenish tinge. The slopes of the surrounding hills are wooded.

From Interlaken the *road along the N side of Lake Brienz* crosses the Aare (on the banks of which, to the right, are a camping site and motel) and winds up the wooded slopes of the *Harder* (funicular: station on left), from which there are extensive views. In 2 km (1 mile) it comes to *Goldswil* (612 m (2008 feet): Hotel Felsenegg, E, 26 b.), a prettily situated little village with a ruined castle surrounded by a beautiful cemetery. Beyond this, on the right, is the *Burgseeli* bathing beach. The road now keeps rather closer to the lake and comes to the village of **Ringgenberg** (599 m (1965 feet): Hotel Alpina, C, 32 b.; Seeburg, D, 50 b.), in a sheltered situation on a terrace above the lake. Here are weathered brown timber houses and a church (1671) standing above the village in the ruins of a castle. Then on, through a short rocky defile, to *Niederried* (580 m (1903 feet): Hotel Bellevue, C, 42 b.), situated amid orchards at the foot of the Augstmatthorn (2140 m – 7021 feet), and *Oberried* (592 m (1942 feet): Hotel Rössli), at the foot of the Rieder Grat (2042 m – 6700 feet).

The road then continues through the little village of *Ebligen* to **Brienz** (569 m (1867 feet): Hotel Lindenhof, C, 80 b., SB; Bären, C, 50 b.; Krone, C, 45 b.), a town of 3000 inhabitants which attracts many summer visitors and has many more

passing through on their way between Lucerne and Interlaken. It is delightfully situated on the lake, with steep wooded slopes rising above the town to the precipitous Brienzer Grat, which reaches its highest point in the Rothorn. The long, straggling little town is the centre of the Oberland craft of woodcarving, with a woodcarving school and the Swiss Violin-Making School (open to visitors). Beside the Protestant church is the house in which the Swiss writer Heinrich Federer (1866–1928) was born. – The Brienzer Rothorn can be climbed with the help of a cog-railway opened in 1892 (steam or diesel driven: 7·5 km (5 miles), 55 minutes). The line runs up through the forest and then climbs more steeply (numerous turns, five tunnels) up the precipitous Planalpfluh to the *Planalp* station (1346 m – 4416 feet). It then continues up the bare valley to the upper station (2252 m – 7390 feet), a few minutes' walk from the *Rothorn-Kulm Hotel* (2270 m (7448 feet): E, 45 b.), from which it is a 15 minutes' climb to the summit of the *Brienzer Rothorn** (2350 m – 7710 feet), with a magnificent prospect of the Appenzell, Uri, Engelberg, Berne and Valais Alps extending from Säntis to the Diablerets. Cableway from Sörenberg. There is a splendid mountain walk (stout footwear required: 4 hours) from the Brienzer Rothorn to the Brünig pass or to the mountain station of Schönbüel (1½ hours).

To the Axalp (9 km – 6 miles). – Take a narrow road which branches off the Lucerne road on the right at the hamlet of *Kienholz*, 2 km (1 mile) from Brienz. The road skirts the E end of the lake at the inflow of the Aare and climbs up the slopes on the S side of the lake, past a turning to the Giessbach (below). It then winds its way up to the **Axalp** (1460–1540 m (4490–5053 feet): Hotel Bellevue, C, 60 b.; good walking and skiing, with ski-lifts), from which there are far-ranging views. From here there is a beautiful footpath into the Upper Giessbach valley, and also a 1¼ hours' walk to the *Hinterburgsee*, a beautiful mountain lake in the Hinterburg nature reserve. – The *Giessbach** (663 m – 2175 feet) can be reached by the road referred to above or by boat to the *Giessbach See* dock (15 minutes from Brienz) and from there either on foot (20 minutes) or by funicular (345 m (1132 feet), 4 minutes). The best

Swiss Open-Air Museum of Rural Life

Ballenberg
ob Brienz

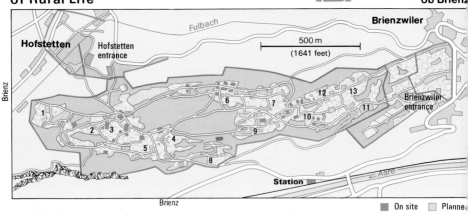

On site   Planne

REGIONAL GROUPS
(As planned: only the numbered items are erected)

1 Jura
No. 211: House from Villnachen (Argau)

2 Central Mittelland

3 Bernese Mittelland
No. 311: "Alter Bären" farmhouse (17th c.) from Rapperswil (Berne)
No. 312: House with stove (18th c.) from Oberwangen (Berne)
No. 321: Farmhouse (early 18th c.) from Madiswil (Berne)
No. 322: Granary (17th c.?) from Kiesen (Berne)
No. 331: Farmhouse (1797) from Ostermundigen (Berne)
No. 332: Granary (18th c.) from Ostermundigen (Berne)
No. 333: "Stöckli" (18th c.) from Detligen (Berne)
No. 334: Journeyman's house (1760) from Detligen (Berne)
No. 341: Barn (1702) from Faulensee (Berne)
No. 352: Granary from Wasen im Emmental (Berne)

4 Rural trades
No. 411: Sawmill (c. 1841) from Rafz (Zurich)
No. 421: Linseed Press
No. 491: Charcoal kiln
No. 492: Lime-burning oven
No. 495: Refuge hut

5 Western Mittelland

6 Eastern Mittelland
No. 611: Half-timbered house (before 1780) from Richterswil (Zurich)

No. 612: Wash-house from Rüschliken (Zurich)
No. 613: Barn from Mennedorf (Zurich)
No. 621: Half-timbered house (17th c.) from Uesslingen (Thurgau); Bread Museum on 2nd floor
No. 622: Granary from Wellhausen (Thurgau)
No. 631: Wine cellar from Schaffhausen with beam-press from Fläsch (Grisons)
No. 641: General-purpose building from Wila (Zurich)

7 Central Switzerland
No. 711: House from Sachseln

8 Ticino

9 Grisons

10 Bernese Oberland
No. 1011: House (1698) from Adelboden (Berne)
No. 1012: Stove for boiling cattle mash from Adelboden (Berne)
No. 1021: House (17th c.) from Matten, near Interlaken (Berne)
No. 1022: Granary (1652) from Niederrieđ (Berne)
No.-1023: Hay loft (1636) from Brienzwiler (Berne)
No. 1024: Turf well from Wimmis (Berne)
No. 1031: Dwelling house (1787) from Brienz (Berne)
No. 1042: Drying oven from Brienzwiler (Berne)
No. 1312: Cheese stove from Hintisberg Alp (Berne)

11 Valais

12 Eastern Switzerland

13 The Alpine pasturelands

view of the Giessbach, which tumbles down from a height of 300 m (984 feet) to the lake in a series of falls over successive ridges of rock on the beautifully wooded hillside, is to be had from the terrace in front of the Parkhotel (C, 120 b., SP). There are footpaths up both banks to the highest of the three bridges, under which the stream emerges from a narrow gorge and plunges into a rock basin 60 m (197 feet) deep.

NE of Brienz by way of Schwanden is the *Swiss Open-Air Museum of Rural Life (car park; bus service from Brienz station; side entrance in Brienzwiler, on the road to Lucerne), a large park covering some 50 hectares (124 acres) of Alpine country on the Ballenberg. A series of regional groups, some still in course of construction, display the traditional way of life in different parts of Switzerland in old houses and other buildings brough here from their original sites, with appro priate furniture, utensils and implements (open daily April–October).

Thurgau

Canton: Thurgau (TG).
Verkehrsbüro des Kantons Thurgau,
c/o Schweizerische Bankgesellschaft,
Rathausplatz 1,
CH-8500 Frauenfeld;
tel. (054) 7 31 28.

The canton of Thurgau in NE Swit zerland lies on the S side of Lake Constance, occupying most of the Swiss shoreline of the lake. It is bounded on the W by the canton of Zurich, on the E by St Gallen. It has an area of 1006 sq. km (388 sq. miles and a population of 185,000. The canton is a region of markedly Pre-Alpine character, with its highest points rising to barely 1000 m (3281 feet). The main source of income is fruit-growing.

HISTORY. – There were many settlements in the canton in Roman times, as is shown by the results of excavation at Arbon (*Arbor Felix*) and Pfyn (*Ad Fines*). Later the area was occupied by Alemannic tribes. In medieval times it was held by the Zähringen and Kyburg families, and from 1264 by the Counts of Habsburg. In 1460 Thurgau was taken over by the Confederates from the excommunicated Duke Sigismund and governed as a "common province". From 1798 to 1803 it was part of the Helvetian Republic; thereafter it became an independent canton.

The cantonal capital is **Frauenfeld** (410 m (1345 feet): pop. 18,000; Hotel Bahnhof, C, 30 b.), situated on the River *Murg* just S of its junction with the *Thur*. In the upper town (rebuilt in uniform style after a fire in the 18th c.), high above the Murg, rears the *Castle*, once the seat of the Confederate *landvögte* (governors), with a massive 12th c. tower. It now houses the Thurgau Cantonal Museum (prehistoric material, history of the town, religious art). In the outlying district of Oberkirch is St Lawrence's church, with fine 14th c. stained glass.

A few kilometres NW of Frauenfeld, above the Thur, is the former Carthusian *monastery of Ittingen*, founded as an Augustinian house in 1152 and taken over by the Carthusians in 1461. Much of the monastery was destroyed by fire in 1524. The cloister dates from about 1540; the church was built in 1549–53 and remodelled in Baroque style in the 18th c.

Tour of Thurgau. – From Frauenfeld road 14 runs E to *Wellhausen*. On a hill 500 m (1641 feet) S is *Wellenberg Castle* (13th c.). – Continuing E, the road crosses the Thur and comes to the busy little town of **Weinfelden** (432 m (1417 feet): pop. 8500; Hotel Thurgauerhof, B, 72 b.), seat of the cantonal parliament and court. Above the vineyards on the slopes of the *Ottenberg* is a castle of 1180 (restored *c.* 1860). – The road continues through *Bürglen* (442 m – 1450 feet), where a 16th–17th c. castle is a prominent landmark, and comes to **Amriswil** (450 m (1476 feet): pop. 8000), a lively little industrial town; a coach museum. – *Hagenwil,* 1·8 km (1 mile) SE, has a charming moated castle (13th–15th c.).

Balcony of Town Hall, Bischofszell

SW of Amriswil, above a loop in the Thur, lies the ancient town of **Bischofszell** (509 m – 1670 feet), with the church of St Pelagius (14th–15th c.), a Town Hall of 1749 and the former Bishop's Palace (16th c.), now a museum. – From here go SW to join road 7 and follow it W to *Münchwilen*, from which a detour can be made a short distance S to *Sirnach* (550 m (1805 feet): pop. 4200), with attractive old half-timbered houses, and *Fischingen* (620 m – 2034 feet) which has a church belonging to the former Benedictine abbey (rebuilt 1685; richly decorated 18th c. interior). From Münchwilen road 7 returns to **Frauenfeld**.

Frauenfeld castle, Thurgau

Rovio, on Lake Lugano

Ticino

Canton: Ticino (TI).

(i) **Ente Ticinese per il Turismo,**
Piazza Nosetto,
CH-6501 Bellinzona;
tel. (092) 25 70 56.

*Ticino (German Tessin), the most southerly of the Swiss cantons, takes its name from the River Ticino, a left-bank tributary of the Po, which rises on the Nufenen pass (Passo della Novena), flows through Lake Maggiore and joins the Po after a course of 248 km (154 miles).

The canton has an area of 2811 sq. km (1085 sq. miles) and a population of some 250,000. Its capital is Bellinzona (see p. 73), situated near the junction of the roads from the St Gotthard (p. 211) and the San Bernardino pass (p. 218). The canton's main sources of revenue are agriculture and tourism. – In the past many German-speaking Swiss and Germans from the Federal Republic have settled in the canton, particularly by the lakes. The indigenous population is almost exclusively Italian-speaking, but with a local dialect.

HISTORY. – The territory of Ticino, occupied in the early historical period by Rhaetians and Lepontii, was later incorporated in the Roman province of Gallia Cisalpina. Between the 5th and 8th c. it was successively occupied by the Goths, the Lombards and the Franks. In the 15th c. the Confederates gradually wrested it from the overlordship of the Dukes of Milan. It became an independent canton in 1803.

PLANT and ANIMAL LIFE. – Along the northern boundaries of Ticino are high Alpine regions with their characteristic plants and animals. Farther S Mediterranean vegetation increasingly predominates, flourishing particularly in the south-facing valleys. By the lakes palms and citrus fruits are found. The animal life, particularly insects and reptiles, also shows clear Mediterranean characteristics.

The markedly southern orientation and the protection from influences from the region N of the Alps which result from Ticino's geographical situation are reflected also is the architecture of the houses and public buildings. In many places the churches are built of natural stone without any external rendering, as in North Italy; and the canton has a rich heritage of Renaissance and Baroque architecture.

*Ascona: p. 58. – Bellinzona: p. 73. – *Locarno: p. 163. – *Lugano: p. 172. – **Lake Lugano: p. 174. – **Lake Maggiore: p. 176.

Ascona, on Lake Maggiore

Toggenburg

Canton: St Gallen (SG).

(i) **Fremdenverkehrsverband des Kantons St Gallen,**
Bahnhofplatz 1A,
CH-9001 St Gallen;
tel. (071) 22 62 62.
Verkehrsverein Ebnat-Kappel,
CH-9642 Ebnat-Kappel;
tel. (074) 3 29 11.
Werbegemeinschaft Obertoggenburg,
CH-9658 Wildhaus;
tel. (074) 5 27 27.

The *Toggenburg district, a region of varied scenery lying S of Thurgau, comprises the Upper Thur valley and its tributary valleys. Once an independent county, it is now part of the canton of St Gallen.

Road 16, going S from *Wil* (p. 211), passes through the pleasant area of **Untertoggenburg**. On the slopes of the hills are handsome farmhouses of Alemannic type, and in the villages are 18th c. "manufacturers' houses" (Fabrikantenhäuser) dating from the period when the region's flourishing textile industry was established.

Beyond Neu-St Johann the road runs through the Starkenbach defile into *Obertoggenburg, a beautiful mountain region between the limestone massifs of Säntis and the Churfirsten which is a popular health and winter sports area. It then goes over the flat-topped Wildhaus pass (1098 m – 3602 feet) and through the beautifully wooded Simmi gorge into the Rhine valley.

To the S of Wil, reached from there on road 16 or from St Gallen on road 8, is **Lichtensteig** (618 m (2028 feet): Hotel Hirschen), an old-world little town (pop. 2200) which is picturesquely situated on a rocky hill above the right bank of the Thur and is the principal place in the Toggenburg region. Handsome old arcaded houses; the Toggenburger Heimatmuseum, a richly stocked local museum; church of St Gallus, in modern style (by W. M. Förderer, 1966–72); Fredy's Mechanical Music Museum (in the house Zur Frohburg). Lichtensteig, like Wattwil and Ebnat-Kappel, has provided homes for numbers of Tibetan refugees.

2 km (1 mile) S of Lichtensteig on road 16 is **Wattwil** (617 m (2024 feet): pop. 9000; Hotel Jakobshof), a long straggling town which is the economic hub of Toggenburg, with a variety of industry (Textile College). The popular Swiss writer Ulrich Bräker (1735–98) worked here as a weaver. On the hillside to the right of the road can be seen the Franciscan nunnery of *St Maria zu den Engeln* (574 m (1883 feet): 17th c.), and opposite it, to the S, *Iberg Castle* (13th c., restored). Road on right via Ricken to Zurich or Glarus.

The road continues up the Thur valley, here wide and fertile, and in 5·5 km (3 miles) reaches **Ebnat-Kappel** (633–650 m (2077–2133 feet): Hotel Traube, C, 70 b.; bypass), actually two towns with a combined population of 5500 inhabitants and a variety of industry which also attracts summer visitors and winter sports enthusiasts (ski-lifts). – Beyond this the

Lichtensteig, in Obertoggenburg

valley closes in. Ahead the Churfirsten (on right) and the Stockberg (on left) come into sight. – At *Krummenau* (716 m – 2349 feet) the valley briefly opens out again. At the far end of the village, on right, is a large parking place near the chair-lift (2025 m – 6644 feet) from *Krümmenschwil* (740 m – 2427 feet) to *Rietbach* (1120 m – 3675 feet), from which there is a ski-lift to the *Wolzenalp* (1456 m – 4777 feet). – Beyond Krummenau the Thur flows under the natural rock bridge known as the Sprung and through the Kesseltobel gorge, with the road running on the hillside high above it. 2·5 km (2 miles) from Krummenau is **Neu-St Johann** (760 m (2494 feet): Hotel Schäfli), a village set amid meadows in a wider part of the valley (summer holiday accommodation, winter sports), with a handsome 17th c. Baroque church belonging to a former Benedictine monastery.

Ascent of Säntis from Neu St-Johann (12 km (7 miles) to lower station of cableway). – A reasonably good road branches off on the left from Neu-St Johann and climbs the slopes above the *Luternbach* valley, with a fine view of Säntis. Reaching the top of the hill in 1·5 km (1 mile), it runs level past the Ennetbühl and then descends gradually to cross the Luternbach gorge. Beyond this a good road winds its way up to **Rietbad** (927 m (3041 feet): Hotel Kurhaus, D, 75 b.), with a well-known spring of sulphurous water (drinking fountain 100 m (328 feet) beyond Kurhotel), at the foot of the *Stockberg* (1784 m (5853 feet): 1 hour; extensive views). – The road now follows a level course through the meadows of a high valley, passing in 1 km (about a ½ mile) the Kurhaus at *Seeben*. It then climbs over the meadows of the *Alp Bernhalde* (1037 m – 3402 feet) and continues through forest to the *Kräzeren pass* (1300 m – 4265 feet). – 500 m (1641 feet) beyond the pass is the inn on the **Schwägalp** (1283 m – 4210 feet), where the road from Urnäsch comes in on the left. 1 km (about a ½ mile) higher up is the lower station (1360 m – 4462 feet) of the cableway to the summit of *Säntis (2504 m (8216 feet): see p. 54).

From Neu-St Johann road 16 continues through the adjoining village of **Nesslau** (762 m (2500 feet); Hotel Sternen, C, 40 b.), also frequented as a summer vacation and winter sports resort. Towering above it to the SW is the *Speer* (1954 m – 6411 feet), which offers a rewarding climb (5 hours).

Higher up the valley is *Germen*, where the road runs through a narrow wooded pass, with the two *Giessen Falls* on the Thur (hydroelectric station). It then winds its way uphill to the little vacation spot of *Stein* (860 m (2823 feet): Hotel Anker)

and continues up through the *Starkenbach pass* (894 m (2933 feet): on right the ruins of *Starkenstein castle*) into the Alpine high valley of *Obertoggenburg, with innumerable farms and huts dotting its green meadow-covered slopes. To the right is the jagged ridge of the Churfirsten; to the left is a first glimpse of the Wildhauser Schafberg. – 5 km (3 miles) from Stein is **Alt-St Johann** (897 m (2943 feet): Hotel Schweizerhof, D, 55 b.; bypass), a popular health and winter sports resort, founded in the 12th c. as the monastery of St John. At the end of the village, on right, is the lower station of a chair-lift (1·5 km (1 mile), 15 minutes) to the *Alp Sellamatt* (1390 m (4561 feet): Schlamatt inn; panoramic views), near which are the *Churfirsten hut* (1450 m – 4757 feet) and the *Iltiosalp* (30 minutes' walk). Good walking and cross-country trekking. – Road 16 continues to **Unterwasser** (927 m (3041 feet): Hotel Säntis, B, 64 b., SB; Sternen, C, 120 b.; bypass), a popular health resort (swimming pool) and winter sports resort in a beautiful sheltered setting between the Säntis chain and the Churfirsten, at the junction where the two streams combine to form the River Thur.

From Unterwasser a narrow mountain road climbs steeply up (2 km (1 mile) N) to the **Alp Kühboden** (1050 m – 3445 feet); from here it is an hour's walk to the charming little *Gräppelensee* (1302 m – 4272 feet).

Another little road runs 3·5 km (2 miles) SE to the *Schwendi-Seen* (1165 m (3822 feet): Touristenhaus Seegüetli), from where there is a road (3·5 km – 2 miles) to Wildhaus.

A funicular 1·2 km (1 mile) long goes up from Unterwasser in 6 minutes to the much-visited *Iltiosalp (1350 m (4429 feet): mountain inn, from

View of the Churfirsten

where there is a magnificent view of the Säntis massif. Excellent skiing (ski-lift to Alp Stöfeli, 1480 m (4856 feet)). From the Iltiosalp a cabin cableway (3450 m (11,319 feet), 8 minutes) runs up to *Chäserrugg* (2250 m (7382 feet): Stöfeli mountain inn). – Footpaths (extensive views) lead E to the *Schwendi-Seen* (30 minutes) and W to the *Alp Sellamatt* (30 minutes). The ascent of the *Hinterrugg* (2309 m – 7575 feet), the highest peak in the *Churfirsten chain, takes 3½ hours.

The main road continues up from Unterwasser in a double hairpin turn and comes in 2·5 km (2 miles) to the hamlet of *Lisighaus* (1056 m (3456 feet): commune of Wildhaus), with the modest house in which the Reformer Ulrich Zwingli (1484–1531) was born. – 3·5 km (2 miles) from Unterwasser is **Wildhaus** (1098 m (3603 feet): Hotel Acker, B, 160 b., SB; Hirschen, C, 130 b., SB; Sonne, C, 50 b., SB), a widely scattered health and winter sports resort (indoor swimming pool; climbing school; holiday courses in hand-weaving; ice-rink, curling rink, cross-country skiing), magnificently situated on an open pass below the S side of the *Wildhauser 'Schafberg* (2384 m – 7822 feet). Chair-lift (to S: 800 m (2625 feet)) to *Oberdorf* (1270 m – 4167 feet), from which another chair-lift (1981 m – 6500 feet) continues up to the *Gamserrugg* (1771 m – 5811 feet), on the *Gamsalp*; also a chair-lift (to NW) to *Gamplüt* (1334 m (4377 feet): two ski-lifts). 1·5 km (1 mile) NE of Wildhaus is a little lake, the *Schönenbodensee* (1104 m (3622 feet): Hotel Schönenboden), with a bathing beach.

From Wildhaus the road goes downhill on a moderate gradient over Alpine meadows flanked by mountains, and then enters the forest and runs more steeply down through the wooded *Simmi gorge* to the *Zollhaus* inn (706 m – 2316 feet). From here it winds its way down the slopes of the *Gamser Berg*, with extensive views (parking place in 200 m (656 feet), on right) and magnificent *vistas of the Rhine valley and the Liechtenstein Alps.

Gams (504 m (1654 feet): Sonnenblick inn) is a trim village with a church above it on higher ground. From here there is a road E to Haag. – Road 16 now turns S along the edge of the wide *Rhine valley* and comes to *Grabs* (482 m (1581 feet): Ochsen inn), a large village surrounded by orchards. Here a steep and narrow mountain road (10 km – 6 miles) turns off on the right and winds its way up the *Grabser*

Berg (Kurhaus Bad Grabser Berg) to the *Kurhaus Voralp*, below the beautiful *Voralpsee* (1116 m – 3662 feet).

From Grabs the road continues along the densely populated valley to the straggling village of **Buchs** (450 m (1476 feet): see p. 193) to join the road from St Margrethen to Chur beneath *Werdenberg castle*. Chur is set picturesquely above a lake.

Valais Alps

Canton: Valais (VS).

ⓘ **Union Valaisanne du Tourisme,**
15 rue de Lausanne,
CH-1950 Sion;
tel. (027) 22 31 61.

The **Valais Alps (German Walliser Alpen, French Alpes Valaisannes) lie between the Upper Rhône valley and the Italian River Dora Baltea. The Swiss-Italian frontier runs along the main ridge of the massif, which belong to the southern Swiss Alps.**

The Matterhorn from Zermatt

The principal valleys in the Valais Alps are accessible on side roads opening off the main road along the Rhône valley. Two important N–S routes run through the massif, over the Great St Bernard (p. 207) to the W and the Simplon pass (p. 229) to the E. Rising to well over 4000 m (13,124 feet), the range includes some of the mightiest peaks in Switzerland, including the **Matterhorn** (4478 m – 14,692 feet) and the Monte Rosa group, with the **Dufourspitze** (4634 m – 15,204 feet), the country's highest mountain. One notable man-made feature is the artificial lake of Grande-Dixence (p. 233), in a grandiose mountain setting.

The beauties of the Valais Alps were discovered by tourists relatively early. The best-known resorts are **Zermatt** (p. 260) and **Saas Fee** (p. 206), but in recent years a number of other resorts such as Verbier (p. 177), Grimentz (p. 226) and Zinal (p. 226) have developed into popular winter sports areas.

Vevey

Canton: Vaud (VD).
Altitude: 383 m (1257 feet). – Population: 16,000.
Post code: CH-1800. – Dialling code: 021.
ⓘ **Association des Intérêts**
de Vevey et Environs,
  5 Place de la Gare;
  tel. 51 48 25.

HOTELS. – *Trois Couronnes*, A, 120 b.; *Du Lac*, B, 90 b., SP; *Comte*, C, 70 b.; *Pavillon* (no rest.), C, 25 b.; *Vieux Vevey*, C, 48 b.; *Pension de Famille*, D, 100 b.; *Des Négociants*, D, 45 b.; *Motel des Quatre Vents*, D, 34 b. – ON MONT PÈLERIN: *Le Mirador Country Club*, A, 150 b., SB; *Du Parc*, B, 150 b., SP.

EVENTS. – A unique wine festival, the *Fête des Vignerons*, is held in Vevey every 25 years (most recently in 1977). – Every Saturday from July to September there is a *Fête folklorique*, with wine-tasting and local culinary specialties.

Vevey lies on Lake Geneva at the mouth of the River Veveyse, with Mont Pèlerin (1084 m – 3557 feet)

and the Pléiades (1364 m – 4475 feet) rearing up behind the town. On the slopes to the N are the famous Lavaux vineyards.

HISTORY. – In Roman times Vevey (*Viviscus*) was the most important port on Lake Geneva. The town received its municipal charter about 1200, and during the Middle Ages it rose to prosperity as a trading station on the road from Burgundy to Piedmont. It began to develop into a major tourist attraction in the 19th c.

SIGHTS. – The central feature of the town is the *Grand'Place*, an unusually large market square on the shores of the lake. At its N end is the colonnaded *Grenette* (Corn Exchange, 1808), and beyond this, near the *Theatre*, is the *Auberge de la Clef*, in which Rousseau stayed in 1730 (commemorative plaque). On the W side of the Grand'Place is the *Jardin du Rivage* (concerts during the season), with the beautiful *Seahorse Fountain*. From the Grand'Place and the long *Quai Perdonnet* to the E there are magnificent views over the lake to the Savoy Alps, with Le Grammont (2172 m – 7126 feet) in the foreground. At the E end of the quay (800 m (2625 feet) long) in front of a small park is an amusing bronze sculpture group, "Première chevauchée de Bacchus" (1930), and a bust of the poetess Anna de Noailles (d. 1933). – To the E, continuous with Vevey, is the little town of **La Tour-de-Peilz** which has a 13th c. castle. In place du Temple is the Freedom fountain,

La Tour-de-Peilz yacht harbour, Vevey

by Gustave Courbet who died here in 1877. Yacht harbour.

In Rue d'Italie, N of Quai Perdonnet, are the *Musée du Vieux-Vevey* (Museum of Old Vevey) and *Musée de la Confrérie des Vignerons* (Museum of the Confraternity of Vintners), closed on Mondays: pre-historic material, fine old furniture, weapons, costumes, history of wine. – In Avenue de la Gare (No. 2), which runs E from the station square, the *Musée Jenisch* (established in 1897: closed Mondays), houses an art collection which includes pictures and sculpture by Swiss artists of the 19th and 20th c. (also special exhibitions) and a small natural history collection. – On a terrace above the railway line (fine views: tourist map) stands the *church of St-Martin* (14th–15th c., with 20th c. stained glass). – On the NW outskirts of the town, near the Lausanne road, is the Y-shaped *Palais Nestlé* (1960), headquarters of the famous Swiss firm.

SURROUNDINGS. – From the hotel colony (alt. 806 m (2644 feet)) on the slopes of *Mont Pèlerin (1084 m – 3557 feet) there are fine views of Lake Geneva, the Rhône valley and the Savoy Alps. It can be reached either by road (12 km (7 miles), via *Corsier*) or by funicular (1·6 km (1 mile), 10 minutes), via *Corseaux* (429 m (1480 feet): swimming pool), where there is a house built by Le Corbusier for his parents in 1924 (museum), and *Chardonne*. – In summer a tourist railway runs between Vevey and Chamby (see p. 180).

Vevey to Blonay (by road 5 km (3 miles), by electric railway 6 km (4 miles) in 20 minutes, to the Pléiades 12 km (7 miles) in 45 minutes). – The road passes the English church and continues up the Route de Blonay, turning left up the hill in 1 km (about a ½ mile). After passing the 18th c. *château de Hauteville* (off the road to the right: beautiful private gardens, with lookouts) it runs through the villages of *St-Légier* (champagne-style wine) and *La Chiésaz*, where the grave of the composer Paul Hindemith (1895–1963) can be seen in the cemetery and where there are a number of houses with humorous external paintings by A. Béguin. Finally the road runs below the massive 12th c. *Château de Blonay*, which has remained in the possession of the Blonay family since it was built. – 5 km (3 miles): **Blonay** (623 m – 2044 feet). Description of village and continuation of road to the *Pléiades*: p. 180.

Along the *corniche road* to **Lausanne** (28 km – 17 miles): p. 135.

Vierwaldstätter See

Cantons: Uri (UR), Schwyz (SZ), Unterwalden (NW) and Lucerne (LU).

ⓘ **Verkehrsverband Zentralschweiz,**
Pilatusstrasse 14,
CH-6002 Luzern;
tel. (041) 23 70 45.
Fremdenverkehrsverband des Kantons Schwyz,
Bahnhofstrasse 32,
CH-6440 Brunnen;
tel. (043) 31 17 77.

Pilatus and Vitznau, on the Vierwaldstätter See

The **Vierwaldstätter See or Lake of the Four Forest Cantons (the three original cantons of Uri, Schwyz and Unterwalden together with the canton of Lucerne) is commonly re-ferred to in English as Lake Lucerne, but is, in fact, only one of the lake's many arms. Lying at an altitude of 437 m (1434 feet), it is the fourth largest of the Swiss lakes (area 113 sq. km (44 sq. miles), length from Lucerne to Flüelen 38 km (24 miles); greatest depth 214 m (702 feet)), but is second to none in magnificence and scenic variety. The great moun-tains with their endless scope for walks and climbs are reflected in the spacious surface of the lake. The famous lookouts of the Rigi, Pilatus and the Stanserhorn are brought within easy reach by mountain** railways and cableways. The beautiful shores of the lake with their southern vegetation offer numerous bathing places. The trim towns and villages provide luxurious or modest accommodation at the visitor's choice. These attractions, plus the lake's associations with the origins of the Swiss Confederation and the legend of William Tell all help make the Lake of the Four Forest Cantons one of the most popular tourist areas in Europe.

The lake begins in the W with the gently beautiful **Luzerner See** (Lake Lucerne), with the *Bucht von Stansstad* (Stansstad Bay) and the **Alpnacher See** to the S and the **Küssnachter See** (Lake Küssnacht) to the NE. Then come the *Weggiser Becken* (Weggis Basin) and, beyond the Rigi and Bürgenstock promontories which reduce the width of the lake to only 825 m (2707 feet), the *Gersauer Becken* (Gersau Basin) and *Buochser Bucht* (Buochs Bay). Running S from Brunnen is the *Urner See* (Lake Uri), a fjord-like strip of water enclosed between massive rock walls, scenically the most magnificent part of the lake.

The area around the Vierwaldstätter See is also of great geological interest, since the geomorphological processes are clearly discernible and the various zones, from the moraine-covered foreland area to the central upthrust of the St Gotthard massif, follow closely upon one another – the narrow zone of nagelfluh (conglomerate) with its strata falling down towards the S (Rigi), the limestones and flysch schists with their steep-sided mountain forms (Bürgenstock) and compressed folds (Axenfluh), the displaced superficial strata (Mythen) and finally, forming a grandiose backdrop, the steeply upthrust or overlapping folds of the Uri Alps with their alternation of different rocks.

BOAT SERVICE from Lucerne to Flüelen: 48 km (30 miles), 3–3½ hours.

The full beauty of the lake and its mountain setting can best be appreciated by taking a boat trip, which will provide a pleasant alternative to the journey by car. Even a one-way trip is worth taking if you can arrange to have your car driven to meet you.

There are also boat services from Lucerne to Küssnacht (15 km (9 miles), 1 hour) and from Lucerne via Kehrsiten-Bürgenstock and Stansstad to Alpnachstad (25 km (16 miles), 1¼–1½ hours). In summer there are services between Lucerne and Brunnen.

*Around the Vierwaldstätter See by road

Lucerne to Flüelen along the N and E sides of the lake (51 km – 32 miles). – Leave **Lucerne** (alt. 438 m (1437 feet): see p. 167) on the Haldenstrasse, going past the Kursaal (on right) and the beautiful lakeside gardens and continuing close to the shore of *Lake Lucerne*. – In 2 km (1 mile) a side road goes off on the right (0.5 km – about a ¼ mile) to the public beach (park, camp site, restaurant). – The road then runs past the *Swiss Transport Museum* (see p. 171) and the Liliputbahn (a miniature steam railway). – Beyond this a road comes in on the right from the beach. Then the Bürgenstock hotels and later the Rigi (p. 203) come into sight.

Seeburg (440 m (1444 feet): New Hotel Seeburg, B, 75 b., bathing beach), an outlying suburb of Lucerne. – Beyond this the road winds its way up to cross the *Megger Berg* (496 m – 1627 feet), with fruit orchards and many houses, past the *Meggenhorn*, a little wooded peninsula on the right. – **Meggen** (483 m (1585 feet): Hotel Balm, C, 30 b., SB), a long straggling village. In *Vorder-Meggen* we find *Schloss Neu-Habsburg* (1869), with the tower of an older castle which was destroyed by the men of Lucerne in 1352; in *Hinter-Meggen* is the parish church (18th and 19th c.). – The road now enters the canton of Schwyz and continues along the NW side of the *Küssnachter See*. – 2 km (1 mile) beyond the village of Merlischachen (444 m – 1457 feet), below the road on the right, is the *Astrid Chapel* (1936), moved here in 1960 from its previous position on the left of the road, commemorating Queen Astrid of the Belgians, who was killed in a car accident here (spot marked by a cross) on 29 August 1935. – The road now descends to **Küssnacht** (440 m (1444 feet): p. 152), from which the main road (No. 2) continues via Arth to Brunnen (p. 92). – The more attractive road via Weggis and Gersau branches off on the right and follows closely to the E side of the Küssnachter See, passing through pleasant countryside below the W side of the Rigi. In 0·5 km (about a ¼ mile) it passes the lower station of the cableway to the Seebodenalp (on left). – In 5 km (3 miles), on right, is the village of *Greppen*

(454 m – 1490 feet). The road now climbs (beautiful view of the lake to the rear) over a hill, with the Hertenstein peninsula to the right, and runs down to a junction where a road (0·8 km – about a ½ mile) goes off on the right to the popular resort of **Weggis**, prettily situated on the lake (440 m (1444 feet): Hotel Albana, B, 100 b.; Alexander, B, 80 b., bathing beach; Parkhotel, B, 105 b., bathing beach; Strandhotel Lützelau, C, 100 b., bathing beach; camping site). From here a beautiful road runs W to the public beach and the Hertenstein peninsula (3 km – 2 miles), and a narrow mountain road climbs 5·5 km (3 miles) E up the slopes of the Rigi (see p. 203. no road to summit). – The main road, bypassing Weggis, runs uphill again. 2·5 km (2 miles) beyond the turning for Weggis the old road comes in on the right. Then follows a beautiful stretch of road, running close to the lake at the foot of the Rigi, with splendid views. To the right can be seen the Bürgenstock (p. 92) and its hotels. – Farther on there is a charming view of the narrowest part of the lake between the two promontories, the Obere and the Untere Nase, and of the Bürgenstock, with the Buochserhorn and Stanserhorn rearing up behind it.

Vitznau (440 m (1444 feet): *Park-Hotel, A, 130 b., SB; Seehotel Vitznauer Hof, B, 100 b., bathing beach; Kreuz, C, 100 b., SP; camping site), a popular summer holiday resort affording extensive views, from which a cog-railway ascends the **Rigi** (35 minutes: see p. 203). (There is another cog-railway up the Rigi from Arth-Goldau, to the E.) – At the far end of the village, on the left, are two cableways, one to *Hinterbergen*, the other to *Weissenfluh* (Wissifluh, 936 m (3071 feet): hotel; pony-trekking), both giving access to fine walking country. – The road continues past the beach and then winds its way around the *Obere Nase*, skirting the shore of the lake or running a little above it, with far-ranging views. – 5 km (3 miles) beyond Vitznau is the dock of a car ferry to Beckenried on the S side of the lake (service every hour, taking 15 minutes).

Gersau (440 m (1444 feet): Hotel Ilge & Mimosa, C, 140 b.; Seehof, D, 35 b., bathing beach), the oldest health resort on the Vierwaldstätter See, in a charming sheltered site. From here a mountain road leads N (5·5 km – 3 miles) to the lower station, at *Gschwend* (1012 m (3320 feet): inn), of a cableway which runs NW to the *Burggeist* guest-house, 20 minutes below the Rigi-Scheidegg peak (1665 m – 5463 feet). – Beyond Gersau the road continues close to the shore or on the wooded slopes above the lake. It passes the old *Kindlimord chapel* (rebuilt 1708), at the foot of the Rigi-Hochfluh (1702 m – 5584 feet), with a view of the two Mythen. Soon after this the Urner See (Lake Uri) comes into view beyond the Treib promontory. – 4 km (2 miles) farther on, to the left, is a cableway up the Urmiberg.

Brunnen (440 m (144 feet): p. 92), where we join the St Gotthard road, coming from Lucerne and Zurich via Arth. The lakeside route from Brunnen to Flüelen follows this road. – At the Wolfsprung Hotel an attractive little mountain road (3 km – 2 miles) goes off on the left via the health resort of *Morschach* (turn left here into a narrow gravel road, past the Rütliblick Hotel) to the *Axenstein* (708 m (2323 feet): see p. 92), with a superb view of both arms of the Vierwaldstätter See. – The route to Flüelen continues on the magnificent *Axenstrasse*, which runs above the steep E shore of the fjord-like *Urner See* (Lake Uri), passing through numerous tunnels and galleries blasted from the rock (it is possible to walk along some stretches of the old road, built in 1863–65). The St Gotthard railway runs parallel to the road, sometimes above it and sometimes below, also passing through many tunnels. On the far side of the lake can be seen the crag known as the Schillerstein and, higher up on the Seelisberg, the Rütli meadow on which the original Swiss Confederation was established. – Just before Sisikon the road enters the canton of Uri.

Sisikon (457 m – 1499 feet), at the mouth of the *Riemenstalden valley*, has a modern church built in 1968. – Beyond this the road continues through more tunnels to the *Tellsplatte Hotel* (512 m – 1680 feet), with a car park and beautiful gardens (view of the massive Urirotstock, 2932 m (9620 feet)). From here a footpath (7 minutes) leads down to the famous **Tell Chapel** (known to have existed since at least 1500; restored 1881, with paintings by Stückelberg), on the spot where William Tell is traditionally supposed to have leapt out of Gessler's ship during a storm. From the hotel a cableway runs up in 4 minutes to the Axen station (825 m – 2707 feet). – 1 km (about a ½ mile) farther on the Axenstrasse enters its last tunnel, with an old gallery (lookout) on the right.

Flüelen (440 m (1444 feet): Hostellerie Sternen, C, 30 b.; Flüelerhof, C, 40 b.), a port and holiday resort at the S end of the Urner See, built on the delta at the mouth of the canalised River *Reuss*, with a handsome church (1913) above the village. Near the station, behind the old church (1665), is the little Schloss Rudenz (14th c. and 1815), which belonged to the Attinghausen family. Cableway up the Eggberge (1440 m – 4725 feet). – The road continues via *Altdorf* to *Isenthal* (see p. 49).

Lucerne to Seelisberg along the W and S sides of the lake (37 km – 23 miles). – Leave **Lucerne** (alt. 438 (1437 feet): p. 167) by Pilatusstrasse and Obergrundstrasse (to left). Just after Paulusplatz a road goes off on the left to *Horw* (445 m (1460 feet): Hotel Waldhaus, C, 30 b.), from which it is possible either to travel SE to *Winkel*, attractively situated in a bay on the lake, or to continue along the shores of the lake to *Hergiswil*. – 500 m (1641 feet) beyond the turning for Horw we join the N 2 motorway and continue on this, at first running below Pilatus (see p. 170) at some distance from the lake, then above the lake, with a beautiful view (to left) of the Rigi, the Bürgenstock and the Stanserhorn.

To the left (motorway exit) is the summer holiday resort of **Hergiswil**, on the lake (445 m (1460 feet): Hotel Belvédère am See, B, 94 b., bathing beach; Pilatus am See, B, 100 b., SB). From *Stalden* (571 m – 1873 feet), above Hergiswil to the W, a cableway ascends in 3 minutes to the Seeblick lookout (724 m – 2375 feet). At *Brunni* (825 m – 2707 feet) 1·5 km (1 mile) farther on, is another cableway which takes 6 minutes to reach the *Alp Gschwänd* (1216 m – 3990 feet), on the N side of Pilatus. – The motorway continues on a beautiful stretch of road above the lake, running along the slopes of the *Lopperberg* (965 m – 3166 feet), an outlier of Pilatus, and comes to a junction where the road to the Brünig pass (see p.

The Schnitzturm, Stansstad

220) diverges to the right. N 2 continues over the channel, only 150 m (492 feet) wide, between the Vierwaldstätter See and the .Alpnacher See to the exit for **Stansstad** (438 m (1437 feet): Hotel Schützen, B, 80 b.; Seehotel Ascheregg, C, 40 b., bathing beach), the port for Stans, a summer holiday resort and the beginning of the road to the Bürgenstock and the road and railway to Engelberg. On the shores of the lake stands the Schnitzturm, a relic of the old fortifications. – 1 km (about a ½ mile) NE on the *Harissenbucht* is a large bathing beach, with a funicular (382 m – 1253 feet) which climbs in 4 minutes to the *Kurhaus Fürigen* (650 m – 2133 feet). – From Stansstad a very attractive road runs E, climbing through the forest, then through the meadows of a high valley and finally through another stretch of forest to the parking place (fee) at the great complex of fine hotels on the ****Bürgenstock** (878 m (2881 feet): see p. 92, a magnificent lookout. – The motorway continues through the fertile valley (fruit orchards) between the Bürgenstock and the Stanserhorn to the exit for **Stans** (455 m (1493 feet): Hotel Regina, C, 25 b.; Motel Rex, D, 55 b.), a little market town (pop. 6000), the capital of the half-canton of Nidwalden, the eastern half of the canton of Unterwalden. In the main square are the parish church (rebuilt in Baroque style 1641–47) and a monument to Arnold von Winkelried, hero of the Battle of Sempach (1386). To the right of the church is a double chapel of 1482 (charnel-house); to the left, above the church, stands the Town Hall (1715). The "Höfli" is a restored medieval secular building. At the lower station of the Stanserhorn funicular

is an interesting historical museum. – A combined funicular and cableway ascends in 25 minutes to the panoramic restaurant on the *Stanserhorn-Kulm* (1849 m – 6067 feet), 5 minutes below the summit of the *Stanserhorn (1901 m – 6237 feet), from which there are superb views of the Uri, Unterwalden and Bernese Alps, the Vierwaldstätter See and the Alpine foreland.

From Stans the road to Seelisberg (Treib) branches off on the left and rejoins the N 2 motorway, which crosses the fertile open valley of the *Engelberger Aa* and then the river. To the left is the Bürgenstock, to the right the Buochserhorn, ahead the Rigi. – Exit for **Buochs** (440 m (1444 feet): Hotel Sonnenheim, D, 40 b.; Krone, D, 50 b.), a village, beautifully situated on the bay of the same name, which attracts many summer visitors; it has a church prominently located on higher ground. From here a good road runs N to *Ennetbürgen*, below the E side of the Bürgenstock (road only as far as the Kurhaus Honegg: beyond this point no through traffic). – Beyond Buochs the road to Seelisberg skirts the lake, with a beautiful view of the Rigi. – At the near end of Beckenried, on left, is the departure point of the *car ferry* to Gersau.

Beckenried (440 m (1444 feet): Hotel Sternen am See, B, 82 b., bathing beach; Edelweiss, D, 50 b., bathing beach; Mond, D, 50 b., bathing beach), a long straggling village at the end of the lakeside road, also popular as a quiet holiday resort. A cableway runs up to the *Klewenalp* (1600 m (5250 feet): Klewenalp-Hotels, D, 70 b.), to the S, from which there is a beautiful view

embracing the lake, the Rigi, the Mythen, the Glarus Alps and the Alpine foreland area with its lakes; good skiing (ski-lifts). – Beyond Beckenried the road to Seelisberg leaves the lake and runs gradually uphill on the slopes of the *Klewenstock* (good skiing), first through an area of meadowland and then over the motorway and through forest. – In 3·5 km (2 miles), on left, is the Roman Catholic mission of *Bethlehem* (687 m – 2254 feet), formerly the Kurhaus Schöneck. – The road then winds its way up, with magnificent views of the lake, to **Emmetten** (762 m – 2500 feet), another straggling village and summer holiday place in a sheltered setting. Beyond this it continues uphill for a short distance and then, near the church, descends steeply into a beautiful green Alpine valley and uphill again on a moderate gradient between the *Niederbauen* (1927 m (6322 feet): on right, a cableway from Emmetten) and the *Stutzberg*. From Emmetten there is a cableway to the *Stockhütte* (1286 m – 4219 feet). – In another 3 km (2 miles) the road winds its way up through forest and then runs down and passes through a tunnel, beyond which there is a picturesque *view of the *Seelisberger See* far below (736 m (2415 feet): bathing beach). Beyond the lake a road branches off on the right to the **Rütli** meadow in the middle of the forest, where tradition has it that the Swiss Confederation was established. Here in 1291 the three "forest cantons" of Schwyz, Uri and Unterwalden joined in an alliance which became the foundation of the "Perpetual League" against the Habsburgs. The Tell legend, which received its classical form in Schiller's drama "William Tell" (1804), was a later addition to the traditional Story. – The road continues to the health resort of **Seelisberg** (804–845 m (2638–2772 feet): Hotel Bellevue, C, 75 b., SP; Löwen, C, 50 b.), situated on a wooded terrace high above the Vierwaldstätter See. – The road passes the pilgrimage chapel of Maria-Sonnenberg (1667) and the funicular to Treib, and then descends through the forest, after which there is a superb *view of the Vierwaldstätter See and the Rigi.

Treib (440 m – 1444 feet), picturesquely set on the tongue of land between the Vierwaldstätter See and the Urner See, was formerly a little trading town and a haven for shipping on the lake. Funicular

The Bernese Alps from the Stanserhorn

Treib, on the Vierwaldstätter See

up to Seelisberg (1149 m (3770 feet), 8 minutes). There is a charming inn, built in 1903 in imitation of the previous inn (1658). Dock. The road ends here.

The motorway SE of Beckenried, opened in 1980, passes through the 9·3 km (5·8 miles) long Seelisberg Tunnel to the S bank of Lake Uri and thence to the St Gotthard road.

Walensee

Cantons: St Gallen (SG) and Glarus (GL).
(i) **Verkehrsverein Weesen,**
Kirchgasse,
CH-8872 Weesen;
tel. (058) 43 12 30.
Verkehrsverein Murg,
CH-8877 Murg;
tel. (085) 4 12 67.
Verkehrsverein Walenstadt,
Seestrasse,
CH-8880 Walenstadt;
tel. (085) 3 55 45.
Verkehrsverein Flumserberge,
CH-8891 Flumserberg;
tel. (085) 3 14 00,

The * Walensee (15 km (9 miles) long, up to 2 km (1 mile) wide, up to 151 m (495 feet) deep) lies at an altitude of 423 m (1388 feet) between the Glarus Alps to the S and the Churfirsten, which tower up on the N to a height of almost 1000 m (3281 feet) above the light green waters of the lake (Hinterrugg 2309 m − 7576 feet).

At the W end of the lake is **Weesen** (431 m (1414 feet): Parkhotel Schwert, C, 40 b.), a charming little town (pop. 1500) and holiday resort. From the shady

lakeside promenade there are very beautiful views. − 1 km (about a ½ mile) E, beyond the wooded detrital fan of the Flibach, is the hamlet of *Fli* or *Fly*.

A little road which branches off the road to Amden at Fli (alternate one-way traffic) runs along the N side of the lake. The road is cut from the rock for most of the way, with two tunnels. After passing the *Muslen falls* and the ruins of *Strahlegg castle* it comes to the little village of **Betlis**, 5 km (3 miles) E of Weesen (520 m; Paradiesli inn; boat service from Weesen), from which a footpath (15 minutes) leads up to the *Seerenbach falls* (inn).

A road NE from Weesen via Fli (6 km (4 miles): views), winds steeply up from the lake with two hairpin turns, to the summer and winter sports resort (several ski-lifts) of **Amden** (911 m (2989 feet): Hotel Rössli, C, 30 b.; Bellevue, D, 50 b., SP), lying high above the lake on sunny Alpine meadows between the *Mattstock* (1939 m (6362 feet): chair-lift, 1400 m (4593 feet) in 15 minutes, to the *Alp Walau*, 1285 m − 4216 feet) and the *Leistkamm* (2105 m (6907 feet): 5 hours). There is a rewarding climb from Amden to the summit of the * *Speer* (1951 m (6401 feet): 3 hours).

The N 3 motorway follows the S side of the lake from the Glarus exit to Walenstadt, with viaducts (electrically heated in winter to prevent icing) and numerous tunnels and galleries.

There is also a slightly longer route via Näfels and the old road over the *Kerenzerberg*. − 3·3 km (2 miles) S of Niederurnen is **Näfels** (440 m (1444 feet): Hotel

The Walensee

Schwert, C, 10 b.), a busy little market town of 4000 inhabitants (mainly Roman Catholic) at the mouth of the Linth valley. The Baroque parish church dates from 1781. The richly appointed Freulerpalast, built in 1642–47 for Colonel Freuler, an officer in the French service, has beautifully panelled rooms with Winterthur stoves and contains the Glarus Cantonal Museum. On the hill once occupied by the castle is a Capuchin friary. A steep road runs 6 km (4 miles) W from Näfels to a charming little lake, the *Obersee* (989 m – 3245 feet).

In Näfels take a road which branches off the Glarus road on the left and crosses the *Linth*. The first place on the road to the Kerenzerberg is *Mollis* (448 m (1470 feet): Bären inn), below the Fronalpstock. It has a number of fine old burghers' houses, including the Zwickyhaus (1621), in Kreuzgasse, and the mansion of Haltli (1784), on the Kerenzerberg road.

Beyond Mollis the road (No. 3, of excellent quality) climbs at a moderate rate, with numerous turns, affording beautiful views to the rear of Näfels and the Linth plain extending to Lake Zurich and bounded on the S by My Hirzli, and to the left of the Weggis chain, Glärnisch and Tödi. In 2 km (1 mile) the *Talblick inn* is passed on the right, after which the road runs through the forest, with the first glimpses of the Walensee. – 5·5 km (3 miles) from Mollis, on the left, is the *Café Kerenzer Berghaus* (730 m – 2395 feet), on the **Kerenzerberg** (1375 m – 4511 feet), with a beautiful ꞏ view of the Walensee and the Churfirsten; to the left, below the Mattstock, is Amden, and at the W end of the lake the village of Weesen. – Here the road reaches its highest point and begins to descend.

Filzbach (720 m (2362 feet): Hotel Seeblick) is a village and health resort, magnificently located on a terrace of meadowland 270 m (886 feet) above the Walensee, under the pyramidal summit of the *Mürtschenstock* (2442 m – 8012 feet). 1¼ hours' walk S is the little *Talalpsee* (1100 m – 3609 feet). A chairlift (1650 m (5414 feet), 14 minutes) ascends from Filzbach to the *Alp Habergschwänd* (1280 m (4200 feet): restaurant).

From Filzbach the road continues gently uphill and circles the *Sallerntobel* gorge, with beautiful views at the *Café Seeblick* (1·5 km – 1 mile) and just before Obstalden. – **Obstalden** (700 m (2297 feet): Hotel Hirschen), in a beautiful setting similar to that of Filzbach, has an old church. Road on right into the *Hüttenberge* (5 km – 3 miles). – The road now winds its way down (views) into the *Merenbach* valley and passes through a short tunnel to join the road along the Walensee at Mühlehorn.

5 km (3 miles) beyond the Glarus exit the N 3 motorway comes to a parking place, and 100 m (328 feet) beyond this, on the left, is the *Walensee* restaurant. – 1 km (about a ½ mile) farther on is an exit (cars only) to the village of *Mühlehorn* (426 m – 1398 feet), at the inflow of the Merenbach into the Walensee. – The road continues along above the lake, traversing two tunnels, and past the Mühlehorn/ Kerenzerberg junction where the road from the Kerenzerberg comes in. The motorway now begins to climb a little. –

In another 1·5 km (1 mile) it comes to the village of **Murg** (430 m (1411 feet): Hotel Rössli), situated below the road (exit only on left) on the alluvial cone of the River Murg, which forms a promontory projecting into the lake. There is a pleasant walk (4–5 hours) up the quiet Alpine valley of the Murg to the three beautiful *Murg-Seen* (1673–1825 m – 5489–5988 feet). On the N side of the lake opposite Murg (motor-boat service), beneath the Leistkamm (2105 m – 6907 feet) at the W end of the Churfirsten massif, is the very attractive little village of *Quinten* (Au inn), with beautiful southern vegetation. Like Terzen and Quarten, the village takes its name from the Latin numbering of ecclesiastical properties in the Middle Ages.

The road continues past parking places on either side, passing above Murg with its camping site, and then descends towards the shore of the lake. – In another 1 km (about a ½ mile), on the left, is the *Rössli* hotel and restaurant, and 1·5 km (1 mile) beyond this, on the right, the *Mühle* hotel.

Oberterzen, above the Walensee

Then comes *Unterterzen* (429 m – 1408 feet), a little industrial town (cement works, match factory, etc.) of 3000 inhabitants. A road goes off on the right and runs up 3 km (2 miles) via *Quarten* (574 m (1883 feet): convalescent home) to **Oberterzen** (662 m (2172 feet): Hotel Gemsli), a health resort and a cross-country skiing base. From here it is a 2½ hours' walk to the three *Seeben-Seen* (1643 m (5391 feet): Kurhaus Seebenalp).

At the far end of Unterterzen the Chur road passes the lower station of a cableway which ascends via Oberterzen to the *Flumserberge*. – 2 km (1 mile) from Unterterzen is *Mols* (432 m (1417 feet): Hotel Schiffahrt), after which the road curves to the right under a wooded spur with the ruins of *Bommerstein Castle*. It then passes a camping site and the Walenstadt bathing beach, at the end of the lake (on left), and before reaching Walenstadt (most of which lies off the road to the left) crosses the *Seez Canal*.

Walenstadt (430 m (1411 feet): pop. 3500; Hotel Churfirsten, D, 28 b.), another popular summer holiday spot, lies 1 km (about a $\frac{1}{2}$ mile) from the E end of the Walensee below the steep rock-faces of the Hinterrugg. From here an attractive mountain road winds its way up to the health resort of *Walenstadtberg* (800–900 m (2625–2953 feet): Kurhaus Alpenblick), 4 km (2 miles) NW, on a terrace of meadowland above the N side of the lake, beneath the jagged peaks of the Churfirsten. 1·5 km (1 mile) farther on is the *Knoblisbühl* sanatorium (982 m – 3222 feet); from where a narrow little road runs up another 2 km (1 mile) to the *Schrina-Hochrugg* restaurant (1313 m – 4308 feet), near which is a temple-like monument to Peace by Karl Bickel.

From Walenstadt the Chur road continues up the broad **Seez valley** below the Alvier massif (on left). To the right, on a projecting spur above Flums, stands the ruined castle of Gräpplang.

Berschis (446 m (1463 feet): bypass). On a wooded crag above the village to the left (easy climb) the *pilgrimage chapel of St George* (592 m (1942 feet): 12th and 15th c.) has wall-paintings (key from priest's house in the village). – Beyond Berschis, at the beginning of the motor-way to Chur, a road branches off on the right, crossing the railway and the Seez canal, to the trim village of **Flums** (444 m (1457 feet): Hotel Bahnhof), at the mouth of the *Schils valley*, with the Weissmeilen (2480 m – 8137 feet) and the curiously shaped Spitzmeilen in the background. By the Seez canal is the church of St Justus, the nave of which was altered in the 17th c. (painted timber ceiling); under the Late Gothic choir (tabernacle of 1488) are the remains of an earlier Carolingian structure. Above the

village are the ruins of the 13th c. *Gräpplang castle* (469 m (1539 feet): hotel), and 15 minutes SW of this is *St James's chapel* (St Jakob), which is partly Romanesque.

From Flums two attractive little roads lead up to the **Flumserberge**, a region of Alpine meadows dotted with huts (Hotels: Gauenpark, B, 64 b., SB; Alpina, C, 51 b.; Cresta, C, 45 b.), visited both in summer and during the winter sports season (several ski-lifts, ice-rink, indoor swimming pool). To the SE, above the E side of the Schilsbach valley, is the *Kleinberg*, with the *Frohe Aussicht* restaurant (900 m – 2953 feet), 4·5 km (3 miles) from Flums; higher up are the *Sässliwiese* (1200 m – 3937 feet) and *Schönhalden* hotels (1494 m (4902 feet): hotel cableway from Saxli). – To the SW, above the W side of the valley, is the *Grossberg*. A good road (11 km – 7 miles) climbs up, passing a number of inns, to **Tannenheim** (1220 m (4003 feet): chair-lift via the *Prodalp*, 1576 m (5171 feet), to *Prodchamm*, c. 2000 m (6562 feet), with restaurant) and the **Alp Tannenboden** (1400 m (4593 feet): cableway from Unterterzen), with several hotels and many chalets. From here a cableway ascends via the *Kreuz* hotel (1610 m – 5282 feet) to the *Maschgenkamm* (Maschgenlücke inn, 1960 m – 6931 feet), on the *Spitzmeilen* (2505 m – 8219 feet).

Winterthur

Canton: Zurich (ZH).
Altitude: 449 m (1473 feet). – Population: 87,000.
Post code: CH-8400. – Dialling code: 052.
ⓘ **Offizielles Verkehrsbüro,**
Bahnhofplatz;
tel. 22 00 88.

HOTELS. – *Garten-Hotel*, B, 85 b.; *Krone*, C, 55 b.; *Römertor*, C, 28 b.; *Zentrum Töss*, C, 32 b.; *Motel Wülflingen*, C, 45 b.; *Winterthur*, D, 83 b.; *Wartmann am Bahnhof*, D, 70 b. – YOUTH HOSTEL. – CAMPING SITE.

Winterthur, the second largest town in the canton of Zurich, lies in a wide basin near the River Töss in the Pre-Alpine region, half-way between the Rhine and Lake Zurich. It

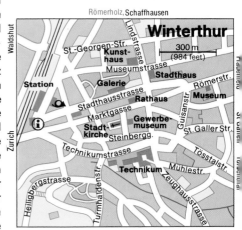

is widely renowned for its engineering industry (Gebrüder Sulzer, Schweizerische Lokomotiv- und Maschinenfabrik, etc.) and its textile factories; Cantonal Technical College.

HISTORY. – Winterthur was founded by the Kyburgs about 1150 as a market village, and received its municipal charter from Rudolf of Habsburg in 1264. Pottery, watchmaking and weaving were early local industries, followed in the 19th c. by engineering.

Parish church, Winterthur

SIGHTS. – The little triangular OLD TOWN still preserves streets of old burghers' houses. The **parish church** (Stadtkirche) was built between 1264 and 1515; the two towers, 65 m (213 feet) high, were added in 1659 and 1794. At Kirchplatz 14 the *Industrial Museum* (Gewerbemuseum), houses a fine collection of applied and decorative art and, from time to time, special exhibitions. In Marktgasse is the **Rathaus** (Town Hall, 18th–19th c.), in the rear wing of which are the *Kellenberger Collection of Watches and Clocks* and the *Briner Collection of Minor Masters.*

The old town is bounded on the N by the *Stadthausstrasse*, which runs E from the station. At No. 6 is the *Galerie Oskar Reinhart*, with a fine collection of works by Swiss, German and Austrian artists of the 18th–20th c., including many Romantics (C. D. Friedrich, K. Blechen, F. Hodler, A. Böcklin, L. Richter, F. G. Kerstling, P. O. Runge, R. F. Wasmann, etc.). At the E end of the Stadthausstrasse we find the **Stadthaus** (by G. Semper, 1865–69; enlarged 1932–34), with the concert hall of the fine Collegium Musicum, founded in 1629.

The *Museum of Art, in the Kunsthaus (Museumstrasse, NW of the Stadthaus), contains pictures by Swiss painters of the 17th–20th c. (including 25 portraits by Anton Graff of Winterthur), works by French artists from the Impressionists onwards (Van Gogh, Bonnard, Vuillard, Maillol) and by German artists (Marées, Corinth, Hofer). Also to be found here are the municipal *coin collection*, a *natural history museum* and the *Municipal Library*. – In the mansion of *Lindengut* (1787), at Römerstrasse 8, is a *Local Museum*, with the collections of the local Historical and Antiquarian Society. – To the N of the town, in Römerholz, is the *Oskar Reinhart Private Collection* (French painting of the 19th c., including works by Corot, Courbet, Daumier Delacroix, Manet, Renoir and Cézanne, and German, Dutch and Spanish old masters)*.

SURROUNDINGS. – To the S of the town is the wooded *Eschenberg* (585 m – 1919 feet), with an outlook tower. Game preserve.

Road 15 (the Rapperswil road) leads S to *Sennhof* (485 m – 1591 feet), from which a road runs W to the *Kyburg*, splendidly situated on a hill (634 m – 2080 feet). The castle, first mentioned in the 11th c., was restored in 1925 and now houses a historical museum; there is a fine view from the keep.

On the Frauenfeld road (No. 1) lies *Oberwinterthur* (445 m – 1460 feet), on the site of the Celtic and Roman settlement of *Vitodurum*. The Romanesque church (12th c.) has 14th c. wall-paintings. In the neighbouring village of *Hegi* is a moated castle of the 15th–18th c. (notable interior). – Road 1 passes under the motorway and comes to the village of *Sulz*. From here an interesting detour can be made to the castle of *Mörsburg*, with a Romanesque chapel (1250) and the museum of the Historical and Antiquarian Society of Winterthur (weapons, domestic utensils; Knights' Hall).

Yverdon

Canton: Vaud (VD).
Altitude: 435 m (1427 feet). – Population: 20,000.
Post code: CH-1400. – Dialling code: 024.
(i) **Association des Intérêts d'Yverdon,**
    1 Avenue Haldimand;
    tel. 21 55 21.

HOTELS. – *De la Prairie*, B, 75 b.; *De Londres*, D, 35 b.; *De l'Ange*, D, 35 b.; *Maison Blanche*, D, 24 b. – YOUTH HOSTEL. – CAMPING SITE.

EVENTS. – *Horse-races* (June–July).

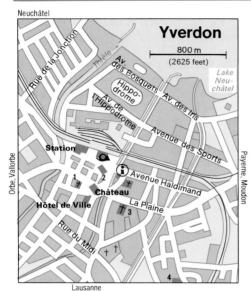

Neuchâtel

Yverdon

800 m
(2625 feet)

Lake Neu-châtel

Rue de la Jonction · *Thièle* · Av. des Bosquets · Hippo-drome · Av. de l'Hippodrome · Av. des Iris · Avenue des Sports

Station

Avenue Haldimand

Château

La Plaine

Hôtel de Ville

Rue du Midi

Orbe, Vallorbe · Payerne, Moudon

Lausanne

1 Parish church　2 Casino　3 German church　4 Centre Thermal

The old-world town of Yverdon, capital of northern Vaud, lies at the SW end of the Lac de Neuchâtel. From ancient times this has been an important traffic junction.

HISTORY. – Yverdon occupies the site of the Roman camp of *Eburodunum*. In the 13th c. the Dukes of Savoy built the massive castle. The famous education-alist Heinrich Pestalozzi ran a school in the castle from 1805 to 1825.

SIGHTS. – The 13th c. **Castle** (*Château*) of the Dukes of Savoy now houses a library, a *Historical Museum* (mementos of Pestalozzi) and a Science Fiction Museum (including the Pierre Versins collection). In the main square stands the *Hôtel de Ville* (Town Hall, 1769–73), on the W side of the square the *parish church* (1755–57).

The *Centre Thermal* (reconstructed 1977) contains the sulphurous spring (34 °C – 93 °F) which was used for curative purposes from Roman times.

SURROUNDINGS. – 7 km (4 miles) SE in the village of *Ursins* is the medieval church of St-Nicolas, built on the foundations of a Roman temple.

14 km (9 miles) SW by way of *Champvent*, with its imposing four-towered 13th c. *castle (no ad-mission), is the little country town of **Orbe** (479 m (1572 feet): pop. 4000), occupying the site of the Roman settlement of *Urba*. From the 7th to the 15th c. this was a fortified Burgundian stronghold. Church of Notre-Dame (15th–16th c.); tower of a castle which was destroyed in the 15th c.; Town Hall (1786).

A few kilometres N of Yverdon, on the W side of the Lac de Neuchâtel, we find the ancient town of

Grandson (439 m (1440 feet): pop. 2000), with a massive five-towered *castle of the 13th and 15th c. (private property, but open to visitors: visit recom-mended – Knights' Hall, armoury, museum, with veteran cars) and the Romanesque **church of St-Jean (12th c.: nave Carolingian, choir Gothic). In the Battle of Grandson on 2 March 1476 the Con-federates won their first victory over Charles the Bold, Duke of Burgundy, who lost the whole of his artillery and a rich treasure (now in the Historical Museum in Berne).

Yverdon to Payerne (30 km – 19 miles). – Leave on a road going E along the SE side of the Lac de Neuchâtel at some distance from the shore (marshy in places), from which there is an attractive view across the lake to Grandson. 19 km (12 miles) from Yverdon is the old-world little town of **Estavayer-le-Lac** (448 m (1470 feet): pop. 2500; Hôtel du Lac, C, 32 b.; bathing beach; Du Port, E, 10 b.; youth hostel; camping site), with arcaded houses, gate towers and the Late Gothic church of St-Laurent (beautiful choir-stalls of 1522). Above the town rears the large *Château de Chenaux* (13th and 15th c.). – 8 km (5 miles) SE of Estavayer is **Payerne** (452 m (1483 feet): Hôtel La Chaumière, E, 28 b.; camping site), a charming little town of 7000 inhabitants which was a frequent residence of the Burgundian kings in the 10th c. It has a former Benedictine abbey founded in the 10th c. by Adelheid, wife of the Emperor Otto I (dissolved 1536), and an 11th c. *church, a three-aisled pillared basilica which is one of the master-pieces of Romanesque architecture in Switzerland (excavations, including the tomb of Queen Bertha, d. before 1000; beautiful capitals; 12th c. wall-paintings in porch; chapterhouse). Adjoining the abbey church is the plain parish church (14th–16th c.: Protestant).

Zermatt

Canton: Valais (VS).
Altitude: 1620 m (5315 feet). – Population: 3000.
Post code: CH-3920. – Dialling code: 028.
ⓘ **Kur- und Verkehrsverein,**
　Zermatt;
　tel. 67 10 31.

HOTELS. – *Mont Cervin-Seilerhaus*, A, 215 b., SB; *Grand Hotel Zermatterhof*, A, 155 b., SB; *National-Bellevue*, B, 160 b., SP, sauna; *Parkhotel/Beau Site*, B, 120 b., SP; *Alex*, B, 110 b., SB; *Nicoletta*, B, 110 b., SB; *Monte Rosa*, B, 99 b.; *Pollux*, B, 65 b.; *Christiania* (no rest.), B, 70 b., SB; *Perren*, C, 120 b.; *Gornergrat*, C, 100 b.; *Schweizerhof*, C, 80 b.; *Biner* (no rest.), C, 80 b., SB; *Aparthotel Hermizeus*, C, 100 b.; *Julen* (with annexe), D, 72 b.; *Dom*, D, 70 b.; *Mischabel*, E, 55 b. – YOUTH HOSTEL. – Two CAMPING SITES.

RECREATION and SPORT. – Tennis (indoor and outdoor courts), swimming, walking; climbing school; heliport (helicopter station) at N end of town.

MOUNTAIN RAILWAYS, CABLEWAYS, etc. – Cog-railway up *Gornergrat* (9·34 km (6 miles), 45 minutes). Cableway from the Gornergrat station (restaurant) to the *Hohtäligrat* (3286 m (10,781 feet): restaurant; view) and *Stockhorn* (3532 m (11,588 feet): upper station 3407 m (11, 178)). – Cableway from Zermatt-Winkelmatten via *Furri* or *Furi* (1886 m (6188 feet): restaurant; to the S, at 1953 m (6408 feet), a "glacier garden") to the *Schwarzsee*, and via *Furri* and *Furgg* (2431 m – 7976 feet) to the *Trockener Steg* (2939 m (9643 feet: large restaurant), on the Upper Theodul glacier (Obertheodulgletscher). From the Trockener Steg there is a ski-lift to the *Furggsattel* (3365 m (11,041 feet): operates in summer as well as winter), on the Italian frontier. There is also a ski-lift via *Gandegg* to the *Theodul pass*, from which there is a lift to the *Testa Grigia* (3480 m – 11,418 feet). Daring* cableway from the Trockener Steg to the N face of the *Kleines Matterhorn* (3820 m – 12,533 feet); a lift to the summit of the Kleines Matterhorn is under construction. Cableway from Furgg to the Schwarzsee. – Funicular (1545 m – 5071 feet long in a tunnel, known as the "Alpine Underground Railway") from the centre of Zermatt to the *Sunnegga hut* (2289 m (7510 feet): restaurant), above Findeln; from there a cableway to *Blauherd* (2580 m (8465 feet): restaurant), and the *Unterrothorn* (3103 m – 10,181 feet); from Blauherd a cableway down to *Gant* (2180 m (7153 feet): ski-lift to the Platte, 2814 m (9233 feet); and from Blauherd a chair-lift (in winter) down to *Findeln* (2164 m – 7100 feet).

Zermatt, with the Matterhorn

WINTER SPORTS. – *Skiing areas* (all above Zermatt, between 2500 and 3500 m (8203 and 11,484 feet); many ski-lifts): Schwarzsee–Trockener Steg–Theodul, Riffelberg–Gornergrat–Stockhorn, Sunnegga–Blauherd–Unterrothorn. – *Summer skiing* on the *Breithorn plateau* (new cableway to Kleines Matterhorn) and the *Rosa plateau* (3500 m – 11,484 feet), on the Theodul pass. – Cross-country skiing and ski-trekking routes. – Two natural ice-rinks, numerous curling rinks.

The mountain village of *Zermatt (from "zur Matte", "on the mountain pasture") is the leading climbing and winter sports capital in the Valais and one of Switzerland's great international resorts. Nestled in a green valley enclosed between steeply scarped mountains, it is dominated by the "mountain of mountains", the huge and gracefully curved pyramid of the** Matterhorn. The Nikolai valley, at the head of which Zermatt lies, is open to cars

only as far as Täsch: Zermatt itself is without motor vehicles (local transport by horse-cabs). Between the old timber houses, weathered brown with age, are numerous hotels, all built in a style adapted to the setting. A cog-railway, several long cableways and numerous ski-lifts bring the various walking, climbing and winter sports areas within easy reach. There are magnificent long ski-runs.

HISTORY. – Until the end of the Middle Ages the glaciers were higher up and the tree-line was about 2600 m (8531 feet) so that the Theodul pass offered a fairly easy route through the mountains, and this was used from Roman times onwards. Zermatt itself is first recorded in 1218 under the Ladin name of *Prato-borgno*. By the 17th c. its hundred or so families had purchased their freedom from the landowners of the Rhône valley and formed a citizen body, to which after 1618 only the 19th c. hotelier Alexandre Seiler was admitted. The mountains around Zermatt were first mastered from 1830 onwards almost exclusively by British climbers, who were the first to climb 31 out of the 39 principal peaks (Breithorn 1830, Monte Rosa 1855, Matterhorn 1865). The famous climbers' hotel, the Monte Rosa, was opened in 1854, the railway from St Niklaus in 1891, the Gornergrat cog-railway in 1898. 1898 also saw the appearance of the first skier, but Zermatt's rise into a great winter sports resort did not really begin until 1927.

ACCESS. – The *road* from Visp, in the Rhône valley, is open to cars only as far as Täsch (30 km – 19 miles), which has a large parking area (fee) at the station. In winter, depending on weather conditions, it may be advisable to take the railway from Visp or St Niklaus. – The *railway* from Visp to Zermatt (the Brig-Visp-Zermatt or BVZ narrow-gauge electric line) runs alongside the road into the Saas valley. – 7 km (4 miles): *Stalden-Saas* (803 m (2635 feet): Hotel Victoria et de la Gare, E, 31 b.), at the junction of the *Saas valley* (through which flows the Saaser Vispa) and the *Nikolai valley* (Matter Vispa). The old timber houses in Valais style cluster round the white parish church, on higher ground. A cableway ascends the E side of the valley to *Staldenried* and the *Gspon* plateau (1893 m – 6211 feet); a road on the W side leads to the mountain village of *Törbel* (1491 m – 4892 feet), 8 km (5 miles) NW. – The Zermatt road now runs up the Nikolai valley through the *Kipfen gorge*. – 16 km (10 miles): **St Niklaus** (1130 m (3708 feet): Hotel La Réserve), the largest village in the Nikolai valley, closely hemmed in by mountains. It has a handsome parish church of 1964 with a medieval tower and three beautiful Baroque altars. – From St Niklaus a narrow and winding road climbs 8 km (5 miles) NE to **Grächen** (1617 m (5305 feet): Hotel Grächerhof & Schönegg, C, 60 b.; Gaedi, C, 50 b.; Elite, C, 48 b.), which stands on a commanding mountain terrace traversed by irrigation channels (*bisses*); it is a village which attracts both summer visitors and winter sports enthusiasts. Indoor swimming pool. Cableway to the *Hannigalp* (2110 m (6923 feet): skiing). – 26 km (16 miles): *Randa* (1410 m (4626 feet): Hotel Dom, D, 32 b.), at the foot of the Mischabel group. – 29 km (18 miles): **Täsch** (1449 m (4757 feet): Hotel Bellevue, C, 52 b.; Walliserhof, C, 68 b.; Täscherhof, C, 40 b.), a picturesque little village. – The peak of the Matterhorn now comes into sight.

SIGHTS. – The life of the resort is primarily on the main street, which runs from the station to the market square, with a charming contrast between hotels or elegant shops and old village houses. In the gardens of the Mont Cervin Hotel is a stone pyramid (1902) with marble plaques of Alexandre Seiler and his wife, to whom the development of Zermatt as a resort was due. Here, too, is the very interesting **Alpine Museum**, with an extensive display of material on the climbing of the mountains around Zermatt. Above this are the guides' and ski school office and the *English church* (1871), built by the Alpine Club (founded 1857), which has the graves of climbers in the churchyard. Farther up the village is the *Monte Rosa Hotel* (1854), for 30 years the headquarters of all climbers in Zermatt, which has preserved much of its original character. A bronze plaque (1925) commemorates Edward Whymper, who made a series of attempts on the Matterhorn between 1860 and 1865. – The trim little *parish church* to the left of the hotel dates from 1576.

Around the market square are the *Gemeindehaus* (communal council house) and six characteristic old village houses, on one of which is a tablet commemorating Whymper's guides, the two Taugwalders (father and son). Here, too, is the charming *Marmot fountain* (1902). The handsome *church* (St Maurice) was rebuilt in 1914, with a tower modelled on that of the earliest church. At the bridge over the Vispa, on a strip of land between that river and its tributary the Triftbach, is the *cemetery*, with the graves of many climbers who met their deaths on the mountains, including Whymper's guide Michel Croz and his companion Hadow. Higher up in the village a few of the old larch-wood storehouses still survive, with large circular slabs of stone on the supporting posts to deter mice.

SURROUNDINGS. – **Ascent of the Gornergrat:** The *cog-railway climbs the E side of the valley, crosses the *Findelnbach* on a high bridge and then runs through the curving Unteralp tunnel. – 4 km (2 miles): *Riffelalp* (2213 m – 7261 feet), with a superb view of the Gabelhorn group. The line continues up the slopes of the Riffelberg in a wide curve, with ever more impressive views of the Matterhorn. – 6 km (4 miles): *Riffelberg* (2582 m (8472 feet): Hotel Riffelberg, D, 60 b.). – 7·5 km (5 miles): *Rotenboden* (2819 m – 9249 feet). A few minutes' walk below the station is the *Riffelsee*, with the pyramidal peak of the Matterhorn mirrored in its water (particularly fine in the morning). – The line then runs high above the

Gorner glacier to the summit station (9 km (6 miles), 3089 m (10,135 feet): Kulmhotel, D, 50 b.), 5 minutes' climb from the famous** **Gornergrat** (3130 m (10,270 feet): observatory), a rocky ridge rearing above the *Gorner glacier* from which there is one of the most magnificent panoramas in the whole of the Alps: in the middle the Matterhorn, with the Breithorn, the Zwillinge ("Twins" – Castor and Pollux), the Lyskamm and Monte Rosa to the left; to the N the peaks of the Mischabel group, including the Dom (4545 m – 14,912 feet), the highest purely Swiss mountain; and to the W the mountains between the Zermatt valley and the Zinal valley.

The** **Matterhorn** (French *Mont Cervin*, Italian *Monte Cervino*: 4478 m (14,692 feet)) was first climbed on 14 July 1865 by a British team consisting of Edward Whymper, Charles Hudson, Lord Francis Douglas and Douglas Hadow, with Michel Croz and the two Peter Taugwalders, father and son, as guides. On the way down, 400 m (1312 feet) below the summit, Hadow slipped and fell on to the Matterhorn glacier, dragging Hudson, Douglas and Croz with him; Whymper and the Taugwalders were saved by the breaking of the rope. The ascent of the Matterhorn from Zermatt is not now regarded as anything out of the ordinary, being achieved by something like 3000 people every summer, but should be attempted only by experienced climbers (4½–6 hours from the Hörnli hut). Whymper climbed the Swiss or Hörnli Ridge; the Italian or SW Ridge was climbed a few days later by a guide named Carrell, the Zmutt Ridge in 1879, the difficult Furgg Ridge in 1911. The W face was climbed in 1927, the ice-covered N face and the S face in 1931 and the E face in 1932; the first winter climb of the N face was made in 1962.

Walks. – There is a very fine walk down from the Gornergrat to Zermatt (3½ hours): first a steep descent (1½ hours) to the *Glacier Findeln* restaurant (2298 m – 7540 feet), from which it is a 45 minutes' walk up the valley to the steeply descending *Findeln glacier; then another hour's walk down to Zermatt by way of the summer village of *Findeln* (2164 m (7100 feet): chair-lift in winter to the Sunnegga hut), where it is still possible to grow corn. – ½–1 hours S of Zermatt are the *Gorner gorges*, through which the Matter Vispa, flowing down from the Gorner glacier, pursues its tumultuous course.

*Zermatt to the Schwarzsee** (3 hours: cableway). – The route follows the left bank of the Vispa and then the Zmuttbach, in ¼ hour crosses the stream (magnificent view of the Matterhorn), and continues by way of the *Zum See* (1763 m – 5784 feet) and *Hermettji* huts (2027 m – 6651 feet) to the **Schwarzseehotel** (2583 m (8475 feet): D, 16 b.), from which there are superb panoramic *views. A few minutes' walk below is the little *Schwarzsee* (2552 m – 8373 feet), with the guides' chapel of *Maria zum See* (18th c.). 2½ hours higher up are the *Belvédère* mountain inn (3263 m (10,706 feet): E, 10 b.) and the *Hörnli hut* (3260 m (10,696 feet): 50 sleeping places), starting-point for the ascent of the Matterhorn. An hour's walk to the NW, lower down, is the Staffelalp.

To the Staffelalp (2¼ hours). – 20 minutes above the Zum See huts on the road to the Schwarzsee take a

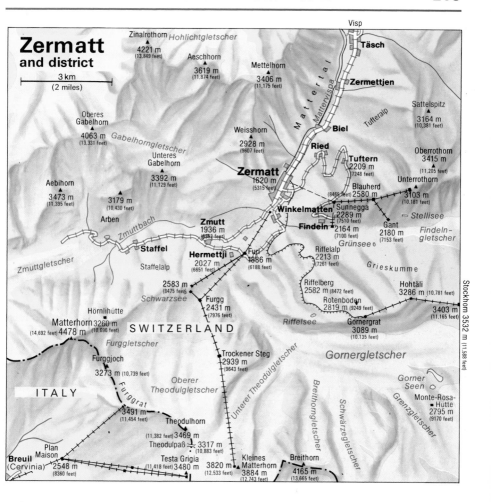

Zermatt and district

3 km (2 miles)

Visp

Täsch

Zinalrothorn 4221 m (13,849 feet)

Hohlichtgletscher

Aeschhorn 3619 m (11,874 feet)

Mettelhorn 3406 m (11,175 feet)

Zermettjen

Sattelspitz 3164 m (10,381 feet)

Oberes Gabelhorn 4063 m (13,331 feet)

Gabelhorngletscher

Weisshorn 2928 m (9607 feet)

Mattertal / Mattervispa

Biel

Tufteralp

Ried

Unteres Gabelhorn 3392 m (11,129 feet)

Zermatt 1620 m (5315 feet)

Tuftern 2209 m (7248 feet)

Oberrothorn 3415 m (11,205 feet)

Aebihorn 3473 m (11,395 feet)

3179 m (10,430 feet)

Blauherd 2580 m (8465 feet)

Unterrothorn 3103 m (10,181 feet)

Arben

Zmuttbach

Zmutt 1936 m (6352 feet)

Winkelmatten

Sunnegga 2289 m (7510 feet)

Stellisee

Findeln 2164 m (7100 feet)

Gant 2180 m (7153 feet)

Findeln-gletscher

Staffel

Staffelalp

Hermettji 2027 m (6651 feet)

Furi 1886 m (6188 feet)

Grünsee

Grieskumme

Riffelalp 2213 m (7261 feet)

Zmuttgletscher

2583 m (8475 feet)

Schwarzsee

Furgg 2431 m (7976 feet)

Riffelberg 2582 m (8472 feet)

Rotenboden 2819 m (9249 feet)

Hohtäli 3286 m (10,781 feet)

3403 m (11,165 feet)

Hörnlihütte

Matterhorn 4478 m (14,692 feet) 3260 m (10,696 feet)

SWITZERLAND

Riffelsee

Gornergrat 3089 m (10,135 feet)

Stockhorn 3532 m (11,588 feet)

Furggletscher

Trockener Steg 2939 m (9643 feet)

Unterer Theodulgletscher

Gornergletscher

Furggjoch 3273 m (10,739 feet)

Furggrat

Oberer Theodulgletscher

Gorner Seen

Breithorngletscher

Monte-Rosa-Hutte 2795 m (9170 feet)

Grenzgletscher

ITALY

Theodulhorn 3469 m (11,382 feet)

Theodulpaß 3317 m (10,883 feet)

Schwärzegletscher

Plan Maison

Breuil (Cervinia) 2548 m (8360 feet)

Testa Grigia 3480 m (11,418 feet)

Kleines Matterhorn 3884 m (12,743 feet)

3820 m (12,533 feet)

Breithorn 4165 m (13,665 feet)

---

road on the right which ascends through beautiful mountain forests, high up on the right bank of the Zmuttbach, to the *Staffelalp (2206 m (7238 feet): restaurant), with a magnificent view of the Matterhorn and the Zmutt glacier, littered with rock debris. The Zmuttbach has been dammed and harnessed to produce electric power.

To the Theodul pass (5–5½ hours, with guide: cableway). – First 1¼ hours to *Hermettji*; then in another 2¼ hours, at the moraine of the *Upper Theodul glacier* (Oberer Theodulgletscher, 2713 m (8901 feet)), either with a rope directly across the much-crevassed glacier to the pass (2 hours) or via the *Gandegg hut* (3029 m (9938 feet): 1 hour) and over the glacier (1¼ hours) to the pass. The **Theodul pass** (*Matterjoch*, 3317 m (10,883 feet)), which was already in use before the 4th c. A.D., lies on the frontier with Italy (magnificent views). From nearby *Testa Grigia* a cableway runs down to *Breuil-Cervinia* in Italy. – *Climbs* from the Theodul pass: the *Breithorn (4165 m (13,665 feet) 3 hours, with guide; fine view); the *Kleines Matterhorn* (3884 m (12,743 feet): cableway).

*Monte Rosa. – From the *Rotenboden* station (2819 m – 9249 feet) on the Gornergrat railway it is a 2 hours' walk to the *Monte Rosa hut* (2795 m – 9170 feet); from there 6–6½ hours, with guide, to the **Dufourspitze* (4634 m – 15,204 feet), the highest peak in the Monte Rosa massif and in Switzerland, with one of the most breathtaking panoramas in the Alps.

Zug

Canton: Zug (ZG).
Altitude: 426 m (1398 feet). – Population: 24,000.
Post code: CH-6300. – Dialling code: 042.

(i) **Verkehrsverband des Kantons Zug,**
Offizielles Verkehrsbüro, Bahnhofstrasse 23;
tel. 21 00 78.

HOTELS. – *City-Hotel Ochsen,* Kolinplatz, C, 60 b.; *Guggital,* Zugerbergstrasse, C, 52 b.; *Rosenberg,* Rosenbergstrasse 38, C, 62 b.; *Löwen au Lac,* Landsgemeindeplatz, D, 35 b.; *Rössli,* Vorstadt 8, D, 30 b.; *Central,* Grabenstrasse 9, E, 20 b. – YOUTH HOSTEL. – CAMP SITE.

RECREATION and SPORTS. – Riding, tennis (indoor and outdoor courts), swimming, fishing, skating, cross-country skiing.

Zug, capital of the canton of the same name, lies at the NE end of the Zuger See (Lake Zug), above which rises the flat-topped ridge of the Zugerberg. The local kirsch (Zuger Kirschwasser) is famous.

SIGHTS. – From the lakeside promenade there is a fine *view of the Rigi, Pilatus and

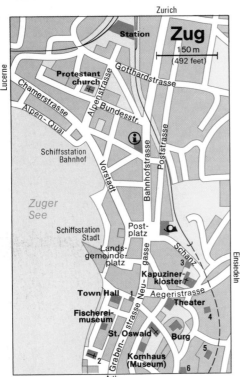

Zurich

Zug
150 m
(492 feet)

Lucerne

Station

Protestant church

Gotthardstrasse

Chamerstrasse

Alpenstrasse

Bundesstr.

Alpen-Quai

Schiffsstation
Bahnhof

Vorstadt

Bahnhofstrasse

Poststrasse

Zuger
See

Schiffsstation
Stadt

Post-
platz

Lands-
gemeinde-
platz

gasse

Schanz

Kapuziner-
kloster

Town Hall

Neu-gasse

Aegeristrasse

Fischerei-
museum

strasse

Theater

St. Oswald

Burg

Graben-

Kornhaus
(Museum)

Einsiedeln

Arth

1 Zytturm (Clock tower)
2 Liebfrauenkapelle (chapel of
   Our Lady)
3 Kapuzinerturm (Capuchin
   tower)

4 Knopfliturm
5 Huwlyerturm
6 Pulverturm (Powder tower)

the Bernese Alps (Eiger, Mönch, Jung-frau). It is a short distance by way of the Fischmarkt into the old town with its handsome burghers' houses and fountains. In the **Rathaus** (Town Hall, completed 1505) is a fine Gothic hall. From here a gateway under the picturesque *Zytturm* ("Time Tower", with an astronomical clock) leads into Kolinplatz with a fountain commemorating Wolfgang Kolin, who fell at the Battle of Arbedo against the Milanese (1422). To the S is the Late Gothic **St Oswald's church** (1478–1545: beautiful doorway, richly decorated interior), and near this the so-called *Burg* (Castle), once the residence of a Habsburg governor.

NE of Kolinplatz is the *Capuchin friary* (Kapuzinerkloster), with a church of 1676. At Aegeristrasse 56 is the *Cantonal Museum of Prehistory*, and in Untergasse a *Fishery Museum* (Fischereimuseum: seen by appointment). On the E side of the town are four towers and remains of walls, relics of the old fortifications. The old *Kornhaus* (Corn Exchange, 15th c.), in the lower part of the old town, now houses a museum of art (occasional special exhibitions).

SURROUNDINGS. – To the SE of the town is the **Zugerberg** (988 m – 3242 feet), with pleasant woodland walks and views of the Alps, particularly from the *Hochwacht*. It can be reached either by the direct road up the hill (9 km – 6 miles) or by driving via *Guggithal* to *Schönegg* (3 km – 2 miles) and taking the funicular (2 km (1 mile), 8 minutes). On the top stands the Zugerberg Hotel (E, 8 b.).

5 km (3 miles) W on the Lucerne road (No. 4) we come to *Cham* (421 m (1381 feet); pop. 6500; Hotel Raben, D, 16 b.), at the junction of several roads. The church, built in 1786, has a slender steeple added in 1853. By the lake is the Schloss St Andreas, with a chapel of 1488 built on Carolingian foundations. – 3 km (2 miles) N of Zug is the little industrial town (textiles) of **Baar** (447 m (1467 feet): Hotel Lindenhof). In the main street are the fine parish church of St Martin (14th c., rebuilt in 1771), with a massive Romanesque tower (Baroque helm roof), and the Town Hall (1676). In the cemetery stands a Late Gothic chapel (1507). An attractive excursion (7 km (4 miles) SE) can be made over a hill covered with fruit-trees and the deep Lorzentobel gorge to the *Höllgrotten* ("Caves of Hell": restaurant), with magnificent stalactitic formations.

To the Ägerisee, Schwyz and Arth (13 km (8 miles) to Oberägeri; 29 km (18 miles) to Schwyz, 4 km (2 miles) more than the main road via Arth). – Leave Zug on a secondary road which runs E to *Thalacker* and crosses the *Lorze gorge* on a high bridge. – 5 km (3 miles): *Nidfurren* (654 m – 2146 feet). The road continues along the E side of the Lorze valley. – 5 km (3 miles): *Unterägeri* (729 m (2392 feet): Hotel Seefeld, C, 70 b.), a busy little village and holiday spot at the N end of the charming **Ägerisee** (725 m (2379 feet): 5·5 km (3 miles) long). The road runs along the NE side of the lake. – 3 km (2 miles): **Oberägeri** (737 m (2418 feet): Hotel Gulm, D, 35 b.), a village of 3500 inhabitants which is also a holiday resort. The road then crosses a low ridge which forms the boundary between the cantons of Zug and Schwyz, and on 15 November 1315 was the scene of the Battle of *Morgarten*, the Swiss Confederates' first victory over the Habsburgs. On the shores of the lake is the Morgarten monument (1908), and on the pass are the Schlachtkapelle (Battle chapel) of 1603 and a defensive tower of 1320. – 7 km (4 miles): **Sattel** (827 m – 2713 feet), on the road from Pfäffikon,

Town Hall, Zug

which continues S to **Schwyz** (9 km (6 miles): bypass): see p. 222. – Alternatively take a road which branches off on the right in Sattel and winds its way down the southern slopes of the Rossberg (fine views of the Rigi and the Mythen), passing through the hamlet of *Ecce Homo* (735 m (2412 feet): chapel of 1667) and the village of *Steinerberg* (629 m (2064 feet): pilgrimage church of 1570), and then continues past the scene of a great landslide at Goldau to **Arth** (11 km – 7 miles).

The beautiful *Zuger See* or *Lake Zug* (alt. 417 m (1368 feet): length 14 km (9 miles), area 38 sq. km (15 sq. miles), greatest depth 198 m (650 feet)) extends S from Zug, its N end surrounded by gentle hills, its S end enclosed between the steep scarps of the Rossberg and the Rigi (see p. 203).

2·5 km (2 miles) S of Zug on the E side of the lake is *Zug-Oberwil* (420 m (1378 feet): Hotel Adler, D, 33 b.), beautifully situated at the foot of the Zugerberg. The road continues along the lower slopes of the hill, with views across the lake to Schloss Buonas (15th and 17th c.), the village of Risch and the long promontory of Kiemen. In 4 km (2 miles) it passes the *Lothenbach* restaurant, where the stream of that name flows into the lake (waterfall) and continues through two short tunnels to **Walchwil** (445 m (1460 feet): Hotel Zugersee, C, 28 b.; Aesch, E, 65 b.), a popular holiday village picturesquely set on the lake amid vineyards and chestnut groves.

The road then enters the canton of Schwyz and continues along the foot of the Rossberg, with magnificent views of the Rigi across the lake; to the right can be seen Immensee, with the "Hohle Gasse" (p. 153). Arth comes into view ahead. – At the S end of the lake is **Arth am See** (420 m (1378 feet): Seehotel Adler, C, 85 b., SB), a town of 3000 inhabitants at an important road junction, with a late 17th c. Baroque church. From the Arth-Goldau station a cog-railway ascends the ** *Rigi* (p. 203). – For the SW shore of the Zuger See and Immensee, see p. 153.

Zurich

Canton: Zurich (ZH).
Altitude: 410 m (1345 feet). – Population: 369,000.
Post code: CH-8000. – Dialling code: 01.
(i) **Schweizerische Verkehrszentrale,**
Bellariastrasse 38,
CH-8027 Zurich;
tel. 2 02 37 37.
Offizielles Verkehrsbüro
(information, accommodation register),
Bahnhofplatz 15, Hauptbahnhof,
tel. 2 11 40 00.
Verkehrsverein Zurich,
Direktion, Kongressbüro,
Bahnhofbrücke 1,
CH-8023 Zurich;
tel. 2 11 12 56.

HOTELS. – ON OR NEAR LAKE: *Baur au Lac*, Talstrasse 1 (Bürkliplatz), A, 225 b., SP; *Eden au Lac*, Utoquai 45, A, 75 b.; *Europe* (no rest.), Dufourstrasse 4, A, 65 b.; *Glärnischhof*, Claridenstrasse 30, B, 130 b.; *Bellerive au Lac*, Utoquai 47, B, 90 b.; *Splügen-schloss*, Splügenstrasse 2, B, 75 b.; *Schifflände*, Schifflände 18, B, 40 b.; *Opera* (no rest.), Dufourstrasse 5,

B, 100 b.; *Excelsior*, Dufourstrasse 24, B, 63 b.; *Helmhaus* (no rest.), Schiffländeplatz 30, B, 50 b.; *Ascot*, Lavaterstrasse 15, at Enge railway station, B, 110 b., SP; *Plaza*, Goethestrasse 18, C, 120 b.; *Ambassador*, Falkenstrasse 6, C, 70 b.; *Neues Schloss*, Stockerstrasse 17, C, 97 b.; *Florida*, Seefeldstrasse 63, C, 150 b.; *Im Park*, Kappelistrasse 41/Seestrasse 220, C, 100 b.; *Seegarten-Bolognese*, Seegartenstrasse 14, C, 40 b.; *Breitinger* (no rest.), Breiteingerstrasse 20, C, 30 b.

IN THE CENTRAL CITY: *Savoy Baur en Ville*, Poststrasse 12, at Paradeplatz, A, 150 b.; *Carlton Elite*, Bahnhofstrasse 41, B, 115 b.; *Storchen*, Weinplatz 2, on the Limmat, B, 115 b.; *Glockenhof*, Sihlstrasse 31, B, 166 b.; *Kindli* (no rest.), Pfalzgasse 1, at Limmathof, B, 35 b.; *Amman* (no rest.), Kirchgasse 4–6, at Grossmünster, B, 37 b.; *Zürcherhof* (no rest.), Zähringerstrasse, 21, B, 50 b.; *Alexander* (no rest.), at Post Office, B, 82 b.; *Scheuble* (no rest.), Mühlgasse 17, B, 110 b.; *Chesa Rustica*, Limmatquai 70, C, 45 b.; *Franziskaner*, Stüssihofstatt 1, C, 42 b.; *City*, Löwenstrasse 34, C, 100 b.; *Seidenhof* (no alcohol), Sihlstrasse 9, C, 142 b.; *Basilea*, Zähringerstrasse 25, C, 75 b.; *Adler*, Rosengasse 10, C, 70 b.; *Goldenes Schwert*, Marktgasse 14, C, 65 b.; *Krone Limmatquai*, Limmatquai 88, D, 38 b.

NEAR THE MAIN STATION: *Schweizerhof*, Bahnhofplatz 7, B, 160 b.; *St Gotthard*, Bahnhofstrasse 87, B, 200 b.; *Continental*, Stampfenbachstrasse 60, B, 250 b.; *Simplon* (no rest.), Schützengasse 16, C, 115 b.; *Central*, Am Central, C, 100 b.; *Trümpy*, Limmatstrasse 5, C, 143 b.; *Du Théâtre* (no rest.), Seilergraben 69, C, 85 b.; *Montana* (no rest.), Konradstrasse 39, C, 60 b.; *Limmathof*, Limmatquai 142, D, 80 b.

E OF STATION AND IN UNIVERSITY QUARTER: *Florhof*, Florhofgasse 4, C, 56 b.; *Rigihof*, Universitätsstrasse 101, C, 115 b.; *Royal* (no rest.), Leonhardstrasse 6, C, 88 b.; *Leoneck,* Leonhardstrasse 1, C, 90 b.; *Poly* (no rest.), Universitätsstrasse 63, C, 65 b.; *Jura*, Stampfenbachstrasse 26, C, 44 b.; *Bristol* (no rest.), Stampfenbachstrasse 34, D, 100 b.

N OF STATION: *Zürich*, Neumühlequai 42, A, 400 b., SB; *Astor*, Weinbergstrasse 44, C, 80 b.; *Waldorf*, Weinbergstrasse 45, C, 70 b.; *Rex* (no rest.), Weinbergstrasse 92, C, 58 b.

W OF STATION: *Nova-Park*, Badenerstrasse 420, B, 1000 b., SB; *Stoller*, Badenerstrasse 357, C, 150 b.; *Goldener Brunnen*, Rotachstrasse 33, C, 40 b.; *Olympia*, Badenerstrasse 324, C, 70 b.; *Limmathaus*, Limmatstrasse 118, D, 100 b.; *Rothaus*, Langstrasse 121, D, 80 b.; *Regina*, Hohlstrasse 18, D, 102 b.

ON SCHAFFHAUSEN ROAD: *Coronado*, Schauffhauserstrasse 137, C, 68 b.; *Krone-Unterstrass*, Schaffhauserstrasse 1, C, 82 b.

ON CHUR ROAD (N 3): *Engematthof*, Engimattstrasse 14, C, 100 b., tennis.

IN OERLIKON: *International*, Am Marktplatz, B, 700 b., SB; *Sternen Oerlikon*, Schaffhauserstrasse 335, C, 80 b.

ON ZÜRICHBERG: *Dolder Grand Hotel*, Kurhausstrasse 65, A, 300 b., SP, tennis, golf; *Waldhaus Dolder*, Kurhausstrasse 20, B, 114 b., SP, tennis, golf; *Sonnenberg*, Aurorastrasse 98, C, 70 b.; *Zürichberg* (no alcohol), Orellistrasse 21, D, 85 b.

Zurich – old town and central city

AT FOOT OF UETLIBERG: *Atlantis Sheraton*, Dölt-schiweg 234, A, 320 b., SB; *Guesthouse Atlantis* (no rest.), Döltschihalde 49, B, 100 b.

AT ZURICH AIRPORT (KLOTEN): *Zürich Hilton*, Hohen-bühlstrasse 10, A, 560 b., SB; *Mövenpick Holiday Inn*, Mittelholzerstrasse 8, B, 576 b., SB; *Welcome-Inn*, Holbergstrasse 1, C, 190 b., SP; *Airport*, Ober-hausenstrasse 30, C, 70 b.

IN REGENSDORF (12 km (7 miles) NW of central city): *Holiday Inn* and *Mövenpick*, Watterstrasse, C, 262 b.; SB.

YOUTH HOSTEL. – Zürich-Wollishofen, Mutschellen-strasse 114, 450 b.

CAMPING SITE. – *Seebucht*, Zürich-Wollishofen, on the lake.

RESTAURANTS. – *Kronenhalle* (popular with artists: Swiss specialties), Rämistrasse 4, near Opera; *Zunfthaus zur Schmiden*, Marktgasse 20, *Zunfthaus zur Waag*, Münsterhof 8, *Zunfthaus zur Saffran*, Limmatquai 54, *Zunfthaus zur Zimmerleuten*, Lim-matquai 40, *Zunfthaus zum Rüden*, Limmatquai 42, *Zunfthaus am Neumarkt*, Neumarkt 5, all excellent; *Baron de la Mouette* (elegant), Mövenpick-Dreikönigshaus, Beethovenstrasse 2; *Conti* (theatri-cal people: French cuisine), Dufourstrasse 1; *Au Premier* (railway buffet: ten restaurants with seating for 2000), at the station; *Widder* (old established), Widdergasse 6; *Le Dézaley* (Vaudois specialties), Römergasse 7, near Grossmünster; *Lindenhofkeller* (friendly atmosphere), Pfalzgasse 4; *Haxenstube* (good plain cooking), Schweizergasse 2; *Mövenpick Paradeplatz*, in Paradeplatz; *Kongresshaus*, Klariden-strasse 3; *Mère Catherine* (country atmosphere),

Rüdenplatz 8; *Augustiner* (good plain cooking) Augustinergasse 25; *Oepfelchammer*, Rindermarkt *Zum Roten Gatter* (French cuisine), Schifflände 6 *Casa Ferlin* (Italian), Stampfenbachstrasse 38; *Com-mercio*, Mühlebachstrasse 2; *Accademia Piceol* (Italian), Rotwandstrasse 48; *Emilio* (Spanish) Müllerstrasse 5; *Hong Kong* (Chinese), See-feldstrasse 60; *Hiltl Vegi*, Sihlstrasse 28, *Gleich* Seefeldstrasse 9, both vegetarian; *Schalom* (kosher) Lavaterstrasse 37; *Bauschänzli*, on Limmat, nea Bürkliplatz (summer only); *Fischstube Zürichhorn* 160 Bellerivestrasse (summer only); and many more.

CAFÉS. – *Sprüngli*, Paradeplatz; *Grand Café*, Lim-matquai and Löwenstrasse; *In Gassen*, In Gassen 6 *Schober*, Napfgasse 4.

EVENTS. – *Sechseläuten* ("Six o'Clock Ringing") with children's and guild processions: April); *Spring Festival* (concerts: April–May); *International June Festival Weeks* (cultural events); *Knabenschiessen* (boys' shooting competition, with fair: second weekend in September, in Albisgütli); exhibitions and trade fairs in Züspa-Hallen, Oerlikon.

SHOPPING. – Zurich's Bahnhofstrasse has long been a particularly attractive shopping area, with elegant shops offering a tempting array of goods (particularly jewelry and watches). Swiss-made souvenirs can be bought in the Schweizer Heimatwerk shops at Rudolf-Brun-Brücke, Bahnhofstrasse 2, Rennweg 14 and the airport. Most of the antique dealers are to be found in the old town, between the Lindenhof and the Grossmünster.

FLEA-MARKET. – In Bürkliplatz, 9 to 4 on Saturday (May–October).

RECREATION and SPORTS. – Sailing on the lake; boating on the Limmat; football stadiums at Letzigrund and Hardturm; covered stadium and open racetrack in Oerlikon; Allmend Sports Hall in Wiedikon; Dolder swimming pool (artificial waves) and ice-rink; municipal swimming pools (indoor) at Sihlporte and in Oerlikon.

*Zurich (German spelling Zürich), Switzerland's largest city and capital of the canton of Zurich, is also the country's economic and cultural hub; but with all its bustling activity it is still one of the handsomest of Swiss towns, with carefully cherished traditions and much to attract and interest the visitor. The town lies at the lower north-western end of Lake Zurich astride the River Limmat, which flows out of the lake at this point, between the Uetliberg on the W and the Zürichberg on the E. It has both a University and the Federal College of Technology. Three of the five major Swiss banks have their head offices in the famous Bahnhofstrasse, one of the finest shopping streets in Europe. Zurich is also a great financial and industrial capital (mainly textiles, engineering and electrical equipment). In addition it is Switzerland's leading tourist attraction, with something like a million visitors a year. A fifth of the country's total national income is earned in Zurich.

One of Europe's most important newspapers, the "Neue Zürcher Zeitung", is published in Zurich. Founded in 1780 by Salomon Gessner, it now has an editorial staff of 100 and a circulation of some 120,000.

Zurich is also the most important focus of communications in Switzerland. It has the country's largest airport; its railway station is on the great international through routes from Vienna and Munich to southern France and Spain and from Stuttgart to Milan; and a number of motorways meet at the city. The motorways all end, however, at the city boundary, since the citizens of Zurich – who have a large say in the matter – have been unable to agree on the line of an urban motorway. As a result all through traffic has to find its way through the city, which can be very time-consuming.

The city of Zurich has a total area of 92 sq. km (36 sq. miles). The population in 1892, before the incorporation of suburban communes, was 87,400. In 1960 the population of the enlarged city had risen to 440,170 – its highest point – but

by 1979 it had fallen to 378,375 (720,000 for the whole urban region). Less than half the resident population belong to the canton of Zurich. Until the end of the 18th c. the population of Zurich was almost entirely Protestant, but by 1979 the proportion of Roman Catholics had reached almost 40%, giving Zurich the largest number of Catholics of any town in Switzerland.

Since 1830 Zurich has been capital of the **canton of Zurich**, the seventh largest of the Swiss cantons in terms of area (1729 sq. km – 668 sq. miles) and the largest of them all in terms of population (1,123,000). Situated in the Swiss Mittelland, it has a green and gentle landscape, reaching its lowest point in the Rhine valley (330 m – 1083 feet) and its highest in the Schnebelhorn (1292 m – 4239 feet). It has much to offer the visitor, with its charming little towns and trim villages, its beautiful countryside and well-kept vineyards.

HISTORY. – The earliest traces of human occupation on the site of Zurich were a Neolithic settlement excavated on the Bauschänzli, the little island in the River Limmat. The Roman fortified settlement of *Turicum* was established on the Lindenhof, where there had been a Roman military station as early as 15 B.C. According to the legendary story the town's patron saints Felix and Regula fled to Zurich with the Theban Legion and were beheaded there; their remains were preserved in the Grossmünster (begun not later than the 9th c.). The works of Hartmann von der Aue and the poems by other medieval minnesingers preserved in the Manesse Manuscript (written in Zurich but now in the University Library, Heidelberg) are a reminder of the great days of chivalry. The development of Zurich into a city state was given a considerable stimulus when the guilds obtained equal rights with the nobility after an assault on the Town Hall in 1336, and in 1351 it became a member of the Confederation. In 1523 Ulrich Zwingli (1484–1531) established the Reformation in Switzerland and made Zurich one of the great cities of the Reformed faith, ranking equally with Wittenberg and Geneva. The town rose to prosperity through its silk and cotton industries; but when a federal state was established in the 19th c. the status of capital passed from Zurich to Berne. In the 18th c. Zurich became influential in intellectual life, with such figures as the theologian Johann Caspar Lavater, the educationalist Heinrich Pestalozzi, the great scholar Johann Jakob Bodmer and the writer Salomon Gessner. During the 19th and 20th c. the town continued to be a pivotal point of liberal thought, and among the notable personalities who stayed here were Gottfried Keller, Conrad Ferdinand Meyer, Georg Büchner, August Bebel, Lenin, James Joyce, C. G. Jung, Ludwig Klages and Thomas Mann. In 1916 the Dadaist school was founded in Zurich. In 1980 and 1981 serious confrontations occurred between young people and police (including the occupation and clearance of a youth centre). In June 1982 the autonomous Youth Centre of Zurich was closed.

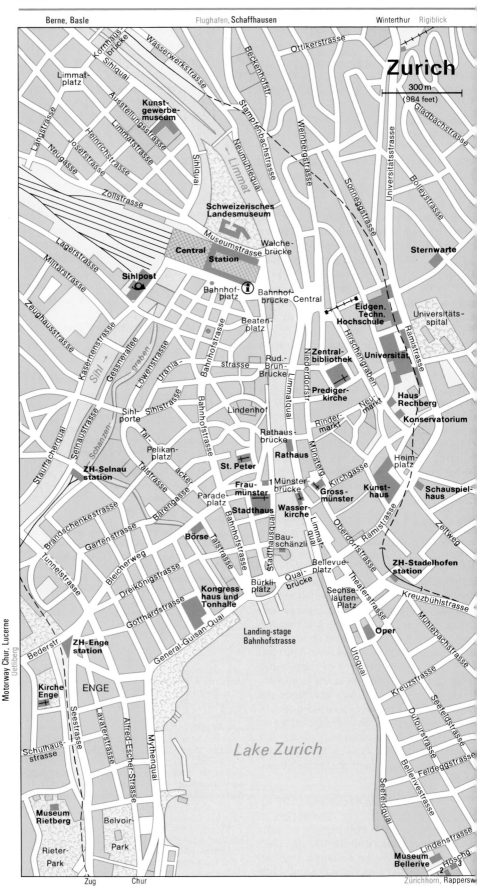

Berne, Basle   Flughafen, Schaffhausen   Winterthur   Rigiblick

Zurich

300 m
(984 feet)

1 Zunfthaus zur Meisen   2 Centre Le Corbusier   3 Studio of Hermann Halle

Museums, Galleries, etc.

Opening Times

Art Gallery (Kunsthaus)
(Painting, sculpture, graphic art: mainly 19th and 20th c.)
Heimplatz 1;
Tue.–Fri. 10–9,
Sat. and Sun. 10–5, Mon. 2–5.
Library
Tue.–Fri. 10–12 and 2–6,
Sat. 10–4,
Closed Sun. and Mon.

Bärengasse Museum of Domestic Life (Wohnmuseum)
(Zurich domestic interiors of the 17th and 18th c.;
Sasha Morgenthaler Puppet Museum)
Bärengasse 22;
Tue.–Sun. 10–12 and 2–5,
Mon. 2–5.

Bellerive Museum
(Applied and decorative art of the past and present)
Höschgasse 3;
Tue., Thu. and Fri 10–5, Wed. 10–9,
Sat. and Sun. 10–12 and 2–5.

Bührle Collection
(French Impressionists, medieval sculpture)
Zollikerstrasse 172;
Tue. and Fri. 2–5.

Central Library (Zentralbibliothek)
Zähringerplatz 6;
Mon.–Fri. 8 a.m. to 8 p.m., Sat. 8–5,
closed Sun.
Exhibitions in choir of Predigerkirche,
Predigerplatz 33;
Tue.–Fri. 1–5, Thu. until 9,
Sat. 10–5,
closed Sun. and Mon.

Federal College of Technology (Eidgenössische Technische Hochschule)
Geological and Mineralogical Collections,
Sonneggstrasse 5;
Mon.–Fri. 10–7, Sat. 10–4,
closed Sun.
Collection of Graphic Art
(entrance in Künstlergasse);
Mon.–Sat. 10–12 and 2–5, exhibitions also Sun. 10–12.

Haus zum Kiel
(Special exhibitions)
Hirschengraben 20;
Tue.–Fri. 2–7, Thu. until 9,
Sat. and Sun. 2–5.

Helmhaus
(Special exhibitions)
Limmatquai 31;
Tue.–Sun. 10–6, Thu. also 8–10,
closed Mon.

INK *(Halle für internationale neue Kunst)*
(Contemporary art)
Limmatstrasse 87;
daily 10–6.

Municipal Collection of Succulents (Städtische Sukkulentensammlung)
(Cactuses and other succulents)
Mythenquai 88;
Daily 9–11.30 and 1.30–4.30.
Guided tours by arrangement.

Municipal Gardens Department Show (Schauhäuser der Stadtgärtnerei)
Sackzelg 25–27;
daily 9–11.30 and 2–5.

Museum of Decorative Arts (Kunstgewerbemuseum)
Ausstellungsstrasse 60;
Tue.–Fri. 10–6, Wed. until 9,
Sat. and Sun. 10–12 and 2–5,
closed Mon.

Museum of the Indian (Indianer-Museum)
(Culture of the North American Indians)
Schulhaus, Feldstrasse 89;
Sat. 2–5, Sun. 10–12.

Rietberg Museum
(Non-European art, particularly India, China and Africa)
Villa Wesendonck,
Gablerstrasse 15;
Tue.–Fri. 10–5, Wed. also 8–10.
Villa Schönberg,
Gablerstrasse 14;
Tue.–Fri. 2–5, Sat. and Sun. 10–5,

Stadthaus
(Special exhibitions)
Mon.–Fri. 8–6,
closed Sat. and Sun.

Strauhof Municipal Gallery
Augustinergasse 9;
Tue.–Fri. 10–6, Thu. until 9,
Sat. 10–4,
closed Sun. and Mon.

Swiss National Museum (Schweizerisches Landesmuseum)
(Swiss culture, art and history)
Museumstrasse 2;
Tue.–Sun. 10–12 and 2–5,
Mon. 2–5.

Thomas Mann Archives
(Manuscripts, study, library)
Schönberggasse 14;
Wed. and Sat. 2–4.

University of Zurich
Archaeological Collection,
Künstlergasse 16 (first floor);
Tue.–Fri. 1–6.
Botanic Garden,
Zollikerstrasse 107;
Mon.–Fri. 7–7,
Sat. and Sun. 8–6,
greenhouses daily 9.30–11.30 and 1–4.
Medical Collection,
Rämistrasse 71;
Wed. and Thu. 2–5, Sat. 10–12.
Museum of Ethnography,
Pelikanstrasse 40.
Tue.–Fri. 10–5, Wed. also 7–9,
Sat. and Sun. 10–?

Palaeontological Museum,
Künstlergasse 16;
Tue.–Fri. 9–5, Sat. and Sun. 10–4.
Zoological Museum,
Künstlergasse 16;
Tue.–Fri. 9–5, Sat. and Sun. 10–4,
closed Mon.

Zunfthaus zur Meisen
(18th c. Swiss ceramics)
Münsterhof 20;
Tue.–Sun. 10–12 and 2–5,
Mon. 2–5.

Sightseeing in Zurich

Zurich is a city best seen on foot, since the main features of interest are concentrated in a fairly small area on both sides of the River Limmat and the N end of Lake Zurich. The pulsating activity of the city is focused on the *Bahnhofstrasse, a street 1200 m (3937 feet) long (most of it for pedestrians only) which extends from the main station to the lake (dock); it is lined with elegant shops (at No. 31 a private watch and clock museum in the Chronométrie Beyer shop), department stores and banks. The middle section of the street was built in 1867 after the filling in of an old moat, the Fröschengraben; the lower part, towards the lake, was built from 1877 on, the upper part from 1885 on. In the lower half is the Paradeplatz, with the palatial headquarters of the *Schweizerische Kreditanstalt* (1876) and the Hotel Savoy Baur en Ville (built 1838, reconstructed 1978). In the 18th c. the cattle market was held in the square; later it became a drill ground. Towards the upper end of Bahnhofstrasse, on the E side (corner of Uraniastrasse), stands the *Urania* observatory; on the W side are the little *Pestalozzi Gardens*, with a bronze statue of Heinrich Pestalozzi (1899).

To the W of the Bahnhofstrasse, extending to the *Sihlporte*, is a district containing many commercial offices and the *Börse* (Stock Exchange). To the E, towards the Limmat, is the "Kleine Stadt" ("Little Town"), the western half of the old town. – A little way NW of Paradeplatz, at Bärengasse 22, is the *Wohnmuseum Bärengasse* (Zurich domestic life of the 17th and 18th c.).

The **Central Station** (*Hauptbahnhof*), built in 1871 on the site of Zurich's first railway station, is still equal to present-day needs. On the S side of the station in the busy *Bahnhofplatz* can be seen a

monument to the Swiss statesman Alfred Escher (d. 1882). Under the square is a pedestrian concourse with a modern shopping area ("Shopville"). On the N side of the station is the Air Terminal (buses to Zurich Airport, 20 min.).

Immediately N of the station is the *Swiss National Museum (Schweizerisches Landesmuseum)*, a large castellated building (1893–98) which contains the country's largest collection of material on the history and culture of Switzerland. Plan, p. 271.

The MAIN DEPARTMENTS in this richly stocked museum are as follows: prehistory and the early historical period; weapons, flags and militaria; goldsmiths' and silversmiths' work; articles in non-ferrous metals and pewter; ceramics and glass; textiles, costume and jewelry; coins and medals; seals; stained glass; sculpture; furniture and domestic interiors; painting and graphic art; clocks, watches and scientific instruments; musical instruments; rural life; craft and industrial antiquities; library; special exhibitions. – Of particular interest and importance are the works of religious art, the unique collection of old stained glass, the *Armoury (famous murals by Hodler), a series of *period rooms from houses of the Gothic to Baroque periods, and the collection of antiquities of the early historical period. A recently acquired treasure is a *celestial globe by Jost Bürg (1552–1632).

Behind the National Museum we find the *Platzpromenade*, a public garden on the triangular spit of land between the Limmat and its tributary the Sihl. To the NW extends the city's large *industrial zone*.

NW of the station on the left bank of the Sihl, at Ausstellungsstrasse 60, is the *Museum of Decorative Arts* (Kunstgewerbemuseum), which from time to time puts on special exhibitions of graphic art, design, architecture and applied art.

Between the Bahnhofstrasse and the left bank of the Limmat extends the WESTERN HALF OF THE OLD TOWN. In this area is to be found the quiet tree-shaded *Lindenhof*, the site of a Roman fort and later of an Imperial stronghold (fine view of the old town from the terrace). To the S of the Lindenhof is **St Peter's church**, Zurich's oldest parish church, with a Late Romanesque choir under the tower (beginning of 13th c.) and a Baroque nave (three-aisled, with galleries) of 1705. It has the largest clock-faces in Europe (1538), 8·7 m (29 feet) in diameter. The great 18th c. preacher and writer J. C. Lavater (1741–1801) was pastor here for

Schweizerisches Landesmuseum
Musée National Suisse

Museo Nazionale Svizzero

Museum Naziunal Svizzer

Swiss National Museum

BASEMENT
10 Special exhibitions
1–13 Old trades and crafts
11a Milling; wine-growing (19th c.)
11b Coachbuilding and blacksmithing (19th c.)
11c Part of a Zurich armoury (16th–17th c.)
11d Casting of non-ferrous metals
11e Bells (12th–18th c.); tower clocks (16th–17th c.)
12a Comb-maker's workshop (19th c.)
12b Cooper's workshop (19th–20th c.)
13 Shoemaker's workshop (19th c.)

GROUND FLOOR

FIRST FLOOR

GROUND FLOOR

FIRST FLOOR

BASEMENT

Main entrance

Cloakroom

Admin.

Stairs up to 2nd and 3rd floors

Balcony

WC

GROUND FLOOR
1a–3 Carolingian and Ottonian art (9th–10th c.); Gothic art, religious and secular (13th–14th c.)
4–9 Heraldry and genealogy; Zurich Arms Roll, etc.; Swiss pewter (16th–19th c.)
14 Council chamber from Mellingen (1467)
15 Cloister (c. 1240)
16–18 Rooms from Fraumünster abbey, Zurich (c. 1500)
19, 21 Transition from Gothic to Renaissance: portraits, furniture (16th c.)
22 Pharmacy (18th c.)
77–80 Temporary exhibitions of prehistory and early history
81 Objects of the Bronze Age (1800–800 B.C.)
82–83 Neolithic material (4th millennium to c. 1800 B.C.); bust of Ferdinand Keller (1800–81), founder of Neolithic archaeology and the theory of pile-dwelling

FIRST FLOOR
23 Stained glass, in particular from Tänikon convent (1558–59); clocks (16th–17th c.); globe from St Gallen abbey (c. 1569); keyed instruments (17th–18th c.)
24 Small room from Valais (15th c.)
25 Drawings, in particular sketches for stained glass (16th c.); bas-relief carving from the Dominican nunnery of Oetenbach, Zurich (1521)
26 Room from Casa Pestalozzi, Chiavenna (1585)
27 Room from Rosenburg, Stans (1602)
28 "Winter room" (bedroom) from Schloss Wiggen, Rorschach (1582); coats of arms (c. 1600)
29 Room from Alter Seidenhof, Zurich (1620)
30 Stained-glass panels (16th c.); wool embroidery; furniture (16th–17th c.); portraits by Samuel Hofmann (1624–32)
31 Painting of the alliance between Louis XIV and the Confederates in 1663; stained glass from the cloisters of the Cistercian nunnery at Rathausen (1591–1623); coin collection from the monastery of Rheinau (1745)
32 Zurich interior (18th c.); Zurich stove (c. 17th c.)
42 Door surround from Zurich (17th c.); special exhibitions
43 "Summer room" from the Lochmann-Haus, Zurich (c. 1660); celestial globe by Jost Bülgi (1594)
44 Upper Chapel: special exhibitions
45 Secular silverware of the late medieval period (to about 1700); gilded drinking-bowls from the convent at Sarnen (14th–15th c.)
46 Stained glass from the cloisters of the former Cistercian nunnery of Rathausen (1591–1623); painted furniture (18th c.); views of Zurich by Conrad Meyer (c. 1656)
47 Special exhibitions of graphic art; tiled stoves (18th c.)
48 Winterthur china (17th c.) and stoves; portraits and stained-glass panels

49 Items of historical interest, canton of Zurich (17th c.); pair of globes by Vincenzo Coronelli (1688); coats of arms (17th c.)
50 Armoury: development of arms and armour in Switzerland from 800 to 1800; Burgundian war: diorama of the battle of Murten (22.6.1476) with about 6000 tin figures
51 Uniforms of the federal army (1815–60)
64 The Swiss in foreign service (1799–1859): uniforms, weapons, orders and decorations; pictures, etc.
66 Late 14th c. helmet (the "Hundsgugel"); Swiss Guards (17th–19th c.)
67 The federal army since 1898
68 Model of the Second Battle of Polotsk during Napoleon's Russian campaign (tin soldiers)
69–70a Military material of the Roman period (1st–4th c. A.D.)
71 Weapons and implements of the Late Iron Age (La Tène, 5th–1st c. B.C.)
72 Domestic objects of the Roman period
73 Cult objects of the Roman period (reconstructions of domestic altars)
74 Models of early medieval refuge forts; jewelry, etc.
75 Coin collection

SECOND FLOOR
(Rooms 33–41 are reached from the first floor by the stairs at Room 47, Rooms 53–57 by the stairs at Rooms 24 and 32)
33 Liturgical utensils: monstrances, chalices, etc. (17th–18th c.)
34 Secular silverware (18th–19th c.)
35–39 Large cases with groups of figures in period costume (18th c.)
35 Furniture, domestic equipment, costumes (Zurich, 18th c.)
36 Music-making in a house of the Rococo period (c. 1760)
37 A reception, c. 1770–80; clockwork model in the form of a bird-cage from western Switzerland
38 Spinning-room from eastern Switzerland; rural costumes and painted furniture
39 Market scene, Zurich (c. 1800)
40–41 Scenes of 19th c. life
40 "Gift temple" with riflemen's cups; table-setting with gold ornaments; sewing-room
41 Large cases with two drawing-rooms of the 1870s
53–57 Town dress of the 18th and 19th c.; collection of footwear, jewelry and fans; smoking and sewing equipment

THIRD FLOOR
(Rooms 59–63, reached from the first floor by the stairs at Rooms 24 and 32)
59–61 Swiss costumes (18th–19th c.), the canton of Zurich being particularly well represented (Room 59)
62 Toys, dolls' houses
63 Toys, particularly dolls; picture showing Glarus costumes by Joseph Reinhart (c. 1790) and watercolour of costumes by Ludwig Vogel (19th c.)

23 years; his house can still be seen at St Peterhofstätt 6.

To the S is the *Münsterhof*, a historic old square. On the *Münsterbrücke* (1838) stands a bronze equestrian statue (by H. Haller, 1937) of Burgomaster Waldmann (beheaded in 1489), under whose rule Zurich reached the peak of its power in the 15th c. On the S side of the square is the **Fraumünster** (restored 1965), a three-aisled pillared basilica with a Gothic nave (13th–15th c.), an Early Gothic transept and a pointed spire. In the imposing Late Romanesque choir are five *stained-glass windows by Marc Chagall (1970). The undercroft contains remains of the crypt of the abbey church founded by the Emperor Ludwig (Louis) the German in 853. The abbey itself was demolished in 1898 to make way for the *Stadthaus*, but the Romanesque and Gothic cloister survives, with paintings of old Zurich legends by P. Bodmer (1928). – On the N side of the Münsterhof (No. 20) is the *Zunfthaus zur Meisen, a magnificent Late Baroque guild-house (by D. Morf, 1752–57) in the style of a French *hôtel* (town mansion) with a *cour d'honneur*, which now houses the Swiss National Museum's ceramic collection. On the W side of the square (No. 8) is another old guild-house, the *Zunfthaus zur Waag* (1636: restaurant).

From here the Stadthausquai leads S past the *Bauschänzli* summer restaurant to *Bürkliplatz* and the **Quaibrücke**, which crosses the outflow of the Limmat to Bellevueplatz on the opposite bank. In Bürkliplatz is the dock for the lake steamers. To the S, in good weather, there is a splendid view over the lake to the Glarus Alps.

From the Weinplatz, with the *Weinbauer fountain* (1909), we cross the Limmat on the *Rathausbrücke* (1878), successor to a series of earlier bridges which for centuries provided the only crossing. Along the banks of the Limmat are well-preserved old burghers' houses. At the E end of the bridge, overhanging the river on the right, is the **Rathaus** (Town Hall, 1694–98), a massive Late Renaissance building, with rich sculptured decoration, in which the cantonal and communal councils meet.

The Limmatquai at night

To the S, along the *Limmatquai*, a popular shopping street, are a number of elegant old guild-houses with richly appointed interiors reflecting the wealth of the guilds which governed the town until 1789: at No. 54 the *Haus zur Saffran* (1719–23), at No. 42 the *Haus zur Rüden* (1660) and at No. 40 the *Haus zur Zimmerleuten* (1709; beautiful oriel window), all now housing restaurants. Immediately S of the Münsterbrücke is the Gothic *Wasserkirche* ("Water Church", 1479–84), once entirely surrounded by the Limmat; bronze statue of Zwingli (1885) in front of the choir. Built on to the N side of the church is the *Helmhaus* (1794), with an open fountain hall, in which special exhibitions are put on by the municipal authorities.

On an open terrace above the river stands Zurich's principal church, the **Grossmünster** (Protestant), which dominates the city with its twin towers (domed tops added in 1782). Built between the 11th and the 13th c., it is a Romanesque three-aisled galleried basilica with an aisleless chancel over a crypt of about 1100. The upper levels of the towers date from 1487. On the upper part of the S tower, on the side facing the river, is a seated figure of Charlemagne (copy: original in the crypt), who is believed to have founded the house of secular canons to which the church originally belonged; on the N side of the N tower is a figure of the Reformer Heinrich Bullinger. Notable features of the church are the two modern bronze doors (1935–36), the sculptured Romanesque capitals, remains of Gothic wall-paintings and the Late Romanesque cloister. In the choir are three vividly coloured stained-glass windows designed by Augusto Giacometti (1933). In the crypt is the badly weathered statue of Charlemagne from the S tower. From 1519 until his death in the Battle of

Kappel in 1531 the great Reformer Ulrich Zwingli was a secular priest in the Grossmünster. His residence was close by, at Kirchgasse 13.

A walk through the EASTERN PART OF THE OLD TOWN is full of charm and interest, with many excellent antique shops adding to its attractions. Going N up Münstergasse, we come to the Napfgasse, with the *Brunnenturm*, headquarters of the Lombard money-changers in the 14th and 15th c. In the *Spiegelgasse* is a house (No. 17) in which Lenin lived in 1917. In this street, too, was the cabaret in which Hans Arp and Tristan Tzara launched the Dadaist movement in 1916. The Spiegelgasse runs E into Neumarkt, in which are (No. 5) the *Shoemakers' Guild-House* (1742: now the Theater am Neumarkt) and (No. 27, set back from the street: commemorative plaque), the birthplace of the great Swiss writer *Gottfried Keller* (1819–90), who was Chief Clerk of the canton of Zurich from 1861 to 1876. Close by, at Rindermarkt 12, is the Oepfelchammer restaurant, a favourite haunt of his. The house in which he died is at Zeltweg 27, SE of Heimplatz. – To the N of Neumarkt stands the *Predigerkirche* (1611–14), the Preachers' (i.e. Dominicans') Church, an Early Baroque building with a Neo-Gothic tower which now houses the Cantonal Archives. Adjoining the church, the *Central Library* (Zentralbibliothek) occupies the site of the old Dominican monastery. – To the E of Neumarkt, at the corner of Hirschengraben and Künstlergasse, is the *Haus zum Rechberg* (1759), Zurich's finest Rococo building and most important 18th c. secular building, occupied in 1799 by French and allied generals and in 1815 by the Emperor Francis I of Austria. To the SE is the *Zurich Conservatoire* (Konservatorium).

A short distance S of the Conservatoire is the Heimplatz, on the SW side of which we find the *Art Gallery (Kunsthaus), with an important collection of pictures and sculpture from antiquity to the present day. To the right of the entrance can be seen a large piece of bronze sculpture, the "Porte de l'Enfer" ("Gate of Hell", 1880–1917), by Rodin. The Gallery, run by the Zurich Society of Arts with the aid of a public subsidy, was established in 1896; the present buildings were erected in 1925, with considerable extensions in 1954–58 and 1976. In addition to Swiss painters such as Hodler, Koller, Füssli (Fuseli) and Böcklin, the French Impressionists and 20th c. German painters are well represented (Monet, Cézanne, Picasso, Kokoschka, Lipchitz, Haller, Giacometti, etc.). There is also a fine collection of graphic art. A Dadaist collection has many exhibits.

Facing the Art Gallery, on the SE side of the square, is the *Haus zum Pfauen* (House of the Peacock: built 1888–89, reconstructed 1976–78), with the **Schauspielhaus** (Theatre), one of the most renowned of German-language theatres, completely remodelled in the recent rebuilding: see plan below.

From 1642 to 1833 Zurich was surrounded by a ring of ramparts and bastions. After the demolition of these fortifications the moats were filled in, and the town was able to expand beyond its former limits. The monumental complexes of the University and the College of Technology are the result of this wave of building activity in the 19th and 20th c. – From the Heimplatz the *Rämistrasse*, coming from the Bellevueplatz, continues up to a terrace on which stands the **University** (founded 1833, rebuilt 1911–14), with a 64 m (210 feet) high tower. The University buildings contain a number of museums and collections. Extensive new University buildings on the Irschel, in the Unterstrass district, were brought into use in 1978. Zurich is the largest Swiss university, with some 12,500 matriculated students.

Immediately N of the University is situated the **Federal College of Technology** (*Eidgenössische Technische Hochschule*), founded in 1855, which now has some 7000 students. It was built by Gottfried Semper in 1860–64 and enlarged between 1915 and 1925. The complex includes the *Federal Observatory* (Sternwarte) and an important *collection of graphic art* (special exhibitions). There is a recent extension to the College on the Hönggerberg to the NW of the town. From the NW corner of the main complex a funicular descends to the Limmatquai.

To the S of the University, at Schönbergstrasse 15, is the *Haus Zum oberen Schönenberg*, built about 1665 and

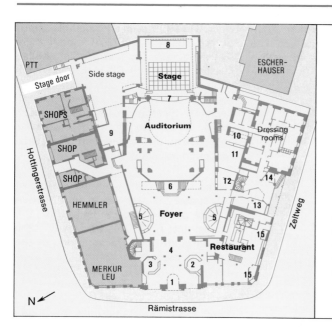

Schauspielhaus, Zurich

GROUND-FLOOR PLAN

1   Entrance
2   Box office
3   Shop (books, etc.)
4   Smoking foyer
5   Cloakrooms
6   Stairs to gallery
7   Orchestra pit
8   Raised podium
9   Store
10 Workshops
11 Properties
12 Rest rooms (men)
13 Rest rooms (women)
14 Entrance for actors and staff
15 Entrances to restaurant

occupied from 1756–83 by Johann Jakob Bodmer (1697–1783), a leading Swiss representative of the Enlightenment, who entertained Goethe, Klopstock and Wieland here. Since 1960 it has housed the *Thomas Mann Archives*, containing all the papers left by the North German novelist (d. 1955).

At the junction of the Rämistrasse with the Utoquai is the spacious *Bellevueplatz*, from which a lakeside promenade offering extensive views runs S along the E side of *Lake Zurich under the name of *Utoquai*, and farther on *Seefeldquai*. To the left stands the neo-Baroque **Opera-House** (Oper), designed by the Viennese architects Fellner and Helmer and built within the space of 20 months in 1890–91. 1·5 km (1 mile) from the Bellevueplatz is the beautiful **Zürichhorn Park** (dock; summer restaurant). At Höschgasse 3 is the *Bellerive Museum* (applied and decorative art), and at No. 8 the *Centre Le Corbusier* (in the Heidi-Weber-Haus, 1967), a forum for community action. Close by, in the Bellerivestrasse, we find the *Studio of Hermann Haller* (sculptor, 1880–1950), with a collection of his work and the urn containing his ashes. Near the Zürichhorn restaurant is a gigantic piece of mechanical sculpture by Jean Tinguely, "Heureka" (1964: operates in summer at 11 and 5).

Some 800 m (2625 feet) E of the Zürichhorn Park, at Zollikerstrasse 172, is the *E. G. Bührle Collection*, one of the richest private collections of European art, mainly assembled by the industrialist Emil G. Bührle (d. 1965) and notable particularly for its 19th and 20th c. French pictures. – To the N (entrance 107 Zollikerstrasse) is the new University *Botanic Garden* (1974), with more than $1\frac{1}{2}$ million plants.

The lakeside promenade which follows the W side of the lake from the Bürkliplatz bears the names of *General-Guisan-Quai* and, farther S, *Mythenquai*. Near the dock used by the lake steamers stands the **Congress Hall** (*Kongresshaus*, 1939), which is built on to the older **Concert Hall** (*Tonhalle*, 1895), and is one of the major focal points of Zurich's social life with its concerts, conferences and festive occasions of all kinds. On the Mythenquai are the headquarters of a number of large insurance corporations, and above it is *Belvoir Park*, with old trees, subtropical plants and a restaurant. Above this again, beyond the Seestrasse, we find *Rieter Park*, at the N end of which, in the Gablerstrasse, is the *Rietberg Museum*, housed in a Neo-classical villa modelled on the Villa Albani in Rome. It was built in 1857 for a German industrialist, Otto Wesendonck, and became the meeting-place of the intellectual élite of Zurich, including Wagner and Conrad Ferdinand Meyer. The villa was acquired by the city of Zurich in 1952, and now contains the fine collection of

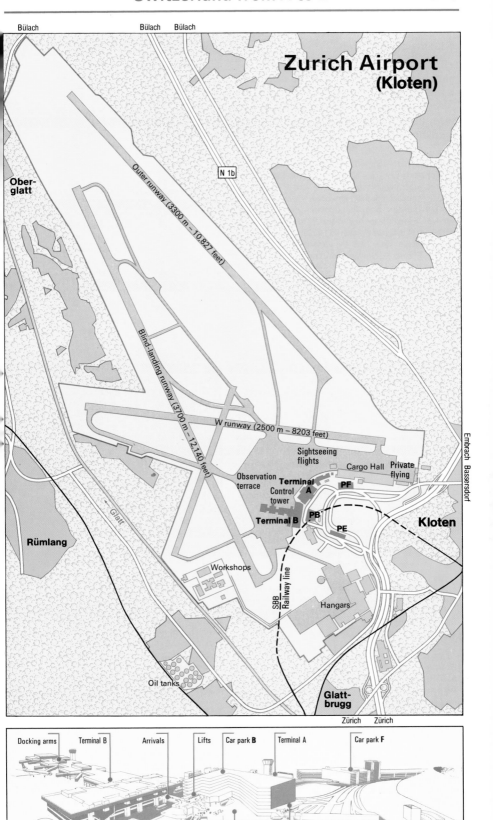

Bülach   Bülach   Bülach

Zurich Airport
(Kloten)

Ober-
glatt

N 1b

Outer runway (3300 m – 10.827 feet)

Blind-landing runway (3700 m – 12.140 feet)

W runway (2500 m – 8203 feet)

Sightseeing
flights

Cargo Hall   Private
flying

Observation
terrace

Control
tower

Terminal
A

PF

Terminal B   PB

PE

Kloten

Rümlang

Glatt

Embrach Bassersdorf

Workshops

SBB Railway line

Hangars

Oil tanks

Glatt-
brugg

Zürich   Zürich

Docking arms   Terminal B   Arrivals   Lifts   Car park **B**   Terminal A   Car park **F**

Platform   Concourse   Airport Plaza   Bus station   **Airport Railway station**

African and Asian art assembled by Baron Eduard von der Heydt.

Farther along the Mythenquai, at No. 88, is the *Municipal Collection of Succulents*. – At Seestrasse 203 the *Muraltengut* has reception rooms used by the Zurich municipal council.

SURROUNDINGS. – To the E of the city is the **Zürichberg** (679 m – 2228 feet), a wooded hill with houses reaching far up its slopes and a number of restaurants commanding extensive views. From the Central Station and Paradeplatz there are tram services (respectively Nos. 5 and 6) to the *Zoo, one of the finest in Europe (opened 1929), with more than 2000 animals. Near here are various sports facilities and the *Fluntern Cemetery*, with the grave of the Irish writer James Joyce (1882–1949). – From the Römerhofplatz a funicular 1328 m (4357 feet) long serves the *Waldhaus Dolder* (548 m (1798 feet): hotel), from which it is possible to continue on foot to the Dolder Grand Hotel, the golf-course, the artificial ice-rink and the swimming pool (artificial waves). – From Winterthurerstrasse another shorter funicular ascends to the *Rigiblick* (586 m – 1923 feet).

To the SW of the city is the *Uetliberg (871 m – 2858 feet), the most northerly hill in the Albis ridge. The *Uetlibergbahn*, a mountain railway, runs from Selnau station to the upper station at 816 m (2677 feet), from which it is a 10 minutes' walk to the summit (restaurant). In clear weather there is a superb view from the outlook tower of the Valais, Bernese and Glarus Alps, with the Black Forest to the N and Säntis to the E. From here there is an easy ridge walk of just over an hour to the *Felsenegg* (790 m – 2592 feet), from which a cableway descends to *Adliswil*. The return to Zurich is by the Sihltalbahn (Zürich-Selnau to Sihlbrugg).

From the Stadelhofen station in Zurich the Forchbahn, an electric railway, runs SE via *Forch* to *Esslingen* in the Zurich Oberland. There are many marked trails in the countryside around Forch.

The passenger-ship services on *Lake Zurich (see below) make possible a variety of attractive day and half-day trips. Information from Zürichsee-Schiffahrtsgesellschaft, Mythenquai 33 (tel. 45 10 33).

11 km (7 miles) N of the central city (reached by rail – Holiday Card valid – or by bus from the Central Station), at *Kloten* (432 m – 1417 feet), is *Zurich Airport, which ranks among the ten largest airports in Europe. It is the headquarters of the Swiss national airline, Swissair, with large hangars and the head office at Balsberg. See plan, p. 275.

The total area of the airport is some 725 hectares (1791 acres). Construction began in 1946, and by 1948 two runways were ready for service. There were major extensions in 1958 and 1971, and further developments are planned. There are now three runways in service, each 60 m (197 feet) wide; the longest is the blind-landing runway (3700 m – 12,140 feet). There are two terminals equipped with shops, restaurants and service facilities – **Terminal A** (with multi-storey *car park F*) for Eastern Europe, Germany, Austria, Israel and charter flights, and **Terminal B** (with *car park B* and radiating arms surmounted by an

observation deck) for inter-continental flights, Western Europe and domestic flights. On the second floor of car park B is a large *shopping area*, with a bank and a post office. Under the *Airport Plaza* is the new **Railway Station Concourse**, and under this again, 18 m (59 feet) below ground level, four railway lines with 420 m (1378 feet) of platforms. Beside car park B is the *Bus Station*. NE of Terminal A are the departure point for sightseeing flights and the large *Cargo Hall*. To the S are the *hangars*, and at the S end of the blind-landing runway the workshops. – The airport has a total staff of some 15,000, including some 2500 technical staff. On the busiest days there are more than 500 aircraft arrivals and departures. – Flight information: tel. (01) 8 12 71 11.

W of Zurich, to the S of the Berne motorway, are two small industrial towns now part of the city. 8 km (5 miles) W is *Schlieren* (pop. 12,500; Hotel Tivoli, C, 90 b.; Salmen, C, 80 b.), with factories manufacturing trucks and elevators. 12 km (7 miles) W is **Dietikon** (pop. 25,000: Hotel Krone, B, 36 b.; Hotel Sommerau-Ticino, C, 120 b.

Regensberg

18 km (11 miles) NW of Zurich, on an eastern spur of the Lägern hills, lies *Regensberg (612 m (2008 feet): pop. 500; Krone inn), one of the best-preserved medieval towns in the country, founded about 1245 by the Barons of Regensberg. The round tower (21 m (69 feet) high) of the old castle (16th–17th c.) and the 57 m (187 feet) deep draw-well (the deepest in Switzerland) in the upper ward date from the original structure. The church, originally 13th c., was rebuilt in 1506. Among the carefully restored old burghers' houses the half-timbered ''Rote Rose'' house (1540), with the Rose Museum of the painter Lotte Günthard, is particularly notable.

15 km (9 miles) E of Zurich, on the NE shore of the *Greifensee* (area 8·6 sq. km (3 sq. miles), depth 34 m (112 feet): nature reserve), the sleepy old town of **Greifensee** (437 m (1434 feet): pop. 5500; Alte Kanzlei restaurant) has a castle which was once the seat of the provincial governor Salomon Landolt. The church (*c.* 1330), in High Gothic style, has an unusual triangular plan. – 5 km (3 miles) SE of Greifensee is the town of **Uster** (pop. 23,000; Hotel Illuster, B, 120 b.).

Lake Zurich

Cantons: Zurich (ZH), St Gallen (SG) and Schwyz (SZ).

ⓘ **Verkehrsverband Zürichsee
und Umgebung** (VVZU),
Mythenquai 333,
CH-8038 Zurich;
tel. (01) 45 10 33.

BOAT SERVICES. – The Zürichsee-Schiffahrtsgesellschaft (Mythenquai 333, CH-8038 Zürich) runs regular services (modern passenger ships and also older steamers) to places on both sides of the lake as far as Rapperswil (Easter to October), and in the main season also to the Obersee.

*Lake Zurich (in German Zürichsee),
which was gouged out by the Linth
glacier during the last Ice Age,
extends for a total length of 39 km
(24 miles) from NW to SE in a
beautiful Pre-Alpine setting. With a
maximum width of 4 km (2 miles), it
has an area of 88 sq. km (34 sq. miles)
(Unterer See 68 sq. km (26 sq. miles),
Obersee 20 sq. km (8 sq. miles)) and a
depth of up to 143 m (469 feet). Its
principal tributary river, the Linth,
rises in Glarus, flows through the
Walensee and continues to Lake
Zurich as a canal. The lake is drained
at the NW end by the Limmat, which
flows into the Aare. Although the
lake lies in a densely populated
region, with something like a million
inhabitants of the cantons of Zurich,
St Gallen and Schwyz living on its
shores, a third of its shoreline is still
freely accessible.*

The *NE shore* of the lake, with an almost continuous succession of attractive towns and villages lying below vineyards and orchards and a whole string of beaches, is popularly known as the "Gold Coast" because of the many wealthy people who have houses here.

The first place beyond Zurich (see above) is **Küsnacht** (427 m (1401 feet): Hotel Ermitage, B, 46 b.; Sonne, D, 30 b.), a town of 12,000 inhabitants with a church first mentioned in the records in 1188 (present building 15th c.; wall-paintings in choir), the "Höchhus" (a 13th c. tower house) and a former commandery of the Knights of St John, now a teachers' training college.

3 km (2 miles) SE is *Erlenbach* (415 m (1362 feet): Hotel Erlibacherhof, C, 34 b.;

Freihof, C, 30 b.), beautifully set at the foot of the vineyards belonging to the "Zur Schipf" estate (sumptuous banqueting hall in the house), with Mariahalde, a handsome country house in Neo-classical style (1770).

5 km (3 miles) beyond this we come to the chief town of the district, **Meilen** (423 m (1388 feet): pop. 10,000). The church (Protestant) was given to Einsiedeln abbey by the Emperor Otto the Great in 965; the choir dates in its present form from 1493 to 1495. In the Seehof C. F. Meyer completed his novel "Jürg Jenatsch" between 1872 and 1875. From here a steep road (5 km – 3 miles) runs up to the *Pfannenstiel* (853 m – 2799 feet), the highest peak on the N side of the lake, from which there are extensive views. Car ferry to Horgen on the S side of the lake.

7 km (4 miles) SE is **Stäfa** (417 m (1368 feet): Hotel Zur Metzg, D, 43 b.), the largest commune on the N side of the lake (pop. 7000), which takes in *Uerikon*, *Oetikon* and numerous small hamlets. In the cemetery is the grave of the German writer Ernst Wiechert (1887–1950). In Uerikon, on the lake, are two old manor-houses and a 16th c. chapel.

9 km (6 miles) E of Stäfa is *Rapperswil* (p. 190), where the road from Winterthur comes in on the left. From here a causeway 930 m (3051 feet) long runs across between the main part of Lake Zurich and the Obersee (to left) to the peninsula of **Hurden**. Here there is a fishing village much frequented by summer visitors (chapel of 1497), and *Pfäffikon*, from which it is possible to return to Zurich either by the lakeside road or by the motorway.

Adjoining Rapperswil, the industrial district of *Jona* lies the fertile area at the mouth of the River Jona. Here also are the former Cistercian nunnery of *Wurmsbach* (16th–17th c.), now occupied by a girls' boarding-school, and the 15th c. church of *St Dionys*, with wall-paintings of the same date. The road then continues along the N side of the Obersee (canton of St Gallen) to *Schmerikon* (415 m – 1362 feet), at the E end of the lake. 1·5 km (1 mile) E, in the Linth plain, we reach the trim little town of *Uznach* (414 m – 1358 feet), with the Kreuzkirche (1494–1505) and a cemetery chapel of 1679. Near the town stands the modern Benedictine missionary house of *St Otmarsberg*. From the road junction at Kaltbrunn, to the SE, it is possible to continue either N via Ricken to *Wattwil* (p. 247) or S via Näfels to *Glarus* (p. 137).

From Zurich road 3 follows the *SW shore* of the lake past a long string of old villages and modern villas surrounded by gardens, with many beaches. In 6 km (4 miles) it reaches **Kilchberg** (427 m (1401 feet): Hotel Schenkel), on the hillside to the right of the road. This was the home of the Swiss writer Conrad Ferdinand Meyer (1825–98) from 1875 onwards, and the German novelist Thomas Mann (1875–1955) and his wife (d. 1980) spent the last years of their lives here. Their graves are in the churchyard, on the S side of the little church, in which the German philosophers F. W. Foerster (1869–1966) and L. Klages (1872–1956) are also buried. – Beyond this is the village of *Rüschlikon* (435 m – 1427 feet). 3 km (2 miles) farther on is *Thalwil* (438 m (1437 feet): Hotel Thalwilerhof, D, 50 b.), an industrial town (silk) of 13,000 inhabitants.

5 km (3 miles) beyond Thalwil is **Horgen** (411 m (1348 feet): Seehotel Meierhof, B, 230 b., SB), a long, straggling industrial town (pop. 16,000) with a Baroque church of 1782 (fine frescoes of 1875). Car ferry to Meilen, on the N side of the lake. The road then passes the village of *Käpfnach* (415 m – 1362 feet), to the right, and the attractive Au peninsula (Hotel Halbinsel Au) on the left, and comes in 5·5 km (3 miles) to **Wädenswil** (411 m (1348 feet): Hôtel du Lac, D, 36 b.), an industrial town of 15,000 inhabitants. Above the town the Neues Schloss (1818) houses the Federal Fruit-Growing, Viticultural and Horticultural Research Station. From here a road branches off on the right over the *Hirzel-Höhe* (750 m – 2461 feet) to Sihlbrugg

(13 km – 8 miles). – 4 km (2 miles) beyond this is **Richterswil** (411 m (1348 feet): Hotel Drei Könige), beautifully set on the lake. Above the village are two churches, from the terraces of which there are fine views. A road on the right climbs 3 km (2 miles) SE to *Wollerau* (507 m – 1663 feet), with a Neo-classical church (1787), and then winds its way steeply up for another 3 km (2 miles) (fine views) to *Schindellegi*.

The road now enters the canton of Schwyz and continues along the side of the lake, which here attains its greatest width (4 km – 2 miles). In 1·8 km (1 mile) it comes to *Bäch* (Hotel Bachau), beyond which is *Freienbach* (416 m – 1365 feet), with a Baroque church. View of the islets of Ufenau and Lützelau to the left, and of the Toggenburg hills straight ahead. – Then in 2 km (1 mile) the road reaches **Pfäffikon** (415 m (1362 feet): pop. 4000; Hotel Sternen), at the S end of the causeway over the lake, with the castle (13th c. tower) which belonged to Einsiedeln abbey. At the N end of the causeway is *Rapperswil* (p. 190).

The road continues along the S side of the lake, known beyond the causeway as the *Oberer Zürichsee* or *Obersee* (Upper Lake), passes the Etzelwerk power station and comes to *Altendorf* (430 m – 1411 feet). – 1·5 km (1 mile) beyond this, off the road to the left, is *Lachen*. On a hill to the right (505 m (1657 feet): road half way up) stands the 15th c. *St John's chapel*, built in the ruins of the old castle of Alt-Rapperswil (destroyed 1350).

Lachen (420 m (1378 feet): Hostellerie Al Porto, C, 44 b.; bypass), attractively situated on the Obersee, has a handsome twin-towered Rococo church (1700–10) designed by the Thumb brothers of Vorarlberg. – NE of Lachen, at the E end of the lake, is *Uznach* (above).

Practical Information

A lane in Grimentz (Valais)

Safety on the Road. Some Reminders for the Holiday Traveller

When to Go

The best time to go to the Pre-Alpine regions is from mid May to the beginning of July; the best season for the mountains is during July, August and the first half of September, when all the passes are open. The summer resorts usually have a season beginning in May and ending about the end of September. The lakes in the S attract their greatest numbers of visitors in spring and autumn. Those who go to Switzerland in May can enjoy the contrast between the spring blossoms in the warmer Pre-Alpine valleys and the wintry conditions still prevailing in the mountains. – The winter sports regions are at their busiest from the end of January to March. The season extends from December to the beginning or end of April, depending on altitude.

Weather

Switzerland is divided by the main ridge of the Alps into two different climatic regions. To the N of the Alpine chain the climate is temperate, with a gradual transition from maritime influences in the W to a more continental régime in the E,

while in the southern half of the country, particularly in Ticino and Grisons, Mediterranean influences are already perceptible. In the Alps themselves weather conditions depend on altitude and the prevailing air currents, and show marked local differences. A phenomenon characteristic of the mountain regions is the temperature reversal which can occur in winter, when the valleys are filled with cold air flowing down from higher levels, often accompanied by heavy cloud formation, while clear, sunny and relatively warm weather prevails on the mountains. The presence of low pressure on the N side of the Alps and high pressure to the S gives rise to the *föhn*, a warm, dry fall wind which brings with it a sharp rise in temperature (up to 10 °C – 50 °F), rapid melting of the snow and usually very clear air affording long-distance views.

For a more detailed account of the climate of Switzerland see pp. 16–17.

Time

Switzerland and the Principality of Liechtenstein observe Central European Time: i.e. they are an hour ahead of Greenwich Mean Time (six hours ahead of New York time). Swiss Summer Time, first introduced in 1981, is an hour ahead of Central European Time (two hours ahead of GMT, seven hours ahead of New York time).

Travel Documents

A valid passport is required. No visa is needed by vacation and business visitors from the United Kingdom (British subjects and British protected persons), Ireland, Commonwealth countries, the United States and many other countries.

Visitors can take a private car, motor-cycle or motor scooter into Switzerland for a temporary stay without customs documents, provided a valid national *driving licence* and the vehicle *registration document* can be produced. An *international insurance certificate* ("green card") should be obtained from the vehicle's normal insurers: visitors from the United Kingdom and Ireland, as members of the EEC, are not required to produce a green card, but since their own insurance covers only the minimum legal requirements it is very desirable to have the fuller protection which the green card affords. Foreign cars must display an oval *international distinguishing sign* of the approved type and design. Failure to comply with this regulation is punishable by a heavy on-the-spot fine.

Since there is no national health service in Switzerland and medical treatment must be paid for, it is advisable to take out insurance cover against personal accident and sickness, as well as loss of, or damage to, luggage and personal effects. Special winter sports policies are obtainable.

Customs Regulations

Visitors to Switzerland may take in, duty-free, personal effects such as clothing, toiletries, sports gear, cameras and amateur movie cameras with appropriate films, musical instruments and camping equipment; provisions for one day's requirements; other goods taken in as gifts up to a value of 100 Swiss francs (with the exception of meat and certain other foodstuffs); and (if over 17 years of age) 2 litres (3½ pints) of alcoholic beverages up to 25°, 1 litre (1½ pints) over 25° and 200 cigarettes *or* 50 cigars *or* 250 grammes (9 ounces) of tobacco (double these quantities of tobacco goods for visitors from outside Europe).

Currency

The unit of currency in Switzerland and Liechtenstein is the **Swiss franc** (German *Schweizer Franken*, French *franc suisse*, Italian *franco svizzero*) of 100 *rappen* or *centimes*.

There are *banknotes* for 10, 20, 50, 100, 500 and 1000 francs and *coins* in denominations of 5, 10 and 20 rappen/centimes and ½, 1, 2 and 5 francs.

There are no restrictions on the import or export of either Swiss or foreign currency. It is advisable to take travellers' checks and a credit card. The standard credit cards are accepted.

Postal Rates

Letters (up to 20 g – 0·7 ounces): to western European countries 0·90 fr. Outside Switzerland (UPU countries) 1·10 fr.

Postcards: to western European countries 0·80 fr. Outside Switzerland 1·10 fr.

Travel in Switzerland

Driving

In the relatively densely populated Alpine foreland regions there is a close network of roads. The roads through towns and villages are sometimes narrow, calling for careful driving. The mountain regions have, of course, a less extensive road system, but the principal valleys are easily accessible.

Swiss roads are classified into **motorways** (highways) (German *Autobahnen*, French *autoroutes*, Italian *autostrade*); Motorways are numbered N (national road) and are divided into classes 1, 2 and 3: they vary from the usual two-lane roadway to 7·6 m (25 feet) wide two-lane roads with limited access points. Motorways are tollroads and an annual toll certificate must be produced by motorists using them.

To join a motorway, follow the green and white signposts, or signposts with the motorway symbol. Vehicles unable to exceed 60 kph (37 mph) and motor cycles under 50 cc are forbidden

Pass roads. – Switzerland has many roads leading over passes, some of them among the most fascinating mountain roads in Europe. The main N–S connections are magnificently engineered, but some of the minor pass roads are very narrow. Most of the passes over the Alps are closed in winter: for information about road conditions dial 163 (anywhere in Switzerland).

On 3 routes cars can be *carried by train* through railway tunnels: see below, p. 288.

Major road tunnels: Grand St Bernard, San Bernardino, St Gotthard.

The **condition of the roads** is usually excellent. The mountain roads are, of course, frequently narrower, with numerous sharp turns; particular care is required on such roads during the summer on account of the many buses.

Driving in Switzerland. – As in the rest of continental Europe, traffic goes on the right, with passing on the left. Road markings and road signs are in accordance with international standards. Within built-up areas vehicles travelling on rails have priority at the intersection or junction of roads of equal importance; otherwise traffic coming from the right has priority. – Drivers and front seat passengers must wear *seat belts*. Children under 12 must not travel in the front seat. – On *mountain roads* ascending vehicles have priority. *Dipped headlights* must be

used in tunnels and galleries at all times. – In the event of a breakdown on a motorway or expressway a *warning triangle* must be set at least 150 m (492 feet) from the vehicle (on other roads 50 m (164 feet)), and the car's flashing warning lights switched on. – Motor cycles must have their low beams on at all times.

The maximum permitted *blood alcohol* level is 0·80% (80 milligrammes of alcohol in 100 millilitres of blood).

Speed limits: 130 km p.h./80 m.p.h. on motorways, **100 km p.h./62 m.p.h.** on other roads, **60 km p.h./37 m.p.h. 50 km p.h./31 m.p.h.** in built-up areas as signposted.

Speed limits should be strictly observed, since there are heavy fines for even minor infringements.

Trailer caravans over 2·10 m (7 feet) wide and 6 m (20 feet) long require a special authorisation, obtainable at the frontier. This allows caravans up to 2·20 m (7 feet) wide and 7 m (23 feet) long (6·50 m (21 feet) on pass roads) to be used.

The limits for **motor caravans** vary according to size and weight: e.g. for a vehicle with a total weight of 4 tons the size limits are 2·50 m (8 feet) by 8 m (26 feet). It is advisable to check the regulations before departure.

Information: *Schweizerische Zolldirektion* (Swiss Customs office), CH-4000 Basle, tel. (061) 23 98 00.

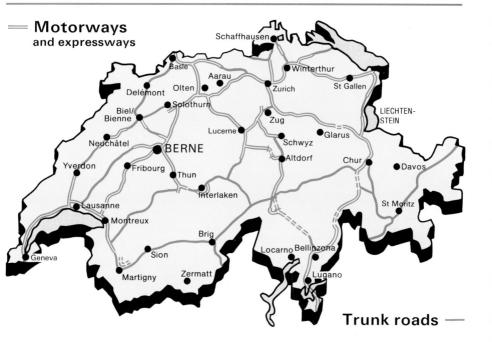

Motorways
and expressways

Schaffhausen
Basle
Aarau
Winterthur
Delémont · Olten
Zurich · St Gallen
Biel/
Bienne · Solothurn
LIECHTEN-
STEIN
Zug
Lucerne
Neuchâtel
Schwyz · Glarus
BERNE
Altdorf
Yverdon
Fribourg · Chur · Davos
Thun
Lausanne · Interlaken
St Moritz
Montreux
Brig
Geneva · Sion
Locarno Bellinzona
Martigny · Zermatt
Lugano

Trunk roads ——

Chains are essential in winter (but must not be used in the principal road tunnels). – **Studded tyres** may be used on vehicles up to 3·5 tons from 1 November to 31 March. Vehicles with such tyres (which must have a plate on the rear indicating this) are subject to a speed limit of 80 km p.h. (50 m.p.h.) and may not use motorways (except on the Thusis–San Bernardino tunnel–Mesocco route).

Buses

The bus services run by the Swiss Post Office (*PTT*) play an important part in the Swiss transport system, particularly in the mountainous regions with more limited rail services. The postal buses serve even the highest Alpine roads. Tickets are sold at all the larger post offices.

The St Gotthard road (S side)

A *Postal Bus Holiday Card* (Postauto-Ferienabonnement), available at a very reasonable rate, covers half-price travel on all regular bus routes in Switzerland (at present some 7500 km (4661 miles)). Holiday cards can also be obtained for particular regions.

● Passes over 1000 m (3281 feet)

1 Col des Etroits
   1153 m (3783 feet)
   Ste-Croix to Fleurier
   Maximum gradient 10%
   open all year

2 Col du Mollendruz
   1180 m (3872 feet)
   Morges to Vallorbe
   Maximum gradient 6%
   open all year

3 Col du Marchairuz
   1447 m (4748 feet)
   Nyon to Le Brassus
   Maximum gradient 13%
   open all year

4 Col de la Givrine
   1228 m (4029 feet)
   Nyon to Morez (France)
   Maximum gradient 7%
   open all year

5 Pas de Morgins
   1369 m (4492 feet)
   Monthey to Evian-les-Bains (France)
   Maximum gradient 14%
   open all year
   Frontier at the top

6 Col de la Forclaz
   1527 m (5010 feet)
   Martigny to Chamonix (France)
   Maximum gradient 8%
   open all year

Mountain Passes in Switzerland

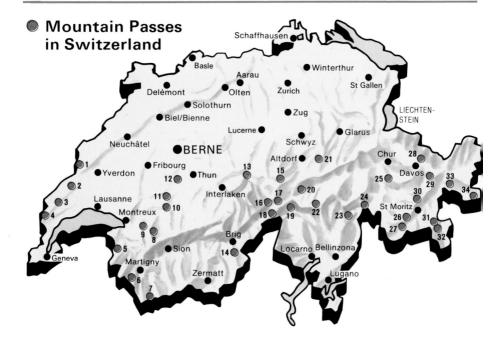

7 Grand St Bernard Pass
2469 m (8101 feet)
Martigny to Aosta (Italy)
Maximum gradient 11%
open June–October
road tunnel available.

8 Col du Pillon
1546 m (5072 feet)
Gstaad to Aigle
Maximum gradient 9%
may be closed at times during January and February

9 Col des Mosses
1445 m (4741 feet)
Château d'Oex to Aigle
Maximum gradient 8%
open all year

10 Saanenmöser Pass
1279 m (4196 feet)
Zweisimmen to Saanen
Maximum gradient 9%
open all year

11 Jaun Pass
1509 m (4951 feet)
Spiez to Bulle
Maximum gradient 10%
open all year

12 Selibühl Pass
1587 m (5207 feet)
Thun to Fribourg
Maximum gradient 11%
open all year

13 Brünig Pass
1007 m (3304 feet)
Lucerne to Brienz
Maximum gradient 8%
open all year

14 Simplon Pass
2005 m (6578 feet)
Brig to Domodossola (Italy)
Maximum gradient 11%
may be closed at times between November and April alternative rail tunnel available

15 Susten Pass
2224 m (7297 feet)
Innertkirchen to Wassen
Maximum gradient 9%
open June to November

16 Grimsel Pass
2165 m (7103 feet)
Gletsch to Innertkirchen
Maximum gradient 11%
open June to October

17 Furka Pass
2431 m (7976 feet)
Gletsch to Andermatt
Maximum gradient 10%
open June to October

18 Nufenen (Novena) Pass
2478 m (8130 feet)
Ulrichen to Airolo
Maximum gradient 10%
open June to October

19 St Gotthard Pass
2108 m (6916 feet)
Andermatt to Airolo
Maximum gradient 10%
open June to October
road tunnel available

20 Oberalp Pass
2044 m (6706 feet)
Andermatt to Disentis
Maximum gradient 10%
open May to November

21 Klausen Pass
1948 m (6391 feet)
Altdorf to Linthal
Maximum gradient 10%
open May to November

22 Lukmanier (Lucomagno) Pass
1020 m (6301 feet)
Disentis to Biasca
Maximum gradient 10%
open May to November

23 San Bernardino Pass
2066 m (6779 feet)
Splügen to Bellinzona
Maximum gradient 10%
open June to November
road tunnel available

24 Splügen (Spluga) Pass
2113 m (6933 feet)
Splügen to Chiavenna (Italy)
Maximum gradient 13%
open June to October;

25 Lenzerheide Pass
1549 m (5082 feet)
Chur to Tiefencastel
Maximum gradient 10%
open all year

26 Julier (Güglia) Pass
2284 m (7494 feet)
Tiefencastel to Silvaplana
Maximum gradient 13%
open all year

27 Maloja Pass
1815 m (5955 feet)
St Moritz to Chiavenna (Italy)
Maximum gradient 9%
open all year

28 Wolfgang Pass
1633 m (5358 feet)
Klosters to Davos
Maximum gradient 10%
open all year

29 Flüela Pass
2383 m (7819 feet)
Davos to Susch
Maximum gradient 10%
open all year

30 Albula Pass
2312 m (7586 feet)
Tiefencastel to La Punt (St Moritz)
Maximum gradient 12%
open May to November

31 Forcola di Livigno
2315 m (7596 feet)
St Moritz to Livigno (Italy)
Maximum gradient 12%
open June to October
Frontier at the top

32 Bernina Pass
2323 m (7622 feet)
St Moritz to Tirano (Italy)
Maximum gradient 12%
closed at night. Also at times during the day
between November and late April

33 Ofen (Fuorn) Pass
2149 m·(7051 feet)
Zernez to Santa Maria i.M.
Maximum gradient 12%
open all year

34 Umbrail Pass
2501 m (8206 feet)
Santa Maria i.M. to Stelvio Pass (Italy)
Maximum gradient 12%
open May to November

Air Services

The airports of Zurich (Kloten) and Geneva (Coitrin) together with the Franco-Swiss airport of Basle/Mulhouse link Switzerland with the international network of air services.

The national airline, **Swissair**, flies on international routes and also on certain domestic routes. There are air services between the following Swiss towns: Basle–Geneva, Basle–Zurich; Geneva–Lugano, Geneva–Zurich; Lugano–Zurich, Berne–Lugano.

Railways

— Main lines
— Branch lines

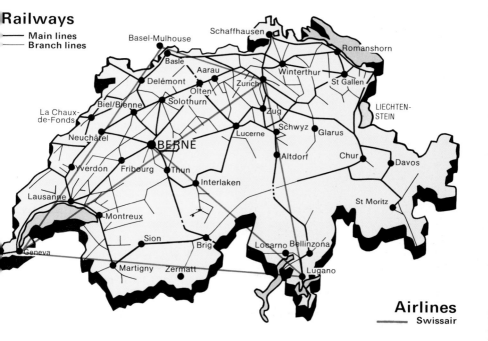

Airlines
— Swissair

Information about pleasure flying from
Aero-Club der Schweiz,
Lidostrasse 5, CH 6006, Lucerne.
Tel. (041) 31 21 21.

Rail Services

The **Swiss Federal Railways**
(*SBB/CFF/FFS*) have a network of some
2900 km (1802 miles), which since 1960
has been fully electrified. In addition there
are a considerable number of privately run
lines, bringing the total length of the
system to some 5000 km (3107 miles).

There are no ticket-takers on Swiss
platforms: tickets are checked on board
the trains.

On Trans-European expresses (TEE) a
supplement is payable in addition to the
fare. – Children under 6 travel free;
between 6 and 16 they pay half fare.

There are **reduced rates** for families, groups, senior
citizens, young people, etc. Other facilities are *Holiday
Tickets* covering specified routes, *Holiday Cards*
allowing unlimited travel for a specified period,
Regional Season Tickets and *Half-Fare Season
Tickets*. – Information from Swiss National Tourist
Office.

Rail Transport of Cars on Alpine Passes

There are railway tunnels under several Alpine passes.
On the following routes cars and trailers can be loaded
on to the train for transport under the pass.

Albula
Cars loaded at Thusis and Samedan.
journey time 1¼ to 1¾ hours.

Lötschberg
Cars loaded at Kandersteg and Goppenstein/Brig.
journey time 15 minutes.

Lötschberg-Simplon
Cars loaded at Kandersteg and Iselle (Italy).
journey time 1½ hours.
Change of trains at Brig

Vitznau-Rigi railway

Säntis cableway

Simplon
Cars loaded at Brig and Iselle (Italy).
journey time 20 minutes.

Motorail

There are motorail services from the Hook of Holland
to Lörrach, near Basle, and from Calais to Mulhouse
(France), 29 km (18 miles) from Basle. There are also
services from 's-Hertogenbosch in Holland to Biasca
and from Brussels (Schaerbeek) to Brig. – Information and booking: Sealink Travel Ltd, P.O. Box 29,
London SW1V 1JX, or through a travel agent.

Bicycle Rentals

Bicycles can be rented at most railway stations in
Switzerland ("Velo am Bahnhof"). There are reductions for railway ticket-holders. – Information
from any Swiss railway station.

Mountain Railways, Cableways, Lifts

These various forms of mountain transport are of great importance in Switzerland, and of particular value to tourists.
Apart from the services they provide for
winter sports enthusiasts they also enable
the older or less strenuously inclined
visitor to enjoy the experience of the
mountain world. There are in all some 400
mountain railways and cableways, sup-
plemented in winter by over 1200 ski-lifts.
Some of the railways and cableways
climb to heights of over 3000 m (9843
feet), such as those up the Kleines
Matterhorn (3820 m – 12,533 feet),
Jungfrau (3457 m – 11,342 feet),
Gornergrat (3407 m – 11,178 feet),
Corvatsch (3298 m – 10,820 feet), Piz
Nair (3025 m – 9925 feet) and Mont Gelé
(3023 m – 9918 feet).

There are the following types: **funicular** (German *Standseilbahn*, French *funiculaire*), in which the cars run on rails and are drawn by a cable. – **rack-railway** (cog-railway) – (*Zahnradbahn, chemin de fer à crémaillère*), with a middle rail fitted with a cog which engages with a pinion on the locomotive. – **cableway** (*Seilschwebebahn* or *Luftseilbahn*, *téléférique* or *télécabine*), with cabins for anything from 4 to 100 passengers suspended from a continuous cable. – **chair-lift** (*Sesselbahn* or *Sessellift*, *télésiège*), with open chairs (sometimes double) suspended from a continuous cable. – **ski-lift** (*Skilift* or *Schlepplift*, *monte-pente*), in which skiers are pulled uphill on their skis attached to a moving cable. – **sledge-lift** (*Schlittenseilbahn, funiculaire à traîneaux*), in which sledges are attached to a cable and drawn uphill. – Many of these facilities operate for only part of the year.

Reductions. – The 'Tele-Check', offering a reduction of 20–30%, and containing coupons to the value of some 130 francs and valid for 3 years, can be bought for some 1000 cableways and lifts throughout Switzerland.

Water Sports and Boat Services

▨ Facilities for water sports

1 Lac de Joux
Alt. 900 m (2953 feet)
Sailing, wind-surfing, fishing

2 Lake Geneva (Lac Léman)
Alt. 372 m (1221 feet)
Regular boat services between many places on the lake
Rental of sailboats and rowboats; water-skiing, fishing
Sailing, wind-surfing and water-skiing lessons

3 Lac de Neuchâtel
Alt. 432 m (1417 feet)
Regular boat services between many places on the lake
Rental of sailboats and rowboats; water-skiing, fishing
Sailing, wind-surfing and canoeing lessons

4 Bieler See/Lac de Bienne
Alt. 432 m (1417 feet)
Regular boat services between many places on the lake
Rental of sailboats and rowboats; water-skiing, fishing
Sailing and wind-surfing lessons

5 Lake Thun (Thuner See)
Alt. 560 m (1837 feet)
Regular boat services between many places on the lake
Rental of sailboats and rowboats; water-skiing, wind-surfing, fishing
Sailing and wind-surfing lessons

6 Lake Brienz (Brienzer See)
Alt. 567 m (1860 feet)
Regular boat services between many places on the lake
Rental of sailboats and rowboats; water-skiing, wind-surfing and fishing
Fishing lessons

7 Sarner See
Alt. 473 m (1552 feet)
Regular boat services between most places on the lake
Rental of motorboats and rowboats; fishing, wind-surfing
Sailing and wind-surfing lessons

8 Vierwaldstätter See (Lake Lucerne)
Alt. 437 m (1434 feet)
Regular boat services between many places on the lake
Rental of sailboats and rowboats: wind-surfing
Sailing and wind-surfing lessons

Facilities for Water Sports

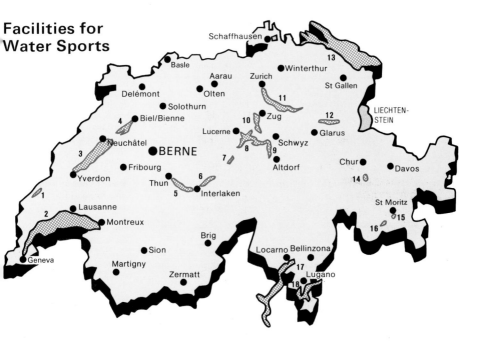

9 Urner See (Lake Uri)
Alt. 437 m (1434 feet)
Regular boat services between many places on the lake
Rental of sailboats and rowboats; wind-surfing

10 Zuger See (Lake Zug)
Alt. 437 m (1434 feet)
Regular boat services between Zug and Arth
Rental of sailboats and rowboats; wind-surfing
Sailing lessons

11 Lake Zurich (Zürichsee)
Alt. 410 m (1345 feet)
Regular boat services between many places on the lake
Rental of sailboats and rowboats; wind-surfing
Sailing and wind-surfing lessons

12 Walensee
Alt. 423 m (1388 feet)
Regular boat services between Weesen and Walenstadt
Rental of sailboats and rowboats; fishing
Sailing, fishing and wind-surfing lessons

13 Lake Constance (Bodensee)
Alt. 395 m (1296 feet)
Regular boat services between many places on the lake
Rental of sailboats and rowboats; wind-surfing and fishing
Sailing, wind-surfing and fishing lessons

14 Heidsee
Alt. 1493 m (4899 feet)
Rental of sailboats; wind-surfing, fishing
Sailing, wind-surfing and fishing lessons

15 St Moritzer See
Alt. 1771 m (5811 feet)
Rental of sailboats; wind-surfing, canoeing
Sailing, wind-surfing and fishing lessons

16 Silser See and Silvaplaner See
Alt. 1795 m (5889 feet)
Regular boat services between certain places on the lake
Sailing, wind-surfing
Wind-surfing lessons

17 Lake Maggiore (Lago Maggiore)
Alt. 194 m (637 feet)
Regular boat services between many places on the lake

Rental of sailboats and rowboats; wind-surfing, water-skiing
Sailing, wind-surfing and water-skiing lessons

18 Lake Lugano (Lago di Lugano)
Alt. 274 m (899 feet)
Regular boat services between many places on the lake
Rental of sailboats and rowboats; wind-surfing, water-skiing
Sailing, wind-surfing and water-skiing lessons

Information: **Union Schweizerischer Yacht-clubs**
(Union of Swiss Yacht Clubs).
Schwarztorstrasse 56,
CH-3007 Berne;
tel. (031) 25 63 33

Schweizerischer Kanuverband
(Swiss Canoeing Federation),
Brünigstrasse 121,
CH-6060 Sarnen;
tel. (041) 66 34 88, a.m.

Fédération Suisse de Ski Nautique
(Swiss Water-Skiing Federation),
25 Route de Florissant,
CH-1206 Genève
tel. (022) 42 74 68

Schweizerischer Ruderverband
(Swiss Rowing Federation),
Postfach 645,
CH-8021 Zürich
tel. (01) 2 34 52 27

Schweizerischer Schwimmverband
(Swiss Swimming Federation),
Haldenstrasse 55,
CH-2501 Biel/Bienne
tel. (032) 41 03 04

Schweizerischer Sportfischer-Verband
(Swiss Angling Federation),
Mühleweg 12,
CH-2543 Lengnau
tel. (065) 8 11 30

Glossary

The following glossary of German topo-graphical terms may be found helpful as a guide to the meaning of names which visitors will encounter frequently on maps, plans and signposts; they may appear either independently or as elements in a longer word.

Allee	avenue, walk
Alm, Alp	Alpine pasture
Anlage	gardens, park
Anstalt	institution
Au(e)	meadow, pasture: island
Auskunft	information
Aussicht	view
Ausstellung	exhibition
Bach	brook, stream
Bad	bath; spa
Bahn	(rail-, cable-) way; lane (in road)
Bahnhof	railway station
Bau	building
Bauernhaus	peasant's house, farmhouse
Bauernhof	farm, farmstead
Becken	basin, pool
Berg	mountain, hill
Bergbahn	mountain railway or cableway: see p. 289
Bibliothek	library
Blick	view
Börse	(stock) exchange
Brücke	bridge
Brunnen	fountain
Bucht	bay
Bühel, Bühl	hill

Bundes-	federal	Mühle	mill
Burg	(fortified) castle	Münster	minister, monastic church; cathedral
Damm	causeway, breakwater		
Denkmal	monument, memorial	Nieder-	lower
Dom	cathedral	Nord	north
Dorf	village	Ober-	upper
Eisenbahn	railway	Oper	opera-house
Fähre	ferry	Ost	east
Fels	rock, crag	Palais, Palast	palace
Flügel	wing	Pfad	path, trail
Flughafen	airport	Pfarrkirche	parish church
Fluh	rock-face	Platz	square
Fluss	river	Post	post office
Forst	forest	PTT	post office
Freilichtmuseum	open-air museum	Quai	quay
Friedhof	cemetery	Quelle	spring, source
Garten	garden	Rathaus	town hall
Gasse	lane, street	Rennbahn	race-track
Gebirge	(range of) mountains or hills	Ruine	ruin
Gemeinde	commune (as an administrative unit)	Rundfunk	radio
		Saal	hall, room
Gericht	court (of law)	Sattel	saddle
Gletscher	glacier	Säule	column
Grab	tomb, grave	SBB	Swiss Federal Railways
Graben	ditch, moat	Schatzkammer	treasury
Grat	(mountain) ridge	Schauspielhaus	theatre
Gebäude	building	Schifflände	dock
Gut	estate; country house, farm	Schlepplift	ski-lift
Hafen	harbour, port	Schloss	castle, palace, country house
Halbinsel	peninsula	Schlucht	gorge
Halde	hillside	Schule	school
Halle	hall	See	lake
Hallenbad	indoor swimming pool	Seilbahn	cableway (either aerial or on rails): see p. 289
Hang	slope, hillside		
Hauptpost	head post office	Seilschwebebahn	aerial cableway
Hauptstrasse	main street	Sesselbahn, Sessel-	
Haus	house	lift	chair-lift
Heide	heath	Sperre	dam, barrage
Heim	home	Spielbank	casino
Heimatmuseum	local or regional museum	Spital	hospital
Hochhaus	multi-storey building, tower block	Spitze	point; peak
		Stadt	town, city
Hochschule	higher educational establish-ment, university	Standseilbahn	funicular
		Stätte	place, site
Hof	courtyard; farm; (royal) court	Stausee	lake formed by dam, reservoir
Höhe	hill, eminence	Steig	path
Höhle	cave	Stein	stone
Holz	wood	Sternwarte	observatory
Hospital	hospital, hospice	Stift	religious house; chapter, col-lege; foundation
Hügel	hill		
Insel	island	Stiftskirche	collegiate church; monastic church
Joch	(mountain) ridge		
Jugendherberge	youth hostel	Stock	massif, rock mass
Kammer	chamber, room	Strand	beach
Kapelle	chapel	Strasse	street, road
Keller	cellar	Süd	south
Kirche	church	Tal	valley
Klamm	gorge	Teich	pond, small lake
Kloster	monastery, convent, monastic house	Theater	theatre
		Tonhalle	concert-hall
Kongresshaus	conference hall	Tor	gate(way)
Krankenhaus	hospital	Turm	tower
Kunsthaus	art gallery, art museum	Ufer	shore, coast
Kurhaus	spa establishment	Universität	university
Kurort	spa, health resort	Unter-	lower
Laube	arcade, loggia	Verkehr	traffic, transport
Luftschwebebahn	(aerial) cableway	Verkehrsbüro,	
Markt(platz)	market (square)	Verkehrsverein	tourist information office
Matte	Alpine meadow	Viertel	quarter, district
Mauer	(masonry) wall	Vita-Parcours	running track
Meer	sea	Vorort, Vorstadt	suburb, outer district
Messe	trade fair	Waage	weigh-station
Moor	moor(land)	Wald	wood, forest
Moos	moss, bog	Wallfahrtskirche	pilgrimage church

Wand	wall, (mountain) face
Wasser	water
Wasserburg, Wasser-schloss	moated castle
Weg	way, road

Weiler	hamlet
West	west
Zahnradbahn	rack-railway (cog-railway)
Zeughaus	arsenal
Zunfthaus	guild-house

Accommodation

Hotels and Inns

The Swiss hotel trade has a long and honourable tradition behind it. Overall, the standard of quality is higher than in other European countries, and even in hotels of the lower categories the accommodation and service are usually among the best of their kind. Outside the larger towns such as Zurich and Geneva, the establishments are mostly of small and medium size.

In many places there are reasonably priced hotels and restaurants which serve no alcohol (*alkoholfrei*). A list of such establishments can be obtained from the *Schweizerische Stiftung für Förderung von Gemeindestuben,* Brandschenkestrasse 36, CH-8039 Zurich, tel. (01) 2 01 20 40.

The following table shows the price ranges for the different categories of hotel.

Official category	In this Guide	Room charge per night in francs one person	two persons
*****	A	105–290	160–420
****	B	85–180	125–340
***	C	42–115	68–210
**	D	32–72	52–125
*	E	27–47	47–84

These are inclusive charges (i.e. including service and taxes). In purely tourist and vacation resorts the rates may be higher, particularly at the height of the season; and it is quite common in such places for hotels to let rooms only with half or full board.

Youth Hostels

Switzerland has some 120 **youth hostels** (German *Jugendherberge*, French *auberge de jeunesse*, Italian *alloggio per giovani*) providing modestly priced accommodation, particularly for young people (with priority for those under 25). During the main holiday season it is advisable to book places in advance; and the maximum period of stay permitted in any one hostel will vary according to the demand for places. Youth hostellers must produce a membership card issued by their national youth hostel association.

Information: **Schweizerischer Bund für Jugendherbergen** (Swiss Youth Hostel Association), Postfach 132, Hochhaus 9, CH-8958 Spreitenbach tel. (056) 71 40 46.

Vacation Houses

Vacation homes and **chalets** can be rented through such agencies as *Inter Home*, Elsastrasse 16, CH-8040 Zurich, and *Uto-Ring*, Beethovenstrasse 20–24, CH-8022 Zurich, or through the Swiss automobile clubs (address on p. 313). A list of vacation homes is published by the *Schweizerische Gemeinnützige Gesellschaft Ferienwohnungen*, Brandschenkestrasse 36, CH-8039 Zurich. Information can also be obtained from the Swiss National Tourist Office.

Holidays on the Farm

This relatively new kind of vacation is now becoming popular in Switzerland, as in other countries. Information about farmhouses providing vacation accommodation can be obtained from the Swiss National Tourist Office.

Camping and Caravanning

Switzerland now has something like 500 camping sites, some 90 of which remain open in winter.

There are special regulations affecting trailer caravans in Switzerland: see p. 284.

Vacations for the Disabled

The *Schweizerischer Invalidenbund*, Froburgstrasse 4, CH-4600 Olten, tel. (062) 21 10 37, publishes a list of Swiss hotels suitable for disabled people. Town guides for disabled persons (Basle, Berne, Lausanne, Lucerne, St Gallen, Zurich) can be obtained from *Pro Infirmis*, Postfach 129, CH-8023 Zürich. In addition information is available from the Schweizerische Arbeitsgemeinschaft für Körperbehinderte.

Food and Drink

Swiss **restaurants** are noted for the excellence of their cuisine, which is as varied as the ethnic composition of the population. The cuisine of the various parts of Switzerland is strongly influenced by that of the neighbouring countries – in the German-speaking cantons by German cooking, in the French-speaking cantons by the "cuisine française", in the Italian-speaking cantons by the "cucina italiana". In addition, however, there are a number of specifically Swiss dishes, mostly using locally produced ingredients such as dairy produce and fish.

The midday meal is usually eaten about 12.30 – called either "dîner" and followed in the evening (7 onwards) by "souper", or "lunch" when the main meal is taken in the evening. Even quite small restaurants provide attentive service, using hot-plates (*réchauds*) to keep the food warm. The station buffets are usually excellent.

The cost of lunch or dinner will range between 10 and 20 francs in the more modest establishments to 20–50 francs in high-class restaurants. To eat à la carte is usually more expensive than to take the fixed-price *menu*, which always provides a very satisfying meal. Many restaurants offer one-course meals which are very good value.

Swiss Specialties

Meat dishes. – The *Berner Platte* is a very nourishing plateful of ham and sausage with sauerkraut or beans. The Mittelland has another very substantial dish, *Gnagi* (slightly salted pigs' trotters), so tender that it is said to melt in the mouth. Favourite Geneva dishes are *pied de porc au madère* (pigs' trotters in madeira sauce) and *gigot d'agneau* (leg of lamb). Zurich has *Gschnetzeltes* (veal stewed with cream) and *Leberspiessli* (calf's liver cooked on a spit, with bacon), Schwyz excellent *Gemsenbraten* (roast chamois), the cantons on the Rhine *Mistkratzerli* or *Güggeli* (young chickens). – Switzerland has a rich assortment of excellent **sausages**. Basle has *Klöpfer* (succulent cervelat sausages), St Gallen *Schüblige* and *Bratwürste*, Appenzell *Pantli* and *Knackerli*. Grisons has a particularly wide variety – *Salsiz* (a small salami), *Beinwurst, Engadinerwurst, Leberwurst* (liver sausage) and *Tiges*, as well as *Bündnerfleisch* (air-dried beef). The canton of Vaud also produces some excellent sausages, including *boutefas, saucissons de Payerne*, liver sausages and sausages made with vegetables. Then there are the *longeoles* of Geneva (pork sausages spiced with caraway and aniseed) and the *Walliser Platte* or "Valais Dish" (cold meat, including dried raw beef). The popular types of sausage in Ticino are *coppa* and *zampone*. – Among favourite Swiss **vegetables** to accompany meat are *Berner Rösti* (sliced potatoes, lightly browned with bacon cubes), gratiné potatoes, aubergines and artichokes. There are also a variety of attractively seasoned salads.

Fish dishes play a large part in the Swiss menu. The country's many lakes and rivers yield a variety of species: *pike* are found in Lake Constance, Lake Geneva, the Lac de Neuchâtel and the Lauerzer See, *trout* in the mountain streams around Arth-Goldau, in Lake Geneva, the Areuse and the mountain streams and lakes of southern Switzerland, *barbel* in the Zuger See, *whitefish* in Lake Constance, *dace, char* and *perch* in Lake Geneva, *bondelles* and *palées* in the Lac de Neuchâtel. Further variety is added by various species of *perch* and *barbel* and by the eels of the mountain lakes. *Blausee trout* are regarded as a particular delicacy.

Pasta is eaten mainly in northern Switzerland, where the influence of German cuisine makes itself felt. In addition to *Spätzli* or *Knöpfli* there is a Zurich speciality, the *Zürcher Topf* (macaroni with minced meat and tomato sauce, cooked in the oven). In southern Switzerland various forms of pasta are popular, including *ravioli*. – Notable among **egg dishes** are the *chucheôles* of Fribourg, which are eaten with sweet mustard.

The Swiss are particularly good at making **cakes and sweets**. Among the most tempting are *Basler Leckerli* (a kind of gingerbread), *Schaffhauser Zungen* ("Schaffhausen tongues"), *Zuger Kirschtorte*, the cream-filled *meringues* (from Meiringen) of the Bernese Oberland, the *bagnolet crème* of the Jura (eaten with raspberries and aniseed biscuits), the *délices* (soda rolls), *croissants, rissoles* (pear tarts), *nougat* and *pralines* of Geneva and the *zabaglione* of Ticino. *Vermicelli*, not the Italian pasta dish but a dessert made of chestnut mousse, is popular all over Switzerland.

A Swiss speciality world renowned for its quality is **chocolate**, in a variety of flavourings.

Cheeses

The excellent dairy products of Switzerland are famed world wide, and the Swiss menu includes a variety of cheese dishes, varying from region to region. *Cheese soups* are particularly popular in central Switzerland; *cheesecakes* (*gâteau* or *salée au fromage, ramequin*) are found all over the country.

The Principal Swiss Cheeses

Appenzeller
Appenzell

A semi-hard cow's-milk cheese, treated with spiced white wine during the maturing process.

Bagnes
Valais

A hard cow's-milk cheese, used in the making of *raclette* (see below).

Brienzer Mutschli
Berne

A hard cow's-milk cheese, usually made on the mountain pastures in summer.

Chaschöl chevra
Grisons

A soft goat's-milk cheese.

Emmentaler
Central Switzerland

A hard cow's-milk cheese, used in *fondue*.

Formaggelli
Ticino

A soft cheese made from ewe's or goat's milk, usually eaten after several days' maturation.

Formaggini
Ticino

A small soft ewe's-milk or goat's-milk cheese.

Goms
Valais

A semi-hard cow's-milk cheese, much used in the making of *raclette*.

Gruyère
Fribourg

A hard cow's-milk cheese, used in *fondue*.

Petit Suisse
Geneva

A fresh cow's-milk cheese.

Reblochon
Geneva

A soft cow's-milk cheese.

Saanen-Hobelkäse
Berne

A hard cow's-milk cheese, used in various cheese dishes or served by itself in thin slices.

Sbrinz
Central Switzerland

A hard cow's-milk cheese, mainly used in the preparation of various cheese dishes.

Schabzieger
Glarus

A hard cow's-milk cheese, with herbs.

Tête de Moine
Jura

A soft cow's-milk cheese.

Tilsiter
Thurgau

A semi-hard cow's-milk cheese.

Toggenburger Ploderkäse
Obertoggenburg

A soft cow's-milk cheese.

Tomme Vaudoise
Vaud

A fresh cow's-milk cheese.

Urserenkäse
Bernese Oberland

A mild soft cow's-milk cheese.

Vacherin Fribourgeois
Fribourg

A semi-hard cow's-milk cheese. There are two types, *Vacherin à fondue* and *Vacherin à la main*.

Vacherin Mont d'Or
Fribourg

A soft cow's-milk cheese, usually eaten after six weeks' maturation.

A selection of Swiss cheeses

Wine-producing Regions of Switzerland

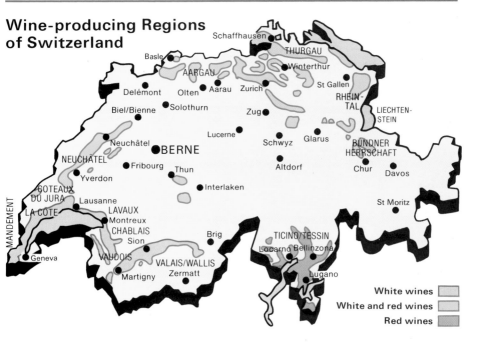

White wines
White and red wines
Red wines

Vero Piora
Ticino

A semi-hard cow's-milk and goat's-milk cheese.

There are also a large number of regional varieties of cheese. *Alpkäse* is made on the mountain pastures in summer, and often toasted at an open fire (*Bratkäsli*). – The process of cheese-making can be observed in the demonstration cheese dairy at Gruyères (see p. 142).

Two cheese dishes which are particularly popular in western Switzerland are *fondue* and *raclette*, both of them invariably accompanied by white wine. – **Fondue** (from French *fondre*, to melt) is made by melting cheese and white wine, flavoured with kirsch and spices, in a special one-handled dish known as a *caquelon*. The dish is then set in the middle of the table over a flame to keep it hot, and each member of the party helps himself by dipping a piece of white bread on a special fork into the common bowl. Anyone who lets his bread fall into the dish is required to pay for the next bottle of wine. – In **raclette** (from French *racler*,

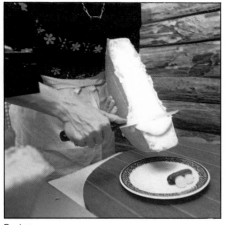

Raclette

to scrape) a large cheese is cut in half and heated until it melts, when the melted cheese is scraped off on to the plate and eaten with a potato in its jacket and various tasty accompaniments.

Wine

Vines are grown in almost all the Swiss cantons, but particularly on the slopes above Lake Geneva and the lakes of the Jura and Ticino and in the wide valleys of the Rhône and the Rhine. Wine has been made in western and southern Switzerland since the 1st c. B.C., in northern Switzerland only since the 7th or 8th c. A.D. Since the end of the 19th c. the area under vines has been considerably reduced. The present output of wine is about 1 million hectolitres, two-thirds of the total being white and the remaining third red (maximum strength 13% of alcohol by volume). Only small quantities of Swiss wine are exported, the imports of wine being many times greater.

Noted Swiss wines. – Lake Geneva, particularly in the Lavaux area (Vaud) between Lausanne and Montreux (from the Chasselas/Gutedel grape): *Dézaley* and *St-Saphorin* (the best), *Pully, Lutry, Epesses; Aigle* and *Yvorne*, from the Chablais area between Montreux and Martigny; and wines from the "Petite Côte" around Morges, the "Côte" from Rolle and the Mandement area (Geneva). – Valais: *Fendant* (from the Chasselas/Gutedel grape), in many different sorts; red *Dôle* (from a mixture of Pinot Noir/Blauburgunder and Gamay grapes); *Johannisberg* (known as "Rhin" or "Petit Rhin", being made from Riesling/Sylvaner grapes); *Ermitage, Amigne, Arvine,*

Vintage time on Lake Geneva

Spirits. – Swiss fruit brandies are of excellent quality – *Kirsch* (the best of which comes from Zug), *Zwetsch* (made from plums), *Enzian* (from the roots of gentian), *Birne* (from pears), *grappa* and *marc* (from the skins of pressed grapes), *Bätzi* (from apples), etc.; *Alpenbitter*, *Kräuterlikör* (Chrüter: a herb liqueur).

Beer. – The two leading Swiss brands are *Feldschlösschen* (Rheinfelden) and *Cardinal* (Fribourg). Beer is often mixed with lemonade to produce a kind of shandy. *Ex-Bier* is non-alcoholic.

Table waters: *Passugger* (Grisons), *Henniez* (Vaud), *Elmer* (Glarus), *Eptinger* (Basel-Land), *Weissenburger* (Berne).

Humagne, Oeil de Perdrix (rosé); *Muscat* and *Malvasier*, two dessert wines made from the Pinot Gris grape ("Strohwein" or "straw wine"); and the very unusual *Heidenwein*, made from the highest vineyards (700–1200 m – 2297–3937 feet) around Visperterminen; after maturing in the cellar for 10–20 years it yields the precious golden-brown *Glacier*. – Bieler See and Lac de Neuchâtel: the slightly sparkling "Bernese lake wines" *Schaffiser* and *Twanner*; *Cortaillod, Auvernier*. – Ticino: *Nostrano* (red, from the Merlot grape); particularly good from Gordola. – Grisons: red wines – *Veltliner* (Valtellina), *Malanser, Jeninser, Maienfelder, Fläscher* (in the Bündner Herrschaft region). – Northern Switzerland: *Meilener, Stäfener, Herrliberger* from Lake Zurich; *Neftenbacher* from the Töss valley; *Karthäuser* (Ittinger), *Steiner, Bachtobler* from Thurgau; *Bernecker, Melser, Wiler* from St Gallen; *Hallauer, Osterfinger, Rheinhalder* from Schaffhausen; *Villiger Schlossberger, Geissberger* from Aargau; *Riehener Schlipfen* from Basle.

In Switzerland white wine is served in small tumblers. – Soon after the wine harvest unfermented *must* (German *Most*, French *moût*) appears in bars and restaurants. – In Vaud there are numerous "wine trails" (*chemins de vignoble*).

Spas

● Health Resorts

1 Rheinfelden
Recommended for rheumatism, metabolism, heart and circulation, gynaecological disorders.

2 Ramsach
Recommended for rheumatism, heart and circulation, metabolism, gynaecological disorders.

3 Schwefelbergbad
Recommended for rheumatism, metabolism, skin conditions.

4 Lenk
Recommended for rheumatism, respiratory organs, gynaecological disorders.

5 Breiten
Recommended for rheumatism, metabolism, respiratory organs, skin conditions.

6 Rietbad
Recommended for rheumatism, heart and circulation, metabolism, gynaecological disorders.

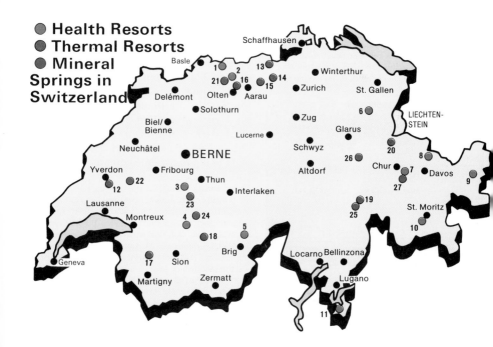

● Health Resorts
● Thermal Resorts
● Mineral Springs in Switzerland

7 Passugg
Recommended for rheumatism, metabolism, respiratory organs.

8 Serneus
Recommended for rheumatism.

9 Bad Scuol, Bad Tarasp-Vulpera
Recommended for respiratory organs, heart and circulation, urinary tract, stomach and intestines, liver and gall bladder, metabolism.

10 St Moritz Bad
Recommended for heart and circulation, urinary tract, stomach and intestines, liver and gall bladder, metabolism.

11 Stabio
Recommended for rheumatism, metabolism, gynaecological disorders.

● Thermal Resorts

12 Yverdon-les-Bains
Water containing sulphur (34 °C – 93 °F). Recommended for rheumatism, metabolism, nervous diseases, respiratory organs.

13 Zurzach
Water containing sodium sulphate, hydrogen carbonate and chloride (40 °C – 105 °F). Recommended for rheumatism, metabolism, heart and circulation.

14 Baden-Ennetbaden
Water containing sulphur, sodium and calcium chloride and sulphate (47 °C – 118 °F). Recommended for rheumatism, metabolism, respiratory organs, heart and circulation.

15 Bad Schinznach
Water containing sulphur, calcium and sodium sulphate and chloride (31 °C – 89 °F). Recommended for rheumatism, metabolism, respiratory organs, heart and circulation, skin conditions.

16 Lostorf
Water containing sulphur, calcium and magnesium sulphate (27 °C – 82 °F). Recommended for rheumatism, metabolism, respiratory organs, heart and circulation.

17 Lavey-les-Bains
Water containing sulphur, sodium sulphate and chloride (radioactive: 62 °C – 145 °F). Recommended for rheumatism, metabolism, respiratory organs, heart and circulation.

18 Leukerbad
Water containing calcium sulphate (42–51 °C – 109–125 °F). Recommended for rheumatism, metabolism, heart and circulation.

19 Vals
Water containing calcium sulphate and hydrogen carbonate (25 °C – 78 °F). Recommended for rheumatism, metabolism, heart and circulation.

20 Bad Ragaz/Valens
Water containing calcium, magnesium, sodium and hydrogen carbonate (37 °C – 100 °F). Recommended for rheumatism, metabolism, heart and circulation.

● Mineral Springs

21 Eptingen

22 Henniez

23 Weissenburg

24 Adelboden

25 Vals

26 Elm

27 Passugg

Castles and Châteaux

(Note: The German *Schloss*, like the French *château*, covers a wide range, from a medieval castle to a Renaissance palace or a large country house. The *Burg* is a fortified medieval castle.)

1 Coppet
Château (17th c.)

2 Crans
Château (18th c.)

3 Nyon
Château (12th/16th c.)

4 Prangins
Château (18th c.)

5 Rolle
Château (13th c.)

6 Morges
Château (13th/16th c.)

7 Vufflens-le-Château
Château (14th/15th c.)

8 Lausanne
Château St-Maire (14th/15th c.)

9 La Tour-de-Peilz
Château (13th c.)

10 Montreux
Château de Chillon (11th/13th c.)

11 Aigle
Château (13th c.)

12 St-Maurice
Château (15th c.)

13 La Sarraz
Château (11th/16th c.)

14 Oron-le-Châtel
Château (13th c.)

15 Gruyères
Château (13th/15th c.)

16 Bulle
Château (13th c.)

17 Romont
Château (13th/16th c.)

18 Lucens
Château (15th/16th c.)

19 Yverdon
Château (13th c.)

20 Grandson
Château (13th/15th c.)

21 Estavayer-le-Lac
Château de Chenaux (13th/15th c.)

22 Murten
Château (13th c.)

23 Gorgier
Château (14th/16th/19th c.)

24 Boudry
Château (16th c.)

25 Neuchâtel
Château (12th/15th/17th c.)

26 Valangin
Château (12th/16th c.)

Castles and Châteaux in Switzerland

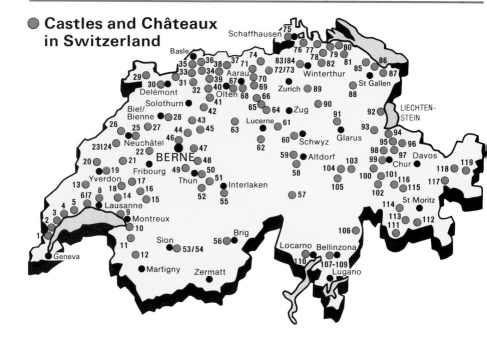

For the Nature-Lover

Climbing

Climbers on the Eiger (Bernese Oberland)

Switzerland is the classic country for mountaineering, which has become increasingly popular as a sport since the middle of the 19th c., when it was pioneered by British climbers at Zermatt. The Swiss Alpine Club, founded in 1863, has built up a network of paths and huts to facilitate access to the mountains; and the central Alps, with numerous peaks rising to over 4000 m (13,124 feet), offer the most magnificent glacier walks and climbs in the whole of the Alps.

There is sometimes a tendency nowadays to under-estimate the importance of proper **equipment**; but this is essential for safe and enjoyable climbing or mountain walking. It is important to have weather-proof (and not too light) clothing, warm underwear, woollen socks, a light waterproof windbreaker and good climbing boots, which must have treaded rubber soles. The rucksack, which should have broad straps, should contain only the most essential requirements (the guides are not required to carry more than 7 kg (15 pounds) in addition to their own equipment). A small reserve of food (biscuits, chocolate, dried fruit, etc.) should always be carried. Other indispensable items are sun-glasses, sunburn cream (and for many people also a lip cream) and adhesive bandages.

The **guides** are subject to control by the Swiss Alpine Club and the cantonal authorities, who issue guides' licences only after testing their competence. The regulations on charges, food, carrying of luggage, etc., vary from canton to canton: it is desirable, therefore, before engaging a guide to ask to see the list of charges and the local regulations and to check that the guide is insured.

Climbing without a guide is now very common; but it should be attempted only by climbers whose own competence on rock and ice, judgment and fitness are not much below those of the professional guides, or who are climbing with experienced Alpine mountaineers. Many accidents occur through a climber's ignorance of the hidden dangers in an apparently easy route, through losing the way when there is a sudden change in the weather or as a result of inadequate equipment. In the high mountains no one should climb alone; but it is also necessary to be wary of uninvited companions, who may give rise to grave difficulties or dangers. – In the climbs mentioned in this Guide the need for a guide is indicated where appropriate.

Glaciers must be crossed early in the day, before the sun softens the snow covering over the crevasses. Even experienced climbers should never tackle a glacier without a guide and a rope.

At altitudes above 4000 m (13,124 feet) or so, and for some people even below this, **mountain sickness** can be a problem. The symptoms are palpitations, dizziness, loss of consciousness and bleeding from the mouth and nose. The best remedies are rest, stimulants and – most effective of all – an immediate descent to a lower altitude.

Weather conditions in the Alps, particularly on their north-western and northern slopes, are the most unreliable in the whole of Central Europe and full of potential danger for the climber. Two generally accepted indications of good weather are a fall in temperature in the evening, when the wind blows down into the valley after blowing up on to the mountains during the day, and a fresh fall of snow on the peaks. The *föhn* (see p. 17), which makes the mountains appear nearer and dark blue in colour, often brings a long period of beautiful weather, though this may change suddenly at any time. Signs of bad weather are the appearance of cirrus clouds moving from W to E (even though they may disappear in the early afternoon), swirls of dust on the roads and driving snow on the ridges and peaks when the weather is otherwise good. In rainy weather there is increased danger of rock falls. In the event of a thunderstorm do not stand under isolated trees, haystacks, etc., in view of the danger of being struck by lightning; come down from the peaks and ridges at once, and keep away from running water.

Weather forecasts are posted up at stations and post offices and given daily on the radio. They can also be obtained by telephone (dial 162).

Alpenglow (German *Alpenglühen*) is the reddish light cast by the setting sun on the rocky and snow-covered summits; in particular it is the afterglow of yellow, purple and violet hues which occurs 5–10 minutes after sunset when there is a slight build-up of clouds in the W and twilight has already fallen in the valleys.

The Climber's Distress Signal

The international Alpine distress signal, for climbers who need help, is a series of six signals given at regular intervals within a minute by whatever means are available (blasts on a whistle, shouts, flashes of a torch, waves of some conspicuous article), followed by a minute's pause, a repetition of the signals, and so on until an answer is received. The answer takes the form of three signals at regular intervals within a minute.

The Swiss Alpine Club has established a large number of rescue stations and reporting posts to ensure that in the event of an accident help can be summoned quickly.

The Swiss Alpine Club (SAC), founded in 1863, maintains some 155 mountain huts, which are open to non-members as well as members of the Club. In some of them there are limited facilities for obtaining food during the summer; in most of them, however, there is no warden, and it is, therefore, necessary to inquire in the valley below about the means of gaining access, and sometimes to take the key with you. The charges for overnight accommodation are posted up in the huts.

Climbing schools. – There are a number of excellently run climbing schools in Switzerland, providing instruction both for beginners and for those who want to learn specialised techniques. In most schools it is also possible to obtain guides. There are such schools, for example, at Wildhaus, Andermatt, Davos, Les Diablerets, Fiesch, La Fouly/Verbier, Grindelwald, Klosters, Pontresina, Meiringen, Kandersteg/Schwarenbach, Arolla and Villars-Chesières.

Information: **Schweizerischer Verband der Bergsteigerschulen**
(Swiss Federation of Climbing Schools),
c/o *Ecole Suisse d'Alpinisme*,
CH-1874 Champéry
tel. (025) 79 14 30.

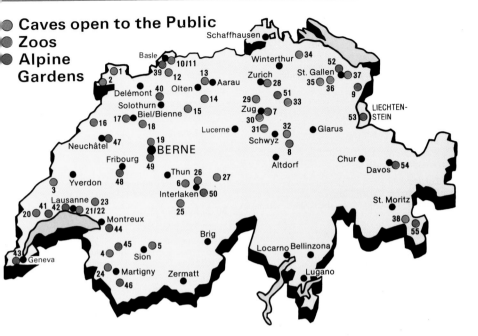

● Caves open to
the Public (Selection)

1 Grotte de Milandre
at Boncourt, NW of Porrentruy
Rock formations, underground river

2 Grotte de Réclère
at Réclère, SW of Porrentruy
Stalactites and stalagmites

3 Grotte de Vallorbe
near Vallorbe
Rock formations, underground river

4 Grotte aux Fées
near St-Maurice
Rock formations, underground river

5 Grotte de St-Léonard
at St-Léonard
Limestone cave, underground lake

6 Beatusböhlen
W of Interlaken
Rock formations, underground river

7 Höllgrotten
NE of Zug
Rock formations

8 Hölloch
near Muotathal, SE of Schwyz
Rock formations, fossils, underground river

9 Kristallhöhle
near Oberriet
Limestone crystals, underground lake

● Zoos and Mini-Zoos
(Selection)

10 Basle
Zoologischer Garten (Zoo)
Animals from all over the world; terrarium, aquarium

11 Basle
Tierpark Lange Erlen (Zoo)
Deer, llamas, etc.

12 Reinach
Tierpark (Zoo)
Deer, birds

13 Roggenhausen
Hirschpark (Deer Park)
Red deer, wild pigs

14 Zofingen
Hirschpark (Deer Park)
Red deer, wild pigs

15 Langenthal
Hirschpark (Deer Park)
Red deer

16 La Chaux-de-Fonds
Parc du Bois
Red deer, ibex, etc.
Vivarium

17 Biel
Tierpark Bötzingenberg (Zoo)
Ibexes

18 Studen
Tierpark Seeteufel (Zoo)
Beasts of prey, aquarium, etc.

19 Berne
Tierpark Dählhölzli (Zoo)
European animals; aquarium, terrarium
Bärengraben (Bear-Pit)

20 Le Vaud
Zoo La Garenne
European animals, birds of prey

21 Lausanne
Vivarium
Reptiles

22 Lausanne
Sauvabelin Deer Park
Red deer, etc.

23 Servion
Zoo
Beasts of prey, red deer

24 **Les Marécottes**
Reno Ranch
Mountain animals, wolves, bears

25 **Mitholz**
Alpenwildpark Riegelsee (Alpine Wild Life Park)
Mountain animals

26 **Interlaken**
Alpenwildpark Harder (Alpine Wild Life Park)
Ibex, marmots

27 **Brienz**
Wildpark (Wild Life Park)
Mountain animals

28 **Zurich**
Zoologischer Garten (Zoo)
Animals from all over the world; aquarium, terrarium

29 **Langnau am Albis**
Wildpark Langenberg (Wild Life Park)
Red deer, wild pigs, bears, etc.

30 **Zug**
Hirsch- und Vogelpark (Deer and Bird Park)
Red deer, exotic birds

31 **Goldau**
Natur- und Tierpark (Nature and Animal Park)
Red deer, wild pigs, etc.

32 **Hoch-Ybrig**
Wildpark (Wild Life Park)
Native animals

33 **Rapperswil**
Knies Kinderzoo (Children's Zoo)
Mini-zoo with dolphinarium

34 **Frauenfeld**
Zoo Plättli
Beasts of prey, monkeys, etc.

35 **Oberglatt**
Vivarium Python
Reptiles

36 **Gossau**
Walter-Zoo
Beasts of prey, monkeys, etc.

37 **St Gallen**
Wildpark Peter und Paul (Wild Life Park)
Native animals

38 **Piz Lagalb**
Alpinarium
Alpine animals

● Alpine Gardens (Selection)

39 **Basle**
Botanischer Garten der Universität
(University Botanic Garden)

40 **Weissenstein**
Juragarten (Jura Garden)

41 **Aubonne**
Arboretum

42 **Lausanne**
Jardin Botanique (Botanic Garden)

43 **Geneva**
Conservatoire et Jardin Botaniques

44 **Rochers de Naye**
Jardin Alpin Rambertia (Alpine Garden)

45 **Pont-de-Nant**
Jardin Botanique Alpin La Thomasia
(Alpine Botanic Garden)

46 **Champex**
Jardin Alpin Floralpe (Alpine Garden)

47 **Neuchâtel**
Jardin Botanique de l'Université
(University Botanic Garden)

48 **Fribourg**
Parc Botanique de l'Université
(University Botanic Park)

49 **Berne**
Botanischer Garten der Universität
(University Botanic Garden)

50 **Schynige Platte**
Alpengarten (Alpine Garden)

51 **Grüningen**
Botanischer Garten, Arboretum
(Botanic Garden and Arboretum)

52 **St Gallen**
Botanischer Garten (Botanic Garden)

53 **Vaduz** (Liechtenstein)
Naturanlage Haberfeld (Nature Park)

54 **Davos**
Alpengarten Schatzalp (Alpine Garden)

55 **Alp Grüm**
Alpengarten (Alpine Garden)

Fishing

Switzerland has a great variety of waters which offer excellent sport to anglers, whether they prefer legering (bottom fishing), spinning or fly fishing. It is necessary to have a fishing licence, usually obtainable from the local tourist information office. – In some places angling courses are run. – Since the regulations about close seasons, minimum size, etc., vary from canton to canton, prospective anglers should enquire locally about these matters.

Information: **Schweizerischer Sportfischer-Verband** (Swiss Angling Federation), Adolf Fink, Mühleweg 12, CH-2543 Lengnau tel. (065) 8 11 30.

Sport

● Golf Courses

1 **Geneva**
18 holes

2 **Lausanne**
18 holes

3 **Aigle**
18 holes

Golf Courses in Switzerland

4 **Villars-sur-Ollon**
18 holes

5 **Verbier**
18 holes

6 **Neuchâtel**
18 holes

7 **Basle**
18 holes

8 **Blumisberg**
18 holes

9 **Gstaad-Saanenland**
9 holes

10 **Interlaken-Unterseen**
18 holes

11 **Crans-sur Sierre**
18 holes

12 **Bad Schinznach**
9 holes

13 **Zurich-Dolder**
9 holes

14 **Breitenloo**
18 holes

15 **Hittnau**
18 holes

16 **Niederbüren**
9 holes

17 **Zumikon**
18 holes

18 **Schönenberg**
18 holes

19 **Lucerne-Dietschiberg**
18 holes

20 **Bürgenstock**
9 holes

21 **Ascona**
18 holes

22 **Lugano-Magliaso**
18 holes

23 **Bad Ragaz**
18 holes

24 **Lenzerheide-Valbella**
18 holes

25 **Arosa**
9 holes

26 **Davos**
18 holes

27 **Samedan**
18 holes

28 **Vulpera**
9 holes

Hang-Gliding

This new sport has become increasingly popular in Switzerland in recent years. There are *hang-gliding schools* at Bernina Suot, Flims Waldhaus, Klosters, Bad Scuol, Malbun (Liechtenstein), Vilters, Wald, Gstaad, Interlaken, Zweisimmen, Bevaix, Fribourg, Les Diablerets, Geneva, Leysin, Morgins and Verbier.

Information: **Schweizerischer Hängegleiter-Verband** (Swiss Hang-Gliding Federation), Postfach 438, CH-6002 Luzern tel. (041) 23 51 01.

Golf course; Bad Ragaz

Other Features of Interest

● Specialised Museums

1 **Geneva**
Car and Motor-cycle Museum

2 **Geneva**
Museum on the History of Science

3 **Geneva**
Watchmaking Museum

4 **Nyon**
Porcelain Museum

5 **Morges**
Doll and Toy Museum

6 **Morges**
Vaudois Military Museum

7 **Lausanne**
Tobacco Pipe Museum

8 **Vevey**
Wine-Growing Museum

9 **Blonay**
Railway Museum

10 **Aigle**
Swiss Salt Museum

11 **Bex**
Le Bouillet Salt-Mine and Museum

12 **St-Maurice**
Military Museum

13 **Gruyères**
Wax Museum

14 **Lucens**
Sherlock Holmes Museum

15 **Vallorbe**
Gyger Railway Museum

16 **L'Auberson**
Baud Museum of Musical Automata

17 **Grandson**
Antique Car Museum

18 **Yverdon**
Science Fiction Museum

19 **Estavayer-le-Lac**
Frog Museum

20 **Boudry**
Museum of Viticulture

21 **Colombier**
Military Museum

22 **Neuchâtel**
Collection of Automata

23 **Le Locle**
Watch and Clock Museum

24 **La Chaux-de-Fonds**
Museum of Rural Life and Crafts

25 **La Chaux-de-Fonds**
Watch and Clock Museum

26 **Ligerz**
Museum of Viticulture

27 **Rizenbach**
Jerisberghof Museum of Rural Life

28 **Berne**
Swiss Alpine Museum

29 **Berne**
Swiss Postal Museum

30 **Berne**
Swiss Riflemen's Museum

31 **Kiesen**
National Dairy Farming Museum

32 **Utzenstorf**
Swiss Hunting Museum

33 **Solothurn**
Artillery Museum

34 **Solothurn**
Arsenal Museum

35 **Seewen**
Museum of Musical Automata

36 **Basle**
Film Museum

37 **Basle**
Rhine Shipping Museum

38 **Basle**
Swiss Fire Service Museum

39 **Basle**
Collection of Musical Instruments

40 **Basle**
Collection on the History of Paper

41 **Basle**
Museum of the History of Pharmacy

42 **Basle**
Museum of Gymnastics and Sport

43 **Riehen**
Toy Museum

44 **Rheinfelden**
Old-Timer Museum

45 **Schönenwerd**
Bally Shoe Museum

46 **Altishofen**
Woodwork Museum

47 **Alberswil**
Farming Museum

48 **Baden**
Power Station Museum

49 **Wohlenschwil**
Museum of Rural Life

50 **Wohlen**
Straw Museum

51 **Lucerne**
Transport Museum

52 **Lucerne**
Glacier Garden Museum

53 **Lucerne**
Wagner Museum, Tribschen

54 **Bürglen**
Tell Museum

55 **Schwyz**
Tower Museum (weapons, etc.)

56 **Goldau**
Rock Fall Museum

57 **Zug**
Bee Museum

Specialised Museums in Switzerland

58 Wädenswil
Museum of Viticulture

59 Wolfhausen
Bühler Two-Wheel Museum

60 Zurich
Police Criminal Museum

61 Zurich
Museum of Time Measurement

62 Zurich
Sasha Doll Museum

63 Zurich
Typewriter Museum

64 Zurich
Tramway Museum

65 Dübendorf
Swiss Air Force Museum

66 Winterthur
Kellenberger Watch and Clock Collection

67 Neftenbach
Wine-Growing Museum

68 Eglisau
Fishery Museum

69 Schleitheim
Plaster Industry Museum

70 Diessenhofen
Museum of Printed Textiles

71 Steckborn
Bernina Sewing-Machine Museum

72 Kreuzlingen
Fire Service Museum

73 Güttingen
Jeannine Doll Museum

74 Amriswil
Collection of Coaches

75 St Gallen
Industrial and Craft Museum

76 Appenzell
Museum of Mechanical Music and Magic

77 Appenzell
Collection of Curios

78 Gossau
Hilti Motor-cycle Museum

79 Lichtensteig
Fredy's Museum of Mechanical Music

80 Unterwasser
Alpine Dairy Farming Museum

81 Sargans
Old-Timer Museum

82 Jenins
Wine-Growing Museum

83 Chur
Collection of Coaches

84 Davos
Mining Museum

85 Gandria
Smuggling Museum

86 Bosco/Gurin
Valais House, Gurin

87 Zermatt
Alpine Museum

88 Sierre
Pewter Museum

● **Swiss Open-Air Museum of Rural Life,**
Ballenberg (Brienz)

Winter Sports

Winter Sports Areas

1 Morgins
Alt. 1343 m (4406 feet)
Cableways to 1922 m (6306 feet)

2 Champéry
Alt. 1052 m (3452 feet)
Cableways to 1800 m (5906 feet)

3 Gruyères-Moléson
Alt. 1110 m (3642 feet)
Cableways to 2002 m (6569 feet)

4 Charmey
Alt. 890 m (2920 feet)
Cableways to 1630 m (5348 feet)

5 Villars-sur-Ollon
Alt. 1256 m (4121 feet)
Cableways to 2118 m (6949 feet)
Leysin
Alt. 1265–1450 m (4150–4757 feet)
Cableways to 2326 m (7632 feet)

6 Saanen
Alt. 1033 m (3389 feet)
Cableways to 2200 m (7218 feet)
Gstaad
Alt. 1050 m (3617 feet)
Cableways to 2000 m (6562 feet)
Helicopter service
Saanenmöser
Alt. 1269 m (4164 feet)
Cableways to 1950 m (6398 feet)
Zweisimmen
Alt. 945 m (3101 feet)
Cableways to 2079 m (6821 feet)
Château-d'Oex
Alt. 990 m (3248 feet)
Cableways to 1630 m (5348 feet)
Les Diablerets
Alt. 1163 m (3816 feet)
Cableways to 2950 m (9679 feet)

7 Salvan/Les Marécottes
Alt. 927–1100 m (3041–3609 feet)
Cableways to 1780 m (5840 feet)

8 Champex
Alt. 1472 m (4830 feet)
Cableways to 2374 m (7789 feet)

9 Verbier
Alt. 1420 m (4659 feet)
Cableways to 3026 m (9928 feet)
Haute-Nendaz
Alt. 1370–1736 m (4495–5696 feet)
Cableways to 2734 m (8970 feet)

10 Lenk
Alt. 1068 m (3504 feet)
Cableways to 2098 m (6884 feet)
Adelboden
Alt. 1357 m (4452 feet)
Cableways to 2200 m (7218 feet)
Kandersteg
Alt. 1170 m (3839 feet)
Cableways to 1947 m (6388 feet)

11 Crans-Montana
Alt. 1500–1680 m (4922–5512 feet)
Cableways to 2943 m (9656 feet)

12 Leikerbad
Alt. 1411 m (4629 feet)
Cableways to 2240 m (8006 feet)

13 Zinal
Alt. 1678 m (5506 feet)
Cableways to 2900 m (9515 feet)

14 Zermatt
Alt. 1630 m (5315 feet)
Cableways to 3820 m (12,533 feet)

15 Saas Fee
Alt. 1562–1679 m (5125–5509 feet)
Cableways to 3100 m (10,171 feet)

16 Stalden
Alt. 803 m (2635 feet)
Cableways to 1893 m (6211 feet)

Winter Sports Areas in Switzerland

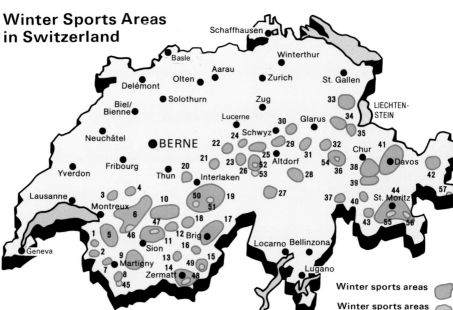

Winter sports areas

Winter sports areas with summer skiing

Skiing in the Swiss mountains

Grächen
Alt. 1617 m (5305 feet)
Cableways to 2110 m (6923 feet)

17 Fiesch
Alt. 1062 m (3484 feet)
Cableways to 2870 m (9416 feet)

18 Wiler im Lötschental
Alt. 1419 m (4656 feet)
Cableways to 2700 m (8859 feet)

19 Lauterbrunnen
Alt. 796 m (2612 feet)
Cableways to 1800 m (5906 feet)
Wengen
Alt. 1276 m (4187 feet)
Cableways to 3454 m (11,333 feet)
Mürren
Alt. 1634 m (5361 feet)
Cableways to 2971 m (9748 feet)
Grindelwald
Alt. 1034 m (3393 feet)
Cableways to 3454 m (11,333 feet)

20 Beatenberg
Alt. 1150 m (3773 feet)
Cableways to 1950 m (6398 feet)

21 Sörenberg
Alt. 1165 m (3822 feet)
Cableways to 2320 m (7612 feet)

22 Melchtal
Alt. 894 m (2933 feet)
Cableways to 1350 m (4429 feet)

23 Melchsee-Frutt
Alt. 1920 m (6300 feet)
Cableways to 2230 m (7317 feet)

24 Stans
Alt. 455 m (1493 feet)
Cableways to 1850 m (6070 feet)

25 Beckenried
Alt. 440 m (1444 feet)
Cableways to 1600 m (5250 feet)

26 Engelberg
Alt. 1020 m (3347 feet)
Cableways to 3020 m (9909 feet)

27 Andermatt
Alt. 1444 m (4738 feet)
Cableways to 2961 m (9715 feet)

28 Disentis
Alt. 1140 m (3740 feet)
Cableways to 3000 m (9843 feet)

29 Muotathal
Alt. 600–870 m (1969–2854 feet)
Cableways to 1922 m (6306 feet)

30 Hoch-Ybrig
Alt. 1038 m (3406 feet)
Cableways to 1856 m (6090 feet)

31 Braunwald
Alt. 1300 m (4265 feet)
Cableways to 1910 m (6267 feet)

32 Elm
Alt. 962 m (3156 feet)
Cableways to 2036 m (6680 feet)

33 Alt St Johann
Alt. 897 m (2943 feet)
Cableways to 1390 m (4561 feet)
Unterwasser
Alt. 927 m (3041 feet)
Cableways to 2250 m (7382 feet)
Wildhaus
Alt. 1098 m (3603 feet)
Cableways to 1771 m (5811 feet)

34 Flumserberge
Alt. 1220–1400 m (4003–4593 feet)
Cableways to 2222 m (7290 feet)

35 Wangs/Bad Ragaz
Alt. 502–520 m (1647–1706 feet)
Cableways to 2227 m (7307 feet)

Skating, *haute école*

36 Flims
Alt. 1070–1103 m (3511–3619 feet)
Cableways to 2678 m (8787 feet)

37 Splügen
Alt. 1450 m (4757 feet)
Cableways to 2160 m (7087 feet)

38 Arosa
Alt. 1740–1890 m (5709–6201 feet)
Cableways to 2653 m (8704 feet)

39 Lenzerheide/Valbella
Alt. 1470–1540 m (4823–5053 feet)
Cableways to 2865 m (9400 feet)

40 Savognin
Alt. 1173 m (3849 feet)
Cableways to 2713 m (8901 feet)

41 Klosters
Alt. 1124–1206 m (3688–3957 feet)
Cableways to 2300 m (7546 feet)
Davos
Alt. 1508–1563 m (4948–5128 feet)
Cableways to 2844 m (9331 feet)

42 Bad Scuol-Tarasp-Vulpera
Alt. 1203–1268 m (3947–4160 feet)
Cableways to 2900 m (9515 feet)

43 Bivio
Alt. 1776 m (5827 feet)
Cableways to 2660 m (8727 feet)

44 Silvaplana
Alt. 1815 m (5955 feet)
Cableways to 3300 m (10,827 feet)
St Moritz
Alt. 1822 m (5978 feet)
Cableways to 3057 m (10,030 feet)
Celerina
Alt. 1724 m (5656 feet)
Cableways to 2955 m (9695 feet)
Pontresina/Bernina
Alt. 1805 m (5922 feet)
Cableways to 2973 m (9754 feet)

⬡ Summer Skiing Areas

45 Bourg-St-Pierre
La Chenalette

46 Les Diablerets
Diablerets glacier

47 Crans-Montana
Glacier de la Plaine Morte

48 Zermatt
Theodul glacier, Breithorn plateau
Little Matterhorn

49 Saas Fee
Egginer Felskinn

50 Mürren
Schilthorn

51 Jungfrau area
Jungfraujoch

52 Engelberg
Titlis

53 Meiringen
Susten Pass

54 Laax
Vorab 3000

55 St Moritz
Corvatsch

56 Pontresina
Diavolezza

57 Münstertal
Stilfser Joch

Folk Traditions

Switzerland has preserved many ancient festivals and traditional ceremonies which are still celebrated with enthusiasm. Among them are a number of survivors from pagan times, in particular old customs connected with the end of winter and the Carnival. Religious festivals and processions are celebrated with great pomp and ceremony.

The strong national consciousness of the Swiss is given expression in the traditional meetings of the *Landsgemeinden* (cantonal assemblies), the shooting contests on the Rütli meadow and other popular events. There are also a number of sports peculiar to Switzerland which have developed out of old peasant sporting contests.

On New Year's Eve, particularly in the German-speaking parts of the country, figures disguised in fancy-dress parade through the streets, symbolising the end of the old year and the time of darkness; and the symbolic struggle between winter and spring is continued far into the new year in the traditional celebrations of the Shrovetide carnival, **Fasnacht**, lasting well into Lent. Atavistic fertility rites and pagan attitudes to nature survive in the numerous masked figures of "wild men" under a variety of names – Butzi, Wildma, Bärzeli, Roitschäggädä, etc. Particularly notable is the Basle carnival, the *Baseler*

Fasnacht, which begins with the "Morgenstraich" at 4 a.m. on the Monday after Ash Wednesday and continues until the following Thursday. The Morgenstraich is a parade through the old town, beginning before daybreak, by the "cliques" or carnival guilds, accompanied by a band of fifes and drums. This is followed on Monday afternoon by the official procession, in which the members of the various cliques wear masks and uniforms. The procession also includes decorated floats with satirical scenes. There is another noisy occasion on Tuesday, when there is a parade by drum and wind bands ("Guggenmusiken"). The Swiss carnival is celebrated later than in some other countries, since it is still related to the old Julian calendar.

Another old spring custom is the *Eieraufleset* ("picking up of eggs"), in which the egg is a fertility symbol representing the victory of spring over winter.

Swiss wrestling (*Schwingen*)

There are also numerous **religious processions**. In Ticino, which reflects the influence of Latin culture, there are *Holy Week processions* in many places, sometimes (e.g. at Mendrisio) including representations of the Passion. – At the beginning of April the ceremony of the *Näfelser Fahrt* is held in Glarus, with the participation of the Capuchins of Näfels – commemorating the victory of the men of Glarus over the Austrians on 9 April 1388. The *Stoos pilgrimage* at Appenzell has a similar origin. At many places in the canton of Lucerne there is an Ascension ride, the *Auffahrtsumritt*, for the blessing of the fields – a ceremony which harks back to pre-Christian traditions. The finest and most impressive religious processions are those celebrated in the predominantly Catholic parts of the country at Corpus Christi, when beautiful old traditional costumes can frequently be seen.

There are also many **historical festivals** reflecting the Swiss love of freedom and readiness to defend their independence. Thus the battles of Morgarten (1315), Sempach (1386), Näfels (1388: see above), Murten (1476) and Dornach (1499) are commemorated by splendid parades in historical costume. Numerous too are the festivals of the riflemen's guilds and military festivals like the *Rütlischiessen* (Rütli shooting contest) in Uri, the *Knabenschiessen* (boys' shooting) in Zurich, the *Ausschiesset* in Thun and the *Wyberschiessen* (women's shooting) in the canton of Lucerne. Perhaps the best-known historical celebration is the Geneva *Escalade*, commemorating the successful defence of the town against a Savoyard attack in 1602. – Living evidence of the Swiss attachment to democracy is provided by the meetings of the **Landsgemeinden** (communal assemblies) at which the citizens elect their representatives by popular vote.

The Swiss **National Day**, which is celebrated throughout the country with torchlight processions, fireworks and shooting contests, is the 1 August, commemorating the occasion in 1291 when representatives of the three original cantons of Schwyz, Uri and Unterwalden met on the Rütli meadow and swore an oath of alliance and mutual defence, thus laying the foundations of the Confederation.

There are also three typically Swiss **sports** – *Schwingen*, *Hornussen* and *Steinstossen*. – *Schwingen* ("swinging") is a form of wrestling in which the contestants seek to throw one another by grasping the short trousers of coarse linen which they wear. – In *Hornussen* one team, the "strikers" (Schläger) are equipped with long (2 m – 7 feet) flexible clubs with hardwood heads, with which they

Playing *Hornussen*

Among old customs reflecting ancient rural traditions the **Älplerfeste** (festivals of the Alpine herdsmen) take a prominent place. At the beginning of summer the *Alpaufzug*, the move up to the mountain pastures, is celebrated. A highlight of this, particularly in the canton of Valais, is the *cow-fights* in which the cattle establish their status within the herd, the winner becoming the leader of the herd for the following year. At the end of summer the cheese produced on the mountain pastures is distributed by lot among the villagers: this is the *Kästeilet* (division of the cheese).

drive the *Hornus*, a disk the size of a man's hand, as far down the field as they can. The object of the defenders (Abtuer) is to catch the disk before it reaches the ground with their large wooden bats. – In *Steinstossen* ("tossing the stone") the object is to throw a large stone weighing 83·5 kg (184 pounds) as far as possible; the record stands at about 3·50 m (11 feet).

In Swiss **folk music** a prominent part is played by *yodelling*. In Switzerland, unlike Bavaria and Austria, yodelling is usually improvised, without any established format. It was originally a means of communicating from one Alpine pasture to another. This was also the original function of the *alphorn*, a horn some 3·50 m (11 feet) long made from a hollowed-out pine stem, whose characteristic melodious sound has astonishing carrying power. Another popular instrument is the accordion (*Schwyzerörgeli* or *Hand-örgeli*), with a chromatic keyboard. Folk bands are often accompanied by "flag-swingers" (*Fahnenschwinger*).

Musicians on the Rigi

In autumn there are numerous *vintage festivals* or *grape festivals* in the wine-producing areas. This is also the season for markets and fairs, among the best known of which are the onion markets of Berne and Biel.

The most popular Swiss card game is *Jass*, played with 36 cards in four suits.

Swiss **folk art** is still very much alive, finding expression particularly in painting, embroidery, woodcarving and hand-weaving.

Swiss folk musicians and flag-swinger

Calendar of Events

(a selection of interesting events)

January	
Many places	Dreikönigssingen (Three Kings singing)
Weiler/Lötschental (VS)	Dreikönigsspiel (Three Kings play)
Schwanden (BE)	Bärzelitag (Bärzeli's Day)
Hallwil (AG)	Bärzelitag
Kandersteg (BE)	Pelzmarti
Schwyz (SZ)	Greiflet
Meisterschwanden (AG)	Meitlisunntig
Pontresina, Samedan, St Moritz (GR)	Schlitteda
Urnäsch (AR)	Silvesterkläuse (New Year celebrations)
Basle (BS)	Vogel Gryff
Finhaut (VS)	St-Sébastien
Carnival	
Altdorf (UR)	Katzenmusik ("Cats' Music")

Carnival, Basle

Carnival and Lent	
Many places	Processions, masquerades
Basle (BS)	Morgenstraich (see p. 309)
Holy Week and Easter	
Many places	Processions
March	
Geneva (GE)	International Automobile Salon
Many places in Grisons	Chalandamarz (1 March)
Glarus (GL)	Fridolinsfeuer (St Fridolin's Fire: 6 March)
April	
Näfels (GL)	Näfelser Fahrt (see p. 309)
Hundwil, Trogen (AR)	Landsgemeinde
Sarnen (OW), Stans (NW)	Landsgemeinde
Montreux (VD)	Golden Rose Television Festival
Zurich (ZH)	Sechseläuten ("Six O'clock Ringing")
Appenzell (AI)	Landsgemeinde
Corpus Christi	
Many places	Processions
May	
Many places	May Day celebrations (first Sunday)

Glarus (GL)	Landsgemeinde
Escholzmatt, Entlebuch, Schüpfheim (LU)	Wyberschiessen
Lausanne (VD)	International Festival of Opera
Zurich (ZH)	Summer Trade Fair
Berne (BE)	International Jazz Festival; Geranium Market
Baden (AG)	Swiss Amateur Film Festival
May—June	
Lausanne (VD)	International Musical Festival
Many places in Valais	Cow-fights
June	
Many places	Alpaufzug
Many places in Valais	Johannisfeuer (Midsummer bonfires)
Murten (FR)	Commemoration of Battle of Murten
Lugano (TI)	Concerti di Lugano
Zurich (ZH)	International Festival; Seenachtsfest (night festival on lake)
Montreux (VD)	Jazz Festival
Berne (BE)	Little Theatre Festival; Dog Show
Locarno (TI)	Flower Parade
Biel (BE)	100 km (62 miles) run; Braderie (fair)
Baar (ZG)	Costume festival
Basle (BS)	Town Festival; Art Fair
Neuchâtel (NE)	Drum and Fife Festival of Western Switzerland
Winterthur (TG)	St Alban's Day
June—July	
Spiez (BE)	Concerts in Schloss
Dornach (SO)	Faust pageant play (every 3–4 years: 1981, etc.)
June—August	
Interlaken (BE)	Musical Festival
June—September	
Intelaken (BE)	William Tell Festival Play
July	
Sempach (LU)	Commemoration of Battle of Sempach
Dornach (SO)	Commemoration of Battle of Dornach (every 5 years)
Villars (VD)	Folk Festival
Lucerne (LU)	Federal Riflemen's Festival; Rowing Regatta on Rotsee
Braunwald (GL)	Music Week
Klosters (GR)	Summer Festival
Kreuzlingen (TG)	Seenachtsfest (night festival on lake)
August	
Everywhere	National Day (1 August)
Many places	Herdsmen's and Älpler festivals
Gstaad (BE)	Yehudi Menuhin Festival
Spiez (BE)	Performances of plays in Schloss
Klosters (GR)	Children's Festival
Mürren (BE)	Village Festival
Leukerbad (VS)	Shepherds' Festival on Gemmi
Saignelégier (JU)	Horse Market
Biel (BE)	Costume festival

Assumption (15 August)

Many places in Catholic parts of country	Processions

August–September

Winterthur (TG)	Musical Festival
Basle (Bs)	Kleinbaslerfest
Langernthal (BL)	Federal Hornus Festival

August–October

Many places	Hornus matches
Ascona (TI)	Music Weeks

September

Zurich (ZH)	Knabenschiessen; Jazz Festival
Montreux, Vevey (VD)	Septembre Musical
Hasliberg (BE)	Chästeilet ("division of cheese") and popular festival
Basle (BS)	Celebration of Reformation and popular festival
Locarno (TI)	Grape Festival
Berne (BE)	Minerals Exchange

September–October

Many places	Vintage festivals

October

Châtel-St-Denis (FR)	Harvest thanksgiving festival
Lausanne (VD)	Festival of Italian Opera
Neuchâtel (NE)	Vintage festival
Locarno (TI)	Chestnut Festival
Biel (BE)	Onion Market

November

Rütli (UR)	Rütlischiessen
Sursee (LU)	Gansabhauet ("cutting down the goose")
Morgarten (ZG)	Commemoration of Battle of Morgarten
Berne (BE)	Onion Market
Zurich (ZH)	Minerals Exchange

December

Many places	Lichtkläuse (around 6 December); masquerades, Silvesterkläuse, etc.
Geneva (GE)	Escalade (12 December)

Headdress worn at New Year celebrations, Urnäsch (AR)

Christmas

Many places	Sternsingen ("Star Singing")

Public Holidays

1 January	New Year's Day
6 January	Epiphany (Three Kings)
Good Friday	
Easter Monday	
1 May	Labour Day
Ascension	
Whit Monday	
Corpus Christi	
(only in cantons with predominantly Catholic population)	
1 August	National Day
1 November	All Saints
Day of Repentance and Prayer 25 and 26 December	

Shopping and Souvenirs

The best-known Swiss products are watches and jewelry. But textiles, St Gallen lace and embroidery and the many-bladed Swiss army knives are other very popular buys.

A good selection of Swiss craft goods can be seen in the showrooms of *Schweizer Heimatwerk* in Zurich and other towns.

Switzerland offers a wide variety of foodstuffs of excellent quality, notably chocolate, cheese and various spirits (e.g. the kirsch of Zug and the herb liqueur of the Grisons, Chrüter), as well as such specialities as the Bündnerfleisch (air-dried beef) and Birnbrot ("pear bread") of the Grisons. Other items are coffee, preserves and various ready-made dishes to be found in rich assortment, particularly in such chain stores as Migros, Coop, etc.

Information

Swiss National Tourist Office

Schweizerische Verkehrszentrale,
Bellariastrasse 38,
CH-8023 **Zurich**
tel. (01) 2 02 37 37.

Swiss National Tourist Office,
Swiss Centre, 1 New Coventry Street,
London W1V 3HG
tel. (01) 734 1921.

Swiss National Tourist Office,
Swiss Center, 608 Fifth Avenue,
New York NY 10020
tel. (0212) 757 5944.

Swiss National Tourist Office,
250 Stockton Street,
San Francisco CA 94108
tel. (0415) 362 2260.

Swiss National Tourist Office,
Commerce Court West, Suite No. 2015,
P.O. Box 215, Commerce Court Postal Station,
Toronto, Ont. M5L 1EB
tel. (0416) 868 0584.

Within Switzerland tourist information can be obtained from local tourist information offices (*Verkehrsbüro, Office Du Tourisme,* etc.).

Automobile Club of Switzerland
Automobil-Club der Schweiz/Automobile-Club de Suisse (ACS).

Head office:
Wasserwerkgasse 39,
CH-3000 **Berne 13**,
tel. (031) 22 47 22

Branch offices in the larger Swiss towns.

Touring Club of Switzerland
Touring-Club der Schweiz/Touring-Club Suisse (TCS)
Head office:
9 rue Pierre-Fatio,
CH-1211 **Genève,**
tel. (022) 37 12 12

Branch offices and information bureaux in the larger Swiss towns.

Diplomatic and Consular Offices in Switzerland

United Kingdom

Embassy
Thunstrasse 50,
CH-3000 **Bern**
tel. (031) 44 50 21-26.

Consulates
37–39 rue de Vermont (6th floor),
CH-1211 **Genève**
tel. (022) 34 38 00 and 33 23 85.

Via Maraini 14A, Loreto,
CH-6900 **Lugano**
tel. (091) 54 54 44.

15 Bourg Dessous,
CH-1814 **La Tour-de-Peilz/Montreux**
tel. (021) 54 12 07.

Dufourstrasse 56,
CH-8008 **Zurich**
tel. (01) 47 15 20-26.

United States of America

Embassy
Jubiläumstrasse 93,
CH-3005 **Berne**
tel. (031) 43 70 11.

Consulates
80 rue de Lausanne,
CH-1200 **Geneva**
tel. (022) 32 70 20.

Zollikerstrasse 141,
CH-8008 **Zurich**
tel. (01) 55 25 66.

Canada

Embassy
Kirchenfeldstrasse 88,
CH-3005 **Bern**
tel. (031) 44 63 81.

Airlines

Swissair

Head office:
Zentralverwaltung Balsberg,
CH-8058 **Zürich** *Flughafen* (Airport)
tel. (01) 8 12 12 12.

Desks at all Swiss commercial airports.

British Airways

Centralbahnplatz 3–4,
Basle
tel. (reservations) (061) 22 40 11.

13 rue de Chantepoulet,
Geneva
tel. (reservations) (022) 31 40 50.

Bahnhofstrasse 100,
Zurich
tel. (reservations) (01) 2 11 40 90.

Swiss Federal Railways
(SBB/CFF/FFS)

Passenger services:
Mittelstrasse 43,
CH-3030 **Berne**
tel. (031) 60 11 11.

Outside Switzerland information about railway services can be obtained from the Swiss National Tourist Office.

Radio Messages for Tourists

In case of emergency, messages for tourists are transmitted by Swiss radio stations. Information from the police and the Automobile Clubs.

Emergency Calls

There are **emergency telephones** on all Swiss motorways and on the most important mountain roads (marked *SOS*).

Police	**117**
Fire Brigade	**118**
Ambulance	**144**
Breakdown service	**140**

International Telephone Dialling Codes

From the United Kingdom to Switzerland and Liechtenstein **010 41**
From the United States to Switzerland and Liechtenstein **011 41**
From Canada to Switzerland and Liechtenstein **011 41**

From Switzerland and Liechtenstein to the United Kingdom **00 44**
From Switzerland and Liechtenstein to the United States **00 1**
From Switzerland and Liechtenstein to Canada **00 1**

In dialling an international call the zero prefixed to the local dialling code should be omitted.

Telephone Information Services in Switzerland

The following numbers can be dialled from anywhere in Switzerland.

Road conditions	**163**
Snow report (Dec.–Mar.)	**120**
Tourist information bulletin (Apr.–Nov.)	**120**
Weather report	**162**

Baedeker's Travel Guides

"The maps and illustrations are lavish. The arrangement of information (alphabetically by city) makes it easy to use the book."

—San Francisco Examiner-Chronicle

What's there to do and see in foreign countries? Travelers who rely on Baedeker, one of the oldest names in travel literature, will miss nothing. Baedeker's bright red, internationally recognized covers open up to reveal fascinating A-Z directories of cities, towns, and regions, complete with their sights, museums, monuments, cathedrals, castles, gardens and ancestral homes—an approach that gives the traveler a quick and easy way to plan a vacation itinerary.

And Baedekers are filled with over 200 full-color photos and detailed maps, including a full-size, fold-out roadmap for easy vacation driving. Baedeker—the premier name in travel for over 140 years.

Please send me the books checked below and fill in order form on reverse side.

☐ **Austria** $14.95
0-13-056127-4

☐ **Caribbean** $14.95
0-13-056143-6

☐ **Egypt** $15.95
0-13-056358-7

☐ **France** $14.95
0-13-055814-1

☐ **Germany** $14.95
0-13-055830-3

☐ **Great Britain** $14.95
0-13-055855-9

☐ **Greece** $14.95
0-13-056002-2

☐ **Israel** $14.95
0-13-056176-2

☐ **Italy** $14.95
0-13-055897-4

☐ **Japan** $15.95
0-13-056382-X

☐ **Loire** $9.95
0-13-056375-7

☐ **Mediterranean Islands** $14.95
0-13-056862-7

☐ **Mexico** $14.95
0-13-056069-3

☐ **Netherlands, Belgium, and Luxembourg** $14.95
0-13-056028-6

☐ **Portugal** $14.95
0-13-056135-5

☐ **Provence/Cote d'Azur** $9.95
0-13-056938-0

☐ **Rhine** $9.95
0-13-056466-4

☐ **Scandinavia** $14.95
0-13-056085-5

☐ **Spain** $14.95
0-13-055913-X

☐ **Switzerland** $14.95
0-13-056044-8

☐ **Tuscany** $9.95
0-13-056482-6

☐ **Yugoslavia** $14.95
0-13-056184-3

Please turn the page for an order form and a list of additional Baedeker Guides.

A series of city guides filled with colour photographs and detailed maps and floor plans from one of the oldest names in travel publishing:

Please send me the books checked below:

☐ **Amsterdam** $10.95
 0-13-057969-6
☐ **Athens**. $10.95
 0-13-057977-7
☐ **Bangkok** $10.95
 0-13-057985-8
☐ **Berlin** $10.95
 0-13-367996-9
☐ **Brussels** $10.95
 0-13-368788-0
☐ **Copenhagen**. $10.95
 0-13-057993-9
☐ **Florence** $10.95
 0-13-369505-0
☐ **Frankfurt**. $10.95
 0-13-369570-0
☐ **Hamburg** $10.95
 0-13-369687-1
☐ **Hong Kong** $10.95
 0-13-058009-0
☐ **Jerusalem** $10.95
 0-13-058017-1
☐ **London** $10.95
 0-13-058025-2

☐ **Madrid** $10.95
 0-13-058033-3
☐ **Moscow** $10.95
 0-13-058041-4
☐ **Munich** $10.95
 0-13-370370-3
☐ **New York** $10.95
 0-13-058058-9
☐ **Paris** $10.95
 0-13-058066-X
☐ **Rome** $10.95
 0-13-058074-0
☐ **San Francisco** $10.95
 0-13-058082-1
☐ **Singapore** $10.95
 0-13-058090-2
☐ **Tokyo** $10.95
 0-13-058108-9
☐ **Venice**. $10.95
 0-13-058116-X
☐ **Vienna**. $10.95
 0-13-371303-2

PRENTICE HALL PRESS

Order Department—Travel Books

200 Old Tappan Road

Old Tappan, New Jersey 07675

In U.S. include $1 postage and handling for 1st book, 25¢ each additional book. Outside U.S. $2 and 50¢ respectively.

Enclosed is my check or money order for $_____

NAME_____

ADDRESS_____

CITY_____STATE_____ZIP_____